7·11·78

Leadership is an act of leadership, a pioneering exploration of the frontiers of scholarship.

James MacGregor Burns rejects our contemporary obsession with power for its own sake — the brute power-wielding of a Hitler or the power-manipulation of a political or corporate boss. He presents instead a theory of leadership as a dynamic reciprocity between ordinary people or "followers," and political and ideological "leaders" that thrives on conflict and demands no consensus. He bases his political-psychological theory on biography, history, and analysis of recent findings in social and behavioral sciences.

Vivid stories of leaders such as Moses, Joan of Arc, Luther, Freud, Wilson, Gandhi, Eleanor and Franklin Roosevelt, and Mao, and of power-wielders such as Stalin, serve as counterpoint to dramatic narratives of leader-follower encounters in parliaments, empires, and revolutions — notably the French, Russian, and Chinese — and leader-follower encounters in individual lives: parent and child, teacher and student, coach and athlete, lovers.

Burns draws on cross-disciplinary sources such as Maslow, Lasswell, and Kohlberg to support his argument that mutual need, empathy, and growth characterize all genuine leadership, whether "transactional" as in congressional bargaining, or "transcending" as in a Gandhi's or Mao's appeal to human need and moral purpose. It is his conclusion that the ultimate test of leadership is intended social change. He spurns elitist ("great man") and anti-elitist (populist) theories alike as ignoring the dialectical relationship between those who "lead" and those who "follow." His is a daring argument of enormous significance to democratic politics.

BOOK

ALSO BY JAMES MACGREGOR BURNS

Edward Kennedy and the Camelot Legacy (1976)

Uncommon Sense (1972)

Roosevelt: The Soldier of Freedom (1970)

Presidential Government: The Crucible of Leadership (1965)

The Deadlock of Democracy: Four-Party Politics in America (1963)

John Kennedy: A Political Profile (1960)

Roosevelt: The Lion and the Fox (1956)

Government by the People (with Jack W. Peltason) (1950)

Congress on Trial (1949)

1817

LEADERSHIP

James MacGregor Burns

HARPER & ROW, PUBLISHERS

NEW YORK, HAGERSTOWN, SAN FRANCISCO, LONDON

FIRST EDITION

Designed by Sidney Feinberg

Library of Congress Cataloging in Publication Data

Burns, James MacGregor.
   Leadership.
   Includes bibliographical references and index.
   1. Leadership.   I. Title.
HM141.B847   301.15'53   76-5117
ISBN 0-06-010588-7

78 79 80 81 82 10 9 8 7 6 5 4 3 2 1

For Joan

. . . a meadow . . . with nesting life
spared by a mower's blade set high
the flowering weeds and grasses strewn
over the field to be raked and dried
by rays from a fire set high in the heaven.

"High Mowing"

CONTENTS

A prince will never lack for legitimate excuses to explain away his breaches of faith. Modern history will furnish innumerable examples of this behavior, showing how the man succeeded best who knew best how to play the fox. But it is a necessary part of this nature that you must conceal it carefully; you must be a great liar and hypocrite. Men are so simple of mind, and so much dominated by their immediate needs, that a deceitful man will always find plenty who are ready to be deceived.

Machiavelli

The Presidency is . . . preeminently a place of moral leadership. All our great Presidents were leaders of thought at times when certain historic ideas in the life of the nation had to be clarified. . . . That is what the office is—a superb opportunity for reapplying, applying in new conditions, the simple rules of human conduct to which we always go back. Without leadership alert and sensitive to change, we are all bogged up or lose our way.

Franklin D. Roosevelt

To link oneself with the masses, one must act in accordance with the needs and wishes of the masses. . . . There are two principles here: one is the actual needs of the masses rather than what we fancy they need, and the other is the wishes of the masses, who must make up their own minds instead of our making up their minds for them. . . . We should pay close attention to the well-being of the masses, from the problems of land and labour to those of fuel, rice, cooking oil and salt. . . . We should help them to proceed from these things to an understanding of the higher tasks which we have put forward. . . . Such is the basic method of leadership.

Mao Tse-tung

PROLOGUE:
THE CRISIS OF LEADERSHIP

One of the most universal cravings of our time is a hunger for compelling and creative leadership. Many of us spent our early years in the eras of the titans—Freud and Einstein, Shaw and Stravinsky, Mao and Gandhi, Churchill and Roosevelt, Stalin and Hitler and Mussolini. Most of these colossi died in the middle years of this century; some lingered on, while a few others—de Gaulle, Nehru, perhaps Kennedy and King—joined the pantheon of leadership. These giants strode across our cultural and intellectual and political horizons. We—followers everywhere—loved or loathed them. We marched for them and fought against them. We died for them and we killed some of them. We could not ignore them.

In the final quarter of our century that life-and-death engagement with leadership has given way to the cult of personality, to a "gee whiz" approach to celebrities. We peer into the private lives of leaders, as though their sleeping habits, eating preferences, sexual practices, dogs, and hobbies carry messages of profound significance. Entire magazines are devoted to trivia about "people" and serious newspapers start off their news stories with a personality anecdote or slant before coming to the essence of the matter. Huge throngs parade in Red Square and in the T'ien An Men Square with giant portraits of men who are not giants. The personality cult—a cult of devils as well as heroes—thrives in both East and West.

The crisis of leadership today is the mediocrity or irresponsibility of so many of the men and women in power, but leadership rarely rises to the full need for it. The fundamental crisis underlying mediocrity is intellectual. If we know all too much about our leaders, we know far too little about *leadership*. We fail to grasp the essence of leadership that is relevant to the modern age and

1

hence we cannot agree even on the standards by which to measure, recruit, and reject it. Is leadership simply innovation—cultural or political? Is it essentially inspiration? Mobilization of followers? Goal setting? Goal fulfillment? Is a leader the definer of values? Satisfier of needs? If leaders require followers, who leads whom from where to where, and why? How do leaders lead followers without being wholly led *by* followers? Leadership is one of the most observed and least understood phenomena on earth.

It was not always so. For two millennia at least, leaders of thought did grapple with the vexing problems of the rulers vs. the ruled. Long before modern sociology Plato analyzed not only philosopher-kings but the influences on rulers of upbringing, social and economic institutions, and responses of followers. Long before today's calls for moral leadership and "profiles in courage," Confucian thinkers were examining the concept of leadership in moral teaching and by example. Long before Gandhi, Christian thinkers were preaching nonviolence. Long before modern biography, Plutarch was writing brilliantly about the lives of a host of Roman and Greek rulers and orators, arguing that philosophers "ought to converse especially with 'men in power,' " and examining questions such as whether "an old man should engage in public affairs." From this biographer Shakespeare borrowed for his *Antony and Cleopatra*.

A rich literature on rulership flourished in the classical and middle ages. Later—for reasons we must examine—the study of rulership and leadership ran into serious intellectual difficulties. Leadership as a concept has dissolved into small and discrete meanings. A recent study turned up 130 definitions of the word. A superabundance of facts about leaders far outruns theories of leadership. The world-famous New York Public Library has tens of thousands of biographies, monographs, and newspaper clippings on individual political leaders, but only one catalogue entry to "political leadership" (referring to an obscure politician of forty years ago).

There is, in short, no school of leadership, intellectual or practical. Does it matter that we lack standards for assessing past, present, and potential leaders? Without a powerful modern philosophical tradition, without theoretical and empirical cumulation, without guiding concepts, and without considered practical experiences, we lack the very foundations for knowledge of a phenomenon—leadership in the arts, the academy, science, politics, the professions, war—that touches and shapes our lives. Without such standards and knowledge we cannot make vital distinctions between types of leaders; we cannot distinguish leaders from rulers, from power wielders, and from despots. Hitler called himself—and was called—the Leader; his grotesque *führerprinzip* is solemnly examined as a doctrine of leadership. But Hitler, once he gained power and crushed all opposition, was no leader—he was a tyrant. A leader and a tyrant are polar opposites.

Although we have no school of leadership, we do have in rich abundance and variety the *makings* of such a school. An immense reservoir of data and analysis and theories has been developed. No central concept of leadership has yet emerged, in part because scholars have worked in separate disciplines and subdisciplines in pursuit of different and often unrelated questions and problems. I believe, however, that the richness of the research and analysis and thoughtful experience, accumulated especially in the past decade or so, enables us now to achieve an intellectual breakthrough. Vitally important but largely unheralded work in humanistic psychology now makes it possible to generalize about the leadership process across cultures and across time. This is the central purpose of this book.

One of the most serious failures in the study of leadership has been the bifurcation between the literature on leadership and the literature on followership. The former deals with the heroic or demonic figures in history, usually through the medium of biography and with the inarticulated major premise that fame is equated with importance. The latter deals with the audiences, the masses, the voters, the people, usually through the medium of studies of mass opinion or of elections; it is premised on the conviction that in the long run, at least, leaders act as agents of their followers. The leadership approach tends often unconsciously to be elitist; it projects heroic figures against the shadowy background of drab, powerless masses. The followership approach tends to be populistic or anti-elitist in ideology; it perceives the masses, even in democratic societies, as linked with small, overlapping circles of conservative politicians, military officers, hierocrats, and businessmen. I describe leadership here as no mere game among elitists and no mere populist response but as a structure of action that engages persons, to varying degrees, throughout the levels and among the interstices of society. Only the inert, the alienated, and the powerless are unengaged.

Surely it is time that the two literatures are brought together, that the roles of leader and follower be united conceptually, that the study of leadership be lifted out of the anecdotal and the eulogistic and placed squarely in the structure and processes of human development and political action. I hope to demonstrate that the processes of leadership must be seen as part of the dynamics of conflict and of power; that leadership is nothing if not linked to collective purpose; that the effectiveness of leaders must be judged not by their press clippings but by actual social change measured by intent and by the satisfaction of human needs and expectations; that political leadership depends on a long chain of biological and social processes, of interaction with structures of political opportunity and closures, of interplay between the calls of moral principles and the recognized necessities of power; that in placing these concepts of political leadership centrally into a theory of historical causation, we will reaffirm the possibilities of human volition and of common standards of justice in the conduct of peoples' affairs.

I will deal with leadership as distinct from mere power-holding and as the opposite of brute power. I will identify two basic types of leadership: the *transactional* and the *transforming*. The relations of most leaders and followers are *transactional*—leaders approach followers with an eye to exchanging one thing for another: jobs for votes, or subsidies for campaign contributions. Such transactions comprise the bulk of the relationships among leaders and followers, especially in groups, legislatures, and parties. *Transforming* leadership, while more complex, is more potent. The transforming leader recognizes and exploits an existing need or demand of a potential follower. But, beyond that, the transforming leader looks for potential motives in followers, seeks to satisfy higher needs, and engages the full person of the follower. The result of transforming leadership is a relationship of mutual stimulation and elevation that converts followers into leaders and may convert leaders into moral agents.

This last concept, *moral leadership,* concerns me the most. By this term I mean, first, that leaders and led have a relationship not only of power but of mutual needs, aspirations, and values; second, that in responding to leaders, followers have adequate knowledge of alternative leaders and programs and the capacity to choose among those alternatives; and, third, that leaders take responsibility for their commitments—if they promise certain kinds of economic, social, and political change, they assume leadership in the bringing about of that change. Moral leadership is not mere preaching, or the uttering of pieties, or the insistence on social conformity. Moral leadership emerges from, and always returns to, the fundamental wants and needs, aspirations, and values of the followers. I mean the kind of leadership that can produce social change that will satisfy followers' authentic needs. I mean less the Ten Commandments than the Golden Rule. But even the Golden Rule is inadequate, for it measures the wants and needs of others simply by our own.

I propose, in short, to move from the usual "practical" questions to the most exacting theoretical and moral ones. Assuming that leaders are neither "born" nor "made," we will look for patterns in the origins and socializing of persons that account for leadership. Using concepts that emphasize the evolving structures of motivations, values, and goals, we will identify distinctive leadership roles and qualities. We will note the interwoven texture of leadership and followership and the vital and concentric rings of secondary, tertiary, and even "lower" leadership at most levels of society, recognizing nevertheless the role of "great leaders," who exercise large influences on the course of history. Searching always for the moral foundations of leadership, we will consider as truly legitimate only those acts of leaders that serve ultimately in some way to help release human potentials now locked in ungratified needs and crushed expectations.

Do skill and genius still matter? Can we distinguish *leaders* from mere power holders? Can we identify forces that enable leaders to act on the basis of common, non-culture-bound needs and values that, in turn, empower leaders to demonstrate genuine moral leadership? Can we deal with these questions across polities and across time? Can we, therefore, apply these concepts of political leadership to wider theories of social change and historical causation?

If we can do these things, we can hope to fashion a general theory of political leadership. And, when we return from moral and causal questions to ways of practical leadership, we might find that there is nothing more practical than sound theory, if we can fashion it.

PART I

LEADERSHIP: POWER AND PURPOSE

THE POWER OF LEADERSHIP

We search eagerly for leadership yet seek to cage and tame it. We recoil from power yet we are bewitched or titillated by it. We devour books on power—power in the office, power in the bedroom, power in the corridors. Connoisseurs of power purport to teach about it—what it is, how to get it, how to use it, how to "gain total control" over "everything around you." We think up new terms for power: clout, wallop, muscle. We measure the power of the aides of Great Men by the number of yards between their offices and that of Number One. If authority made the powerful "giddy, proud, and vain," as Samuel Butler wrote, today it entrances both the seekers of power and the powerless.

Why this preoccupation, this near-obsession, with power? In part because we in this century cannot escape the horror of it. Stalin controlled an apparatus that, year after year and in prison after prison, quietly put to death millions of persons, some of them old comrades and leading Bolsheviks, with hardly a ripple of protest from others. Between teatime and dinner Adolf Hitler could decide whether to release a holocaust of terror and death in an easterly or westerly direction, with stupendous impact on the fate of a continent and a world. On smaller planes of horror, American soldiers have slaughtered women and children cowering in ditches; village tyrants hold serfs and slaves in thrall; revolutionary leaders disperse whole populations into the countryside, where they dig or die; the daughter of Nehru jails her political adversaries—and is jailed in turn.

Then too, striking displays of power stick in our memories; the more subtle interplays between leaders and followers elude us. I have long been haunted by the tale of an encounter with Mtésa, king of Uganda, that John

Speke brought back from his early travels to the source of the Nile. The Englishman was first briefed on court decorum: while the king's subjects groveled before the throne, their faces plastered with dirt, Speke would be allowed to sit on a bundle of grass. Following an interlude of Wasoga minstrels playing on tambira, the visitor was summoned to the court, where women, cows, goats, porcupines, and rats were arrayed for presentation. The king showed an avid interest in the guns Speke had brought. He invited his guest to take potshots at the cows, and great applause broke out when Speke dropped five in a row. Speke reported further:

"The king now loaded one of the carbines I had given him with his own hands, and giving it full-cock to a page, told him to go out and shoot a man in the outer court, which was no sooner accomplished than the little urchin returned to announce his success with a look of glee such as one would see in the face of a boy who had robbed a bird's nest, caught a trout, or done any other boyish trick. The king said to him, 'And did you do it well?' 'Oh, yes, capitally.' " The affair created little interest in the court, Speke said, and no one inquired about the man who had been killed.

It is a story to make one pause. Mtésa was an absolute monarch, but could a man be randomly shot at the whim of the tyrant—indeed, of a boy? Did the victim have no mother or father, no protective brother, no lover, no comrade with whom he had played and hunted?

The case of the nurse of the children of Frederick William, king of Prussia, may be more instructive. Despising the mildly bohemian ways of his oldest son, the king heaped humiliation on him and flogged him in public. When the crown prince fled with a companion, the king had them arrested, falsely told his wife that their son had been executed, beat his children when they intervened in their brother's behalf, and dealt with the companion—the son and grandson of high-ranking generals—by setting aside a life imprisonment sentence imposed by a military court in favor of the death penalty. He forced his son to watch while his friend was beheaded. One of the few persons to stand up to the king was the nurse, who barred his way when he tried to drag his cowering children out from under the table, and she got away with it.

Sheer evil and brute power always seem more fascinating than complex human relationships. Sinners usually outsell saints, at least in Western cultures, and the ruthless exercise of power somehow seems more realistic, moral influence more naive. Above all, sheer massed power seems to have the most impact on history. Such, at least, is this century's bias. Perhaps I exemplify the problem of this distorted perception in my own intellectual development. Growing up in the aftermath of one world war, taking part in a second, studying the records of these and later wars, I have been struck by the sheer physical impact of men's armaments. Living in the age of political titans, I too have assumed that their actual power equaled their reputed power. As a political scientist I have belonged to a "power school" that analyzed the interrelationships of persons on the basis only of power. Perhaps this was fitting for an era of two world wars and scores of lesser ones, the murder of entire cities, bloody revolutions, the unleashing of the inhuman force of the atom.

I fear, however, that we are paying a steep intellectual and political price for our preoccupation with power. Viewing politics *as* power has blinded us to the role of power *in* politics and hence to the pivotal role of leadership. Our failure is partly empirical and psychological. Consider again the story of Mtésa and Speke. It is easy to suspend disbelief and swallow the story whole, enticing as it is. But did the English visitor actually know what happened in the outer court? Was the king staging an act for him? If a man did die, was he an already doomed culprit? If not, would Mtésa later pay a terrible price at the hands of his subjects? Or turn back to the brutality of Frederick William? Was his "absolute" power more important than the moral courage of the nurse who resisted him? So shocking are the acts of tyrants, so rarely reported the acts of defiance, that we forget that even the most despotic are continually frustrated by foot-dragging, quiet sabotage, communications failures, stupidity, even aside from moral resistance and sheer physical circumstance.

Our main hope for disenthralling ourselves from our overemphasis on power lies more in a theoretical, or at least conceptual, effort, than in an empirical one. It lies not only in recognizing that not all human influences are necessarily coercive and exploitative, that not all transactions among persons are mechanical, impersonal, ephemeral. It lies in seeing that the most powerful influences consist of deeply human relationships in which two or more persons *engage* with one another. It lies in a more realistic, a more sophisticated understanding of power, and of the often far more consequential exercise of mutual persuasion, exchange, elevation, and transformation—in short, of leadership. This is not to exorcise power from its pervasive influence in our daily lives; recognizing this kind of power is absolutely indispensable to understanding leadership. But we must recognize the limited reach of "total" or "coercive" power. We must see power—and leadership—as not things but as *relationships*. We must analyze power in a context of human motives and physical constraints. If we can come to grips with these aspects of power, we can hope to comprehend the true nature of leadership—a venture far more intellectually daunting than the study of naked power.

The Two Essentials of Power

We all have *power* to do acts we lack the *motive* to do—to buy a gun and slaughter people, to crush the feelings of loved ones who cannot defend themselves, to drive a car down a crowded city sidewalk, to torture an animal.

We all have the *motives* to do things we do not have the resources to do—to be President or senator, to buy a luxurious yacht, to give away millions to charity, to travel for months on end, to right injustices, to tell off the boss.

The two essentials of power are motive and resource. The two are interrelated. Lacking motive, resource diminishes; lacking resource, motive lies idle. Lacking either one, power collapses. Because both resource and motive are needed, and because both may be in short supply, power is an elusive and limited thing. Human beings, both the agents and the victims of power, for two thousand years or more have tried to penetrate its mysteries, but the nature of power remains elusive. Certainly no one has mastered the secrets of personal power as physicists have penetrated the atom. It is probably just as well.

To understand the nature of leadership requires understanding of the essence of power, for leadership is a special form of power. Forty years ago Bertrand Russell called power the fundamental concept in social science, "in the same sense in which Energy is a fundamental concept in physics." This is a compelling metaphor; it suggests that the source of power may lie in immense reserves of the wants and needs of the wielders and objects of power, just as the winds and the tides, oil and coal, the atom and the sun have been harnessed to supply physical energy. But it is still only a metaphor.

What is power? The "power of A over B," we are told, "is equal to maximum force which A can induce on B minus the maximum resisting force which B can mobilize in the opposite direction." One wonders about the As and the Bs, the Xs and the Ys, in the equations of power. Are they mere croquet balls, knocking other balls and being knocked, in some game of the gods? Or do these As and Xs and the others have wants and needs, ambitions and aspirations, of their own? And what if a ball does not obey a god, just as the children's nurse stood in the autocrat's way? Surely this formula is more physics than power. But the formula offers one vital clue to power: power is a *relationship* among persons.

Power, says Max Weber—he uses the term *Macht*—"is the probability that one actor within a social relationship will be in a position to carry out his own will despite resistance, regardless of the basis on which this probability rests." This formula helps the search for power, since it reminds us that there is no certain relationship between what P (power holder) does and how R (power recipient) responds. Those who have pressed a button and found no light turned on, or who have admonished a child with no palpable effect, welcome the factor of probability. But what controls the *degree* of probability? Motive? Intention? Power resources? Skill? Is P acting on his own, or is he the agent of some other power holder? And what if P orders R to do something to someone else—who then is the *real* power recipient? To answer such questions, P and R and all the other croquet players, mallets, and balls must be put into a broader universe of power relationships—that is, viewed as a *collective* act. Power and leadership become part of a system of social causation.

Essential in a concept of power is the role of *purpose*. This absolutely central value has been inadequately recognized in most theories of power. Power has been defined as the production of intended effects, but the crux of the matter lies in the dimensions of "intent." What is the nature (intensity, persistence, scope) of purpose? How is P's purpose communicated to R—and to what degree is that intent perceived by R as it is by P? Assuming an intent of P, to what extent is there a power relation if P's intent is influenced by P's prior knowledge and anticipation of R's intent? To what extent is intent part of a wider interaction among wants, needs, and values of P and R, before any overt behavior takes place? Few persons have a single intent; if P has more than one, are these intentions deemed equal, hierarchical, or unrelated? These relationships also define the exercise of power as a collective act.

A *psychological* conception of power will help us cut through some of these complexities and provide a basis for understanding the relation of power to leadership. This approach carries on the assumptions above: that power is first of all a *relationship* and not merely an entity to be passed around like a baton or hand grenade; that it involves the *intention* or *purpose* of both power holder and power recipient; and hence that it is *collective,* not merely the behavior of one person. On these assumptions I view the power process as one *in which power holders (P), possessing certain motives and goals, have the capacity to secure changes in the behavior of a respondent (R), human or animal, and in the environment, by utilizing resources in their power base, including factors of skill, relative to the targets of their power-wielding and necessary to secure such changes.* This view of power deals with three elements in the process: the motives and resources of power holders; the motives and resources of power recipients; and the relationship among all these.

The power holder may be the person whose "private motives are displaced onto public objects and rationalized in terms of public interest," to quote Harold Lasswell's classic formula. So accustomed are we to observing persons with power drives or complexes, so sensitive to leaders with the "will to power,'' so exposed to studies finding the source of the power urge in early deprivation, that we tend to assume the power motive to be exclusively that of seeking to dominate the behavior of others. "But must *all* experiences of power have as their ultimate goal the exercise of power over others?" David McClelland demands. He and other psychologists find that persons with high need for power (*''n* Power'') may derive that need for power not only from deprivation but from other experiences. One study indicated that young men watching a film of John F. Kennedy's Inaugural felt strengthened and inspirited by this exposure to an admired leader. Other persons may draw on internal resources as they grow older and learn to exert power against those who constrain them, like children who self-consciously recognize their exercise of power as they resist their mothers' directives. They find "sources of strength in the self to develop the self.''

These and other findings remind us that the power holder has a variety of motives besides that of wielding power over others. They help us correct the traditional picture of single-minded power wielders bent on exerting control over respondents. (Their main motive may be to institute power over *themselves*.) In fact power holders may have as varied motives—of wants, needs, expectations, etc.—as their targets. Some may pursue not power but status, recognition, prestige, and glory, or they may seek power as an intermediate value instrumental to realizing those loftier goals. Some psychologists consider the need to achieve (*''n* Achievement'') a powerful motive, especially in western cultures, and one whose results may be prized more as an *attainment* than as a means of social control. Some use power to collect possessions such as paintings, cars, or jewelry; they may collect wives or mistresses less to dominate them than to love or to display them. Others will use power to seek novelty and excitement. Still others may enjoy the exercise of power mainly because it enables them to exhibit—if only to themselves—their skill and knowledge, their ability to stimulate their own capacities and to master their environment. Those skilled in athletics may enjoy riding horseback or skiing as solitary pastimes, with no one but themselves to admire their skills. The motivational base of this kind of competence has been labeled "effectance" by Robert White.

Still, there *are* the single-minded power wielders who fit the classical images of Machiavelli or Hobbes or Nietzsche, or at least the portraits of the modern power theorists. They consciously exploit their external resources (economic, social, psychological, and institutional) and their "effectance," their training, skill, and competence, to make persons and things do what they want done. The key factor here is indeed "what they want done." The motives of power wielders may or may not coincide with what the respondent wants done;

it is P's intention that controls. Power wielders may or may not recognize respondents' wants and needs; if they do, they may recognize them only to the degree necessary to achieve their goals; and if they must make a choice between satisfying their own purposes and satisfying respondents' needs, they will choose the former. Power wielders are not free agents. They are subject— even slaves—to pressures working on them and in them. But once their will and purpose is forged, it may be controlling. If P wants circuses and R wants bread, the power wielder may manipulate popular demand for bread only to the degree that it helps P achieve circuses. At the "naked power" extremity on the continuum of types of power holders are the practitioners of virtually unbridled power—Hitler, Stalin, and the like—subject always, of course, to empowering and constraining circumstances.

The foundation of this kind of control lies in P's "power base" *as it is relevant to those at the receiving end of power*. The composition of the power base will vary from culture to culture, from situation to situation. Some power holders will have such pervasive control over factors influencing behavior that the imbalance between P's and R's power bases, and between the possibility of realizing P's and R's purposes, will be overwhelming. Nazi death camps and communist "re-education" camps are examples of such overwhelming imbalances. A dictator can put respondents physically in such isolation and under such constraint that they cannot even appeal to the dictator's conscience, if he has one, or to sympathetic opinion outside the camp or outside the country, if such exists. More typical, in most cultures, is the less asymmetric relationship in which P's power base supplies P with extensive control over R but leaves R with various resources for resisting. Prisons, armies, authoritarian families, concentration camps such as the United States relocation centers for Japanese-Americans during World War II, exemplify this kind of imbalance. There is a multitude of power balances in villages, tribes, schools, homes, collectives, businesses, trade unions, cities, in which most persons spend most of their lives.

To define power not as a property or entity or possession but as a *relationship* in which two or more persons tap motivational bases in one another and bring varying resources to bear in the process is to perceive power as drawing a vast range of human behavior into its orbit. The arena of power is no longer the exclusive preserve of a power elite or an establishment or persons clothed with legitimacy. Power is ubiquitous; it permeates human relationships. It exists whether or not it is quested for. It is the glory and the burden of most of humanity. A common, highly asymmetric, and sometimes cruel power relation can exist, for example, when one person is in love with another but the other does not reciprocate. The wants and needs and expectations of the person in love are aroused and engaged by a partner whose resources of attractiveness or desirability are high and whose own cluster of motives is less vulnerable. The person possessed by love can maneuver and struggle but still is a slave to the one loved, as the plight of Philip in Somerset Maugham's marvelously titled *Of Human Bondage* illustrates.

Because power can take such multifarious, ubiquitous, and subtle forms, it is reflected in an infinite number of combinations and particularities in specific contexts. Even so, observers *in* those contexts may perceive their particular "power mix" as the basic and universal type, and they will base elaborate descriptions and theories of power on one model—their own. Even Machiavelli's celebrated portrait of the uses and abuses of power, while relevant to a few other cultures and eras, is essentially culture-bound and irrelevant to a host of other power situations and systems. Thus popular tracts on power—how to win power and influence people—typically are useful only for particular situations and may disable the student of power coping with quite different power constellations.

Still there are ways of breaking power down into certain attributes that allow for some generalization and even theory-building. Robert Dahl's breakdown of the reach and magnitude of power is useful and parsimonious. One dimension is *distribution*—the concentration and dispersion of power among persons of diverse influence in various political, social, and economic locations such as geographical areas, castes and classes, status positions, skill groups, communications centers, and the like. Another dimension is *scope*—the extent to which power is generalized over a wide range or is specialized. Persons who are relatively powerful in relation to one kind of activity, Dahl notes, may be relatively weak in other power relationships. Still another dimension is *domain*—the number and nature of power respondents influenced by power wielders compared to those who are not. These dimensions are not greatly different from Lasswell and Abraham Kaplan's conception of the weight, scope, and domain of power.

A more common way to organize the data of power is in terms of the *size* of the *arena* in which power is exercised. The relation of P and R is, in many studies, typically one of micropower, as Edward Lehman calls it. Most power relations embrace a multiplicity of power holders; the relation is one among many Ps and many Rs. As power holders and respondents multiply, the number of relationships increases geometrically. Macropower, as Lehman contends, has distinct attributes of its own; the complex relations involved in the aggregate are not simply those of micropower extended to a higher plane. Causal interrelations become vastly more complex as a greater number of power actors and power components comes into play. Paradoxically, we may, with modern techniques of fact-gathering and of empirical analysis, gain a better understanding of mass phenomena of power and leadership than of the more intricate and elusive interactions in micropower situations.

Whatever the dimensions or context, the fundamental process remains the same. *Power wielders draw from their power bases resources relevant to their own motives and the motives and resources of others upon whom they exercise power.* The power base may be narrow and weak, or it may consist of ample and multiple resources useful for vast and long-term exercises of power, but the process is the same. Dominated by personal motives, P draws on supporters, on funds, on ideology, on institutions, on old friendships, on political credits, on status, and on his own skills of calculation, judgment, communication, timing, to mobilize those elements that relate to the motives of the persons P wishes to control—even if in the end P overrides their values and goals—just as P mobilizes machines and fuel and manpower and engineering expertise relevant to the tasks of building dams or clearing forests.

Power shows many faces and takes many forms. It may be as visible as the policeman's badge or billy or as veiled as the politician's whisper in the back room. It may exist as an overwhelming presence or as a potential that can be drawn on at will. It may appear in the form of money, sex appeal, authority, administrative regulation, charisma, munitions, staff resources, instruments for torture. But all these resources must have this in common: *they must be relevant to the motivations of the power recipients.* Even the most fearsome of power devices, such as imprisonment or torture or denial of food or water, may not affect the behavior of a masochist or a martyr.

The exception to this qualification is the appalling power totally to dominate a power object physically or mentally through slavery, imprisonment, deportation, hypnotism. This kind of power has two significant implications. One is the expenditure of effort and resources by P to exercise this kind of control; unless power has been inherited, P has invested, over a period of time and through many power-related acts, in power resources that permit exertion of "total" power. The other is the constraint that may tighten when P exercises total psychological or physical control; P may gain power over a limited number of persons or goods at the expense of antagonizing other persons —perhaps millions of them—by threatening and attacking their values. Power can be fully analyzed and measured only by viewing it in the context of multiple human interaction and broad causal relationships.

Leadership and Followership

Leadership is an aspect of power, but it is also a separate and vital process in itself.

Power over other persons, we have noted, is exercised when potential power wielders, motivated to achieve certain goals of their own, marshal in their power base resources (economic, military, institutional, or skill) that enable them to influence the behavior of respondents by activating motives of respondents relevant to those resources and to those goals. This is done in order to realize the purposes of the *power wielders, whether or not these are also the goals of the respondents*. Power wielders also exercise influence by mobilizing their own power base in such a way as to establish direct physical control over others' behavior, as in a war of conquest or through measures of harsh deprivation, but these are highly restricted exercises of power, dependent on certain times, cultures, and personalities, and they are often self-destructive and transitory.

Leadership over human beings is exercised when persons with certain motives and purposes mobilize, in competition or conflict with others, institutional, political, psychological, and other resources so as to arouse, engage, and satisfy the motives of followers. This is done in order to realize goals mutually held by *both* leaders and followers, as in Lenin's calls for peace, bread, and land. In brief, leaders with motive and power bases tap followers' motives in order to realize the purposes of both leaders and followers. Not only must motivation be relevant, as in power generally, but its purposes must be realized and satisfied. Leadership is exercised in a condition of *conflict* or *competition* in which leaders contend in appealing to the motive bases of potential followers. Naked power, on the other hand, admits of no competition or conflict—there is no engagement.

Leaders are a particular kind of power holder. Like power, leadership is relational, collective, and purposeful. Leadership shares with power the central function of achieving purpose. But the reach and domain of leadership are, in the short range at least, more limited than those of power. Leaders do not obliterate followers' motives though they may arouse certain motives and ignore others. They lead other creatures, not things (and lead animals only to the degree that they recognize animal motives—i.e., leading cattle to shelter rather than to slaughter). To control *things*—tools, mineral resources, money, energy—is an act of power, not leadership, for things have no motives. Power wielders may treat people as things. Leaders may not.

All leaders are actual or potential power holders, but not all power holders are leaders.

These definitions of power and of leadership differ from those that others have offered. Lasswell and Kaplan hold that power must be relevant to people's valued things; I hold that it must be relevant to the *power wielder's* valued things and may be relevant to the *recipient's* needs or values only as necessary to exploit them. Kenneth Janda defines power as "the ability to cause other persons to adjust their behavior in conformance with communicated behavior patterns." I agree, assuming that those behavior patterns aid the purpose of the power wielder. According to Andrew McFarland, "If the leader causes changes that he intended, he has exercised power; if the leader causes changes that he did not intend or want, he has exercised influence, but not power. . . ." I dispense with the concept of influence as unnecessary and unparsimonious. For me the leader is a very special, very circumscribed, but potentially the most effective of power holders, judged by the degree of intended "real change" finally achieved. Roderick Bell et al. contend that power is a relationship rather than an entity—an entity being something that "could be smelled and touched, or stored in a keg"; while I agree that power is a relationship, I contend that the relationship is one in which some entity—part of the "power base"—plays an indispensable part, whether that keg is a keg of beer, of dynamite, or of ink.

The crucial variable, again, is *purpose.* Some define leadership as leaders making followers do what *followers* would not otherwise do, or as leaders making followers do what the *leaders* want them to do; I define leadership as leaders inducing followers to act for certain goals that represent the values and the motivations—the wants and needs, the aspirations and expectations—*of both leaders and followers.* And the genius of leadership lies in the manner in which leaders see and act on their own and their followers' values and motivations.

Leadership, unlike naked power-wielding, is thus inseparable from followers' needs and goals. The essence of the leader-follower relation is the interaction of persons with different levels of motivations and of power potential, including skill, in pursuit of a common or at least joint purpose. That interaction, however, takes two fundamentally different forms. The first I will call *transactional* leadership (the nature of which will be developed in Part III). Such leadership occurs when one person takes the initiative in making contact with others for the purpose of an exchange of valued things. The exchange could be economic or political or psychological in nature: a swap of goods or of one good for money; a trading of votes between candidate and citizen or between legislators; hospitality to another person in exchange for willingness to listen to one's troubles. Each party to the bargain is conscious of the power resources and attitudes of the other. Each person recognizes the other as a *person.* Their purposes are related, at least to the extent that the purposes stand within the bargaining process and can be advanced by maintaining that process. But beyond this the relationship does not go. The bargainers have no enduring purpose that holds them together; hence they may go their separate ways. A leadership act took place, but it was not one that binds leader and follower together in a mutual and continuing pursuit of a higher purpose.

Contrast this with *transforming* leadership. Such leadership occurs when one or more persons *engage* with others in such a way that leaders and followers raise one another to higher levels of motivation and morality. (The nature of this motivation and this morality will be developed in Part II.) Their purposes, which might have started out as separate but related, as in the case of transactional leadership, become fused. Power bases are linked not as counterweights but as mutual support for common purpose. Various names are used for such leadership, some of them derisory: elevating, mobilizing, inspiring, exalting, uplifting, preaching, exhorting, evangelizing. The relationship can be moralistic, of course. But transforming leadership ultimately becomes *moral* in that it raises the level of human conduct and ethical aspiration of both leader and led, and thus it has a transforming effect on both. Perhaps the best modern example is Gandhi, who aroused and elevated the hopes and demands of millions of Indians and whose life and personality were enhanced in the process. Transcending leadership is dynamic leadership in the sense that the leaders throw themselves into a relationship with followers who will feel "elevated" by it and often become more active themselves, thereby creating new cadres of leaders. Transcending leadership is leadership *engagé*. Naked power-wielding can be neither transactional nor transforming; only leadership can be.

Leaders and followers may be inseparable in function, but they are not the same. The leader takes the initiative in making the leader-led connection; it is the leader who creates the links that allow communication and exchange to take place. An office seeker does this in accosting a voter on the street, but if the voter espies and accosts the politician, the voter is assuming a leadership function, at least for that brief moment. The leader is more skillful in evaluating followers' motives, anticipating their responses to an initiative, and estimating their power bases, than the reverse. Leaders continue to take the major part in maintaining and effectuating the relationship with followers and will have the major role in ultimately carrying out the combined purpose of leaders and followers. Finally, and most important by far, leaders address themselves to followers' wants, needs, and other motivations, as well as to their own, and thus they serve as an *independent force in changing the makeup of the followers' motive base through gratifying their motives.*

Certain forms of power and certain forms of leadership are near-extremes on the power continuum. One is the kind of absolute power that, Lord Acton felt, "corrupts absolutely." It also coerces absolutely. The essence of this kind of power is the capacity of power wielders, given the necessary motivation, to override the motive and power bases of their targets. Such power objectifies its victims; it literally turns them into objects, like the inadvertent weapon tester in Mtésa's court. Such power wielders, as well, are objectified and dehumanized. Hitler, according to Richard Hughes, saw the universe as containing no persons other than himself, only "things." The ordinary citizen in Russia, says a Soviet linguist and dissident, does not identify with his government. "With us, it is there, like the wind, like a wall, like the sky. It is something permanent, unchangeable. So the individual acquiesces, does not dream of changing it— except a few, few people. . . ."

At the other extreme is leadership so sensitive to the motives of potential followers that the roles of leader and follower become virtually interdependent. Whether the leadership relationship is transactional or transforming, in it motives, values, and goals of leader and led have merged. It may appear that at the other extreme from the raw power relationship, dramatized in works like Arthur Koestler's *Darkness at Noon* and George Orwell's *1984,* is the extreme of leadership-led merger dramatized in novels about persons utterly dependent on parents, wives, or lovers. Analytically these extreme types of relationships are not very perplexing. To watch one person absolutely dominate another is horrifying; to watch one person disappear, his motives and values submerged into those of another to the point of loss of individuality, is saddening. But puzzling out the nature of these extreme relationships is not intellectually challenging because each in its own way lacks the qualities of complexity and conflict. Submersion of one personality in another is not genuine merger based on mutual respect. Such submersion is an example of brute power subtly applied, perhaps with the acquiescence of the victim.

More complex are relationships that lie between these poles of brute power and wholly reciprocal leadership-followership. Here empirical and theoretical questions still perplex both the analysts and the practitioners of power. One of these concerns the sheer measurement of power (or leadership). Traditionally we measure power resources by calculating each one and adding them up: constituency support plus access to leadership plus financial resources plus skill plus "popularity" plus access to information, etc., all in relation to the strength of opposing forces, similarly computed. But these calculations omit the vital factor of motivation and purpose and hence fall of their own weight. Another controversial measurement device is *reputation.* Researchers seek to learn from informed observers their estimates of the power or leadership role and resources of visible *community* leaders (projecting this into national arenas of power is a formidable task). Major questions arise as to the reliability of the estimates, the degree of agreement between interviewer and interviewee over their definition of power and leadership, the transferability of power from one area of decision-making to another. Another device for studying power and leadership is *linkage theory,* which requires elaborate mapping of communication and other in-terrelations among power holders in different spheres, such as the economic and the military. The difficulty here is that communication, which may ex-pedite the processes of power and leadership, is not a substitute for them.

My own measurement of power and leadership is simpler in concept but no less demanding of analysis: *power and leadership are measured by the degree of production of intended effects.* This need not be a theoretical exer-cise. Indeed, in ordinary political life, the power resources and the motivations of presidents and prime ministers and political parties are measured by the ex-tent to which presidential promises and party programs are carried out. Note that the variables are the double ones of *intent* (a function of motivation) and of *capacity* (a function of power base), but the test of the extent and quality of power and leadership is the degree of *actual accomplishment* of the promised change.

Other complexities in the study of power and leadership are equally serious. One is the extent to which power and leadership are exercised not by positive action but by *inaction* or *nondecision.* Another is that power and lead-ership are often exercised not directly on targets but indirectly, and perhaps through multiple channels, on multiple targets. We must ask not only whether P has the power to do X to R, but whether P can induce or force R to do Y to Z. The existence of power and leadership in the form of a stream of multiple direct and indirect forces operating over time must be seen as part of the broader sequences of historical causation. Finally, we must acknowledge the knotty problem of events of history that are beyond the control of identifiable persons capable of foreseeing developments and powerful enough to influence them and hence to be held accountable for them. We can only agree with C. Wright Mills that these are matters of fate rather than power or leadership.

We do well to approach these and other complexities of power and leader-ship with some humility as well as a measure of boldness. We can reject the "gee whiz" approach to power that often takes the form of the automatic presumption of "elite control" of communities, groups, institutions, entire na-tions. Certain concepts and techniques of the "elitist" school of power are in-dispensable in social and political analysis, but "elitism" is often used as a concept that *presupposes* the existence of the very degree and kind of power that is to be estimated and analyzed. Such "elite theorists" commit the gross error of equating power and leadership with the assumed power bases of pre-conceived leaders and power holders, without considering the crucial role of *motivations* of leaders and followers. Every good detective knows that one must look for the motive as well as the weapon.

What Leadership Is Not: Closing the Intellectual Gap

It may seem puzzling that after centuries of experience with rulers as power wielders, with royal and ecclesiastical and military authority, humankind should have made such limited progress in developing propositions about *leadership*—propositions that focus on the role of the ruled, the power recipients, and the followers. The first, and primary, explanation lies in a blind alley in the history of political thought; a second, in an inadequacy of empirical data. Plato's parable of the ship epitomizes the first.

"Imagine then," said Plato, "a fleet or a ship in which there is a captain who is taller and stronger than any of the crew, but he is a little deaf and has a similar infirmity in sight, and his knowledge of navigation is not much better." A furious quarrel breaks out among the crew; everyone thinks he has a right to steer, no matter how untrained in navigation. The sailors throng around the captain, begging him to commit the helm to them; when he refuses, they take over the ship and make free with the stores. "Him who is their partisan and cleverly aids them in their plot . . . they compliment with the name of sailor, pilot, able seaman . . . but that the true pilot must pay attention to the year and seasons and sky and wind . . . and that he must and will be the steerer, whether other people like it or not—the possibility of this union of authority with the steerer's art has never seriously entered into their thoughts. . . ." And the true pilot, Plato added, would be dismissed as a prater, a stargazer, a good-for-nothing.

Plato was apotheosizing a certain kind of authority—that of the true philosopher, artist, expert. Yet in derogating the sailors who would dismiss the navigator he was defending the status of philosopher-kings and of those in their courts. He was also ignoring the rightful concerns of the crew—their suspicion of experts, their difficulties with *this* expert, their doubts about *his* destination for the ship, their own needs and aspirations and destinations. For centuries after Plato his kind of expert embodied authority, but scientific revolutions later brought much learned authority under attack. It was discovered that captains and navigators pretended to an intellectual authority that often turned out to be false. Doctors and scientists and theologians are still treated as "authority" though their expertise may be challenged, their doctrines overturned, and the purposes to which they lend their expertise may be found to diverge from the public's own purposes.

For philosophers and kings, however, authority came to stand for much more than expertise. It was the intellectual and often the legal buttress of the power of the father in the family, the priest in the community, the feudal lord in the barony, the king in the nation-state, the Pope in Western Christendom. Authority was seen as deriving from God or, later, from the innate nature of man. Authority was even more fundamental than the state for it was the source and the legitimation of state power. In the tumultuous Western world the power of authority was the means of preserving order; it was necessary in an "unquiet world," Hooker said. It would compel men to regulate their conduct, Hobbes wrote. Church and state combined to furbish authority. It carried formal legitimacy, religious sanction, and physical force.

Typically authority was perceived and used as a *property*. Rulers were symbolically invested with authority through things—crowns, scepters, maces, scrolls, robes, badges. Such rulers were objects of awe for their subjects, until rivals seized the armaments of office or substituted their own. To the extent that authority was a *relationship* between monarch and subjects it was a relationship of gross inequality, of the ruler and the ruled. But authority was sharply distinguished from naked power, force, coercion. Rulers must be *legitimate*. They must inherit or assume office through carefully established procedures; they must assume certain responsibilities under God, and for the people.

Authority, in short, was legitimated power. But it was legitimated by tradition, religious sanction, rights of succession, and procedures, not by mandate of the people. Authority was quite one-sided. Rulers had the right to command, subjects the obligation to obey. Only a few complained. The fundamental need of the people was for order and security; obedience seemed a fair exchange for survival. In the seventeenth and eighteenth centuries, however, the concept of authority was undermined. Thinkers and preachers, riding new intellectual currents of innovation and iconoclasm, rebelled against the old canons of authority that were founded so often in the past, the dead, or the patriarchs. Spreading through Europe and America, powerful new doctrines proclaimed the rights of individuals against rulers, set forth goals and values beyond those of simple order or security, and called for liberty, equality, fraternity, even the pursuit of happiness.

Authority did not crumble under the impact of these forces; revolutionary disturbances and excesses like the French terror confirmed its importance. But it could not be re-established on the old foundations, for now it was supposed to be derived from the people and hence ultimately lie in their hands—at least in the hands of those people who were not poor, slaves, or women. A new secular basis of authority was needed. In response, the old "substantive" authority gave way to procedural. Since the citizenry now embodied authority, since the people had to be protected against themselves, and since authority had to be protected against shifting majorities and volatile popular movements, constitutions were adopted to safeguard the people against themselves. Under the constitutions, authority was concentrated in judges, legislative upper chambers, local governments, in doctrines of due process, protection of property, and in judicial review.

The upshot was this: the doctrine of authority came into the modern age devitalized, fragmentized, and trivialized; it became a captive of the right, even of fascism. Mussolini substituted authority, order, and justice for liberty, equality, fraternity. Hannah Arendt in this century could mourn that the entire concept of leadership had lost its validity; almost everyone could agree that the concept had been emptied of meaning and definition. The loss was not simply of a stricken concept—doctrines, like empires, grow, flourish, and decline—but of authority that was not transformed into a doctrine suitable for the new age. No new, democratized, and radicalized doctrine arose to salvage the authentic and the relevant in authority and link these strengths to a doctrine of leadership that recognized the vital need for qualities of integrity, authenticity, initiative, and moral resolve. Max Weber, Carl Friedrich, and others tried to pump new vitality and relevance into the concept, without marked success; Vilfredo Pareto's famous concept of the "circulation of the elites" focused chiefly on the problem of bringing fresh talent or expertise to the top. They, like the shapers of the grand tradition in earlier centuries, typically looked at the ruler-ruled relationship from the top down, not upward from the peasant's sward or the worker's bench. In the end, in a more democratic age, authority was never turned on its head.

The resulting intellectual gap—that is, the absence of a doctrine of leadership with the power and sweep of the old doctrine of authority but now emphasizing the influence of followers on leaders—was especially evident in America. The pilgrims' voyage to Plymouth in 1620 has been contrasted with Plato's parable of the ship most arrestingly by Norman Jacobson. The goal of the settlers was Virginia but they lost their way. Facing rebellion, and with their authority undermined, the leaders had to grant the demands of the rest of the party for a compact among all the members. Under this declaration no person or group was empowered to assume authority, nor was any one person seen as commanding special expertise. The compact idea was restated in the Declaration of Independence. By the time of the constitutional convention of 1787, however, in the wake of Shays' rebellion in Massachusetts, the Federalist leadership had become fearful of popular unrest and of electoral majorities that represented the turbulent masses. Under the new constitution, authority was derived from the people, but direct popular action was frustrated by an elaborate system of federalism, separation of powers, and checks and balances.

What would happen in a nation that made the people sovereign, that elevated Jeffersonian and Jacksonian and Lincolnian leaders who orated about government by the people, but a nation that hedged in popular majorities *and their leaders* with checks and balances that constituted probably the most elaborate and well-calculated barriers in constitutional history? As usual, the Americans tried to have the best of both ways. They maintained their system of restraints on leaders almost intact, but they encouraged the emergence of a powerful executive, especially in the twentieth century. American Marxists contended that not leaders but technicians—simple administrative functionaries, in Engels' words, "watching over the true interests of society"—would run the state. American Progressives looked on leadership as "bossism" and sponsored successfully such anti-leadership devices as the initiative, referendum and recall, and the destruction of parties. The failure was also intellectual. Historians and political scientists admired individual leaders, especially Presidents, who could break through legislative and judicial barriers. Some of them—notably Woodrow Wilson—moralized about the need for leaders in education and politics. No one advanced a grand theory of *leadership*.

Perhaps such a theory was impossible in any event, in the absence of hard and detailed data about the people, the public, the masses, the voters, the followers. Earlier thinkers had by no means ignored the psychology of the ruler's subjects. Hobbes and Locke, Rousseau and Bentham, and others, had offered some remarkable insights into human nature. These insights were based on observation and speculation, not on scientific data. In recent decades advances in theories of opinion formation, the revolution in the technique and technology of analyzing public attitudes, aspirations and goals in depth, and above all the impressive work of psychologists in analyzing the formation, structure, qualities, and change in persons' opinions, attitudes, values, wants, needs, and aspirations, have made possible an understanding of followers' response to leadership impossible only half a century ago. Cross-cultural research and analysis in popular motives and values at last permits us to avoid parochial notions of authority and power and to identify broad patterns of leadership-followership interaction as part of a broader concept of social causation. At last we can hope to close the intellectual gap between the fecund canons of authority and a new and general theory of leadership.

Such a general theory demands the best of several disciplines. Historians and biographers typically focus on the "unique" person with more or less idiosyncratic qualities and traits confronting particular sets of problems and situations over time. Psychologists scrutinize genetic factors, early intrafamily relationships, widening arcs of personal interaction, changing constellations of attitudes and motivations. Sociologists view the developing personality as it moves through a series of social contexts—family, school, neighborhood, workplace—and undergoes powerful socializing forces in the process. Political scientists emphasize the social and political institutions impinging on developing leaders, changes in political leaders as they learn from their experience, the eventual impact of leadership on policy and on history. And most of these various investigators wander into one another's fields, pouncing on insights, borrowing data, filching concepts.

We, too, will poach as required, but the initial emphasis will be heavily dependent on theories of personality development. As a political scientist I am sensitive to the impact of social and political entities—of homes, schools, regimens, constitutions, and political systems. I see that leaders operate in many contexts for many purposes. Why then is my central emphasis on "psychology"? The principal limitation of institutional or systemic analysis is that the kind of transferability of power or leadership that we can assess in gross terms (the influence of Indian Brahmins, the electoral power of a steel union, the discipline of the British Labour party) is not directly transferable to the calculating of influences on, or the influence of, particular leaders at particular times in particular circumstances. The power of the institution must be translated into discernible forces that immediately influence the behavior of leaders. In the past the exercise has often been fruitless because we lacked deep understanding of motivational forces. Modern developmental theory and data can help us to grasp the psychological forces immediately working on or in leaders and the dynamic psychological factors moving persons to new levels of motivation and morality.

The study of leadership in general will be advanced by looking at leaders in particular. The development of certain leaders or rulers is described not in order to "solve" leadership problems or necessarily to predict what kind of leader a person might become, but to raise questions inherent in the complexity of leadership processes. In singling out, among others, four twentieth-century "makers of history," Woodrow Wilson, Mahatma Gandhi, Nikolai Lenin, and Adolf Hitler—the first two of these leaders in my sense, the third a leader whose theory of leadership had a fatal flaw, the fourth an absolute wielder of brutal power—we can compare the origins and development of four men who took different routes to power and exercised power in different ways. We will note in these cases and others that authoritarian rulers can emerge from relatively benign circumstances, and democratic leaders from less benign ones. This will only enhance our sense of humility, complexity, and mystery (useful intellectual inhibitions in the explorations of leadership).

We might also note, in shunning simplistic theories, that the German crown prince who was endlessly mortified and savagely punished by his wrathful father grew up to be Frederick the Great, one of the most masterful—by contemporary standards—constructive and successful rulers in recent times. He who had been abused by power bore it with equanimity. "The passions of princes," Frederick wrote toward the end, "are restrained only by exhaustion."

2

THE STRUCTURE
OF MORAL LEADERSHIP

"We have many wants," Plato said, and society and government arose out of these needs as people began to exchange things that they made. Necessity is the mother of invention, Plato went on. "Now the first and greatest necessity is food, which is the condition of life and existence. . . . The second is a dwelling, and the third clothing and the like. . . ." Once a family had these things, then "noble cakes and loaves" would be served up on a mat of reeds or clean leaves, the parents "reclining the while upon beds strewn with yew or myrtle. And they and their children will feast, drinking of the wine which they have made, wearing garlands on their heads, and hymning the praises of the gods, in happy converse with one another. . . ."

With these words Plato posed a question that has challenged philosophers and scientists to this day: whether people the world over share common wants and needs. As some wants are satisfied are other—"higher"—wants created? Are wants and needs arranged in roughly the same hierarchies in most or all cultures? Common sense tells us that any person, whether Eskimo or Hottentot, Zuni or Kpelle, Brooklynite or East End Londoner, puts first things first—breathing before eating, human life above property, basic nourishment before the "sauces and sweets" that Plato proposed as the climax of the meal. The same would seem to be true of "higher needs"—for survival needs before social acceptance, and social needs—love and esteem—before aesthetic. Yet anthropologists have identified countless cultures with the most remarkable varieties of wants and needs. Consider the assumed top priority of sheer survival. Some societies kill their infants to protect their food reserves. In others, men kill themselves (Wall Street, 1929) when they lose their property. In India women burned themselves on funeral pyres when they lost their husbands.

29

For students of leadership an even more urgent question arises. Supposing we could find species-wide commonalities among hierarchies of wants and needs, could we also find common stages and levels of moral development and reasoning emerging out of those wants and needs? If so, we could assume common foundations for leadership. If we define leadership as not merely a property or activity of leaders but as *relationship* between leaders and a multitude of followers of many types, if we see leaders as interacting with followers in a great merging of motivations and purposes of both, and if in turn we find that many of those motivations and purposes are common to vast numbers of humankind in many cultures, then could we expect to identify patterns of leadership behavior permitting plausible generalizations about the ways in which leaders generally behave?

During the last decade or so, researches in the field of moral development have uncovered remarkable uniformities in hierarchies of moral reasoning across a number of cultures. The research is far from complete; certain cultural relativists hold that the findings and implications are overgeneralized; and it is alleged that the values considered to be universal have in fact a Western bias. But, as Harry Girvetz has said: "In rejecting moral dogmatism are we to be driven to moral skepticism?" Identification of leadership patterns does not depend on finding absolutely universal motives and values. Universal patterns simply assume strong probabilities that most leaders in interacting with followers will behave in similar ways most of the time. In dealing with the structure of moral leadership in this chapter, we will be summarizing more extensive findings to be presented more fully in the next chapter. Here we must note how levels of wants and needs and other motivations, combined with hierarchies of values, and sharpened by conflict, undergird the dynamics of leadership.

> *Erst kommt das Fressen, dann Kommt die Moral.*
> First comes the belly, then morality.
>
> Bertolt Brecht, Three-Penny Opera

The Power and Sources of Values

Like Plato, we can see the role of power and values in every-day life.

A thousand years ago, according to Soviet Armenian legend, Moslem invaders tried to find a way to lower the water level of Lake Sevan. Their aim was to make a land attack on an island fortress and monastery in the lake, located halfway between the Black Sea and the lower Caspian. In the 1930s Soviet engineers accomplished this feat not for military but for economic purposes; by tapping the lake's waters they were able to create new farmland and to generate electric power for local industrial development. They succeeded, but the lowered water level caused extensive ecological and aesthetic damage. Forty years later Soviet construction crews were digging a huge, thirty-mile tunnel from a nearby river to replenish the lake.

"When we were poor," a local water power official observed, "Lake Sevan helped us to stand on our feet. But when we became richer, we began to think how we had to help Sevan, this beauty of nature."

In New York City not long ago a construction crew, chain saws in hand, suddenly appeared on East 63rd Street and fell upon a dozen or so spreading sycamores. The tearing, growling noise of the saws brought residents to their windows. One woman hurled a plastic bag filled with water at a foreman; another woman burst into tears as she watched. She was not propitiated by the setting up of some potted trees where the sycamores had stood.

"They were beautiful old trees, so old, so fresh," she said later, "you looked up at them and regardless of your depression, you simply thought, oh isn't that lovely."

"I'll tell you, to be very honest, I was mad," the foreman said. "We're poor people, but we're human beings." Pointing to the replacement trees, he added: "You see what the poor people do for the rich people."

"I must study politics and war, that my sons may have liberty to study mathematics and philosophy," John Adams said. "My sons ought to study mathematics and philosophy, geography, natural history and naval architecture, in order to give their children a right to study painting, poetry, music, architecture, statuary, tapestry and porcelain." A Thai boy scout, recruited to combat "communism," bespoke the value he was scheduled to embrace. "Once we get trained, we are united. So it is very difficult for other types of ideas to come in. We stress love of our king, of our country, of religion." Oh, there was no ideology, he added; they did not mention Communism, "but it works automatically."

We must not put groups or societies into conceptual straitjackets. Sometimes the people seem to "skip" a level and advance to a higher one apparently inappropriate to present need. In the 1976 electoral revolt against Indira Gandhi and the Congress party, India voted against suppressors of liberty despite the emphasis of the Congress party on basic needs for food, shelter, and land. Ordinarily, however, economic want and social disarray are stultifying, causing people's aspirations to turn downward and inward; only after physical survival and economic security are assured do people turn to higher needs and hopes.

The long relationship between Franklin D. Roosevelt and Joseph P. Kennedy illustrates the complex interplay of power and values, and suggests that ultimately the role of values may be crucial, even in the "practical" relationships of leaders. Both were Harvard men, but otherwise their backgrounds contrasted sharply: Roosevelt the product of a benign, secure and small patrician world on the banks of the Hudson, Kennedy of the striving, competitive, vulnerable world of the Irish immigrant on the urban East Coast. The two men were thrown into a personal confrontation in World War I when Roosevelt, the assistant secretary of the navy, asked Kennedy, assistant manager of the Fore River shipyard in Massachusetts, to deliver several battleships Fore River had built for the Argentine government. Kennedy refused to release the ships because the Argentinians had not yet paid the bill. After appealing in vain to Kennedy's sense of patriotism in wartime, Roosevelt threatened to have the navy tow the ships away. Kennedy left fuming and defeated; he was so upset on leaving Roosevelt's office, he admitted later, that "I broke down and cried."

More than two decades later, during another great European war, Kennedy and Roosevelt confronted each other once again, under a very different set of circumstances. Having joined the Roosevelt bandwagon well before the Chicago convention of 1932, Kennedy had headed the Securities and Exchange Commission and the Maritime Commission and then eagerly accepted an appointment by Roosevelt as ambassador to Britain. But as Europe plunged into war, disquieting reports trickled into Washington about the ambassador's "defeatist" view of Britain's ability to withstand Nazi attack and about his veiled but pungent criticism of Roosevelt and his administration. As the 1940 presidential campaign got under way, Kennedy seemed to hold a pivotal political position. To fight off a hard drive by Wendell Willkie, Roosevelt was picking out a tortuous path between the interventionists and the America Firsters. A resignation by such a prominent Roosevelt ambassador as Kennedy and a return home to join Willkie's "crusade"—or even a Kennedy warning against the administration's "interventionism"—might have tipped the scales in favor of the Republicans. Kennedy's conspicuous Catholicism gave him considerable leverage with the Irish and other ethnic voters who might be pivotal in some of the Northeastern states. He could help the President a lot—or hurt him a lot.

The problem for the President was to persuade Kennedy either to remain in London or to declare for Roosevelt with the right kind of endorsement. First Roosevelt directed that Kennedy be ordered to remain at his post, but when Kennedy threatened to release a statement critical of the administration if not allowed home, the President granted his envoy home leave, with repeated instructions not to say a word about politics or diplomacy on the way back to America. Presidential agents intercepted Kennedy at LaGuardia Field and in effect cordoned him off from Willkie emissaries who had hoped to bring the ambassador into the Republican campaign. A red carpet awaited Kennedy at the

White House, where Roosevelt greeted him effusively and invited him to talk. The ambassador proceeded to pour out his grievances against the State Department and against the White House for asking him to perform favors and then not reciprocating. Roosevelt made no defense of his subordinates or of himself. On the contrary, he nodded understandingly, adding that he knew exactly how Kennedy felt and promising that State Department bureaucrats would not be permitted to treat old and valued envoys so outrageously in the future. The President even—or so the ambassador was led to believe—made some ''offer'' to Kennedy of the Democratic party nomination in 1944. The carrot was dangled, but so perhaps was the stick—according to a British secret service agent, Roosevelt brought out transcripts of Kennedy's London denunciations of the President. Now his chief asked him to support him publicly for re-election, and Kennedy gave in. A few nights later Kennedy endorsed Roosevelt in a nationwide radio address. The President defeated Willkie, and after the election, Kennedy resigned in expectation of another presidential appointment. No word came from the White House. A year later, after Pearl Harbor, Kennedy volunteered his services for an important war job, but he never received one. Roosevelt exerted the power of *inaction*.

Leadership in the shaping of private and public opinion, leadership of reform and revolutionary movements—that is, transformational leadership—seems to take on significant and collective proportions historically, but at the time and point of action leadership is intensely individual and personal. Leadership becomes a matter of all-too-human motivation and goals, of conflict and competition that seem to be dominated by the petty quest for esteem and prestige. In the battle of the battleships Kennedy and Roosevelt seemed to be engaged in a naked power fight, and the bigger battalions—in this case, battleships—won. Roosevelt finally got his way not by appealing to Kennedy's motives of patriotism or personal advancement; he got it through direct exercise of power. In the crux Kennedy had no recourse. Conceivably he might have appealed to the head of Bethlehem Steel, who owned the Fore River yard, but Bethlehem would hardly have challenged the administration in time of war. Or he might have appealed to shipyard workers to cordon off the battleships against the navy, but the workers hardly shared Kennedy's obsession with cash on the barrelhead. Kennedy built warships but Roosevelt disposed of them. No wonder Kennedy cried.

Roosevelt's bringing Kennedy back into camp in 1940 is a contrasting kind of power-wielding. Once again Roosevelt seemed to exert his will, but this time Kennedy had considerable freedom of choice. The President could try to exploit the ambassador's motives of self-esteem and patriotism, but Kennedy could achieve self-esteem through the esteem of others beside Roosevelt—of the Willkieites, for example—and he had his own notion of patriotism. If Roosevelt blocked his hopes of becoming a wartime czar, Kennedy had other means of achieving recognition.

What ultimately dominated World War II politics and strategy, however, was the moral issue of aid to the allies who were fighting Nazism. It was because Roosevelt's fundamental values were deeply humane and democratic that he was able, despite his earlier compromises and evasions, to act when action was imperative. Within a few weeks of his re-election in 1940 he was hard at work on a program—Lend Lease—that was to have an extraordinary impact on war and post-war outcomes. Testifying on the Lend Lease bill before the House Foreign Affairs committee, Kennedy was so inconclusive and self-contradictory that he gave no clear lead to friend or foe. Kennedy never seemed to see a transcending moral issue in the war. Because Roosevelt did, he was able to act with moral impact—to act with power.

Clearly the leader who commands compelling causes has an extraordinary potential influence over followers. Followers armed by moral inspiration, mobilized and purposeful, become zealots and leaders in their own right. How do values come to hold such power over certain leaders? What theories of human development cast light on the sources of such values in both leaders and followers? Do some leaders respond to followers' values without sharing them?

The need for social esteem, we have noted, is a powerful one. Mature leaders may have such a voracious need for affection that they seek it and accept it from every source, without discrimination; Lyndon B. Johnson seemed to want every member of the Senate to love him when he was majority leader and every American to love him when he was President. No matter how strong this longing for unanimity, however, almost all leaders, at least at the national level, must settle for far less than universal affection. They must be willing *to make enemies*—to deny themselves the affection of their adversaries. They must accept conflict. They must be willing and able to be unloved. It is hard to pick one's friends, harder to pick one's enemies.

On what basis is the decision *not* to win friends made? The calculus may seem purely pragmatic; leaders may need to win only enough support to gain a party nomination, build an electoral majority, put a bill through the legislature, bring off a revolution. But even in the most practical terms leaders must decide what side they will take, which group they will lead, what party they will utilize, what kind of revolution they will command. They will, in short, be influenced by considerations of *purpose* or *value* that may lie beyond calculations of personal advancement. Can we trace the origins of the shaping and sharing of values back to various needs of childhood, or is purpose and influence built into the potential leader by social and political processes only during later

years? Is it in some measure independent of psychological need and environmental cause—objectively based in process of mind? How deep are the roots of
values held strongly by leaders and the led?

The roots lie very deep, entwined with guilt feelings that arise out of the
child's early confrontation with parental authority, too deep to disentangle them
completely. In Freudian theory the superego develops as part of the resolution
of Oedipal conflicts, as the child internalizes prohibitions expressed in the form
of parental chidings and warnings. In need of urgent instant gratification, anxious also to identify with the parents and gain their affection, the child learns to
evade parental displeasure and punishment by repressing the behavior that
would invoke these penalties. Typically the superego manifested itself in feelings of conscience early in childhood. Jean Piaget noted that children internalized rules and standards so automatically that they grew literal and absolutist about them; rules they saw as ends—almost as objects—in themselves, to
be responded to indiscriminately. In some persons these moralistic rigidities
carried on into later years without adequate transformation of rule into values.
In most cases they were altered by socializing forces.

Out of these elemental but powerful influences of the superego values
emerge. The question is how the child makes the transition from rules dictated
by Oedipal and other conflict, articulated and enforced by parents, and internalized by the child to the shaping of values. This question has divided the
analysts. Freud doubted that the early configurations of conscience and standards could be substantially changed in adult life, except perhaps through psychoanalysis, for they were determined by an iron law of biological and child-
parent relations. Carl Jung criticized the "Viennese idea of sexuality with all
its vague omnipotence," the notion that the brain was merely an appendage of
the genital glands, and the entire mechanistic approach to causation. Persons,
Jung insisted, acted not only in response to causal (i.e., mechanistic) forces but
to ends or aims (*fines*) as well. Julian Huxley wrote that the evolution of "the
primitive super-ego" into a "more rational and less cruel mechanism" is "the
central ethical problem confronting every human individual." Erik Erikson
said: "The great governor of initiative is conscience. . . . But . . . the conscience of the child can be primitive, cruel, and uncompromising. . . ." Talcott Parsons contended that Freud's view while correct was too narrow, that not
only moral standards but all the components of the common culture become
rooted in personality structure.

Of these views on the origins of values, Freud's theory of Oedipal conflict, as applied to broader social processes, and Jung's concern with ends, or
purposes, are together most useful to students of leadership, for they make possible a concept of values forged and hardened by *conflict*.

Conflict and Consciousness

Leadership is a process of morality to the degree that leaders engage with followers on the basis of shared motives and values and goals—on the basis, that is, of the followers' "true" needs as well as those of leaders: psychological, economic, safety, spiritual, sexual, aesthetic, or physical. Friends, relatives, teachers, officials, politicians, ministers, and others will supply a variety of initiatives, but only the followers themselves can ultimately define their own true needs. And they can do so only when they have been exposed to the competing diagnoses, claims, and values of would-be leaders, only when the followers can make an informed choice among competing "prescriptions," only when—in the political arena at least—followers have had full opportunity to perceive, comprehend, evaluate, and finally experience alternatives offered by those professing to be their "true" representatives. Ultimately the moral legitimacy of transformational leadership, and to a lesser degree transactional leadership, is grounded in *conscious choice among real alternatives*. Hence leadership assumes competition and conflict, and brute power denies it.

Conflict has become the stepchild of political thought. Philosophical concern with conflict reaches back to Hobbes and even Heraclitus, and men who spurred revolutions in Western thought—Machiavelli and Hegel, Marx and Freud—recognized the vital role of conflict in the relations among persons or in the ambivalences within them. The seventeenth-century foes of absolute monarchy, the eighteenth-century Scottish moralists, the nineteenth-century Social Darwinists—these and other schools of thought dealt directly with questions of power and conflict, and indirectly at least with the nature of leadership. The theories of Pareto, Durkheim, Weber, and others, while not centrally concerned with problems of social conflict, "contain many concepts, assumptions, and hypotheses which greatly influenced later writers who did attempt to deal with conflict in general." Georg Simmel and others carried theories of conflict into the twentieth century.

It was, curiously, in this same century—an epoch of the bloodiest world wars, mightiest revolutions, and most savage civil wars—that social science, at least in the West, became most entranced with doctrines of harmony, adjustment, and stability. Perhaps this was the result of relative affluence, or of the need to unify people to conduct total war or consolidate revolutions, or of the co-option of scholars to advise on mitigating hostility among interest groups such as labor and management or racial groups such as blacks and whites. Whatever the cause, the "static bias" afflicted scholarly research with a tendency to look on conflict as an aberration, if not a perversion, of the agreeable and harmonious interactions that were seen as actually making up organized society. More recently Western scholarship has shown a quickened interest in the role of conflict in establishing boundaries, channeling hostility, counteracting social ossification, invigorating class and group interests, encouraging innovation, and defining and empowering leadership.

The static bias among scholars doubtless encouraged and reflected the pronouncements of political authority. Communist leaders apotheosized conflict as the engine of the process of overthrowing bourgeois regimes and then banned both the profession and the utilization of conflict in the new "classless" societies. Western leaders, especially in the United States, make a virtual fetish of "national unity," "party harmony," and foreign policy bipartisanship even while they indulge in—and virtually live off—contested elections and divisive policy issues. Jefferson proclaimed at his first Inaugural, "We are all Federalists, we are all Republicans." Few American presidents have aroused and inflamed popular attitudes as divisively as Franklin D. Roosevelt with his assaults on conservatives in both parties, his New Deal innovations, and his efforts to pack the Supreme Court and purge the Democratic party, yet few American presidents have devoted so many addresses to sermonlike calls for transcending differences and behaving as one nation and one people.

The potential for conflict permeates the relations of humankind, and that potential is a force for health and growth as well as for destruction and barbarism. No group can be wholly harmonious, as Simmel said, for such a group would be empty of process and structure. The smooth interaction of people is continually threatened by disparate rates of change, technological innovation, mass deprivation, competition for scarce resources, and other ineluctable social forces and by ambivalences, tensions, and conflicts within individuals' personalities. One can imagine a society—in ancient Egypt, perhaps, or in an isolated rural area today—in which the division of labor, the barriers against external influence, the structure of the family, the organization of the value system, the acceptance of authority, and the decision-making by leaders all interact smoothly and amiably with one another. But the vision of such a society would be useful only as an imaginary construct at one end of a continuum from cohesion to conflict. Indeed, the closer, the more intimate the relations within a group, the more hostility as well as harmony may be generated. The smaller the cooperative group—even if united by language and thrown closely together by living arrangements—"the easier it is for them to be mutually irritated and to flare up in anger," Bronislaw Malinowski said. Some conflict over valued goals and objects is almost inevitable. Even small, isolated societies cannot indefinitely dike off the impact of internal changes such as alteration of the birth rate or the disruption caused by various forms of innovation.

The question, then, is not the inevitability of conflict but the function of leadership in expressing, shaping, and curbing it. Leadership as conceptualized here is grounded in the seedbed of conflict. Conflict is intrinsically compelling; it galvanizes, prods, motivates people. Every person, group, and society has latent tension and hostility, forming a variety of psychological and political patterns across social situations. Leadership acts as an inciting and triggering force in the conversion of conflicting demands, values, and goals into significant behavior. Since leaders have an interest of their own, whether opportunistic or ideological or both, in expressing and exploiting followers' wants, needs, and aspirations, they act as catalytic agents in arousing followers' consciousness. They discern signs of dissatisfaction, deprivation, and strain; they take the initiative in making connections with their followers; they plumb the character and intensity of their potential for mobilization; they articulate grievances and wants; and they act for followers in their dealings with other clusters of followers.

Conflicts vary in origin—in and between nations, races, regions, religions, economic enterprises, labor unions, communities, kinship groups, families, and individuals themselves. Conflicts show various degrees and qualities of persistence, direction, intensity, volatility, latency, scope. The last alone may be pivotal; the outcome of every conflict, E. E. Schattschneider wrote, "is determined by the *scope* of its contagion. The number of people involved in any conflict determines what happens; every change in the number of participants . . . affects the results . . . . The moral of this is: If a fight starts, watch the crowd, because the crowd plays the decisive role." But it is leadership that draws the crowd into the incident, that changes the number of participants, that closely affects the manner of the spread of the conflict, that constitutes the main "processes" of relating the wider public to the conflict.

The root causes of conflict are as varied as their origins. No one has described these causes as cogently as James Madison.

> The latent causes of faction are thus sown in the nature of man; and we see them every where brought into different degrees of activity, according to the different circumstances of civil society. A zeal for different opinions concerning religion, concerning government and many other points, as well of speculation as of practice; an attachment to different leaders ambitiously contending for preeminence and power; or to persons of other descriptions whose fortunes have been interesting to the human passions, have in turn divided mankind into parties, inflamed them with mutual animosity, and rendered them much more disposed to vex and oppress each other, than to co-operate for their common good. So strong is this propensity of mankind to fall into mutual animosities, that where no substantial occasion presents itself, the most frivolous and fanciful distinctions have

been sufficient to kindle their unfriendly passions, and excite their most violent conflicts. But the most common and durable source of factions, has been the various and unequal distribution of property.

Not only "attachment to different leaders" but all these forces for conflict are expressed and channeled through many different types of leaders "ambitiously contending for pre-eminence and power."

Leaders, whatever their professions of harmony, do not shun conflict; they confront it, exploit it, ultimately embody it. Standing at the points of contact among latent conflict groups, they can take various roles, sometimes acting directly for their followers, sometimes bargaining with others, sometimes overriding certain motives of followers and summoning others into play. The smaller and more homogeneous the group for which they act, the more probable that they will have to deal with the leaders of other groups with opposing needs and values. The larger, more heterogeneous their collection of followers, the more probable that they will have to embrace competing interests and goals within their constituency. At the same time, their marginality supplies them with a double leverage, since in their status as leaders they are expected by their followers and by other leaders to deviate, to innovate, and to mediate between the claims of their groups and those of others.

But leaders shape as well as express and mediate conflict. They do this largely by influencing the intensity and scope of conflict. Within limits they can soften or sharpen the claims and demands of their followers, as they calculate their own political resources in dealing with competing leaders within their own constituencies and outside. They can amplify the voice and pressure of their followers, to the benefit of their bargaining power perhaps, but at the possible price of freedom to maneuver—less freedom to protect themselves against their followers—as they play in games of broader stakes. Similarly, they can narrow or broaden the scope of conflict as they seek to limit or multiply the number of entrants into a specific political arena.

Franklin Roosevelt demonstrated the fine art of controlling entry in the presidential nomination race in 1940. There was widespread uncertainty as to whether he would run for a third term. He himself was following the development of public opinion at the same time that he was influencing it. Leaders in his own party were divided; onetime stalwarts like James A. Farley and Cordell Hull opposed a third term. It was supposed that FDR would discourage Democrats from entering the nomination race. On the contrary, he welcomed them. Secondary figures like Joseph Kennedy, coming to the Oval Office to sound out Roosevelt on his intentions and on their own chances, found themselves flattered and rated as serious and deserving possibilities. The effect was to broaden the field of possible adversaries and hence divide and weaken the opposition. FDR had little trouble winning the nomination.

The essential strategy of leadership in mobilizing power is to recognize the arrays of motives and goals in potential followers, to appeal to those motives by words and action, and to strengthen those motives and goals in order to increase the power of leadership, thereby changing the environment within which both followers and leaders act. Conflict—disagreement over goals within an array of followers, fear of outsiders, competition for scarce resources—immensely invigorates the mobilization of consensus and dissensus. But the fundamental process is a more elusive one; it is, in large part, *to make conscious what lies unconscious among followers.*

The purposeful awakening of persons into a state of political consciousness is a familiar problem for philosophers and psychologists and one that has stimulated thought in other disciplines. For the student of leadership the concept of political consciousness is as primitive as it is fertile. That ''conflict produces consciousness'' was fundamental in the doctrine of Hegel, Marx, and other nineteenth-century theorists, but they differed over the cardinal question: consciousness of *what?* They recognized the essential human needs but differed as to the nature of those needs. Feuerbach, an intellectual leader of the young Marx, conceived humanity as imbued with real, tangible, solid needs arising from Nature. Marx compared human consciousness with that of animals, which had no consciousness of the world as something objective and real apart from the animal's own existence and needs. But *human* labor, rather than leading to direct satisfaction of need, generates human consciousness and self-consciousness. Thus the early Marx had some understanding of the variety and inexhaustibility of human needs.

It was a marvelous insight, but Marx came to be identified with the doctrine that *true* consciousness, to be achieved through unremitting conflict, was always of *class*. Felt, palpable human needs, however, did not seem to be translated into a rising class consciousness in the capitalist environment of the mid-nineteenth century. Marx and Engels railed at the ''false consciousness'' of religion and nationalism and the other diversions and superficialities that seemed to engage men who were caught in the iron grip of material deprivation. The progress toward class consciousness was slow, irregular, uneven. The almost automatic movement toward revolution, emerging out of the ''spontaneous class-organization of the proletariat,'' simply did not come about in the great bourgeois societies; ultimately revolution would need to be spurred by militant leadership and iron party discipline.

In the fiery intellectual and political conflict of the nineteenth century both Marxists and their adversaries assumed too much about the central springs of human behavior without knowing enough about motivation or the complex relations between motives and behavior. Few perceived that if people did not behave the way they were supposed to, the fault might lie in the suppositions rather than in the people. One of the suppositions was that ultimately humans would respond rationally and "realistically" to "objective" social conditions. But what was real and rational? If Marx had turned Hegel's dialectic of ideas on its head, Freud turned Marx's Consciousness upside down. Freud was drawn to the function of the unconscious rather than the conscious or the preconscious; for him the unconscious was the "true psychic reality," betrayed by dreams, fantasies, accidents, and curious slips of the tongue. Consciousness and related concepts of alienation and identity have continued to be variously defined and heatedly debated. During the ferment of the 1960s that reached across the Western world, young people were urged to "expand consciousness" and "consciousness-raising" became something of a fad and a profession.

If the first task of leadership is to bring to consciousness the followers' sense of their own needs, values, and purposes, the question remains: consciousness of what? Which of these motives and goals are to be tapped? Leaders, for example, can make followers more conscious of aspects of their *identity* (sexual, communal, ethnic, class, national, ideological). Georges Sorel argued that only through leadership and conflict, including "terrifying violence," could the working class become conscious of its true identity—and hence of its power. But to what extent was Sorel imposing his own values and goals on workers who might have very different, even idiosyncratic, ones? We return to the dilemma: to what degree do leaders, through their command of personal influence, substitute their own motives and goals for those of the followers? Should they whip up chauvinism, feelings of ethnic superiority, regional prejudice, economic rivalry? What must they accept among followers as being durable and valid rather than false and transient? And we return to the surmise here: leaders with relevant motives and goals of their own respond to followers' needs and wants and goals in such a way as to meet those motivations and to bring changes consonant with those of both leaders and followers, and with the values of both.

The Elevating Power of Leadership

Mobilized and shaped by gifted leadership, sharpened and strengthened by conflict, values can be the source of vital change. The question is: at what level of need or stage of morality do leaders operate to elevate their followers? At levels of safety and security, followers tend to conform to group expectations and to support and justify the social order. At a certain stage Kohlberg finds a "law and order" orientation toward authority, fixed rules, and maintenance of the social order for its own sake. At a higher stage Simpson found a significant relation between tendencies toward self-esteem and positive law values (belief that the authority for judgments rests in the laws and norms humans have developed collectively). This is the level of "social contract morality."

At the highest stage of moral development persons are guided by near-universal ethical principles of justice such as equality of human rights and respect for individual dignity. This stage sets the opportunity for rare and creative leadership. Politicians who operate at the lower and middle levels of need and moral development are easily understood, but what kind of leadership reaches into the need and value structures, mobilizing and directing support for such values as justice and empathy?

First, it is the kind of leadership that *operates at need and value levels higher than those of the potential follower* (but not so much higher as to lose contact). This kind of leadership need be neither doctrinaire nor indoctrinative (in the ordinary sense of preaching). In its most effective form it appeals to the higher, more general and comprehensive values that express followers' more fundamental and enduring needs. The appeal may be more potent when a polity faces danger from outside, as from an invasion, or from inside, as in social breakdown, civil war, or natural catastrophe. "If inefficiencies and corruption of governmental and social leadership go beyond 'normal,' if demands are constantly frustrated by incapacities, which can be readily laid at some human door, if all of this is compounded by a rising consciousness of discrimination and sense of justice," according to a four-nation study, "then people can experience great and often very sudden transformation of values, or those values that were subdued can become the basis for vigorous action." No single force, such as economic conditions, predetermines change, this study concluded; other factors—notably the quality of leadership—intervene, so the role of values in social change varies from culture to culture. Among the nations studied (India, Poland, the United States, Yugoslavia) similarities were found in leaders' espousal of innovative change, economic development, and the norms of selflessness (commitment to the general welfare) and honesty.

Second, it is the kind of leadership that *can exploit conflict and tension within persons' value structures*. Contradictions can be expected among competing substantive values, such as liberty and equality, or between those values and moral values like honesty, or between terminal values and instrumental values. "All contemporary theories in social psychology would probably agree that a necessary prerequisite to cognitive change is the presence of some state of imbalance within the system," Rokeach says.

Leaders may simply help a follower see these types of contradictions, or they might actively arouse a sense of dissatisfaction by making the followers aware of contradictions in or inconsistencies between values and behavior. The more contradictions challenge self-conceptions, according to Rokeach, the more dissatisfaction will be aroused. And such dissatisfactions are the source of changes that the leader can influence. There is an implication in Rokeach that the contradictions in themselves cause change, simply on the basis of self-cognition. Typically, however, an outside influence is required in the form of a leader, preferably "one step above." Rokeach bases much of his analysis on experimental situations in which the subjects are exposed to close direction and restraint—certainly a context of manipulation if not of leadership. Autonomous cognition usually is not enough to enable persons to break out of their imprisoning value structures. Experimenters may assume a leadership role.

Given the right conditions of value conflict, leaders hold enhanced influence at the higher levels of the need and value hierarchies. They can appeal to the more widely and deeply held values, such as justice, liberty, and brotherhood. They can expose followers to the broader values that contradict narrower ones or inconsistent behavior. They can redefine aspirations and gratifications to help followers see their stake in new, program-oriented social movements. Most important, they can gratify lower needs so that higher motivations will arise to elevate the conscience of men and women. To be sure, leadership may be frustrated and weakened at the higher levels as well as the lower. Potential support may thin out when immediate parochial needs and values threaten to weaken higher, more general ones. Substantive values, such as liberty or equality, may compete with one another, and, however logically compelling the leader's value priorities may look, they may not co-exist so harmoniously in the political arena. Perhaps the most disruptive force in competitive politics is conflict between *modal values* such as fair play and due process and *end-values* such as equality. Roosevelt's court-packing plan, with its use of dubious means to attain high ends, is a case in point. Some of those believing in equal opportunity today may also believe in certain modes of conduct— endless debate, for example, or elaborate procedures for judicial review—that make the attainment of equal opportunity far less certain.

The potential for influence through leadership is usually immense. The essence of leadership in any polity is the recognition of real need, the uncovering and exploiting of contradictions among values and between values and practice, the realigning of values, the reorganization of institutions where necessary, and the governance of change. Essentially the leader's task is consciousness-raising on a wide plane. "Values exist only when there is consciousness," Susanne Langer has said. "Where nothing is felt, nothing matters." The leader's fundamental act is to induce people to be aware or conscious of what they feel—to feel their true needs so strongly, to define their values so meaningfully, that they can be moved to purposeful action.

A congruence between the need and value hierarchies would produce a powerful potential for the exercise of purposeful leadership. When these hierarchies are combined with stage theories—for example, Erikson's eight psychosocial stages of man, with its emphasis on trust versus mistrust, autonomy versus shame, role experimentation versus negative identity—leadership, with its capacity to exploit tension and conflict, finds an even more durable foundation. While both Maslow's and Kohlberg's hierarchies imply *uni-directionality* and *irreversibility*—persons move through the levels at varying rates of speed but in only one direction—we know that people can and do regress. Still, for four values in particular—the end-values of equality, freedom, and a world of beauty (Rokeach's "terminal" values) and the instrumental value of self-control—the long-term changes have been documented in several studies as leading toward heavier impact of values. These findings suggest one of the most vital aspects of leadership: it cannot influence people "downward" on the need or value hierarchy without a reinforcing environment. The functioning of some persons at the levels of principle or self-actualization would not easily regress to the conventional level (e.g., need for social esteem). *Stasis* operates to prevent slippage to an earlier stage. If leaders reflecting more widely and deeply held values compete for support among followers who are moving toward more socially responsible levels in the hierarchies, leadership itself tends to move on to still broader and "higher" values.

This phenomenon provides the theoretical foundation for Gunnar Myrdal's brilliant analysis of the likely course of the conflict between egalitarian values and practice in the United States. Just as most persons strive for some coherence and consistency within their value hierarchies, so value systems in whole societies, reflecting the cognitive-affective-behavioral factors described above, tend toward some structuring. As societies, like persons, confront challenges, crises, and conflict, there is a tendency toward consistency. A rough hierarchy of values develops as lower and higher priorities develop (or are assigned) in circumstances where people cannot equally embrace all the end-values and modal values that they might wish. In the process of the moral criticism that men make upon each other, Myrdal notes, "the valuations of the higher and more general planes—referring to *all* human beings and *not* to specific small groups—are regularly invoked by one party or the other, simply because they are held in common among all groups in society, and also because of the supreme prestige they are traditionally awarded. . . . Specific attitudes and forms of behavior are then reconciled to the more general moral principles. . . .'' There are, of course, limits to the tendency toward congruency in societies—and probably in persons as well. The four-nation study found an unexpectedly high degree of conflict *within* the countries studied, not merely conflict among the countries. At societal levels, however, such conflict is not random but assumes some kind of form and persistence. And conflict, as we understand it here, is necessary for leadership and, indeed, for higher levels of coherence, in a kind of dialectical and synthesis response.

In a famous distinction Max Weber contrasted the "ethic of responsibility" with the "ethic of ultimate ends." The latter measured persons' behavior by the extent of their adherence to good ends or high purposes; the former measured action by persons' capacity to take a calculating, prudential, rationalistic approach, making choices in terms of not one supreme value or value hierarchy alone but many values, attitudes, and interests, seeing the implication of choice for the means of attaining it—the price paid to achieve it, the relation of one goal to another, the direct and indirect effects of different goals for different persons and interests, all in a context of specificity and immediacy, and with an eye to actual *consequences* rather than lofty intent.

This dualism is of course oversimplified; most leaders and followers shift back and forth from specific, self-involved values to broader, public-involved ones. But the perception of dualism poses sharply the dilemmas facing leaders who embrace and respond to popular needs and values. The ethic of responsibility, whatever its appeal to moral rationalists like Weber, opened the floodgates to such a variety of discrete, multiple, relativistic, individualistic values as to allow a person observing this ethic to legitimate an enormous variety of actions. This ethic, by extension, permitted expedient, opportunistic, and highly self-serving action because the concept of responsibility could easily be stretched to authorize the kind of opportunism that we associate, for example, with nineteenth-century "rugged individualism." If leaders are encouraged to follow immediate, specific, calculable interests, they can end up serving their narrow, short-run interests alone, rationalizing the consequences in terms of responsibility to themselves, to their families, or to a relatively narrow group. Leaders holding this ethic, or representing persons holding this ethic, would act amid such a plethora of responsibilities as to legitimate both high-minded and self-serving behavior, action both for broad, general interests and for parochial ones, action that might be self-limiting contrasted with action that in the long run might be self-fulfilling (by the standards of the highest level of moral development). Worse, leaders might lack useful standards for distinguishing between the two sets of alternatives.

By the same token, Weber's ethic of ultimate ends emphasizes the demands of an overriding, millenarian kind of value system at the expense of the far more typical situation (at least in pluralistic societies) in which choices must be made among a number of compelling end-values, modal values, and instrumental values. And the ethic of responsibility could rather be seen as the day-to-day measured application of the "ethic of ultimate ends" to complex circumstance.

For the study of leadership, the dichotomy is not between Weber's two ethics but between the leader's commitment to a number of overriding, general welfare-oriented values on the one hand and his encouragement of, and entanglement in, a host of lesser values and "responsibilities" on the other. The four-nation study notes the "most important motivational distinction among leaders desiring change—the distinction between those who see progress primarily in terms of political opportunity and those who nurse a feeling of social injustice arising out of the gap between the economically deprived and the privileged," even though no consistent relationship seemed to explain it. The great bulk of leadership activity consists of the day-to-day interaction of leaders and followers characterized by the processes described above. But the ultimate test of moral leadership is its capacity to transcend the claims of the multiplicity of everyday wants and needs and expectations, to respond to the higher levels of moral development, and to relate leadership behavior—its roles, choices, style, commitments—to a set of reasoned, relatively explicit, conscious values.

PART II

ORIGINS

OF

LEADERSHIP

3

THE PSYCHOLOGICAL MATRIX
OF LEADERSHIP

The key to understanding leadership lies in recent findings and concepts in psychology. For the student of leadership this field is filled with hazards as well as riches. Psychological theories that have verged on a "biologistic" view of leadership, drawing on studies of animal behavior, have tended to misconceive leadership as simply control or rulership. Thus we hear much about the "pecking order" established through threatening behavior intended to control or monopolize females, food, and territory. Rigid hierarchies of coercion and deference would seem to bar leadership from animal life.

Extended observation of primates has suggested, on the other hand, that animals too indulge in various forms of leadership. In one experiment designed explicitly to answer the question whether leaders needed followers, a chimpanzee was shown some food hidden under leaves and grass and then led back to rejoin his group. Soon he was trying to persuade the others to follow him to the food. He rushed from one follower to another, grimacing, tapping him on the shoulder, screaming, and sometimes grabbing a companion and dragging him toward the food. All this, according to the observer (at the Delta Regional Primate Research Center), "suggested that group cohesion was strong and the *'leader' was as dependent upon the group for getting to the food as they were dependent on him in knowing precisely where to go.''*

When a chimpanzee was acquainted with the food location, put back into the cage, and then freed without the others, he tried to release his fellows before running for the food and he whimpered or screamed or isolated himself if he could not release them. When two "leaders" were each apprized of a different cache, they were able somehow to inform each other of the relative value of the two caches so the other chimpanzee would go first to the larger lot. And they seemed to know how to attract followers, partly by walking in tandem or whimpering or tugging an arm, but also by moving off independently in a consistent direction.

These are only the more dramatic of many findings about animal behavior that suggest leadership in some fashion. A study of goat behavior concluded that the phenomena of dominance and leadership were not correlated but the result of two separate learning processes. Studies of "imprinting" by Lorenz and others found that "following responses" were set at intervals early in an animal's life and tend to persist. "Finder" bees are known to communicate the location of food by indicating the nature and direction of the food through variations in buzzing and flower scents exuded from their body. Some of these behaviors are genetically determined, but others seem to be learning experiences based on recognizing leaders with dominant influence as well as knowing the right cues.

Another, quite different biological emphasis in the study of leadership is the assumption of male leadership, especially at the higher levels of power. Over the centuries femininity has been stereotyped as dependent, submissive and conforming, and hence women have been seen as lacking in leadership qualities. In some cultures, in consequence, women are cut off from power positions as well as from the stepping stones and access routes that reach toward leadership. Discrimination by men may be less crucial or less lasting than the consciousness of women themselves of their subordinate or "outgroup" status in politics, though the one has influenced the other. Women in lower political offices, such as convention delegates, saw their roles more as "representative" and less as independent than did male delegates. This leadership bias persists despite the political influence of the likes of Eleanor Roosevelt, Golda Meir, Indira Gandhi, or Margaret Thatcher. The male bias is reflected in the false conception of leadership as mere command or control. As leadership comes properly to be seen as a process of leaders engaging and mobilizing the human needs and aspirations of followers, women will be more readily recognized as leaders and men will change their own leadership styles.

The psychological approach to leadership has its own biases. One of these is the common view that the critical influences on the shaping of leaders lie almost wholly in their early years. Another is a common reliance on psychoanalysis and psychobiography, which are inescapably culture-bound. Psychoanalysis is a peculiarly Western invention and practice. It follows certain assumptions, perceptions, and methods. It may ignore or misperceive psychological motives or cultural attitudes—or even vagrant and idiosyncratic behaviors—that could be major sources of influence of leadership in other cultures. It may focus on pathology, on the abnormal, and fail to grasp the dimensions and dynamics of normality or even healthy genius. Analysts may look for configurations that are crucial in their own cultures but nonexistent or misleading in others. Some societies, as Kenneth Keniston points out, may "create" stages of life that do not exist in other cultures, or they may "stop" human development in some sectors earlier than other cultures do. Transcultural changes in development certainly do occur, but adequate data and interpretation are lacking. If a "Western" approach made possible a unified theoretical, conceptual, and methodological analysis, we might at least benefit to some degree from our parochialism, but in fact Western analysts are fundamentally divided in their assumptions and methods.

Our knowledge of the early psychological experiences of famous leaders also is limited by the paucity of data. The little we have is pieced together from the memories of childhood friends and witnesses, from the few fugitive documents that families choose to allow scholars to examine, from memoirs or other autobiographical accounts of the eminent persons themselves. Memories of early years are woefully, even perversely, limited and distorted. If the truths that can be found naked on the battlefield later put on their uniforms (as military historians like to say), the recollections of doting cousins, proud and overly protective descendants, and hometown chauvinists erect a eulogistic camouflage of their own. It is the task of the trained analyst—the psychobiographer or the history-oriented psychoanalyst—to sift through this dross. But this suggests another difficulty; in the absence of detailed, dependable information, even such portraits—especially of their subjects' early years—tend to be speculative and generalized. The more subtle and specialized the accounts of the early years of eminent persons, the more debatable the implications for leadership in general.

By far the most critical bias in the "great man" theory of leadership is neither cultural nor sexual. It is the assumption that "great men" *do* make history, that the causes of real, intended social change can be traced back to the purposes and decisions of the most visible actors on the political stage. Various versions of this theory have long been popular in folklore, with its imputation of mythic, transforming power to kings, princes, warriors, and various demigods within and outside the mortal realm. Carlyle's heroes, Nietzsche's great blond beast, Hegel's evoker and carrier of the spirit of the times, Sidney Hook's "event-making man," and contemporary concepts of elitism exemplify the range and variety of this kind of theory. Most of us are captive to this general bias, if only as a result of the enormous focus on political celebrities in the mass media. For this reason, and because it is easier to look for heroes and scapegoats than to probe for complex and obscure causal forces, some assume that the lives of the "greats" carry more clues to the understanding of society, history, and current events than the lives of the great mass of people, of the subleaders and the followers. The truth of this assumption as a general proposition has never been demonstrated. Nor has that of the opposite assumption—that history is made by masses of people acting through "leaders" who are merely agents for the "popular" or "majority" will. Nor has a third assumption, that history is forged in the crucible of class struggle rising out of consciousness of relative social and economic deprivation. The study of leadership cannot, in my view, ride on any single existing theory of historical causation; rather the study of leadership should contribute to developing more sophisticated theories of causation.

Political leadership is ubiquitous and pervasive. In most societies leadership is not confined to a tiny, omnipotent elite but includes the behavior of much larger but not yet defined populations. I assume this because it seems more fitting to cast a wide net for possible actors than to restrict one's analytical universe to a predetermined category. This is not to assume that rule by a Hitler or leadership by a Gandhi is to be seen as different only in degree from, or to be equated conceptually with, that of a Brown Shirt corporal or a village wise man. The famous may have a marked and rare capacity to respond to motivations and values of themselves and others, to persuade and manipulate with skill, to relate ends and means. That is why we can find insights in studying the Lenins, Wilsons, and Maos. It is one thing to say that they have special qualities, but something else to say that they control historical processes. Thus Hitler must have been responding to overwhelming motives in deliberately and persistently, year after year, destroying captive European Jews and Russian Slavs by the millions. The motives of an extermination camp commander cannot automatically be equated with the demonic will, much less the political skill, of the führer. But the local rule of the camp commander is still significant in the total historical process.

That power as sheer *domination* is pervasive in this century of Hitler and Stalin is obvious, as perhaps it was in every other. Is *leadership,* as it is defined in this book? Power lies deep in our origins. It has long been manifest in animal behavior. In primates domination is by far the most common trait, but even at this stage, as noted above, there are tendencies toward leadership. Domination usually takes the form of a clear-cut hierarchy, with mature adult males at the top, young adult males next in line, then male orphans and other miscellaneous males, with females highly subordinated. The hierarchy of power is enforced occasionally by fighting, but much of the deference seems automatic, a result of learning experiences.

To see the ubiquity and pervasiveness of power and leadership in the relationships of mother and daughter, teacher and schoolchildren, coach and athlete, master and apprentice, minister and congregation, sergeant and rifleman, party chieftain and card-carrying member, propagandist and believer, is to see power wielders, leaders, and followers in continuous interaction in virtually every sphere of human society. This does not mean that the apparent leader is necessarily or exclusively the "real" leader or the effective leader. Leaders lead in such a way, as we will have many occasions to note, as to anticipate responses of followers, and followers and leaders may exchange places. Rulers never exchange places with followers. The leadership-followership process must be viewed as a totality of interactive roles before we can identify the forces and processes at work and hence assess the role of leadership in the historical process.

The pervasiveness of power and leadership opens up a large problem and a larger opportunity. The problem is that we must supplement our data on the "greats" (national or local) with aggregative, cumulative data on the personal, social, and political influences operating on large numbers of subleaders and followers. The opportunity is this: if we can generalize with any success, and if we can make inferences from data gathered at one level about phenomena at another level, we may, partially at least, compensate for the noncomparability, unreliability, and narrow focus of the information we have on individual great leaders. Even more, we can hope to build the foundations of a more general theory of the role of leadership in the processes of historical causation.

The Cocoon of Personality

Despite its limitations, psychobiography, which depends on a psychoanalytic approach to biographical data, can be an indispensable tool in analyzing the shaping influences on leadership. Like all tools, it must be used cautiously, and adjusted to the task at hand. There is a difference between amateur or "pop" psychiatry (sometimes hardly more than voyeurism) and serious exploration of the linkage between the dynamics of personality development and the character of the leadership of prominent men and women. Gandhi, Lenin, and Hitler, among others, have been subjected to brilliant psychobiographical analysis.

Our knowledge of Gandhi's early life, for example, cannot answer all the fascinating questions about his complex motives and aspirations. But it does provide clues, in large part as a result of his own autobiographical efforts to analyze his motives and behavior, and of Erikson's pioneering and probing studies.

Like most eminent rebels, Mohandas Gandhi came from an upper-class family. His father was the appointed prime minister of the small principality of Porbandar. The family belonged to the Vaisyas caste, of farmers and merchants, and to a subcaste of commercial and ascetic proclivities. The father had considerable political influence, subject of course to the British Raj, but the family managed to safeguard a reputation for integrity and independence. Born in 1869, Gandhi grew up in an elegantly seedy home with his parents, brothers and sisters, and five uncles and their families. In this crowded setting, an Indian biographer observed, Mohandas learned the power of mutual tolerance. He later remembered his father as truthful, brave, and generous but also as short-tempered and overly given to "carnal pleasures." The father had married for the fourth time when he was over forty—twice the age of his bride—and Mohandas was the last of their issue.

His relation to his parents was complex. As the last child of a young mother and an aging patriarch, Erik Erikson observed, Gandhi had a central place in the family, yet he feared his father and felt unable to live up to the masculine ideal. "Gandhi," Victor Wolfenstein says, "was torn between . . . a desire to submit to his father (and his own superego, the internal manifestation of his father's moral standards) and a desire to replace him in his mother's eyes." When his father was away the boy would banish the portrait of the local ruling prince from its usual stool and install himself in its place; he even scattered utensils of worship.

His mother left him the memory of sheer saintliness. She presided over a highly regulated home, and she combined her deep religiosity with a merry, commonsense approach to practical matters even in the court, where she was something of a favorite. She impressed her son with her indomitable fasting; to keep two or three consecutive fasts was nothing to her, he recalled proudly, and not even illness was allowed to interrupt the ceremony. In his *Autobiography* Gandhi told of the time during one *Chaturmas,* an extended period of semi-fasting, when she had vowed not to have food at all until the sun came out; it was the rainy season, and the children, after waiting endlessly, finally rushed in to announce the sun's appearance, but already it had faded away. "That does not matter," she said cheerfully. "God did not want me to eat today."

A century later, peering through the lenses of ignorance, myth, and hero worship, we cannot dependably recreate those early years of Mohandas Gandhi. But we can see that he loved as well as feared his father. His early relations with his father left him with intense guilt feelings that took the form of shame over his own "carnality." His relations with his youthful mother and patriarchal father may have intensified his emotional malaise through Oedipal conflict. His mother, given to obsessive religiosity, tried to distribute her affection equitably among the children, but to him her love may have seemed diffuse and unpredictable.

Even in his preschool years Gandhi seems to have had feelings of insecurity about his appearance—his sharp facial features, big ears, small frame—his physical prowess, and his manliness. But strong, healthy counterbalancing tendencies came into play. Erikson argues convincingly that the boy probably harbored an early sense of originality and even superiority; that he experimented with and overcame the levels of shame and doubt, guilt and inferiority; that his parents allowed him about as much freedom as he needed; and that his first real rebuff came after childhood, in his adolescent years. Perhaps it came when he dropped out of college after a few months. Little of his future power and purpose was forecast in his early life.

Half a year after Gandhi was born into one of the prominent families of Porbandar, a rising young teacher and educational administrator in a small provincial Russian city became the father of a second son, christened Vladimir Ilyich Ulyanov, later to be known as Lenin. His first name meant Ruler of the World.

So idyllic seemed the world of the Ulyanovs, so happy their reminiscences, that the historian Bertram Wolfe warned off "psychological" theorists. There was nothing to account for fashionable explanations of the great revolutionaries, he said, nothing to support the formula of mother or father fixation, no unhappy family life, maladjusted childhood, youthful rebellion in the home, no traces of lack of self-esteem due to failure at school or in sports, "no sign of queerness or abnormality." Lenin's parents were both of the middle or upper middle class, the father through dutiful and efficient work as inspector and builder of schools, the mother because her father was a doctor and a prosperous landowner. Ulyanov, dedicated to his work, loyal to the czar, orthodox in religion, and self-protective in his bureaucratic world in Simbirsk, won promotion to the prized rank of state councillor with the status of a minor noble.

They were a secure and affluent family—and seemingly a most contented one. The father was devoted, benevolent, attentive; he assisted with the early schooling at home, played chess with his sons, tolerated the pranks and mediated the quarrels among his six children. The mother was resourceful and steady; she taught her children to play the piano, led them in singing, and helped them put out a weekly magazine. The children paired off naturally; Vladimir was especially close to his older brother Alexander and for a time acted as his imitator and virtual slave. Summers the family spent on their paternal grandfather's estate near Kazan, where Vladimir splashed in the river, picked mushrooms, and roamed the manor's one thousand acres—but had no contact with the peasants laboring on those acres.

The undaunted psychologists have raised questions nonetheless. They noted that the father was away a great deal on official duties—sometimes for weeks on end—and they wondered how his comings and goings may have stirred the undercurrents of family life, especially for Vladimir, who identified with his father. "The high moral rectitude of the father undoubtedly resulted in an unusually demanding superego for the son," Wolfenstein has speculated, "so that young Lenin probably was unable to think or express the feelings of resentment which seem sure to have followed his father's absences and disciplining without experiencing guilt as a consequence." The second son seemed as secure—even strident and self-assured—within the family as he seemed shy and unaggressive outside. But Vladimir was slow in learning to walk and accompanied the process by much falling down and loud wailing. Did this have long-run consequences—in nurturing Lenin's later mistrustfulness, for example? Was the (seemingly) sudden change in his older brother's life, with the shocking consequence of his execution for opposition to the czar, a clue that the early psychological relationship among the Ulyanovs had grown tight and strained behind the facade of that happy tranquil life? Or did the secure family life given Lenin a psychic strength that, counterpoised against later events, made him the self-assured revolutionary he became?

We have no persuasive answers. It does seem clear, however, that scholars should give as much attention to healthy and sustaining relationships in the lives of leaders as they have given to the grimmer evidence of tragedy and deviance. Perhaps they should explore the positive even more.

With Adolf Hitler, on the other hand, there is little redeeming evidence of a happy, fulfilling early life despite Hitler's attempt at camouflage. "Today it seemed to me providential that Fate should have chosen Braunau on the Inn as my birthplace," Adolf Hitler wrote in *Mein Kampf*. "In this little town on the Inn, gilded by the rays of German martyrdom, Bavarian by blood, technically Austrian, lived my parents in the late eighties of the past century; my father a dutiful civil servant, my mother giving all her being to the household, and devoted above all to us children in eternal, loving care. . . ." This glimpse of a serene little family is fascinating, all the more so because it is false. Hitler was probably depicting his own real childhood when, purportedly describing the drab, impoverished life of children in a "worker's" family, he said: "It ends badly if the man goes his own way from the beginning and the woman, for the children's sake, opposes him. Then there is fighting and quarreling, and, as the man grows estranged from his wife, he becomes more intimate with alcohol. He is drunk every Saturday, and, with her instinct of self-preservation for herself and her children, the woman has to fight to get even a few pennies out of him. . . . When at length he comes home on Sunday or even Monday night, drunk and brutal, but always parted from his last cent, such scenes often occur that God have mercy!''

Psychoanalysts have concluded that as a child Hitler saw, or thought he saw, his father assault and rape his mother. The conclusion is based on what is known of the family circumstances, Hitler's later behavior, and repeated references in his writings to a squalid family life that he claimed to have witnessed in Vienna—a family life he would have had little opportunity to observe. The father, outwardly a stiff, correct, prickly official, metamorphosed at home, according to extensive evidence, into a petty tyrant who bullied and beat his wife and children. From the führer's behavior in later years—his frequent reference to Germany as the motherland (in contrast to the more usual term, fatherland), his feminizing of certain German neuter nouns, his identification of his father with Austria and his rage over the alleged hostility of Austria to Germany and later the "rape" of his motherland by predatory Jews and the aggressive Allies, his alleged indulgence in certain sexual perversions—from all this and other evidence it may be inferred that he had repressed his anguish over traumatic childhood experiences only to project them into the political arena in later struggles.

In some respects his was a classical Oedipal situation. Hitler's father was twenty-three years older than the boy's mother. She was a comely woman who had lost two or three babies, fretted over Adolf's health, lavished affection on him, and overprotected her son. In the evenings the close relationship would break off when her husband returned with his threats and demands. "The more he hated his father," Walter Langer concluded, "the more dependent he became upon the affection and love of his mother, and the more she loved him the more afraid he became of his father's vengeance should his secret be discovered." And if the boy felt that his mother had submitted sexually to his father—had even invited the assault or at least acquiesced in it—he would have felt a sense of betrayal. He would have suffered from anxiety and guilt feelings toward his father and from resentment and ambivalence toward the mother who had submitted to the attack. These are clues to his later punishment of Austria (the father) and *Germany* (the mother who had deserted him). Hence the planned destruction of the Germany that "is no longer worthy of me."

Oedipal feelings seem to have been combined with an almost unbearable doubt about his own worth. Hitler was a small, unattractive, somewhat sickly child who was dwarfed by his dignified, uniformed father. The deaths of brothers and sisters doubtless caused him added anxiety. Even in his early years he evidently had more than the average boy's insecurity over his masculinity; not only was it threatened by his father but (according to the Russian autopsy of

May 1945), he had a condition of monorchidism (one undescended testicle). This condition, Robert Waite says, is neither uncommon nor in itself pathogenic; but ''it may become so if, as in Hitler's case, there are other infantile disorders and a badly disturbed parent-child relationship.'' His mother, it is believed, demanded absolute cleanliness and tidiness and subjected her son to rigorous toilet training; in later years Hitler oscillated between utter fastidiousness and fascinations with filth—with stench and dung and dirt.

These explosive psychological forces dominated Hitler's sexual deviation and his political extremism in his adult years. He did not marry; his intimate friendships with women were marked by such perverse behavior on Hitler's part that the relation was usually broken off, with Hitler's partner in torment; all the women involved committed suicide or attempted to do so. The later reports of his friends and lovers and his own talk and actions—his self-degradation in courting women, his carrying around a riding whip, his castration anxiety, his fascination with decapitation and with blood in general (including his own)—point to enormous guilt, insecurity, and damaged self-esteem in Hitler's childhood. Whether his anxieties affected a nation's destiny or simply produced a bizarre case study for psychoanalysts' files would depend not on these personal tensions alone but on the degree to which they fed a sickness in the German society.

There are parallels in the early experiences of both ''great leaders'' and notorious rulers or power wielders despite the contrary uses they made of their resources. All three described above, in their widely different social environments, as children felt especially close to their mothers, who served as objects of strong affect and as anchors of emotional stability. All showed varying combinations of love and hatred for their fathers, who in all cases held positions of esteem or at least status in their communities. At least two of the children in one respect or another were markedly ''slow learners'' and were subject to feelings of insecurity and lack of self-esteem. Lenin may have incurred less psychic damage in his boyhood, but his relations with his parents resemble significantly those of the others.

One could speculate that the common inclusive childhood experience for all these monumental figures was intense positive attachment to one parent coupled with some intensely negative attachment to the other or an intensely traumatic and negative youthful experience. Could it be the tension between emotional demands, the conflict engendered that must be resolved, plus uncommon talent and energy, that makes the need for power so compelling? What were the controlling factors that would direct one person toward raw power-wielding and another to reciprocal leadership? We know little about the source of these distinctions, in part because we have not tended to make such distinctions in our power theory. What leads some to moral leadership and others to amoral or immoral power-wielding? This is a frontier that scholarship must explore.

The differences, too, in the three childhoods also leap to the eye. It is difficult to compare Oedipal influences when the mothers of two of the boys were much younger than their husbands and one was a contemporary. Relations with siblings varied significantly. And although resemblances seemed striking in certain respects, especially in the relation of child to mother, differences emerge on a closer look. The mothers varied considerably in their status, roles, and psychic security. Note too the contrast between Lenin's apparent admiration for his father and Hitler's apparent loathing of his. The sense of insecurity and damaged self-esteem, however powerful, must have taken many forms; thus Lenin's lack of motor skills may have had less impact on his personality than Gandhi's difficulties in college had on his. The three vary widely in severity of psychic stress, from Lenin, the least strained, to Gandhi to Hitler.

Tension, conflict, and insecurity have marked the early lives of other leaders as well. The dominant trait of Bismarck, builder of modern Germany, was his will to power, to master men and events. Stress and guilt in his early years seem to have been related less to his father than to his mother. "She wished that I should learn much and become much, and it often appeared to me that she was hard, cold toward me," he recalled when he was in his early thirties. "As a small child I hated her, later I successfully deceived her with falsehoods. One only learns the value of the mother for the child when it is too late, when she is dead. . . . Nowhere perhaps have I sinned more grievously than against my parents, above all against my mother. I really loved my father. . . ." But he had guilt feelings toward his father as well as his mother. "How often did I repay his truly boundless, unselfish, good-natured tenderness for me with coldness and bad grace. Even more frequently I made a pretense of loving him, not wanting to violate my own code of propriety, when innerly I felt hard and unloving because of his apparent weaknesses. . . ." Perhaps it was Bismarck's parents who suffered from psychic stress!

Or consider Kurt Schumacher, a compatriot of Bismarck's eighty years later, who also developed an intense drive toward power. His stern father was often away, and the son was smothered in affection by his mother and several older sisters. The loss of an arm when he was a child doubtless brought him special solicitude. "Neither his father nor any other male—teacher, relative, or friend—appears to have had any significant influence on his early character formation," according to Lewis Edinger. But "he may have developed an increasing disposition to rebel against all his female attention, at the same time that he continued to accept it, by asserting his masculinity and independence in spheres he conceived to be outside the feminine realm. . . ." Schumacher's biographer believes that in the end he, like Wilson, was defeated politically by his moralistic dogmatism, by his lack of resilience and flexibility in the face of new conditions.

Eleanor Roosevelt's early years were a desperate period of desertion and loneliness. Her mother she found cold and severe, but she adored her father, who betrayed her again and again in his strange, unexplained departures and long absences. Then came the ultimate desertions: her mother died when she was eight, her father when she was ten. After his death she wanted only "to live in a dream world in which I was the heroine and my father the hero." She grew up full of fears—of dogs, horses, snakes, of the dark, of being buried alive, of being scolded, of being disliked—and with her back in a brace. She was raised in a gloomy house by a benevolent grandmother and by formidable nurses and governesses. A young brother died when she was nine. Later she felt deserted by her husband—and in turn she rejected him sexually. Yet she survived to become the serene, poised, compassionate, immensely capable first lady of the Roosevelt years and of the United Nations. Did she succeed because of or in spite of the unhappiness and insecurity of her early life?

Consider Richard Nixon, the second of five brothers, two of whom died of illness in the home when Nixon was in his teens. Bruce Mazlish speculates that Nixon, who himself barely escaped death on one or two occasions, may have grown up with a feeling of survivor's guilt over his brothers' deaths and that his mother's long absence to take his ailing brother to a drier climate may have left the boy with a sense of insecurity and even betrayal. But Nixon turned out to be a very different type of political leader from Wilson, Schumacher, and Eleanor Roosevelt—a man who could build his career on anti-Communism and then lead his nation into involvement with the People's Republic of China, who could campaign on the issue of law and order and create the lawlessness of Watergate. Could his amoral, self-pitying justification for impeachable offenses be traced to insecurities and self-doubt in his childhood years?

Viewing some of the formative influences in the early lives of great leaders, one is struck by the acuteness of the insights of many psychobiographers and others even while recognizing the absence of systematic explanatory theory. Cumulative and comparative analysis of a large number of leaders should eventually provide stronger foundations for generalizations and hypotheses. We may come to understand better the powerful influences of family, school, and adolescent experience. But these studies will always be inadequate; they tend to overemphasize the early years of noted leaders and play down the potent effects of political learning, successes, and failures, of political and institutional context, during leaders' middle and late years. And they slight the role of *followers* who closely mold the behavior of leaders. To be sure, historians and journalists are now searching the records for evidence of the motives and feelings of "ordinary" men and women, as Studs Terkel has done, taping the testimony of contemporaries about their work, their concerns, their setbacks, and their dreams. But we must know much more about the hitherto nameless persons who comprise the followers of leaders if we are to develop adequate understanding of the reciprocal relationship.

Path-breaking work in psychology and related fields is gradually producing cumulative data, comparative analysis, and fruitful hypotheses that enable us to explore the motivations and behavior of persons in collectivities and hence to advance new propositions about the sources of leadership. Twenty-four hundred years after Plato, psychologists are looking systematically at the motives dominating the collective and reciprocal relationships of leaders and followers.

The Wellsprings of Want

The original sources of leadership and followership lie in vast pools of human wants and in the transformation of wants into needs, social aspirations, collective expectations, and political demands. Human beings embody these wants and other motives from birth. At the moment infants are expelled from the calm warmth and dependence of the uterus into the shocking, bewildering world of light and sound, of touching and prodding, of deprivation and fulfillment, they begin the lifelong process of stimulus and response that will culminate for some in skills and motivations for leadership. Biological endowments generate tendencies to respond in certain ways to stimuli. These endowments, the product of millennia of genetic mutations, have much in common among infants in all cultures, but each child also possesses a unique inheritance in its own singular genetic mix. The child is different in genetic makeup not only from all other children but from both parents and all the child's forebears.

The genetic inheritance initiates the series of openings and closures of life chances—mechanisms powerful enough to have a direct impact on evolving personality no matter how strong the cultural, social, and political mediators. Thus a girl born into a society that legally or culturally debars females from political participation and leadership will find no means of solving this problem (assuming it *is* a problem for her) beyond the traditional resort to influence in harem, boudoir, or court. A boy who is born with an undescended testicle, as Hitler is said to have been, or a club foot, like the abolitionist politician Thaddeus Stevens, and who grows up in a male-oriented society may to some degree seek to compensate for this biological accident all through life. Powerful glandular, motor, and neural attributes can dominate and control life careers despite the continuing play of family, social, and cultural influences. In some circumstances biology *is* destiny, political and otherwise. But much more typically the genetic and the environmental act together to produce endless new patterns and individualities. Since we are concerned with all the human materials that may be sources of the processes that culminate in leadership, we must consider biological processes. They are the genesis of wants and needs; biology ordinarily helps shape but does not predetermine destiny.

The long and complex process of leadership begins with infants' drives, direct expressions of their biological constitution. This is the force that makes them as one with their fellows. The "absolutely dependable motives," Otto Klineberg notes, are hunger, thirst, rest and sleep, elimination, breathing, activity, and sensory hunger; these drives are universal to all persons in all human cultures (though they are not exclusively human). This is not an exhaustive list of drives; psychologists have not agreed on such a list, just as they variously use the terms drives, motives, and (less often now) instincts to characterize the phenomena. They do agree that these are elemental forces that shape infants' physiological development and affect their psychological makeup. Sometimes these forces directly influence the potential for leadership. In certain societies, John Nash notes, "the satisfaction of some basic needs is so time-consuming an operation that little remains for investment in derived needs." This is the case with sheer hunger. It is not unusual in poverty-stricken countries to encounter political leaders who, in their speech, deportment, and ideology, bear the psychic scars of lack of food in their childhood—or of the desperate scramble to procure it.

The biologically determined drives do not operate in anarchic concatenation but in an intensifying sequence of interlocking biological and psychological factors. Freud described the stages of psychosexual development as oral, anal, phallic (or Oedipal), latent, and genital. The oral phase is one of almost total dependency of child on mother; the extent and longevity of this dependency may affect the nature of the passage of the child through later phases. The anal stage embraces both the physiological tension and satisfaction of elimination and both the erotic pleasures and the fears of toilet training; the severity of the training may affect the child's adult behavior. During the Oedipal phase the child gravitates into the restricted but highly socialized milieu of triangular relations among father, mother, and child. Associated with each of these stages, Erikson contends, are characteristic dilemmas between self and others that give rise to lasting character traits. Thus Erikson sees tendencies toward basic trust or mistrust emerging from the oral-sensory stage, toward autonomy or self-doubt from the muscular-anal stage, toward initiative or guilt from the locomotor-genital stage. Children's personalities begin to develop according to predetermined steps as, in growing, they perceive and engage widening arcs of social life.

For our purposes, alas, Freudian emphasis on the interplay of biological and early family (especially Oedipal) influences on individual socialization and personal development, while necessary, is by no means adequate. Indispensable though that emphasis is to any theory of personality, classic psychoanalytical theory fails to provide an adequate explanation of the dynamic biologic and social interaction in personal growth or of healthy or rational potentials in human beings. Radical behaviorism associated with B. F. Skinner, on the other hand, minimizes the role of motive and emphasizes external reinforcing determinants in the form of reward or reward-denial and short-run social conditioning in controlled environments at the expense of both the significant internal and the more generalized external influences that shape personality in multidimensional contexts over the long run. Neither approach lends itself to our need for a comprehensive approach to understanding of the mass popular base to which political leadership appeals.

Most of these theories ignore or underplay the force that may be the most important in shaping most leaders: *learning*. Learning from experience, learning from people, learning from successes and failures, learning from leaders and followers: personality is formed in these reactions to stimuli in social environments. Albert Bandura and Richard Walters have shown that behavior is learned not only by conditioning but by imitating persons with whom the learner identifies and whom he takes as models. The social environment becomes a vast maze of rewards and punishments that reinforce certain responses and extinguish others. The learning experience of each leader is so unique that fruitful generalization becomes impossible. Hence, cutting across all cultures, we turn back to the basic forces that provide clues to the understanding of sources of leadership.

Human wants are biological imperatives; they are the most widely distributed, intensely felt, and "absolutely dependable" motives. By wants we mean the palpable tissue demands in their simplest and most powerful state, expressed in the phenomena of persons directly and consciously feeling the lack of air or warmth or food or drink. The feeling of want is highly subjective, internal, and autonomous, as with a day-old infant wanting nourishment; the want stems from a drive, a tissue necessity, born into the child. Wants are biological requirements of the human system. They apply, in varying mixtures and degrees of intensity, to all human beings.

Here we must make a vital distinction between *wants* and *needs*. The concepts are often confused; some of the elements of "want" set forth above are often labeled "need," and needs are often seen as subsuming wants. (James Davies has literally equated the two concepts in his pioneering study of human nature in politics.) These concepts, both important, we sharply differentiate here. *Need* in longtime English usage implies a more socialized, collective, objective phenomenon, in the sense of persons requiring something needful in *the view of others* as well as of themselves. *Wants* are subjective, genetic, biological, organic, self-activating, inescapable. I *want* sweets but I *need* vitamins, so I am told.

The distinction is worth pondering. The want is direct, conscious, internal, physiological, and to a degree undiscriminating; thus the tissue requirements of liquid are satisfied by potable liquid in almost any form. Even at the stage of want a person will begin to choose—the infant may prefer milk to whiskey—but the preference stems much more from inherited dispositions than from cultural influences. The physical structure of the person comes into play—motor abilities, for example, and sensory perceptual tendencies—and these abilities are increasingly tested by environmental cues, responses, and resistances.

Wants, the great energizers, serve more as sources of action than guides to action. Motives are "pushed" by generalized drives and other body-bound forces and "pulled" by more specific wants, needs, aspirations, goals, and values. Children say "I want . . ." before they say "I want to . . ." The main source of action, though, is still the response to internal requirements.

Another distinction between wants and needs has profound implications for our conception of political leadership. As subjectively felt *wants,* with their impetus toward direct and conscious action to satisfy those wants, give way more and more to socially influenced *needs* defined increasingly by others than the self (in a process described below) a vital element of personal volition and purpose is eroded. "In contrast with objective need," according to M. Brewster Smith, "is subjective wish, desire, or want, all of which are motivational terms that find their home in a metapsychological framework of meaningful human action. They assume the peculiar human property of *intentionality*. . . ." The wanting person will be subjected more and more intensively to leaders in various guises—parents and siblings and teachers and peers—who will seek, consciously or not, to substitute their conceptions of need.

A political leader, Hanna Pitkin wrote, "must not be found persistently at odds with the wishes of the represented without good reason in terms of their interest, without a good explanation of why their wishes are not in accord with their interest." But what is that wish, what is that "real" interest, if it is crushed under the burden of needs leaders impose on their followers? Authentic wants express an autonomy and an individuality within a person that should not be hammered into nonexistence by social forces or manipulated to death by political "leaders." The wellsprings of want before contamination or purification—this is the source the leader must recognize even though wants will be, to some degree, "socialized" by later influences.

Just as biological inheritance may have a direct, pervasive influence on persons' behavior throughout their lives, a powerful *physiological* need in the early formative years may have a continuing impact on political behavior, especially on leadership and followership. Long-standing deprivation of a physiological need, even if later satisfied, Jeanne Knutson notes, will leave its imprint on the character of persons. "Overwhelmingly preoccupied with physical survival," she observes, "they do not have enough psychic energy remaining to become mentally or physically concerned with their environment." Their attitude toward others is marked by distrust and hostility. Evidence is scattered but suggestive. In Knutson's study of several hundred teachers, hospital employees, and wood and paper processors in Oregon, those who had shown greater physiological needs tended to exhibit more anxiety, dogmatism, and close-mindedness and a greater sense of being threatened than the rest of the sample. Psychic, social, and political isolates are not materials of which great leadership—or perhaps even great followership—can be formed. The physiologically deprived scored low on the Woodward-Roper Participation Scale, based on such activities as voting and contributing money to politics, and also on Knutson's Index of Leadership, based both on offices held since school and on the persons' assessment of their role in relationships. "Though individuals in this group may participate in some political activities," Knutson concludes, "the likelihood exists that they will not assume positions of even informal leadership among their peers. By their scores on other measures, such non-participation becomes understandable—to be inconspicuous is a necessary concomitant of safety."

These conclusions are drawn from explorations in an affluent Western nation. The same kind of physiological deprivation that inhibits self-confidence and political participation and leadership in one society might have opposite effects in another. Extreme want could destroy persons or convert them into true believers passionately intent on winning power in order to help their fellow sufferers, to gain for themselves the material and psychic goods they once sorely lacked, or to avenge themselves on the agents of deprivation and exploitation. Knutson notes Maslow's point that a political leader, even though president of the country and surrounded by all the comforts that civilization can offer, will continue to react as do those who experience the hunger and the cold, if the leader has been severely deprived in his formative years.

What the absence of gratification *actually does* to a person—for example, poor nutrition's causing a proneness to ill health—is important in itself. Equally significant is what a person *perceives* as lacking and hence reacts to—for example, the perception that others have food when I do not. Combined, these two factors can have a powerful effect. Physiological needs can be especially relevant to political leadership when they are seen as relative deprivation. Revolution usually breaks out after the frustration of rising expectations, amid a general view that the possibility of bettering conditions actually exists. Or, in another society, one poor boy, depending on his interpretation of his experience, may become a beneficent captain of industry sympathetic to his employees because he remembers "how it was," while another rejects the class out of which he struggled to get to the top.

According to Maslow and others, needs are arrayed on a hierarchical basis, ranging from physiological needs to safety needs (including the desire for freedom from fear and insecurity and harm), to the need for affection and belongingness (including the sense of being involved and accepted in a group), to the need for esteem, and to other needs higher in the pyramid or ladder.

Once physiological needs are alleviated, the next pressing need, for *safety* and *security,* becomes the priority. The child shows a preference for routine or rhythm, a world he can count on, one in which all-powerful parents shield him against harm. Persons with safety needs are likely to react to political events with attitudes of uncertainty and insecurity when dealing with normal political processes and with a yearning for a leader who may serve as a guide and simplifier. Describing the loss of identity evident in one man in a small group he studied intensively, Robert Lane reported: "In religion, national origin, political party, class status, and even sexual matters, Rapuano shows signs of ambivalent identification or loss of identity. I would argue that the most likely intellectual development for a man where nothing is anchored, nothing, including his concept of himself, is secure, is to put a high premium on stability, order, decisiveness, rationality. This is, I think, what has happened to Rapuano. Since confusion about himself, combined with ambivalence about political matters, and uncertainty about his occupational future are constantly framing questions in his own mind, and have made him chronically worried and badly ulcerous, he cannot bear more confusion and indecisiveness in his world—such confusion as may appear in legislative processes. . . . Finding it difficult himself to decide on policy matters, he insists that the President have the powers for quick decision." Maslow too concludes that the needs of persons lacking security in the early years "often find specific expression in a search for a protector, or a stronger person on whom he may depend, perhaps a Fuehrer." Perhaps the most marked characteristic is a low sense of political efficacy. Knutson's

Oregon study found that the security-deprived regard political activity as futile even though it is the citizen's duty to participate. They score higher on the index of political participation than do the physiologically deprived, but their participation is still low. And their potential for *leadership* is also limited, Knutson concludes. "Their insecurities keep them from desiring the social prominence which is a feature of public office and of leadership roles generally. Tending to view the world as threatening and the phenomena which surround them as unmanageable, persons who operate on this need level are likely to react with dogmatism and intolerance of ambiguity—to be inflexible and fearful in situations of crisis."

The need for affection and belongingness—the third need in Maslow's hierarchy—has long been considered a stimulus toward political participation and leadership. Whether in a nation of joiners, such as the United States, or in nations with strong political movements, as in Asia or Europe, the chance to take part in countless local clubs and associations or to enjoy the brotherhood of a militant, participatory cause is likely to attract many who are not necessarily seeking power or leadership but who crave a comradeship and acceptance that they have felt has been denied to them. Here again, however, deprivation of affection in early years can have varied impacts on later behavior. Children starved for love may indeed seek abundant compensating affection through social and political groups, and they will learn how to offer affection in order to receive it. Studies have shown a close relation between acceptance of self and acceptance of others.

In studying first-term members of the Connecticut legislature, James David Barber identified a type of legislator he classified as the Spectator—a person of "modest achievement, limited skills, and restricted ambitions, political and otherwise," short on competence for political leadership but long on availability. The Spectator wanted to stay in the legislature but not to be intensely active or to be a leader. His main pleasures seemed to stem from being approved, loved, and appreciated; he hated to be left out, rejected, or abused. His goal was clearly affection and approval rather than leadership and power.

This powerful need for affection and belongingness, combined with the effect of social influences and political forces, helps produce a variety of forms of leadership. A passion for affection and acceptance could manifest itself in leadership in small groups, where the warmth of close, stable, and affective relations may compensate for the deprivation of affection in childhood. Whether the group was involved in activities supporting the status quo or in revolutionary violence might be irrelevant to the participant as long as personal need was gratified. Or the quest for affection or belonging might lead to participation in highly structured bureaucratic organizations, where a sense of belonging would be persistent and dependable even if superficial or artificial. Or that quest could be expressed in participation in mass movements or in small conspiratorial sects wherein the membership's common sense of mission, persecution, and danger (especially in the face of official disapproval or suppression) could produce feelings of solidarity and mutual support powerful enough to appease the yearnings resulting from earlier deprivation. Affection or belonging needs can also serve as a source of different types of *followers*, among them passive followers who offer leaders undiscriminating support in order to gain access or affection, "participatory" followers who in effect exchange their support on a selective and bargaining basis but who also wish to feel part of the leadership group, and close followers of great men, who are really subleaders but are still dependent on their leader's involvement with *them*.

This last kind of dependence can be intense. President Wilson decided at one point to sack his personal secretary, Joseph P. Tumulty. Then he received a desperate letter from Tumulty. "I had hoped with all my heart that I might remain in close association with you. . . . To think of leaving you at this time . . . wounds me more deeply than I can tell you. . . . I dread the misconstruction that will be placed upon my departure and its reflection upon my loyalty. . . . You cannot know what this means to me and to mine. I am grateful for having been associated so closely with so great a man. I am heart-sick that the end should be like this." Wilson relented, but his compassion was short-lived. The next time Tumulty aroused his leader's ire, Wilson banished him from his circle.

The Transmutation of Need

It is in the transformation of human wants into needs that leadership first occurs. The wanting child is responding to a generalized drive shaped in the mother's womb. The child will want drink but will consume nutritionless liquid as well as milk, will want food but will eat poisoned candy as well as rice, will want to explore but will touch a scorching andiron as readily as a rubber ball. Parents who insist on milk and rice and rubber balls are substituting their own conceptions of the infant's needs for those of the child, and they do so in the pursuit of aims and values that the parents, rather than the child, establish. This is the initial act of leadership.

If wants are drives experienced as feelings of longing, needs are wants influenced by the environment. When environments change because of longtime shifts in the climate, for example, wants must yield to the new circumstances or the wanting creature will yield to biological imperatives. "Creatures that go on wanting things that interfere with fulfilling their needs or do not come to want the things they need are likely in the very long run to have their genes dropped from the genetic pool of the species,'' Brewster Smith observes. It is the act of deliberate and selective ''socializing''—the influencing in terms of group values of another person's wants—that brings the conscious leadership process into play. The leader—parent, teacher, doctor, priest, schoolmate—chooses to encourage certain wants and discourage others. Drives and wants remain the basic energizers, the main ''pushers,'' but the targets toward which the wants are directed become more focused as wants give way to needs. The child's want for food becomes, under the parents' guidance, a need for nutrition; the child's want for freedom from pain becomes, under the doctor's examination, a need for medicine (which the child would not take voluntarily). The leaders are those who closely influence stimulation and transformation of wants. There is a feedback effect in the push-pull of wants and needs: wants energize and broadly direct needs, but needs focus and channel wants. As needs ''educate'' wants, persons may come to want what they need.

Because needs are broadly shaped by both impersonal environmental forces and by persons who are themselves caught in the grip of circumstance, psychological and social needs manifest themselves in historical necessity. Hannah Arendt referred to those ''who desired liberation from their masters and from necessity, the great master of their masters'' and to the ''most powerful necessity we know'' as the ''life process that permeates our bodies.'' Franklin D. Roosevelt reiterated that ''necessitous men are not free men.'' Within the working of iron necessity, however, there is some play at the joints, and this provides the margin for leadership. Leaders are distinguished by their quality of *not* necessarily responding to the wants of ''followers,'' but to wants transformed into needs. Leaders respond to subjective wants and later to more objective needs as the leaders define those wants and needs. Followers' definitions of wants and needs will also change in the continuing interplay with leadership.

We can generalize across cultures about fundamental human needs and their implications for leadership in two significant respects: in the *frustration* of needs and—paradoxically—in their *gratification*.

Needs can be frustrated by environmental circumstance, such as climate-caused famine, or by the inaction of those who could fulfill needs. Such unfulfilled needs become the most powerful of motives. No one is more enslaved—at the level of bodily need—than persons wild with thirst, deep in pain, desperate with hunger, fighting for air. No matter that their own bodies imprison them; the tyranny of deprivation controls. The more acute and powerful the need, the more persons are drawn down to the most bodily motives. A person wracked by hunger will fight for air before seeking food; a person wild with thirst will flee a burning cottage before seeking drink. Those who died in the stifling Black Hole of Calcutta evidently fought for air rather than water. In some circumstances an awful hierarchy of deprivation assumes mastery.

At the more benign level of mere starvation, responses to need frustration can vary considerably. In laboratory starvation experiments, subjects typically become obsessed with the thought of food for a time and then settle into apathy and resignation. Lethargy may extend to politics. As a rudimentary example, Davies suggests that "an individual who is very hungry is *un*able to turn his attention to political concerns at the very time when his political action may get him some food." But the actual behavior of the deprived group may depend largely on the nature of leadership within the group, or on leadership in the community and nation. During the French Revolution, at a time when workers spent the bulk of their income on food and sometimes on bread alone, the housewives of Paris exerted intense pressure in face-to-face confrontation with the Jacobin leadership in Paris; the women would not be put off long by excuses and promises, and they became usually an unseen but powerful presence in revolutionary councils. Throughout history food deprivation has led to fierce competition for limited resources, to massive migrations, wars of conquest, revolutions, and civil strife, as well as to egalitarian ideologies and movements.

Common sense would suggest that the placating of needs would turn people's interests inward and would lower the intensity of their public concern and involvement. Yet if the frustration of physiological needs is politically significant, far more consequential is the *gratification* of such needs. The vital aspect of this hierarchy for Maslow and for students of leadership is its dynamic quality: as lower needs are satisfied, higher needs come into play. "Bread before Bach"—but the gratification of hunger automatically brings an end to that sequence and encourages the pursuit of higher needs. Maslow's theory need not be accepted literally; it is imprecise, and confirming empirical studies are limited. But they do exist, and the influence of a rough hierarchy of needs has also been supported by historical experience. The physical deprivation of the Great Depression did not activate American workers politically; rather they became less and less militant as they huddled in their homes or in breadlines. It was not the deprivation that directly mobilized workers but Roosevelt's forceful leadership during his first thirty months in office. It was in 1935, not in 1931 or 1933, that industrial workers, their immediate needs somewhat satisfied, felt secure enough to throw their collective weight into the economic struggle over industrial unionism.

The needs themselves have direct implications for politics. The powerful "lower" need for safety or security—for order and predictability, for protection against invasion, war, catastrophe, disease, threats to motherland or to home, crime in the streets—puts heavy pressure on government to perform. Karen Horney conceived the phenomenon largely in individual terms, as feelings of insecurity (especially on the part of infants and children) in the face of a dangerous and hostile environment, resulting, in turn, in neurotic needs for affection, approval, and prestige. This kind of individual need for security may closely influence the personality and attitudes of individual political leaders, but the *safety* needs rising from a sense of collective insecurity can influence whole populations. To be sure, political response may not be all that direct or positive. "People generally do not turn to politics," Davies notes, "to satisfy hunger and to gain love, self-esteem, and self-actualization; they go to the food market, pursue members of the opposite sex, show friends what they have done, and lose themselves in handicrafts, fishing or contemplation—with rarely a thought about politics. If achievement of these goals is *threatened* by other individuals or groups too powerful to be dealt with privately, people then turn to politics to secure these ends." When the achievement of these goals *does* seem to be threatened, political leadership is called into play. Moreover, the need for safety may be combined with other basic needs, such as hunger, to produce a multiplier demand. Such a combination helps explain such episodes as the massacres and other terrors of the French Revolution and the ferocity of combat in the Chinese and Russian civil wars and revolutions.

The political consequences of sexual need are less clear. For Freud's heavy emphasis on the primacy of sex certain theorists have substituted a much blander concept of affection and belonging. What the need theorists have gained in subtlety and proportion they have lost in the analytical power and promise of the study of sexuality. The exploration of sexual motivation in laboratory studies of learning processes, however, has been less extensive than the analysis of hunger, thirst, and pain. Moreover, neither before nor after procreation is sex crucial to the survival of the individual; sexual abstention does not cause death, though some may consider it a condition worse than death. Its varied use as a sign of personal interest and creativity provides, as M. Brewster Smith has suggested, a good reason why it *can* be more relevant to personality development than the obligatory needs.

As species-wide behavior, sex may no longer even be necessary for survival, considering the growing possibilities of medical implantation and other developments. The satisfaction of the need for sex has, as individual behavior, led to some of the more interesting political episodes in history; as aggregate behavior it has made possible the continuation of the social and political system. Between the extremes of macroanalysis and microanalysis, knowledge of the politics of sex is limited, despite the pioneering work of Harold Lasswell and others. We know that observers of a great orator swaying a crowd sense an almost orgasmic relation between leaders and followers, but this kind of phenomenon is rather murky.

A crucial element, as one moves up the ladder of the "lower needs," is the change in the extent and character of leadership influence. To a degree, followers' needs become less egoistic and short-run and more consciously and deliberately defined as they move out of the gross restraints rising from hunger, perceived threats to survival, and withdrawal of affection and as they cultivate and become engaged with a broader, more diverse culture-and-leadership-influenced set of needs. Leaders may shape the manifestations of more basic needs as well. In the endless interplay between leaders and followers, each will be motivated by needs but these needs may sharply differ. Followers may respond to a leader's concern or shift support to other leaders who promise to show even more concern. They may follow a Winston Churchill with enthusiasm during a time of compelling need for survival and later reject him when social and economic needs—which he showed little promise of meeting—seemed likely to be paramount.

The manifestations of these various needs will of course vary widely from culture to culture. But proponents of need-hierarchy theory contend that all cultures share a basic hierarchy, which may vary superficially. If so, the implications for leadership are significant. It will be recalled that the *frustration* of the lower needs merely intensifies the motivation to realize them. Only gifted and purposeful leadership can prevent that motive intensification from leading to even greater frustration, privatization, apathy, neurosis, and other forms of social disarray. But the *gratification* of needs places an even greater burden on leadership—above all, to raise its own goals as the needs of followers are transmuted into higher and higher searches for individual and social fulfillment.

The Hierarchies of Need and Value

Children progress from the received morality of the cave, the herd, the tribe, the family, to the broader, more consciously conceived values that will guide and strengthen them in wider collectivities. Early morality lays the basis for ideological attachments that may grip the adult leader and follower. One thinks of Woodrow Wilson's "Presbyterian conscience," instilled in him in his father's church and manse and still influencing his personal behavior—and hence history—during his presidential years. "Moralities sooner or later outlive themselves," Erikson concludes, "ethics never: this is what the need for identity and for fidelity, reborn with each generation, seems to point to. Morality in the moralistic sense can be predicted to be predicated on superstitions and irrational inner mechanisms which, in fact, ever again undermine the ethical fiber of generations; but old morality is expendable only where new and more universal ethics prevail." If the origin of the leader's value system lies in childhood conscience, adolescence and adulthood bring new overtures and new closures as norms are interpreted and applied in ever-widening, ever more differentiated social collectivities.

Theories of personal development that can help explain the lifelong process of forming social and political values must differentiate measurably among stages of personal development and fulfillment. They must make possible broader explorations of the human potential both for individual self-realization and for civic virtue and even for aesthetic standards—for an almost indefinite expansion and realization of people's human and generous possibilities. They must be holistic in avoiding reduction of explanation to simple and single causes; discriminatory in distinguishing between levels of behavior; developmental in analyzing long-term personal and social change. A. H. Maslow's theory, viewed in a broader sequence of wants, needs, hopes, and expectations, meets this test; so does that of Lawrence Kohlberg.

Basing his concepts on data drawn from Taiwan, Mexico, Turkey, Yucatan, and the United States, and building on Piaget, Kohlberg identifies six stages of moral development. In the first two—the "preconventional level"—the pre-adolescent is oriented toward punishment, defers to superior power, and sees proper actions as those that satisfy needs, mainly one's own. In the next two stages—the "conventional level"—the emphasis is on conformity and acceptability to gain approval, and this merges into a concern with authority and fixed rules, even with maintenance of the given social order for its own sake. In the last two stages—the "postconventional level"—the moral orientation is more principled. At the lower of these two stages there is greater awareness of the role of procedural rules in group and individual norms. These rules and values are shared by a *social transaction or contract for overall utility:* "the greatest good for the greatest number." This orientation shades into the final (sixth) stage, where there is focus on general ethical standards, on principles that are "logical, comprehensive, universal, and consistent." These are the more general or universal values noted above—those of liberty, equality, dignity, justice, and human rights.

It is in the congruence of the levels of need and other motivations, and of the stages of moral development, that leadership is animated, politicized, and enlivened with moral purpose.

"How about the word 'democracy.' What does that mean?" the interviewer asks Judith, ten years old.

"Democracy . . . oh. Well, democracy is really a kind of—well, what the people have—well, I can't explain it!"

"Say the words that come to your mind."

"Well, democracy is sort of what the people should have . . . well, you should have democracy and be . . . well, it's like . . . uh!"

"You're not exactly sure what it is?"

"I'm not exactly sure, but in a way I am—it's what the people should have, they should have democracy, like be a good citizen, or something like that—I can't explain it."

"Uh huh—it's something good at any rate."

"Yes."

"You're not completely sure about the details."

"No, I'm not."

Judith's fuzziness, no doubt, results in part from her youth and stage of development. She is very young to be adept at such abstraction. She has grown up in a society that itself lacks a sure sense of its political values and the institutions that serve them. Her confusion also stems from the plight of the youngster passing through a congeries of situations, cliques, and roles that bring with them threats to the youth's self-identity and set of norms. Moving into adolescence, youths may come to reject the easy, imitative, deferential allegiance of childhood to national symbols and leaders. But what to put in their place? The adolescent mind, Erikson says, is essentially a mind of the moratorium, "a psychosocial stage between childhood and adulthood, and between the morality learned by the child, and the ethics to be developed by the adult." It is not always easy to recall, Erikson says elsewhere, "that in spite of the similarity of adolescent 'symptoms' and episodes to neurotic and psychotic symptoms and episodes, adolescence is not an affliction but a normative crisis, i.e., a normal phase of increased conflict characterized by a seeming fluctuation in ego strength as well as by a high growth potential." While the plight of the adolescent may not be critical in many cultures, or even among most adolescents in Western cultures, the typical condition is one of confusion and of spasmodic, helter-skelter change. This personal confusion may well reflect the broader confusion in Western cultures about the nature of values and their function in political life.

The concept of value is so crucial to our concept of leadership here that we must establish definitions. Values have a special potency because they embrace separate but closely interrelated phenomena. Values indicate desirable or preferred *end-states* or collective goals or explicit purposes, and values are *standards* in terms of which specific criteria may be established and choices made among alternatives. Thus social equality can be both a goal and a standard by which to measure policies, practices, other goals. We will use the term *end-values* to designate these two intertwined meanings of values as goals and standards. Values are also defined as *modes of conduct,* such as prudence, honor, courage, civility, honesty, fairness. Modes sometimes are goals in themselves but they are always means by which political and other human enterprises should be conducted, and thus we will call these *modal values.* Some values are both ends in themselves—intrinsic values—and the means of achieving further end-states—extrinsic or instrumental values—as in the case of a young man who goes to college to get a job but values the education for its own sake, the colonial people who embrace nationalism and achieve only independence but never give up nationalism after independence is gained, and the student who prizes high grades in themselves as satisfying and stimulating but also as a means of getting a better job.

End-values as goals and as standards, modal values as modes of behavior, and instrumental and intrinsic values that represent both means and ends—all these are a formidable arsenal for any leader who can command them. If leaders believe in the goal of equality, measure questions of public policy by egalitarian standards, monitor their own and their adversaries' behavior by canons of civility and honor, and favor a value such as fraternity because it also leads to the end-state of equality, they can summon wide support from followers with many different values; but to the degree that these actions are controversial, they can also arouse intense opposition and conflict.

Are values mere motives, or do they have an independent (and thus stronger) arousing and directing power? Students of the subject disagree; sometimes values are treated as being merely another kind of motive. If so, the difference in degree amounts to a difference in kind. "Values have a strong motivational component as well as cognitive, affective, and behavioral components," Milton Rokeach says. Compared to cognitive certitudes ("it's raining outside") values are internalized so deeply that they define personality and behavior as well as consciously and unconsciously held attitudes. They become an expression of both *conscience* and *consciousness.* Hence holders of values will often follow the dictates of those values in the absence of incentives, sanctions, or even witnesses—like the girl who returns a lost wallet when she knows no one saw her pick it up, or politicians who defend free speech when it is guaranteed to lose them votes. A test of adherence to values is the willingness to apply principles or standards to oneself as well as others.

Phenomena so powerful hardly develop randomly or in a fit of absentmindedness, nor do they spring full-clothed from the brow of Jove. Yet the source of these potent and palpable forces has long been in dispute. As a "practical" matter, parents, teachers, ministers, and other keepers of parochial and general liturgies, codes, and moralities over the millennia have sought to instill the "right" values, including especially modal values like honesty, in the young and seemingly pliable. These deliberate efforts have had mixed results; some recent evidence suggests that the more obvious and formal and *external* the efforts at teaching values, without effectively reaching internalization, the more meager the results. Moral behavior is more closely related to affective response, to degrees of love and affection for the parents, studies indicated, than to external stimuli such as expectations and practices of concrete reward and punishment. Perhaps the official norm definers and standard setters influence the "lower-level" value retailers—parents, teachers, etc., who have influence on followers—in the familiar two-step process (i.e., newspaper editorial influence, taxi driver who influences customer). But the practical, grass-roots teachers of morals are often the first to see and to admit the limits on their influence.

How, then, account for the strong grip of certain end-values and modal values on large numbers of persons? Value setters are established throughout society and are all the more influential because they are implicit, taken for granted, and thus not overtly concerned with reforming their fellow human beings. Both Piaget and Kohlberg have raised fundamental questions about this process in development evolution.

And why do children move from a "lower" stage to a "higher" stage in moral outlook? Why, if they are born into a lower stage, do they not remain locked into it, captive to cultural forces, prisoners of their "lower" wants and needs? Some of course do remain so, but many do not. For those who move on, the motive force is composed both of those peers who may demonstrate higher intrinsic modes of moral reasoning and of others—in school, church, social status, or peer group—who have moved one step beyond the learner in the hierarchy. Children tend to prefer levels of moral thinking above their own stage of development, studies indicated, but they did not comprehend what they preferred if it was more than one stage above their own.

There is considerable slippage in the communication of values. It is unlikely that leaders who serve as "value communicators" convey the precise values adumbrated from official purveyors on high—except perhaps in wars or other crises. Aaron did not interpret the Ten Commandments as Moses handed them down. Usually they exact a price in serving as transmitters, modifying values as they express or impart them. Paul's codification of the values of Jesus changed them powerfully. But this role may make the assimilation of values more expeditious and effective, even insidious in its possible distortion. Different types of leaders exercise influence at different stages: parents during the earlier years, teachers later, peers and preachers and political leaders at others. Fathers may instill values as authority figures more than as mealtime or bedtime preachers, mothers as suppliers and withholders of affection rather than as in-house purveyors of official doctrine.

Precisely which peers or cultural heroes—playmates, schoolmates, older siblings, parents, surrogates, teachers, scoutmasters, village elders, folk heroes—exercise how much influence over value formation cannot be ascertained with much precision; in any event, those forms of influence vary from culture to culture. The political culture itself establishes dominant and less dominant values. For our purpose, several factors must be kept in mind. The cumulative influence of leaders on value formation is considerable but not total. The movement of children through stages of moral development, and their receptivity to influence at any stage, still turns significantly on their individual experience and on their skills. Widening activities and broadening knowledge are in themselves forces for change. But cognitive development is in turn dependent on the direct, the two-step, and the multi-step flows of influence from peers and others. Through participatory experience the evolving persons "hook in" cognitively and morally with influential persons around them, but on others' terms as well as their own.

The psychological processes are multiple and complex. Children must develop some sense of guilt, or at least a sense of empathy, as they make value judgments about "fairness" and "honesty" at higher and higher levels above the primitive levels of morality. They learn how to imitate parents and others, but their imitation is selective, based on original and autonomous want. A sense of reciprocity grows, changing in form at different stages. In Kohlberg's first stage of moral development, the "most primitive form of reciprocity is that based on power and punishment, i.e., the reciprocity of obedience and freedom from punishment." In the next higher stages come literal exchange and then a recognition that positive social relationships are systems of reciprocity based on gratitude, empathy, and mutual expectations. At the highest stage the child is appealing not to the palpable rules of the social order but to the abstract conception of justice that lies beyond those rules—"it isn't fair!"

As children participate more widely in home, school, and play groups, confront diverse personalities, exchange confidences, and take part in group decisions, they are drawn more and more into new roles. Ultimately young people move into wider educational, occupational, legal, and political milieus. But not all do, or they do so on different terms. "One index of differential opportunities for participation in the social structures of government and of work or economy," according to Kohlberg, "is that of socioeconomic status. It is abundantly clear that the lower class cannot and does not feel as much sense of power in, and responsibility for, the institutions of government and economy as does the middle class.''

Qualities of leadership emerge out of these imitative, selective, and role-taking or empathetic processes. As persons gain in experience, knowledge and understanding, imitation, intentionality, and capacity for higher moral judgment, and as they grow more skillful in accommodation and role-taking, they gain in the capacity for leadership that draws from understanding of others' needs, roles, and values and expresses fundamental principles and purposes. Distinctions emerge between leader and follower, for leaders must comprehend many roles and followers fewer; leaders must accommodate followers' wants and needs without sacrificing basic principle (otherwise they would not be leaders); they must mediate group conflict without becoming mere referees or conciliators without purpose of their own; they must be ''with'' their followers but also ''above'' them. But the leader's main strength is the ability to operate close enough to the followers to draw them up to the leader's level of moral development.

Leaders do not neatly array themselves in stages any more than followers do. In a study of high school teachers in California, Elizabeth Simpson found a group of men and women who tended to be moderate-to-left in political beliefs, above average in interest and political participation, generally optimistic about the resolvability of social problems, advocates of the values of freedom, responsibility, law and order, and fairness, but nevertheless prone to conventional as well as postconventional thinking, in Kohlberg's definition. They viewed the functions of law as more the prohibition of undesirable acts than ''the prescription of facilitating behavior as standards and guidance, or a *beneficial* and *rational* approach to the assistance of human beings based on a principled belief in what is right or just.'' Most felt that the law could be broken under certain conditions, to be sure, but when asked the functions of law in the abstract, they responded on the basis of prohibition and control to a much larger degree than might have been expected from their ages and social class. Still, on balance, these teachers, in their collective shaping of the curriculum, their control of readings and discussions, their role as authority figures, their unconscious projections of attitudes—but not, we can presume, in formal preachings and moralizings—were helping to draw students up through the levels of moral development.

It is still in many ways a mystery how the child or adolescent is propelled from one level to another. As we have seen, some do not change; they remain indefinitely in a stage of deference, of conformity, of simplistic norm-observance, of a literal following of rules. But among those who do move from preconventional to postconventional levels our future political leadership will be recruited. Again a fruitful explanation lies in Maslow's need theory, with its emphasis on the dynamic influence of lower and higher needs. Simpson has found a congruence between Maslow's developmental need sequence and Kohlberg's scheme of the motivational aspects of moral development. She sees Maslow's lowest need level—physiological and security needs—as related to Kohlberg's stages of both punishment by others and manipulation of goods and rewards by others; Maslow's belongingness needs as apposite to Kohlberg's norm levels of disapproval by others and censure by legitimate authorities; and Maslow's esteem needs—both self-esteem and social esteem—as congruent with Kohlberg's norm of community respect and disrespect, self-criticism and self-condemnation. Simpson sees an even more meaningful correspondence between the more opportunistic, reward-and-punishment, self-regarding, conformist attitudes and behaviors and the survival and belongingness needs at the bottom and middle levels of both Kohlberg's and Maslow's hierarchies; and between Maslow's need for self-esteem and efficacy and Kohlberg's emphasis on higher, less expedient, less self-involved values at the top of the two hierarchies.

Not every adolescent—not even every adolescent leader—spends much time contemplating the "higher" values. Most go about their business in a blissful state of unconcern about such portentous matters. A study of Italian youth less than a decade and a half after the end of World War II found the vast majority stating they had little or no interest in national and international matters; those that were interested often held views highly contradictory one with the other. Similar results probably would be obtained from studies of most Western societies. Youth groups in authoritarian societies may behave in a more ideological fashion, but even so one can presume that much of their behavior is motivated by lesser needs and values. In most societies those who assume leadership of school activities, peer groups, athletic teams, and the like do so spontaneously, perhaps without awareness of their leadership behavior. At the very least these activities may be a form of learning formal leadership roles; they may also be fraught with implications for the purposes and values of leaders and followers.

The study of leadership among groups of children and adolescents has traditionally emphasized the situationist and opportunistic character of leadership—that is, the witting or unwitting response of the potential leader to opportunities for leadership rising from transitory or persisting situations. Forty years ago, after experimenting with systematically varied combinations of leaders and followers among Japanese schoolchildren, K. Toki concluded that the specific requirements of the moment (rather than internalized normative standards, for example) determined the nature of the leadership in most cases. Especially significant was the set of results in his manipulation of leader absence from the group. When the leader was removed the group deteriorated, as one might expect, but it deteriorated in different ways depending on the physical extent of the removal, its duration, and the availability of a leader-substitute. Removal of a follower from the group had no perceptible effect on its structure.

Different situations tend to produce different leaders in similarly structured situations. William Whyte noted that the leader of a street-corner gang did not deal with his followers as if it were an undifferentiated group. He quotes a secondary leader: "On any corner you would find not only a leader but probably a couple of lieutenants. They could be leaders themselves, but they let the man lead them. You would say, 'They let him lead because they like the way he does things.' Sure, but he leans upon them for his authority. Many times you find fellows on a corner that stay in the background until some situation comes up, and then they will take over and call the shots. Things like that can change fast sometimes. . . ." The leader is the focal point for the organization of the group, Whyte concludes. In the absence of the leader its cohesion disintegrates and the group becomes a collection of smaller groups.

These findings could be multiplied almost endlessly; they have indeed become a staple of small-group leadership studies. This emphasis on *situation* in sociological and some psychological literature poses again the old problem of the influence of the personal compared with the environmental (class, school, community). Fred Greenstein notes the distinction that has occasionally been made in contemporary anthropology between the old culture-and-personality literature, which was especially concerned with early childhood socialization and its effects on personality formation, and the new culture-and-personality literature, which emphasizes systematic exploration of persons' cognitive maps of their environment. "At base, these divisions between old and new are an artifact of the history of research. Human beings at whatever stage of the lifelong socialization process, are not divided into self-contained compartments of personality versus cognitions, 'specifically political' versus 'non-political but politically relevant' development. What has been adventitiously separated needs to be pulled together. But in the present instance this will call for a good bit of careful conceptualization. We need sets of distinctions which 'carve at the joints' for thinking about what intervenes between personality socialization and political systems." Socialization processes to which we now turn may help make these distinctions.

4

THE SOCIAL SOURCES OF LEADERSHIP

The nuclear family is a tiny political system—a small *Leviathan,* Hobbes called it—and a primitive leadership system. In all cultures the origins of political attention and comprehension lie largely in the early childhood years. "The entire man is, so to speak, to be seen in the cradle of the child," Tocqueville said. We "must watch the infant in his mother's arms, we must see the first images that the external world casts upon the dark mirror of his mind, the first occurrences that he witnesses; we must hear the first words which awaken the sleeping powers of thought, and stand by his earliest efforts if we would understand the prejudices, the habits, and the passions which will later rule his life."

Cues provoke the flickering, widening interest of the child: a family reaction to a caste incident in India; a Communist parade in Peking; a class-oriented remark in Buenos Aires; a Republican uncle in Philadelphia; a Nazi song; the British flag flying in Durham; a tribal ceremony in Uganda; a religious service in Dublin; a family grouped around a television set waiting for the President to speak. Symbols of the dominant ideologies flow in around the child. Subtly or not, the child is rewarded for compliance, punished for deviance—by standards established by the *parents*.

The most common experience of humankind is close association with a parent or parents during the first several years of life. We can generalize across cultures about this experience that exists everywhere despite extended kinship systems in many cultures. The mother or mother-substitute, the chief nurturant figure, is the main object of identification and attachment, a relationship whose importance has been debated. The influence of need-reducing maternal feeding, by breast or otherwise, combined with daily household routines, makes the functioning mother a desired and satisfying object for the child. The infant may develop a keen sensitivity to the emotional behavior of its mother and to any intrusion that interrupts the intimate relationship. A powerful symbiotic relationship may develop, the strength of which is only slowly weakened by wider influences.

In most cultures the father becomes more important as the child grows older. The inclusion of the father creates a tiny social system. Much has been made, in Darwinian and Freudian theory, of the primal horde in which the violent and jealous father keeps all females for himself and drives away his sons until the brothers band together to kill and even devour their father; much has been made, too, of the tendency of the child to manage its feelings toward a punitive parent—usually the father—by displacing the punitiveness onto other targets (a result of which can be propensity toward the formation of an authoritarian personality). But the most common effect of the father's heightening intervention is the creation of a small, dynamic organization based on the interplay of two generations and two sexes. "Any group needs unity of leadership." Theodore Lidz says, reflecting long-held group theory in social psychology, "but the family contains two leaders—a father and a mother. Unity of direction and organization requires a coalition between the parents that is possible because of the different but interrelated functions of a father and a mother." The parental coalition gives unity of direction to the child.

A crucial aspect of the leadership system is the imbalance or asymmetry in early power relationships. Even children who escape classical Oedipal influences may envy the parents' status and power in family rivalry over scarce resources such as care, affection, and food, but the parents' near-monopoly of rewards and punishments is all but controlling. There are natural tendencies in almost all societies, Lawrence Kohlberg hypothesizes, for the child to see the father as the dominant authority, but the political influence of the father on the child is probably less marked in the American culture than in some others.

The Family as Imperium

This powerful little imperium of parents and child is neither closed not static. "For man's psychosocial survival," Erik Erikson says, "is safeguarded only by vital virtues which develop in the interplay of successive and overlapping generations, living together in organized settings. Here, living together means more than incidental proximity. It means that the individual's life-stages are 'inter-living,' cogwheeling with the stages of others which move him along as he moves them." No matter how heavy the impact of the parents' personality and example, the child moves increasingly from the near-captivity of parental influence to ego-defensiveness and ego-assertion of its own. Under Erikson's epigenetic principle the child develops by encountering and overcoming critical tasks in phases. The child plays, experiments—and again Erikson captures that crucial quality. "Play is to the child what thinking, planning, and blue-printing are to the adult, a trial universe in which conditions are simplified and methods exploratory, so that past failures can be thought through, expectations tested. The rules of play cannot be altogether imposed by the will of adults: toys and playmates are the child's equals. . . ." It is children's exploratory curiosity that releases them from bondage to their parents and heads them toward the assimilation of new experiences, learning, skills, and values, depending in part on how parents respond to that curiosity. As Jean Piaget and his collaborators and disciples have demonstrated, the child, by constantly adapting to new experiences and reaching out for more, develops intelligence, language, reasoning— and these impel the child to more play, exploration, and learning. These developments help move children from the status of passive *followers* to that of potential *leaders,* who at least act on their own needs and goals and at the most share leadership in the nuclear family.

The buzzing confusion begins to take form. Children learn to see people as members of racial, caste, class, geographical, occupational, or language groups. They learn from other people not only to identify but to identify with or against the people in such social categories. The earliest primitive set of childrens' values ("they have to be taught") is based largely on "we" versus "them." These early identifications and loyalties can show an impressive strength and persistence throughout a person's life. "It is remarkable to witness the endurance of nationalism, group identifications, and partisan loyalties," Richard Dawson and Kenneth Prewitt observe, "even in the face of extensive pressure toward change." A battery of cultural and institutional influences reinforce the process. In most cultures, family, neighborhood, village, urban enclave, and church or temple exist as mutual supports. Solidarity and acceptance are the price of psychic, social, and even physical survival.

From infancy, childhood, and adolescence, an individual passes through a series of social systems that may themselves be evolving and changing. The coalitions and conflicts that are Oedipal in the eye of the psychoanalyst may, in the view of the sociologist or cultural anthropologist, be socially conditioned and structured. The eye of the beholder may govern what is seen. The behavior that one discipline sees as a product of conflict among id, ego, and superego is to another a product of conditioning by the father as provider of social cues and as link and mediator with the outside world, and by the mother as provider of nurturant, indiscriminate love. However variously perceived, the process operates, as John Dollard reminds us, in a life that is one connected whole: one person who is captive to the tangle of influences operating *on* that person and *within* that person.

Against the enormous pressure of these socializing forces is ranged adolescent deviance and rebellion, creating a tension central to the study of leadership. Conflict is at least as crucial to politics as consensus. For many cultures the potential for deviance has been minimal. Over vast stretches of time and space societies have maintained themselves in unchanging configurations of social and religious and political institutions despite—or sometimes because of—external threats and pressures. New ranks of parents have transmitted the political culture to new ranks of children and adolescents. Religious sects have initiated the young into the majesty and mystery of their ancient practices. Youth groups—Boy Scouts, Young Patriots' Leagues, Red Pioneers—have encapsulated the dominant symbols of patriotism, motherland, nationhood. Puberty rites and tribal rituals have celebrated the transition to adulthood within a set tradition or value system. Socialization is essentially a conserving and hence a conservative force in its maintenance of existing social distinctions and institutions.

But the political culture *does* change, and the mechanics and dynamics of this change set the stage for later leadership emergence and conflict. Few societies are immune in the long run to fundamental economic and social changes that bring in their wake forces of social and geographical mobility that massively alter the flow of political change in families and communities. Population movements caused by war, poverty, and natural disasters transplant and recreate whole communities. Some localities and indeed regions—Russia's Georgia, the Scottish Highlands, the American, German, French, and Indian "Souths"—may escape nationalizing trends for longer periods and finally succumb. Other separatist communities may exist as tiny enclaves cut off from the great city that encircles them, as in the case of Oscar Lewis' rural culture in Mexico City, but eventually the isolation is penetrated, to some degree at least.

Even families in static communities seemingly untouched by social and economic change may develop major discontinuities, influenced by imbalance in maternal or paternal domination, by the absence of mother, father, or both parents, by substitution of "constellations of 'significant others' in the early learning process," as Kenneth Langton notes. Or the parents may simply disagree on political issues, although in most cultures the wife conforms to her husband's value preferences or at least maintains neutrality. When they do differ the children face cross-pressures. Sometimes they may resolve the conflict by adopting a neutral position; sometimes the mother or the father (or some other member in an extended kinship group) may exert the stronger pull. Intergenerational conflict may be sharper over questions of political process or structure—civil disobedience, for example—than over specific policy issues. Change and intrafamily conflict proceed hand in hand.

Authoritarian or overprotective parents evidently have a special influence on the shape of adolescent thinking. Findings of studies are, as usual, mixed, but there is evidence that short-run conformity may be gained at the expense of subsequent rebellion. In a study of five nations—Britain, Germany, Mexico, Italy, and the United States—Gabriel Almond and Sidney Verba concluded that American children took part more freely and critically in family decisions, and hence rebellion in these families probably was less frequent. Parental overprotection in France, Belgium, and Holland was found to arouse political distrust and disaffection among high school and university students. A Caribbean study showed a decrease in offspring agreement with parents' party preferences as family authoritarianism increased, except for the most highly authoritarian group. A Cambridge, Massachusetts, study reported that the children of parents who try to exercise stricter control over their teenage children are those who most often move away from the political preferences of their parents. The family is an imperium, but like all such domains it has its boundaries.

Political Schooling

The child's society is found in the home, the village road or the front stoop, the schoolroom or the city playground. But in recent decades, in most cultures, formal schooling has come to be seen as central in shaping political attitudes and behavior. Fifty years ago Charles Merriam, on the basis of a survey of eight Western nations, called the school the major instrument in shaping civic education; four decades later two investigators concluded: "The public school is the most important and effective instrument of political socialization in the United States." And Almond and Verba in their five-nation study maintained that no other variable compared with the educational in influence on political attitudes. These views are disputed, and some researchers are more impressed by the sheer variety of socializing forces, by the impact on classroom learning of predispositions formed in the home environment, and by direct learning from experiences and events—a learning that goes on long after school.

Obviously much depends on the child, the school, and aspects of the school and the culture involved: the class and caste heterogeneity of the student bodies, the curricula and school quality, and on the extent of the authority of these schools as agencies of national values, or of regional or community mores, and of religious doctrine. The formal classroom training and classroom teaching may be the least of the school's political influence. In one study, the number of civics courses taken by a group of American students seemed to have little effect on their political interest, knowledge, and sense of efficacy. As every teacher knows, the pedagogue's influence is a limited one, except in special circumstances. Younger children are more impressionable than older, but the political attitudes of the younger will be more diffused and inchoate. The older may be more resistant, but when reached they may be more politically focused and effective. Classroom teaching in a politically mobilized and indoctrinated society may have strong impact because it reinforces much wider, more intensive efforts in the society at large. Thus in Imperial Japan pupils took part in ceremonial assemblies in which the Imperial Rescript on Education was read, the Imperial Portraits exhibited, the flag raised, and the entire undertaking carried through with a protocol that was at once grave and moving. Students joined in pilgrimages to shrines. But even in authoritarian societies resistances may develop. Soviet principles of pedagogy leave no doubt that education is an instrument of the state, and textbooks, songbooks, and technical manuals follow the prescribed line, but Soviet students, one study showed, become politically apathetic "from sheer overwhelming boredom aroused by the dogmatism and repetitiveness of all political communication sponsored by the regime, whether in the classroom, the Komsomol, or the mass media.'' Indoctrination is not uniformly irresistible.

And children are not mere sponges, soaking up cultural influences that they mingle with psychological ones; in most cases they are generators of ideas that they in turn project into their environment. What they *are* shapes to a large degree their capacity to learn what is offered, their selectivity, and the way in which they integrate their knowledge and apply it in specific social and political situations.

The powerful influence of peer groups in molding social attitudes is as evident to the casual observer as it is in the findings of numberless studies. The price of group membership is conformity to prevailing norms, whether in urban high schools or in the Soviet Union or in an elite college like Bennington, where a classic study demonstrated that acceptance by prestigious peer groups required allegiance to liberal norms (doubtless an early example of radical chic). Peers may reinforce or attack home and classroom norms; much depends on the degree of heterogeneity in schools and the extent to which students are segregated—in classroom, luncheon hall, or athletic field—into class, sex, and racial groupings. Association with peers may also help a child move from parental control to more autonomous values and choices as children move from restricted family environments into ever-widening transforming social systems.

Process influences the *content* of adolescent views on politics—especially views on political participation and leadership, loyalty, dissent, or rebellion, apathy or involvement. Whatever the nature of personal youthful rebellion against parental or school authority, however, the earliest external political responses are conforming. Children are encouraged, first of all, to be patriots. In the United States—and there is reason to think that the situation is comparable in most other societies—schoolchildren see theirs as the best country, one that is clearly superior to all others. This attachment is stable, Robert Hess and Judith Torney report, and shows virtually no change through the years of elementary school. When pressed, children cannot explain what their country means; they just love it. "Sally, would you rather be an American or an Englishman?" the interviewer asks. "I'd rather be an American because I like America better, because we have freedom and I know more people here." Ninety-five percent of a sample of American children agreed that the American flag is the best flag in the world.

Not only do youngsters love their country, they admire the people who run it. In a New Haven survey of fourth- through eighth-grade children of widely diverse social background, virtually all described their political leaders as helpful, benevolent, and good. Little of the cynicism of adult years was evident. Chicago schoolchildren perceived their leaders and governmental institutions as competent, infallible, trustworthy. If pressed to name a famous political leader they did *not* want to be like, most listed a foreign political leader such as Khrushchev. "This early faith in political authority figures seems to be general among young children in this country," Hess and Torney find. They have reason to believe that it is characteristic of other countries as well. Since early learning strongly affects later learning, this acceptance of authority is a potential long-run influence toward followers' acceptance of leadership in their adult years.

The American schoolchild has a hierarchical view of government. The President looms as far more important and far better known personally than legislators, judges, or mayors (except where certain persons may be unusually visible and popular, as happened in the case of the mayor of New Haven). Indeed, this sense of hierarchy is shared by adults. Beyond this, some children see the vice president, governors, and mayors as essentially the President's helpers. The President pays the governors, a fifth-grade boy observed, and the governors pay the mayors. The President bosses Congress and gives it jobs to do; legislators are helpers to executives at all levels. Theirs is a vertical structure; they do not see lateral or countervailing or parallel structures of governmental authority (e.g., the Supreme Court, Congress, the President). Most schoolchildren have benevolent attitudes toward most authority figures.

But the magic is in the image of President—perhaps mainly in the image of any *President,* for "the President of China" received (as of 1960) high ratings too. Certainly the political authority the youngster perceives and idealizes in the United States is that of the President. He outranks even the visible corner cop in the child's emerging civic consciousness. The President is a very personal image, much as God is to the child. The concept of the presidency as a cluster of roles develops later. At first the institution of government is seen as personal; "the government is like the President, but he [the government] isn't actually a President," says one primary schoolboy. School-children know the President's name, they have some idea of what he does. They believe that the President is friendly, helpful, personally available by telephone call or visit. "Judy, do you know of anyone in the United States government?" "Well, the President." "What do you know about the President?" "Well, that a . . . oh, dear . . . he . . . ah, makes laws and a . . . and ah . . . well, he tries to do good." And the President helps the schoolchild make sense of the rest of the government.

The most dramatic manifestation of this attitude toward the highest political leader in the United States comes in response to the death of a President. In the wake of John Kennedy's assassination schoolchildren shared with adults the kind of intense experience of watching the funeral and the mourning nation on television, the resulting shock, grief, and sense of vacancy similar to that experienced in the loss of a parent; among both children and adults there was a marked incidence of headache, sleeplessness, loss of appetite, and the like. Schoolchildren felt they *knew* President Kennedy. And they did know him. Most of the youngsters in a Detroit survey remembered the President mainly in personal terms; they mentioned his courage, friendliness, kindness, and so on. But many others remembered him as *President*—especially his stands on civil rights and peace. "He made peace because he did not want war," a nine-year-old said. The older the schoolchildren, the more they remembered Kennedy for political rather than merely personal reasons. Some of the upper-grade children listed key programs and specific policies. To them he was more than a symbol; he was a concrete political figure, a leader.

The President as idealized father may have been exaggerated but the cognitive and substantive content of the image of the President has been underestimated. Slowly a transfer of perception of authority figures takes place. The sizable overlap of the images of the father and of the President, the Chicago study concludes, begins to diminish as the schoolchild gains information about the role demands of the presidential office. In effect, Robert Hess and David Easton report, the child is "learning to see differences among adults in terms of role definitions (what they should be like) as well as in terms of role performance (what kind of person they really are)." The youngsters are acquiring, in short, some sophistication in perceiving and measuring their leaders.

Knowledge about different leaders comes to different children in different sequences. While American schoolchildren grow to awareness of the President before other executives, and of executives before legislators, and of national and local levels of government before state levels, their comprehension of political *parties* and their differences develops relatively late. The parties are seen in terms of personalities rather than issues. Children wear party campaign buttons with relish; the contests between candidates seem rather like football matches. Younger schoolchildren are more likely to view the parties as partners rather than as competitive foes. But as the school years pass the party image sharpens, party identification hardens, and understanding of the competition grows. These tendencies may, however, be dwindling now with the decline of party identification and salience in the United States. Campaign insignia were rare in the 1976 campaign and not only for cited reasons of economy. An understanding of *issues* comes still later than the understanding of leaders or parties, and these are largely perceived in a context of leadership and political institutions.

Socio-economic status seems to have some influence on perceptions. In general, schoolchildren of lower socio-economic status are less politicized than children of upper economic status. They are more deferential toward political leaders than are higher status peers; thus they are more likely to accept authority figures as trustworthy, less likely to question their motives, more acquiescent in political institutions. An exception is the children of rebellious or discontented minorities who are seeking redress and who come to view the neighborhood policeman and the politician as enemies or, at the least, as accommodating defenders of the status quo. As for sex differences, boys in the United States (as typically in other countries) at least at the elementary level show greater political interest and possess more political information than do girls, who seem more oriented toward personality figures. These social differences may reflect the biases of researchers, but even more they bespeak cultural influences.

Such are some findings, heavily canted toward the American experience, and probably toward the male experience, about the early social influences on the youths who will be, in different ways, the followers of the future—and the leaders as well. What about those who will come to function *primarily* as leaders? Their emergence will be the product of long and complex processes—psychological, social, and political. But even in the childhood years the road toward leadership roles takes some form and direction. Taking that road may require a sense of *political efficacy,* defined as persons' confidence that they have the competence to take part in politics and that political leaders will listen to them and respond to them. This feeling, like general political awareness, develops early; third-grade children have already begun to develop a sense of political efficacy, and this feeling tends to increase, at least in a nationwide American sample, to about the eighth grade. During these early years a high sense of political efficacy tends to be positively associated with the child's greater ego strength, family and school interest in politics, higher socio-economic status, and participation in school activities. After the early years of increasing confidence in one's competence, schoolchildren may separate as they move through different groups and experiences. As the child feels some emergent sense of mastery of the political world, David Easton and Jack Dennis note, "he begins to carve out a small piece of political authority for himself—at his own level of consciousness. He is still far away from any actual role that he normally would have in the political process. Even so he begins to feel his political power when it still involves a high degree of projection to those around him and to his future role as an adult member of the system." Most of the schoolchildren who feel politically efficacious will become great "leader-followers," and out of this group much of the political leadership of the future will be recruited.

The growth of a feeling of political efficacy, however tortuous and uneven, and of self-esteem, is ultimately a source of leadership only if coupled with a sense of purpose. For youth, as Erikson says, "makes an important step toward parenthood and adult responsibility in learning to take *leadership* as well as to assume *followership* . . . among peers and to develop what often amounts to an astonishing foresight in the functions thus assumed. Such foresight can be, as it were, ahead of the individual's overall maturity precisely because the prevailing ideology provides a framework for an orientation in leadership. By the same token, the common 'cause' permits others to follow and to obey (and the leader himself to obey higher leaders) and thus to replace the parent images set up in the infantile superego with the hierarchy of leader-images inhabiting the available gallery of ideals—a process as typical for delinquent gangs as for any highly motivated group." Youngsters may not only respond to adults and peers in ways that are shaped by family and culture, they may develop increasingly a sense of purpose, however crude and inchoate, that will help create a *self* that will enable them as leaders to fashion influences *on* society rather than merely being agents *of* it.

Mohandas Gandhi's account of his early life reflects the development of self and purpose. After his childhood years the family moved to Rajkat, where his father served as prime minister. Mohandas began his most serious schooling in the West during his adolescence. In his childhood Gandhi had been betrothed three times—his first two fiancées died before he even learned of the arrangements—and was finally married at the age of thirteen. He spent part of each day at school dreaming about—and feeling guilty that he dreamed about—the carnal pleasures of the evening to come. Nor did his relations with his father follow the usual generational sequence. After the prime minister was badly hurt in a carriage accident on the way to his son's wedding, Mohandas nursed him. Teenager, husband, adult—he was all three. Still, young Gandhi endured ordinary developmental and generational crises.

School meant time away from home, peer associations outside the family, and temptation. Sheik Mehtab, who was everything Mohandas was not— a Moslem, a meat eater, a natural athlete, a smoker—talked Mohandas into eating meat, on the ground that Indians could never overcome the British overlord unless they too developed the hardy physiques of the rulers. The two sneaked down to the river and tried some leathery goat meat; afterward Gandhi had a nightmare during which he felt as though "a live goat were bleating" inside him. Yet he continued to eat meat for a year.

Sheik also took him to a brothel, solicitously providing instruction and even prepaying the bill. The result was mortifying. "I sat near the woman on her bed," Gandhi remembered years later, "but I was tongue-tied. She naturally lost patience with me and showed me the door, with abuses and insults." He felt as though his manhood had been rejected. His lust in marriage afforded him little reassurance about his virility, since loss of semen was seen in his culture as a drain on mental vitality. He was haunted by fears—fears of the dark, fears of thieves and ghosts and serpents. He dreaded talking to fellow students lest they make fun of him. Astonished when he won prizes, he had little regard for his abilities; he was acutely sensitive to criticism. He even made a half-hearted try at suicide. Conscience and moral frailty seemed locked in a titanic battle within him. He ate meat; he smoked; he lied to his parents; he even stole a bit of gold from his brother's armlet—yet he clung to his traditional, family-derived image of probity.

Gandhi's father personified his conscience. When Mohandas stole the gold he dared not speak to the old man, who was on his sickbed; rather he wrote out his confession on a slip of paper. His father said nothing, but "pearl-drops trickled down his cheeks." One evening not long after, Mohandas was massaging his stricken father when an uncle came in to relieve him. Mohandas happily went straight to his marital bed only to be informed a few minutes later that his father had suddenly died. A terrible feeling of guilt fell on the boy; he felt he had lost his father *because of his lust*. "It is a blot I have never been able to efface or forget," he wrote in his autobiography. His father's death seemed to wound him much more than did the death of his child-wife's baby not long after.

His father's death, Erikson says in *Gandhi's Truth,* "represents in

Gandhi's life what, following Kierkegaard, I have come to call 'the curse' in the lives of spiritual innovators with a similarly precocious and relentless conscience. It is indicative of an aspect of childhood or youth which comes to represent an account that can never be settled and remains an existential debt all the rest of a lifetime. . . . . In Gandhi's case the 'feminine' service to his father would have served to deny the boyish wish to replace the (aging) father in the possession of the (young) mother and the youthful intention to outdo him as a leader in later life. Thus the pattern would be set for a style of leadership which can defeat a superior adversary only nonviolently and with the express intent of saving him as well as those whom he oppressed. . . ."

These psychological influences on Gandhi's future leadership were intertwined with powerful social influences. Mohandas was born into the Vaishnava faith with its powerful doctrine of righteousness combined with a measure of tolerance and eclecticism. He read deeply of the *Ramayana* with its stories of soldiers and kings, heroic deeds and martial combat, and learned to overcome his youthful fears of danger. He learned toleration of all branches of Hinduism and its sister religions from listening to his father talk with his Moslem and Parsi friends. Only for Christianity did he have an aversion. The tale of Shravana, who carried his blind parents on his shoulders during a pilgrimage, and the play in which Harishchandra followed truth through all ordeals inspired him. By the time he left on the long trip to London (without his wife) at the age of nineteen he was ready for training for adulthood and leadership roles. The self and a sense of purpose were emerging.

For the young Adolf Hitler, purpose meant a ferocious commitment of self that would come to be distorted into destructive power roles and abdication of any potential for transforming leadership after he won total authority. Though his early school years had been a time of relative calm and security, when he did fairly well in his courses and made friends, he came into increasing conflict with his Austrian father, who wanted his son to become a civil servant like himself; he intended that Adolf go to technical high school rather than to the more humanistic and prestigious *Gymnasium;* he was appalled that the boy wanted to become a painter, an artist. His son challenged him on all these counts, and his grades deteriorated. During this period, Hitler claimed later, he became a pan-German nationalist and unionist and a political and artistic revolutionary who "learned to understand and grasp the meaning of history." At the height of the conflict between them the father collapsed and died in the street. The event, Walter Langer feels, must have reinforced the guilt Adolf felt over his siblings' deaths, especially those of his brothers. Not long afterward he failed his entrance examination for the Academy of Art in Vienna.

Then his mother died of cancer of the breast. "I had honored my father, but my mother I had loved." Less than a year later he was again denied admission to the art academy, and soon afterward he was turned down by the School of Architecture. Alone and penniless, he decided in 1908 to go to Vienna to "overcome all obstacles" in that international, cosmopolitan, bohemian city. It was the city of an ancient monarchy and of massive socialist and trade-union movements. It harbored a sizable Jewish population and an especially large number of Jewish students, along with polyglot elements drawn from the hinterland south and east. A host of sects, coteries, and cabals—radicals and reactionaries, monarchists and anarchists, clerics and freethinkers, liberals and anti-Semites—jousted in press debates and parliamentary struggles.

For five years Hitler lived in tiny rented rooms, in dismal homes for men, or in mere flophouses. Occasionally he earned a few kronen as a day laborer or by peddling his water colors; most of the time he was jobless, a vagrant living mainly on charity. He remembered it as the most wretched period of his life. Vienna nevertheless became his political schoolhouse. It denied him security and comfort, but it gave him purpose. He had ample time to read tracts and newspapers and to take part in the heated political debates that occupied the time of the jobless. "In this period," he wrote in *Mein Kampf,* "there took shape within me a world picture and a philosophy which became the granite foundation of all my acts." He learned to hate Austrians, trade unionists, monarchists, socialists, Marxists, and—above all—Jews.

This outcast, his greasy clothes virtually falling from his gaunt body, made the Jews the target of his frustrations. They were physically and morally unclean, white slavers, the scum of the earth—yet they controlled much of the press, finance, and education. They became an underclass that lifted him up. His credo was essentially negative except for all things Germanic. But within this cauldron of hate developed the rudiments of his later ideology. He visited the houses of parliament and scoffed at the yawning deputies and unheard speakers. He came to fear rule by the mob, for the mob was what he knew best. "Mustn't our principle of parliamentary majorities lead to the demolition of any idea of leadership?" he asked. The masses were stupid and cowardly. The true leader would not bargain with majorities or haggle with parliamentarians but would keep himself free for creative achievement. The majority could never replace the ruler.

Lenin also found purpose in tragedy and in discipline. Like Hitler and Gandhi he lost his father at an early age. His life had been serene and generally happy through his early adolescence. He did well in his studies in school and read deeply of Tolstoy, Turgenev, and Pushkin. When his older brother Alexander left to study at the University of St. Petersburg, Vladimir took on heavier family responsibilities—and he went through a period of mild adolescent rebellion in school and at home. Then, when he was sixteen, his father suddenly died. Vladimir seemed to suppress his grief, with the help of his indomitable mother; he said later, though, that he gave up religion during this period. He continued to excel in his schoolwork.

At the university his older brother had continued his studies, not even returning home for their father's funeral. But he too was deeply affected by his father's death and may even have contemplated suicide. Victor Wolfenstein concludes that both brothers had feelings of guilt over their father's death, that Alexander "wanted to die as atonement for his sins, to pay for his aggressive impulses toward his father," that his young brother's suppression of grief reinforced the guilt engendered by his aggressive feelings against his father. Following this reasoning Alexander's guilt feelings could have taken the form of a patricidal wish to kill the Father of all Russians, the czar. In any event, he became involved in a bungled effort to assassinate Czar Alexander III. Quickly apprehended, he confessed without remorse or plea for mercy and indeed seemed eager to serve the role of martyr to dramatize his messianic vision. Despite his mother's desperate efforts to obtain clemency, Alexander was hanged.

Vladimir again showed remarkable self-control. He remained in school and graduated with a gold medal for ability and deportment; he gained admission to Kazan University as a law student with the help of an influential friend of his father. But something had changed in Vladimir's soul. The university, itself the scene of much student turmoil, served as catalyst. He was arrested following a student demonstration and banished from the university. After he had spent an interval at home reading a good deal of Marx and a summons to action by Chernyshevsky entitled *What Is to Be Done?*, his mother wangled permission for him to take the law examinations for admission to the University of St. Petersburg. He passed brilliantly, completed the required law courses in record time, and settled down briefly as a junior attorney in Samara. But he was bored, and in 1893 he left again for St. Petersburg, center of rising revolutionary activity. His sense of purpose had hardened.

Self-esteem, Social Role, and Empathy

Two powerful influences play on adolescents, drawing some of them into positions of potential leadership and keeping others out. One is a continuing need for self-esteem, closely related to the perception of esteem by others. The second is a developing need and capacity for social role-taking. Alfred Adler related these two psychological dynamics in a theory that considered personal motivation toward power and the development of the capacity for empathy as the shaping influences on personality. According to Adler, human beings strive toward power to overcome and compensate for inevitable childhood feelings of inferiority, impotence, and dependence on adults by achieving a sense of self-esteem. Yet this striving cannot occur in a vacuum. As they grow, children also develop a sense of their social role as members of families, communities, and larger social groups. This social consciousness, which Adler defined as "social interest," enables individuals to identify their own striving for self-esteem with the striving of larger groups in society. Thus the striving for self-esteem and the evolution of a sense of human empathy work in harmony to bring out the potential for leadership.

The need for self-esteem—for a high individual valuation of one's own worth—is affected by, though not necessarily congruent with, adolescents' need to be esteemed by persons whose good opinion they value. A. H. Maslow reports that all persons, save for a few pathological exceptions, have a need for "stable, firmly based, usually high evaluation of themselves, for self-respect or self-esteem, and for the esteem of others." He classifies this need into two subsets: first, "the desire for strength, for achievement, for adequacy, for mastery and competence, for confidence in the face of the world, and for independence and freedom," and second, "the desire for reputation or prestige (defining it as respect or esteem from other people), status, dominance, recognition, attention, importance, or appreciation." The need, as evidently in the case of Woodrow Wilson, may rise in early years out of insecurity about parental affection and regard for the child. Alexander and Juliette George analyze Wilson's childhood fears that he was ugly and stupid—and that his father so regarded him—as leading to his later unappeasable need for affection and power; the chief immediate result was evidently a craving for esteem from others that could bolster self-esteem. A deeper source of esteem need is the gap between ego level and aspired achievement level; William James defined self-esteem as the numerator *success* over the denominator *pretension*. In Maslow's formulation, self-esteem need comes into play as the "lower" needs for safety and affection are met.

The buttressing of self-esteem goes through a continuing process of challenge and reinforcement. Much depends on the schoolchildren's expectations of the esteem in which they will be held—expectations that are formed in the widening sphere of family and school life in childhood and early adolescence. "The person who is disappointed in himself, in his status in the eyes of the world," Robert Lane says, "is also disappointed about the world that sees him this way. . . ." In tests self-esteem increases with success and decreases, at least momentarily, with failure. Expectation and realization (or nonfulfillment) feed on each other, leading to altered expectations for the future. The young person's evaluation of achievement is also a factor; "persons who are highly oriented to achievement and who are anxious to avoid failure," Walter Mischel notes, "may react quite differently to failure experiences than do people who are low in achievement striving." Self-esteem seems to be related positively to parental self-esteem. It is related positively to a feeling of competence and efficacy and responds to teacher expectations in school. Will a child's school seek to overcome the psychic and social deprivations that may affect learning and behavior? At one pole are the schools designed to investigate and remedy poor student performance in a systematic fashion, some in traditional schools with serious goals, others in "alternative" *public* schools that offer academic options. At the other pole stand the schools that bar entrance to large numbers of youngsters or perpetuate and reinforce within the school the existing social and economic inequalities by assuming a necessary link between low achievement and social inequality.

The British public (private) school system of the late nineteenth century stood close to this latter pole. Eton supplied 75—over one-fourth—of the 284 cabinet ministers who held office during the period 1868–1955. And in 1884 Eton employed twenty-eight classics masters, six mathematics teachers, one historian, no science teacher, and no modern language teacher. The English public schools taught values that their graduates would exemplify in public service: self-discipline, teamwork, group loyalty, amateurism, a balance between tradition and efficiency, and in general a restrained but muscular Christianity. The schools also taught habits of superiority: a controlled and lofty attitude, an aura of command, and at least a facade of crisp decisiveness. The public schools also graduated men—the elite schools were all male—who were not educated to recognize the great scientific and technological developments of the late nineteenth century, or the need for expert theory, or the threat of Nazism, or the vital necessity for innovation and creativity. Yet, by almost every test, the Britain of Victoria and Edward VII and the recent Georges was one of the least badly governed nations of the modern age.

The public schools were both inclusive and rigorously exclusive: inclusive in opening their doors to sons of the commercial and managerial classes, exclusive in barring boys of working-class background. Their great feat was to recruit talented middle-class youths and convert them into a class of gentlemen and ultimately into an executive and bureaucratic elite that could work with aristocrats in the services and in cabinet and parliament. Most of the headmasters were of middle-class origin, and the teaching seemed designed to perpetuate an aristocratic ethos and way of life rather than to train rulers to govern a nation and an empire. There is little evidence, however, that this was a plan or a plot of the aristocracy. The striking aspect of the public school was the "unconscious" engineering that led to magnificent social opportunities for a chosen few males of the middle class and helped reinforce social deprivation and political frustration for Britain's working classes.

Most schools in most developed societies have a far more mixed effect than do British public schools on adolescents' sense of self-esteem. The self-confidence, competence, and ease with which adolescents play a variety of roles in school differs according to class background and school expectations related to background. Schools in varying degrees in various societies foster social mobility, as did the American public schools for the children of early-twentieth-century European immigrants, but, to summarize a vast amount of analysis, their general effect in contemporary American society is more to confirm than to mitigate the already existing social inequalities in the family and community. Children are channeled into stratified courses, programs, schools (such as vocational schools), "tracks," and other routes that shape, enhance, or limit their life chances. Thus the "liberal arts" program, with its heavier demands on the student's capacity to handle a variety of subjects and to play appropriate roles in the different social milieus that surround the teaching of these subjects, would in itself influence middle-class and working-class youths.

Clearly the family and the school serve as powerful agencies of manpower allocation, in Parsons' phrase, since they directly affect the reciprocal pattern of role relationships, with its structure of expectation, realization, and feedback. But for the child in school, even more than for the child in the family, the allocation process in many societies is affected by countless factors, with various implications for leadership. These include the informal status network that provides the athlete from a working-class background, for example, a degree of prestige that opens up new expectations, roles, and channels of upward mobility. Intelligence (defined as the capacity to do well in school), which can put the child into social opening or closure, is closely affected by school response to socio-economic status. Children may have higher expectations and aspirations for role opportunities than the social context objectively would seem to warrant; but their very aspirations and resulting actions can modify the structure of social opportunities. And they may belong not to a monolithic, rigid social system but to plural structures that set up alternative opportunities to choose or bargain among.

Self-esteem, or lack of it, affects the roles children play or from which they desist. The urgent need for self-esteem rises at a time when, in most cultures, schoolchildren are exposed to widening and diverging congeries of persons or groups whom they value. In the period before school that Piaget describes as preoperational, children do not develop significantly an ability to perceive and adjust to the roles of others in relation to their own role. "The growing and developing youths, faced with this physiological revolution within them," Erikson says, referring to bodily maturation, "and with tangible adult tasks ahead of them are now primarily concerned with what they appear to be in the eyes of others as compared with what they feel they are, and with the question of how to connect the roles and skills cultivated earlier with the occupational prototypes of the day." Role confusion is caused by doubts over one's sexual or occupational identity. Is a boy masculine in identity or feminine, as the culture perceives these to be? Is a girl to be a housewife like her mother or a doctor like her father?

Role enactment is a central link between social behavior and political leadership; it is also an overworked and much abused concept. As in the case of the concept of *esteem* we must distinguish between an "outer" (structural, social) and an "inner" (processual, psychological) influence. We must distinguish, that is, between role as a set of structurally given demands emerging from given social positions, as a set of influences "outside" persons, of demands *on* them, reinforcing and blocking their movement through social and political space, and, on the other hand, role as persons' perceptions and definitions of their place in sets of social relationships, of "what someone in his social position is supposed to think and do about it," of demands of the role *in* them. A father expects his daughter to be a counterpart of his passive, accommodating wife; the daughter longs to be a doctor like her father. Demands—inner and outer—must be distinguished from acts or behavior. All three concepts are separate but related, both in theory and in practice. Role-*taking*—as the application of empathy—is a different matter.

Children enter school with continuing feeling and orientation toward their parents, the lawgivers and sentinels. Parents retain this role even as children gain some distance from them. Then come new confrontations, often with blinding speed. By the fourth grade the self-contained classroom may have been abandoned; shared team-teaching may be common. Children confront teachers, severally and individually, who pursue separate roles—a gym instructor, a math teacher, a vice principal concerned with discipline—as they seek to exact roles from youths. Children may move from classroom to classroom, each with its fresh combination of teachers, peers, and role requirements. Outside the school they mingle with shifting clusters of peers. Youths encounter some situations in which females are sharply segregated from males, some in which they are mixed. They may be on a high track or a low track, with all whites or all blacks. As they are exposed to a broad diversity—and decide whether to value or fear or oppose or simply accept others—they are drawn into the playing of new roles. Unlike role enactment, a test of effective role-*taking* is the development of the child's capacity to take the part of others and to know that others are able to empathize in response. Thus, in order to play the role of son appropriately, a son imitates the role of his father toward him in his own relationships with others.

The nature of the roles enacted will obviously vary enormously from person to person and from culture to culture. The important question is *scope*—opportunity to encounter and respond to and receive esteem from wide gradations of valued groups. Some children, protected by homogeneous school and social settings, have fewer such stimuli. Opportunity for such broad experience is one of the primary justifications for the American public school system.

The adolescent who can recognize, adjust to, reconcile, mediate among, and cope with shifting mixes of role requirements is a person with at least a latent capacity to thrive in a variegated social and political environment and to demonstrate some potential ability for political leadership in a pluralized, complex, and open society. In more traditional or developing societies the role demands might be lineal, monistic, and overpoweringly cumulative. Role in family, role with teacher, role in occupation, role in relation to opposite sex, and role in ritual may all be so congruent as to make children unable to cope with diversity of persons or roles. The country bumpkin ricocheting from group to group in the city is the storied example; other examples are members of narrowly parochial groups within urban communities and adolescents in a child-centered affluent suburban community.

Young "misfits" may simply be persons who reject the role demands and the expectations placed on them by others. They may force a change on the part of those who are trying to change the "misfits" or, more likely, they will be expelled or will seek to escape by dropping out or shifting to another school. They may remain, either in a state of "apathetic conformity," as Daniel Levinson suggests, or in outright opposition, expressed either in open confrontation or quiet sabotage. The upwardly mobile misfit whose expectations exceed the limitations of the role offered may develop a private life of individual achievement in which the role and expectations are both intervals. Role demands are real and complex, not idealized or ritualized; role expectations *of* them on the part of parents, teachers, peer groups, social classes, ethnic groupings—both positive and negative—may put children in a situation of role cross-pressures or conflict that may paralyze them psychologically, strand them socially, frustrate them politically. Too severe competition may be as paralyzing as too limited demands. At the other end of the spectrum, persons may feel a growing sense of competence as they resolve role conflicts and exploit role opportunities—a sense of competence that will in turn augment their motivation for leadership in complex environments. At the highest level, their role enactment, rather than expressing a static definition of self, may also become role-*taking* and reflect genuine capacity for *empathy*—the vital leadership quality of entering into another person's feelings and perspectives. That is the beginning of moral leadership.

Role behavior continually modifies personality as new roles are assumed. Or, as William James put it years ago, a man has as many different social selves as there are distinct groups of persons about whose opinion he cares. In the development of purpose and the management of these selves lie potentials for the morality of power, which is genuine leadership.

If all children possessed the same need for esteem from others and were equally capable of empathic social role-taking, society would be evenly balanced, if dull. In fact, of course, the manifestations of the need to compensate for unfulfilled wants varies widely in most cultures. Jeanne Knutson found a direct relation between the need for esteem and low socio-economic status. Other findings cast doubt on this relationship, but most agree that influences of family, schools, and other institutions are all affected by socio-economic status and the rewards and deprivations that come with it. We can assume at least a relation between the need for esteem and a feeling of deprivation or insecurity as to others' esteem for oneself; the manner in which persons respond to this condition will affect their behavior. From a study of American public school children, using a limited sample, Stanley Coopersmith concluded that "differences in styles of responding to oneself, to other persons, and to impersonal objects reveal that persons with high, medium, and low self-esteem adapt to events in markedly different ways." A greater tendency toward distrust and a greater feeling of vulnerability lead the youth to turn inward.

Summing up a good deal of psychological investigation, Bernard Bass finds that persons with high self-esteem appear "more likely to change others, to lead others, rather than to be changed by others or to conform readily." Reviewing a host of studies of the relations between self-esteem and assessments of successful leadership, Ralph Melvin Stogdill concluded that "leaders rate higher than their followers in self-confidence and self-esteem." James David Barber found that legislative leaders tended to be either very high or very low in self-esteem, with few in between. But, across the whole range of studies, correlations between self-esteem and leadership *objectively measured* often were not high, with the implication that other significant factors were involved, and that leaders and followers were not all that different.

One of these factors is the purposeful building of social esteem and self-esteem in order to enhance leadership potential. In the case of British public schools, the educational leaders who shaped the social structure of education may pervasively affect later political leadership without wholly intending to do so, or at least without clear conception as to their ultimate effect on society (e.g., imperial ventures versus social welfare programs). Social recruitment merely sets the stage for political recruitment, a process that in turn may counteract the effect of the social channeling. Too, a society can establish a relatively rigid *social* hierarchy without achieving a political one. It is easier to exclude a workingman's son from a London club than from the English cabinet, to bar a peasant's son from a provincial social elite than from wartime command of a regiment.

All this is aside from a *conscious* effort to build political channels to the top, as in the case of the British labor movement, the early leaders of which fashioned routes to Downing Street that did not run through Eton or Harrow or Oxbridge. In most societies the sources of political leadership are unequally distributed, but in some the social outsider may join a messianic sect, a mass movement, or a revolutionary cell and thus compete for leadership and power with the insider. The same lack of self-esteem, moreover, that may cripple persons from seizing opportunities in certain social and political settings may motivate them in others. Social status, Prewitt reminds us, is a useful but not a necessary condition for political power.

A more fundamental ambiguity as to the impact of low self-esteem on leadership is involved pointedly in the life of a man who consciously devoted himself to the study and practice of leadership, Woodrow Wilson.

Psychobiographers have argued convincingly that Wilson's self-esteem was so damaged in youth that he spent his life in a relentless and consuming search for the moral approbation and personal loyalty of family and friends. Alexander and Juliette George summarize the "crushing feelings" of inadequacy: "Had he as a boy felt unimportant? Then anything he or anyone else could do to convince him that he was uniquely qualified to accomplish great things—perhaps even something immortal—would be a balm. Had his father ridiculed his intellectual capacities and made him feel mediocre? Then anything he or anyone else could do to help him feel that he had superior ability and infallible judgment in matters in which he chose to exercise leadership would relieve him—temporarily. Had he grown up in a stern Calvinist atmosphere, subjected to disquisitions on the natural immorality of man in general and his own immorality in particular? Then he must convince himself always of his superior virtue. Had he, as a child, been overwhelmed by feelings of helplessness and weakness in relation to the masterful adults about him? Then as a man, he must impose his will on others and never permit himself to be subjugated."

When young Thomas Woodrow Wilson came down late one morning to a wedding breakfast, according to a family story, his father elaborately apologized to the guests. Tommy had been so excited at discovering another hair in his mustache, he said, that he had been delayed in his dressing. A painful flush passed over the boy's face, a cousin remembers. But he never openly rebelled against his father; it would have been a hopeless encounter. The "Doctor," as members of his flock addressed him, a big, handsome man of commanding presence, was a dominant figure in the community and a potentate at home, a man of eloquent sermons in the pulpit and a caustic wit in his manse. The son—at least in the boy's own eyes—was homely, backward, worthless.

Tommy did not learn the written alphabet until he was nine, enter school until ten, or learn to read easily until eleven—all this despite the Doctor's intensive effort to teach the boy at home and to inspire him in church. Later he would make his son rewrite his compositions three or four or five times in an effort at perfection. But Tommy, like Gandhi much earlier, did badly both in studies and in sports. He barely won admission to Davidson College and then left within a year, following some sort of physical or emotional collapse, which led to fifteen months of nursing and desultory reading at home. This was the first of the breakdowns that in various forms would afflict him every few years until the climactic prostration of 1919.

We cannot know for sure what was happening inside the quiet manse. Doubtless the Doctor was frustrated by his son's apparent obtuseness. Perhaps the boy seemed to him a rival for the mother's affection. We can only speculate. But it does seem evident that "Tommy" was an object to be pushed and prodded into a predetermined mold and, when the object refused to fit the mold, the target of his father's hardly veiled hostility. The Doctor's message was clearly, "To the extent you perform according to my standards, I will grant guarded approval"—a message that precluded the development of intrinsic self-esteem.

Tommy variously loved and hated, feared and admired his father. The Doctor could be stern and exacting; he could also be playful, merry, and affectionate. Later the son would speak of his strong love for and tender devotion to his father; he not only repressed any overt hostility toward his father but he transformed it into an unusual caring for him until the end of his life. He loved his mother, a retiring, domiciliated woman, and he was attached to his older sisters, who probably served as a bridge to the passionate literary friendships Wilson conducted with middle-aged women in his later years.

But the psychic scars were deep and lasting. The need to compensate for damaged self-esteem lay at the source of Wilson's moralistic, messianic dogmatism and his quest for personal power in his later years. Wilson's break with friends and supporters at Princeton, his repudiation of the Democratic leaders in New Jersey, his love-hate relationship with aides and officials in his administration, and above all his "unyielding" position on the League of Nations—all these and other strained postures and violent ruptures could be seen as part of a pattern of rigidity and dogmatism stemming in turn from repressed aggression against his father and, later, other authority figures. It was this pattern that many of Wilson's contemporaries were reacting against; not only Lloyd George and Clemenceau (who said that Wilson talked like Jesus Christ but acted like Lloyd George) but Sigmund Freud, who also felt he identified with Christ; John Maynard Keynes, who summed him up at Versailles as a bumbling, sermonizing Don Quixote outwitted by the foxes; and William Allen White, who called for someone to come and, with a good whack, release the "festering rage" in Wilson's underconsciousness.

Still, there is the "other Wilson," a man of strong self-esteem and genuine affection for other persons, individually and collectively. This is the Wilson who as a student at Princeton fulfilled himself intellectually and emotionally; who conducted a brilliant career of teaching and writing marked by the offers of a half dozen university presidencies and capped by his appointment at Princeton; who infused his alma mater with a new sense of purpose and excitement and left a lasting imprint of reform; who outmaneuvered the party bosses in New Jersey and put through his reform program; who led his minority party to national victory in 1912, as he would again in 1916; who took personal command of his legislative program in Washington, forged coalitions with improbable allies, overrode or outflanked the opposition, and substantially carried out his promises to the voters; who showed consummate strategic flexibility in reorienting the Democratic party from the essentially rural, individualistic, and conservative organization of 1912 to the more liberal, collectivist, and urban-minded movement of 1916; who usually showed a rare capacity to inspire men as he persuaded them; who, more than any other President, brought to the White House an explicit and considered concept of political leadership; and who acted not just as a channelizer or catalyst of social forces but as a creative leader who, in his educational policies, his governorship, his party and legislative direction, and in his campaign for a new international organization, refashioned his political world.

His well-publicized intransigence over the League of Nations issue in 1919–1920 has fortified the image of Wilson as a stubborn and dogmatic man. Here, too, history plays its tricks; the heroic man of principle, enshrined even in a Hollywood film of the 1940s, became the narrow, rigid figure of the 1950s and, by the 1960s, the imperialistic agent of corporate capitalism. (A future verdict may shift the image again.) It may be perceived that Wilson, whatever his blunders and inflexibilities, did make concessions to the opposition —especially to the internationalist Republicans as personified by William Howard Taft—but that he could never have won the support of Henry Cabot Lodge, the leader of the conservative Republicans entrenched in the congressional system of power. Through endless compromises with an insatiable adversary he would have lost the issue he wanted to take to the American people in his swing across the country in 1919 and in the election of 1920. Losing in the short run, he might salvage a cause to which the people could rally in the future, rather than yield the vital principle of collective security and thus lose both the League *and* the issue.

Wilson's handling of the issue cannot be separated from the short-run congressional and electoral conditions of 1919–1920 and surely it cannot be separated from the long-run strategies of the 1920s and the 1930s, when the dire prophecies of the "martyred President" would come true, when a new surge of internationalism would follow on Hitler's conquests, and the ground would be laid for American participation in a new world organization.

Still, the question remains as to why this masterful politician failed so badly in realizing his immediate and cherished goal—American membership in the League of Nations. In analyzing this puzzle it is helpful to recall that, while low self-esteem may disable some potential leaders, it may compel others to seek fame and glory in order to overcome doubts about one's worth. This seems to have been the case with Wilson. "He needed his friends to confirm his faith," the Georges conclude, "—so easily shaken by outer attack because so savagely preyed upon from within—in his great destiny, in his human worth. He needed their tributes to his selfless idealism, particularly when the detractors rudely stripped away his carefully wrought rationalizations." In provoking the opposition of men like Lodge, he may have been demonstrating a need to overcome them in order to prove his prowess as a leader. No sooner had he obtained a particular leadership role, Robert Tucker observes, "than he would take advantage of it to espouse and strive to put through new ideas, new departures in policy, new programs which, if successful, would bring greater glory and possibly, also, open the way to a still higher leadership role with its still greater opportunities for further leadership success." Not a bad definition of leadership!

Wilson himself might say that he did finally prove his leadership quality—twenty-five years later. Others would answer that the world could not afford the delay. At the very least, Wilson's life demonstrates to the student of leadership that we cannot unravel the mysteries of the rise and fall of a great man unless we analyze not only the psychological and social influences operating in him in his early years, but the political forces that he both encounters and generates in his middle and later life.

5

THE CRUCIBLES OF
POLITICAL LEADERSHIP

Sigmund Freud, before going to sleep one evening when he was seven or eight years old, "disregarded the rules which modesty lays down and obeyed the calls of nature in my parents' bedroom while they were present. In the course of his reprimand, my father let fall the words: *'The boy will come to nothing.'* This must have been a frightful blow [*Kränkung,* insult] to my ambition, for references to this scene are still constantly recurring in my dreams and are always linked with an enumeration of my achievements and successes, as though I wanted to say: *'You see, I have come to something.'* "

It would be gratifying if political leaders could probe the sources of their ambitions as neatly and dramatically as Freud analyzed his own. Even if they could—or even if we could identify relatively clear psychological sources of behavior with some assurance—we still could not generalize about the political motivations of the great numbers of political leaders in a variety of cultures. The sources of political leadership lie deep, as we have seen, in the biological, psychological, and social forces that play on the child and adolescent. We know that the early influences propelling persons toward leadership roles are closely affected by parental attitudes and behavior, peer relations, schooling, and youthful orientation toward leaders and leadership positions. Many of these influences are not sufficient in themselves to propel persons into leadership channels; the influences may produce political activists, dutiful citizens, or ideological fanatics. Early personal and social dispositions must be linked to political interest and activity, and these to political careers, if leadership is to be achieved.

The linkage consists of an array of *political motives* applied to a *structure of political opportunity*. Motive without a structure of openings and closures would produce motion without direction (if not anarchy). Opportunity without motivation—a phenomenon sometimes discernible in heirs to the throne—could produce a desiccated political order. Psychologists have raised a vast literature on psychological and social motivation as well as a sizable body of findings on political motivation. But the treatment of ambition has been left largely to writers of fiction. Horatio Alger, Jr.'s economic heroes have their counterparts in novels about young Welshmen climbing out of the mines and up the social and political ladder, novels about proletarians, upward-mobiles, outlanders, and others who made it to the top. More recently scientific work on the personal needs for *achievement* has been expanding.

Analysis of the nature of political ambition has been handicapped by a venerable tradition of defining political ambition as simply the quest for power, to the exclusion of other motives. Such a definition lends itself to drama in both fiction and social science, but more extensive analysis suggests that political leadership emerges from a broader set of motivations. Some distinction, Philip E. Vernon has proposed, should be made between dominance and leadership, as there are probably many persons who wish to dominate without wishing to exercise responsible leadership, while in many types of leadership, persuasiveness, sensitivity to group attitudes, and acceptance of responsibility for meeting group desires are more significant than a desire to dominate. (Dominance as I use the word means raw power-wielding.)

For the study of leadership the crucial distinction is between the quest for *individual recognition and self-advancement,* regardless of its social and political consequences, and the quest for the kind of status and power that can be used to *advance collective purposes* that transcend the needs and ambitions of the individual. Alfred Adler developed a theory of personality that emphasized the unique capacity of human beings to identify with other human beings; the development of this sense of empathy in people enables them to identify their personal striving for advancement with the striving of the community toward progress, enlisting individual human energies for the pursuit of the common good. A. H. Maslow, a student of Adler who expanded this theory, divided the series of needs that make up individual motivation toward power into two subsidiary sets of needs, as we will note, distinguishing between achievement and fame.

The Spur of Ambition

When Gandhi as a young law student in London was asked why he had come to England his answer was emphatic: "Ambition!" For a young Indian of high aspiration, London was a series of frustrations. He felt later that he had failed as a public speaker and—far worse—that he had made himself look ridiculous. He wore top hat, monocle, silk shirt, and spats; he took dancing and violin lessons; he tried to socialize with young women, but his social graces were limited; the lessons did not go well; he feared the Englishwomen with their aggressive ways (and he did not let on that he had a wife in India). But he passed his bar examinations, enrolled in the high court, and departed for India only to find himself virtually without clients. He traveled to South Africa to seize a legal opportunity, and stayed more than twenty years. There Gandhi first encountered systematic racial discrimination and hatred—and there, in response, he rehearsed the role of leadership in civil disobedience that he was to play years later in his homeland. There his ambition became an instrumental motive, a means to the end of destroying injustice. When he was ordered by the judge to take off his turban in court, he walked out rather than obey. In a first-class compartment on a train to Pretoria a European entered, looked Gandhi over, then summoned officials who ordered him into the van compartment. Gandhi refused and was ejected from the train. On a stagecoach he was ordered to sit on the coachbox rather than inside with the white passengers; when the insults persisted and Gandhi protested, the burly driver cursed him and boxed his ears. He was turned away from hotels, knocked into the gutter by a policeman, and barely escaped a lynching at the hands of one racist mob. The young graduate of the Inner Temple who had affected frock coat and shiny boots was, after all, just a "coolie barrister." The night his train steamed on to Pretoria without him, Gandhi sat in the icy-cold waiting room and experienced his moment of truth. Should he fight for his rights or return to India? To go back, he decided, would be cowardice. "The hardship to which I was subjected was superficial—only a symptom of the deep disease of color prejudice." He must root out the disease. He went on to Pretoria.

"There is every reason to believe," Erik Erikson says, "that the central identity which here found its historical time and place was the conviction that among the Indians in South Africa he was *the only person equipped by fate* to reform a situation which under no conditions could be tolerated."

Not only were Indians in South Africa subordinated to whites, and blacks subordinate to both; the Indians were divided among themselves. At the top were Moslem tradesmen who gained from condescending whites a little social advantage as "Arabs." Hindu and Parsi clerks occupied a lower social stratum, with waiters and house servants below them. At the bottom were "coolies," indentured laborers who had been brought from India to work the mines and fields in a condition of semi-slavery. Indians were further divided by their origin or religion into Hindus, Moslems, Gujaratis, Madrasis, Christians, and other identities. How unite such a people, in a foreign land?

Gandhi had been slow to develop even a personal strategy; sometimes he gave in to the authorities, sometimes he stood up to them, sometimes he skirmished. He was half lawyer, half rebel. To the English he was simply another coolie. But out of his own humiliations, out of the plight of the Indians who came daily to his law office, out of his reading of Ruskin, Thoreau, Tolstoy, and others, Gandhi gradually shaped a political strategy. Indians must unite and organize politically. They must dramatize their plight through demonstrations, confrontations, noncompliance, passive resistance. Gandhi and his associates learned how to raise money, to put out propaganda, and to influence government through wire-pulling or direct pressure. Arrested, the protesters, Gandhi among them, packed the jails. He organized a great march—a forerunner of tactics in India—and was arrested three times; each time he posted bail and made his way back.

This was the period of Gandhi's young manhood. He made his commitment to *Satyagraha,* truth-force, with its enormous potential for self-expression, tolerance, militancy, self-discipline, equality. He had found his identity as well as his ideology, and his great potential began to be realized. The once timorous, insecure lawyer was transformed into a determined, shrewd, flexible strategist of political action, with a growing sense of competence and efficacy and a comprehensive and compelling set of values. In South Africa Gandhi became a *leader.*

For Adolf Hitler, ambition was essentially terminal. While he claimed to seek power for the sake of the salvation of his country and for the purification of the Nordic race, this was self-deception. He identified the goal wholly with his own dominance and was willing to destroy his people for the sake of his own power. Hitler's ambition probably was forged at the military hospital in Pomerania where he lay gassed and wounded at the end of the World War I. "Now I knew that everything was lost," he wrote later of these "terrible days and even worse nights." He fell into periods of depression and withdrawal punctuated by fits of weeping. The fate of vanquished Germany and his sense of defeat seemed to merge—as the hope of victory and his own power merged later—and perhaps too, as Walter Langer suggests, he was reacting to the defeat of Germany as if it were a rape of himself as well as of his real and simulated mother (in *Mein Kampf* he was still referring to Germany as "she"). While he lay in the hospital alternating between hysteria and depression, sailors were mutinying at Kiel. Some came to the hospital with a red flag and a call to revolution. When a pastor told the patients a few days later that the kaiser had quit Germany for exile Hitler seemed to realize the full dimensions of defeat. "Once again everything went black before my eyes, and I tottered and groped my way back to the place where we slept, and buried my burning head in the blankets and the pillows.''

During these nights, he said later, hatred grew for the betrayers of Germany. He vowed to know neither rest nor peace until the ''November criminals'' were overthrown. As he wrote in *Mein Kampf*, he resolved to become a political leader so that he could punish the traitors who had stayed at home and stabbed his motherland in the back. Probably the decision did not come so abruptly, yet this period must have been crucial for him. Otherwise we cannot begin to explain the emergence of the führer: the fact that this man, not yet thirty, after years of drifting and vagrancy in Munich and four years of routine, almost mindless service in the army, little formal education, no political connections, no job or vocation to return to, virtually no practical experience, and with only a pastiche of hazy political dogmas—this man in five years would shape a political strategy, an ideological program, and a style of popular control that would within a decade bring him to the absolute rule of Germany and, for a brief time, the mastery of half the world. There comes to mind no other world power wielder of recent times who established his style of rule so quickly and surely.

Returning to Munich, where he had volunteered for service, he fell in again with the ultranationalists and racist agitators he had known before the war. Soon he was serving as an undercover agent for the List Regiment. His real political education began as he spied on political gatherings and was indoctrinated in political ideology through courses conducted by the army. In the fall of 1919 he investigated the German Workers' Party, one of the many tiny groups hatched in the steamy political incubator of Munich. Impressed by its program and certain that he could improve its organization and tactics, he joined and became the seventh member of the executive committee. He soon took control of the party.

Before 1933 Hitler was less an innovator than a master amalgamator of party organization, propaganda techniques, and political credo. In the intense political competition of Munich he found that he could draw increasingly big crowds and hold them spellbound; that he could out-argue the opposition or, failing that, subdue them with his armed followers; that he had an intuitive grasp of the role of banners, posters, insignia, pageantry, and other devices and symbols that would excite his audiences; and that his solitary dominance of the party was superior to collective direction by the executive committee. Politics became his vocation and his avocation in large part because he was good at it and had been good at little else.

Most remarkable was his doctrinal consistency. To read his speeches of the beginning of the 1920s is to read the speeches he gave for the next quarter century. The outrage of Versailles, the evils of stock-exchange capitalism, the threat of Russian Bolshevism, the need for a strong central government, the power principle, a spate of social welfare (rather than radically socialist) measures, Aryan supremacy, and—first, last, and always—the wickedness and menace of the Jews: all these would become only too well known in later years. Hitler could hardly be accused of deceit; his plans and goals were laid out for all the world to see in his speeches, in party programs, and in *Mein Kampf*. So rapid was Hitler's rise, so marked his early successes, that he had only to learn the need for patience. This lesson he was taught in his attempted putsch in Munich in November 1923. Incarcerated in comfortable conditions in Landsberg fortress prison, where he wrote *Mein Kampf*, he decided to wait until events turned his way. The economic distress and political convulsion of the early 1930s was the context he needed for the consolidation of brute power.

Lenin's ambition also was shaped during early manhood, and he also adhered to his strategy, if not his tactics, with remarkable tenacity during the ensuing years. Was he a raw power wielder or a leader? In St. Petersburg in the fall of 1893 he threw himself into revolutionary study and action. During the next decade he underwent a persisting crisis of identity and self-definition, Victor Wolfenstein argues, and perhaps it was the combination of guilt over his father's death and simmering, barely suppressed wrath over his brother's execution that steeled Lenin's will during this period. His early indoctrination in Marx shaped his intellectual perceptions and judgments. But the most commanding influence in Lenin's steadfast pursuit of the vocation of revolutionary leadership was doubtless the vocation itself and his almost immediate success at it.

He systematically interrogated St. Petersburg's workers on their living conditions, factory comrades, and political views, and he compiled statistics to support his study of the development of capitalism in Russia. He built up and indoctrinated a network of study groups that doubled as revolutionary cells. Hunted and harassed by the police, he learned to elude them with various disguises and subterfuges. When he was finally tracked down by the police and exiled to Siberia, he simply continued his revolutionary profession by intensive reading and correspondence, and he resumed his revolutionary activity in Russia on his release, traveling extensively in Europe, in the closed world of revolutionary agitation and conspiracy. In Paris, where he ran a school for activists, he became a teacher and preacher of revolution. He learned that he was more effective as a pamphleteer than as a speaker but that his simple, blunt, hammerlike oratory could on occasion cut through the fog of Jesuitical argumentation to arouse his working-class listeners. He exhibited an extraordinary self-discipline, emotional and intellectual. He preached and practiced the doctrine that revolutionary duty must override personal friendships, sentiment, love. He subordinated his marriage and his love affairs to the cause.

Lenin was not yet thirty-two years old when he set forth his theory of revolutionary action in *What Is to Be Done?* This tract, Bertram Wolfe says, contained, either in germ or fully developed, virtually all the doctrines on politics and party organization that would later be known as Leninism. An attack on both gradualists and terrorists, the thick pamphlet argued that the masses by their own efforts and spontaneity could arrive only at a "trade union consciousness," that the revolution could be achieved only through the leadership of a disciplined, militant vanguard—and hence that the revolution could not wait on the slow workings of history, Marxist or otherwise.

Out of the long, turgid argument, illuminated by gleams of insight and clogged by pedantic strictures against his adversaries, emerged a central concept that was to take command of Lenin's strategy and to help shape Russian and world history. This was his concept of leadership—leadership of the masses by the party, leadership of the party by one man—who else but Lenin? There had of course been leaders of the movement, but, as Adam Ulam notes, "that a decision could be reached without a discussion, that people could simply be commandeered to do this or that job, that the Party cells were expected to report to and obey the center, all those things presaged a vast and new development."

For Lenin and his party the vocation of revolution had become the strategy of leadership. (I will describe revolutionary power in Chapter 8 not only as leadership but as transforming moral leadership.) Lenin was to rule for only a few years but he had time to employ means characteristic of brutal power-wielding. Conflict, an essential of leadership, came to be suppressed (though chiefly under Lenin's disciples). The merger of leader and led, postulated in Communist revolutionary theory, was subverted into dominance of the led by the leaders. Lenin's demand for obedience and one-man control had come to a logical conclusion. The feudal system was not wholly transformed, but the feudal leaders were replaced. But Lenin was a leader, if a contradictory one, until he became a brute power wielder. If he had had as many years as Mao, the balance of leader and power wielder would perhaps have been revealed.

The love of fame, Alexander Hamilton said, is "the ruling passion of the noblest minds." If ambition is a ceaseless spur, we must know more about its consequences. In these three cases, Hitler fulfilled his own ambitions—until the apocalyptic ending—but pulled down the nation he promised to lead to glory.

Gandhi's ambitions for India have not yet been realized. The instrument of Lenin's ambition—the disciplined party—has been used for purposes abhorrent to Leninism as a liberating force.

The Need for Gratification

Maslow identifies two sets of needs power requires: the desire for strength, achievement, adequacy, mastery and competence, autonomy and freedom; and the desire for reputation or prestige, status, dominance, recognition, attention and appreciation—the desire for skill, in effect, and the desire for fame. (These needs, he notes, have been relatively stressed by Adler and relatively neglected by Freud.) Ambition for political power is only one—and often among the less important—of a wide range of need-resolving motivations. As Jeanne Knutson points out, the acquisition of power is connected directly to only one of Maslow's values—dominance—and "many types of political activity may be high in status, attention, importance, et cetera, but have little undivided power which is associated with the role (nevertheless satisfying). . . ."

Politicians, too, may overestimate ambition for power and underestimate the need for status and recognition. When Mother Garvey, in Edwin O'Connor's *The Last Hurrah,* visits Charlie Hennessey in an effort to build a coalition against Frank Skeffington, he assumes that the loquacious Hennessey is interested in power, or at least power to acquire boodle. "Come in with us," he beseeches Charlie. "Come and join with us like the smart man that you are. We'll lick the murderer together, the both of us, and carve him up like a Christmas turkey!" But Charlie seems unmoved. "Ah my dear man, winning's not everything!" he exclaims. "No no no! The thing is to take the matter to the people, to let them know what's going on, to fight the good fight, to tell the truth! Marvellous! I'll be in my sound-truck on every corner in the city every night of the campaign, lashing away at them all! Skeffington and the rest of them! The big boys against Skeffington are just as bad and worse! I'll stand on the side lines and harass away, harass away! Marvellous! They fear it. They fear it more each year. One man telling the truth to the people! A time-bomb!" As crazy as a bedbug, Garvey thought morosely—but Hennessey was not crazy, only differently motivated.

The question—ambition for what?—need not be left to the realm of speculation or fiction. Rufus Browning and Herbert Jacob, in a study of politicians in a middle-size eastern city and two counties of Louisiana, sought to evaluate the importance of the desire for power in the quest for political office. They posed two questions: how strongly were politicians motivated to power compared with nonpoliticians and to what extent did characteristics of the political system affect their motivation? They proceeded on the assumption, drawn from previous studies, that measures of motivation were associated with a wide range of variables important in recruitment and other behavior (risk-taking, class background, dependency, consistency, sensitivity to opportunities to influence others). "Simply being a politician does not entail a distinctive concern for power, or for achievement or affiliation," they concluded from their findings. The data for the eastern city and the Louisiana parishes suggested that "relatively plentiful opportunities for power and achievement in the economic arena channel strongly motivated men into economic rather than political activity; that in communities where politics and political issues are at the center of attention and interest, men attracted to politics are likely to be more strongly power and achievement-motivated than in communities where politics commands only peripheral interest; that political systems that offer upward political mobility attract men with relatively strong achievement and power motivation; and that concentration in a political system on matters of strictly party or factional organization and power, to the near exclusion of public policy concerns, tends to keep men with strong affiliative needs out of politics."

All this is not to minimize the role of political ambition but to place it in a wider context—indeed, to enhance its importance, for now we conceive ambition in its broadest sense as springing out of a host of motives that come into play with differing force depending on roles taken in different cultures and different situations. One generalization seems safe on the basis of both systematic and casual observation: *the most potent sources of political motivation—the key elements of political ambition—are unfulfilled esteem needs* (both self-esteem and esteem by others). Both power wielders and leaders have such needs. "Because persons with a need for esteem have moved a considerable way up the need hierarchy towards self-actualization," Knutson notes, "they are especially likely to be active in their social political environment, and to be found in leadership positions." And James David Barber believes that the decisive step of candidacy for office, involving great personal risk and sharp change in one's life and commitments, "is most likely to be taken by two kinds of people: those who have such *high* self-esteem that they can manage relatively easily the threats and strains and anxieties involved in this change; and those who have such *low* self-esteem that they are ready to do this extraordinary thing to raise it." However, self-esteem is likely to vary sharply in its ingredients from culture to culture.

This potent need for esteem, for prestige, for reputation, for admiration—this need that dwarfs even as it produces the ambition for power—is evident in the careers of "great men," whether brutal power wielders or leaders. It is evident especially in the effects of damaged self-esteem—in Woodrow

Wilson's insecurity over his father's love for him; in Karl Schumacher's need to prove his superiority in spite of his physical impediments and stresses; in Thaddeus Stevens' sensitivity over his origins, his absentee father, his physical deformation; in the discrimination practiced against both Disraeli and Gandhi in their early years; in Bismarck's ambivalent feelings toward his mother and in his hypochondria.

Desire for esteem is not always pathological: some persons simply have large appetites. It is an old observation of those who watch presidents, premiers, and princes that many power holders, at least in nontotalitarian nations, relish the trappings at least as much as the substance of power. Still there are persons, of whom Bismarck was an example, whose dominant characteristic is an unremitting drive to master other persons and events: the will to power. Others are concerned with influencing events for the sake of gratifying the needs of others. The crucial question becomes the nature of the linkage between their attempts at self-gratification or other gratification, their achievement of gratification, and their consequent impact on history.

Most important for its implications for leadership, self-esteem is not simply a generalized force but relates to specific expectations and realizations about specific behaviors and outcomes in specific situations. Franklin Roosevelt's capacity for shrewd manipulation of political rivals like John L. Lewis, Huey Long, and Joseph P. Kennedy rose in good part from a strong sense of self-esteem and of political competence proved again and again in political combat—an esteem shared by himself and his many admirers. Self-esteem is a mixed and ambivalent factor in human personality, one whose expression varies depending on the social context. Woodrow Wilson's sense of inadequacy could not have influenced *all* aspects of his life or he would have rejected the vocation of political leadership.

Biographers tend to stress the visible, dramatic, and conflict-ridden behaviors of "the great"—behaviors that speak sharply of psychological and social deprivations and disturbances. These behaviors make for stirring accounts in the press, and they are seized upon and relished. Nor are the "great men" themselves averse to interpretations that suggest that their driving ambition and compulsive behavior are really not their fault but reflect the traumas of their lives and hard times. Yet the hallmark of most leaders in most cultures is not uncontrollable ambition or irrational, immoral, or aggressive behavior but prudence, calculation, and management; otherwise, in most cultures, they would not be leaders, or they would be leaders only symbolically rather than functionally. The way in which persons cope with their problems is their most revealing aspect. Politicians who reveal neuroses or emotions too nakedly— who weep in public in societies that disesteem public demonstrations of feeling (except for special occasions reserved for sentiment), as Muskie did in New Hampshire in 1972, or who lose control before a hostile audience and indulge in a violent harangue, as did Robert La Follette, Sr., toward the end of his career—are typically blocked off from the channels of power by societies that esteem restraint and civility. We must gauge not only the projective thrust of ambition but the political response to it and the political controls over it.

Thus we see ambitious politicians curbing their burning frustration as they patiently deal with allies and adversaries; we see the divisive vote seeker patching up coalitions and practicing the arts of consensus; we see the politician of strong opinions trying to keep an open mind and to get a grip on the facts; we see ideologues striving to maintain a little distance from their cause so that they can see themselves and their commitments from positions of some detachment. Consider Franklin Roosevelt. He was a man of strong feelings who knew when to be silent and when to speak out. He had a receptivity to facts, a fingertip sensitivity to the moods and motivations of allies and adversaries, a capacity to deceive and dissimulate, and such a good (and well-disguised) intelligence network that he usually had an apperception of reality that his political rivals could not surpass. He was free, in Erwin Hargrove's view, from anxieties that could cripple his cognitive and emotional functioning. He could make political errors, as perhaps in his effort to pack the Supreme Court and to oust his conservative opponents from Congress, but he met defeat with such apparent aplomb and he recovered politically with such adroitness that he seemed damaged neither in his own esteem nor in that of most of the voters. Indeed, Roosevelt in his second term was caught in a tangle of events—his political setbacks, the recession of the late 1930s, his inability to overcome the depression, his helplessness in the face of Nazi aggression in Europe—that might have destroyed a fanatic or "true believer." Somehow he not only recovered politically, won a third term in office, and presided over an altered political situation, but he never, even in the depths of his political troubles, exhibited more than a mild anxiety, a half-humorous exasperation, and an expedient blowing off of steam. Somehow Roosevelt's sense of security managed to live harmoniously with a towering ambition; once he had been drawn into electoral politics in 1910 he ran for virtually every office he found physically and politically within his reach—in 1912, 1914, 1920, 1928, 1930, 1932, 1936, 1940, and 1944.

The eternal quest for office that Roosevelt and myriad other politicians have exemplified is traced by some to neurotic feelings of insecurity and deprivation. But that quest can also be seen, depending on the leader involved, as exhibiting a feeling of self-confidence and self-efficacy that reflects healthy motivation toward *self-actualization,* a term coined by Kurt Goldstein and later given broader currency by Maslow. Self-actualization is to Maslow a complex class of "higher" needs, a need less imperative than that for sheer survival, less related to brute physical and psychological needs, a need more healthy psychologically, tending toward more creativity and a better balance between individual and collective claims, a continuing striving for efficacy in a series of challenges and tasks. It represents motivation to *become* those positive qualities that are a potential growth of the self. Unlike the more basic needs such as those for safety and affection, self-actualization, Maslow notes, is "intrinsic growth of what is already in the organism, or more accurately of what *is* the organism itself." Development proceeds from within rather than without. And self-actualizers, Knutson adds, may possess a flexibility, an ability to assess the personality needs of others as well as of oneself, and an open-mindedness (cognitively, not normatively) that is likely to make for successful leadership.

This kind of self-actualization—this need to grow and achieve, to fulfill oneself and respect others' needs—embraces also a feeling of competence and confidence in one's own performance. Robert White has suggested that a competence or "effectance" motive may even be intrinsic because it satisfies an innate need to cope with the environment. Underlying all the powerful personal and social influences working on the potential leader is the sheer sense of political skill, of being effective in politics as others are in, say, teaching and tennis. There is a natural tendency for persons to develop skills appropriate to politics in order to realize political ambition. But the reverse is also true: political skills facilitate the recruitment of persons into politics. The reason may be no more than sheer love of the game for which the person has an aptitude. Ambition feeds on skill.

These simple observations have important implications. For one thing, they mean that political skill itself becomes a power factor, that "the greater the actor's skill, the less his initial need for a favorable position or a manipulable environment, and the greater the likelihood that *he himself* will contribute to making his subsequent position favorable and his environment manipulable," as Fred Greenstein has said. Too, they mean, assuming that skills are unequally distributed or learned, that, in Harold Lasswell's phrase, there is a *skill struggle* as well as a class struggle, with significant impact on who gets what and when. The nature of that impact turns on the situation in which skill is exercised and on the purposes to which it is harnessed. The nature of these skills will vary with the situation, but one talent all leaders must possess—the capacity to perceive needs of followers in relationship to their own, to help followers move toward fuller self-realization and self-actualization along with the leaders themselves.

Just as self-actualizers are potential leaders at all levels—because of their capacity to grow, their flexibility, their creativity, their competence—the concept of self-actualization is a powerful one for understanding the processes of leadership. Its applicability to leadership has been stultified, however, by an overemphasis on *self*-actualization rather than mutual actualization with others. The view of Maslow himself is almost "biologistic," Brewster Smith has complained, as in Maslow's statement that man "demonstrates *in his own nature* a pressure toward fuller and fuller Being, more and more perfect actualization of his humanness in exactly the same naturalistic, scientific sense that an acorn may be said to be 'pressing toward' being an oak tree, or that a tiger can be observed to 'push toward' being tigerish. . . ." Humanistic psychologists have seen self-actualization rising less from internal factors than from the interplay of the self-actualized with other persons, accompanied by a steady rise in tolerant understanding of other persons, an open and inclusive attitude toward them, an ability to assess themselves in a "reflexive self-awareness," and a relatively rational and orderly approach to problems.

I suggest that the most marked characteristic of self-actualizers as potential leaders goes beyond Maslow's self-actualization; it is their capacity to *learn* from others and from the environment—the capacity *to be taught*. That capacity calls for an ability to listen and be guided by others without being threatened by them, to be dependent on others but not overly dependent, to judge other persons with both affection and discrimination, to possess enough autonomy to be creative without rejecting the external influences that make for growth and relevance. Self-actualization ultimately means the ability *to lead by being led*.

It is this kind of self-actualization that enables leaders to comprehend the needs of potential followers, to enter into their perspectives, and to act on popular needs such as those for material help and for security and esteem. Because leaders themselves are continually going through self-actualization processes, they are able to rise with their followers, usually one step ahead of them, to respond to their transformed needs and thus to help followers move into self-actualization processes. As the expression of needs becomes more purposeful—that is, as that expression becomes less subjective, egoistic, body-bound, direct and immediate, as it becomes more related to socially sanctioned aims and collective goals and values—leaders help transform followers' needs into positive *hopes* and *aspirations*. Hopes emerge from needs but are closely influenced by leaders who arouse or dampen them. Hope (looking forward with desire and with belief in possibility) can readily be escalated into aspiration (eagerly and ambitiously desirous of a higher goal) by leadership and other socializing influences. Studies of aspiration levels suggest that such levels are affected by leaders—for example, by the way in which experiment conductors influence aspiration levels by the phrasing of questions—as well as by more subjective factors such as anticipation of success. Leaders, of course, can also play on fears of failure.

Leaders can, in turn, help convert hopes and aspirations into sanctioned *expectations*. Expectations carry more psychological and political force than hopes and aspirations. They are more purposeful, focused, and affect-laden; the expectation is directed toward more specific and explicit goals, ones that are valued by the builder of expectations. As entitlements they carry a greater air of legitimacy; people expect what is rightfully theirs and are provoked or outraged when they do not receive it. And they widen the margin of the perceived probable. All these factors, and especially the last, have two further effects. They cultivate a situation in which heightened expectations, confronted with lowered or zero realization, combine to produce an extreme sense of deprivation in people. Thus theories of revolution have stressed as a critical condition the broadening gap between what people expect and what they get. Violence becomes increasingly probable, James Davies argues, when any basic need that has come to be routinely satisfied suddenly becomes unfulfilled. Revolution occurs, Ted Robert Gurr contends, when major segments of society perceive a discrepancy between their "value expectations" and the "value capabilities of the environment." Expectations are closely influenced by what leaders hold out as necessary, desirable, deserved, and possible.

Leadership plays an even more consequential role in converting economic and social expectation into *political demands,* that is, specific claims asserted directly against government. This step might seem a logical and almost inescapable culmination of the long process of the conversion of wants into needs, needs into hopes and aspirations, aspirations into expectations. But the sequence may not be this neat. Persons may not define their needs or aspirations in a way that relates to government. They may not define needs that are indeed even resolvable by government. They may perceive needs as related to government when the governors—especially bureaucrats—do not perceive those needs in the same light. A study of migrant poor in a number of Latin American cities offers a case in point. The clear and present "objective" needs of the migrants, as defined by middle-class standards, were to improve their living conditions by acquiring better housing, having water piped into their homes, securing a legal and dependable supply of electricity (many obtained electricity illegally), and the like. But in Mexico City fewer than one in ten *migrants* regarded improvement of living conditions as their most important concern. Almost half were more concerned about improving the economic situation or having steady work; education and health were also major concerns.

What persons demand of government will be affected by leadership in several ways. Leaders at the grass roots—teachers, priests, community activists, village elders—will closely influence persons' perceptions of their own needs, as against "objective" definition of their needs by observers. Political activists and practitioners will take the lead in mobilizing support behind certain demands and not behind others (depending on the ambition and ideology of those activists and politicians) and in organizing support that can be converted into pressures *on* government and *in* government in diverse ways and for diverse goals. And leaders, in vying for support among followers, will compete among themselves in their efforts to identify followers' fundamental wants and needs that can be mobilized and directed in support of the regime or against it, in protection of the status quo or in reformist or revolutionary action.

Aroused wants and needs, heightened aspirations and expectations, powerfully supported demands—and then, perhaps, disappointed expectations or rejected demands—these are all materials for political leadership. In these processes leaders have a central part in shaping, articulating, and targeting popular demands. But typically their ability to shape and redirect is limited, for they are dealing not with transient popular opinions or one-day fads but with demands emerging directly from powerful motivations based deeply and dispersed widely among humans. It is only when leadership itself is seen as pervading virtually every level and sector of society, rather than being limited to the formal institutions of government, that one can say with confidence that it is mainly in the crucible of leadership that the transmutation of "lower" needs into "higher" and the refinement of political demands take place.

Openings and Closures: The Structure of Political Opportunity

If ambition, in all its gross and subtle forms, is a powerful spur to leadership, we must recognize that leaders are not merely the product of potent social and psychological influences; they are cognitive, fact-gathering, calculating creatures who link their goals—and even subordinate them—to the reality of the structures of political opportunity around them. Motivation toward particular ends impels a person to seek office. But the structure, risk, and opportunity of various offices—the political context—shape the outcome of this motivation. They have a dynamic of their own.

The structure and the dynamic vary from polity to polity. In a sheikdom persons outside a small cluster of royal and princely families will expect to be excluded from formal political leadership; their hopes for political office will lie in minor bureaucratic opportunities. In a one-party system opportunity will be channeled through formal, circumscribed career lines, but the one party may provide multiple points of access. In a developing nation the military may offer the best chance for political advancement. In a more pluralistic society the access routes may be tangled and "nonpolitical"; thus there may be many possibilities for "lateral" entrance into politics from business, trade unions, religious organizations, the professions, sports, or organized crime. The structure of political openings and closures may vary slowly over time; contrast the circumscribed routes in England before the Great Reform Act of 1832 and the opportunities available to aspirants in the middle class later in the century, and contrast that with the openings available to trade unionists after further enfranchisements and the rise of a strong labor movement.

We can begin with a simple bipolarity: career-minded persons, usually rather flexible about the specific political career they will follow, confronting institutionalized and rather unchanging (but not unchangeable) structures of political offices. Whatever the intensity of their ambition, they will calculate their chances in terms of possible access points and advancement channels. This operation would appear to be a rather simple one, but in fact it is full of complexities and pitfalls. For political offices are not passive receptacles to be filled from an assembly line. They take on a kind of life of their own as they arouse or diminish certain expectations from those filling them and from other persons involved. They serve as stepping-stones to other offices, immobilize political careers, and even destroy them.

The British parliament notably exemplifies an institution that has preserved a structure and continuity over the centuries while responding to the ambitions of nascent political leaders emerging from changing social backgrounds. In the great, slow flux of British political life it has served as a focus of political ambition and a means of ordering channels of political advancement. For "several centuries," Lewis Namier wrote, "the dream of English youth and manhood of the nation-forming class has remained unchanged; it has been fixed and focused on the House of Commons, a modified, socialized arena for battle, drive, and dominion." To be out of Parliament was to be out of the world.

The organization of parliamentary office established the channels through which political ambition flowed. Whatever their capacity to gain seats—through adhering to the king's party or employing money or currying favor with great political families and notable national leaders—it was a *parliamentary seat* that had to be secured. Not only was a seat useful in itself—for reasons of prestige or income or even to escape creditors—but it was often the stepping-stone to the House of Lords, administrative sinecures, and military commissions. "You must make a figure there," Lord Chesterfield wrote his son in 1749, "if you would make a figure in your country." The target was a chamber of 558 members, the vast majority elected from England, only a few score from Scotland and Wales. Within England parliamentary representation, reflecting the distribution of wealth and population, was weighted toward the south. Almost one-third of the English parliamentary boroughs were seaports. The overrepresented southern counties included a host of "rotten boroughs" with tiny populations—a source both of corruption and of a "substantial surplus for national purposes," in Namier's words, "and it was there that seats were found for professional politicians, civil servants, and big merchants, *i.e.* for the administrative and commercial classes concentrated in London. At present the national as against the local type of candidate is planted out in the constituencies by the party organizations; in the eighteenth century this was done with the help of rotten or corrupt boroughs."

In the mid-nineteenth century Parliament remained the focus of British political ambition. The suffrage had been broadened moderately but the channels to political influence had not been; seats were still expensive and wealthy landowners still dominated the selection process in many counties. Only as the first Reform Bill and (especially) the Second Reform Bill had a chance to widen both the selection process and people's ambitions and expectations did new political forces move into the venerable Commons and ultimately into the upper chamber. Once the floodgates were opened the structure of access to the lower house changed steadily, except of course for women, whose suffragette leaders were compelled to agitate outside the system for the right to vote inside the system. Largely under Liberal party leadership local political associations and caucuses were formed, party officials hired, party work professionalized, political discipline tightened. "In order to win the masses," Max Weber said, "it became necessary to call into being a tremendous apparatus of apparently democratic associations."

Many cabinet members of middle-class origin were of course educated in public schools along with sons of the landed elite, only to take on the veneer and sometimes the doctrines of the old landed aristocracy; still, the social sources of political leadership were inexorably broadened. The process continued. By the end of the century, labor constituencies were gaining representation, first in the Liberal party and later in autonomous political organizations. A host of authentic toilers and sons of toilers made it to the House of Commons, though less often into the inner corridors of power. As Labour moved from its narrow trade-union emphasis of the early years into its role as a national party depending on coalitions of interests, it became the vehicle for left-oriented middle-class leadership to rise to power. But through all this the formal structure of opportunity remained largely unchanged. Some local offices—such as mayor of Birmingham in Joseph Chamberlain's years—offered a modicum of prestige and power, but businessmen, trade unionists, press lords, and the like had their eye on the main ladder of political power. Parliament remained the goal, if only as a stepping-stone to ministry and cabinet.

Russia after the Revolution, in contrast to Britain, witnessed a dramatic overturn in the political opportunity structure, but perhaps with less profound change and consequence than many had expected. The highest positions of state, once mainly restricted to aristocrats and the upper middle class, were to be thrown open to the masses. The more proletarian the applicant, the higher were the formal credentials. The Soviet governmental system, like the American, established a layercake of opportunities at the local, regional, republic, and national levels. A far more formidable pyramid of opportunity was created in the Communist party. The base comprised six or seven million party members. At the next level were many tens of thousands of party functionaries and activists. Stalin in the 1930s spoke of "100,000 to 150,000 of the lower rank who are the Party's non-commissioned officers." Above them lay a cadre of perhaps 50,000 party leaders of the middle rank and important bureaucrats such as factory directors, judges, division chiefs, high municipal officials, and some scientific, technical, and professional people. From here the structure of opportunity narrowed sharply to what Raymond Bauer, Alex Inkeles, and Clyde Kluckhohn have called the several thousand persons in the "top elite" but not the "ruling elite." The latter is a clearly defined pyramid of power: perhaps two thousand key party and government officials, topped in turn by several hundred members of the Central Committee of the Communist party, by a dozen or so leaders in the party presidium or awaiting entrance, by a small collegial group surrounding the general secretary, and finally by Number One himself.

The framing of the American Constitution in 1787 and the establishment of a new national government had a profound impact on the structure of opportunity. Not only were two national legislative chambers created, as in Britain, but a potentially strong executive and a national judicial system set up a host of political opportunities. The presidency and the cabinet and key presidential appointments became the focus of politicians' ambitions, along with, ultimately, several hundred legislative seats and a considerable number of prized federal judgeships. This layer of opportunity perched on top of the existing state and local structure; in contrast to Britain, the state and local offices served both as targets in themselves and as important stepping-stones to national executive and legislative office. This development was not fortuitous—the Constitution framers "planned it that way." A seat in Congress under the Articles of Confederation, Alexander Hamilton told the New York ratifying convention, had been so little an object of ambition that "it has been difficult to find men who were willing to suffer the mortification to which so feeble a government exposed them'' but the new government would be ready for the ''accomplishment of great purposes. . . .''

The mere existence of a plethora of state, county, and local offices had an independent effect of its own: it created a wealth of opportunities for men (and, to a modest degree, women) from many socio-economic, ethnic, and racial groupings. Almost anyone could run for city council, town selectman, county commissioner, and various judicial and law-enforcement offices, and almost anyone did. Educational qualifications were not always required. The opportunity structure absorbed and molded the ambitions of leaders from the stream of immigration into the country. In contrast to the narrowed political channels in Britain, offices in the United States were too numerous and accessible to filter out all the low-income, polyglot elements.

The structure of opportunity is not composed of offices in the narrow sense alone. Around each significant position a political substructure of leadership and followership develops as office seekers build political support to win nomination and election or to bring political pressure on executives or legislators making administrative appointments. The campaign for office may be fought out in the party arena, in which case the candidate will mobilize support from party leaders, convention delegates, and the like. Or, at the other extreme, candidates may build their own personal organizations that will operate through the party system or bypass it as expediency dictates. In either case new substructures of opportunity will be created as positions in the parties or in candidates' personal organizations became valued in themselves. All this broadens the already variegated structure of opportunity in the United States.

To see the array of openings and closures through the eyes of the aspiring, calculating office seeker is to glimpse both the mechanics and dynamics of the process. The positions sit there, established by constitutional or legislative action and occupied by officeholders, many of whom are eyeing other possibilities. Office seekers typically act like investors: they calculate risks and possibilities. What options will be given up, either in politics or outside? How desirable is the office in terms of pay, perquisites, prestige, power, career advancement? What will be the price of seeking it, financial and otherwise, in obligations to others, strain of endless errand-running, wear and tear on family relationships, erosion of privacy? What ''cushions'' exist to ease a fall out of favor? Since achieving office is a very public act in most polities, investors must make their calculations amid a stream of good and bad advice from friends, family, party officials, pundits, and self-appointed political counselors.

All this would seem the natural and eternal order of things, but the structure of openings and closures, and the cognitive and affective response of the office seeker, have major systemic effects. The capacity to calculate opportunities will be a significant factor in the shaping of leadership. To note a rational—in the sense of calculating—response to an array of openings is not to propose that the response is infallible; doubtless the miscalculations outnumber the correct estimates, as more seekers fall by the wayside than achieve their goals. The calculating, investing approach does suggest the likelihood that a certain type of person and politician will take risks, and will take risks successfully, more than will others. Absorbed as we are in the type of persons who rule us, we must observe also those who have *not* gained office: to what extent, for example, were they unwilling or unable to choose politics as a vocation because of the repellent aspects of campaigning and officeholding—financial cost, boredom, lack of privacy—as well as the personal and social influences acting on them and in them? In competitive societies the investing, calculating, transacting, risk-taking quality of politics may attract individualistic, entrepreneurial types of personalities who bring to politics the ethics and the practices of laissez-faire capitalism—with crucial implications for policy-making and political leadership.

The nature of both the array of positions and the calculation of aspirants, moreover, establishes a subsystem of career routes within the overall structure of opportunity. It comes to be accepted that certain kinds of aspirants will seek certain kinds of office. In many cultures the aspirant will be expected to start at the bottom and work up; in others, "inferior" officeholders will not be expected to attain top leadership but rather will be ignored or shunted aside in favor of lateral entrants. Certain offices will be expected to lead to other offices for several reasons: because they serve constituencies that are part of, or congruent with, constituencies of higher officials (as in the cases of a state representative running for state senator in an American state or a governor running for United States senator) and hence the candidate's constituencies are seen as deliverable or convertible; because the skills acquired in one office are seen as being relevant to another; or because the office seeker is expected to rise up the ladder of power.

Calculations of the interrelation of office opportunity may become rather sophisticated. In England the possession of a "safe seat" may make for a longevity in office that in turn has implications for membership in ministry and cabinet. In the United States, with its proliferation of state, national, and local offices, the aspirant may size up offices in terms of the opportunity they afford to try for a higher office without risking the lower. Governors with a four-year term may try for senator or President halfway through their term. Senators can seek the presidency with impunity during the second or fourth year of their six-year term; this circumstance has been known to affect the availability—or at least the timing of the availability—of a number of senators interested in a presidential nomination. Politicians can play a defensive game of staggered elections. It is said that some United States senators oppose a change from two-year to four-year terms for representatives because they fear that representatives with four-year terms would be tempted to take a "free chance" at midterm to unseat senators coming up for re-election.

Too, the structure of offices makes for varying degrees of collectivity and individuality among politicians. In a situation of congruent constituencies and relatively strong party support and solidarity among the voters, office seekers will tend to campaign—potentially to govern—in a large degree of mutual dependence and unity. The tendency here will be toward discipline and team-work. Politicians with less visibility or appeal may attach their fortunes to more successful politicians—hence the phenomenon of coattail-riding. A different structure of elections and offices—one that gives politicians separate and non-congruent constituencies, with overlapping terms—makes seeking and holding office less a collective or cooperative act than an individualistic one, with office seekers thrown onto their own political resources. In this situation candidates exercise coattail avoidance as they shuck off unpopular candidates who, they fear, might taint their own campaign effort.

Influential officeholders may manipulate the channels of opportunity in order to minimize threats to their own position. In New England congressional districts essentially dominated by the Democratic party, the incumbents have little fear of a successful Republican party challenge to their seats; the main threat lies in ambitious young rivals who might attack through the Democratic primary. Congressmen have used their influence to encourage potential opposition to run for state legislative office. The art of offering incentives outside the district and disincentives within, of helping to build up a rising politician for an out-of-district race without unduly building up future opposition *within* the district—these are means of exploiting what has been called the "steam kettle effect" of redirecting political pressure into safe channels.

So the structure of openings is also a structure of closures. A Trotsky or a Bukharin can ultimately find no secure position at the top because the Bolshevik party and the power system allow collective leadership in name but usually not in fact. A Boulanger arouses exuberant support when he campaigns through France, but he cannot find a firm lodgement in the existing parliamentary system. A Daniel Webster wins a variety of illustrious offices but he cannot make Massachusetts, with its divisions among the Whigs, a stepping-stone to his supreme goal of the presidency. Those who are filtered out by the system are not necessarily blocked from power; they may change the system to find a place in it, in the fashion of Latin American generals or Greek dictators, or they may turn to extralegal or revolutionary opportunities.

Political leadership is a product of personal drives, social influences, political motivations, job skills, the structure of career possibilities. These forces not only shape the rising politician but influence one another. Thus the need for esteem from others motivates the political tyro to run for office, but the office and the career possibilities in turn shape the esteem received. Leadership is fired in the forge of ambition and opportunity.

Viewing the structure of office opportunity through Western "pluralist" eyes, we see elected and appointive positions as the objects of an individualistic, competitive scramble for advancement. Whatever the political impact and even dynamism of the offices, they are essentially targets to be aimed at by aspirants. In less individualistic cultures, however, the relation between office and aspirant may be reversed; leadership positions tend to have an autonomous thrust of their own, in the sense that benefactors and guardians of these positions actively recruit potential leaders and indoctrinate and motivate them for established positions.

The most striking example of this kind of leadership opportunity has been the education of princes. The claims and requirements of the throne were considered clear; the task was to fit the prince for his future vocation. Antonine emperors carefully selected and prepared their successors in order to help stabilize the Roman imperial succession. Centuries later, in *The Education of a Christian Prince,* Erasmus offered elaborate advice on the practical and theoretical aspects of the training of hereditary leaders. A real prince must be a Christian philosopher. The tutor must instill in the young prince Christian principles and moral values but no ideas incompatible with his future position. "It is fruitless to attempt advice on the theory of government until you have freed the prince's mind from those most common, and yet most truly false, opinions of the common people," Erasmus cautioned. No government by public opinion poll here! Above all the prince must be educated in the nature of his future tasks. "All other men take great pains to get previous knowledge of the professions which they follow," Erasmus noted. "How much more care should the prince take to get an early knowledge of the theory of government!" The prince is also warned against the way of flatterers. Juan de Mariana laid out a full set of instructions for the education of a king, including his exercise, food, clothing, and companions.

The literature on the education of princes became so voluminous as to amount to a genre in itself. Machiavelli's *Prince* is the most celebrated example. A prescriptive society, however, prepares both princes and commoners who will exercise authority. During four dynasties stretching over a millennium Confucian China was largely ruled by a highly trained civil service. Confucian education was directly and explicitly linked to the recruitment needs of the state. An elaborate examination system catered to the abilities and upbringing of the prestigious country families, but there was an effort to broaden the system to include talented commoners that resulted in considerable occupational and social mobility over several generations. Scholars of lower-class origin could make it to the top, but only by first learning and practicing gentlemanly dress and manners. Motivation for public careers was intense, since scholars— especially those in government—stood near the top of the social scale, below only the imperial and noble classes. Public office was saturated in magic and ritual and was directly linked to the moral and political doctrine of the state.

Confucian China and Victorian England appear to have been remarkably similar in the organization of political opportunity. "Both systems," Rupert Wilkinson says, "taught morals by teaching manners: both moulded behavior through etiquette, through aesthetic appeals to 'good form.' Similarly, both systems pursued an amateur ideal, the notion that manners (signifying virtue) and classical culture (signifying a well-tuned mind) were better credentials for leadership than any amount of expert, practical training." And both served the landed gentry, though the Confucian more than the English. In fact, access to the top was far more restricted in China even than in Britain. Oxford, Cambridge, and a dozen public schools served as recruiting agencies for British government, especially for the Foreign Office and the diplomatic service. The nineteenth century saw a large influx of middle-class boys into these schools, where they mixed with sons of aristocrats and took on upper-class accents, dress, and manners. The situation varied with the prestige of the department they were to enter. Many of the civil servants in the Home Office came from the "minor" boarding schools, but two-thirds of all the Foreign Office attachés during the five years before World War I were Old Etonians.

Throughout most of the nineteenth century talented working-class youths had virtually no opportunity to attain higher positions in the more exclusive enclaves of the English bureaucracy. Many middle-class youths did find room at the top—but with what effect? Perhaps they served as leavening among the aristocracy, but despite the recruitment of talented middle-class youths, comradeship and competition on the playing fields of Eton doubtless produced more victories for aristocratic than for middle-class styles and values. This tendency might not have been critical for Confucian China, but Britain in the nineteenth century had entered on an age of advancing technology and intensifying social problems. The lack of emphasis on science in the public schools and the teaching of history and languages by rote (discussed in Chapter 4), the elevation of traditional elitist canons of behavior, the bias in favor of rural values, the deification of gentlemanly sport, the near-absolute ignorance of working-class life—all these demonstrated the significance of restricted access to office opportunity. On the other hand, the rising bourgeois classes learned some of the aristocracy's values—noblesse oblige, honor, courage—and had to shed some of the individualistic and pecuniary values they brought from their own social backgrounds.

Training for political leadership in the United States has been marked more by pious injunction than realistic effort. The American intellectual tradition is too inchoate, the Jefferson-Jackson myth of equal opportunity too potent, the fear of political indoctrination in private schools too strong, the appeals of commerce and the professions too persuasive, for private schools to serve as clear and effective channels of recruitment for leadership. For every Roosevelt or Kennedy who rose through exclusive educational institutions there have been many more Hardings, Trumans, and Johnsons who found other channels of advancement. A number of prestigious private schools exhorted youths to enter public service but supplied little political training or preparation. Groton, for example, at the turn of the century emphasized the ancient languages of Greece and Rome, taught European but little American history, and drilled the boys instead of educating them. Its headmaster, Endicott Peabody, preached the need for entering into politics in order to purify it, but his exhortations against political dishonesty and compromise failed to deal with the tough questions of expediency and accommodation that would confront the American politician. Franklin Roosevelt probably won success despite his Groton education rather than because of it. A number of Grotonians, such as Sumner Welles and Dean Acheson, went on to notable careers in public service, but not because they won elections or got along with most of the politicians who did.

Leaders of the developing nations in the twentieth century have not missed certain implications of the older nations' experience. In some cases the old colonial institutions for educating native youths for government service have been kept intact; in others new educational systems for political leadership have been established. The object in each case has been the same: to recruit politically reliable talent into the opportunity structure. The process has not been without tension—for example, between traditionalist political leaders and younger, more specialized graduates of universities and training schools moving into key administrative and technical positions. The need of a national army, if only for purposes of national prestige and unification, establishes an alternative channel for talent. In most cases able youths are channeled through state schools and universities under extensive government control. In Indonesia two universities in the 1960s were supplying about 90 percent of college graduates in government employment; most of the graduates flocked to and stayed in central government, facilitating nationhood but draining political and administrative talent from outlying rural areas. In the Philippines formal schooling seems to be a precondition to success not only in the civil service but in winning elective office. In the Soviet Union, as in other authoritarian nations, a monolithic and heavily politicized educational system has been used to recruit and train political leaders as well as to indoctrinate the masses.

How conscious and calculated are these efforts to organize and control the channels of recruitment into the opportunity structure? The answer varies with the nation, depending largely on the extent of its ideological unity and the degree of central control of its political and social processes. Evidently the English public schools were not intended to be recruiting agencies; the concatenation of historical circumstances produced this result. In other nations schools and universities have not been wholly tractable instruments for mobilizing new leaders to serve existing leadership. Even when political control of the university is tight, the response of students and teachers may be wayward and refractory and the long-run effect of leadership indoctrination may be incalculable and even self-defeating. In any event, the intensive effort to indoctrinate future leaders and to control recruitment channels emphasizes again that the formal structure of opportunity is not a cluster of inert targets of ambition. It has a life and impact of its own as it interacts with psychological and social influences on aspiring leaders.

The Creation of Followers

The people do not rule, according to Schumpeter. The democratic method is "that institutional arrangement for arriving at political decisions in which individuals acquire the power to decide by means of a competitive struggle for the people's vote." In many ways Gandhi exemplified this elitist type of leadership, both in his appeal to the Indian masses and in his incitement of, and heavy demands on, his immediate circle of followers. The difference lay in Gandhi's complete involvement with his followers. In putting his disciples to work, "giving direction to their capacity to care, and multiplying miraculously both their practical gifts and their sense of participation," in Erikson's words, he created followers who were also leaders, "aspirants for highest political power," and the makers of modern India. The shaping of the leader-follower by Gandhi and by all other effective leaders suggests the inadequacy of the conventional distinction between leaders and followers; it also forces us to examine in more depth the complex interrelation of different kinds of leaders, subleaders (or cadres), and followers.

To begin to sort out the channels of interaction among leaders and followers, we may think in terms of activators, the activated (respondents), and the nature of the response—ultimately its function, however small, in changing an existing structure of interaction. Activation consists of any initial act that stimulates a response; if no response results from an activation effort, activation does not take place. Activation so defined covers a vast range of acts, from long-term arousal of expectations to precipitating an immediate response—a landlord's warning to a tenant, a speech by a prime minister or president, preelection comments by a bartender, a church group circulating a petition, revolutionary appeals to the masses, the offer of a handshake by a campaigner to a bystander, propagandistic appeals across national boundaries, the politically motivated confrontation by Red Guards, a college teacher's lectures or assignments, a get-out-the-vote campaign, proselytizing by an anticolonial, nationalistic party in the rural areas of a developing nation, the "kindling power" of a Huey Long, a Boulanger, or a Demosthenes.

We can discern general patterns of activation: (1) face-to-face conversations and other interactions in which an activator may be all the more effective, as Paul Lazarsfeld suggested, because of the apparently nonpurposeful, nonpropagandistic nature of his comments, a knowledge of the followers and the kind of appeal that might be influential, an ability to be flexible and to try another approach if the first encounters resistance, the faith or trust the followers may have in the activator; (2) activation in the context of membership in groups and associations ranging from small social groups such as the family, to work groups or school classes, to larger, more formal associations like trade unions, ethnic associations, and business organizations; (3) efforts by political parties, popular movements, revolutionary organizations, and other groups contending for power to arouse support among the mass of people; (4) strategies by which established regimes retain or expand their hold on followers who make up some kind of electorate; (5) appeals by public and private communicators to foreign governments and populations. The *context* of activation is a key factor; an established party appealing for support to voters, many of whom dependably, almost "blindly," support (or oppose) that party, is in a different position from a new party or an antiregime movement.

The activated followers are generally even more diverse than the activators (leaders); indeed, it is the contrary assumption—that one follower is necessarily like another (because the follower is in the same family, labor union, ethnic group, party cell, occupational category)—that has led to so much attempted activation that finds either no response or unanticipated responses. One way to sort out the multitude of followers is to place them in their psychological, social, and political settings. Followers exist in diverse degrees of latency and of potential incitement; they hold beliefs, attitudes, needs, and values of varying intensity. Norman Nie, Bingham Powell, and Kenneth Prewitt began their five-nation study (Germany, Italy, Mexico, the United States, the United Kingdom) by identifying five attitude sets considered relevant to their investigation: (1) sense of citizen duty; (2) basic information about politics; (3) perceived stake in political outcomes; (4) sense of political efficacy; and (5) attentiveness to political matters.

Knowledge of events, and apperception of reality, will range along a broad psychological continuum. Persons may already be attentive to political stimuli and thus excitable, or enormous effort may be necessary to gain their attention in the first place. They may be so protected or imprisoned by sets of attitudes, needs, and norms that efforts at certain kinds of political activation would be doomed to failure. Or they may be ripe for mobilization, as in the case of some adolescents or college students. Each of these psychological forces is a cluster of characteristics. The quality of intensity of opinion alone, as V. O. Key suggests, may cover a variety of concerns. "Intensity may rest on a sense of group identification. It may flow from naked and immediate self-interest. It may emerge from an attachment to community values. It may be simply an assurance founded on knowledge. It may come from an anxiety about threats to an ordered course of existence." It would be doubtful, Key added, that intensity had the same meaning from person to person, situation to situation, or issue to issue.

A second way to perceive types of followers is in their social and psychological matrix. Some of the environmental settings long considered significant to political participation are family, school, class, status group, work group, residence (especially urban or rural), and political party; studies abound of correlations between participation and occupation, sex, income, race, religion, age, and other categories. One of the most consistent findings, at least in western nations, is that the extent of participation varies directly with more education, higher socio-economic status, greater age, male sex, and settled residence. Followers, embedded in their settings, can be activated only by stimuli that take context into account—an obvious fact but one sometimes forgotten by politicians and publicists who expect too much from appeals to artificial, autonomous, perhaps "reasonable" persons somehow standing outside the personal and social attributes of their family, class, church, sex, or neighborhood.

And persons' entrenchment in these settings must be seen not as a matter of mere "membership" but as a role fixed by attitudes, expectations, and claims by other group members whose esteem they value.

Followers also have *political* contexts. They hold all degrees of identification, attachment, affiliation, membership, loyalty, and disposition to activity in parties and organized interests. They belong to various political systems (with registration and voting arrangements that facilitate political participation or discourage it) of regimes that seek to mobilize them politically or suppress or channel political participation. They directly elect some of their leaders, indirectly choose others, and have no significant influence over still others. They may have a choice between fiercely competitive candidates and parties, or they may exist in noncompetitive, one-party districts where the election results are foreordained. The dominant politics may be heavily value-laden and ideological or pragmatic and "practical."

Out of these countless varieties of activations, playing on endless varieties of followers in their diverse settings, emerge patterns of political participation. It has been customary to assume that persons involved in the election process can be divided into two simple categories—voters and nonvoters—with numerous subcategories. But it has long been evident that voters take part in some elections and not others, vote for or against certain candidates and ignore others on the same ballot, bring a list of preferred candidates to the polls and faithfully vote the list or vote utterly at random, spoil their ballot deliberately or not, or perhaps simply take part, under pressure from an authoritarian regime and amid pageantry and symbolism, in a ceremonial performance the outcome of which everyone knows almost to the exact percentile.

The voter-nonvoter dichotomy is of limited value in itself. It does not cover much of the range of participation from those who merely vote to those who are intensely active in politics or the many gradations in between. Key distinguishes between the attentive and inattentive public—between, that is, the relatively small, interested, informed public that directs a stream of influences on leaders, and the mass public that pays some regard to political matters but has to be shaken out of its latency and shocked or propagandized or persuaded into paying attention and participating. Lazarsfeld stresses the role of local influentials in activating persons and influencing their political participation. Others have distinguished degrees of participation more precisely. Lester Milbrath divides the electorate into "spectators," "transitional activists," and "gladiatorial activists." In a hierarchy of increased participation, he sees spectators as those who expose themselves to political stimuli, vote, start a political discussion, try to persuade another to vote a certain way, or wear a political button; persons in the second group contact a political leader or public official, give money to a party or candidate, attend a political meeting; "gladiators" give time to a political campaign, attend a political caucus, raise political money, run for office, and—at the top of the hierarchy—hold public or party office.

These are useful categories as long as we keep in mind that persons are actually arrayed along a flexible range in which clear distinctions are difficult to make. Voting can encompass a wide range of behavior, as we have noted; so can attending a political meeting (actively or passively, vocally or acquiescently, rebelliously or trustingly) or talking to another voter or even serving in public office (acting independently, serving certain interests supinely, etc.). Time is a key factor: last year's nonparticipant may be this year's activist; this year's aroused citizen may be disgusted by the results and become next year's apathetic. There is a constant flux and heave in the political world that is hard to capture and label.

Most important, the vast majority are both activators and respondents, leaders and followers, at the same time or at different times. Voting studies have identified a "two-step" flow of communication and influence. Persons who changed their voting intentions during campaigns cited friends and family members as sources of influence more often than those who stuck to their voting decision throughout the campaign. The influencers or activators turned out to be persons with relatively high exposure to opinion media. Serving as transmission belts, the activators were both leaders and followers. Everyday observation supports this; we know that certain persons—a house-to-house canvasser, a sidewalk demonstrator, a party ward leader—appear in sets of leader-follower relations that are difficult to separate out. Indeed, the flow of influence is not two-way but *multiple;* national leaders and parties indoctrinate cadres, who in turn activate local opinion leaders, who in turn appeal to the wants and needs of potential supporters.

Conclusions on leader-follower relations have been drawn largely from experience and research in Western nations, but non-Western experience shows parallels. The two-step flow of influence is formalized in China, for example, where Communist party leaders maintain a "mass line process" with working-level cadres, as do the cadres with the general population. To make sure that the political line both emanated from the masses and went to the masses, Mao wrote in 1945, "close contact must be established not only between the Party and the masses outside the Party (the class and the people), but first of all between the leading bodies of the Party and the masses within the Party (the cadres and the membership)." Traditional representative bodies have been abolished or bypassed as the party demanded that the mass line call for an organic, intuitive relationship between cadres and masses rather than bureaucratic or legal controls. Enormous emphasis has been placed on soliciting mass discussion and opinion as a means of both directing the people and tapping its energies and commitment. The famous *tatzupao* (huge handwritten placards posted or paraded conspicuously), for example, are supposed to express mass opinion as well as reflect cadre indoctrination. Just where central direction leaves off and local "democratization" begins is not easy to judge—as in all politics—but the dominating mode of Chinese central command and control should not obscure the reciprocal relation between political authority and the people as a whole or the symbolic relation between cadres and masses—in short, the complex interaction in which party officials must activate, mobilize, and direct popular energies but must also anticipate and adjust to popular response and resistance.

These patterns of political participation, of activation and mobilization, of leader-follower interaction, are hardly novel; they have been well documented in research in many countries. But out of these findings emerges a conclusion and problem of profound importance for the study of political leadership: in most polities there is no clear or sharp line between the roles of leader and follower. And in no society are there leaders without followers or followers without leaders. Moreover, leaders and followers exchange roles over time and in different political settings. Many persons are leaders and followers at the same time. Leaders have a special role as activators, initiators, mobilizers. Personal influence flows in many directions, vertically and horizontally, through complex networks of two-step and multi-step processes. It was once assumed that certain political activity—voting, persuading others to vote, attending meetings, contacting government officials—tended to be concentrated in the hands of limited numbers of activists. But important research by Sidney Verba and Norman Nie reveals that, in the United States at least, the overlap of activism was by no means complete; various types of "followers" engaged in different types of political activity with the result that "the different modes influence leaders in different ways" and the impact on leaders of different kinds of political activity by different sets of people is powerful indeed.

One can still discount the significance of all this if one holds the fixed conviction that humankind is divided into small, intensely active, knowledgeable, and united elites on the one hand and a great mass of persons in a state of ignorance, inactivity, and low motivation on the other. A good deal of research and analysis has rejected this simplistic dichotomy. Vast areas of ignorance, inattention, and nonparticipation are always uncovered in such studies, but this typically is not true of most of the citizenry. Key summarized an enormous range of research when he concluded simply that (American) "voters are not fools."

Still, Key was referring to *voters*. If the processes of leadership and fol-lowership are hard to separate out, a most important dichotomy does exist be-tween those who participate in some degree as leaders or followers and those who participate not at all. The latter are the apathetics, the anomics, the alien-ated, and the excluded—the political outsiders or isolates. They are latent fol-lowers, unrealized, dormant.

Those who are isolated from the political process by the deliberate actions or inactions of the controllers of access and entrance differ from *those who exclude themselves,* for whatever reason. The first group has long been barred from political office, polls, associations, and activity in democracies and dicta-torships, monarchies and republics; they are the poor, the landless, the female, the young, the criminal, the sick, the feebleminded, the religious or racial mi-nority group member, and the heretic and the infidel. The means used to exclude them are ingenious and varied: outright coercion by the regime or by groups encourged by the regime; constitutional and legal provisions excluding certain categories of the population; impossible registration requirements; legal obstacles, often in the guise of protecting some "higher" value such as na-tional security, law and order, or defense against internal subversion. Some-times exclusion is rationalized with the cloak of plausibility, as in the case of failure to provide effective absentee registration and voting arrangements for the hospitalized, shut-ins, or soldiers overseas. Yet democratic societies are gradually moving to include more of those previously excluded—the poor, the female (only recently in Switzerland), the black, the immigrants, the young.

Most numerous among the self-excluding in most societies are the *apa-thetic,* who shun political participation because politics is at the periphery of their lives (if even there). They may be so immersed in private troubles, de-manding careers, peripatetic jobs, or segregated social enclaves, such as disaf-fected racial minorities or bohemian subcultures, that politics cannot be impor-tant to them. They may be totally involved with staying alive, remaining free from attack or starvation. Rarely are they able to connect what happens "out there," Herbert McClosky notes, with the events of their own lives. Or their apathy may be somewhat more cognitively grounded; some apathetics see poli-tics as obscure, dull, and pointless because their political environment—in the absence of arousing issues, perhaps, or of competitive parties or inspiring lead-ership—is obscure, dull, and pointless. It has been conjectured that not only those with great frustration but those with little frustration are likely to be apa-thetic; the former may be immobilized by politics and the latter bored to death by it. For such apathetics it is not themselves but the system that is apathetic.

The *alienated* reject politics because they feel politics has rejected them. They believe that, whether or not they vote, an establishment or a few insiders or the System will make the decisions. They see no meaningful difference between the parties or between the candidates. Government seems too remote and complex for them to see and touch, much less master. They suspect that the system serves them ill for the benefit of a small elite. They reject politics or participation in it. Such alienated persons are not merely apathetic; they are negative and resistant.

The *anomic* lack feelings of self-efficacy, purpose, roots, belonging. They feel normless, aimless, powerless. In L. Srole's five dimensions of anomia, anomic persons are seen to sense that political leaders are indifferent to their needs; to see the social order as fickle and unpredictable; to fear that they and their kind are not realizing life-goals and even retreating from those already reached; to have lost a sense of the meaning of life; and to see the framework of their immediate personal relationships as neither predictive nor supportive.

In his worldwide study of human concerns Hadley Cantril found apathy at its desperate extreme among the people of India, "who were found to be still unaware of their problems; who were too depressed to have many ambitions for themselves; who were unaware, too, of the possibilities of action at the national level to improve their welfare; whose passivity derives in large part from an ancient and widespread fatalism which still makes it possible for millions upon millions of Indians to accept their wretched lot. . . ." If the apathetic are unaroused by politics, and if the alienated feel rejected by politics, the anomic feel rejected by themselves. Doubtless the feeling of anomie is exacerbated by the social or political environment—by a widening gap between the social conditions of the masses and the official norms, in Marxist terms, or by a conflict between political systems with resulting social disintegration, in Robert Merton's term—but the origin of anomie lies deep in the anomic's psychological growth.

Given the great variety of the apathetic, the alienated, and the anomic, given too the immense diversity of psychological, social, and political nonparticipants, is it fair to conclude that these persons are truly political *isolates?* Granted, perhaps, that they will not become politically active on their own volition, cannot they be motivated and activated by some form of leadership? Obviously some of the isolates are borderline cases and can be induced, however transiently, to commit a political act. In India persons aroused by the sterilization program struck back at the Congress party. But the essential quality of isolates is that they are indeed isolated, beyond the reach of normal political activation. There is a world of difference between relatively passive, unmotivated persons who are potential participants, susceptible to whatever form of political stimulation that is relevant to them, and the hardcore isolates. For in the former case there is a potential of which certain types of leaders will be aware, a potential that can be realized under certain relatively calculable circumstances. But no technique or mechanism is available to the average leader to reach the utterly bored and apathetic; they are still in this condition, after all, despite repeated overtures in the past. No political appeal can easily move the alienated; political appeals by "power-hungry, insincere, dishonest politicians" are part of their alienation in the first place, and more appeals may only increase the alienation. And the anomic are the most removed of all; since the sources of their condition are social and psychological, the only influences that could motivate them politically would have to reach deep into their intrapsychic selves, and few politicians would know how to do this or would consider it worth the effort.

Time may make a difference. Over long periods the isolates may enter the political arena and participants may leave it as social and psychological conditions change. Institutional and legal arrangements may also be slowly modified. Beginning with the granting of a limited franchise in England, Norway, and Belgium in the early nineteenth century, the suffrage has been extended incrementally in the Western nations until by the mid-twentieth century it met the basic democratic requirements in most Western-type democracies: it was universal, secret, and equal. In some nations political participation came to be required; nonvoters, for example, were subjected to penalties. Winning the right to vote in Britain was only in part the result of efforts by leaders of the voteless; at least as important was the leadership of parties such as the Whigs and, later, the Conservatives, of politicians like Disraeli, who saw advantages for themselves if new voting blocs entered the electorate, and of reformers who acted out of libertarian and egalitarian impulses.

Exceptional leadership may also make a difference in transforming dormant into active followers. The leadership of men like Lenin, Gandhi, and Mao brought literally hundreds of millions of men and women out of political isolation and into a new kind of political participation. Heroic, transcending, transforming leadership excites the previously bored and apathetic; it recreates a political connection with the alienated; it reaches even to the wants and needs of the anomic and shapes their motivation. Militant anticolonial regimes in emerging nations mobilize tribal and rural people hitherto far beyond the potential of political activation. Revolutionary parties and movements enlist mass memberships and assemble recruits and drill them in the political arena. Heroic leaders and competitive parties within the democracies reach out to the bored and disaffected and give new meaning to issues and causes. But all this calls for uncommon leadership, and uncommon leadership is just that.

PART III

TRANSFORMING

LEADERSHIP

6

INTELLECTUAL LEADERSHIP:
IDEAS AS MORAL POWER

Napoleon is said to have coined the term *ideologue* in a fit of pique at the captious theoreticians of Paris. But the men Napoleon scorned as *ideologues* were not ideologists in today's sense of the word. They were *intellectuals*—a term that would come into fashion in France a century later, during another time of trouble. Confusion about the term has disrupted and inflamed discourse over the role of the intellectual. What is this creature? Metaphysician? Dreamer? Mystic? Utopian? Evangelicist? Dilettante? Goal setter? Detached contemplator? Joiner of thought and action? Raymond Aron found so many definitions that he virtually gave up the term. Joseph Schumpeter was almost willing to settle for Wellington's gibe, the "scribbling set."

The ambiguity rises in part from a failure to distinguish between the intellectual as a relatively autonomous and detached figure and the intellectual as a person hovering in a particular cultural milieu or social class. An intellectual is, in the first sense, a devotee of ideas, knowledge, values. "Intellect," Richard Hofstadter wrote, "is the critical, creative, and contemplative side of mind. Whereas intelligence seeks to grasp, manipulate, re-order, adjust, intellect examines, ponders, wonders, theorizes, criticizes, imagines." An intellectual is something more: a person concerned critically with values, purposes, ends that transcend immediate practical needs. By this definition the person who deals with analytical ideas and data alone is a theorist; the one who works only with normative ideas is a moralist; the person who deals with both and unites them through disciplined imagination is an intellectual. Some scholars regard value as corrupting the critical sense; they argue for moral detachment. But moral detachment is itself at best a modal value and one hostile to the concerns of the free mind.

141

Intellectual leaders deal with both analytical and normative ideas and they bring both to bear on their environment. However transcendent their theories and values, intellectual leaders are not detached from their social milieus; typically they seek to change it. "The actual definition of an intellectual," according to J. P. Nettl, "must . . . include not only a certain type of thinking but also a relationship to socio-structural dissent, at least potentially." Some intellectuals—perhaps long after their time—pervasively influence the intellectual temper of an epoch and the thinking and the actions of politicians. The concept of intellectual *leadership* brings in the role of *conscious purpose* drawn from values. The intellectual may be a mandarin; the intellectual leader cannot be. Intellectual leadership is *transforming* leadership.

But intellectuals, like intellectual leaders, cannot stand outside society, for they are a response to needs of society. Even the rudimentary societies "have a place for the intellectual functions which are expressed in art and interpretative speculation," according to Edward A. Shils. More advanced societies require intellectuals to explain the nature of evil; "to interpret the society's past experiences; to instruct the youth in the traditions and skills of the society; to facilitate and guide the aesthetic and religious experiences of various sectors of the society. . . ." The needs that give rise to functional intellectual roles, Shils notes, also impel intellectual creativity.

The catalyst that converts these generalized needs into specific intellectual leadership is *conflict*. A remarkable number of eighteenth- and nineteenth-century intellectuals seem to have been driven by internal conflict that expressed itself in emotional breakdown, withdrawal, or alienation. David Hume, following a kind of intellectual orgy at the age of eighteen, experienced hysterical symptoms, hypochondria, and melancholia that marked a long breakdown. Voltaire went through a period of intellectual and emotional crisis. Fourier as a boy was steeped in sexual guilt and later lived as a quarrelsome, erratic recluse (many great thinkers, male and female, have been bachelors). Saint-Simon was alleged to have been so stubborn and willful as a youth that his father had him imprisoned for contumely; he grew up to be an adventurer, a libertine, a rebel, and a thinker. John Stuart Mill in his early years experienced a period of extreme melancholia and purposelessness (though he may, in retrospect, have exaggerated it). Comte suffered repeated psychic breakdowns in which he flung knives and acted out grandiose fantasies. Weber and Mannheim would undergo their own individual emotional ordeals.

We cannot psychoanalyze these thinkers a century or so later; neither can we ignore the suffering and tension that in some cases must have thrust on them new perceptions of the world. More important, and probably more ascertainable, was the emergence of intellectuals like these in periods of moral and social conflict. Educated men and women in eighteenth-century France in particular were profoundly divided over questions of man's relation to God, the nature of Nature, the legitimacy of tradition and custom, the place of man in the universe, the relation of reason and the passions, the inevitability of evil, the natural rights of man, and the philosophical and practical questions that flowed from these concerns. Perhaps the life of the intellectual—especially that of the intellectual leader—is inherently conflict-ridden, embracing the tension between the pure and the applied, the negative and the affirmative, the analytical and the prophetic, the relationist and the absolutist, the classical and the rationalist—what has been called the "quarrel of the ancients and the moderns." But the expression of these conflicts is quickened, blunted, transformed, repressed, magnified by the social and political environment. Eighteenth-century France, early and mid-nineteenth-century England, late eighteenth-century America, and the early twentieth-century "reform" eras in the United States were times of social conflict during which intellectual leaders were drawn into the arenas of political combat.

Intellectuals at the Tension Points

Of the French thinkers of the eighteenth century's epoch of tumultuous intellectual combat and excitement, we will be mistaken if we assume, as so many have, that the *philosophes* held thoughtlessly optimistic views of human nature and its potential for reason and for good. On the contrary, this was an issue that deeply perplexed these thinkers and about which they agonized in their discussions and correspondence. They were not merely the children of the optimism of the early Renaissance, with its newfound faith in man's rational and moral potential. They were heirs to a much longer tradition of extreme skepticism, sometimes of unrelieved pessimism, about the nature of man—a tradition going back to the Greeks but culminating in the "counter-renaissance" of Machiavelli, Luther, Montaigne, and then again in the works of Hobbes, Pascal, La Rochefoucauld, Racine. Men were naturally given to hatred and envy, Spinoza said. Men are "more wicked than beasts," according to Pufendorf, and could not live without law. Man's irrationality, uncontrollable passion, inordinate selfishness, vanity, and hypocrisy—all these in varying combinations and degrees made up a dominant theme of eighteenth-century thought. It was not, after all, a century for easy optimism.

The *philosophes* had few illusions about man as he *was;* they had high hopes about man as he *could be.* That is why so many think them and the American moral leaders of the golden age to have been naive. "The optimism of the Age of Enlightenment was, for the most part, not about human nature,"

Lester Crocker writes, "but about what could be done with human beings, through the process of science, through education and government, and in general, through the rational reconstruction of society." The crucial effort of Enlightenment thinkers, he notes, was to control corrupt self-interest through rational self-interest. Years later Reinhold Niebuhr and others would renew the attack and argue that liberals especially should give up their naive optimism about human reason and goodness and pay more attention to human selfishness and original sin.

To control the spring of human action by using that spring to control itself; to devise institutions that would draw from the best in human nature to subdue the worst; to alter the social context of people's lives so that the impulses of rationality and tolerance and generosity could overcome the thrust of unreason, cruelty, and selfishness: all this fused into a compelling idea. United as they were about the major ills of society, however, the intellectual leaders of eighteenth-century France—the *philosophes,* the Encyclopedists, the writers of the Enlightenment (terms that are by no means interchangeable)—divided over the means to accomplish such high ends. Given their premises they could argue for a totalitarian system or for anarchy; they could argue for violent revolution or for gradual change. In fact few *philosophes* argued for any of these extremes; they were mainly moderate men. But between those extreme alternatives, which had a logic of their own however perverse, lay a shadowy world of hopes and alternatives and possibilities about the kind of society they would like to see arise in place of *l'infame.* Most of the *philosophes* directed their hopes toward this shadowland without clearly specifying the ends they sought or the means through which their ends could be realized. Above all they failed to recognize the hobbling chains of history and human nature. If a new kind of man could be created in a social milieu of reformed and broadened education, enlightened government, and benign social arrangements—and on this general proposition most of the *philosophes* were agreed—how could that milieu be fashioned out of the existing passions and depravities of man and his benighted, infamous, and hypocritical institutions? Would not any new social system be so freighted with the existing deep-seated ills of society as to be compromised and perverted even as it was being shaped? How could the past be exorcised, the slate wiped clean?

The *philosophes'* hopes on this score rested largely on their view of man's capacity for enlightened self-interest. Self-interest could be realized, under Physiocratic doctrine, through a system that would protect every person's interests and rights; and out of the conflict and compromise among all these individual interests a just society would emerge. Or self-interest could be achieved, in Rousseauean terms, through protection and enhancement and consolidation of the combined general interests of mankind. Each of these doctrines had implications for economic and political arrangements, the first for a system of private enterprise and the representation of discrete interests in government through a legislature composed of locally chosen representatives responding to such interests, the second for collective—communal, mercantilist, or even socialistic—decision-making in the economy and for the expression of a supreme general interest in government through a powerful executive.

These and many other notions floated in the intellectual shadowland of late eighteenth-century France. The *philosophes* were profoundly divided over the means of achieving a just society and the assumptions underlying such a society. Despite endless discussion of the nature of man and society, of human good and human evil, they came up with few clearly drawn sets of alternatives in which general ends were explicitly defined, instrumental means (political strategies, governmental structures, constitutional allotments of power) were set forth, and specific means (administrative arrangements or precise educational reforms) were spelled out. All these ends and most of these means were elaborately analyzed, but they were left—as systemic choices—in an intellectually disheveled condition.

Hence it was easy, toward the end of the eighteenth century, for an intellectual son of the *philosophes* like Robespierre to borrow eclectically from the prevailing wisdom. From Montesquieu he drew a theory of representation asserting that the legislative assembly represented the "essence of sovereignty." From Rousseau he drew a theory of popular sovereignty declaring that the state was a single will, a common entity, an expression of the social contract embodying Rousseau's faith that "each uniting with all will nevertheless obey only himself." From the countless projects for educational reform he drew his proposal for a system of national education in which children from the age of five would be enlightened and regenerated and made capable of sustaining the new society. At this point—during the first phases of the Revolution—Robespierre as intellectual leader was a social reformer and benign revolutionary. He called for the abolition of the death penalty and condemned the "frightful doctrine of denunciation" and other instruments of terror.

The *philosophes* were *hommes engagés.* The conflicts within them conjoined with the intellectual and social conflicts around them to draw them into the tension points of their time and place. They were embattled but not lonely men. The portrait of the remote and withdrawn thinker has been as overdrawn as that of the starving poet in the garret. Intellectuals—especially intellectual leaders—need company. They need disciples to sustain them, patrons to subsidize them, lovers to cherish them, adversaries to exchange hate with, and, above all, ways of communicating their ideas to intellectual circles and beyond.

Religious orders, universities, royal courts, and think tanks over the centuries have variously provided intellectuals with protected places to think and discourse. The social and intellectual habitat of the *philosophe* was the *salon*. Here he exchanged ideas, news, quips, and gossip with theorists like Diderot and Rousseau, Condorcet or lesser lights, or perhaps with foreign celebrities like Hume, Franklin, or Priestley. "If you were a *philosophe*," Kingsley Martin observed, "you would be wise to maintain your reputation in an older world at Madame Geoffrin's on Monday or Wednesday, you would certainly call on Mademoiselle de Lespinasse (who received almost every evening between five and nine), you could discuss Helvétius' books (for he always wrote them in public) with their author on Tuesday; on Friday you could visit Madame Necker, and you would miss the best part of the week's entertainment if you did not dine with Holbach on Sunday or Thursday."

Brilliant and formidable ladies reigned over these affairs; they selected the guests, set the tone of the occasion, arbitrated quarrels, and sometimes set boundaries to the discussion. They wielded influence not only as hostesses but as discoverers, befrienders, and patrons of intellectuals. They arranged for sinecures for their favorites and intrigued for honors; it was said that at one point Madame Lambert had created half the living members of the Academy. A significant change occurred in the salon during the century. Earlier it had been of an exclusive, even aristocratic character; like its Italian model it was run by ladies in or close to royal circles. The house intellectuals were largely dependent on aristocratic recognition and patronage, even for their food and lodgings. Later in the century, as the *philosophes* gained wider sources of support, they were able to set their own criteria for intellectual discourse in the salons and to broaden the company so that a wandering ne'er-do-well, socially inept and humorless—Rousseau is the best example—could be admitted and listened to.

The salon was always a tiny world set apart. It prized wit, cleverness, charm, and intellectual audacity more than intellectual substance or the kind of political commentary that came to grips with the social reality of eighteenth-century France. The need to please the hostess was no small part of it. "Women accustom us to discuss with charm and clarity the driest and thorniest subjects," Diderot noted. "We talk to them unceasingly; we wish them to listen; we are afraid of tiring or boring them; hence we develop a particular method of explaining ourselves easily, and this passes from conversation into style." Despite Montesquieu's complaint too that "the society of women corrupts the morals and forms the taste," the main difficulty lay with the *philosophes* themselves. Night after night they met in their coteries, exchanged epigrams, criticized one another's works, and made the judgments that ultimately would establish literary reputations. The literature that emerged, according to Lewis Coser, was "eminently a literature of sociability, a literature of playfulness, liveliness, and sparkle—but also a literature that too often eschewed exploration of the deeply personal and the philosophically profound." The salons were both incubators and legitimators of ideas, but they had the air of an intellectual charade acted out by a self-chosen few.

If the *philosophes* were separated from the social cauldron around them, there was a reason more portentous than salons and their ladies. This was censorship. The penalty for writing or printing unauthorized books was severe: by an edict of 1757, the death penalty. Swarms of policemen, spies, and informers infiltrated printing shops, booksellers, cafés, and libraries; eventually even the sale of books in once-privileged noble mansions was supervised. Printers, writers, and mere readers of banned books were occasionally handed long prison sentences. To be sure, the policing was erratic and inefficient, and authors were often protected in high places. Banning of a book inevitably whetted the appetites of those who heard about it. Clandestine presses were busy in France, and books were smuggled in from abroad. Forty-three editions of Voltaire's forbidden *Candide* were printed before the Revolution. But censorship had its effects. In particular, the higher prices of pirated books made them less available to the poorer members of the literate middle classes.

Thus censorship, as Coser suggests, became "an unintentional but powerful agency of alienation." Writers were embittered by both the capriciousness of the censors and the hostility of the regime that lay behind it. Yet the *philosophes* were alienated from the society around them doubtless as much by their own propensities as intellectuals as by external restraint. The *philosophes* felt they formed a distinct and special class. When a man is truly intellectual, they believed, he was by that commitment, in Charles Frankel's words, performing a social function and engaging in a species of social action. D'Alembert, one of the leading *philosophes,* said: "Happy are men of letters if they recognize at last that the surest way of making themselves respectable is to live united and almost shut up among themselves; that by this union they will come, without any trouble, to give the law to the rest of the nation in all affairs of taste and philosophy." Ernst Cassirer may be correct in putting down Taine's objections that the Encyclopedists were Utopian doctrinaires who constructed synthetic societies without regard to historical reality. For the Encyclopedists—and the *philosophes* in general—had a voracious appetite for data, experiment, experience. They were also intensely interested in practical reforms of education, penology, law, and administration. What was lacking was a grasp of the political strategies and broad institutional means that could connect their grand theories of reason, progress, and justice and the reforms necessary to fulfill theory, with the needs and hopes and the capabilities and potentials of the common man.

Tocqueville recognized the problem when he looked back on the eighteenth century from the vantage point of the nineteenth. Describing in *The Old Regime and the French Revolution* how "men of letters took the lead in politics and the consequences" of it, he concluded that the revolutionaries were much like the writers of abstract books: they had "the same fondness for broad generalizations, cut-and-dried legislative systems, and a pedantic symmetry; the same contempt for hard facts; the same taste for reshaping institutions on novel, ingenious, original lines; the same desire to reconstruct the entire constitution according to the rules of logic and a preconceived system instead of trying to rectify its faulty parts. The result was nothing short of disastrous; for what is a merit in the writer may well be a vice in the statesman and the very qualities which go to make great literature can lead to catastrophic revolutions." With hindsight Tocqueville could know what the French intellectuals of the eighteenth century could not—that the cauldron would overflow, destroying their hopes and compromising their doctrines yet opening up immense opportunities for the future.

Liberty and Power

The English experience was notably different from that of the French. Rarely have intellectuals exercised more striking influence over the political ideas of an entire society and a whole epoch than did the English thinkers of the seventeenth century. They too speculated on the nature of man and on other philosophical questions that were to occupy the great French writers. They joined with thinkers across the channel in grappling with the paramount question of finding a new secular basis of authority following the collapse of the traditional arguments for churchly and princely power. But the English concentrated their attention on what seemed to them the single most urgent and critical problem: the defense of liberty against governmental power. That defense called for constant vigil since liberty was ever under threat from the power-hungry. The "Interest of Freedom," Marchamont Nedham wrote in the mid-1650s, "is a Virgin that everyone seeks to deflower." Without representative government "so great is the Lust of mankind after dominion, there follows a rape upon the first opportunity."

So the examination of power and the pursuit of liberty followed on a palpable need, a need felt by lord and commoner alike as England went through its experiments with absolute rule, republican government, a lord protector, restoration, and an imported and tamed monarch. Algernon Sydney summed up two centuries of hard thought and harder experience when he wrote in 1698: "Men are so subject to vices, and passions, that they stand in need of some restraints in every condition; but especially when they are in power. The rage of a private man may be pernicious to one or few of his neighbors; but the fury of an unlimited prince would drive whole nations into ruin. And those very men, who have lived modestly when they had little power, have often proved the most savage of monsters when they thought nothing able to resist their rage.'' Much earlier Hobbes had written that men had a perpetual and restless desire of power after power that ceased only in death.

Perhaps the most remarkable aspect of this search for the means of protecting personal liberty against political power was the number of brilliant thinkers who directly confronted the problem but were themselves, over the centuries, virtually forgotten. The "fame rule"—that the coverage of political leaders decreases geometrically as one descends from the figures of first importance to those of the second and third rank—is equally true for intellectual leaders. The vital ideas of the "greats" come through to us: Filmer and his theory that English government must be both arbitrary and royal, Hobbes and his belief in absolute sovereignty, Locke and his defense of parliamentary government. In fact the major analysis and the theoretical formulation of the problem of liberty and power were both well under way before Locke wrote. Today the names of Charles Herle and H. Ferne, of Philip Hunton and Charles Dallison, of John Lambert and Marchamont Nedham, hardly dwell on schoolboys' lips even in England. Charles I would be known, and perhaps his able defense of the need of shared power between king and Parliament, but not the names of the two brain trusters who wrote his defense, Viscount Falkland and Sir John Colepeper. There are hundreds of books and articles about Locke and Hobbes, but the number dwindles to dozens or less for the secondary figures, to still fewer for the tertiary thinkers, and to hardly a handful concerning the publicists, jurists, ecclesiastics, parliamentarians, patrons, academics, and printers who formed the structure of support and dissent, conflict and communication, within which new ideas were incubated, molded, and disseminated.

If the need for such ideas was acute, and if the intellectual response was a collective one, the English scene during the seventeenth century presented an environment of conflict in which new ideas flourished. W. B. Gwyn has noted that during the years before the accession of James I and the outbreak of the Civil War there was a "poverty of ideas" in both the royal and the parliamentary camps. The English were even slow to take up new ideas of sovereignty and fundamental law that were developing in France in the sixteenth century. "However, once the Civil War broke out, political and constitutional thought was to flourish in England as never before and to furnish herself, her colonies, and her neighbors with a stock of ideas, many of which continue to be the currency of constitutional discussion to this day.'' It was the outbreak of open conflict between king and Parliament that sharpened intellectual wits and forced disputants to relate their proposals for the control of power to fundamental alternatives in the Western tradition. The divisions were deep not only between monarchists and parliamentarians but among Presbyterians, Independents, and Levellers. Political thinkers embodied and reflected the conflicts of the time. Hobbes was a tutor to aristocratic rulers, a combative thinker with a bent for long and sometimes humiliating wrangles, a disturber of the peace whose work was suspected of atheism, an anti-parliamentary theorist who fled to the Continent when he felt Parliament threatened his life. His eternal quest for authority probably bespoke an internal need for control and order as well as a reaction against the disorder around him. Locke was the son of a strict Puritan engaged in the service of the popular party. "From the time I knew anything," the philosopher would write later, "I found myself in a storm which has continued to this time." His school, Westminster, was at the headquarters of the parliamentary movement; his university, Oxford, was one of the battlefronts of the political and intellectual struggle of the time. He became tutor and adviser to Lord Ashley, later the Earl of Shaftesbury, and was soon deeply engaged in the plots and counterplots surrounding Shaftesbury's turbulent career. Locke too found it prudent to retire to the Continent, where he did some of his most lasting work. He was, in Peter Laslett's words, a "meticulous and practiced controversialist." Other thinkers of the time were similarly engaged; some of the best writing was done in prisons.

The towering achievement of the English thinkers was the application of their intellectual resources to one of the most demanding and perplexing problems facing political philosophers seeking to puzzle out the relation between liberty and power. This question concerned the way in which various arrangements for distributing power within governments, combined with certain methods for representing social classes, estates, or other entities in government, could best maximize individual liberty without crippling the effectiveness of government in realizing government's fundamental aim, the maintenance of justice and order.

We are so used today to the operation of mixed and separated constitutional arrangements, whatever their awkwardness in practice or their occasional breakdown, that the intellectual foundations of these systems are somewhat taken for granted. For the intellectual innovators of the seventeenth century the theoretical and practical problems were formidable. The thinkers were dealing with two distinct but related systems of government. One was a system of mixed government, or balanced constitution, that would preserve liberty and check power by balancing the basic classes of society—typically the monarchical, aristocratic, and popular groupings—against one another. The other was a system of separation of powers that would divide the functions of government among different parts or agencies of the government so that each branch would be restricted to the exercise of its proper function. The difficulty lay not simply in understanding how each of these arrangements would work in quite different and eternally changing societies, for what purposes, and tested by what standards. Nor did it lie mainly in the fact that each arrangement came in a variety of alternative combinations—thus the executive, the legislature, and the judiciary could be separated in many different ways, and further separations could be created within branches (as in the division of a legislature into two chambers). The main intellectual labor came in puzzling out how each of the alternative arrangements—mixed government and separation of powers, each in its many versions—related to the other at a time when Englishmen were busily sorting through models of government in their effort to defend liberty against power.

For the intellectual leaders of the seventeenth century, developing the theory of mixed government was the easier of the two tasks since they could exploit the intellectual capital of many centuries of hard thought on the question. Plato had emphasized the need of mixed government in order to achieve balance, harmony, and compromise among social classes. Aristotle had seen the value of a wider balance of classes but agreed with Plato about the importance of each class having a proportionate share in government; "proportion is as necessary to a constitution as it is (let us say) to a nose." Polybius and other Romans had carried the debate further; and after the ancient doctrines of mixed government had spread to medieval Europe, Aquinas had reaffirmed the Aristotelian notion of mixed government founded in monarchy, aristocracy, and democracy. The existence of king, lords, and commons and the estates they embodied provided English thinkers with an immediate and tangible field of interests and institutions in which further to develop the theory of a mixed constitution.

Working out the theory and the mechanics of the separation of powers, however, sorely tested the English thinkers. The mechanical problems were fearsome; how literally does one draw the line between the making of law and the executing of law? What executive decision-making powers should be less subject to legislative control (foreign policy-making)? What decisions had to be ratified by Parliament? There was the larger problem of the extent to which the different agencies or branches of government should be independent of one another and interdependent on one another: a workable compromise had to be found between absolute separation and absolute merger. Not surprisingly the debate was marked by misinterpretations of the great thinkers, misperception of opposing arguments, misreadings of experience, and mixed values and standards.

What happened, in effect, was the intellectual grafting of the theory of divided powers onto the theory of mixed and balanced classes, the grafting of separated agencies of government onto a system of cooperating and countervailing estates. The separation of powers, as M. J. C. Vile has noted, thus became a subordinate though essential element in the theory of the balanced constitution. "This subordinate theory was, however, capable of a life of its own, rejecting the class basis of the theory of the balanced constitution, and emerging as a theory of constitutionalism which, overtly at any rate, was based exclusively upon a functional approach to the division of power, recognizing only the right of the democratic branch of government in the making of law, relegating the 'ruler' to a purely executive role, and, insofar as the aristocratic element was recognized at all, assimilating it to the judiciary."

It was a tribute to the caliber of the intellectual leadership of seventeenth-century England that the century that followed was alive with continuing debate and analysis and was at the same time a period of muted passions, gradual governmental innovation, and relative political calm. While seventeenth-century discourse had taken place in heated pamphlets, tracts, and broadsheets, much of the political discourse of eighteenth-century England erupted in face-to-face confrontations in coffee-houses. London alone offered more than two thousand of these houses at mid-century. Far more democratic than the aristocratic salon of Paris, the coffee-house attracted men of different ranks, who stayed as long as they wished—to talk, to read, or to be read to. One entered the house by paying a penny at the bar; a stranger could take any vacant seat and listen to the talk of poets, politicians, and playwrights and perhaps speak up, engage others in conversation, or remain silent.

More exclusive than the coffee-houses were the London clubs that catered to special intellectual interests. Sometimes clubmen met in closed-off parts of coffee-houses, sometimes in taverns or at the homes of members. Only later did they have their own discreet and comfortable sanctuaries along St. James's and elsewhere. Here intellect was often married to power, as writers and ministers of the crown met weekly or monthly to discuss political affairs and even plan government actions. Some clubs took on markedly Tory or Whig tendencies and became themselves targets of sharp controversy. It was in such clubs that Daniel Defoe and Jonathan Swift sharpened their pens and came to exercise a pervasive influence on the thinking of their times. And it was in such coffee-houses and clubs that theorist and practitioner, government minister and academic critic, preacher and pamphleteer argued and perhaps shaped the practical applications of the ideas of the great intellectual leaders of an earlier century.

◆

If the influence of intellectual leadership is hard to measure in general terms, we can gain a firmer understanding of the causal role of collective intellectual leadership, operating through a known structure of discourse and decisively affecting political actions, by analyzing the process in a more focused situation. The experience of the American colonialists and constitutionalists offers an almost unparalleled opportunity to study the effect of political ideas addressed to a broad problem of cardinal importance, transplanted across three thousand miles of ocean, and directed in a known context to a series of political and constitutional decisions that would shape the destiny of a new nation for decades to come.

Circumstances seemed to collaborate to make eighteenth-century America a cockpit for the intellectual and political battle of "liberty against power." The heirs of the men and women who had forsaken England to defend their political and religious liberty would not readily surrender that liberty on a new continent. The multiplicity of religions—members of eighteen different sects were listed in a 1775 census of religion—and of doctrinal divisions within sects provided ample provocation for disputation on the meaning of liberty and the authority of establishments. The colonies experimented with various political arrangements under the Crown and with different forms of representation in their own colonial systems. And the never-ending debate drew heavily from classical, English, and continental thinkers and from the practical experiences of men of commerce, law, and government.

Liberty against power—this would seem to be a glib and even misleading way of formulating the paramount issue. But eighteenth-century Americans knew what they were about. Just as these students of Machiavelli and Hobbes held a realistic view of man's perversity and frailty, so they knew that power was necessary and inevitable. But power was also expansionist, aggressive, cunning, corrupt, and eternally seeking to "trespass on men's rights and liberties." American thinkers did not conceive of power as a means of advancing or protecting liberty. Power and liberty were opposites. Indeed, the natural prey of power was liberty. Both power and liberty were legitimate; but, as Bernard Bailyn has written, their spheres were innately antagonistic: "The one was brutal, ceaselessly active, and heedless; the other was delicate, passive, and sensitive." Madison noted that in Europe charters of liberty had been granted by power but in America charters of power were granted by liberty.

How subdue the voracious, crafty, and inescapable beast of power? England was the Americans' model. Sharing with their British brethren fundamental assumptions about natural law and man's inalienable rights, Americans watched admiringly the manner in which the English constitutionalists seemed to achieve a governmental balance of powers among executive, lords, and commons—a balance founded in turn on a social equilibrium among the monarchy, the aristocracy, and the common people. But Americans lacked—they proudly spurned—the monarchical and aristocratic classes that made the British system work. What would they do, a Tory critic sneered, *invent* a collection of marquises and barons—perhaps out of heroes well known for burning pamphlets and tarring and feathering opponents? Americans were divided over the issue. Some, like Franklin and Paine, would carry the republican principle to its logical end and depend on the prudence and wisdom of the people acting through a single, strong legislative chamber, with frequent rotation of executive office. Others would restrict the ballot, create lifetime appointments, or otherwise subdue the fury of popular passion and ignorance.

In their search for a solution to this riddle Americans had three advantages. One was their common schooling in the teachings of the leading English and continental intellectuals. Here too the single influence of particular thinkers—especially Locke—has been exaggerated. If any single influence predominated, it was probably his; but the intellectual leaders in the colonies had read too their Plato, Aristotle, Vergil, Cicero, Cato, Plutarch, Sidney, Pufendorf, and Bolingbroke. They had also read—or learned from at second or third hand—a host of thinkers hardly remembered today, men such as John Somier, Thomas Gordon, John Trenchard, Benjamin Hoadley. They also had their own intellectuals: the celebrated Franklin and the lesser known John Wise, Jonathan Mayhew, Richard Bland. All these men wrote a generation or two before the era of the immortals of 1776 and 1787; the immortals could not have done without them.

The most practical advantage for American political thinkers was a rich array of the means of circulating their ideas. They could print pamphlets, which would usually be reprinted in London and would quickly provoke rebuttal pamphlets by English Tories. They could write newspaper articles that would often be reprinted in local weeklies throughout the colonies. In a crisis they could turn to the broadside peddled on street corners as a ready way of alerting friends. To reach a mass audience they could write for one of the many almanacs. On civic occasions they could offer an oration, which might be printed later. They could pen letters—and they did so indefatigably. Some could use the pulpit; churches in the colonies, especially in the North, seemed to have few inhibitions about political and even flammatory sermons. Pastors indeed were expected to preach on the religious implications of political contests. Anyone could dignify his plea by making it an official remonstrance or appeal to king and Parliament, and a host of resolutions, petitions, declarations, and grand jury charges were shipped across the Atlantic after suitable hometown publicity.

Another advantage was the immersion of early American political thinkers in political experience as well as philosophy. John Adams was a veteran (admittedly a rather bruised one) of factional Massachusetts politics, a leader of colonial protests against England, and later a diplomatic agent for the pre-1789 confederation. Jefferson, a Renaissance man with intellectual and practical interests in science, invention, architecture, politics, education, and philosophy, served as a Virginia legislator, a Continental congressman, governor of Virginia, and minister to France. Madison was a Virginia assemblyman and a Continental congressman, Hamilton a military man, John Dickinson a man of wide affairs. Franklin was the most practical of practical men. But the practitioners still sought to learn from the theorists, ancient and recent, and there was a lively exchange between the "thinkers" in pulpit and academe and the "practical men" of law, politics, and commerce.

Out of the clash of ideas widely disseminated and debated there came—in the crises of secession, revolution, and constitution-building—a grand solution to the dilemma of protecting liberty against power in a government needing internal checks and balances and lacking a grounding in social classes and estates. The solution was to establish *within* government a balance of powers that exploited cross-splitting divisions among men, and to do so by contriving selection processes, terms of office, and powers of position so that the natural disharmonies of persons would be converted into friction and conflict in government. Thus the rulers could go about their business of securing order and acting for the general welfare but would not be capable of concerting their powers and energies against the people's liberty. To erect such a government in a system of balanced statuses, as in England, was one thing; conflict in such circumstances was so traditional, predictable, and moderate (typically) that equilibrium was assured. To discern that among a "free" people without royalty or aristocracy the thrust of economic and sectional power would also be dispersed and controlled and hence that government would not threaten republican liberty—this took a revolution in thought that represented intellectual leadership at its apogee.

Such an intellectual leader was James Madison, and no one summarized the strategy of checks and balances more persuasively than the constitutionalist from Virginia. He clearly discerned the evolving needs of the American people, and his political experience and political reading had left him with no illusions as to the nature of man. He analyzed the political situation in terms of a conflict theory—the tendency of popular governments toward the violence of faction, with resulting confusion, instability, and injustice. He examined the root causes of faction and found them not in superficial or ephemeral forces but "sown in the nature of man." These forces erupted in religious, political, leadership, and above all economic conflict, but "so strong is this propensity of mankind to fall into mutual animosities, that where no substantial occasion presents itself, the most frivolous and fanciful distinctions have been sufficient to kindle their unfriendly passions and excite their most violent conflicts." Because factionalism was so puissant it could not be subdued by devices such as "destroying the liberty which is essential to its existence" or by giving "every citizen the same opinions, the same passions, and the same interests." Such notions were impractical or worse than the disease itself.

No, the strategy of protecting liberty against power must be as potent as the forces to be curbed. The *causes* of faction could not be removed; only its *effects* could be. The problem must be solved "by so contriving the interior structure of the government as that its several constituent parts may, by their mutual relations, be the means of keeping each other in their proper places." But this device would not work unless each department of government had a will of its own. How create those opposing and conflicting wills? By making the departments respond to conflicting and opposing constituencies. "The great security against a gradual concentration of the several powers in the same department, consists in giving to those who administer each department the necessary constitutional means and personal motives to resist encroachments of the others. . . . Ambition must be made to counteract ambition. The interest of the man must be connected with the constitutional rights of the place." Granted, Madison added ruefully, that all this was a reflection on human nature. "But what is government itself, but the greatest of all reflections on human nature? If men were angels, no government would be necessary." If men are to rule over men, the government must be able to control the governed *and* to control itself.

So sagaciously did Madison state the problem, so compellingly did Hamilton, Adams, and the others conceive, execute, and defend their strategy, that later generations have spoken of an explosion of political genius in 1776 and (especially) in 1787. If we stand back, however, we can see the American Constitution as the culmination of thinking that had its sources in centuries of hard political thought and analysis, in direct political experience, and in the special human needs and political circumstances of the American colonies. Not only was the 1787 "solution" the culmination of a "continuous, unbroken line of intellectual development and political experience," as Bailyn has called it, bridging the worlds of classical antiquity, seventeenth-century English and continental thought, and Madisonian analysis. It was a classic, perhaps even an unparalleled example of the power of political leadership by intellectuals in a situation where their understanding of human nature was firm and realistic, their grasp of earlier thinking broad and acute, their capacity to learn from their own and others' experiences discriminating, the nature of the theoretical and practical problems clearly delineated, and the time and circumstances ripe for a philosophical and operational resolution of the problem—the problem of curbing power and protecting the people's liberties.

Intellectuals and the Nature of Liberty

Even as we marvel at the sweep and power of John Locke's theories of government, the innovative but little-known thinkers who preceded him, and the brilliant theorist-practitioners who applied English liberal thought to the crisis conditions of America, we must note failures of intellectual leadership that closely affected political thought and action deep into the nineteenth and twentieth centuries. Not only did the intellectual leaders of the seventeenth century meet difficulty in reconciling the doctrine of mixed or balanced government with the very different doctrine of the separation of powers; not only was it hard to apply either doctrine to societies undergoing rapid political change; the intellectual problem lay far deeper. The massive, articulate major premise of these thinkers was the protection of individual civil and political liberty against public power. Their conclusion was a limited government stabilized by a mixed constitution or by the separation of powers or by a combination of the two. These devices would protect the individual against oppression by a monarch, by an established church, by an aristocracy, or by other individuals.

The inarticulated larger question concerned the capacity of people collectively to expand their liberties *through the use of governmental power* rather than merely to defend their private liberties *against* it. It was a question of the ability of common as well as uncommon people to use public agencies both negatively to curb the citadels of private power (such as churches, aristocracies, and rural oligarchies that threatened their liberties) and positively to fashion political, economic, and social institutions and processes that could expand their liberty in the broadest sense—their opportunity to gain education, nutrition, health, employment. We cannot fault seventeenth-century thinkers for failing to conquer intellectual problems that still perplex and thwart us three centuries later. The problem was that in their pursuit of "negative" liberty the liberal intellectuals were helping to shape institutions that would have the most direct influence on the manner in which "negative" and "positive" liberty was examined, generated, and distributed. Each of the two great arrangements of government that occupied the practical minds of the theorists could be applied in a fashion to limit or maximize the two kinds of liberty. Under "pure" separation of powers the legislature that monopolized lawmaking power could be established in a way that would directly reflect popular interests (through, say, the manner of electing legislators) or it could be organized to block them (through, say, direct crown influence over members of parliament). A mixed government could combine executive, legislative, and judicial power in a manner that would reflect popular majorities or in a manner that would protect the retention and exercise of power by minority groups and established leadership elements.

The intellectual leaders of the seventeenth century were confronting vital questions of political leadership and power without recognizing the immense stakes that would be involved in future political and societal arrangements. In effect they were engaged in applying theories of leadership without seeing the broadest implications of leadership or even employing—much less conceptualizing—the term. Their views were compelling enough for their time and place, and the historic circumstances on another continent were ripe enough for their views to have a profound and generally positive effect on the American Constitution makers; only later would Americans face their own intellectual and political Armageddon. But in England historic circumstances were beginning to shift radically even as the ideas of the seventeenth century were being applied in the eighteenth. For that later century witnessed, in the tortuous course of the industrial revolution, the massive growth of a form of power that would have an enormous impact on liberty, one far surpassing that of ecclesiastic and other "private" powers of the past. This was capitalistic power, the rapidly growing control of satisfactions and deprivations, centered in the hands of private entrepreneurs. How would English intellectual leadership respond to these new circumstances?

The epistemological and analytical burden was enormous. The intellectual leaders of the time simply did not "see" the nature of liberty as we do in modern times; they could not easily shake off the mental carry-over from centuries of human experience with oppressive power. To carve out and to legitimate a place for private liberty—political, social, and economic (principally the defense of one's right to personal private property)—virtually exhausted the intellectual resources of the day. But intellectual leaders would have had to do much more than this to grapple with new potentials of positive and collective liberty. They would have needed to explore the potential resources of the state in education, housing, health, and employment for developing and maximizing real opportunity for the common man; eventually they would have had to deal with the implications of radical equality of opportunity for sweeping concepts of equality of condition.

That was the conceptual challenge; the task of thinking through the requirements of governmental and political institution-building was also intellectually daunting. The generating and expanding of positive liberty could not take place until a political system was created that could mobilize potential popular support for positive liberty, link that support with governmental institutions, and create a system of government to respond to aroused popular wants and needs and to make and enforce decisions that ultimately would respond to those pressures. Such a political system required at least three things: a populace with mass political power, a means of linking that power to the government, and a structure within government that could enact and enforce relevant laws and decisions. The question was whether the intellectual leaders of eighteenth-century Britain, drawing on the intellectual resources of earlier centuries without being overwhelmed by them, could imaginatively explore such problems and opportunities and at least pose alternative ways of dealing with them, at the same time redefining and presumably broadening the concept of liberty. In general the intellectual leaders of the eighteenth century failed to do this.

What happened instead was the slow, piecemeal, hit-or-miss creation of institutions by practical men of affairs aided or abetted by theorists, most of them hardly known or remembered today. The first of the institutions to be developed was cabinet government. While theorists were still arguing the niceties of separated power and balanced government, men of affairs were creating and legitimating a means of linking legislative and executive action. Not only did Montesquieu, Blackstone, and many others miss the potential significance of the cabinet for unified and effective government, but the cabinet system itself came under attack from those still entranced by the doctrine of limited government and separated power. "We see the same men with the power of creating offices, and the power of furnishing salaries," wrote John Cartwright, a veteran advocate of the separation of powers; "with the power of forming schemes of expense, and the power of voting themselves the money; with the power of plunging their country into war whenever it may suit their corrupt views, and the power of granting themselves the supplies. Can faction, in the lust of dominion, want more?" Neither France nor America had such a system, he added; in those countries men would not be found "skipping, like harlequins, from the cabinet to the legislature, from the legislature to the cabinet."

A cabinet could suppress rather than encourage liberty for commoners, depending on how it was linked to popular aspirations. By the dawn of the nineteenth century there was considerable agitation for an extension of the right to vote—an agitation that in England would culminate, in this epoch, in the Great Reform Bill of 1830. Defenders of negative liberty and divided government saw the implications of a broadened franchise for the allegedly "delicate" balances and harmonies. Conservatives who simply feared the democratization of government and society were also vociferous. It cannot be said that these critics were answered by theorists who recognized the need for positive liberty that could be sustained in the long run only by a populace aware of the possibilities of positive liberty and of the mass electoral rights necessary to it. Many who favored the separation of powers well understood its capacity to deadlock government, but there was no intellectual conflict between them and those who wanted or understood the necessity for change, because the latter did not see the link between active, popular government and social change. Once again political theory was lagging behind the pace of actual change.

And the pace of social change seemed to be quickening as millions of English men, women, and children either poured into the turbid cities that spread out around mill, dock, and mine or converted their cottages into tiny factories. What philosopher of the new century could draw and complete the magic circle of theory encompassing a revised definition of liberty, an expanded vision of the benign potential of government, and a compassionate understanding of the need of mass political agitation and organization? One might have expected that Jeremy Bentham, with his "felicific calculus" of the greatest happiness for the greatest number and his attack on traditional laws and institutions, might have advanced an intellectual system embracing mass needs, rationalized government, and popular action. He did frame general rules that would establish a maximum of free choice and practical liberties for the great number of Englishmen, and as the years passed he endorsed parliamentary reform, the secret ballot, universal suffrage, and majority rule. But Bentham held a crabbed and negative view of the possibilities of government. The essential purpose of the state was to administer punishments and sanctions to actions that were inimical to the greatest happiness of the greatest number. "All government is in itself one vast evil," he wrote. Government might liberate man from ancient, obsolete bonds, but it would not in itself generate economic and social liberties for the masses. How could this thinker, with his fertile proposals for penal reform, for a "frigidarium" (to keep foods from rotting), for new schools, and for various gimmicks—how could he have such a negative view of government? That view sprang from his most fundamental values, especially his concept of liberty. Both a slave to and a prophet of the prevailing doctrine of atomistic individualism and laissez-faire, he viewed liberty as essentially a protection from government (except, to a limited degree, in education) and had little vision of the state as a moral or cultural agency and its possibilities of enlarging man's potential for freedom and self-fulfillment.

To a remarkable degree John Stuart Mill, a youthful disciple of Bentham, devoted his own intellectual life to the definition and analysis of individual liberty and to its defense from oppression and intolerance. His *On Liberty* still stands as the classic treatment of the subject. No one surpassed Mill in defining the political sphere within which government must not intrude—the sphere of

self-regarding action that did not harm others. Mill, too, was a political reformer; he endorsed proportional representation, woman's rights, compulsory
education, heavy death taxes, and other ideas far advanced for the time. His
concept of liberty, nevertheless, was inadequate to the economic and social
deprivations, needs, and opportunities of middle nineteenth-century England.
On Liberty was marked by ambiguities and inconsistencies, as Gertrude Himmelfarb has suggested. Mill's concept of liberty, while less negative than
Bentham's, glimpsed but never embraced the enlargement of freedom through
action by the state. His social generosity and compassion were always tempered
by a fear of the great uneducated multitude—perhaps a majority of the voters
dominated by trade unionists—seizing the machinery of government and
engulfing the liberties of free men. That compassion led him to make enough
exceptions to his own principles to establish him as a traditional figure in England's slow movement toward positive liberalism and a vague brand of socialism. But Mill did not exert the kind of intellectual leadership that ultimately
would bring meaningful freedom to urban, industrial man.

Who would close the circle? Not Walter Bagehot, with his astringent analysis of cabinet government—"a hyphen which joins, a buckle that fastens"—
coupled with a fear of the masses that surpassed Mill's and with an old-
fashioned dependence on a lower-class deference that was sure to erode in the
democratizing milieu of urban Britain. Not Lord Acton, whose normative
beginning and ending point was liberty, which he defined as obedience to moral
law and which he held to be threatened not by absolute monarchy but by
absolute democracy directed by lower-class levellers who were restrained—but
perhaps only temporarily—by a sense of deference. It was late in the century
before the extension of the suffrage, the rise of a mass-based party system, and
a redefined concept of liberty fell into a creative conjunction. An Oxford philosopher, T. H. Green, taught an idealistic metaphysics that supplied the intellectual underpinning for the transition from laissez-faire to governmental planning and control. On the premise that every injury to the well-being of the
individual was a public injury, Green saw that individual liberty could be
enlarged through expansion of government's positive role in health, housing,
mine and mill regulation, and, above all, education. But the closing of the intellectual circle was accomplished mainly by a host of lesser-known thinkers
rising out of the Chartist, radical, socialist, labor, and other social and political
movements.

These thinkers, whose intellectual roots went down to the early Levellers
and Diggers, had long recognized the social implications of the negative concept of liberty; they had fought for the poor man's right to vote; they had no
inhibitions about the use of power to broaden the liberty of the common man—

provided the right people ran the government. By the last decade or two of the nineteenth-century the questions faced by the labor, liberal, and socialist thinkers of Britain were less concerned with broad ideology and general strategy than with social data and analysis, industrial organization, political tactics, and government administration. Much of the burden of analysis was shouldered by the remarkable collection of thinkers who called themselves Fabians. Spurning direct political action, they set themselves to the cerebral task of accumulating and closely analyzing social data and to long—and long-winded—discussions of their implications. Their political tactic was the penetration, through speeches, books, and pamphlets, of the organizations and entities—trade unions, socialist and reform societies, ministerial and municipal councils, and London drawing rooms—that lay close to the networks of power. Disentangling the precise influence of the Fabians from that of Comtean positivists, Christian and non-Christian socialists, trade unionists, anarchists, land reformers, Henry George disciples, and a multitude of others is all but impossible. But that the Fabian influence, based mainly on the indefatigable gathering and merciless dissemination of facts disagreeable to the Victorian mind, was profound cannot be gainsaid. Despite their leaden prose leavened occasionally by Shavian wit, despite their lovers' quarrels, their emotional and physical remoteness from the working class, their tiny size, and their inexperience in politics, men and women like Beatrice and Sidney Webb and G. B. Shaw acted at a decisive moment of British history to integrate the concepts of liberty and equality and to comprehend the implications of their ideas for political action and government structure.

Beatrice Webb exulted over the "behind the scenes intellectual leadership" for which she felt her husband Sidney had an especial talent. She felt that their home was becoming the intellectual headquarters of the labor movement. H. G. Wells, who long was impatient with his fellow Fabians and later broke with them, disagreed about the effectiveness of the little band. "Measure with your eye this little meeting, this little hall," he said to the Fabians, "look at that little stall of not very powerful Tracts: think of the scattered members, one here, one there." Then, he urged, "go out into the Strand. Note the size of the buildings and the business places, note the glare of the advertisements, note the abundance of traffic and the multitude of people." That was the very world, he concluded, "whose very foundations you are attempting to change. How does this little dribble of activities look then?" Both Beatrice Webb and H. G. Wells exaggerated, but in the conflict between venerable institutions and intellectually powerful ideas, it was mainly Wells' institutions that would give way.

The Intellectual Test of Transforming Power

The test of intellectual leadership in facing such problems as the relationship of liberty and power is a stern and demanding one. That test, in the world of politics, is more than the supplying of ideas to politicians and parties in order to help them gain power or frame policy. It is more than the capacity of intellectuals to exert direct personal influence on government and politics. These are important functions, but they are not the ultimate test of political leadership by intellectuals. That test is the capacity to conceive values or purpose in such a way that ends and means are linked analytically and creatively and that the implications of certain values for political action and governmental organization are clarified. The test is one of *transforming* power. This was precisely the measure of the grand accomplishment of the American Founding Fathers in framing a structure of government and (at least by implication in *The Federalist* and other writings) a strategy of political action ideal for protecting the kind of *negative* liberty—liberty from oppressive government—that they valued.

In an industrializing nation, how long would it take for intellectual and political leaders to frame a doctrine of *positive* liberty to be achieved through a government responding to popular needs and capable of responding to those needs? One of the major components of a system of positive liberty—majority rule by a coalition of farmers, small debtors, artisans, frontierspeople, and others among the less affluent—came into being with astonishing rapidity with the victory of Jefferson in 1800 and his triumphant re-election four years later. The politician-philosopher built a majority coalition through his broad appeal and the failings of his Federalist opponents, and he proved the essential temperateness of majority rule by favoring moderate policies and bringing what he called "Republican Federalists" into his camp during his presidency. He exerted presidential leadership on policy, attacked the courts as havens for holdovers from a previous, now minority, Federalist party, and wielded formidable influence in Congress through his Republican followers there.

Yet as an intellectual concept majority rule did not take firm hold in nineteenth-century America. Jefferson was more effective at practicing it than rationalizing it, and no intellectual leader stepped forward to provide a body of theory and exegesis that would relate the doctrine of majority rule to Enlightenment ideas, British political thought and practice, and American circumstance and possibilities. On the contrary, the most important act of intellectual leadership in the last century was performed by a towering anti-majoritarian, John C. Calhoun, who wished to build even more checks and balances into the Madisonian model in order to defend his way of life, his section, and its peculiar institution. Calhoun and other anti-majoritarians, therefore, tapped in the growing nation a deep well of feeling against majority rule. This was remarkable, as Louis Hartz suggested, because the nation was so united around liberal "Lockean" doctrine that no majority would be so opposed to a substantial minority as to wish to destroy it. But the very liberalism that restrained the minority had given rise to a vast neurotic fear of what the majority might do. "What must be accounted one of the tamest, mildest, and most unimaginative majorities in modern political history has been bound down by a set of restrictions that betray fanatical terror," Hartz has written. "The American majority has been an amiable shepherd dog kept forever on a lion's leash." The Jacksonian movement, which further alarmed anti-majoritarian Whigs, was more effective in gaining and wielding practical political power than in provoking a powerful intellectual defense of majority rule.

Both the Jeffersonian and the Jacksonian movements, furthermore, operated from an essentially negative conception of liberty; they were more effective in attacking courts and banks and other aristocratic and Whig sanctuaries than in seeing and realizing more positive purposes for government. With the intensely rapid industrialization that came in the middle and later years of the century, the question was whether intellectual leaders in the United States would grapple more successfully than had their British counterparts with the need to transform the real foundations of the concept of liberty. A number of factors dimmed this possibility. In the wake of the Darwinian revolution of thought Americans were attracted to a brand of "social" Darwinism that encouraged doctrines of open competition, individualism, and laissez-faire. A nascent labor movement, constantly being reshaped by heavy immigration from abroad and by drain-offs of labor to the western frontier, found more immediate success in "joining" capitalist ethos and practice through various forms of business unionism than in militant and ideological action. The socialist and other radical movements could not find a grounding in the political culture of the late nineteenth-century. As usual the reformers were divided among civil service advocates, anti-saloon enthusiasts, pure food supporters, trustbusters, money tinkerers, and countless others.

Some of the most gifted intellectual leadership was displayed by conservative, libertarian individualists. Social Darwinist William Graham Sumner synthesized the Protestant ethic, Ricardian economics, and the doctrine of natural selection and advanced a theory of social determinism that, as Richard Hofstadter suggested, left little role for government other than defending the property of men and the honor of women. Jurist Stephen J. Field combined Darwinism, classical economics, and Spencerian individualism in opinions and decisions (as in *Lochner vs. New York*—a New York statute limiting bakers' working hours), that invalidated social legislation and dimmed hopes that the states might innovate in the harnessing of a socially disruptive industrialism. Andrew Carnegie, author of *Triumphant Democracy,* decried excessive egalitarianism and practiced a ruthless kind of competition while he preached a curious combination of rugged individualism and the social obligation of capitalistic trustees for the poor. Dominating this intellectual scene was Herbert Spencer himself. The apogee of the concept of negative liberty must have been reached in the fall of 1882 when the famous Englishman journeyed to America, was attended by reporters and hotel managers, and was feted at a banquet at Delmonico's and fulsomely praised by Sumner, Carl Schurz, Henry Ward Beecher, and other leaders of American thought, business, and politics.

In a landscape almost barren of thinkers who might recognize the possibilities and necessities of positive liberty, one intellectual stands out. This was Lester Ward, sociologist and social critic. Ever concerned about the ends of government, Ward turned social Darwinism on its head by arguing that, compared to the purposeless evolution of animals, human evolution could be decisively modified by purposive action. He contended that man, unlike animals, could purposefully transform his environment; that competition in nature and in human society could be more wasteful than productive; that negative liberty was appropriate for earlier eras of authoritarian rule but not for a time of representative government. Hence there was a positive and even a planning role for government. A champion of the masses who believed that intellectuals must lead, Ward nevertheless did not fashion a political strategy worthy of his sociology. Always a somewhat isolated thinker, he did not command the backing of a school of intellectual disciples that might have affected more forcefully the political thought of late nineteenth-century America.

Only in the first decade or so of the new century, with the coming to power and influence of muckrakers, reformers, and progressives, of Square Deal Republicans, New Freedom Democrats, and La Follette Progressives, did the American nation begin to confront the need for enlarging men's liberties through collective action on the part of government. But that collective action came haltingly and erratically, in part because intellectual leadership was inadequate to the task. In many areas it has not yet come and intellectual leadership is only beginning to find a resolution. The United States simply did not possess a body of social and political thought that could lend adequate direction, substance, and legitimacy to a systematic attack on industrial and urban ills. Government action was piecemeal, discrete, and feeble. Few thinkers of that day—and this—seemed motivated or able to develop a comprehensive theory that could supply the intellectual foundations for a theory that would unite purpose, politics, and government.

One of the few was Woodrow Wilson. After a brief flirtation with some of Bagehot's literary theories of government, with their anti-popular and anti-majoritarian thrust, the young political scientist soon fashioned a body of theory that would direct and sustain him until the end of his life. He was the first of the post-Civil War American writers, according to Austin Ranney, to advance the doctrine that responsible party government would be the best way of organizing democracy in the United States. He became a firm majoritarian; no group of men, Wilson said, "less than the majority has a right to tell me how I have got to live in America." He had not heard of any group of trustees, he added, "in whose hands I am willing to lodge the liberties of America in trust." He wanted a party system strong enough to unite the divided government, to present clear alternatives to the voters, and to put up a vigorous opposition to the party in power. Above all Wilson was devoted to the vocation of *leadership* as an elevating force. Great and gifted leadership, he argued, could not be found in Congress with its fragmented power and tiny baronies. Nor could it be found, he contended at first, in the President, who was usually the lackluster product of a compromised nominating convention. As his own ideas matured, and as he observed the activist presidency of Theodore Roosevelt, Wilson embraced the doctrine of vigorous presidential leadership grounded in a responsible and democratic party system. And he viewed all these institutions in terms of purpose, principle, and policy. With leaders, he wrote, "whose leadership was earned in an open war of principle against principle . . . parties from the necessities of the case have definite policies. . . . *No leaders, no principles; no principles, no parties."*

To few men are given the opportunity to demonstrate the kind of leadership they had called for at the lectern, and few men—even for a time—have acquitted themselves as well as Wilson did. But in the end he was defeated by the very forces of fragmentation and mutual frustration that he had attacked—and by his own *hubris.* He had tried to realign his party, and the party he left in the 1920s drifted toward a bleak and churlish conservatism from which it did not emerge until the New Deal. He had preached the need for strong parties to carry out the principles of the winning majority, and the party he left was so feeble that it suffered one of its worst defeats in history in 1920. This episode involved one of the supreme tests of leadership, and we will return to it later; here one can hypothesize that Wilson, aside from his errors in dealing with other leaders, demanded of his party, of the structure of leadership around and beneath him, and of his followers, a response that was not intellectually and politically possible in the America of this century's second decade.

Twenty years after Woodrow Wilson's first election as President his one-time lieutenant and longtime admirer, Franklin D. Roosevelt, won the presidency at the nadir of the nation's worst depression. The people and the new administration were in desperate need of intellectual leadership that could define the economic failure, set new directions, and above all advance a new definition of liberty. Much has been made of the new President's use of a brains trust that served as a fertile source of policy innovation. But perhaps the most significant aspect of the brain trusters was the absence (in comparison, say, with the Fabians) of a body of developed and sophisticated thought concerning the nature of liberty under modern conditions and the economic and political means necessary to fulfill it, perhaps because there was no group in American society that combined political commitment with tough intellectual sophistication. Gathered around Roosevelt, or at least claiming some kind of access to him, were trustbusters and economic collectivists, budget balancers and deficit spenders, economic nationalists and Wilsonian internationalists, social planners and Jeffersonian individualists, business regulators and business subsidizers and business atomizers. Roosevelt's vaunted experimentation was as much a necessary response to this intellectual melange as a reflection of his own intellectual habits. It was significant and poignant that the intellectual with whom Roosevelt most needed to make contact, John Maynard Keynes, eluded him until late in the New Deal.

In the end it was the harsh pressures of depression and war, far more than the force of intellectual leadership, that brought Roosevelt to a striking redefinition of liberty. Confronting in Hitler an adversary who had his own compelling definition of freedom, and confronting the stirrings at home and abroad of peoples who wanted to know what the war was being waged *for,* Roosevelt proclaimed an economic bill of rights to supplement and expand the first bill of a century and a half earlier. And the President was quite explicit; arguing that "necessitous men are not free men," he said that the American people "had accepted, so to speak, a second Bill of Rights under which a new basis of security and prosperity can be established for all." The specifics—jobs, food, clothing, homes, medical care, education, social security, all to be secured through the help of government if necessary—flowed naturally from this new definition of liberty.

Why had Americans taken so long to introduce a doctrine that had become dominant in Britain generations earlier? Why, for example, did the nation have to wait until thirty years after Wilson's first Inaugural for the first really sophisticated elaborations and defenses of majority rule (those by Henry Steele Commager and Max Lerner)? For many reasons, not the least of which was the failure of intellectual leadership. In reflecting on the role of "labour's intellectuals" in Britain, Royden Harrison noted that the success of any intellectual school in politics depended on the presence of certain characteristics. "First, the leading spirits must be bound together by close ties of personal friendship extending over many years. . . . Second, the school must arrive at principles which have such fecundity that they can supply and replenish legislative programmes. Third, they must be able to create at least that minimum of organization without which they cannot popularize their principles'' such as command over journals and platforms. ''Fourth, they must be able to win the confidence of powerful and dissatisfied groups interested in change'' while retaining at least some access to the highest circles of established power. ''Fifth, they must be able to promote direct political action either through the 'permeation' of existing parties or by means of their 'own' candidate or both.''

To scan this list is to see how handicapped Americans were by the condition of their intellectual leadership. Perhaps it was appropriate that, in the land of a bastardized pragmatism derived from Peirce and Dewey and James, Americans would have to be taught—belatedly and inadequately—by the harsh teacher Experience. But Experience, however wise, is a response to leadership by others, while intellectual leadership at its best anticipates, mediates, and ultimately subdues Experience with the weapons of imagination and intelligence.

7

REFORM LEADERSHIP

Skill in exploiting power resources is in itself a vital power resource for leaders. This simple fact is sometimes obscured in our elaborate studies of the historical, psychological, and intellectual sources of leadership. But one might command ample financial resources, vast popularity, a solid political base, and a grasp of public needs and still lack political vision or skill in political management. One might have these resources as President of the United States and fritter them away in handling crises or challenges such as Versailles, the Depression, Vietnam, Watergate. *Real* leaders—leaders who teach and are taught by their followers—acquire many of their skills in everyday experience, in on-the-job training, in dealing with other leaders and with followers.

Of all the kinds of leadership that require exceptional political skill, the leadership of reform movements must be among the most exacting. Revolutionary leadership demands commitment, persistence, courage, perhaps selflessness and even self-abnegation (the ultimate sacrifice for solipsistic leadership). Pragmatic, transactional leadership requires a shrewd eye for opportunity, a good hand at bargaining, persuading, reciprocating. Reform may need these qualities, but it demands much more. Since reform efforts usually require the participation of a large number of allies with various reform and nonreform goals of their own, reform leaders must deal with endless divisions within their own ranks. While revolutionaries usually recognize the need for leadership, an anti-leadership doctrine often characterizes and taunts reform programs.

Questions of strategy may be even more demanding of reform leaders. To what degree should reformers arouse popular hopes that may in turn be transformed into popular expectations and demands that run far beyond the leaders' specific aims? Should reform leaders cooperate or even merge with existing parties, create new parties, or shun parties altogether and thereby keep their ranks undefiled and their position uncompromised? How can upper-class and middle-class reformers work with left-wing, unionist, or radical groups that may have different, even anti-reform goals as well as mutual ones? Should reformers press ahead on one dramatic issue such as electoral reform or on a package of political, social, and economic issues? Should reformers with imposing goals seek to achieve them by working through existing institutions or seek to change the institutions in order to accommodate the reforms at the risk of alienating supporters of the institutional status quo? Franklin Roosevelt faced—and perhaps misjudged—this question when he decided to reform (his foes said "purge") the Democratic party in 1938. But a generation earlier the Liberals challenged the power of the House of Lords in order to realize some of their other goals, and they won.

Reform leadership by definition usually implies moral leadership, and this imposes a special burden. It means that reformers must not follow improper means in trying to achieve moral ends, on the ground that the means can taint and pervert the ends. Taking moral leadership means that one also must *win;* a strong success ethic attaches to reform, at least in some Western nations. It was Wilson's *failure* to bring the United States into the League of Nations, not his high sounding moralistic platitudes, that has given him such a bad historical press. Recently the newly installed governor of a large American state tried to get the Speaker of its lower house replaced because the Speaker seemed unfit to handle the governor's legislative program—and because of his well-known moral lapses. It was the kind of action that would have been hailed as an act of high moral courage had the governor won; he lost, so he was called a bumbling quixotic.

The very nature of reform narrows the strategic choices. "The reformer operates on parts where the revolutionist operates on wholes," H. M. Kallen notes. "The reformer seeks modifications harmonious with existing trends and consistent with prevailing principles and movements. The revolutionist seeks redirections, arrest or reversal of movements and mutation of principles. . . . It is this insistent exclusive particularism which distinguishes the reformer from the revolutionary as a psychological type. . . ." Reform leaders, however gradualist in instinct, must be willing to transform society, or parts of it, if that is necessary to realize moral principles. Most perplexing is the question of why some persons become brilliant and effective reformers and others fail—or why some, like Wilson, first succeed and then fail, or, like Charles Grey, fail and then succeed.

We may take Grey as an early and archetypal reformer. Born in 1764 at

Fallodon, an old country house perched midway between the moors and the sea, in Northumberland, longtime theater of battle for marauding Scots and English, he became, at the death of an older brother, eldest son of a general who was to win the title of first Earl Grey of Howick for his service in the American revolutionary war. Young Charles seemed to be enchanted with his early boyhood life spent near hills and sea, but that was not to last long. At six he was sent on a four-day posting to school at Marylebone, where he stayed in bad health and utter misery for three years. On his first day out of doors his nurse took him to Tyburn to watch a group of Jews hanged for forgery. Thrust up on top of a grenadier so that he would see all, he witnessed death contortions that never left his mind; in his old age he would wake up sweating from the nightmare memory.

At nine he graduated from Marylebone and went on to Eton. "It was here," G. M. Trevelyan says, that "he first touched the great world of politics and fashion, to which Eton was then an antechamber," but, though he was something of a social and academic success, he evidently was not happy at Eton. It was not until fifty years after his graduation that he returned to his old school for the first time, and he sent none of his several sons there, on the ground that he had learned nothing of importance at the school. Eton not only lacked masters and courses that might have given the boys some glimmering of the merging economic and social problems of the country, but even its training in the great world of politics and fashion was narrowly focused. Essentially Eton educated future statesmen, as J. R. M. Butler noted, in the art of "winning and retaining the confidence of an assembly of some six hundred gentlemen," which meant oratory of a very special type, eloquent, rounded, and lofty, "appealing to the sense of honour and responsibility of a privileged class." Grey was somewhat happier at Trinity College, Cambridge, where there was neither profound learning nor intellectual ferment, but at least there were liberal-minded friends who may have influenced his later ideas. The traditional Grand Tour of France, Switzerland, and Italy followed.

Grey was still on his tour when in 1786, at the age of twenty-two, he was chosen a member of Parliament in a Northumberland by-election. If the practice of the day was followed, Grey's family in effect bought him the seat by heavy spending for the entertainment of a few electors. The young man entered Parliament unencumbered by strong political convictions, platform, or personal promises. He moved naturally into Brooks (the Whigs' club), into Devonshire and other great Whig houses, and into the orbit of Charles Fox. The Whigs were then a party in the old sense of the word, a shifting band of parliamentary leaders and lieutenants with ties to coteries of country aristocrats, squires, and gentry and to city businessmen. Under Fox they pursued a tactic of opportunistic coalition-making in Parliament and of labyrinthine involvement with court politics; they were generally blundering in opposition and showed little potential for greatness in office. In figure, voice, education, and manner, Addington noted, Grey seemed the equal of any member of the House. Others saw a different man—ambitious, mercurial, violent-tempered. He was all these, at different times deeply involved politically and then withdrawing goomily to Howick, honorable and high-minded but capable of lying for reasons of state, liberal in spirit but narrow in his party views, feverishly active and languidly diffident, fastidiously aristocratic in manner and even less democratic, many said, than his Tory adversaries. He lacked a comprehensive philosophical doctrine or reasoned political strategy. Yet this man would, late in his life, display a consummate grasp of the art of parliamentary leadership in one of the most exacting political situations—the struggle over the Great Reform Bill of 1832.

Great Britain: The Insistent Particularists

The single great animating issue for English reformers of the late eighteenth and early nineteenth centuries was electoral reform. Other questions—notably the slave trade and Catholic emancipation—were charged with high feeling, but men of liberal tendencies felt that to overcome the rotten boroughs was to seize the lever that would bring about a general improvement of society. Through half a century of tumult, beginning with English reaction to the American and French revolutions, stretching through the long wars cold and hot with France, the rising social and economic discontent in Britain, and hard political repression, and culminating in the English reaction to the French revolution of 1830, the "one strand which runs through the whole web, and gives it a unity," according to Butler, "is the faith in Reform of a section of the Whig party, at times the merest remnant. . . . " So strongly did the political currents appear to be running toward reform that, in retrospect, the question is not whether significant electoral change would be achieved in Britain but when. For the English had the unusual options of two great opportunities for reform, one in the late 1770s and one a half century later. The protest in coffee-houses and taverns in the late 1760s against an oppressive king and a corrupt Commons, the founding in 1769 of the Society of Supporters of the Bill of Rights, and the sharpening of discontent with the mismanagement of the war in America led to a spate of proposals for improvement that included electoral reform. In 1782 none other than William Pitt proposed in Commons the appointment of a committee to inquire into the condition of parliamentary representation.

One reason for the failure of reform in the 1770s and 1780s was the absence of a fundamental feeling of need for the bill—a feeling of need that would outlast the seesaw of ministries. The main need expressed was for better management and less corruption, and once the obvious grievances were removed by other means, as Butler notes, "there seemed no crying need for Reform while England was still primarily agricultural." Conflict did not yet exist in ways that would make reform the fulcrum of combat; rather the various issues of the day split leaders into multiple and shifting configurations. Many leaders found it more expedient to identify and mobilize conflict between Englishmen and Frenchmen over the many inflammable issues that divided the two nations than to cultivate a conflict among Englishmen that might jeopardize "national unity"—and their own careers.

Grey was among those who waited for more propitious circumstances. He did take one step toward reform in the 1790s. Responding to encouragement from the "Friends of the People," an association of reform-minded gentlemen that he himself had founded to press solely for parliamentary electoral reform, Grey in 1792 gave notice of a bill to reform Parliament to be introduced in the next session. He quoted Pitt's earlier recognition of the need for fairer representation only to encounter, as he sat down on his bench, an angry Pitt warning of anarchy and questioning the patriotism of the Friends of the People. As soon as Pitt had finished Fox leaped up to support Grey and, as Trevelyan says, the split in the Whig party had begun. Hardening states of conflict over repression in the following decades made prospects of reform seem more and more forlorn. Pitt drew up a royal proclamation on sedition that seemed to apply as much to the genteel Friends of the People as it did to the corresponding societies inflamed by Tom Paine and other radicals.

As the British recoiled more and more from the mounting ferocity of the French Revolution, the government turned to repression to quell the reform instinct and England entered a long period of bleak and sterile politics. In the absence of great and ordered domestic issues, Grey's political fortunes rose and fell. He joined a coalition "ministry of all the talents" which undertook illegalization of the slave trade, and on Fox's death he became the Whig party and parliamentary leader. He then lost his Northumberland seat to an aristocratic family that had turned on him and surprised him with an opposition candidate. He had his choice of other constituencies, only to be relieved of the need by the death of his father and his own subsequent elevation to the House of Lords. Here he felt cut off from his old supportive colleagues as he patiently waited for the nation to survive the passions of the Napoleonic wars and the postwar repression and to return to the domestic battles of old.

It was an extraordinary conjunction of forces and events that rescued England from its miasma, reform from its torpidity, and Grey from his political quiescence. By the late 1820s economic and social forces were overrunning the old electoral and constitutional fixtures. The expansion of industry and the modernization of transport were helping to produce a working class increasingly militant and articulate under conditions of boom and bust, a growing body of industrial employers and tradesmen angry over their exclusion from political power, small employers resentful of the pensions, sinecures, and court recognition of the older rich, and tenant farmers without share in the county franchise or county favors. A rising tide of democratic feeling reflected the political needs and expectations of these groups. And they were better organized now—middle class and upper working class in a host of political unions and working-class dissidents in societies of their own. As debate over reform mounted, these associations drew together in national groupings in support of national spokesmen.

The axis of conflict was shifting, too. The coming to power of Wellington in 1828 served as a catalytic agent in realigning a de facto four-party system—Wellington and Canning Tories, Grey and Brougham Whigs—into a rough semblance of two relatively coherent parties. To be sure, Wellington dished the Whigs by carrying through the Catholic emancipation for which the Whigs had labored for many years—but at the price of a split in the Tory ranks. By staying out of Wellington's cabinet despite his personal friendship for him, Grey helped transform the lines of conflict and at the same time protected his own isolation. There was always the possibility that some combination of Whigs and Tories under liberal Tory leadership might support a token reform bill that would split the ranks of the reformers. By withdrawing and waiting Grey helped to avert this possibility. Instead Wellington broke his own party into factions and helped bring the Whigs into office in 1830.

The struggle of parties, leaders, and interests was also a struggle over ideas. The central value for the Whigs was liberty. All paid lip service to this venerable ideal; the question was its meaning—of which the Whigs had little doubt. In Pitt's reaction to the French Revolution and Napoleon's conquests they had had a frightening glimpse of what their own government could do in repressing civil liberty. Englishmen had been flogged, jailed, transported, and hanged for seditious utterances—that is, utterances critical of the Tory government. The Whig conception of liberty was naturally a restricted one; it called for government tolerance of individual opinion, conscience and dissent, and it did not attack the broader question of government protection and cultivation of social and economic freedom. The popular definition of the day was indicated when tens of thousands at mass meetings sang the Reform Bill hymn:

> . . . By union, justice, reason, law
> We'll gain the birthright of our sires.

And thus we raise from sea to sea
Our sacred watchword, Liberty!

Grey wrote to a friend that the preservation of the Whig party in Parliament was of the utmost importance, for that party was "really in practice the only defense for the liberties of the country."

Rising needs and expectations, shifting planes of conflict, values that served as guides to action—these forces, however powerful, could not produce real political change without the catalyst of rare and gifted leadership—and this is what Grey provided in the crux. Gone were the diffidence, the withdrawals, the depressions, and the uncertainties of earlier years. "He had foreseen at thirty the necessity of the measure which he carried at seventy," a historian wrote later with only a slight hyperbole. "He seemed to be raised up to carry Reform."

In conception Grey's strategy was simple: to unite the cabinet, the Whig party, and the country behind a strong reform bill. "Bit by bit Reform," he told the Lords, would leave the question "in as unsettled a condition as before"—by which he meant that expectations would have been raised and then left unsatisfied, thereby playing into the hands of the radicals who wanted immediate universal suffrage. But this strategy was enormously difficult to implement because of the forces arrayed on the right and on the left. Not only did most of the Tories hotly oppose the bill—indeed, they were shocked by its bold provisions for making a clean sweep of the "borough-mongers" and granting the vote to small property holders—but many conservative Whigs, alarmed by the bill, were reluctant to support it. On the left in Grey's reform ministry were most of his close associates in the Whig party, including his son-in-law. Balancing right and left is a standard posture for a coalition leader, but Grey had to deal with two other forces that made his trapeze act even more delicate: a somewhat capricious monarch who could hardly stomach the reform bill but feared disorder and revolution even more, and a House of Lords generally opposed to the bill and goaded into fiery resistance by diehards in the church establishment.

Grey's leadership was by no means a solo performance; he was surrounded by a remarkable group of ministers who themselves carried great weight with Parliament and with the people; and he was prodded from the left by an equally remarkable array of men representing the middle-class and working-class political unions of the nation. Lord John Russell, an old and unswerving supporter of reform; Grey's son-in-law, "Radical Jack" Durham (John George Lambton, first Earl Durham), who took a strong reform posture and had a grievous falling-out with Grey during one of the Reform Bill crises;

the ambitious, opportunistic, somewhat demagogic (as he appeared to moderate eyes) Lord Brougham with his grudging acceptance of Grey as the reform leader; the venerable Lord Holland, who time and again leant a steadying hand—these were only the more visible leaders of a group of talented Whigs that emerged from the earlier period of Tory repression and lost Whig directions.

Maintaining a steady bombardment of Crown and Parliament from outside was a group of "secondary" leaders who collectively may have played a more important role than the ministry itself. Francis Place, reared by a brutal father in a poverty-seared family, had somehow won an education, established himself as a skilled craftsman, and had gone on to become adept in Westminster politics, a spokesman for the political unions, and a source of both information and pressure on reform ministers. He was a coalition builder at the grass roots, constantly seeking to unite middle-class and working-class forces behind reform. George Grote, banker and historian, had access to circles other reformers could not penetrate. William Cobbett, son of a laborer, ex-soldier, passionate lover (as Butler notes) of the very soil of England, carried his agitation for parliamentary reform through his own newspaper and through a dramatic speaking tour of the country. To the left of him stood Henry Hunt, a fiery orator scorned by his foes as a sheer demagogue but skillful enough to arouse the masses in support of reform and to make his own way into Parliament, where he attacked Grey's bill as inadequate for the working class. A brooding intellectual presence—and often a physical one—for most of these men was James B. Mill, who was both a theoretician and a strategist of radical action and was now involved in the climactic political and intellectual act of his life.

Supporting these leaders were great numbers of Englishmen mobilized in their political unions and other organizations and acting through their immediate spokesmen. This was the age of the mass meeting, when great orators could reach the eyes and ears of tens of thousands gathered before them, where the crowd was not a passive spectator but was capable of trading sentiments with the speakers (urging them to "print it" when the oratory was too long-winded) and constantly voted with its feet by joining or deserting the throng. This was the age of large deputations organized at meetings and sent into Parliament to confront members in their own redoubts, the age of highly political caricaturists, most notably John Doyle ("HB"), who, while cool enough himself to parliamentary reform, was able to reduce the complexities and obscurities of guerrilla warfare in Parliament to sharp little scenes showing the interplay of party and personality.

In these circumstances all Grey had to do was to hew to the middle of his coalition and insist on a strong bill, and the structure of political forces sustained him. Time and again the bill was imperiled by a skittish king, an obdurate Lords, and vacillating allies in the ministry and among the backbenchers, but Grey's unswerving purpose and skillful mediation always seemed to mobilize basic forces that sustained his hand when the outcome lay in the balance. When the Reform Bill finally became law in 1832 after countless exigencies, he lived up to Horace Kallen's definition of the reformer as an "exclusive particularist." After passage of the Great Reform Act Grey presided for two more years over an increasingly divided Whig ministry. But, as Trevelyan noted, the great legislative achievements of those years—slavery abolition, the factory act, the India bill, the new poor law—were not his personal achievement. The Whigs were moving beyond the reach of their reform coalition, and when Lord John Russell took a divisive position on Church of Ireland revenues and "upset the reform coach," Grey seemed happy to resign and to retire to Howick. The year Grey resigned, 1834, the House of Commons burned to the ground; the new building, housing a moderately reformed Parliament, embodied Grey's legacy of leadership.

Does quality of leadership make much difference in political reform movements such as these, with their shifting social foundations and cross-cutting lines of cleavage? If Grey's timing, steadiness of purpose, and mediatory skills helped supply the crucial margin of victory in the strategy of the Great Reform Bill, the fate of the Chartists a decade later suggests a possible outcome should reformers lack unifying leadership and hold to a doctrine of anti-leadership.

Disenchanted and angered by the middle-class bias of the reform act, leaders of the working class and other elements that made up the Chartist ranks proposed to move on swiftly to sweeping electoral and parliamentary reform. The Charter was explicit enough: suffrage for all males over twenty-one, the secret ballot, equal electoral districts, payment of members of Parliament, abolition of their property qualifications, and annual parliaments. Lacking the vote and much leverage within the existing parties, the Chartists planned to stimulate such pressure on Parliament from the outside that this predominantly aristocratic and upper-middle class body would grant all these demands.

Another outgrowth of the dissatisfaction with the 1832 act was a determination on the part of working-class leaders to make their own way without the help of celebrities. Speaking of earlier 'upsurges of popular radicalism,'' F. C. Mather noted that in advocating manhood suffrage and other reforms, "their adherents had sometimes allowed themselves to fall under the sway of dominant personalities, usually drawn from a higher social class. . . . The London Working Men's Association, instituted in 1836, was a political movement launched and conducted by working men and animated by a conscious repudiation of leadership. . . ." William Lovett, its principal founder, referred scornfully to the tendency of the working class to defer to lords or M.P.s or esquires. The working classes, he said "were always looking up to leadership of one description or another. . . . In fact, the masses, in their political organizations, were taught to look up to 'great men' . . . rather than to great principles." On taking the chair at the formulation meeting of the Charter before three thousand working men at the Crown and Anchor, in the Strand, London, in 1837, Robert Hartwell said: "I express gratification that you placed a working man in the chair, rather than running after a man with a high-sounding title or of great ability but little honesty. This great mass meeting will remove the stigma from the working classes that they do not attend meetings to support their principles, but to gaze on a 'lion' or to applaud and swallow the dogmas he may give utterance to."

The disdain for "great man" leadership helped draw from the ranks of the working class an exceptional cadre of grass-roots leadership—men such as Henry Hetherington, a compositor who became a brilliant pamphleteer in defense of free speech; James Watson, born in Yorkshire of working-class parents who taught him to read and write, later a writer and itinerant preacher who was jailed three times for his freethinking; Lovett, a ropemaker turned cabinetmaker, one of the early founders of co-operative shops and perhaps the most respected of the London leaders; and a number of Irish activists who fired the movement with their zeal but were often at loggerheads with the London leadership. The Chartists did not enjoy the kind of farsighted leadership that could transcend divisions in the movement and fashion a strategy for victory. Perhaps the movement was too divided for such leadership; it was always an alliance of strong regional groupings with weak federation in London. There were endless and unresolved differences over tactics, such as the issue of resort to—or threat of—taking up arms. The leaders differed over the knotty question of whether to fight simply for Chartist political aims or for the social purposes that political reform was supposed to help achieve. Nor did the Chartists achieve coalition with potential allies outside the movement; they deliberately kept their distance from middle-class groups, and they positively hated the Anti-Corn League and its narrow goal.

Yet the Chartist leaders were superb mobilizers of working-class sentiment and action. They pamphleted and leafleted indefatigably. They staged dramatic mass meetings. They drew up a petition that was signed by over a million persons, weighed six hundred pounds, and was two miles long. More important, they immensely augmented the feeling of class consciousness among British workers—a feeling that would closely influence British politics for more than a century. And they mobilized for action thousands of followers who fluctuated in their participation but who gave the movement color and force, as Asa Briggs noted, and who became subjects of history, not merely its objects.

Perhaps the final failure of the Chartist movement in Parliament and in the desperate general strike that followed lay mainly in the overambitiousness of its aims; perhaps it should have established a priority among its six goals and concentrated its resources behind one or two of them. Or perhaps its timing was poor; possibly Britain needed a whole generation, rather than a few years, to adapt to the Great Reform Act, to make it anachronistic, and to move on to the next great reform effort. If such was the case, the Anti-Corn League—a very different kind of reform group—used just the right tactics in securing the abolition of grain tariffs that seemed to have become a fixture in British economic and social policy.

The Anti-Corn League was everything that the Chartists were not— pridefully middle-class and willing to use the "wealth, organization and moral power which were associated with the adjective''; determined on the one specific aim of corn law repeal; and eager for, and dependent on, leadership by national celebrities. The league's timing was superb. Grain tariffs had existed for decades, even centuries; at the point when the tariffs were becoming obviously outmoded by commercial and social developments, the league organized rapidly, mobilized support in the right channels of influence, after some frustration witnessed the collapse of its opposition, saw repeal voted in Parliament, and disappeared. At the beginning of 1842 the league raised fifty thousand pounds to carry on its reform agitation, and the report on its spending during that year suggests the intensity of the league's effort to influence public opinion: over nine million tracts printed and distributed; 650 lectures given; over 150 deputations sent to borough and county meetings; over 400,000 tracts published in magazines as advertisements; and large sums paid for hiring rooms for lectures, for printing, placarding, rent, taxes, and wages. The league showed a flair for moral passion combined with public-relations techniques; thus it assembled seven hundred clergymen to bear witness, on the basis of their ministrations to the poor in the slums, to the baneful effect of poverty on the religious life of the masses. All this effort did not have an immediate impact; indeed, the league's strength declined for a year or two at the height of its campaign, but the work told off in later years.

The cardinal difference between the Chartists and the Anti-Corn League was in the caliber of the political leadership. The league possessed in its great national spokesman, Richard Cobden, a man who combined eloquence with a command of facts in statistical array; year after year he confronted Peel across the floor of the House of Commons with morality and figures until the day came when the prime minister, listening to Cobden's outpouring of lucid reasoning, crumpled up the notes he was taking and, turning to a colleague, whispered: ''You must answer this. I cannot.'' Peel's public switch to free trade and repeal of the corn laws followed not long after. So effective had the league been that large sections of both Whigs and Tories came over to the cause. The league had leadership in depth; John Bright was only the most notable of a large group of national spokesmen and local "missionaries" who inundated Britain with appeals.

The tests of political leadership within single-cause reform movements such as the Anti-Corn League or the causes that agitated British politics later in the century—temperance, education, municipal reform, anti-imperialism—were always far more exacting for leaders conducting the external rather than the internal politics of the reform movements. Within the movement the leader's problem was essentially tactical: developing better methods of propagandizing, mobilizing, and organizing; concerting leaders and followers behind the single issue without being diverted to related causes; balancing centrist and sectional tendencies within the movement; protecting one's own status against rivals; building coalitions within and between parties. Reformers could always fall back on Kallen's "insistent exclusive particularism" and operate within narrow and easily definable areas. External relations called for a more complex and far-sighted leadership. Maintaining connections with parallel reform movements intent on different but related issues (i.e., church and education reform) without either yielding too much to the other reformers or alienating them; bringing pressure to bear on government without being unduly compromised by the closer connection; and, above all, fashioning contacts between reform movements and one or both of the two major parties without surrendering the reform impetus to the party's homogenizing tendencies—all this demanded a political and intellectual comprehension beyond the capacities of many reform leaders.

Reformers who were also party leaders faced a harsher test. The Liberal party drew much of its strength in the middle and late nineteenth century from its ready espousal of popular reforms. It was a tempting strategy, for the reforms were usually relevant to Liberal doctrine or impulses, the ready-made issues were developed and publicized by reform groups without major cost to the party, and the single-issue spokesmen usually had close and benevolent ties to sections of the Liberal party. But there was a price to pay. The party tended to become a grab-bag of mutually inconsistent, or at least competitive, projects; it lost identity and credibility as a national party; the passionate adherence to particular causes among so many leaders and followers aroused turmoil within the party; and the greater the support a particular reform group brought to the Liberal party, the greater its potential for abstinence or desertion or other genteel forms of political bargaining and blackmail.

Few among the Liberal leaders supported the grab-bag strategy. What did develop was a more sophisticated doctrine of the single organizing or galvanizing reform that could rally the whole party. The theory was that the galvanizing issue was of such overriding importance that other diverse interests within the party might be persuaded to subordinate their own causes to it, at least for a time. Gladstone came to believe in this strategy and became a master of it. In a letter to Bright in 1873 he defined the need for some issue that would generate "a *positive* force to carry us onward as a body" and that, if "worked into certain shapes," might "greatly help to mould the rest, at least for the time." Joseph Chamberlain opposed this strategy. He believed in programmatic politics—in simultaneously promoting and agitating many reforms, in teaching the connection among them, in establishing priorities among them as guides to government action, in reaching and organizing the masses behind a general-purpose instrument such as the National Liberal Federation. This question was never entirely resolved within the Liberal party and may have contributed to its decline; it was Labour that became the essentially programmatic and potentially transforming party in British politics.

Russia: Reform from Above

It has long been observed that social and political reforms—even those that ultimately shake the foundations of the existing order—are often launched from leadership echelons at the top of the social structure, not from the middle or lower levels. The examples of Lord Grey and Disraeli in England, the two Roosevelts in America, and Bismarck in Germany could be matched in scores of other polities. Reared typically in an ethic of noblesse oblige and public service, freed of the economic want that pits persons against their fellows, touched often by feelings of guilt at having privileges that others do not share, and fearful perhaps that those privileges would be threatened unless the masses received concessions in time, the aristocratic or patrician reformer is one of the archetypes of the modern epoch. Sometimes he moves far ahead of many of the middle-class and working-class influences around him, and the poignant spectacle of the affluent, highbrow reformer vainly peddling his political wares to phlegmatic peasants or hostile factory workers *for their benefit* is all too familiar.

History affords no more dramatic and melancholy case of the noble reformer than that of Alexander II of Russia, the Great Liberator, the Czar of Freedom. Coming to the throne during his nation's humiliation and demoralization following the Crimean War, Alexander recognized that Russia must modernize to survive and in one stunning decision ordered legal emancipation of the serfs. His emancipation of the serfs is considered to be the most significant and portentous political act in Russian history from the time of Peter the Great until the coming of the Revolution. What was the eventual outcome of this striking act of reform leadership? Like most noble reformers, Alexander believed that to reform was to preserve. What he hoped to preserve was an order whose essential components had been well summarized in the time of Alexander's father, Nicholas I, as Orthodoxy, autocracy, and nationalism. Within seventy years of Alexander's emancipation of the serfs, Orthodoxy had yielded to atheistic Communism, the czarist autocracy had been obliterated, and Russian nationalism had been ignominiously rebuffed by Japan and by Germany. Failure of reform leadership could scarcely have been more nearly complete.

Alexander was hardly born or reared to be a reformer. He grew up in the shadow of his father, whose rule provided one of the bleakest chapters in the history of Russian autocracy. The father exacted absolute obedience from the son; the boy held the father in awe and dreaded his rebukes for his failings. The emperor was "more than a father," Alexander told his mother. "For me *he* was the *personification of our dear fatherland.*" His tutors were Western in education and outlook, but the court atmosphere was paternal and militaristic. Affable and indolent as a boy, the czarevitch tended to lapse into inaction in the face of obstacle and frustration. Alexander traveled widely in Russia and Europe; how much he learned on these rapid trips, surrounded as he was by protective court officials and burdened by receptions, inspections, and the demands of local hospitality and church attendance, is conjectural. He grew up to be a man of contrasts. He remained charming and kindly in his domestic role, but in the face of the exigencies of state his manner turned forced and awkward; then he became, as someone observed, a "bad copy" of his father. He was tenderhearted toward friends and toward soldiers, but he governed in the repressive tradition of the czars. Later he was dependent on his ministers, but he hired, heeded, ignored, and sacked subordinates unpredictably.

In legend Alexander issued his great act of emancipation as a sudden commandment from on high, and he acted almost single-handedly. In fact, the act was responsive to forces playing on the Crown from outside and from within; the decision was a collective one. For decades Western ideas of individualism, modernity, and liberalism had been trickling into Russia, mainly through the agency of traveled and educated cosmopolites. Russians could not but be impressed by English, French, and German technological advances, both industrial and military. Western ideas had permeated sections of the bureaucracy, the gentry, and the court itself. These ideas were hotly resisted by Slavophile leaders who, as William Chamberlin noted, "exalted patriarchal, believing peasant Russia against the individualistic, urbanized, sceptical West" and championed Russian Orthodoxy over Roman Catholicism and Protestantism. But Russia's eternal backwardness was a painful reminder to liberals, and even more to nationalists, that the country must modernize to survive.

Alexander had special concerns. He had been exposed to Western ideas; he had some glimmerings of the need for moderate reform to avert unrest, radicalism, and revolution; but above all he was dismayed by the weaknesses of his army that Crimea had advertised to his subjects at home and his adversaries abroad. His military advisers—especially his brilliant minister of war, Dmitrii Miliutin—were warning him that serfdom stood squarely in the way of building a modern, mobile, combat-ready army. It was largely for reasons of state power that the young czar decided on his great act of reform.

He had considerable support from the leadership of key sectors of the polity. Within court circles his aunt, Elena Pavlovna, not only gave him strong encouragement—she revealed to him that Nicholas had hoped his son would succeed where he had failed and emancipate the serfs—but she rallied support within the bureaucracy and among the gentry and the intelligentsia. Intellectuals, devotees variously of Western liberal thinkers and of Frenchmen Saint-Simon, Fourier, and Proudhon, had long favored emancipation. The gentry—the landowners who held millions of peasants in serfdom—were divided. The vast majority either clung to the whole structure of serfdom or would accept emancipation only on terms that would protect their social hegemony and their economic power. Like most dominating classes, they equated the national welfare with their own interests. A significant and influential number of the gentry, however, aware of the backwardness of the agrarian economy, educated by tutors and travel in the West, sharing liberal ideas, and fearing the radical implications of serfdom for a slowly urbanizing and industrializing economy, were ready for emancipation. At the base of the social pyramid was the peasant, the *muzhik,* stolid, illiterate, servile—patronized and protected when he behaved, chastised and brutalized when he did not. Occasional peasant uprisings, mercilessly suppressed, had raised the specter of revolution.

Aware of the problems and potentials, Alexander acted secretly and deviously. In a manifesto on the conclusion of the Crimean peace agreement in 1856 he had promised the Russian people the prospect of enjoying the fruits of their labor. His words were so ambiguous, however, that cynics scoffed at them and gentry leaders were apprehensive. A few days later, in a famous address to leaders of the Moscow gentry, the czar discounted rumors of his intention to emancipate the serfs, at least at present, but then added enigmatically: "But, of course, you understand yourselves that the existing order of serfdom cannot remain unchanged. It is better to begin to abolish bondage from above than to wait for the time when it will begin to abolish itself spontaneously from below.'' The czar's genteel blackmail seemed to produce little response from the gentry leadership. Forced back on the resources of his court and bureaucracy, the czar established a secret committee on emancipation headed by his brother, Grand Duke Constantine, a supporter of reform. The committee planned a ten-year transition for a process it did not dare call emancipation but referred to as the ''betterment in the condition of the serfs.'' During the committee's proceedings Alexander, under heavy pressure from noble and gentry partisans of reform, shifted to the notion of speedy emancipation.

The announcement in December 1857 of the government's plan to proceed with emancipation planning had two immediate results: it unloosed a flood of hopes and expectations and it polarized attitudes in both bureaucracy and gentry. The act of liberating the serfs and granting them the legal right to acquire property, to take up trades, and to marry was relatively easy; the difficulty was in securing the peasants' social, economic, and political rights. A cluster of onerous and perplexing questions arose concerning the extent of land holdings to be granted to former serfs, compensation to the former landowners and the peasants' share of that compensation, village self-government, and the extent to which the landowners' powers over the peasants would be surrendered to an equally repressive body, the village commune. The resolution of these and other questions would shape the socio-economic structure of Russia for decades.

The czar of Russia, with a few bureaucrats, a large and disaffected body of gentry, meager economic resources, and near-primitive social data and understanding, was embarked on the leadership of a profound transformation from the top—and the task was an insuperable one. Alexander himself was erratic, irresolute, and suspicious. He had much to be suspicious about; his efforts were sabotaged by some of the bureaucratic leaders, and among those landowners working on the implementation of emancipation were avowed opponents of reform. ''The normal channels of communication and administration flowed through the state bureaucracy and the provincial gentry; yet separately neither of these possessed the leadership, organization or spirit to plan and carry out the Tsar's wishes,'' Alfred Rieber notes. Animosity between bureaucracy and gentry further thwarted reform. The czar spurned proposals that a representative body be established to rally gentry backing for his reform, doubtless because he recognized that such a body would want some control over the substance and process of reform.

In the end emancipation stood as a symbolic act of historic importance. It granted legal rights that had some significance in themselves; it altered the relations of gentry and peasant; but it did not transform the social and economic foundations of agrarian life and thus generate significant liberalization or modernization of Russian society. "The peasant," E. Lampert concludes, "was left subject to a system of enforced contracts which proved a no less fatal source of bondage than his previous condition. Instead of receiving what he considered to be his freedom, he had merely been provoked to demand it. There is scarcely a more striking example in Russian history of the dominant role of the economic factor in the enslavement of man than this substitution of economic dependence for legal compulsion. . . ." Observant Russians were not unaware of the failure; a government commission acknowledged twelve years after emancipation that the condition of the vast majority of the peasants was either the same or considerably deteriorated. The peasants were liberated but they were not free; they were not equal.

This failure of a reform-minded but vacillating leader, a divided bureaucracy, an upper class resistant to effective reform—this failure is nothing new in the annals of human miscalculation, social frustration, and defeat. The failure of reform leadership in Russia, however, had more basic causes. One was the misperception of the peasants'—and the nation's—needs. Slavophiles contended that the *muzhik* needed a mystical union with his land, his church, and his nation, liberals that he needed political and civil liberties, the gentry that he needed order and security. "No, no!" Turgenev has his minor aristocrat say to the young nihilist Bazarov, "I don't want to believe that you gentlemen have a true knowledge of the Russian people, that you are representative of its needs, its aspirations! No, the Russian people is not such as you imagine it. It considers its traditions sacred; it is patriarchal, it cannot live without faith." But if "true freedom" was the aim, what the Russian peasants needed were the conditions that would convert legal emancipation into human fulfillment: literacy, land, agricultural technology, better roads, health services, education, nutrition, political influence. Only a handful of liberals and a number of radicals were thinking in these terms in mid-century Russia.

A second factor was a structure of social and political conflict that discouraged the posing, confronting, and resolving of fundamental political issues. The great myth of the Russian state was the mystic union of czar and people. Returning from a tour of the provinces, Alexander wrote: "The bond which in Russia ties the sovereign to the people gives us our strength and God willing let none weaken it." This genuine and deeply felt sympathy of the czar tended not only to place him above the political battle but to disrupt the battle lines themselves. Official and semi-official opinion, Lampert notes, sought to deny or explain away the existence of real social antagonisms in Russia. Liberals and even radicals deemed it necessary to pay obeisance to the czar, even in their protests; hence conflict too could be organized or obliterated from above. No political parties worthy of the name existed; group interests were ill represented; amorphous movements groped through the political miasma. Creative forms of conflict were also discouraged by censorship that throttled press discussion and dissent, by repressive laws that exiled Protestants in droves, and by the spies and informers who infested liberal and radical organizations.

A third and crucial factor in the frustration of reform by leadership from above was the absence of a sense of overriding purpose or transcending value. Alexander rejected consistency and adherence to principle lest it curb his freedom of choice. Many of his advisers were consciously anti-idealistic, relativistic, pragmatic. There was much talk of grand principle but little observance of it. Thus, when Alexander liberated the serfs mainly for reasons of state power and military efficiency, he was rejecting a guiding purpose such as genuine political liberty or social opportunity that could have served as a standard in shaping the day-to-day decisions concerning the relation of reform to lasting popular needs. A more coherent sense of purpose at least would have made clear the gap between the noble ideals of reform and the ultimate paucity of concrete social change and human betterment.

Alexander II reigned for two decades after his great act of liberation, but one can doubt that he ever understood the failure of reform from above. Nor could he understand why the extremists, and even the responsible liberals and radicals, came to distrust him. There were repeated attempts against his life. "What have these wretches against me," he cried out. "Why do they hunt me down like a wild beast?" It seemed all the stranger because other legal reforms had followed the liberation of the serfs. In March 1881 the czar, escorted by cossacks, was driving back to the winter palace on the snowy streets of St. Petersburg when a man threw a packet of nitroglycerin behind the carriage. The czar emerged from the shattered vehicle unscathed; typically he refused to leave the scene until he had looked after the condition of the wounded guards. A second assassin threw another packet and blew the Liberator to pieces.

A cardinal weakness of reform leadership from above is its volatility over time. Alexander II was succeeded by his son, Alexander III, who was as Orthodox, autocratic, and nationalistic as his grandfather had been three decades before. A political blight almost instantly fell on the country. The new czar was served by his former tutor, now chief procurator of the Holy Synod, Pobedonostšev, a zealous and indefatigable monarchist, a foe of reform and an anti-constitutionalist, who called for absolutist leadership even though, according to Robert Byrnes, "he saw the history of Russia as the history of the state as it was affected by blind, organic, historical forces." When Alexander III read that Bismarck had condemned parliamentary regimes as obstructionist and had expressed the hope that Russia would remain absolutist, the new czar had written on the dispatch: "All this is true and just. May God will that every Russian, particularly our ministers, shall understand our situation as clearly as does Prince Bismarck and shall not strive to achieve unattainable fantasies and lousy [*parshyvyi*] liberalism.'' The czar did not camouflage his autocratic instincts. Shortly after his succession he issued a manifesto, written by Pobedonostšev, that proclaimed his complete faith in the strength and truth of absolute power wielded ''for the good of the people.''

Alexander III's rejection of his father's posture as Czar of Freedom meant that, if any reform leadership were to be exercised in late nineteenth-century Russia, the task would have to be assumed mainly by the nation's liberals. To this day it is hard to define Russian liberalism confidently or to identify Russian liberals of the period. As in the West, liberalism embraced standpatters, gradualists, activists, and persons farther to the left; but the liberal scene in Russia was complicated by the number of Slavophiles, populists, economists, and others who shared certain liberal goals and variously collaborated with liberals politically. In terms of their significance for reform leadership, an essential distinction once again must be made among those who wished to gain protection *against* government through the safeguarding of individual civil and legal rights, those who favored the extension of political rights and more democratic representation, and those who were mainly concerned with the social and economic reforms that would help meet the needs of the peasants and workers. This range of substantive positions embraced a variety of political strategies, from seeking reform gradually within existing institutions, to establishing a constitutional system with a presentable and respectable parliament and strong local government, and to peaceful overthrow of the existing system.

Liberals were to be found in the court and the bureaucracy, among businessmen, and inevitably among the intelligentsia, but their main social base was in the gentry. ''Education, worldliness, and access to the state made the nobility the only class in nineteenth century Russia that dared engage in politics,'' George Fischer observes. The gentry had long served as the main recruiting ground for the military and civil administration, and its influence rose to a peak when Alexander II called on the landowning aristocracy to take part in preparing the procedures for emancipation. During the remainder of the century, however, the social and economic power of the gentry declined as a result of the financial impact of emancipation, the world agricultural crisis, and the new state policy of favoring large-scale industry. As the gentry, stripped of the special advantages it had long received from the Crown and aroused by liberal oppositionists, faced the specter of loss of political power, it turned increasingly to the institution of local government in which it had long predominated. That institution was the *zemstvo,* which typically consisted of an elected assembly of delegates meeting annually and a continuing, salaried executive board elected from the assembly. Since representation was proportional to land ownership rather than "movable wealth," the large landowners had the whip hand in the *zemstvos* and effectively closed off peasantry and small-town bourgeois from power. Inevitably the gentry liberals turned to this system of semi-autonomous local government as a means of bypassing and ultimately confronting czarist power. But the effort met considerable frustration. In the three decades following emancipation the central government peeled major financial, educational, and judicial powers away from the *zemstvos*. For some years following emancipation reform leaders forsook the *zemstvos* because of the declining power of the assemblies, but from the late 1870s until the 1905 revolution liberals turned to the assemblies as the central means of gaining their objectives.

Liberal reform leaders had little else to work with. They lacked a strong organization and an uncensored means of communication. They had no national parliament within which they could attack conservative incumbents and rally the forces of protest. They had no national, organized party that could carry their message into the small towns and villages. They had to build the very instruments that in turn might open the gateways to national recognition and even authority. Viewed today, a century later, their plight seems poignant and hopeless. They were faced with the task of building almost anew the liberal institutions and processes that had been the embodiment and carrier of liberal reform in the West. Western nations had had two or three centuries for this process; as the nineteenth century came to an end, we know now, Russian liberals had two or three decades. They thought they had more time.

Major forces seemed to be working in the liberals' favor. The harshness of Alexander III's regime and—despite high hopes—that of Nicholas II, who succeeded him in 1894, aroused among workers, peasants, and intelligentsia the resentment that forms the seedbed of liberal and radical protest. Industrialization was producing conflict over economic questions and the rudimentary organization of workers. New leadership was developing in *zemstvos*, professions, and universities. Radical movements were springing up on the left and threatening to outflank the liberals, and this was in part an advantage; the liberals could seek concessions on the grounds that the alternative was far more menacing to the czarist regime.

Liberal reform leaders did secure some notable gains. Under their influence the *zemstvos*, overstepping the narrow borders of their official jurisdiction, began to challenge the government on important national problems. They took the initiative in forming secret study groups and a liberal organ, *Liberation*. They founded a new organization, the Union of Liberation—which, to be sure, dared act only in a clandestine fashion. They helped organize secret discussions and conferences to consider the government's illiberal actions and policies.

Aided by the disastrous war with Japan, Bloody Sunday, and the revolutionary tide of 1905, the liberals helped establish the twin foundations of reformist government: a liberal party, in the form of the Constitutional Democratic (or Kadet) party, and the Duma, a parliament with some independent power.

Was it ever possible for reform leaders to secure a ''Western'' parliamentary and party regime and avert the social and political holocaust of 1917? Historians will ever speculate and divide on the question. Aside even from the impact of Russia's ''backwardness,'' its uneven industrial and agricultural development, and the lack of literacy and education among its peasants, however, it seems probable that liberal reform leadership in Russia never had the vision or the vitality necessary to lead such an enormous social and political transformation. Its cardinal failing was its inability on the whole to recognize the basic needs of the Russian masses. Liberals earlier in the century were struggling for civil protection *from* government when they should also—in terms of the few decades allowed them—have been working for such positive reforms as general enfranchisement of the masses and parliamentary institutions. They were fighting for narrow political reforms when the great need of the peasants, especially after the terrible famine of 1891, was bread and land, and that of the workers, social legislation and economic security. There was not the long interaction among reform tendencies, political organization (especially parties) and parliamentary institution-building that had characterized the slow and erratic growth of democratic regimes in the west. This misperception of popular needs stemmed to a marked degree from the values that dominated nineteenth-century liberalism in Russia. Early in the century many Russian liberals were under the spell of Adam Smith; they sought largely to lift the hand of the state from private enterprise. As the decades passed, liberal doctrine took a more positive direction and concentrated on the political reforms that might eventually make possible social and economic reforms. But even after the turn of the century reform manifestos were still emphasizing civil liberties, legal rights, and political reforms at a time when the basic needs of the people were running far ahead of such reforms.

Both these tendencies of liberal reform leadership were related to a third: the absence of a meaningful structure of conflict embracing liberals and conservatives, autocrats and radicals. Instead of organizing around lines of conflict in defense of the autocracy and in opposition to it, all but the radical groups were linked with the government and to some degree dependent on it. Liberals received concessions and favors from the Crown and had enormous difficulty confronting it. The organization of conflict was made more difficult by the government's repressive policies—its heavy censorship and its overreaction to even mild liberal reform proposals. These circumstances often left the liberal reform leadership in a position curiously like the reformist autocrat trying to reform the nation and its institutions from the top rather than conducting the battle in the factories and peasant huts as well.

Reform leaders in nineteenth-century Russia, like those in many other countries, prided themselves on being pragmatists. In the beginning particularly, as Fischer points out, the liberals operated ad hoc, "truly deserving in this period the appellation 'empiricists par excellence'." Later the liberal reform leaders became more doctrinal, but they did not overcome their tendency to concentrate on immediate and discrete reforms. It was Nicholas II who denounced the "senseless dreams" of liberal reformers (a reference to a modest proposal for *zemstvo* participation in internal administration). The alternative to dreams was always "small deeds"—and the liberal reform generally opted for the latter. "Small deeds" was the Russian version of the particularism that has characterized reform leadership in other countries. In the final decades of the czardom liberals moved from small deeds to senseless dreams in the face of the rising power of revolutionary parties. But it was much, much too late for the reformers.

Reform in America:
Dilemmas of Transforming Leadership

How to mobilize persons of reform instincts but of diverse and volatile predispositions behind a considered reform effort; how to connect one reform cause with related but seemingly separate ones; how above all to deal as reformers with politicians and parties and governments that reflect more mixed and general needs and attitudes—these questions challenged American reformers as they had British reformers. Many Americans were caught and even intoxicated by the reform spirit in the 1830s and 1840s, just as the British and other Europeans were. "In the history of the world the doctrine of Reform had never such scope as at the present hour," Ralph Waldo Emerson told the Mechanics' Apprentices' Library Association in Boston in 1841, ". . . not a kingdom, town, statute, rite, calling, man, or woman, but is threatened by the new spirit. . . . The demon of reform has a secret door into the heart of every law-maker of every inhabitant of every city. . . . What is a man born for but to be a Reformer, a Re-maker of what man has made . . . ?" In style and doctrine American reformers were not far behind their brethren abroad, Allan Nevins notes: "America where Neal Dow strove for Prohibition, and Elizabeth Cady Stanton for women's rights, and Robert Rantoul for the ten-hour day, and Horace Mann for better schools, and James G. Birney for emancipation, and

Horace Greeley for free homesteads, and Theodore Parker for a purer religion; America which Jefferson had taught to believe in the indefinite perfectibility of mankind.'' Many of these causes had a special, native American flavor.

Some reform leaders were well aware of the political dilemmas they faced. On the pace of reform Wendell Phillips wrote: ''The reformer is careless of numbers, disregards popularity, and deals only with ideas, conscience, and common sense. He feels, with Copernicus, that as God waited long for an interpreter, so he can wait for his followers. He neither expects nor is overanxious for immediate success. The politician dwells in an everlasting NOW. His motto is 'Success'—his aim, votes. His object is not absolute right, but, like Solon's laws, as much right as the people will sanction. His office is not to instruct public opinion, but to represent it. Thus, in England, Cobden, the reformer, created sentiment, and Peel, the politician, stereotyped it into statutes.'' In 1853 a reform convention met in the Bowery to fuse all the reform groups into one grand organization; on the same evening a woman's rights convention, an abolition convention, and a world temperance convention were held in New York, and each proceeded to argue furiously with itself and to eject ''visiting'' reformers who threatened to divide the convention on ''side issues.'' As the years wore on the tendency of reformers to join several causes and to hold their ''cause'' conventions in the same city at the same time produced some trend toward unity—or at least cooperation.

The abolitionist movement embraced both single-issue enthusiasts and multi-issue unifiers, both gradualists and immediatists, and hence it embodied a deep dualism among reformers. William Lloyd Garrison was at once a leader of a political movement and the epitome of the theological, often evangelistic, approach to the structure of slavery in the South. When in the first issue of his *The Liberator* he cried out that ''I *will* be harsh as truth, and as uncompromising as justice,'' that ''I will not equivocate—I will not excuse—I will not retreat a single inch'' he was forecasting the moral absolutism that would characterize both the ends and the means of those calling for immediate emancipation without compensation. So intent was Garrison on the single, overriding issue of slavery, whatever his other instincts and interests, that he labeled the Constitution (borrowing from Shaker founder Ann Lee's characterization of marriage) ''a covenant with death and an agreement with hell'' and demanded the breakup of the Union. He seemed not to care whether the South seceded from the North or vice versa. He would not so much extirpate slavery as extrude it, cast it into the outer darkness and out of his consciousness—and conscience. He would not engage in group collaboration with other reform groups and certainly not in organized party action, as this would compromise the purity of his reformism. "They treat ideas as ignorant persons do cherries," James Russell Lowell said of the abolitionists. "They think them unwholesome unless they are swallowed stone and all."

Many abolitionists rejected such single-issue purism, and increasingly they did so during the course of the 1840s and 1850s. Exploiting the rising feeling in the North, they perfected group tactics, organized third-party ventures, threw their weight into major-party politics, and then in the mid-1850s turned to the most audacious of political strategies in America: the founding of a new party that would challenge both of the old parties and seek to replace one of them. The abolitionists did not forsake their old principles or their morality. Senator Charles Sumner of Massachusetts could contend that "true politics" was simply "morals applied to public affairs." But Sumner was also effective in the arts of coalition and compromise, and he and other antislavery leaders, such as Thaddeus Stevens of Pennsylvania, were able to win legislative office.

In the end the abolitionists helped produce a catalytic political situation in which a new antislavery party, the Republicans, overcame a divided opposition and elected their own man President. They won with a moderate, Abraham Lincoln, but a moderate keenly aware of the moral force that the abolitionists provided the new party. Should he forget, the reformers were quick to exert leverage on him. The President bore the affliction of reform moralism with his usual fortitude, but he took their measure. "They are utterly lawless—the unhandiest devils in the world to deal with," Lincoln said of the radicals, "—but after all, their faces are set Zionwards." If the minds of the abolitionists were rigid and doctrinaire, one reason was probably their difficulty in reaching two prime targets, the slaves and their masters. This, Richard Hofstadter concluded, may have caused them to be "driven inward intellectually" with the result that their thinking had become increasingly theological and millennial.

Finally emancipation, Appomattox, reunion. What would the reforming abolitionists do with their victory? Following the war, at a meeting of the National Anti-Slavery Society, Garrison proposed that the society be dissolved, for its purpose had been achieved with the passage of the Thirteenth Amendment. This proposal precipitated a break with his onetime fervent disciple, Wendell Phillips, who demanded a positive and comprehensive reconstruction policy toward the freedmen. The society not only voted to stay in existence but chose Phillips president. He now had a political base from which he proceeded to shape his own reconstruction program calling not simply for the end of black bondage but for land, education, and the ballot for the Negro. That the "negative" freedom of emancipation would prove a chimera unless it were underpinned by social and economic and psychological freedom was not uniquely the doctrine of the Boston radical. A commission established during the war by the War Department on the urging of Republican leaders had called for legal, political, and economic guarantees for the freedmen—indeed, had called for the confiscation of plantation lands in the South and their redistribution among emancipated Negroes and poor whites. A number of Radical Republican leaders endorsed the idea. Forty acres and a hut, Stevens said, would be more valuable than the right to vote.

Much depended now on whether the bulk of the prewar reformers would rally to a program for genuine reconstruction. They would not. In rejecting positive federal action to protect the political liberty and economic security of former slaves, the reformers decisively enfeebled the willingness and capacity of Republican presidents and congresses to bring about fundamental change in the South and to discourage the re-establishment of white oligarchies. It was to be expected that conservatives, moderates, and old-time Southern leaders would reject policies that might truly reconstruct the foundations of Negro life in the South; it was the steady desertion of the old causes by reformers that marked the blighting of white and black hopes for Negro opportunity in the South.

The reasons for the reformers' retreat tell us something of the restraints on their leadership. The great number of reformers perceived the needs of society in a special and restricted way. The scandals of the Grant administration had aroused their deep-seated revulsion against corruption and chicanery. That revulsion sprang from moralistic Christian precepts about individual honesty and responsibility, from a class bias against the grubbier parvenus who fed at the public trough, and from a fervent belief in the inviolability of private property. Most reformers had little understanding or sympathy for the more basic needs of the people—especially those of workers subject to boom and bust and to low wages and long hours even in good times, and those of farmers vulnerable to drought, transportation monopolies, middlemen, and the continual flux of costs and income. Concentrated mainly in upper-class urban areas, the reformers were indeed cut off from the mass of Americans in breeding, in education, in moral credo, and in social status. Above all the reformers believed in economic individualism and laissez-faire and could not countenance, even if they otherwise desired, comprehensive government action to help the freedmen. How could those who exalted private property tolerate compulsory land redistribution?

And even if they favored social values relevant to popular attitudes and black needs the reformers lacked the political skills and resources to influence government. Adept at exciting and mobilizing reform instincts within their own middle-class circles, they typically failed to extend their appeal to lower-class and working-class people who were rebelling against low incomes and blighted opportunity or to poor farmers who were increasingly restive under the harsh agrarian circumstances of late nineteenth-century America. These groups the liberal reformers designated as the "dangerous classes"—a designation encompassing immigrants, anarchists, socialists, strikers, social reformers, demagogues, agitators, rioters. The ties between liberal reformers and their potentially powerful ally, union labor, were especially frail. The reformers acknowledged that workers had grievances but felt that "their leaders, instead of teaching them the basic identity of interests between capital and labor, harangued them with wild charges against employers and whipped up dangerous class hatreds," according to John Sproat. "Instead of advising workers to wait patiently for 'natural laws' to rectify temporary imbalances in the economy, agitators urged their ignorant charges to demand 'unnatural' concessions from businessmen."

Nor did liberal reformers find it possible to turn to the classic means of alliance with other groups in a general-interest mechanism—the political party—for they feared and disliked party. The whole idea of party spirit, party discipline, party spoils, and sordid party combat offended their morality, their individualism, their purism. The New York Reform Club from the start banned from membership anyone who could be called a political worker. Young reformers like Theodore Roosevelt or Henry Cabot Lodge who tried to improve their party from within were chastized as trimmers and opportunists. To be sure, reform leaders saw parties as both necessary and inevitable in a democracy, but they should be run sedately and disinterestedly by gentlemen; otherwise parties should be exposed and shunned. Party spirit should always yield to "true public spirit." One influential reform leader, Moorfield Storey, advanced the interesting theory that parties were useful during eras of deep conflict but not during ordinary times, when they could not achieve even so simple an aim as honest government.

When the compulsions of American politics—especially the need to win the presidency or a majority in Congress—forced reform leaders to turn to major-party or third-party politics, they were usually ineffective and even inept. In 1872, repelled by cronyism and corruption in the first Grant administration, liberal Republicans decided to hold a separate convention and launch a reform ticket against the general's re-election. Most of the leading reformers attended a large conclave in Cincinnati where, amid much optimism, they greeted with cheers reformer Carl Schurz's prediction that out of their efforts would come "a Government which the best people of the country will be proud of." But while the best people were declaiming and platform-writing and planning to nominate an impeccable reform leader—a Massachusetts Adams, no less—

other delegates were indulging in the very "tricky manipulation" and mean, political trading that Schurz in his keynote deplored. Those delegates secured the nomination for a man of questionable reform standing, Horace Greeley, and they did so in a convention-floor power play on a late ballot. The "true" reform leaders were shocked at the outcome; Greeley had supported almost every reform fad, from Fourierism to anti-tea drinking, but not the respectable reforms like civil service and free trade; and in Cincinnati he promptly chose as his running mate a Missouri spoilsman, Senator B. Gratz Brown, who had helped deliver votes to Greeley out of the convention's trading rooms. The Democrats later nominated Greeley in their own convention, but Grant easily defeated him in the fall.

In later years reform leaders became somewhat more adept at party politics, or at least at balance-of-power politics within the two-party system. Liberal Republicans bolted the ticket of James G. Blaine, who on his record and promises probably deserved better of them, to support a Democrat after their own hearts, Grover Cleveland. And Cleveland in office turned out to be their kind of liberal: a money pincher, a tariff reducer, a civil service advocate, and above all a laissez-faire conservative. Liberal reformers won other victories; the very narrowness of their program gave their cause an intensity and persistence that made some kind of breakthrough inevitable on issues like civil service reform, but that kind of reform seemed increasingly irrelevant to the needs and hopes of millions of Americans in factory and field.

"True politics" is simply "morals applied to public affairs." During the first decade of the twentieth century reform leaders were increasingly aware of the thorny dilemmas implicit in Sumner's definition. Events of the 1880s and 1890s—the agrarian revolt, massive immigration, labor protest and violence, the Populist capture of the Democratic party—had simply washed over and around the narrow boundaries of genteel, gradualist, issue-by-issue reform. Many of the old reforms had not been legislated into federal or state law; those that had been, such as anti-spoils and anti-corruption measures, usually had limited impact; even reforms that had been vigorously pursued were hardly purifying American democracy. And now by chance, not by the efforts of reform leaders, a kind of reformer was in the White House in the person of Theodore Roosevelt, the man who years earlier had made a separate peace with the Grand Old Party. TR was keeping one foot in the ranks of the old guard, the other in the reform movement. He was impartial at least in his hatreds; hardly a day passed that he did not rail at the mossbacks among the old guard or at the fools and idiots among the reformers, and he played each off against the other. It was a heady but perplexing decade for reformers: the nation seemed intoxicated with new ideas. However, actual reforms—and the actual application of legislated reforms—came haltingly. Toward the end of the decade, when Roosevelt gave way to the genial nonreformer William Howard Taft, the agenda of reform was far from nearing adoption.

And that agenda was longer than ever. The investigative reporting of the decade by Ida Tarbell, Lincoln Steffens, and others; the explosion of semi-popular journals that publicized the evils of child labor, meatpacking, plunderers of public lands, malefactors of great wealth, and the new power of the newly rich; and the rise of a large class of professional, middle-class persons who acted out of a sense of loss of status and alienation provided both a steady supply of scandals and exposés and a vast market of those prone to indignation.

So the old question was more urgent than ever: given the continuing fragmentation and dispersal of power in the American political system, given the pragmatic and often conservative tendencies of American politicians, given, too, the still-pervasive power of doctrines of economic individualism, liberty against government, and laissez-faire; but also given now the impetus of reform feeling among millions of Americans, what kinds of strategies could reform leaders devise to maximize the influence of the new spirit?

Many reform leaders approached this question with an instinct not to use organized power but to shun it. The Progressive community, Hofstadter notes, was divided "between those who proposed an aggressive and uncompromising struggle against organization as such and those who proposed to meet it by counterorganization, by increasing specialism and leadership, and by the assumption of new responsibilities." Anti-organization reformers sought mainly to dissolve concentrated power in big corporations, labor unions, and political parties and machines in order that the citizen's individualism and sense of personal responsibility could have free play. It was not enough, journalist William Allen White contended, to break the machine; it was necessary to create a state of affairs in which machines would not be necessary at all: the "modern movement in America politics was bristling with rampant, militant, unhampered men crowding out of the mass for individual elbow-room." Closely allied to this view was the notion that politics could be conducted as a rational exchange of views among individuals rather than as a continuing conflict among persons in organized groups. The citizen contributed to the public welfare not by acting on his own—or society's—palpable needs but through "disinterested reflection upon the needs of the community," as Hofstadter put it. This effort to rise above deeply felt, "selfish," collective need was in effect an effort to banish collective conflict—that is, conflict among organized groups or parties.

Another way to exorcise collective and systemic conflict was by the old reform device of identifying individual reform issues, developing organization behind such issues, and letting the organization die when the reform was either accomplished or abandoned. M. I. Ostrogorski pushed this idea a step further by urging single-issue parties that would form and re-form around individual issues as these issues rose, flourished, and declined. Voters, "instead of being jumbled together in an ill-assorted compound and kept mechanically in the fixed grooves of permanent parties," would "be able to combine and re-combine at will, according to their natural affinities, in homogeneous categories." Ostrogorski perceived democracy as an atomistic enterprise in which isolated persons engaged in the rational discussion of public affairs, far above the passions of the multitude.

But the most powerful impulse among the reform leaders was the democratization and ultimately the purification of party. And by the early twentieth century the device that seemingly would democratize parties was at hand: the direct primary. This was not a new device, but it took on immense popularity during the muckraking era as a result of a peculiar historical development that was to have an extraordinary impact on American political institutions. Since the days of Jackson, American parties had nominated their candidates in conventions. This procedure worked relatively well as long as the two major parties were relatively competitive with each other; while the convention could easily be dominated by city bosses and corporate money, any party that allowed itself to become conspicuously controlled by "vested interests" ran the risk of public disapproval and loss of the next election. Democracy *between* the parties, in short, was a safeguard against lapses in democracy *within* the parties. Much depended on vigorous party competition, but the national party balance was badly upset in the election of 1896, when voters became polarized on geographic lines: McKinley won lopsidedly in the north and east, and Bryan won heavily in the south and much of the west. The imbalance persisted acutely for the next decade or so. Exploiting their regional monopolies, party bosses could defy the public by nominating men they could control—or so it seemed to the reform leaders. The primary election was Reform's answer, and in the reformist mood of the progressive era, this "people's instrument" for choosing candidates was quickly adopted by a number of states. What most of the reformers did not understand, however, was that in thwarting bad party leaders they were also thwarting good ones; in pulverizing "boss control" they were damping the possibilities of democratic, creative, and imaginative party leadership.

Other reform leaders understood this and wanted it. To them party, like most organizations, was irremediably corrupt and undemocratic. Under a banner proclaiming that "the only cure for democracy is more democracy" they backed such reforms as the initiative, the referendum, and recall, all of which were designed to allow the citizenry to bypass party leadership and directly influence the processes and decisions of government. The reformers discouraged straight party-ticket voting by eliminating the form of ballot that made it easy to vote for an entire party slate with one **X**. They strengthened civil service laws against the onslaught of the patronage mongers. In many localities they established the nonpartisan ballot, which shifted the axis of conflict from the familiar two-party battle to a multi-sided struggle among a host of "independent," often obscure candidates. Some states voted to institute cross-filing, under which candidates could run for more than one party nomination; and they legalized procedures whereby Democrats could easily vote in Republican primaries and vice versa. All these efforts varied considerably from state to state; under the leadership of Hiram Johnson California all but abolished its party system.

Some reformers and intellectuals saw dangers in the destruction of a party system that, whatever its failings, for decades had organized conflict and consensus effectively. But, obsessed as most of them were with democratizing the parties, they failed to sense the potential conflict between making parties more representative of their rank and file and making them more competitive with each other at every level of government. Democracy *within* the party was still out of kilter with democracy—or competition—*between* parties. Few saw this vital contradiction. One result of the reform dilemma was that some progressive leaders leaped right over the possible regeneration of parties and called for a leadership essentially independent of party. Some, like Henry Jones Ford, called for more presidential leadership, on the ground that the only kind of party leadership possible in the United States was through presidential leadership. "The greatness of the presidency," Ford wrote, "is the work of the people, breaking through the constitutional form. . . ." He saw the party serving as a link between executive and legislative, but the "situation is such that the extension of executive authority is still the only practical method of advancing popular rule." Others, like Herbert Croly, acting out of the Hamiltonian tradition of executive authority, argued that "Progressive democracy needs executive leadership" and that such leadership, better than any parliamentary or legalistic system, "organizes and vitalizes the rule of the majority." He was highly critical of the quality of the actual party system and had few hopes for it, though theoretically he believed in it. Woodrow Wilson was one of the few who developed a thorough comprehension of the potential role of party, but he, too, in theory and in practice, turned to the concepts of direct executive leadership of the popular majority.

The upshot was that reform leaders approached the most critical epochs in modern American history without a theoretically convincing and practically operational theory of the relation of reform ideals and politics to the organization of political power, without a political strategy that could maximize reform influence, and without a clear sense of the interrelation of reform ends and means with the political environment. This explains why reform and reform leadership could play such an indispensable part in Roosevelt's New Deal even though they lacked a durable base; and it explains why decades after the Liberal Republican movement reformers had still not come to terms with the reality of American politics. It helps explain why Roosevelt had no dependable and organized majority to fall back on but rather had to build ad hoc alliances as he went along, dramatizing individual issues by lifting them out of ordinary debate and applying to them his own special techniques of persuasion. One result of this situation was that reform seemed to die with Roosevelt and had to be resurrected in new alliances and combinations as his successors tried to push major reform legislation through Congress. Not only were such combinations not representative, they fell to pieces as the individual issues were resolved or obscured. The great dilemmas of reform leadership in America persisted as Harry Truman, John Kennedy, and Jimmy Carter each tried to fashion or refashion leadership coalitions wide and strong enough to support their programs.

As we reflect on these cases of reform leadership in England, Russia, and America, two aspects stand out. One is the tendency of members of the nobility, aristocracy, gentry, and higher bourgeoisie to take the lead in reforming the very system that seems to shore up their positions of privilege. Not among these groups but among the working class, peasantry, lower middle-class, and sections of the gentry and other higher classes, does one find the most obdurate and fearful responses to the changes that are proposed mainly for the benefit of the great number of people or the masses. This long observed tendency—to which literally hundreds of other examples would attest—is often ascribed to the comfortable lives of the rich and well-born, to their broader vistas resulting from their cosmopolitan friendships, education, and travel, to their resources of time and money, to their sense of noblesse oblige, to their feeling of guilt over their affluent lives. A more fundamental cause, I think, is the satisfaction and hence the extinction of their basic security and material needs, allowing other, higher needs and aspirations and demands of conscience to come into play. While narrower class attitudes and social interests influence many of the rich and well-born to resist reform, the psychological and cultural forces are strong enough in many societies to make patrician reformers a vital element in reform leadership. Revolution too has attracted the high-born and the rich, but has typically been more dependent on recruitment from workers and peasants.

The other tendency is the failure of reform leadership to achieve the actual (real) social change proportionate to the transformations that the leaders promised, and in the name of which reform was promised. Reform leaders may act on the benevolent notion that true politics is simply morals applied to public affairs, but they find in the heat of battle that true politics is the everyday scuffling and swapping in governmental and political marketplaces. Because reform leaders typically accept the political and social structures within which they act, their reform efforts are inevitably compromised, and usually inhibited, by the tenacious inertia of existing institutions. Far-reaching change in the end is carried through less by reform leaders, vital though their role is, than by politicians who see their political ambitions entangled in the reform effort. Reform is ever poised between the transforming and the transactional—transforming in spirit and posture, transactional in process and results. Revolutionary leaders understand this. They seek to evade or minimize transactional processes and costs—and thus they incur other costs on their own.

8

REVOLUTIONARY LEADERSHIP

"C'est une révolte," Louis XVI exclaimed when the Duc de la Rochefoucauld-Liancourt told him that royal troops had defected in the face of a popular attack and the Bastille had fallen. *"Non, Sire, c'est une révolution,"* the duke responded. In this exchange the old astronomical meaning of revolution—the revolving motion of the stars following a preordained course beyond the power of human beings to change—had been brought down to earth, Hannah Arendt remarks, and transformed into the irresistible movement that no man could arrest.

The dialogue had broader implication. The beleaguered and bewildered king doubtless surmised that the storming of the Bastille was merely the latest of those popular outbreaks that had struck at royal regimes since time immemorial without reaching the jugular of kingly power. Perhaps the duke sensed that this was something far more profound than an uprising, that this was the trigger that would detonate a larger explosion that would in turn precipitate some kind of collective effort, in the name of some kind of overriding purpose, to transform the system of class and status, the alignment of popular attitudes and expectations, and the pattern of political power.

Two centuries later, in a more cynical age, the surmise of Louis XVI might seem more justified. For, in the wake of cruel disillusionment with the long-term results of the Bolshevik seizure of power, some had concluded that revolutions were games conducted by elites over the heads of the masses, palace struggles projected onto a broader landscape but with no more enduring meaning than coups d'état in a banana republic and at most the replacement of one set of rulers with another—all with little impact on the lives and the hopes of the millions who watched the drama with no sense of involvement and no stake in the outcome. At best the leaders altered their behavior to adjust to the predictable responses of their followers; at worst the leaders made their decisions without regard to the people, and if some *sans culottes* later raised objections, such protest could be overcome by blandishments from the authorities and by various forms of outright manipulation.

In its broadest meaning revolution is a complete and pervasive transformation of an entire social system. It means the birth of a radical new ideology; the rise of a movement bent on transforming society on the basis of that ideology; overthrow of the established government; creation of a new political system; reconstruction of the economy, education, communications, law, medicine; and the confirmation and perhaps deification of a new leadership. The "pure" form of revolution is rare in practice. Also rare is the revolutionary leader who helps initiate a revolution, lasts through the whole revolutionary cycle of struggle, victory, and consolidation of power, and directs the process of social transformation. The French Revolution devoured its leaders. Lenin enjoyed just a few years of rulership. Only Mao, Fidel Castro, and perhaps a few others have experienced as transforming forces the revolutions they helped to start. More often other leaders come to the fore to play their parts during the succeeding stages of the revolutionary cycle.

Of all the stages in a transforming revolution, the birth of the idea or vision that impels the revolution and its adoption by a decisive number of persons are probably the most crucial steps toward transformation, save perhaps for the actual physical capture of state power. The source of that idea or that vision in a leader, or in a small group of leaders, may be as mysterious as the origin of the sparks of creativity in an artist or writer. The spread of the new gospel—like that by the small band of persecuted Christians—is equally mysterious.

But we know some of the requirements for success. The leaders must be absolutely dedicated to the cause and able to demonstrate that commitment by giving time and effort to it, risking their lives, undergoing imprisonment, exile, persecution, and continual hardship. Thus Castro and his small band experienced constant privation. This commitment, which may end in martyrdom, must survive all defeats and setbacks. Too, the revolution, like all genuine leadership, must address the wants and needs and aspirations of the populace—motives that may not be felt by followers at the time but can be mobilized through propaganda and political action. Further, a revolution requires *conflict*, as does all leadership. But revolutionary conflict is more extreme; it is dramatized in the characters of saints and devils, heroes and villains. As the lines become more sharply drawn between the establishment or elite and the poor and the rebelling, doctrine and purpose are hardened in the crucible. Finally, there must be a powerful sense of mission, of end-values, of transcending purpose.

These processes can be summarized in a phrase: the raising of social and political *consciousness* on the part of both leaders and followers.

We will follow the course of three revolutions, noting the interplay of human wants and needs, power, conflict, consciousness, and values, leading to diverse forms of change. Revolutionary leadership, perhaps more than other leadership forms, is collective, relying in this age, even more than reform leadership does, on movements, parties, and political organizations. We will note the simple, dire needs that impelled masses of people to revolt and the variations in the courses of the revolutions in several quite different environments.

Few leaders would seem so ill-suited for revolutionary leadership as Martin Luther, for he acted without party and organization; his strength lay in the collective strength of a following he hardly knew. Yet few leaders have aroused consciousness so dramatically or had such a shattering impact on the political and religious attitudes of his era. For most of his life Luther was a poor monk with no political base and an uncertain ecclesiastical one, with no military protection—and in frequent peril to his life and freedom. He had virtually no training in history, politics, or geography and lacked understanding of the historical background, the political arrangements, and the strategic dispositions of the very forces he assaulted so thunderously. He was no ordinary propagandist: he had little concern for others' opinions, no political program worthy of the name to propose, and no gift for organization. He was neither a learned theologian nor a trained philosopher. Fundamentally conservative, he struggled to return to first principles rather than create new and revolutionary ones. Yet he created a revolution whose resonance still echoes in our own time.

What Luther had was more powerful than formal learning or political artifice. He had an absolute, fanatical conviction that carried almost everything before it. And he had the good fortune to live in an era ripe for ideological change, one in which the art of communication had been modernized and the voice of a lone monk could be heard in many lands.

Like many ideological subversives, Luther went back to original principles and sources—in this case to the Bible itself. He consumed it, preached it, translated it. He apotheosized individual conscience, the sanctity of the inner man, the direct, personal relation between God and man. He would sweep away the vast papal establishment with its unbridled exploitation of commerce in indulgences and excommunication, its cynical flouting of the same restrictions it laid down on the devout, its departure from the teaching of the Scriptures. Restoring man's inner grace seemed hardly a manifesto for political leadership, but it meant the reform or abolition of indulgences, and this was a threat to the economic foundations of the papacy. And so Luther confronted papal legates, emperors, kings, and cardinals. He would not retreat, he would not bargain and adjust; he did not know the language—nor perhaps the arithmetic—of calculation. Excommunicated, he burned the Bull of Excommunication—and the decretals, the heart of papal law. Summoned before the emperor at the Diet of Worms and ordered to recant, he said no—and may have added, "Here I stand. I can do no other. So help me God. Amen."

What produced such passion and zeal? Luther's father, the son of a peasant, had risen in the world to become the operator of a small copper mine; he disliked priests and preferred that Martin become a lawyer rather than a monk. Some have seen Luther's early years as being crucial to his later development. There is some evidence that discipline in the family was harsh, to the point that Martin ran away briefly; was his later rebellion against the Holy Father in Rome simply a projection of early hostility against the stern, overworked father at home? On the other hand, child and parents were much involved with one another and dependent on one another; do early Oedipal relations explain the later Luther? Or is the rebellious Luther to be traced back to even more fundamental psychological factors, such as those Erik Erikson has explored so brilliantly in his study of the young man? Marxist historians stress rather the interaction between the youth growing up in an upwardly mobile family and the busy, trading, profit-making environment of northern Germany. And philosophers and theologians stress the reasoning, cognitive influences—especially during Luther's sojourn in "pagan" Rome and his encounters with the ordinary German people during his long walking journeys from monastery to monastery.

In a few short years—almost overnight, it seemed later—he was transformed from a beggarly monk to a powerful preacher and a brilliant writer and popularizer. At first the main communication was by word of mouth. He acquired a knowledge of human nature, Richard Friedenthal says; "his language became richer; so did his conception of life in the towns and villages and on the roads, reflecting as it did all the varied social strata which filled the Germany of those days to bursting point with unrest, dissension and hope. Politics were hammered out on the roads; in the towns, where everybody knew everybody, people were usually more reticent. Conversations on the highroads—between a peasant and a nobleman, a mendicant friar and an abbot on horseback, a brothel keeper and a university scholar—were the sources from which sprang the inflammatory writings and dialogues that reflect the tumult of the times so much more truly than the dull records of meetings of diets and their evasive announcements."

But perhaps more than ever before the impetus toward reform moved by the printed word. Literacy was spreading rapidly and printing presses were springing up to meet the new demand. Four thousand copies of Luther's *On Improving the Christian Estate* were sold in a few weeks—an astounding sale for that time. Printers in at least a score of cities published his sermons as fast as they could get their hands on them. Woodcuts, many of them carrying Luther's countenance, dramatized the new teachings. Militant psalms became the war songs of the Reformation. The Bible, of course, was the bestseller.

Later it would be said about Martin Luther, as about all great leaders, that he was merely a catalyst of social change, a trigger for historic forces that had piled up and were waiting to burst into flame. Certainly many forces were coming into concatenation during the early sixteenth century. Cultivated by Erasmus and other thinkers, humanism was bursting into full bloom. Rebelliousness against Rome was sharply on the increase. Popular comprehension of political and religious actions was intensifying. Political tumult and violence were spreading. Luther responded to these forces, but he was not a passive receptacle. He spoke vernacular German so he could communicate with the people; he translated the Bible into German and enormously magnified his power to reach the common man in Germany and across western Europe. He examined his printed sermons and did not hesitate to chastise the craftsmen for slovenly printing and shoddy paper. Yet he led public opinion mainly because of the image of courage and independence that he created; all the rhetoric and the technique would have come to little if Luther had not stood uncompromising and incorruptible. Like many other revolutions, his would in some respects ultimately turn conservative and even reactionary. But there is no gainsaying its explosive revolutionary implications.

In setting off in men's minds a series of insurrections that shook the foundations of theological and political power throughout western Europe, Luther showed himself to be a master preacher and propagandist. He was not an organizer, a collective leader, a revolutionary strategist. He was more of a prophet than a politician. Master organizers would follow, and then the religious and political armies would march. The revolutionary reformism of the sixteenth century led to the "enlightened" rationalism of the next two centuries—and, in the two centuries after that, to the revolutions that would topple the regimes of the West and then the East.

France: The Maelstrom of Leadership

One of these revolutions came in Bourbon France in the 1790s. Some have seen that social paroxysm as a great drama that simply led to the replacement of the Bourbons by the Bonapartes. Yet the more that historians have dug into police records and other archives, in Paris and other cities, the more it has become evident that, in Paris at least, this was a revolution in the classic sense. Though the first steps toward revolution were taken by aristocrats and higher bourgeoisie, new leaders emerged from the masses, defied or ignored the celebrated leaders of the upheaval, and exerted a crucial influence on decisions.

In the 1780s France displayed what have come to be seen as classic conditions for revolution: a monarchy that was weak when it should have been firm, resolute when it might have compromised; a concretized structure of aristocratic, corporate, and guild rights that defied the reform efforts of the king's ministers; little access for middle-class talent to the channels of prestige and power; fiscal chaos; simmering conflict among Crown, aristocracy, and higher bourgeoisie and, more important, within each of those entities a huge, suffering underclass (in addition to intellectuals and publicists) inspired by Rousseau and the *philosophes* and intoxicated by the American Revolution and its aura of success. Following a deceptive period of relative calm, events escalated at the end of the decade. The Assembly of Notables, which had last met a century and a half before, was convened by the king in 1787 in the hope that this collection of reformers would ease the growing tension. The venture failed. Sharpened conflict arose between the king and the old, unrepresentative parliaments, and the parliaments were suspended in the spring of 1788. The first Estates-General to be held in France for 175 years was convoked on a broadly representative basis (exclusive, of course, of women and the poor). The Estates-General assembled in Versailles in May 1789 amid splendid pageantry, with the six hundred deputies of the third estate, clad in bourgeois simplicity, marching in, followed by nobles festooned in color, priests in black, and finally by Louis and Marie-Antoinette and their retinue.

Louis had no significant program of reform, and the assembly deteriorated into petty squabbles and deadlock. Then came stunning climaxes: a trial of strength as nobles and clergy insisted on the autonomy—and the veto power—of their separate estates while commons held that it was all one national assembly; the invoking of a new right, the general will of the people, in the third-estate demand for a national assembly that it would dominate; the king's barring the entrance of third-estate deputies to the hall, followed by the deputies' swearing their celebrated oath of the tennis court, binding themselves as national assembly members to continue to meet; vacillations by Louis in the face of this affront to royal authority; his sudden dismissal of Necker, his reform minister; the strange Great Fear in the countryside; turbulence in Paris; and then the sudden, savage assault on the Bastille.

All but the last of these proceedings seemed to be dominated by leaders of the three estates who knew how to talk, negotiate, dramatize, compose declarations, and compromise—dominated, that is, by persons who had always been good at this sort of thing because they were educated, presentable, amenable, plausible, reasonable. During the "first phase" of the Revolution the under classes and their leaders were hardly heard from. Even so, they could not be ignored. Jacqueries were a potent folk memory in France. Paris had seen bread riots in 1752 and in 1775. During the half century before the Revolution, strikes were not infrequent—strikes of stocking-frame weavers, journeymen hatters, bookbinders, furriers, locksmiths, stonemasons, porters, bakers. The "lunatics" and "criminals" who stormed the Bastille, as conservative historians later pictured them, were almost all small tradesmen, artisans, and wage earners.

An incident in April 1789, termed by some the first significant outbreak of the Revolution and by others the last outbreak of the old regime, illuminated the character of crowd action. A wallpaper manufacturer named Réveillon, widely known as a kindly employer and good citizen, was rumored to have lamented publicly that the day had come when working people could not make do on fifteen *sous* a day. Several hundred *sans culottes* gathered near the Bastille and hanged Réveillon in effigy; then the mob, swelling in numbers, went on a two-day rampage, sacking shops and houses (including Réveillon's), standing up to the guard under direct fire, and fighting back despite heavy losses. Later it was charged that the crowd and its leaders came mainly from outside the arena of battle, but investigation revealed that most of the rioters were from the neighborhood. Nor were the rioters "brigands," as the historian Taine later charged; nor were they bribed; nor were they tools of outside forces.

Leaders had simply risen spontaneously in the crowd as it mobilized in the streets. They were catalysts to the action of others. We do not know the shape and structure of that leadership, its origin and identity, its persistence and potency, for there were no reporters and no documents left by crowd leaders. Analysts of crowd behavior later used the lurid accounts of Parisian mobs to support their tendentious theories of mass action. Thus Gustave Le Bon: "The leader has most often started as one of the led. He has himself been hypnotised by the idea, whose apostle he has since become. It has taken possession of him." The leaders, Le Bon went on, were recruited from the ranks of the "morbidly nervous, excitable, half-deranged persons who are bordering on madness." Careful investigation has thrown doubt on this explanation of the behavior of the Paris crowds.

The source of the volcanic energy and drive of those mobs was fundamental: it was hunger. The average Parisian worker lived on the edge of disaster; in the eighteenth century he would normally spend about half his income on bread. Families were abnormally vulnerable to any increase in its price and to the effects of drought, insect infestation, middleman gouging, work stoppages, transportation breakdowns, government harassment. The proportion of income spent on bread to maintain the normal consumption of an average Parisian builder's laborer rose from about 50 percent in August 1788 to over 80 percent between February and July 1789, when bread prices soared in the months immediately preceding the assault on the Bastille. Rumors and reports of actual scarcities of bread provoked fear and anger among the *sans culottes*. It is not surprising that women were active in street action; they could not vote, could not serve in the army, could not express their distress in national assemblies— but they could and did move into the streets. George Rudé agrees that "the primary and most constant motive impelling revolutionary crowds during this period was the concern for the provision of cheap and plentiful food." In the countryside peasants suffered from other miseries and hatreds—including disdain for the canaille in the capital. Driven by the mysterious Great Fear, peasants attacked châteaux and gangs of vagrants roamed the countryside, pillaging and burning.

In the period of reform, celebration, and relative calm that followed the summer tumult of 1789, Louis, seen now as freed from the embrace of his nefarious advisers, was greeted by joyous crowds as Father of the French and "king of a free people." He espoused the *tricolore* (the white of the Bourbons united to the red and blue of Paris, symbolizing gradual reformism), recognized the National Assembly as legislative sovereign, and accepted Lafayette as commander-in-chief of the new civic guard. The National Assembly resolution to "abolish the feudal regime entirely" was not carried out, but it did revoke exemptions from taxation, abolish property-in-office, and open all employments in the public service to all, without distinction of birth. Even with exceptions, compensations, and compromises, it opened the way for further reform of the financial, administrative, and judicial arrangements—and for reform of the Church as well. The use of martial law was restricted. A uniform national tariff was decreed. Church property was nationalized. Wars of conquest were renounced, the nobility "abolished," and local government reorganized.

A truce seemed to have been declared among the warring elements of French life, though the position of the Crown remained anomalous.

Since the assembly's power was now considered supreme, the king's assent to reform was not legally necessary, but the moderates in control preferred some device by which the king might accept or even promulgate the decrees. Because of a brief bread crisis in Paris in the early fall (and for other reasons) they urged a reluctant king to leave Versailles for Paris. But Louis did not wish to remove. Women set off from the central markets of Paris for Versailles, dragging cannon through the rain and mud; in Versailles with sympathetic deputies they gained an interview with the king. He did not respond to their pleas, but when he learned that the national guard of Paris was on the march he agreed to return to Paris. A vast and triumphant procession of soldiers, nobles, deputies, and women escorted the royal carriage into the city.

With an abundant late harvest and the monarch a kind of hostage, France enjoyed some months of social peace. A towering question now confronted the political leaders of France (as it would later revolutionary generations): whether legal, constitutional, administrative, and financial reform could cut deeply enough into institutional structure to initiate and sustain real social change. The pace of rising wants, needs, expectations, and demands would far exceed the actual social impact of reformism. Few societies have been given much time to conduct this fateful contest.

The liberal political reforms and egalitarian social changes would require broad popular support, but social conflict had been exacerbated by the revolutionary developments. Within each class or estate, order or group, deep-seated conflicts abounded. There was no united "upper class" ranged against the poor and the peasant, and there was no united group of "lower class" republicans. Some nobles were militant Jacobins; some *sans culottes* were fanatical royalists. The urban population did tend to unite against the rural, but there were divisions between craftsmen and journeymen, factory owners and labor. In the Catholic Church parish priests tended to be far more sympathetic to revolutionary ideas than were the bishops, and the clergy were split over major issues of doctrine and organization. Established business interests, enjoying monopolies and other privileges from the Crown, were pitted against rising entrepreneurs who demanded freedom to produce, buy, and sell. On the left, radicals fought among themselves over doctrinal and strategic questions.

Most decisive for the course of the Revolution was a rising hostility between revolutionary and counterrevolutionary forces in the whole of Europe. The revolutionary spirit has never stopped at national boundaries, and the firebrands of Paris were inflaming radical leaders in Belgium, Holland, Austria, Poland, Ireland, and elsewhere. French revolutionaries joined hands with their counterparts abroad, and so did French monarchists. There was no conspiracy on either side, nor even highly coordinated action. But the more the Paris revolutionaries threatened Louis XVI, the more the friends of monarchy rallied to support the man they otherwise condemned; the more foreign leaders talked about invading France to salvage the monarchy, the more the Revolution was converted into a national effort, threats from abroad were perceived as attacks on *la patrie,* and revolutionary leaders in Paris viewed the opponents of revolution as disloyal and subversive.

Six weeks after the fall of the Bastille, the National Assembly proclaimed the Declaration of the Rights of Man. The assembly, debating during the political upheaval of the famous summer of 1789, overrode objections that its ringing covenants might raise expectations that could not be fulfilled. The declaration, in R. R. Palmer's estimate, was a political act of the first magnitude, "a powerful ethical affirmation denying the moral foundations of the old order." It was far more akin to the Virginia Declaration of 1776 than to the American Declaration of Independence, which was mainly a lawyer's listing of grievances (though it came to symbolize far more than that).

On the face of it, the Declaration was several things: the raising of a standard, the setting of a direction, the statement of ethical goals. Following a prolix preamble, the declaration laid out a series of postulations: Men are born and remain free and equal in rights. The aim of all political association is to preserve the natural and imprescriptible rights of man—liberty, property, security, and resistance to oppression. Liberty consists in the ability to do whatever does not harm another. Free communication of thought and opinion is one of the most precious of the rights of man. All citizens, being equal in the eyes of the law, are equally admissible to all public dignities, offices, and employments, according to their capacity and with no other distinction than that of their virtues and talents.

These propositions made an uncompromising commitment to the individual liberty that constituted the supreme value for which the bourgeois revolutions of the seventeenth and eighteenth centuries were fought. But the declaration was ambivalent, even schizophrenic on this matter. Almost every promise of individual liberty was compromised by a balancing commitment to the demands of organized society. Social distinctions might exist if they were "based on common utility." Since the principle of all sovereignty rested essentially in the nation, no person could exercise authority that did not emanate from the nation "expressly." No man might be disturbed for his opinions, "even in religion," provided that their manifestation did not trouble public order as established by law. Every citizen might speak, write, and print freely but "on his own responsibility for abuse of this liberty in cases determined by law." The implicit conflict in values divided practice and theory throughout the revolutionary era. In 1793, on the eve of the Terror, the draft of a new declaration drew a sharp distinction between the individual and society in a proviso that "any individual who usurps the sovereignty of the people shall be instantly put to death by free men." Saint-Just aptly summed up the dichotomy: "Liberty will not be terrible for those who submit to the law." Otherwise the second declaration was a more egalitarian document than the first and stressed to a greater degree the obligation to meet the social and economic needs of the people, though property rights remained a fundamental commitment in both declarations.

The French declaration would serve as both trumpet call and historic archetype for generations of radicals and revolutionaries. Musket fire by hungry men in the streets of Paris, more than the volleys of the minutemen on Lexington Green, were the true shots "heard round the world." The sad truth of the matter, according to Hannah Arendt, "is that the French Revolution, which ended in disaster, has made world history, while the American Revolution, so triumphantly successful, has remained an event of little more than local importance." But if the French Revolution bequeathed the noble concepts of liberty and equality to the leaders of humanity everywhere, it also left the poisoned legacy of conflict between these values. The half-starved *sans culottes* and the land-hungry peasants, mobilized politically by their own leaders, wanted government to live up to its egalitarian credo by satisfying their economic and social needs. They were eager for "liberty" mainly to the degree that it would protect them from private and public oppression and enable them to bring pressure on the authorities to provide jobs, requisition bread, control inflation, and improve working conditions.

For the middle-class men who largely composed the leadership of the revolutionary movement, the value priority was just the reverse. As children of the Enlightenment, students of the *philosophes,* members of a libertarian middle class hostile to economic controls on property and business, and ferocious individualists, they valued above all liberty as they defined it. As revolutionists they were compassionate toward the poor, but efforts to meet economic and social needs must not be undertaken at the expense of liberty.

Underlying this conflict between ends was an even more serious question: What was the revolution for? Was it essentially an effort to create institutions of popular democracy that could involve the people in participatory democracy and let them shape their own destinies as long as those institutions lasted? Or was it to meet the immediate needs of the people, to solve tangible economic and social problems? True freedom, in Arendt's view, was very much the former, and that kind of freedom was being corrupted by the revolutionists who transformed the rights of man into the rights of *sans culottes,* who made real freedom give way to necessity. In an uprising of *les malheureux,* Arendt argues, the consequence was impotence, the principle rage, the conscious aim not freedom but happiness.

This bleak view of social revolution has been sharply questioned. The search was not for happiness as such but for subsistence and freedom from despair. If revolutions are regarded as perverted by the intrusion of necessitous classes and their problems, to what remedies can the needy and the hungry resort? Is the creation of a popular, participatory democracy (or republic) the ultimate definition of freedom? Or is it in fact one of the means—or proximate ends—that are vital to ultimate ends such as liberty, equality, justice, security, happiness? Must political liberty and social welfare always be so dichotomous? Arendt dramatized a dilemma of revolution—indeed, of all reform—a dilemma that would reappear in the Russian and Chinese upheavals in the most portentous form. It is extraordinarily difficult to sort out the interrelationship of immediate practical means, institutional structures, and ultimate goals in a revolutionary situation—and the role of leadership in the linkage of these, amid the chaos, frustration, and opportunism of revolution.

Certainly a full grasp of the interrelationship of means and ends in all their complexity was beyond the capacity of the French revolutionary leaders, who could at best regret their failure to achieve freedom, as in the case of Robespierre, who in his last speech predicted, "we shall perish because, in the history of mankind, we missed the moment to found freedom." Events were in the saddle, and these events were shaped far less by the conspicuous public figures in the assembly than by the leaders of the local sections and by street crowds. In June 1792, following renewed conflict between the king and the assembly, two armed columns accompanied by a huge crowd carrying weapons and banners gathered before the assembly; their orator, a customs clerk, was admitted to the chamber and demanded the destruction of executive power. On the way back the mob invaded the royal palace, badgered the king and queen, and forced Louis to don the cap of liberty. Royalists reacted vehemently to this insult to the crown, and this led to more polarization, which in turn was sharpened by stepped-up fears of foreign invasion.

In August the formidable Paris crowd, mobilized by its own leadership, invaded the Tuileries and assaulted and took the palace. This episode and the ensuing "suspension of the king" formed a turning point in the Revolution. Previously there had been a rough balance of power between royal and revolutionary authority; now the contest was mainly between the leaders of the assembly and the leaders of the Paris communes, sections, and crowds.

Perhaps in the circumstances the revolutionary leadership was bound to move toward violence and dictatorship. The old Jacobin elements in the National Assembly were still under the leadership of Jacques Pierre Brissot, the poor son of a pastry cook, a onetime reformist journalist posed against Robespierre, who as a committed and single-minded revolutionary held the confidence of the people in the streets, and George Jacques Danton, a onetime solicitor's clerk who had gained by purchase a prized position at the bar of the select Court of the King's Councils. Danton's strength lay in his personification of the revolution in arms against the counterrevolutionaries at home and abroad. During the following weeks the assembly's security committee (which eventually evolved into the dread Committee of Public Safety) and the Paris communard leaders vied with each other to impose censorship, hunt down suspects, and requisition arms for distribution to patriots. In September crowds invaded Paris and slaughtered more than a thousand men and women.

For some months Brissotins skirmished with Montagnards (men of the mountain; so named for their position in the highest seats of the assembly on the left), with Jacobins serving as a kind of caucus for the Montagnards and finally expelling Brissot himself from membership. Formerly, Brissot said, "disorganizers were real revolutionaries, for a republican had to be a disorganizer. But today the disorganizers are counterrevolutionaries. They are anarchists and levellers." Popular pressure intensified to dispose of the king, who was seen as a continual rallying point for royalist counterrevolution. A young fanatic, Antoine de Saint-Just, demanded the killing of the king less because he was guilty of crime than because he was the *enemy* and should be executed under the laws of war. Brissotins who urged moderation or delay were attacked as secret royalists. Louis was beheaded on January 21, 1793.

Without a royalist opposition at home, revolutionary leaders moved strongly to the left. Soldiers in the field were instructed to institute reforms wherever they conquered territory abroad—a move that inflamed foreign monarchs who faced protest in their own domains. France declared war on England and Spain; in a few months it would be technically at war with all major foreign nations except the United States and Switzerland (considered to be sister republics). The pace of fanaticism accelerated. Suspecting foreign plots in Paris, the leaders created a revolutionary tribunal with extraordinary prosecutory powers. They ruled that all rebels taken in arms were to be executed within twenty-four hours on the decision of the military; they set up local revolutionary committees and established the Committee of Public Safety, made up of the hardcore leadership of the Revolution. The Convention, the supreme constituent power elected by universal male suffrage, was now accused of tolerating disloyalty; after a commission of twelve had been appointed to investigate plots against it, the Montagnards managed to purge the Convention of some of its moderate leadership and to consolidate their direction of the Revolution. A few weeks later Jean Paul Marat, an early hero of the Revolution and a leader of the Convention purge, was stabbed to death in his health bath by Charlotte Corday.

If Charlotte Corday was acting on her own theory of leadership—that the killing would deter the extremists and encourage the moderates—her act of July 1793 was utterly self-defeating. It helped precipitate the year of the Terror.

Continued bad news from the fronts strengthened the hands of the *enragés*. Continuing pressures from the *sans culottes,* combined with a paranoid reaction to foreign threats, created an atmosphere of fear and hatred. Hoarding was made a capital crime. A new Law of Suspects decreed the immediate arrest of anyone who might be suspected of political disloyalty; eventually 300,000 persons were imprisoned under its provisions. Marie-Antoinette was executed. The tumbrel steadily made its rounds in Paris; in some of the provinces the carnage was still worse. In Lyons, in a horrifying foretoken of mass murder in a later century, victims by the hundreds were forced to stand by open ditches and were fired on by cannon.

Then the revolutionary leadership began to turn on itself. Brissot and a score of his associates were given a rump trial and guillotined. Power shifted back and forth among the Montagnards and in the Convention, claiming victims with every lunge. The Hébertistes on the left were isolated, identified, and guillotined; then the Dantonists on the right. Control moved so rapidly to the extremes that men who once ruled as flaming radicals suddenly found themselves stigmatized as counterrevolutionaries. By July 1794 it was Robespierre's turn and then Saint-Just's. Shortly the Terror was over, its survivors sated; soon after the pendulum was swinging away from revolution and toward reaction.

It is often said that the French Revolution devoured its own children; or that the Revolution was a mighty torrent that first pulled them down to vengeance and terror. Both metaphors suggest that the leaders lost control and became puppets of some impersonal fate or of historical necessity. Viewed more closely, those celebrated and notorious leaders seem not so much victims of fate as agents of popular subleaders who mediated between them and the masses. The revolutionary leaders found their political footings in a number of institutions such as the National Assembly, the Jacobin Society, the Committee of Public Safety, the communes, the Paris sections. All leaders must find such footings, but these foundations usually have some strength, dependability, and durability. In Paris in the 1790s the institutions themselves were under attack and would collapse along with the leaders who occupied them.

The main cause of the extremism was the Paris crowd and its leaders. At virtually every major turn of events in the later years of the Revolution—as in the earlier ones—it was the leader of the *sans culottes* who took the decisive initiatives. It was the leadership of the crowd that repeatedly confronted or invaded the assembly or the Convention; that time and again attacked revolutionary leaders for their failure to deal with food prices and shortages; that had an insatiable appetite for more heads to be held dripping before the spectators; that assembled before the Hotel de Ville and shouted to the *procureur* of the commune, ''We don't want promises—we want bread and we want it now!'';

and that often took the law into its own hands, committing its own massacres when the authorities seemed reluctant. The crowd remained militant because of its *need*. Despite all the promises, the food crisis continued; because of all the promises, the food expectation soared. *Sans culottes* were once again shouting for bread but living on rice that could hardly be cooked for lack of fuel.

Because the revolutionary leaders could not satisfy this need, because they felt guilty and helpless before the populist thrust of the crowd, fearing confrontation and invasions they could not face down, and because men on the left tend to be vulnerable to men on *their* left, the crucible of revolutionary extremism—unrecorded, except in police records—was crowd leadership. And if the revolution seemed to lose its way, it was in part because revolutionary leaders were able to construct neither institutions that could satisfy basic needs nor ideologies that could interrelate the middle-class credo of individual liberty and working-class demands for equality and welfare. M. J. Sydenham concludes that the true tragedy was that "the revolutionaries respected popular authority sincerely but never managed to embody it in any free institutions which could command general support and obedience." The revolutionary impulse had succumbed to a derangement of leadership.

Russia: The Vocation of Leadership

The fifty years before the Russian Revolution comprise perhaps the most remarkable of those periods, few in number, when a group of men and women made a conscious effort to understand the processes of history and to locate the levers of social action. Theirs was a singular academy. Scattered from London to New York to remote provinces of Siberia, hounded by the police, spied on by infiltrators, driven from city to city by the authorities, forced into exile but often escaping and returning, the Marxist revolutionaries conducted a frenetic continental dialogue on the most fundamental questions of social conflict and change. They went to school to one another through fugitive meetings; in their raggedy-thin newspapers they denounced, boycotted, split hairs, and ruptured and repaired relations, all the while arguing the finer points of revolutionary theory with Jesuitical fervor. The purpose of their journalistic organs, Donald Treadgold notes, "was completely serious; every article, every word of every issue was in dead earnest." Collectively they presented a world view, a grand strategy, and a tactical plan.

The intellectual and political leadership of this band of revolutionary thinkers, polemicists, and activists at least rivaled the burst of creative thought of the English theorists of the seventeenth century and the Americans of the eighteenth. There was one central difference. The English and American constitutionalists proposed to curb and stabilize the leadership of popular regimes; the European revolutionaries—above all, Lenin—sought a leadership strategy that could mobilize the masses and direct them into the channels of political action history had decreed.

Intellectually the European revolutionaries drew from, and were constrained by, one of the most powerful doctrines ever to sweep the Western world. Karl Marx's *Das Kapital,* first published in 1867 in German, appeared in Russia five years later in one of its earliest translations. This work was heady drink for intellectuals—Plekhanov, Lenin, Martov, and others of the middle-class intelligentsia—who thirsted for an explanation of history and a theory of economic development that could serve as an invitation to revolution. Marxism became their bible of inspiration, a fount of theory, and a guide to action. Like all bibles, the great book had its ambiguities, and furious controversies broke out concerning the implication of Marxist doctrine for strategies of political leadership—indeed, whether political leadership was necessary at all.

The pivotal question for revolutionaries in Russia was whether Marx, and later Marx and Engels, had provided them not only with a sweeping theory of class conflict but with a strategy of political action, and of political leadership, that flowed directly from the master doctrine. It was clear from Marx that some kind of political movement would emerge out of the working class as the proletariat was pounded by the "modes and means of production" into a solid and weighty mass. "Against the collective power of the propertied classes," Marx and Engels proclaimed, "the working class cannot act as a class except by constituting itself into a political party distinct from, and opposed to, all old parties formed from the propertied classes," and this was "indispensable in order to ensure the triumph of the social revolution, and its ultimate end, the abolition of classes." But what kind of party? A small cadre of middle-class intellectuals? A broad coalition of liberal, left, and revolutionary forces? A party of workers and peasants plus intellectuals? And how would the party be led, if indeed it need be led at all? By rank-and-file workers and peasants? By outside leaders—students, intellectuals, professional revolutionaries? Some combination of these and others? And what would be the nature and extent of that leadership?

On these questions Marx and Engels took a minimal, or at least highly flexible, view of the role of party. They were familiar with the political operations of small leagues and associations, of which they were sometime members, and with the rising mass party, the German Social Democratic Workers party, with the nascent labor party in Britain, the agrarian and labor politics of America, and of course the international federation of workers organizations, the First International of 1864–1872. They believed that a workers' party should have a radical program distinct from those of other parties, but otherwise they did not hold explicit and consistent views about party organization and strategy. They seemed to believe in a moderate degree of party centralization. They preferred a broadly based workers' party, but the coalitional aspect of the party depended to a large degree on the political circumstances, especially the balance of "democratic" and authoritarian control.

Marx and Engels were more concerned about the state of working-class consciousness than that of working-class political organization. To them, as Rossana Rossanda says, revolution was "nothing but the product, simultaneously, of a material situation (the confrontation between classes), its political translation (the crisis of the institutions of power), and the formation of a consciousness." With such consciousness everything was possible; without it, nothing. Through the iron laws of history workers were subjugated, oppressed, alienated from their work, isolated from other classes. Revolutionary consciousness was forged above all in conflict, as class organized against class. But it was not entirely clear in Marx whether consciousness was a kind of natural, internal, objectified growth or a force shaped by deliberate human action.

This ambiguity in turn led to a political question of prime practical importance: Could the proletariat be counted on to generate its own revolutionary organization out of its rising consciousness or must that consciousness be stirred, awakened, quickened, sharpened by leaders outside the proletariat? This was the issue of "spontaneity." Some revolutionary leaders believed it was un-Marxist and undemocratic to seek to hasten a natural and necessary process. Lenin violently disagreed. He advanced a second theory of revolutionary strategy. The history of all countries demonstrated, he said, that the working class left to itself could not develop revolutionary militance on its own but only trade-union consciousness and that the spontaneous development of the working-class movement meant the ideological enslavement of the workers to the bourgeoisie.

These maxims, delivered like hammer blows, were at the heart of Lenin's tract *What Is to Be Done?* Over and over again he returned to his central point: the workers would be diverted by the immediate temptations of reform, trade unionism, bourgeois compromise. Communism would be completely overwhelmed by spontaneity. The result would be the kind of opportunism that brings small reforms instead of transforming social action. This process would simply strengthen the bourgeoisie. "Hence," Lenin said, "our task, the task of Social-Democracy, is to *combat spontaneity,* to *divert* the labour movement, with its spontaneous trade-union striving, from under the wing of the bourgeoisie, and to bring it under the wing of revolutionary Social-Democracy."

What Is to Be Done? was in fact a tract on the theory and practice of political leadership—one of the most influential ever written and one ultimately to be ranked with Machiavelli. Its essential thesis was that the proletariat as a whole must take the lead in the coming revolutionary convulsion. Who would lead the proletariat? Lenin derided those who held that a new social order would come about because of "elemental outbursts" among the masses. "Our grandfathers," Lenin wrote, "in their old-fashioned wisdom used to say: 'Any fool can bring forth children,' and today the 'modern Socialists' . . . in their wisdom say: 'Any fool can help the spontaneous birth of a new social order.' " No, leadership of the revolution was the task of a small, secret, highly organized party led by a disciplined cadre of trained, trusted, and tried revolutionists. It was a question not of the crowd versus leadership but of good leaders versus bad leaders.

This manual on revolutionary leadership evaded many thorny questions—questions about the relationship of revolutionary minded workers with their fellows and with their leaders, about the institutional forms in which leader-follower linkages would be organized, about the nature of the restraints on the party leaders, and about the relation between the manner of seizing state power and of wielding it later. But the tract gained enormous force from its grounding in a comprehensive theory of revolution. The heart of that theory was the role of conflict. The revolutionary working-class element would gain proletarian consciousness not from natural forces but because the leadership demonstrated that the essence of the revolutionary movement was the struggle for power, that class antagonisms were irreconcilable, that there was no middle course between bourgeois power and proletarian power. As a tactical matter Lenin proposed to abjure alliances and coalitions and deliberately narrow the base of the movement in order to make it leaner, harder, more ideological, more revolutionary. Thus his theory of proletarian leadership, built on class conflict, became a theory of political power.

But if Lenin's strategy of leadership was well grounded in a theory of history and social conflict, it was not linked firmly to an understanding of human needs and values. Like virtually all the moderate reform leaders and the social revolutionaries, Lenin was convinced that he knew what the masses wanted—or at least what they needed. Reformers by the turn of the century were still emphasizing the negative goals of liberation from autocracy: civil liberty, voting rights, fair representation. Leninist revolutionaries pounded away on the importance of social and economic freedoms such as improved working conditions, but they were not clear about these ends and how they would be achieved. Lenin's clarity and honesty about his instrumental end of revolution compared with his haziness about ultimate ends—and especially about the relations of his ends and means—would haunt the Leninist party for decades to come.

History dilates and dramatizes and canonizes the feats of political thinkers and leaders who later win power; history acknowledges the roles of the winners' lieutenants and the winners' main adversaries; history neglects the subsidiary forces, important though they may have been—the myriad groupings that structure political conflict, the sporadic movements, the third and fourth and fifth parties. Lenin's main adversaries, at least in the contest over the authoritative rendition of Marxist theory, were those Social Democrats who for both practical and theoretical reasons opposed his political leadership and strategy. Some twenty Marxist groups had joined in 1895 under the leadership of Lenin, Martov, and others in the Fighting Union for the Liberation of the Working Classes; three years later a few delegates, barely escaping the police net, formed the Russian Social Democratic Workers party, with a constitution, a parliament elected by universal franchise, and freedom of speech and press as their immediate ends and socialist ownership of the means of production, including land, as their ultimate goal. In calling for such specific goals as the eight-hour day and agrarian reform and for such apocalyptic ones as the crushing of capitalism and rule by the proletariat, the conference exhibited the combination of practical appeal and theoretical ambiguity that characterized many Russian revolutionaries. Lenin was not present at the founding conference (he had been exiled in 1895), but he followed the proceedings closely and soon engaged in disputation with the founders over questions both petty and ideological.

All the teeming conflicts within the Marxist revolutionary movement in Russia seemed to erupt in 1903 during the Second Party Congress, which began in Brussels but, after bouts with fleas and the Belgian police, moved to London. Among the approximately fifty delegates only four were "real" workers. Lenin was very much there on this occasion and played a leading role in dividing the meeting over doctrine and strategy. The "unity" conference broke up after ferocious wrangling and left the party divided into two wings: the Bolsheviks, so named because they won a close majority during the voting, and the Mensheviks, or minority. The immediate issue was the control of *Iskra,* the party journal-in-exile, which Lenin wanted to take over; the basic issue was revolutionary strategy. The Mensheviks generally believed that, in conformity with the Marxist stages of history, the autocracy must be superseded by a bourgeois regime, followed by a "significant interval of time," after which the real revolution, the social revolution, could take place. Mensheviks did not fear this "interval." It would be a time of bourgeois reform and civil liberty, a time when the workers could grow stronger in number and in power. Lenin flatly disagreed. The social revolution could come about only as a result of armed revolution and insurrectionary military action, he believed, not through cooperation with trade unions and liberals.

Amidst all the doctrinal ambiguity and infighting the question came down to one of leadership, of activism, of giving history a shove. To Lenin the paramount issue was that "the outcome of the revolution depends on whether the working class will play the part of a subsidiary to the bourgeoisie, a subsidiary that is powerful in the force of its onslaught against Autocracy but important politically, or whether it will play the part of leader of the people's revolution." The Mensheviks, he said scornfully, "march with a will, but lead badly."

Other groups threatened to take the leadership. Somewhere to the left of the divided Social Democrats were the Social Revolutionaries, also founded at the turn of the century by a gathering of factions. Contrary to orthodox Marxist doctrine, Social Revolutionary leaders proposed to move immediately to socialism on the fall of the autocracy. They adhered to a vaguely populist doctrine that called for a program of communal ownership by the peasants (who would take a central role in the revolution) and that decried Marxist "state socialism" as no better than the existing "state capitalism." Believing also in terror as a tactic, the Social Revolutionaries sponsored a series of spectacular assassinations and armed robberies, or "expropriations." Somewhere to the right were the liberal leaders, heir to the great reformist tradition of nineteenth-century Russia. During the ferment of the 1890s the liberals had turned away from their devotion to practical needs and toward more radical, long-run goals under the leadership of P. N. Miliukov. This eminent professor of history, educated in Western ideas and influenced by rationalist thinkers such as Kant, Locke, Hume, and Marx, had moved so strongly to the left that thrice he was imprisoned by the czarist government. He sought coalition with other liberal and leftist forces, but he could not carry the liberal movement, freighted as it was with a narrow political reformism, beyond its absorption with immediate improvements or toward action for fundamental social and economic change. Lenin scorned the liberals—indeed hated them, as being incorrigibly bourgeois. Never, he said, would liberals jump the track of their class and property interests. They wanted both the czar and freedom; they could not have both. He would not accept their political aid. Perhaps Lenin feared the liberals as possible competitors for leadership of the working class—a role they had assumed in Western nations—but he seemed almost as hostile to economists and other moderate elements.

All these and other forces and personalities came into collision in 1905.

War had broken out with Japan the previous year; the Russians were decisively beaten in a series of land battles and were humiliated when a large fleet of the imperial navy, after majestically steaming halfway around the world, was demolished in a few hours in the Straits of Tsushima. Once again czardom had failed in its most elemental and sacred duty; once again political turmoil was precipitated not by the wrangling revolutionaries but by national defeat and mortification. On a Sunday in 1905 an orderly crowd of workers, bearing both petitions for the czar and portraits of him, were met by bullets from the czar's guards. Following Bloody Sunday, liberal, labor, and revolutionary groups burst into new agitation. While the regime moved with elephantine slowness to head off protest, liberals called for a constituent assembly, peasant organizations met and protested, *zemstvos* leaders demanded sweeping political reforms, and strikes erupted in industrial areas. A Social Revolutionary assassinated the czar's uncle.

Lenin, in exile as usual, showered the Social Democrats with advice. Belatedly he made his way back to Russia, where he spent frustrating months hounded and nearly isolated by the police. If, as Lenin said later, 1905 was a "great rehearsal," the Bolshevik leader had only a small role on the revolutionary stage; indeed, he returned only after most of the major events had taken place. Still distrusting "spontaneity," he hardly knew how to deal with the unexpected fruit of the revolution—the soviets that sprang up in St. Petersburg and elsewhere mainly under Menshevik influence. The Bolsheviks had a part, but not a leading one, in uprisings toward the end of 1905; these were crushed, and Lenin, rejecting Social Democratic repudiation of terrorism, advised his followers to stage hit-and-run attacks and "expropriations" against banks and government offices. Lenin hated or distrusted the forces behind the revolution: the Kadets, who were weak and cowardly but also won elections; the terrorists; the intelligentsia; the Mensheviks, who were behind the soviets; even the workers and their spontaneity. More and more his hopes turned to the peasants and their revolutionary potential.

After 1905 the stage seemed set in Russia for an epochal struggle between reform and revolutionary leadership. In October 1905 the czar had issued a manifesto converting Russia into a constitutional monarchy. The liberal leader Miliukov greeted the czar's manifesto, with its guarantee of political and civil liberty, as both a great victory and a new stage in the struggle. The 1905 revolution had jolted Nicholas and hardly fortified his faith, small at best, in the possibilities of a constitutional democracy.

Some historians have concluded that it was not a fair contest, that the reform leaders never had the time and the political resources necessary for the generating of steady social change. The country lacked the infrastructure for a liberal reforming regime. The *zemstvos* had not developed into effective parliamentary institutions. An array of parties had emerged from the turn-of-the-century political upheavals, but they were badly organized and led. The wooden bureaucracy of the old regime rumbled along, hardly affected by the turmoil. Most Russians were still illiterate; few had practice in the contrivances and contrarieties of self-government. The liberals, according to Michael T. Florinsky, "had still to learn the subtle art of compromise essential to the successful working of the complex mechanics of representative government." Revolutionaries felt no such need. A young firebrand named Trotsky, who had emerged as a brilliant leader of St. Petersburg radicals, summed up 1905: *La révolution est morte, vive la révolution.*

The prospects of liberal reform in a constitutional monarchy did not seem so bleak to contemporaries. The natives had been undergoing, at forced draft, many of the socio-economic changes that had underlain the liberal constitution-building of other societies—industrial mobilization, urbanization, a growing middle class, a vigorous press, trade unionism, social diversification. Able leaders were still emerging from centers of theoretical and practical liberalism. The new parties and their leaders seemed promising, if untutored. When a real parliament, composed of the State Duma as the lower, "popular" chamber and the State Council as the higher, was established by a manifesto of February 1906, it was clear that the czar had made real if grudging concessions to democracy. The electoral arrangements of the lower house, to be sure, would underrepresent the masses (especially city dwellers and industrial workers) while the czar retained an absolute veto over legislation. But this did not unduly discourage reform leaders. Most liberal regimes had started with gross underrepresentation of the people. After all, the "Queen of Parliaments," in London, still comprised in 1905 a strong House of Lords and a House of Commons that underrepresented the lower orders, and it was exposed to significant influence from the throne. In Russia the growth of constitutional democracy, with all its implications for restricted and stabilized leadership, depended on whether the revolutionary changes of 1905–1906 were the prelude to continuous liberalization and democratization of governmental processes in the years ahead.

Most revolutionary leaders had no doubt on this score. To them the bourgeois phase was but one stage that history had to pass through before the objective conditions of social revolution could come into play. Some Social Revolutionary leaders proposed to leap over the capitalistic phase and advance at once toward the socialist, via revolution. Lenin rebutted this strategy. To claim that Russia could skip the period of capitalist development was sheer nonsense, he said. The Social Revolutionaries failed to understand that "even the redistribution of all the land available in accordance with the peasants' wishes will not in the least contribute to the destruction of capitalism, but, on the contrary, will only stimulate the development of capitalism and will accelerate the process of class cleavage among the peasants themselves.'' For Lenin and the other revolutionaries the need of a capitalist phase poised the poignant question: would revolution come in their time?

The broader, the more decisive and consistent the bourgeois revolution, Lenin said, the more certain the struggle of the proletariat against the bourgeoisie. The bourgeois revolution in Russia hardly appeared decisive or consistent although its early months did seem auspicious. Witte, the czar's reluctant choice for president of the new council of ministers, purged the bureaucracy of some conservatives—notably the formidable Pobedonostšev—and made a genuine effort to broaden the cabinet to include liberal and *zemstvos* organizations. Duma elections, duly held, resulted in a sweeping victory for the Constitutional Democratic party and a labor coalition. Not a single outright conservative was elected, and the large peasant contingent turned out to be unexpectedly radical. The Duma proceeded immediately to demand the classic political reforms that Russian liberals had been urging for decades: universal suffrage, direct vote, parliamentary supremacy, land reform.

The mild swing to the left, however, proved too much for the czar's vulnerabilities and for the embryonic institutions of liberal government. Witte, attacked from all directions, quit and was succeeded by a bureaucratic lackey to the Crown. The czar rejected liberal leaders' demands for political reforms. Conflicts in bewildering variety broke out in a chamber representing a broad range of splinter parties, many of them intransigent, and within ten weeks the first Duma was dissolved. When two hundred left-wing deputies urged passive obstruction to the government by tax and draft resistance, they were arrested, convicted, and jailed, thereby inaugurating a decade of repression. Later Dumas, elected by a restricted vote, were increasingly conservative. Many Social Revolutionary leaders fled the country, and the Social Democrats, with most of their leaders in exile or underground, dissolved into small groups.

If the liberal reform leadership of Russia did not distinguish itself during this period, neither did the revolutionary. Both the Social Revolutionaries and the Social Democrats boycotted the 1906 election, thereby helping in the Constitutional Democratic party victory. Both revolutionary parties reversed their tactic in the 1907 election of the second Duma, returning 65 Social Democrats and 34 Social Revolutionaries. Lenin, as implacable as ever in his hatred for liberal reformers, led the revolutionaries in concentrating attacks on the Constitutional Democrats. As a result of this bombardment from the left, financial and other support from the Crown for ultrarightists, and a strong conservative trend in public opinion, the number of Kadets in the new Duma was halved. Undermining the liberal leadership was fundamental to Lenin's strategy, but the revolutionary leaders did not gain as the liberals declined. Fratricidal quarrels erupted in Lenin's party as the dreary years of pursuit and exile continued. Lenin was attacked for his dogmatic and dictatorial ways; even the small band of Bolsheviks was infested by police spies; and czardom seemed to be winning a new lease on power as the liberal and left opposition faltered.

Only a more general convulsion, not internal revolution, seemed likely to overturn the regime. That convulsion began in 1914. Lenin was on vacation when war broke out; he had had no warning that world conflict was imminent. For years he had expected a climactic war among the capitalistic nations; for years, too, he had expected that good socialists in all lands would transcend their chauvinistic instincts and join hands across flaming borders to organize against imperialistic war. He could not believe the reports that came to him— good socialists in the German Reichstag and in other parliaments voting to support the war! This outbreak of radical patriotism left Lenin more isolated than ever. By now he was a despised and discredited figure in most socialist circles. He had lost good friends and allies; in 1914 he was close to being censured by the international socialist movement. In retrospect, however, Adam Ulam observes, "his very isolation in those years and the virulence of attacks upon him were to become the main reasons for his greatness in 1917. There was then nobody to share with him the leadership of the extremist course. The legendary trouble-maker and dogmatist became the only man to suit the violent and impatient mood of the last stage of the Revolution." The trials of the prewar and war years provided him with the final edge of titanic self-assurance that enabled him to lead and command the strong-minded men around him.

Lenin was still in exile in Zurich when, to his enormous excitement, news came in the early weeks of 1917 of strikes and disorder sweeping Russia and then of the czar's abdication. The old regime had simply collapsed. At first Lenin misperceived the situation; he thought that the Revolution was the work of the French and English embassies, and then, not knowing the extent of the cataclysm, he feared that the czar would launch a counterrevolution and regain power. He burned with eagerness to return, and in a brilliant feat of political warfare on the part of the Germans, he was given the famous "sealed train" so that he could bring his "pacifist" ideas and his revolutionary zeal back into the homeland of the kaiser's disintegrating enemy. Lenin returned to a capital that was in tumult and division yet was heady with freedom. Parties, cliques, and sects seemed hopelessly divided among and within themselves. In the teeth of adversaries and skeptics Lenin flung out his "April theses"—perhaps the most striking act of leadership of his entire career. He made no concessions to liberals, Mensheviks, or Social Revolutionaries. The attack on the provisional government must be intensified. Most important, the party must change its name to "Communist," immediately begin confiscating estates and distributing land to the peasants, and set up a new *Internationale* that would exclude Mensheviks and moderates. The theses came as a bombshell. Was Lenin repudiating Marxism and demanding an immediate *socialist* revolution?

The April theses were the first move—perhaps the most decisive move—in a resolute assumption of revolutionary leadership on Lenin's part. His primacy in the party councils was not assured; many rivals were coming to the top in the flux of revolution. Every day brought new crises, intractable problems, practical choices—and no decision could be made without endless oratory over Marxist doctrine. Lenin's tactics changed from day to day. Most of the time he was preparing and prodding his followers toward direct action against the provisional government. At other times—especially during July, when a "spontaneous" eruption of workers and soldiers threatened to force the pace unduly—Lenin had to restrain revolutionary tendencies. Accused of having taken "German gold" as well as free transportation from the kaiser, he was in hiding during most of this period; communication was poor; fundamental policy differences divided Lenin from many of his associates. His old associates and rivals, Zinoviev and Kamenev, insisted that to move ahead directly to revolutionary action would be premature and suicidal. Even with Trotsky, who generally was his closest supporter, Lenin had his differences. "Lenin concentrated exclusively on the end to be attained," Isaac Deutscher notes. "Trotsky paid more regard to its political context, to the moods of the masses, and to the need to win over the hesitant elements, who might respond to the Soviet's but not to the party's call."

Fall 1917. The Kerensky government, in warding off a military threat, had allowed the Red Guards to rearm and their chiefs to be freed. In September the Bolsheviks gained a majority in the Petrograd soviet and shortly afterwards in the Moscow. In October Lenin, still pressing for action and fearful that moderate elements would thwart him, created a military revolutionary committee to prepare an armed uprising. The left Social Revolutionaries, led by an eighteen-year-old youth, were allied with the Bolsheviks. Lenin, more impatient than ever, pressed for action in the face of pleas for delay on the part of his closest associates. But it seemed, as Ulam has noted, that some of the Bolsheviks Lenin prodded "felt almost fatalistically that they *had* to risk everything rather than to repudiate their leader." Events came to a sudden climax; the provisional government was so impotent, the political void so wide, that the Bolsheviks with hardly more than an armed rabble, and despite blunders and mishaps, were able to take over the government. Within hours Lenin was writing the first Bolshevik decrees—on peace and on land.

The judgment of history, which favors winners over losers, is that Lenin demonstrated masterly leadership in 1917. The explanations of this success vary. Was it his command of Marxist revolutionary theory? While such doctrine, in its prediction of capitalist breakdown and proletarian triumph, was a general source of reassurance and broad direction for Lenin, he showed, for a theorist, a remarkable capacity to flout doctrine in the face of concrete difficulties. At one time he seemed almost to embrace anarchism, at another time, terrorism—both anathema to the true word. He seemed to change his attitude repeatedly on the old and classic question of the two stages of revolution. He talked the Marxist language of a broad working-class coalition for revolution but moved far in advance of proletarian opinion.

Others have attributed Lenin's success to his iron self-discipline, aura of command, and absolute self-confidence. Lenin often acted among his associates and followers like a benevolently authoritarian father; he was psychologically, according to Victor Wolfenstein, filling a father's role. "Consciously Lenin may not have aspired to be the leader of Russian Social Democracy, but unconsciously he could not bear to be anything but the leader," Wolfenstein says. Relations with peers are enormously difficult for the person aspiring to supreme leadership. "But when he is the leader himself, when he can act as a father to his revolutionary children, the gratifications outweigh the strains. . . ." He becomes a leader "who is powerful and righteous, whom the 'children' love, fear, and respect. . . ." The leader manages his ambivalent feelings toward followers by impersonalization, that is, by setting up objective rules and procedures and by maintaining centralized control over his followers, often through a disciplined party. Lenin used both these devices.

Political factors were perhaps more significant than ideological or psychological factors. One of these was Lenin's perception of the real needs of the Russian masses, especially the peasants. At a time when liberal reformers were demanding civil liberties and political rights for the people, the Bolshevik leader recognized that most peasants and workers wanted the kind of economic improvement and social change that, in the Communist view, was the indispensable foundation of authentic freedom. At a time (during the spring and summer months of 1917) when the "bourgeois" government assumed that the old patriotic instincts (or at least those of self-defense) of the Russian peasant, worker, and soldier were behind the war, Lenin saw that the protest increasingly was not against the faulty prosecution of the war, as many liberals felt, *but against the war itself*. Bolshevik promises of bread, land, and peace, proclaimed from thousands of platforms, tracts, and banners, went straight to the heart of the human needs of Russia.

Equally important in Lenin's strategy of leadership was a theory of conflict that helped him to draw the political battle lines in a manner appropriate to the revolutionary situation. While the liberal reformer was ever intent on widening his group or party coalition so that moderates, liberals, and leftists could outnumber the opposition in elections and assemblies, Lenin usually spurned such bargaining and brokerage.

Part of the reason was temperamental; even more it lay in Lenin's conscious decision to build a small, selective party vanguard that would more than make up in discipline and élan for the flabby majorities of brokering parliamentarians. He believed that revolutionary strategy called for re-establishing the lines of conflict so that the *intensity* of loyal support would be increased even though—and because—the *breadth* of the support was narrowed. Contemporaries of Lenin marveled, even as historians have, at his willingness and indeed insistence on rejecting support when he seemed desperately in need of it. On the eve of the October Revolution, when other leaders were ready to join the Bolsheviks if only out of opportunism, Lenin was losing some of his close associates and making little effort to win moderate support.

Both Lenin's perception of need and his sharpening of conflict were linked with the *values* he embraced. As a disciple of Marxist socialism he was also a son of the Enlightenment. Although his concept of freedom owed much to the doctrine of liberty, equality, and fraternity that had inspired earlier revolutions, there always seemed to be some question whether these ultimate values predominated over the instrumental value of revolution by itself. What finally distinguished Lenin from others was not his set of ultimate values—many other leaders shared them—but his consecration to the *vocation of revolutionary leadership*. He refused to subordinate the means of achieving the revolution to the kind of freedom the revolution was supposed to achieve. Not only did he make concessions to peasant land hunger that contradicted the collectivist doctrine fundamental to socialism, but his means of achieving power (and later of holding it) violated those individual liberties and political freedoms that were supposed to be part of the Communist value system. Thus there developed between Lenin's ultimate and proximate ends a distortion that would have fateful impact on the nature of the Soviet regime.

That price would be paid later. In 1917 Lenin was a professional among professionals. His fashioning of the party as vanguard was deliberate and principled. On the very eve of the uprising he was analyzing and teaching revolutionary method: "Never *play* with an uprising, but once it has begun, be firm in the knowledge that you have *to carry it through to the end*. . . . Once the uprising has begun, one must act with the utmost *decisiveness* . . . and go over *to the offensive*. . . . One must strive *daily* for at least small victories . . . in order to maintain at all costs *moral superiority*." He had taught the vocation of leadership in a school for revolutionaries in France, in countless letters and tracts, and before party committees and conferences. Now he embodied it.

He was, in Archilochus's (and Isaiah Berlin's) term, both a fox who "knows many things" and a hedgehog who "knows one big thing." In his foxlike, shifting tactics he was often no more impressive than many of the other leaders of the day; he made his share of mistakes and miscalculations. It was in the big thing he knew, the one big thing he preached and fought and dared mightily for, that he showed the wisdom of the hedgehog. This was that in Russia the masses wanted a kind of economic and social freedom, as he defined it, that neither czarist reformers nor liberal constitutionalists could ever supply. But his dedication to revolution gripped him far more than his devotion to freedom. He was a theorist, but a theorist of logistics and means, not of intrinsic values and ends. Thus the instrumental means of conflict and control of conflict became an ultimate end dominating all others. The probability that this kind of means could pervert the end of freedom by becoming the end itself was the one big thing that Lenin did not know.

China: The Cult of Leadership

The distinguishing characteristic of Chinese Communism, John W. Lewis wrote, is the leadership doctrine by which the party elite rules China. That doctrine has been dismissed by those who see Communist leadership in China as a simple process of bullying the masses into submission or brainwashing them into adulation. In fact revolutionary leadership in China has been remarkably effective in practice and surprisingly anomalous in its theoretical underpinnings. Effective in practice because the leadership has welded seven hundred million persons into a solidarity unmatched at least since the high noon of imperial rule; anomalous because the leadership has continued to celebrate Marxism while violating its most fundamental precepts concerning the nature of revolutionary action, because the Chinese Communists have developed the most elaborate theories of struggle and conflict—far more sophisticated than Marx's theories—even while they glorified harmony, and because men who genuinely shunned careerism and opportunism ended up as masters of one quarter of the people of the globe.

The vital nexus between the very European-oriented Marx and the embattled leaders of peasants in the Chinese hinterland was Lenin. During World War I he had found time to write a small tract, *Imperialism, The Highest Stage of Capitalism*—neither a very original nor a profound book, but one brilliantly timed to appeal to colonial peoples drawn into the world economic orbit by the war and experiencing rising nationalistic feelings of their own. As usual, Lenin argued from Marxist premises: "The more capitalism, the more the need of raw materials is felt. . . . The more feverishly the hunt for raw materials proceeds throughout the whole world, the more desperate becomes the struggle for the acquisition of colonies." The flag followed investment and Great Power wars followed the flag. The masses in the colonial countries were perforce the comrades of the workers of the West; all must join to overthrow rule by the international class of bourgeois.

This was heady doctrine for aspiring nationalists and revolutionaries. At the end of World War I China seemed to be the traumatized giant of Asia. The nation had undergone two decades of abortive reform and revolution not wholly unlike the experience of European nations. Ten years before Russia, China too had been humiliated by Japanese arms. Two thousand years of imperial rule were threatened by military defeat, penetration by Japan and other nations, and the slow spread of technology and liberal ideas from the West. The Manchu regime had been jarred into sporadic attempts at reform in education, the civil service, and the opium trade; Confucius, it was contended, had himself been something of a reformer. A constitution was even adopted in 1908, but it seemed to confirm the emperor's authority rather than curb it. These and other reform efforts failed largely because, in Fred Greene's words, the "Chinese government lacked the vigorous and farsighted leadership required to control the country, minimize violence, and institute the changes deemed necessary." There was an experiment with provincial assemblies that somewhat resembled the Russia *zemstvos*—and had about as much long-run success.

A leadership that plays with reform without pressing it and controlling it arouses expectations and unleashes forces that further unsettle the foundations of the regime. In one three-year period, seven major efforts were made to overthrow the Manchu regime by military force. Unable to gain major political reforms under imperial rule, Chinese reformers at home and overseas were drawn increasingly to the prospect of overthrowing the emperor. One of the most prominent of these reform leaders was Sun Yat-sen. Born near Macao and Canton in 1866, the son of an impoverished jack-of-all-trades, Sun was educated and indoctrinated into Christianity in a British mission school in Hawaii; later he trained as a doctor in British Hong Kong and practiced medicine in Portuguese Macao, becoming active politically at the same time. When an insurrection broke out in the Hankow area late in 1911 and spread rapidly through southern China, Sun was abroad; he returned home to help lead the uprising. The old regime, headed by the six-year-old boy emperor, simply collapsed. At the beginning of 1912 Sun took office in Nanking as provisional president of the new republic.

The way now seemed open for the Westernized, liberal leadership of

China to carry through the economic, social, and political reforms that had been dammed up by the Manchus. Leader of the strongest party in the new legislature, the Kuomintang, Sun was widely regarded as the intellectual and inspirational leader of the reform and revolutionary forces. But Sun, lacking the organizing talents that Lenin was to demonstrate after 1917, seemed unable to exert control in the volatile, turbulent, and diffused politics of his huge country. Rival leaders both at the center and in the provinces harried Sun, and he soon yielded his provisional office to a rival. There followed years of rampant warlordism, conflict between the southern and northern parts of the country, diplomatic and economic intervention from abroad, rival governments in the various "capitals," government disintegration, and deepening misery for the peasantry. Repeatedly Sun was forced to flee for his safety. Although his prestige remained high, he could not extend revolutionary influence much beyond the Canton government, of which he became president in 1921. He turned to the United States and other Western nations for diplomatic and financial help, but in vain. Then he turned to the new Bolshevik regime in Russia—and it responded.

There ensued one of the most remarkable leadership coalitions in political history. The Soviet had reasons of realpolitik to ally with the Kuomintang because it needed a stable regime to the east as it faced the Western counter-revolutionary thrusts of the early twenties. It had even better ideological reasons because under Marxist doctrine China, not having passed through the phase of bourgeois-democratic revolution, was not ready for Communism. Moscow was happy to assist in this task. The extraordinary factor was not the familiar strategy of international Communism but the lengths to which the Russians went in order to maintain their alliance with the Chinese Nationalists. Soviet advisers (notably the fabled Michael Borodin) counseled the disorganized Kuomintang on party structure, propaganda techniques, military organization, and centralized government. And—far more awkward and complicated—the Communists in Moscow had to hold in check their own comrades, the Communist party of China. That party had been founded in 1921 by a small group of men who had arisen out of the explosive nationalism of the post-World War I years and the disenchantment with the Kuomintang. Its early leaders, notably Li Ta-chao and Ch'en Tu-hsiu, both professors at Peking University, had been educated in the Western intellectual tradition and had only recently been exposed to Marxist teachings. Discussions of the powerful doctrine first centered in Marxist-Leninist study groups at the University of Peking; then Ch'en stimulated activity in other cities through his ex-students. Advised and encouraged by Russian agents, twelve Chinese Marxists held the first congress of the Chinese Communist party in Shanghai in July 1921.

Several years of confusion and frustration followed. Ch'en, head of the party, agreed with Moscow that the Chinese proletariat was too undeveloped for revolutionary action. But what was the Communist party to do while the Kremlin's agents were devoting themselves to modernizing and indoctrinating the Kuomintang? The Chinese Communists were themselves divided between those who favored an independent course and those who wished to work within the Kuomintang in order to strengthen its left wing. There was little chance of changing Moscow's line, for grand strategy in China had become entangled in the intensifying rivalry between Stalin and Trotsky.

At first the Bolshevik leaders had been in broad agreement that, by standard Marxist-Leninist theory, Communists could support nationalistic movements that were seeking to overthrow *ancien régimes*. It was hoped that after the Kuomintang had seized control of more and more of China, the left-wing forces in the Kuomintang and eventually the Chinese Communists would shove the Nationalists aside and assume power. The Nationalists, Stalin said, "have to be utilized to the end, squeezed out like a lemon, and then thrown away," and Bukharin even envisaged that Canton, the capital of revolutionary China, might become "a kind of 'Red Moscow' for the awakening masses of the Asiatic colonies." The Kremlin's tactics, Ulam notes, foresaw an eventual October Revolution for China, but the difficulty with this scheme was that Chiang Kai-shek had read about the Russian Revolution and was determined to be a *successful* Kornilov. And for a time he was. Rivals of Stalin feared that the Kuomintang would double-cross the Kremlin first, though Trotsky himself was slow in expressing doubts about the policy. The Chinese Communists were remarkably submissive to Bolshevik strategic direction, but they were apprehensive. The Chinese party feared that the death of Sun Yat-sen in 1925 and the rising influence of Chiang in the Kuomintang portended a swing toward the right. And the Nationalists for their part had little confidence in the steadfastness of their allies on the left.

The unstable equilibrium collapsed in 1926. In the summer the Nationalists under Chiang launched a major offensive toward the north from Canton to seize the valley of the Yangtze and its great cities of Hankow, Nanking, and Shanghai. The left wing of the Kuomintang with its Communist allies had gained control of Hankow and the whole Wuhan area several hundred miles up the river from Nanking and had developed extensive support among peasants and unionized workers. When the Hankow leaders challenged Chiang for control of the Nationalist movement, Chiang, after taking Nanking and Shanghai in March 1927, turned on his old left-wing allies. Ordered by Moscow to put up no resistance, the Communists in Shanghai were easy game. Many of their leaders were executed. Faced with ambiguous instructions from Moscow,

Borodin and other Russian advisers quit the Hankow regime. The Communists launched a series of unsuccessful attacks in the Chinese hinterland. Chiang remained in command of a victorious, reunified Kuomintang; the Chinese Communists were left in disarray and defeat.

In fact the Kuomintang was losing in its success and the Communists winning in their failure. With the ties with the Kuomintang broken, new leaders could come to the fore. One of these was Mao Tse-tung. Mao was born in 1893 in Hunan province, the son of a poor peasant who was in the process of raising himself, through trading in grain, to the status of a rich peasant. His mother was illiterate and a devout Buddhist, in which faith the boy was raised. From an early age Mao came into frequent conflict with his father—over what fundamental issue is not clear. That conflict led to speculation later that Mao's revolutionary activities had their origin in his hostility to his father. An equally plausible explanation is that he was caught in an ambiguous class position because of his father's rising status—or that he had to work on the land part-time from the age of six and full-time from the age of thirteen. At sixteen, defying his father, he left home to attend primary school. He managed to continue his education and his reading of Western classics and Chinese tales of heroism, winning a diploma from the normal school in Changsha.

Mao traveled to Peking in the fall of 1918 to work at the university. Thus began one of the decisive periods in Mao's intellectual development. In Peking he was exposed to the ideas of professors Li and Ch'en, Communist party leaders, and other radical intellectuals and to the intense nationalism of the students. In Peking Mao's status was lowly, for he was merely a librarian's assistant under Li and he shared a room with eight other Hunan students. It is said that when he tried to ask a question of Hu Shih, that eminent philosopher of pragmatism would not deign to answer a mere library assistant. Mao joined student societies and Marxist study groups and soon was caught up in the revolutionary ferment of the university city. By 1920 he was a committed Marxist.

But what kind of Marxist? Chinese revolutionaries, even more acutely than Russian revolutionaries, faced the formidable task of applying Marxist theory to a "backward" agrarian and colonial nation at a time when the urban proletariat in that nation was neither large in number nor wholly revolutionary in mood. As in Russia, an enormous amount of energy was spent on debating the role of bourgeois, proletariat, and peasantry, and especially the interrelations of their leaderships, in the mammoth task of the social transformation of China. Here again Lenin served as the vital nexus, for he was the theoretical opportunist, changing his views on the question of "stages" and "classes" but always insisting on the need for revolutionary leadership and disciplined organization. In this respect Mao was a super-Leninist. During the early 1920s

Mao's revolutionary doctrine was unformed as his boundless energy and revolutionary commitment brought him increasing influence in Communist circles; certainly he had little difficulty in following Moscow's line of cooperation with the Kuomintang.

In 1924 Mao returned to Hunan province largely for reasons of health, both bodily and political. This was a second major step in his rise as revolutionary leader. He had unhappy memories of peasant life in his own village, and he still looked on the peasantry as more a source of revolutionary support than of revolutionary leadership. To his surprise he discovered that the peasants of Hunan were aroused over foreign slights to China and their own rural grievances. Mao's famous "Report of an Investigation into the Peasant Movement in Hunan" reflected his excitement over the newfound militance of the peasants. "In a very short time," he wrote, "several hundred million peasants in China's central, southern, and northern provinces will rise like a tornado or tempest—a force so extraordinarily swift and violent that no power, however great, will be able to suppress it. They will break through all the trammels that now bind them and push forward along the road to liberation. They will send all imperialists, warlords, corrupt officials, local bullies, and evil gentry to their graves. All revolutionary parties and all revolutionary comrades will stand before them to be tested, to be accepted or rejected by them. To march at their head and lead them? To follow in the rear, gesticulating at them and criticizing them? To face them as opponents? Every Chinese is free to choose among the three." The peasants, Mao argued, not only could organize and exercise revolutionary leadership; they *had* done so. Had the peasants committed excesses? Well, a "revolution is not the same as inviting people to dinner or writing an essay or painting a picture or embroidering a flower." Mao rejected the Confucian virtues of manners (a Western modal value). A revolution was a revolution, an act of violence whereby one class shatters the authority of another.

The peasants as vanguard of the revolution—certainly this was a departure from Marxist orthodoxy. Mao made clear that proletarian action also was necessary to revolution, but his own commitment had been made. The "very short time" before the promised peasant revolt stretched into years of defeat and frustration. Following Chiang's onslaught on the Communists in 1927 and Stalin's demand for revolutionary military action, Mao directed the Autumn Harvest uprisings in Hunan. When these collapsed he was blamed, ousted from his leadership position, and driven out of Hunan.

Mao and his close associate Chu Teh journeyed to the east and found safety in the isolated mountain area of Kiangsi. Here Mao, with Chu Teh as his military commander, was able to rehearse techniques of party leadership, propaganda, self-criticism, and peasant mobilization that he would later apply to much wider arenas. The rehearsal was to be short, for Chiang, leader of the victorious Kuomintang, now began a series of "extermination campaigns" against the Communists. Mao's Red Army evaded the Nationalist effort at encirclement; a ragged body of 120,000 men and women began the fabled Long March to Shenshi Province and safety. By the end of the march the army was reduced to about 10,000 soldiers—and Mao had won wide recognition as the unchallengeable leader of Chinese Communism.

In Shenshi Province Mao established the political base for his ultimate bid for the revolutionary capture of power, and it was there that he demonstrated his capacity to follow flexible tactics in consolidating as well as gaining power. Orthodox Marxist doctrine called for socialization of land and the collective management of agriculture, but Mao developed a program of progressive taxation and land reform instead. That doctrine condemned "adventurism," but Mao benefited from, if he did not concur in, the famous (and temporary) kidnapping of Chiang Kai-shek in Sian. That doctrine called for the urban proletariat to serve as the vanguard of revolution, but Mao built his movement squarely on the peasantry. Orthodox doctrine denied that bourgeois, peasants, and proletariat could jointly effect fundamental transformation, but the Yenan Communists established a united-front strategy of unity among those classes. To be sure, the posture of the Communists on a united front was crucially influenced by the Japanese aggression of the 1930s, but as a doctrinal matter the Communists did not need to take the highly patriotic and nationalistic position that they did assume. And the party under Mao's leadership followed such a moderate policy toward land-owning peasants, landlords, and business interests generally that not only some Americans but many Chinese concluded that the Communists were essentially "agrarian reformers."

The stupendous events of the 1930s and 1940s—the widening Japanese aggression; the American and British wartime alliance with Nationalist China following Pearl Harbor; the faltering defense against the Japanese, with both Nationalists and Communists conserving their forces for the postwar showdown; belated and almost poignant efforts by the Kuomintang to institute political reforms; abortive American attempts to head off Chinese civil war; the all-out effort of Chiang against the Communists and his early successes in 1947; then the Communist counteroffensive, the rallying of the peasants, the pinching off of Nationalist-controlled cities, and finally the capture of the cities by the revolutionaries—these events largely played into Mao's hands much as the cataclysmic events of World War I had helped produce the Bolshevik capture of power. The Chinese Communists quickly consolidated their control over the country, except for Formosa. The People's Republic of China was proclaimed on October 1, 1949. Mao continued to exhibit the political pragmatism that had characterized his seizing and wielding of power. But if pragmatism alone had been the key, rivals might have replaced him; his leadership was rooted in more solid ground.

Mao's decisive move, both for the success of Chinese Communism and for his own leadership, was his rejection of important criteria of Marxist orthodoxy and his turning to the peasants as the motive force for revolution. The idea was hardly original with him; other Chinese politicians, Communist and non-Communist, had been "going to the country" for millennia. And, after all, Marx was the product of an essentially urban culture; China was essentially rural. Mao was brilliantly successful not merely because of his skills as propagandist and organizer but because he was far more attuned than were his rivals to the *needs* of the "agrarian masses." With a class status somewhat above that of the peasant, he had labored in the fields as a boy, and the combination of this experience and revolutionary doctrine made it easier for him later to go to the peasantry. He studied the peasants in a conscious effort to analyze their discontent and their revolutionary potential. In working up his report on the Hunan peasants, and in other studies, he investigated cross-sections of groups of ordinary Chinese to ascertain their material conditions, opinions, and preferences for alternative courses of action. He was always concerned about "concrete problems"—food, land, tenantry, suppression of women—and their implications for individual character and political action. It had long been recognized that the peasantry would supply supporting forces for revolutionary action; Mao saw it also as a source of revolutionary leadership. If one of the supreme qualities of the gifted political leader is to understand not only the needs of potential followers but the way in which those needs could be activated and channeled, Mao's experience, perception, and analysis gave him an unparalleled opportunity to mobilize and lead.

Mao came to recognize the potential and the indispensability of social and political conflict in Chinese society and the relation of conflict to leadership and power. He was at once a victim of conflict, an exploiter of conflict, and a grand theorist of conflict. It was above all in the analysis and management of conflict that he showed his mastery of the strategy of political leadership. As a boy Mao had escaped from clashes with his father at home only to meet hostility from his higher-status schoolmates because of his gawky ways and frayed clothes. At Peking University he was an underling, in a party headed by intellectuals he had limited academic credentials, and in a movement dominated by intellectuals he was not primarily a Marxist theoretician. He suffered the price of civil conflict: he lost many comrades. His first wife and a younger sister were executed by the Kuomintang in 1930, and much later he lost a son in the Korean

War. Countless friends and followers were executed by his foes; he would execute—or cause to be executed—countless landlords and counterrevolutionaries. In one of his earliest known writings he discussed the ordinarily rather benign subject of physical education. "In order to civilize the mind one must first make savage the body. If the body is made savage, then the civilized mind will follow. . . . Exercise should be savage and rude." He mentioned great battles and feats of heroes: "all this is savage and rude and has nothing to do with delicacy."

His matured theory of conflict was remarkably explicit and comprehensive, far more searching in its psychological and philosophical bases than Lenin's. Mao's began with a concept of the omnipresence of dualism and contradiction. Dualisms were fundamental contrasting pairs such as action and inaction, the old and the new, cooperation and conflict, life and death, the present and the future, the pure and the impure, the *yin* and the *yang*. These dualisms exist within as well as among individuals. To the extent that they relate to the material forces of production and to class relationships, they characterize the class structure of society.

Contradictions would continue indefinitely, even in a socialist or Communist society. "As long as contradictions exist between the subjective and the objective, between the advanced and the backward, and between the productive forces and the conditions of production, the contradiction between materialism and idealism will continue in a socialist or communist society and will manifest itself in various forms. . . . Not everybody will be perfect. . . . There will still be good people and bad," people who were relatively correct and incorrect in their thinking.

The theory of contradictions emphasized not only the opposites but a kind of Hegelian "law of the unity of opposites." Mao wrote: "A contradictory aspect cannot exist in isolation. Without the other aspect that is opposed to it, each aspect loses the condition of its existence." Without life there would be no death, without "above" no "below," without fortune no misfortune. He went on to a series of social opposites that were "interconnected, and interpenetrated, interpermeated, and interdependent": landlords and tenant peasants, bourgeois and proletariat, imperialist nations and colonies, and so on.

Mao distinguished between antagonistic and nonantagonistic (i.e., nonclass related) contradictions like those found among workers or among peasants. But it was the antagonistic contradiction that was the stuff of fundamental conflict and struggle. This doctrine, at the heart of both Hegelian and Marxist philosophy, Mao embellished and applied to the social and political circumstances of Chinese agrarian life. If the struggle grew to the point of intense antagonism, a "dialectical reversal" might take place; for example, rulers might

be forced to change places with the ruled. Mao's argument became rather tortured, but three implications came through strongly: Political conflict was necessary to social change. Conflict could be managed by leaders. Conflict could
be contrived by leaders. Basic in Mao's thinking was that conflict is essential
for transformation and ultimate unity. "Extraordinary about this manner of
thinking is its simplicity," according to Franz Schurmann. "Having accepted
a few philosophical premises from Marxism-Leninism, it then proceeds to
combine ideas into a never-ending series of dualities."

Resolution may lead to new contradictions and new conflict. Since in
Mao's view many contradictions exist, of which one dominant contradiction—the economic—shapes the others, the cardinal responsiblity of leadership is to identify the dominant contradiction at each point of the historical process and to work out a central line to resolve it. This gives leadership
considerable scope for action. Leaders are not pale reflectors of major social
conflicts; they play up some, play down others, ignore still others. They run the
risk that other leaders responding to human needs will challenge them. In a
pluralistic system, on the other hand, transactional leaders are more at the
mercy of conflict in the groups and interests which they acknowledge or ignore.

We have been referring to Mao, "the leader," etc.; in fact this has been
shorthand for the whole leadership hierarchy, and we have no reason to contradict a basic view in this volume of leadership as a collective enterprise. Mao
was always surrounded by a slowly shifting hierarchy of powerful leaders, of
whom one was his third wife, party activist Chiang Ch'ing. Institutionalized in
the massive Chinese Communist party, the leadership structure radiated out to
all the major institutions of the Chinese nation and through party hierarchies to
the Communist cells at the grass roots. The party followed the usual Communist pattern: national congress, central committee, politburo, central secretariat,
elaborate provincial and local organs, and a picked, disciplined, dues-paying
membership. The party established the usual agencies for organization, propaganda, party finance, research, and the like. The party of course controlled
all means of mass propaganda and put special emphasis on oral and face-to-face
persuasion. Old and new techniques of persuasion—isolation of the audience
for maximum impact, arousal of emotional tension, simplification of the issues—were designed to raise the consciousness of the masses and to politicize
them until they became grass-roots ideologists.

In one respect, however, Mao and the other leaders went far beyond the
standard Communist utilization of the party as an instrument of top leadership.
Mao was the first Chinese leader, according to Lewis, to forge in action a
steady line based not on authority but on the "reciprocal and organized rela-

tionship between political leaders and the general Chinese population.'' Mao was explicit and forthright about this. Learn from one's subordinates! he urged party leaders. ''We should never pretend to know what we don't know, we should not feel ashamed to ask and learn from people below, and we should listen carefully to the views of the cadres at the lower levels. Be a pupil before you become a teacher; learn from the cadres at the lower levels before you issue orders.'' Cadres were carefully instructed as to how to carry out this doctrine of ''from the masses, to the masses.'' Wishes and complaints were to be collected, sorted out, summed up, and related to the official line of policies in order to transmit the reactions upward to the political leadership, so that they could be related to government and party policy, which in turn might be modified accordingly. The explanations of the new policies would then be carried back to the people. This dialectical process would go on indefinitely.

The result of this process of leadership-followership interaction was one of the most powerful leadership systems in history. To the extent that the attitudes of the masses influenced party policy—and the influence, however exaggerated in the official pieties, was significant—followers became leaders. Hence the Chinese Communist party constituted, in Schurmann's words, ''an organization made up of leaders whose one great purpose in life is to lead—at all levels of the structure.'' Party leadership at every level dictated a way of life: public, visible, collective, and highly demanding of time, energy, and personal commitment. Endless time was devoted to criticism, self-criticism, ''struggle meetings,'' and ''rectification'' campaigns that came to be seen in the West as ''brainwashing techniques'' that substituted group purpose for individual thought. The Chinese Communist party has been by no means free of serious problems—aging leadership, lack of upward mobility in the top ranks, friction between ideologists and technicians, for example—but the strength and durability of the party as a leadership system are impressive. Without its effectiveness in mobilizing the leadership potential in the ''masses'' the party could hardly have survived the enormous pressures of the Cultural Revolution.

One of the most interesting problems of strategy faced by the Communist leadership was how to deal with the elite they replaced, in particular the upper-class intellectuals, the cultivated, often Western-educated professionals. Essentially these privileged persons were seen as a threat. Their perquisites and many of their possessions were taken away; they were humbled by scrutiny and reeducation; their children were sent to the country to labor with the peasants. Some sent their children abroad to stay. Others submitted to the Communist power reluctantly; many became converts to the new movement, convinced that the comfort of the few had properly been sacrificed to the greater good of millions previously oppressed. But the essentially anti-intellectual bias of the regime remained, for the curious, skeptical, doubting, independent, even detached approach of the intellectual was and still is alien to this fervent, interdependent, disciplined, and essentially religious revolutionary movement.

It remains only to ask what values this past leadership system serves, and here, as with the Bolsheviks, the answer is not wholly clear. The Chinese Communists have been brilliant fashioners of political institutions; they have made contributions to Communist theory and doctrine; they have produced immense ideological, political, and, to a striking degree, cultural and social changes in China. Theirs has been a transforming revolution. But they have been far more effective in their theories of means and proximate ends than in their elaboration of the ultimate purposes that all these efforts are to serve. Much can be inferred, of course, from party promises and programs and from the economic and social programs that the regime has instituted in the past quarter century. The egalitarian ends are visible. But on the exacting questions of the priorities and interrelations among supreme ends—especially in the issue of individual liberties and collective rights in a totalitarian society—the revolutionary leadership has been less intelligible and positive. And as long as this is the case, the ultimate success of revolutionary leadership is impossible to measure. Chinese revolutionary leaders had no historical tradition of civil liberties, in theory or in practice, to build upon, and they did not create one.

What can be said broadly of revolutionary leadership? It is passionate, dedicated, single-minded, ruthless, self-assured, courageous, tireless, usually humorless, often cruel. It is always based on a chiliastic political theology, but it remains flexible in its uses of theology in practice. It is committed to conflict. It rests on a belief in angels and devils and salvation. It does not tolerate heretics. It requires a prophet but it needs institutional support and collective leadership to survive. Its source is leadership sparking the dry tinder of human wants and needs, leadership that is frustrated by oppression, wide popular discontent, and the failure of reformism. Its success rests on a powerful value system, on responsiveness to popular need, and on systematic suppression of dissent. It is egalitarian in theory but not always in practice. It qualifies as leadership when it is reciprocal in a situation of open conflict and as brute power when it is not. The leadership of the French Revolution deteriorated to become mere terrorism, though its early ethical vision survived its own demise to become inspiration to future generations. The leadership of the Russian Revolution subverted reformism; it has survived by meeting the needs of the Russian masses for social order, material welfare, and national pride. The leadership of the Chinese Revolution has been the most transforming of the three, but it, too, has its massive cruelties and its victims.

The humane end-values of revolution are often widely shared by all classes; that is one of the strengths of revolutionaries. It is the lack of modal values—the inhumanity and irresponsibility with which the struggle is conducted—that produces fear and counterrevolution. The American Revolution left few deep scars because of the essential fidelity and even civility of revolutionary leaders like Washington and Adams. Revolutions seem to produce first generations of leaders who not only represent but embody the higher ends of the cause; who else could have led their revolutions than Lenin, Mao, Bolivar, Castro, Ho Chi Minh? The test is the second generation of leadership—the Jeffersons, Nehrus—and the extent to which the original human purposes of revolution have been perverted in the drive for power.

It was this test that Stalin failed. Like Woodrow Wilson, he was compelled to create an idealized image of himself as a defense against his fears of being seen as unworthy, and this idealized image in turn compelled him to demand and feed on flattery of him as a towering political and even intellectual leader. But Lenin had left him with a flawed inheritance that, in the final analysis, stressed revolutionary means over revolutionary ends. Even without that inheritance, the Georgian could hardly have overcome the effects of his own harsh and psychologically scarring early years, and the burden of centuries of oppression in Russia. He helped his people realize their direst need, in 1941 and 1942, of survival. But he could never recognize their higher needs of innovation, creativity, and free expression. Once he had consolidated his power and coldly destroyed a multitude of old comrades and adversaries like his mortal enemy, Adolf Hitler, he was not a leader but a despot.

9

HEROES AND IDEOLOGUES

During one of his travels before the turn of the century, Sigmund Freud visited the lonely church of San Pietro in Vincoli in Rome and came face to face with Michelangelo's statue of Moses. Years later, haunted by his first impression of the masterpiece, he returned to the church and, day after day over a three-week period, studied the statue, measured it, and sketched it, lingering for hours over its detail. He noted precisely how Moses held the tablets against his side, how he turned his cold and wrathful face toward those who were worshiping the Golden Calf; how his long beard flowed to one side; and Freud reflected at length on the significance of all this. Moses was not giving vent to his passion against the idol-worshipers, Freud concluded, but rather was controlling that passion in a great effort.

Yet so unsure was Freud of his conclusions that he waited years before publishing them and then did so anonymously. His biographer Ernest Jones speculated that Freud had identified himself with Moses and was seeking to emulate the victory over passion that Michelangelo had caught in his "stupendous" work because Freud at this time was trying to control his own wrath over his backsliding disciples, Adler and the others, as Moses was over the backsliding idol-worshipers. Freud himself later admitted that the work was a "love-child" that took him years to legitimate. Toward the end of his long life he published *Moses and Monotheism,* in which he dwelt on Moses as a great man acting in the network of determining historical causes.

Moses was one of the first of the towering "charismatic" leaders. He influenced history in two ways, Freud noted: through his personality and through the idea for which he stood. Freud captured both the essence of Moses' greatness and an ambiguity in the concept of charisma that has clouded understanding of the "hero in history" to this day. Is the charismatic leader the spiritual and political father of his people, the source of authority, the lawgiver, the statesman, the mobilizer of popular support for the religious and political ideas that he defines and embraces? Or is he the idol and ikon, the miracle worker, the prophet, the magic man, the "personality" who arouses his people not because of the substance of his rule or his ideas but because of the halo effect of his magic? Moses was all of these and more; he was prophet but also, as Martin Buber observed, "leader of the people, as legislator." Moses is brought up a prince; he has revelations; he casts a tree into the bitter waters of Marah to make them sweet; he smites the rock and water gushes out. Yet as God's agent he proclaims laws and values so explicit in form and so universal in meeting human needs that they have powerfully influenced Western political thought and behavior. Rare is the leader who can serve as both idol and ideologue, both hero and lawgiver.

In the late 1420s, out of the flowered pasturelands and mystic oakwoods of the Meuse valley, there suddenly emerged an astonishing charismatic figure, who would become a heroine but no lawgiver. The birth of Joan of Arc (as she came to be called) in a poor peasant home, her insistence on confronting military men who had little time for peasants, and much less for an eighteen-year-old farm girl, her bold summons to the Dauphin to act like a king, her courage in battle, her martyrdom and subsequent rehabilitation and (much later) canonization—all this is the stuff out of which heroes are fashioned. The angelic voices she said she heard gave her a sense of conviction and confidence that, for a brief year, carried almost everything opposing her. Her fame battened on conflict. The English and their French allies viewed her as a camp follower or mere prostitute, perhaps even a secret agent or sorceress. The Church feared the example she set with her "voices." Historians still debate the extent to which the legendary leader existed in history, but recognize her "voices" and "visions" as in accord with a common hallucinatory pattern.

The forces that sustained Joan during her life—and sustained the legend after her burning—were the followers who gathered around her in battle and in the streets through which she and her small retinue proceeded, beneath fluttering pennants. For the common people, this was the age of revelation and of worship of the Virgin, and Joan met both these psychic needs. During this time other maidens heard voices that commanded them, but no peasant girl had the audacity and steadfastness, and the opportunity and sheer luck, that turned Joan into an object of idolatry among the masses and of fear and hatred in the royal and ecclesiastical establishments. Her persecution and fiery "crucifixion"—so like the fate of an earlier heretic—and the lasting hope for her resurrection branded her name on the popular consciousness and the pages of history alike.

The question remains: did Joan's heroic leadership have any permanent effect? She entered a period of official obscurity after her death, only to be rescued by a posthumous "retrial" and rehabilitation that was more a response to the power politics of the day than to popular demand. Her military mission of expelling the English from France was only partly accomplished. But, as a child of the common people, she inspired a lasting populist feeling; as a champion of French patriotism at a time when a nascent nationalism was beginning to fashion the France we know today, she left a poignant and glowing image that the French have refurbished in critical times. The French will always commemorate her, says Lightbody, because, "as a soldier in humanity's war of liberation, she expressed their needs and underlying wishes." But Joan left no heritage in the form of political doctrine, institution-making, or fundamental law. Still fought over by rival factions, as she was in her last months, she remains more a hero of history than a maker of it.

Heroic Leadership

Max Weber concluded that societies passed through a sequence of three "pure" types of authority: the charismatic, the rational-legal, and the traditional. The miraculous, transcending leadership of a religious savior such as Christ or Muhammad was followed by a period in which charisma was routinized and bureaucratized and authority was exercised through legal and "rational" institutions and practices. In time this system evolved into a traditionalist society in which authority was legitimated by usage, precedent, and custom. As this society became more traditionbound and static, the seeds were sown for the birth of a new charismatic leadership and authority. And so the cycle proceeded. Russia seemed to fit Weber's model. The archetypes of traditionalist rule there were the czars, James Davies notes, "who presumed to be exercising power according to long-established custom but for practical purposes recognized no superior earthly authority." Confronted by a delegation of churchmen exhorting him to appoint someone head of the state church, Peter the Great pointed to himself and said, "Here is your patriarch."

The concept of charisma has fertilized the study of leadership. Its very ambiguity has enabled it to be captured by scholars in different disciplines and applied to a variety of situations. The term itself means the endowment of divine grace, but Weber did not make clear whether this gift of grace was a quality possessed by leaders independent of society or a quality dependent on its recognition by followers. The term has taken on a number of different but overlapping meanings: leaders' magical qualities; an emotional bond between leader and led; dependence on a father figure by the masses; popular assumptions that a leader is powerful, omniscient, and virtuous; imputation of enormous supernatural power to leaders (or secular power, or both); and simply popular support for a leader that verges on love. The word has been so overburdened as to collapse under close analysis. It has also become cheapened. Lyndon Johnson would complain that his trouble was that he lacked "charisma" (a word he pronounced with a soft "ch"—to the derision of the intelligentsia).

It is impossible to restore the word to analytic duty; hence I will use the term *heroic leadership* to mean the following: belief in leaders because of their personage alone, aside from their tested capacities, experience, or stand on issues; faith in the leaders' capacity to overcome obstacles and crises; readiness to grant to leaders the powers to handle crises; mass support for such leaders expressed directly—through votes, applause, letters, shaking hands—rather than through intermediaries or institutions. Heroic leadership is not simply a quality or entity possessed by someone; it is a *type of relationship* between leader and led. A crucial aspect of this relationship is the absence of conflict. "Instead of acquiring insight into their deep-lying motives, people seek some release from their conflicts by projecting their fears, aggressions, and aspirations onto some social objects which allow a symbolic solution," Daniel Katz notes. Heroic leadership provides the *symbolic* solution of internal and external conflict.

Heroic leaders—in contrast with leaders who are merely enjoying popular favor—usually arise in societies undergoing profound crisis. Existing mechanisms of conflict resolution have broken down; traditions, established authority, old legitimations, customary ways of doing things—all are under heavy strain. Mass alienation and social atomization are rising. Intense psychological and material needs go unfulfilled. Long-held values are ready to be replaced or transformed. A variety of secondary leaders come to the fore to raise expectations and sharpen demands. In short, a crisis in trust and legitimacy overwhelms the system's rulers, ideology, and institutions. Then there appears a leader or leadership group, equipped with rare gifts of compassion and competence—dynamic, resourceful, responsive—that rebels against authority and tradition.

Of numerous instances of the rise of such leadership, the case of the Mahdi of the Sudan is one of the most striking. The eighteenth and early nineteenth centuries saw the emergence of powerful religious movements with heavy puritanical overtones in the borderlands of the imperial Ottoman domain, in Arabia, Libya, and especially the Sudan. Society was becoming atomized as traditional Islamic belief systems became fragmented. "Foreign" invaders and conquerors further threatened old loyalties by seeking to impose "alien" legal and penal ways on native populations. A host of religious proselytizers exploited and abetted the unrest. It had long been a popular myth that "the guided one" would come to save the Islamic community.

Muhammad Ahmad was born the son of a poor Dongolese boatbuilder. Orphaned in his early years, he was sent to live with an uncle. "As a child he displayed unusual motivation and a prodigious mind that enabled him to recite the entire Qur'an at the age of nine." Denied an education at the prestigious university of Al-Azhar, he remained in the Sudan and lived as an ascetic in an established order. Becoming in time a full-time proselytizer with a reputation for great piety, humility, and asceticism, he turned against the established rulers, accusing them of impious practices such as music and dancing. Expelled from his order, he joined a rival one and soon became its head. He declared himself the Mahdi on the claim that during a vision the Prophet Muhammad had appointed him successor of Allah's apostle.

The message of the new Mahdi was direct and explicit: a return to puritanical Islam, a rejection of sinful pursuits in favor of perpetual asceticism. The government saw this as a political as well as a religious threat and dispatched an army to put down the usurper and his followers. The defeat of this army and a series of victories in succeeding months brought more recruits to the Mahdi's cause. But his main strength seemed to lie in the force of his message, his ability to adapt it to the needs of different classes and groups, his promise of salvation to believers who fell in battle, and his ability to win sophisticated theological debates with the opposition. He won world renown—and opprobrium in Britain—when his forces took Khartoum and slew the British hero General Charles Gordon. The Mahdi himself died not long after the fall of Khartoum. The succession proceeded peacefully for a time, but it was challenged later, and the dramatic episode came to an end when the British under Kitchener reconquered the Sudan.

The extent of actual change brought about by the Mahdi remains a subject of debate. The extent of "value transformation" in itself could not be measured, though it is noteworthy that more than ten thousand of the Mahdi's followers threw themselves against the British machine guns in the last big stand. "At the zenith of his power, the leader died without an opportunity to see through the process of rebuilding (routinization) that had barely started," Richard Dekmejian and Margaret Wyszomirski conclude. "As a result, the task of the comprehensive, spiritual-social reconstruction of Sudanese society that the Mahdi intended never became a reality. In other words, the crucial social integration and spiritual homogenization of the tribal Sudanese was aborted." One can question whether lasting social transformation would have taken place even if the Mahdi had lived, given the theological emphasis of his message and the puritanical, anti-modern cast of his doctrine. The Mahdi was not, in the end, an agent for social change.

Heroic leadership plays a vital role in transitional or developing societies, where even the more idolatrous form of heroic leadership may meet the special needs of both leaders and followers. The idols are usually motivated by powerful needs for affection, esteem, and self-actualization. They want and need an audience, and an audience needs them. Followers flock to see such heroes, crowd in to touch their hands or the hems of their garments. The spectators are moved by their own needs—by their need to overcome their frustrations through projecting their fears, hopes, and aggressions onto heroes who can provide at least symbolic solutions; by their need for identification with the mighty and the awesome; by their need for esteem from performers who bestow recognition and flattery on them—and thus by their need for self-esteem. The heroes personalize movements and symbolize ideas. In some elections in "new nations" illiterate persons who cannot recognize the name of a candidate or a party, and perhaps not even a party device such as a cow, can still decide by choosing from small balls bearing the likenesses of the candidates.

The idolatrous form of heroic leadership can serve, in Robert C. Tucker's words, as "essentially a fulcrum of the transition from colonial-ruled traditional society to politically independent modern society." Lucian W. Pye noted, in his study of Burmese transitional politics, that questions of personal loyalty and identification are central and the bond between idolized leader and follower is generally an affective and emotional one. Symbols of national unity and personal support overshadow policy issues. It is far easier, according to Pye, to communicate emotional and personal support than substantive government programs. But this kind of relationship, Pye points out, is "likely to wear thin"; expectations are built up that are hard for idolized leaders to follow.

"The people believe that just because I am important there is nothing that I can't do," one Burmese politician complained. "If I don't do something for them they say that I am either mean to them or that I am a weak leader and they should find another. Our people have no idea at all how hard it is to do anything."

The question remains whether the hero can do anything more for idol-worshipers than incite and appease emotional or psychological needs. This may be important—for some spectators all-important—for the psychic investment of the "follower" in the "leader" may be very high while the reverse relationship may be slight. The effect on the hero-worshiper's life or happiness may be insubstantial and fleeting, while the performer easily moves on to new audiences. The cardinal question is whether the idolized hero can help develop in "new nations" the political movements or parties that convert personal followings into durable ones, personal affect and symbol into policy and program. The record is mixed. Some of the Roman emperors who claimed—or had imputed to them—godlike powers had little interest in identifying with or responding to the lasting "real needs" of their people. Muhammad was an idolized religious leader but, like Moses, he left a legacy of social and political values—including that of equality (except between the sexes)—that helped shape Islamic thought and behavior. Napoleon encouraged a cult of personality but, like Moses, he bequeathed France a legal code. Atatürk, often envisioned as a "charismatic" leader because of his courage and his narrow escapes, was even more a cautious, calculating leader—"an organization man thrown into a charismatic situation," Dankwart A. Rustow labeled him. Nkrumah—handsome, graceful, warm, responsive, of voice "both deep and melodious"—viewed himself as a cross between Gandhi and Lenin in the tradition of great "thinker-politicians." An article in the Ghana press proclaimed that Nkrumah had "revealed himself like a Moses—yea, a greater Moses. . . . With the support of all African leaders he will help to lead his people across the Red Sea of imperialist massacre and suffering." But in the end, David Apter says, "Nkrumah lacked the imagination and skill to develop a country. He was a revolutionary without a plan—a visionary, but not a builder."

The "developed" nations are by no means free of hero-idolatry. A poem in *Pravda* in 1936 sang to Stalin:

> O, thou great leader of the peoples/ Thou who gavest man his life/
> Thou who fructified the lands. . . . O, father . . . Thou art the sun. . . .

And a poem in *Women of China* (Peking) in 1961 praised Mao Tse-tung:

> You are rain for the planting season, Breeze for the hottest noon/
> You are the red sun that never sets. . . .

In the United States the "jumpers" of 1960 hopped up and down, screaming in frenzy, as John F. Kennedy and his entourage approached during the presidential campaign of that year. One can doubt that these teenagers and subteenagers were whooping it up for Kennedy because of his stand on old-age pensions or on Latin America policy. Over the succeeding decade pictures of John and Jacqueline Kennedy decorated the front covers of literally tens of millions of copies of popular magazines. He was handsome, with a boyish grin, but in

1960 Kennedy had little connection with the basic needs, expectations, and values of the young people. Kennedy's appearance and performance titillated them; that was enough.

Some years before this phenomenon, a California longshoreman-philosopher, Eric Hoffer, was analyzing "true believers" as he had seen and read about them. He dissected the groups that seemed most susceptible to leadership that "articulates and justifies the resentment dammed up in the souls of the frustrated": the misfits, the inordinately selfish, the bored, the sinners, and the different varieties of the poor. He was more interested in the led—the kind of people he watched and listened to daily—than the leaders. He noted that the "total surrender of a distinct self" is a prerequisite for the attainment of both unity and self-sacrifice; that to the frustrated, "freedom from responsibility is more attractive than freedom from restraint"; that they surrendered to leaders because leaders could take them away from their unwanted selves. People lost themselves in mass movements to escape individual responsibility—to be free of freedom.

The "escape from freedom" is also an escape from conflict; the spectator can love the performer without hating anyone else. (It is easier not to choose up sides.) The halo surrounding Number One bathes the political landscape in a glow of harmony and consent. Purpose, which needs to be sharpened in conflict, is also lacking. While emotional needs in hero and spectator may be deeply involved, no central purpose, no collective intent other than short-run psychic dependency and gratification unites performer and spectator. And if there is no transcending purpose, there is no real change that can be related to or measured by original purpose.

Idolized heroes are not, then, authentic leaders because no true relationship exists between them and the spectators—no relationship characterized by deeply held motives, shared goals, rational conflict, *and* lasting influence in the form of change.

Ideological Leadership

In sharp contrast with the idolized hero, ideological leaders dedicate themselves to explicit goals that require substantial social change and to organizing and leading political movements that pursue these goals. Ideological leaders may have personal needs of esteem and actualization that are as compelling as those of the idol, but these leaders embody and personify collective goals so intensely that other human wants and needs and aspirations—those of both the leaders and the led—may be swallowed in the *purposes of the movement*. The leaders, at least, have "thrown themselves" into a transcending cause and quest. Their relations with their followers are close psychologically, politically, organizationally. Relations of leaders and led, and of one cause to a competing or threatening one, are ridden with conflict—with actual or potential conflict inside the movement over specific strategies and goals, and with constant conflict with opposing ideologies. The ultimate success of the leaders is tested not by peoples' delight in a performance or personality but by *actual social change* measured by the ideologists' purposes, programs, and values.

Ideology has become as ambiguous and debased a word as charisma. The term was born in conflict and has been somewhat suspect ever since. From their lofty positions in the National Institute the French oracles of the 1790s issued their pronunciamentos attacking the false abstract doctrines of the great philosophers and theologians of prerevolutionary times. In place of the ideas that served the old regime they advanced the new "science of ideas," which they called *ideology,* through the study of which all ideas could be reduced to their origin in sensation. This new philosophical breed and their revolutionary ideas did not escape the watchful eye of Napoleon, who as emperor concluded that these visionaries, with no understanding of practical statecraft, were a threat to political order and to him. With a wave of his hand he reorganized the institute and extinguished the Second Class of Moral and Political Sciences, in which most of the *ideologues* were clustered. The term survived, but it has had its ups and downs. The word became fashionable in the years before World War II, when formidable ideologies seemed at war with one another—Soviet communism, German Nazism, democratic socialism, and an amorphous ideology of liberal democracy. Following the war the "end of ideology" was proclaimed by pundits in the United States. In this pragmatic age the term has come to stand for everything that is doctrinaire, abstract, opinionated, rigid, and unrealistic. Yet the concept represents a significant strategy of thinking—and of leadership—and it needs to be salvaged.

The crucial quality of ideology is that it combines both *what* one believes—one's belief system, value structure, *Weltanschauung*—and *how* one came to hold certain beliefs, the lenses through which one regards the world, the ideas and experience and motivation one brings to the process of sorting out and evaluating the stream of phenomena that one perceives. This dualism is well captured in part by Arthur Schlesinger—"By ideology I mean a body of systematic and rigid dogma by which people seek to understand the world—and to preserve or transform it"—and by Zbigniew Brzezinski: "Ideology that combines action—and since its object is society, it must be political action—with a consciousness both of purpose and of the general thrust of history." Soviet Communist ideology, especially in the years after the revolution, illustrates this dualism. For our purposes we can think of ideology as a set of major values and modes of cognition and perception, seated in congruent need and value hierarchies, all of which relate to one another and to social and economic forces and institutions in varying degrees of reinforcement and antagonism. So defined, political ideology embraces both persons' theories of reality, modes of truth, etc., *and* those potent "isms" that have possessed peoples' imaginations and overturned ancient customs, societies, and elites as well as fortified them.

To define ideology in this fashion is to present a pure model but a model that may be useful as a diagnostic instrument. The striking aspect of this model is the full congruence of the key elements of ideology: *cognition, conflict, consciousness, value,* and *purpose.* What leaders and followers see in their environment and in one another; the conflict with opposing ideologies that draws them together; their social and historical consciousness; the values that hold moral significance for them; the social and political purposes that emerge from such ideology—all these mutually fortify one another. A movement of followers possessing these qualities obviously provides an enormously powerful base for leadership that expresses and embodies it.

In the context of ideology so conceptualized the structure of values, the lines of conflict, and the alignment of leadership are sharply defined and deeply etched in society. To the extent of the rulers' power, dissident or hostile or incongruent values in the ideology are proscribed and cast into outer darkness. Leadership within the system becomes a direct expression of the dominant ideology. Leaders may depart from orthodoxy but only for the purpose of "tactical" deviations that do not challenge the value system. Expressed conflict is shifted from inside the polity to its external relations. As conflict sharpens between ideological systems, leadership becomes the mobilizer and articulator of international rivalry.

The extent of congruence "in real life" within apparently ideological societies should not be overstated, as the four-nation study has shown. In the matter of gross international differences, the study found "no clear association between political system or ideology and the social values" measured. It was difficult to find correspondence between a national value profile and a distinctive feature of a country's social structure, perhaps because the internal differences in values largely outweigh the international ones. But this finding suggested, according to the study, "that the socialization of political leadership is largely a process that takes place *below* the national level, and that the forces of socialization are sufficiently diversified within nations so that leader's values are not easily identified as 'Made in the USA,' or in Poland, Yugoslavia or India." This conclusion coincides with the weight put in this work on leadership roles *throughout the socialization process* rather than merely at the top.

Ultimately, as Robert E. Lane has said, political ideology deals with the questions, Who will be the rulers? How will the rulers be selected? By what principles will they govern? The last question leads to others: How does the ideology embrace the major values of life? To what extent is the ideology "normative, ethical, moral in tone and comment"? What kinds of moralities or philosophies does it *oppose?* An ideological movement united (by definition) behind high moral purpose and united by conflict with opposing ideologies is a powerful causal force; it is, as Willard Mullins has pointed out, "an active agent of historical change." It is transforming leadership.

The test of leadership in all its forms—whether idolatrous or ideological or somewhere in between, whether institutionalized through political parties, movements behind causes, politicized interests, or organized personal followings—is the realization of purpose measured by popular needs manifested in social and human values. Leaders can operate off the "skin" of public opinion—off surges of transient opinion, the applause of idolizing spectators, the bubbling up of passing social and political fads, trumped-up foreign crises, and exaggerated dangers to national security—without recognizing the persisting, widespread, and intensive needs and goals that motivate followers and that are there for the evoking by leaders. Ultimately the effectiveness of leaders as *leaders* will be tested by the achievement of purpose in the form of real and intended social change. The revolutionary, intellectual, and reformist processes through which social purpose is realized are varied and fascinating, but ultimately the forcing-house of change will be the conversion of leaders' and followers' motives, demands, and values into reservoirs of realizable, operational *power* for leaders at all levels.

Most leaders combine both ideological and charismatic qualities, and great leaders combine them creatively. Such a leader was Mao Tse-tung. He fulfilled his necessary role as hero, father figure, cult object, idol. Even more, he understood the Chinese masses' need to worship leaders as a reflection of their dependency needs—needs probably rising out of their childhood circumstances and conditions of life. Part of his general conception of leadership as a powerful leader-follower relationship was his view that the leader serves a *psychic* need for followers, as do followers for leaders. Following the Cultural Revolution Mao told Edgar Snow that the Chinese people had probably gone too far in imputing magical powers to his Thoughts, but, he continued, a personality cult is needed at certain times, for in human affairs one thing will always exist: "the desire to be worshipped and the desire to worship." Part of Mao's brilliance as a leader was his awareness of the peculiar needs of the leader as well as those of the followers.

Leadership as Transformation

The leader's ultimate role in social change, however, turns largely on his ideological leadership, including the degree to which he makes his appeal as idol and hero serve his purposes and those of his followers. Evidently there was never any serious danger that Mao would succumb to hero-worship; he was too detached, too calculating, too self-protective, and too *ideological*. "It is permissible to arouse emotions [in others]," he once wrote, "but not ever to give vent to them." Comradeship was at the heart of Leninist notions of leadership, but Mao, like many other great leaders, clung to ideology rather than hero worshippers when he felt he had to make the choice.

That Mao would ultimately make hero-worship serve the needs and purposes of ideology was demonstrated by the advent of the Cultural Revolution. Further "revolution" at this time might not have seemed necessary even to an ideologist; a decade after its final military victory the ideological triumph of Chinese Communism seemed complete. Political, governmental, and legal institutions were abolished or reorganized to meet ideological needs so that the new "superstructure" would express the new values and goals of the masses. The values and goals of Communism were proclaimed by party theologians and echoed in schools and colleges, newspapers and radio, wall posters and mass meetings. The authorities condemned all art forms that did not serve the political education of the masses on the grounds that nonpolitical art was an illusion, that all art reflected class feeling, and that the proletariat must have its own revolutionary art. History was rearranged and rewritten to fit the needs of the new order. Chinese Communist ideology hardly questioned itself, though a limited amount of mass criticism of ways and means was permitted. "The true, the good, and the beautiful always exist in comparison with the false, the evil, and the ugly," Mao said, "and grow in struggle with the latter." Ideologies easily separate the saints from the devils.

But it was precisely on the grounds of ideology that Mao was not satisfied. His supreme aim of an egalitarian, classless society was not being realized fast enough. He was joined by other leaders, especially his wife Chiang Ch'ing, a former actress interested in culture who later claimed, as quoted in Roxane Witke's *Comrade Chiang Ch'ing,* that she had "convinced the Chairman (as she had argued for years) of the compelling need to gain the upper hand ideologically by vigorously promoting proletarian supremacy in the arts." Mao was particularly concerned that the growth of the socialist superstructure was being blocked by "revisionists," those party leaders, bureaucrats, and intellectuals who were allegedly trying to restore capitalist attitudes and institutions. Mao blamed the revisionists for the increasing bureaucratization of the Communist party and the rise of a bureaucratic elite cut off from the masses. To build a socialist superstructure, the next stage in China's advance toward Communism, the party bureaucrats would have to be overthrown.

He began with a magic gesture. On July 16, 1966, the seventy-two-year-old chairman of the Chinese Communist party plunged into the fast-moving current of the Yangtze River and swam fifteen kilometers in one hour, allegedly breaking all Olympic records. It was a consummate symbolic gesture by the now legendary leader of eight hundred million Chinese. Swimming in the great river amidst thousands of other bobbing heads, he was in effect inviting China's younger generation to join him in launching a new revolution, "advancing in the teeth of great storms and waves." Mao knew what he was about. "It was I who started the fire," he said a few months after the swim. "As I see it, shocking people is good. For many years I thought about how to administer to the revisionists in the party a shock . . . and finally I conceived this."

Mao's emphasis on conflict in these statements was significant. His grand strategy in the Cultural Revolution was to inspire, legitimize, and guide a mass movement of shifting composition, constantly enlarging the arena of action, much as he had done earlier as a guerrilla leader in the Chinese countryside. The heart of that strategy was the managing, channeling, and manipulating of political *conflict* between the mass movement and the party bureaucracy to serve his own ends and those of the masses—ends that he believed to be identical. Mao's strategy of conflict was founded on Leninist Communism with its emphasis on the dialectic, on contradictions, on antagonisms that pervade society. Conflict was employed both to buttress the leadership and to undermine the opposition. Mao's strategy was also implemented through his celebrated writings on revolutionary theory and practice, his most direct and powerful ideological link with the needs and aspirations of the masses.

There was some wonderment in foreign capitals—especially in Moscow, one may surmise—that Mao might initiate a mass movement from below to accomplish his goals rather than simply remove his opponents from power and reform the bureaucracy by decree from above. The explanation refers us to our earlier consideration of Mao's basic philosophy of leadership. He possessed almost absolute confidence in the ultimate capacity of the masses to help solve problems, achieve social change, and finally create a Communist society. He was still committed to the "mass line," to his doctrine of leadership "from the masses, to the masses," and to his concept of democratic centralism. This concept differed from Lenin's original notion, which applied essentially to leadership within the vanguard party. The essence of the Cultural Revolution was the unique interaction between Mao's centralist leadership and the mass action of his revolutionary followers. The Cultural Revolution was the ultimate expression of Mao's political credo.

Mao's leadership was based on his interconnected roles, played masterfully in the Cultural Revolution, of ideological leader, initiator of broad policies, and political broker and mediator. He had always stressed collective leadership in the party as he had in the years of guerrilla war. Partly to allow his successors to be trained and partly to concentrate on broader questions of ideology and policy, the chairman relinquished direct control of the Chinese government in 1959, withdrawing more and more from party administration. Over the years he had delegated wide authority to Liu Shao-ch'i, Lin Piao, Chou En-lai, and others. Regaining supremacy during the Cultural Revolution, he once again shared power with his associates, and not only with radical leaders but with Defense Minister Lin Piao, who had led a self-contained cultural revolution within the People's Liberation Army under Mao's guidance.

Mao's tactics in the Cultural Revolution were much like those he had used before with success: to act slowly and cautiously until there was "suitable climate and soil" for decisive action; to test the opposition and maneuver them into exposing themselves; to exploit the "negative example" of his opponents to gain support; to divide the opposition and "concentrate superior forces to destroy the enemy forces one by one." All this required an uncanny ability to hone in on and champion—while shrewdly exploiting and manipulating—the needs and motivations of other leaders, followers, and foes. Mao's "genius in understanding the emotions of others," as Lucian Pye has called it, enabled him to occupy the classic role of the great leader, which is to comprehend not only the existing needs of followers but to mobilize within them newer motivations and aspirations that would in the future furnish a popular foundation for the kind of leadership Mao hoped to supply. That kind of leadership is transforming leadership.

And that was Mao's kind of leadership. He was shocked by the anti-leadership attitudes (especially of younger Communists) and by a formal proposal from the Shanghai People's Council asking for the elimination of all chiefs on the ground that all leaders were, or became, agents of reaction and revisionism. "This is extreme anarchy," Mao responded; "it is most reactionary. . . . Actually, there always have to be chiefs." And without "chiefs," we may add, there will be no transformation.

PART IV

TRANSACTIONAL LEADERSHIP

10

OPINION LEADERSHIP: THE MISSING PIECE OF THE PUZZLE

Few political analysts have more closely observed conditions of social disorganization, popular apathy, political ignorance, and electoral disarray than the late V. O. Key, Jr. In conducting research for his incomparable study of Southern politics during the 1940s, he uncovered a state-by-state pattern of one-party domination, political fragmentation, issueless conflict, statewide and county demagoguery, Dixie-style personalism, and—first, last, and always—exclusion from power of the poor in general and the Negro in particular. Later, during the 1950s, Key studied public opinion data on Americans as a whole, dealing mainly with findings from the Eisenhower years, a time of relative smugness and blandness in the presidency coupled with the political hysteria engendered by Senator Joe McCarthy's hunt for domestic Communists. It might be expected that this political scientist, drawing up his final conclusions during a period of his own declining health, would come to the judgment fashionable in liberal circles that American democracy was vegetating if not decaying, that the masses were pulling their elected representatives down to a level of drab mediocrity on the one hand or fanatical witch-hunting on the other, that the great public was not only uninformed and apathetic but intolerant and anti-civil libertarian.

He did not. On the contrary, Key ended his last book with the observation that, in the United States at least, "voters are not fools." Both "vote switchers" and party standpatters acted fairly rationally. He had, however, to admit that there was a missing piece in the puzzle of what constitutes a democracy; that ingredient was the role and behavior of leaders and activists.

We must ask why this piece of the puzzle has been missing, at least to students of public opinion. The answer lies in part in the transactional theory of

257

the relationship of leader and follower. This theory, as it applies to the role of public opinion in that relationship, conceives of leader and follower as exchanging gratifications in a political marketplace. They are bargainers seeking to maximize their political and psychic profits. In this marketplace the bargaining is restricted in scope because the process works only in easily identifiable, calculable, tangible, measurable properties. Up to this point the theory coincides with the classic "exchange theory" of sociology. But transactional theory, as I define it, must lead to short-lived relationships because sellers and buyers cannot repeat the identical exchange; both must move on to new types and levels of gratifications. Most important, the transactional gratification itself may be a superficial and trivial one.

In the world of public opinion these transactions may not be tangible, like exchange of a political office for electoral support. The relationships are often likely to be "psychic," however: leader communicates with follower in a manner designed to elicit follower's response; follower responds in a manner likely to produce further leader initiatives; leader appeals to presumed follower motivations; follower responds; leader arouses further expectations and closes in on the transaction itself, and so the exchange process continues. The transactions initially may consist of gestures, smiles, applause, promises, opinion polls, letters and later take more tangible form, such as followers' votes for leaders in an election and leaders' votes for followers in a legislature.

It is possible that transactional opinion leaders will appeal to fundamental, enduring, and authentic wants, to deeply seated latent needs, and even to followers' convictions about morality and justice. Opinion leadership and followership in the context of the marketplace, however, does not readily lend itself to such substantial appeal or to creative, self-fulfilling responses as characterize transforming leadership. For the marketplace is just that—a mart. It is a place of quick connections and quick fixes. It is a place of multiple leaders and followers, a place where leaders can move from follower to follower in search of gratification and followers can respond in the same way to leaders. The moods and styles are quick; they assure reciprocity, flexibility, substitutability of buyers and of sellers, volatility of relationships. *Adaptability* is the rule—to the extent that leaders become hardly distinguishable from followers. Relationships are dominated by quick calculations of cost-benefits.

This kind of opinion leadership and followership is more likely to be found in Western-style liberal democracies than in more authoritarian regimes. It is both epitomized and made operational in most Western-style-enterprise attitude and opinion research through public opinion polls and academic surveys. Kenneth B. Clark has passed severe judgment on aspects of this enterprise: "Most social psychology is still primarily concerned with the investigation of isolated, trivial, and convenient problems rather than with those problems directly related to urgent social realities. . . . Opinion research, while concerned with some of the ingredients of power, takes no stand upon them, nor does it concern itself with the consequences of opinion in action. It may ask how many persons are willing to live next door to a Negro and how many have no opinion. It does not usually investigate what such persons actually do in a given situation nor does it explore the means of social change that would alter or sustain the direction of their behavior. . . ." Television rating surveys are also often criticized for tending to reinforce mediocrity and ignoring the preferences of diverse opinion minorities.

Arousal: The Mobilization of Political Opinion

The transactional theory of opinion leadership applies only to part of the opinion formation system, even in Western liberal democracies. The "free market" of public opinion, even in the United States, is a limited one. The degree of stability and even viscosity in public opinion is also impressive, and not only in bypassed hamlets where opinion stimuli rarely reach. Socializing tendencies of family and tribe, school, church, and workplace that we considered earlier can hold persons in a viselike grip. Shared values will intensify with continued exchange among group members in the absence of external opinion, as in medieval monasteries and Amish communities. Close friendships within groups stabilize opinions even further. Separatism may be ethnocentric or paranoid; it may also be based on the most careful calculations of self-interest and institutional survival.

The effectiveness of separatism depends on the relevance of institutions and other social mechanisms to the needs and attitudes of their members. If classes, groups, and regions are "sealed off" against external communication, internal communication will promote conformity or consensus. In groups open to the outer world, cohesive internal opinion may serve to reinforce the external and thus multiply its influence on its own members. The training of soldiers, priests, and revolutionaries is an example of this. Conditions that ease the transmission of communications, Elihu Katz and Paul Lazarsfeld note, occur "first, in the mere frequency of association with peers; second, in association with others who share a particular norm or standard; third, in being a member of a group which supplements and reinforces the mass media message; fourth, in belonging to a social group which has 'hooked up' a human communications system of its own with that of the mass media; and finally, in being 'near' enough to an appropriate social outlet to give expression to a motivated social action."

What social forces can break through the powerful psychological and institutional barriers that enforce conformity, consensus, and stability? Only those forces that can "hook up" with latent opinion sources that serve as potential rallying points behind those barriers for both consensual and competitive leadership. Television, for example, can reach into isolated homes and awaken wants for more possessions, or it can stimulate empathy, as it did when it disseminated a film of police dogs attacking civil rights demonstrators.

The potential for conflict is multifold. Psychological relationships between parents and child and among siblings make for fundamental tensions that can link up with external, socially generated conflict. Even in stable and affluent societies a person's passage through a series of shifting wants, needs, expectations, social attitudes, and political opinions creates a series of changing responses and counterresponses among classes, groups, and sections within society. The division of labor, for example, fosters roles that, under certain conditions, can come into conflict (management and workers, policemen and juveniles).

Leadership, especially in its transactional form, has a central role in all this. Clusters of opposing opinion, as Key has suggested, form foundations of support for opposing leadership cliques while competing leaders in turn cultivate the cleavages that sustain them. The distribution of conflict may take various forms, and the shape of leadership may follow suit, but leadership in turn chisels and enlarges or narrows the cleavages among subleaders and followers. The relations between leaders and opinion are obviously complex—so complex, according to Key, "that they can probably never be disentangled into their component elements. . . ." He continues: "The points of contact in political conflict tend to be principally between the opposing centers of leadership in the formal and informal political apparatus. . . . It is also in the relations between the opposing centers of leadership that the composition or settlement of conflict occurs." Leadership conflict and coalition, in turn, shape popular opinion.

The functions of leadership appear even more complex when one considers their varying relations to conflict and consensus, depending on the context within which a particular leadership is perceived. Thus the leader of a small and homogeneous group may simply exercise "headship" in the sense that the members of the group are so unified (whatever the potential conflict in the group) that the head of the group may serve only a simple representative function—the group is "re-presented" in him. If, however, this group exists in a more heterogeneous context, it is likely in some respects to come into some form of conflict with other groups or with the doctrines and leaders prevailing in the larger entity. Thus the leader who is a focus of consensus in one context is a source of conflict in another—for example, a general of an army projected into a political situation. A leader typically is not limited to these two roles but acts for, and mediates among, a great variety of differing and perhaps clashing groups—the army general relates differently to recruits and to fellow officers and seeks to reconcile black soldiers and Ku Klux Klan members on the same post. The most difficult problem most leaders face is reconciling divergent groups of which the same person may in effect be leader. As a result conflict takes place *within* such leaders as well as among the groups, classes, or constituencies sustaining them.

The extent to which political conflict is reflected and stabilized within one leader or leadership group depends on the extent to which the social forces in conflict are polarized in situations where types of conflict reinforce rather than offset each other. A proletariat holding strongly nationalistic and religious doctrines in opposition to external elements—Irish Catholics in Ulster, for example, or the French in Quebec—inevitably will nourish leadership in almost total opposition to the "ruling" forces. It would be difficult for leaders to embrace such competing forces within themselves—"to contain multitudes," as Walt Whitman said—though doubtless some leaders have tried. But in the typically heterogeneous society the lines of conflict cross one another rather than converge. The same leader may be a follower's *bête noire* one month and hero the next—but on different issues.

In discussing the effects of variegated opinion clusters on political leadership, Key notes that "one must seek the bearing of a multiplicity of political cleavages on the nature of the political order. Individuals can hold inconsistent opinions with no great personal discomfort. The political leader, though, must contrive some way to enact social welfare legislation to benefit his constituents without at the same time outraging them by the necessary levy of taxes. He must also, if he is a legislator, so conduct himself that he may tomorrow approach for support his enemy of today." The man in the street may escape some of the burden of conflict by the mechanism of "perceptual distortion"—seeing agreement among leaders or between leaders and followers where it does not exist. The leader may resort to this also, but perhaps at the expense of his political career. There are other ways, as Robert Lane and David Sears have suggested, of reducing "dissonance," depending on the strength of opinion belief and leadership support, but the burden on the leader would seem heavier than on the follower.

To dwell on the *structure* of consensus and conflict that characterizes interleadership relations and leader-follower relations in most societies would be to risk overemphasizing the stabilizing forces. Aspiring and competing leaders do have an impact on political opinions, but they arouse and activate attitudes that are there in latent forms; they mold popular wants and demands even as they respond to them. The public consists not of a great gray mass but of an immense variety of persons ranging from the passive (but potentially mobilizable) to the relatively active. We can sort out the political behaviors of these types of "leaders" and "followers" by defining and analyzing clusters of leadership-followership interaction measured by intensity, scope, and degree of activity—that is, by looking for major types of leaders and major types of followers and scrutinizing their interrelation.

The most visible and often the most consequential type of leader is the person who has major objectives—ideological, programmatic, policy, career, or immediately self-serving—and who seeks to activate, mobilize, and motivate all persons relative to their purposes. Except in an absolutely totalitarian, monolithic, and regimented society—in which case they would not be acting as "leaders" in our definition—these persons make leadership decisions in a context of anticipated reactions by other leaders (allied or competing, "higher" or "lower," etc.) and by participants of all types.

A second cluster of leaders consists of persons *who control the formal media of communication* of every type and to some degree at every level, from national newspaper or television network to the news crier in the village square or the picketer with a sign. Seemingly free from the "constituency pressures" that sharply restrict elected political leaders, the media managers operate in a web of constraints and anticipated reactions from financial subsidizers (mainly advertisers), rivals competing for the identical audience, and the readers, listeners, and observers they hope to retain or attract—though their control is sharply affected by the extent of their monopolistic position in the communications system. The electronic media in addition must respond in certain ways to governmental monitors (e.g., the fairness doctrine). Media managers lead public opinion in two ways: by manipulation, distortion, or "objective" presentation of what is considered "straight news" and by open and intended influencing of opinion through acknowledged editorializing, choice of columnists and commentators, selection of letters from readers, and so on. Thus the owner of a publishing empire and the editor who lays out the front page of *Le Monde* each has a singular and identifiable part in opinion-making.

A third cluster of leadership comprises the transactional "opinion leaders" who mediate between the mass media and the mass public. Opinion leadership, according to Katz and Lazarsfeld, "is leadership at its simplest: it is casually exercised, sometimes unwitting and unbeknown, within the smallest grouping of friends, family members, and neighbors. It is not leadership on the high level of a Churchill, nor of a local politico, nor even of a local social elite. It is at quite the opposite extreme: it is the almost invisible, certainly inconspicuous, form of leadership at the person-to-person level of ordinary, intimate, informal, everyday contact. . . ." Opinion leaders are ubiquitous, at least in the American setting; they are found in virtually every social stratum, but they also communicate across class and group boundaries. Opinion leaders could be the neighborhood druggist, the local taxi driver, a shop foreman, or indeed someone with no particular status but with the capacity to purvey information and ideas. They may be all the more effective because they seem to have no ostensible special purpose in passing on ideas and information. They know how to "personalize" their influence by adjusting what they say to the interests and biases of whomever they are communicating with, and they have both the time and proximity to engulf their listener in a stream of disguised propaganda or influence. A pioneering study of the 1940 presidential campaign indicated that the effect of the mass media was small compared to that of personal influence—or at least that the flow of information and ideas from mass media opinion leaders was monitored and changed by secondary opinion leaders in passing on the content to the less attentive public.

Opinion leadership takes many different forms in different polities. The person who can read in an Indian village of illiterates—indeed, any person who reads or quotes from the provincial paper that comes into the village—is a gatekeeper at a critical point in the channel of information and opinion. In the village of Kalos in Greece one of the two men in the community who could read was a teacher who received a newspaper and passed on to interested illiterates those parts of its contents as he wished. Members of an ethnic enclave in a large city may be highly dependent on their "ambassador" to the larger community, an ambassador who in turn communicates to them, in words or symbols they understand, the laws, mores, news, and controversy of the metropolis or the nation. Authoritarian polities are not unaware of the uses of opinion leadership—or of the criteria for effective personal influence. The Russian Communist party's model for an agitator, according to Alex Inkeles, was "the man who knows not only how each person in his shop works, but also how he lives, what his family is like, what his living conditions are, and whether or not he needs advice on one or another personal problem." Within the family the party line can be selectively interpreted as befits the needs and attitudes of the individual member.

The public, like the leaders, can be divided into three broad groupings, selected somewhat arbitrarily from the infinite range of types from the more active to the most passive. The more active have been designated the "attentive public"—people who are relatively interested in politics, aware of significant political issues, exposed to political information, conscious of competing political leadership, active to at least a small degree in party or group politics, concerned about the outcomes of elections and about the ultimate effectiveness of actions by government. A second grouping of the general public—let us call them the "semi-actives"—is a rather amorphous element that is aware of highly publicized candidates and issues and is drawn into political awareness and debate; these people tend to vote, at least in the more significant elections and for the more visible candidates. A third grouping is the "latent public," which typically does not pay attention to politics and does not vote or otherwise take part in political activity but always has the potential of being drawn into political awareness and activity—perhaps in response to especially stirring political leadership but more often as a result of traumas like wars, depressions, external threats, domestic crises, and sharpened fears of conspiratorial plots. Frightened, goaded, or persuaded into political activity, the latent public may behave in a manner that cannot be predicted, and its involvement may be fleeting and of low intensity.

The interactions and transactions over time of all these types of leaders and all these types of followers constitute a structure of political opinion leadership. In that structure leaders have their usual initiating, triggering, and catalyzing roles, but the "opinion leaders" at all levels also serve as relays and channels for opinion. Followers are variously attentive, semi-active, or passive, but the behavior of leaders of all types is conditioned by their anticipation of how other leaders and followers, in general, will respond. Analysts have found a "two-step flow" in communication from the highly visible formal leaders, such as presidents and prime ministers, and from the influential media, to the local opinion leaders, and from the latter to the ultimate recipients of ideas and information. Actually the steps are *multifold,* as in the case of an influential bartender who passes on something he has seen on television to a customer who then returns home and passes the message on to his wife. The researchers of the "two-step flow" acknowledge the real complexity when they refer to "the respondents of our original sample, their influentials, their influentials' influentials and their influentials' influentials' influentials." They add: "And with all that, we have hardly begun."

The structure is complex, but networks of interaction are discernible. The flow of opinion may move horizontally within class or status enclaves or vertically across them, but usually the flow will follow friendship or kinship patterns, gossip lines, work teams, and intragroup and intergroup interactions of cooperation and exchange. In some cultures the flow will be more from higher-status person to lower-status person than the reverse, more from old to young than the reverse (in public affairs but not in cultural matters such as films and popular songs). The flow of opinion will follow conflict lines too, as persons with clashing ideas come into some kind of confrontation or rival candidates communicate in the press, in formal debates, or on a street corner.

Once again we confront the essence of transactional opinion leadership: most leaders are followers, and most followers are leaders. Hence we must question simplistic views of systems made up of some kind of compact leadership or elite set off against a vast and amorphous public. Even Key, with his more sophisticated concept of many types of leaders and many subpublics, speaks of public opinion as a "system of dikes which channel public action or which fix a range of discretion within which government may act or within which debate at official levels may proceed." A more appropriate comparison might be made with a river bed along which the flow of opinion is both constrained by and bursts through natural banks and retaining walls, a river bed full of small channels and of rocks and fallen logs that interrupt the flow, a river bed subject to tides and winds.

Aggregation: The Alignment of Opinion

An oft-related story tells of a Frenchman sitting in a café who suddenly hears a disturbance outside. He jumps to his feet and cries, "There goes the mob. I am their leader. I must follow them!" The story contains a profound truth about the apparent paradox of leadership: the fact that leaders are followers and that we must distinguish the leadership *of* opinion from leadership *by* opinion. The story also reminds us of the duality of leadership. Persons are often perceived to be leaders simply because they reflect the needs and attitudes of their followers—or because they *differ* with their followers and seek to change their opinions. If they seek to mirror their followers' attitudes they are like the Frenchman in the café—his followers are his leaders. Unless they are willing to carry their representation of followers to the point of conflict with other groups of followers or with society as a whole, they may be viewed as persons with particular and individualistic goals, seeking their own advancement by gratifying group needs and attitudes. This is one of the simplest forms of transactional opinion leadership.

More typically, public opinion is an expression of conflict over *goals;* indeed, to some students of public opinion the subject cannot be separated from the concept of conflict. William Albig sees the opinion process as the interaction occurring within a group on a controversial issue; Kimball Young sees opinions as really beliefs about a controversial topic or with respect to the valuative interpretation or moral meaning of certain facts; and Clarence Schettler emphasizes interaction and conflict in the formation of public opinion.

In the competition to arouse public support in the ongoing conflict over goals, the paradox of leaders as followers and the duality of transactional opinion leadership as self-interest and as broader interest become all the more visible and significant. Leaders today have the advantages of modern social science and technology both in identifying and measuring followers' opinions and in consolidating or changing those opinions. It would be impossible in one volume to summarize the countless ways in which, in different polities, opinion leaders try to gauge and influence the attitudes of their followers—nor is it necessary. The techniques of persuasion of propagandists, "hidden persuaders," media experts, missionaries, and the like are fascinating technically but intellectually unchallenging unless they are related to broader questions of power, value, and responsibility—to the question especially of the extent to which transactional opinion leaders, in responding to the advice of media experts that they cater to volatile and superficial attitudes of followers, repudiate their own personal, doctrinal, and party commitments. In general, techniques of persuasion are matters of tactical choice; decisions about their use turn almost entirely on the availability and cost of propaganda technology, the cultural and political context in which persuasion is being attempted, and the technical skills and judgment of the opinion influencers and their advisers.

The *strategic* problems are far more perplexing. How do leaders of political opinion "bank" support in such a way that it will be available for future struggles? Political leaders are greedy; and they are insecure. They need to maximize their support, ensure its continued existence, and at the same time minimize the political cost of these endeavors. Opinion leadership of small groups and local geographical enclaves is relatively simple on this score; tactical shrewdness and persistence may be enough, with little need for aggregation. As leaders of opinion reach out to broader, more variegated publics and confront the cleavages and conflicts inherent in these publics they face the problem of economy or parsimony: how can they aggregate public opinion to support their ambitions and purposes without suffering undue costs that include the threat of failure?

One strategy is *the organization of a large personal following,* a following so devoted to the leader that it overwhelms the internal conflicts that might otherwise fragment it. This may involve a strategic leader response to the hero-worship phenomenon. Latin America has offered some prime examples of this strategy at work. The politics of *personalismo* has embraced the organization of political opinion around compelling and colorful personalities; the subordination of political parties and platforms to a leader's personal organization, which offers them unswerving and uncritical support; and, if the leader wins office, the establishment in government of a personalized structure with essentially a "patrón relationship between leaders and followers." Political personalism is a promising strategy for dynamic, charismatic leadership; its great weakness for those interested in realizing political goals and achieving real social change is that the movement rises and falls with the success of a less than immortal leader. Hence it is no substitute for transforming leadership.

Parties are usually able to transfer support from leaders to successors within the party; personal leadership usually cannot be so transferred. There was some indication that the support of Getulio Vargas, president of Brazil for twenty years between 1930 and 1954, had been transferred to a successor, but closer inspection revealed that Vargas and his successor each had to build his own personal following, which turned out to be not transferable even within the same party—or, indeed, within the same political family. Similarly, the personal support of Juan D. Perón in Argentina could not be shifted at will; only the return of Perón from exile could re-establish the personalist relationship. Another example comes from the United States civil rights movement and organizations like the Southern Christian Leadership Conference, whose highly personal leadership under Martin Luther King, Jr., could not after his assassination be effectively transferred. As a strategy of opinion leadership, personalism may be a useful way station for developing societies that lack an established party system or dependable channels of access to leadership positions, but in most large and heterogeneous societies personalism provides too frail a basis for continuing leadership and leadership succession, at least in the eyes of subleaders, activists, and followers committed to a long-run effort to achieve major social change.

An alternative strategy for aggregating political opinion as a foundation for political leadership is *the mobilization of support by socio-economic class*. A class-based strategy would seem simple on the face of it. Since virtually all societies harbor significant differences in income and property, and since these tendencies seem to persist over decades and even centuries, and since the haves and the have-nots would seem to have a natural antipathy toward each other as they compete for limited resources, at least two political groupings would seem to be available to political leaders skilled at making appeals to proletariat (or working classes) on the one hand or to bourgeois (or upper classes) on the other. Since most political issues, government decisions, and ultimate administrative actions have major implications for the distribution or redistribution of goods and income, it would not seem difficult for political leaders to find a secure footing in one of the two opposing camps.

In fact the difficulties are formidable. Potential followers do not necessarily perceive the possibilities that politicians might expect them to; among lower-income, less-educated, and less-involved groups in particular, class-oriented political issues are not easily grasped or related to daily life. The "masses" may simply not be aware of the "objective" conditions that others see. In other cases they may be aware of—they may have full *cognition* of—their objective class position or status, but they may feel that nothing *need* be done about it (their situation is ordained by God or fate or their enemies or their own incapacities), that nothing *can* be done about it (they are trapped by ineluctable circumstance), or that something can or should be done about it but not by government or political leadership. Such was the status of many Southern pre-civil rights blacks.

Members of higher socio-economic classes may be similarly uninformed, unmotivated, passive, isolated, or hopeless, even in defense of their property and income. For them conflict may be cross-cutting rather than reinforcing. In situations where members of classes do perceive their class status and wish to act on that perception, further impediments to class action remain. They may be highly sensitive to non-class-oriented issues (such as religion, region, race, foreign relations, ethnic attachment) that instead of reinforcing class consciousness (as they may do in certain circumstances) muddy and deaden it. Members of repressed lower-status groups may be aware of the nature of the class (or racial) position and aware of the possibilities for change. In such situations, civil rights leadership can galvanize the group to act as in the American South. But in such cases the potential must have been nurtured by leadership before action can be possible—a combination of transactional and transforming leadership. Even if members of classes are brought to a high pitch of class consciousness and class conflict, there may still be a gap between their attitudes and their willingness to act politically—and often to face serious personal risk—in response to those attitudes. In short, the seemingly logical chain (or interactions and interlocks) from "objective" class position to subjective class position, to class awareness, to perception of relation of class to politics and political leadership, to full class consciousness, and to meaningful class political action in support of leaders—that chain is broken or can be broken in many of its presumed linkages.

A third strategy for the aggregation and stabilization of political opinion in support of leadership is the use of the *political party*. Parties vary widely in their desire and capacity to influence the political opinions of their own members and activists and those of the voters they seek to retain or win over. A zealous, disciplined, ideological, and programmatic party with extensive participation, operating in a context of relatively unstructured public opinion, presumably has more transforming influence than an old and settled party that has largely adjusted to existing political institutions and structures of public opinion. In either case, however, and in the many types of parties that lie between these poles, purposeful leadership within the party is able to use party symbolism and machinery to activate and stabilize opinion. With older parties, merely seizing control of the party label ("Democratic" or "Republican," "Socialist" or "Christian Democrat") and presenting new proposals and ideas under the name and rubric of that party will result in support—or at least the lack of opposition—from a great many party members. The new ideas take on a kind of legitimacy from the party identification alone.

The process is mainly a transactional one. The great body of party opinion is open to some stimulus and movement at the hands of a party leader who can use the party symbolism and mechanism to bring about change in rank-and-file attitudes. Party leaders must to some degree adapt themselves to party tradition, expectations, and claims in seeking to wield influence for change. Once having achieved change, the party leaders can assume a certain stability of party attitudes as they seek to publicize or effectuate the new policy. Thus, under the leadership of Roosevelt and other New Dealers, the Democratic party came to support a program of social security; once that kind of support was insured, Roosevelt and subsequent party leaders could go on to new concepts of public welfare-ism with a large and dependable reservoir of support within the party.

The interaction may be rather subtle, especially in nations with poorly organized party systems and ill-defined linkages between party leadership and party rank and file. "Given the nature of the party as an instrument and the kinds of broad issues with which it is associated in the minds of its followers," Key notes, "one should not necessarily expect an immediate articulation in time or a precise congruence in fit between the opinions of party identifiers and party leadership. Yet of the capacity of mass opinion to bring party to its service in the long run there can be little doubt." Party leadership does not slavishly represent either partisan or mass opinion. It can expect a certain salutary misperception by the "mass" of leadership positions, combined usually with a faith in the leadership based on expectations that the leaders ultimately will satisfy the needs and wants of party members.

So subtle indeed are the transactions not only between leader and rank and file but between all degrees of leadership and followership within the party—quite aside from demands and pressures from outside party ranks—that it usually takes leaders a long time so to consolidate their position in the party that they in turn can use the party for social and political ends. The same concessions they had made in order to win backing within the party, the explicit or implicit trades they arranged, may return to haunt them when as leaders they seek leverage within the party. In most cases this condition makes for gradualism in changes of party opinion and behavior; in certain circumstances, however, leadership can thwart incrementalism. Leaders may have so dominated the founding or early growth of a party that it becomes almost inseparable from their personality and program, and they can use it as virtually their personal instrument—as in the case of Luis Muñoz Marín and the Popular Democratic party in Puerto Rico—though this kind of development may lead to overpersonalism in the party. Or leaders may rise through the parliamentary party and thus hold positions that enable them to influence party policy intimately without being overly dependent on the party rank and file; British ministers have often exemplified this relationship. Or leaders may be brought in—or may push their way in—from far outside the party and exert leverage on party opinion and policy without having had to give forfeits to the party rank and file.

Such was the achievement of Wendell Willkie in 1940 when, after a short and brilliant campaign, he won the Republican presidential nomination and found himself the captain of a great and historic party that had to go along with his view of election exigencies despite grumbling in the ranks. Willkie preached government economy; few could match the political economy with which he had suddenly seized the organization, apparatus, name, symbolism, and appeal of an established party. Jimmy Carter also "came in from the cold" to capture the Democratic party nomination in 1976, but he went on to win in November and thus inherited both the brokerage problems of transactional leadership and the moral dilemmas of transforming leadership.

In shaping political opinion how much scope and initiative is left in the hands of leaders? In developing nations, where mass opinion may be amorphous and volatile, leaders like Nkrumah or Muñoz Marín may have considerable leeway in the manner in which they seek to mobilize and align popular attitudes. In the more mature and stabilized polities, leaders may operate under narrower restraints. It may seem much easier and certainly safer to seek marginally aggregative changes for playing the same old transactional politics of stabilized party and parliamentary politics than to repudiate the existing system, seek to realign popular support in radically different ways, and run the risk of breaking a party instead of remaking it. What makes the latter an especially formidable act is the tendency of the rank and file and of rank-and-file leaders to cling to existing political attitudes and arrangements. The realignment of support is peculiarly a responsibility of leadership, and only bold and gifted leadership can accomplish it.

At great junctures of history the need for realignment may seem evident to some, but a nation may lack the intellectual and institutional resources for drastic change. It was clear in the 1930s that France suffered from a dangerous immobilism or *stasis* in its multi-party system, with its "hair-trigger" parliamentary coalitions that exploded under pressure. Some leaders like Georges Mandel spoke up for a strong central executive that would take clear stands on issues and bring about a two-party system by forcing parties to align either for or against the executive leadership. In the mid-1930s Léon Blum and his associates took a small step in this direction by fashioning a Popular Front of the Radical, Socialist, and Communist parties, but the coalition collapsed under the pressure of rising German power, the Spanish Civil War, economic crisis, and other developments. In postwar France Charles de Gaulle founded and then deserted the *Rassemblement du peuple français.* Later he helped fashion a new constitutional system in which executive power predominated, but whether this change would convert the pluralistic party system into a two-party system polarized around competition for the top executive office seemed doubtful years after de Gaulle's venture.

British party leaders during the past century have acted in political contexts that allowed more rewarding efforts to gather opinion behind leaders. Conservative party leadership showed the way. During a period of urbanization and suburbanization when the effects of the Industrial Revolution were coming to a peak, the Tories accepted the inevitability of enfranchisement and political participation by the middle-class and working-class masses, generally supported the enfranchising legislation, and managed to retain the support of large sections not only of the middle classes but of the working class as well. Study after study has shown that through a century of vast domestic and international change the self-styled Tories have managed to hang on to roughly one-third of the working-class vote. Socialists and Labourites have been appalled and astonished by the failure of so many working-class people to vote their apparent self-interest. "Once again the proletariat has discredited itself terribly," Engels wrote to Marx as he watched the returns from factory districts following the general election of 1868. Some rationalized that the working-class "defections" comprised simply a "deferential vote" still enamored of crown and aristocracy, but analysis of the vote showed that many workers voted Tory because they felt that the Conservatives could govern the nation more effectively, at least on problems outside the orbit of domestic economic affairs. The Liberal party leadership also showed some capacity for re-aggregation of political opinion and party support, especially in the efforts of the "Birmingham Caucus" and Joseph Chamberlain to build a stronger constituency organization within the party.

It can be argued that both the Conservative and the Liberal efforts at re-aggregation were essentially only shrewd efforts to maximize popular support through moderate changes or minor concessions in party appeal and organization. The decisions of British Labour leaders following World War I are perhaps a better example of a strategy of realigning party support. Although

Labour had struck off in an independent direction around the turn of the century, Labourites and Liberals as a practical matter had been cooperating, especially during wartime. Some in both parties hailed the new coalition tactics in the hope that cooperation would benefit both sides. On the other hand, there was disillusionment on each side; trade-union membership and Labour militancy had grown during World War I, and, while the Liberal party leadership saw advantages in continued alliance with Labour, many of the constituency leaders and parties were opposed. What was probably decisive in this balance of conditions was a growing sense of class consciousness in Labour ranks, a sharpened set of wants, goals, and expectations, and the vision of party leaders such as Arthur Henderson who saw the possibilities of independent Labour party action based on a clear appeal to working-class ideology and interests. Labour's subsequent replacement of the Liberals as the second—and on several occasions the first—party of Britain seemed to vindicate this strategy.

In no large nation has the role of political leadership in the aggregating and realigning of public opinion been more intricate and puzzling than in the United States. The reasons for this are at least twofold: Americans have on the whole failed to embrace sets of strong and intense political doctrines that could serve as a foundation for purposeful and consistent behavior by rival sets of leadership; and powerful regional forces in the United States, combined with a system of federalism that left extensive governmental authority in the hands of state leaders (including representatives of states and localities in Congress), made aggregation of opinion slow and difficult and realignment of voters uneven and spotty. These and related forces have produced less the vigorous expression and significant exercise of leadership than its frustration.

The early decades of the nineteenth century witnessed the growth and flowering of a mass-based, two-party system in the United States. The early parties centered in legislative leaders and local notables were transformed through the raising of great national issues and the dramatic expansion of the suffrage into nationwide parties based firmly in state and local party organizations and invigorated by new party institutions such as caucuses and conventions. The chief leaders of this great party-building process were Jefferson and Jackson, but equally important were a host of party unifiers such as Clay in the Whig party and Van Buren in the Democratic party who were skilled in building interregional and intergroup alliances. By the 1840s American parties had the key characteristics of a stable, mature, and participatory politics: they were well organized, competitive, and directly representative of the voters. And the two parties divided over meaningful national issues that shaped public opinion, such as tariffs, the banking system, and government subsidy of internal improvements.

In those decades American political development followed the classic path that would later be seen as characteristic of developing polities. Public opinion was aggregated in national parties after first aligning around meaningful individuals, interests, and issues. The critical test of leaders and followers would be their capacity to *reshape* opinions and *realign* popular support as new problems and issues challenged the nation. Such reshaping and realigning are not matters merely of shifts in party balance but of basic, organic change. Realignments, according to Walter Burnham, "are themselves constituent acts: they arise from emergent tensions in society which, not adequately controlled by the organization or outputs of party politics as usual, escalate to a flash point; they are issue-oriented phenomena, centrally associated with these tensions and more or less leading to resolution adjustments; they result in significant transformations in the general shape of policy''; and they shape the roles of institutional elites.

Clearly the first and most portentous strategic decision leaders must make if they wish to aggregate and align opinion on a grand scale is whether or not to work through political parties. It may be tempting *not* to follow a strategy of parties. Leaders then can make a direct appeal to potential followers, build their following and their organization as they wish, coalesce with other groups as events and conditions suggest, pressure and lobby the government from the outside, and stick to their goal toward the realization of which they mobilize all their resources. Countless examples of strikingly successful independent political action could be cited. One of the most notable was the Anti-Saloon League, which cowed both major parties, focused intense pressure on legislators and other government officials, and accomplished the rare feat of putting across a constitutional amendment that denied Americans liquor. To follow party strategy, on the other hand, requires an effective appeal to rank-and-file partisans and their leaders, a watering down of program and principle in order to be acceptable to leaders of a major party, toleration of coalition and compromise with dubious-looking party factions, and in general a willingness to subordinate one's zealously supported cause to the general interests of the party.

In the long run, however, the lure of party is usually irresistible. Party offers the leader of a cause a large body of troops, experienced rank-and-file leadership, and a tested standing with a substantial portion of the electorate. Party also brings the leader of opinion or candidate into a direct relation with the election process through which opinion can be converted into votes, government policy, and social and economic change. To opt for the party route does not, of course, settle the strategic questions that face the leaders and transactors of opinion. They will have to decide whether to throw their lot with one or another of the major parties or perhaps work through both or all of them. Or they may choose to capture a minor party or establish a new party that could be transformed into a major threat to the existing dominant parties, as in the case of the British Labourites. Such strategic choices will be decisively influenced by the peculiar combinations of popular needs and goals, electoral patterns, intraparty organization and interparty competition, and realignment potentials that dominate specific polities.

Voting: The Conversion of Opinion

"How does this vague, fluctuating, complex thing we call public opinion—omnipotent yet indeterminate, a sovereign to whose voice everyone listens, yet whose words, because he speaks with so many tongues as the waves of a boisterous sea, it is so hard to catch—how does public opinion express itself in America . . . ?" Lord Bryce asked. The best index to public opinion in the United States and other Western democracies, Bryce felt, was election results. With the advent of polling and other techniques of measuring opinion, students of the subject have less confidence than Bryce in the extent to which elections mirror popular attitudes with any exactitude. Elections are more important than polls, however, as a link between opinion and government action; elections are both a rough reflection of opinion and a *decision*.

For political leaders an election is an opportunity to convert realigned political support into government office, status, and power. They must bring together aggregations of political attitudes and election processes. Public opinion, as they see it, is a congeries of existing and potential attitudes in all conditions of consensus and cross-cutting cleavage, as vague and fluctuating in appearance as Bryce noted. The election system, moreover, is never neutral. Even the most elaborate attempts to produce elections that perfectly mirror public opinion produce some distortion, if only as a result of mechanical problems; more important, the theoretical basis on which the election arrangements are established has profound consequences for the conversion of public opinion into government policy and action. The Weimar Republic, with its mathematically impressive system of transferring and pooling votes in order to reflect every ripple of public opinion, was incapable of identifying and acting on the aggregated and unifying—as against the proportionate and plural—attitudes that might have made survival of the republic possible. In France, under certain constitutions, the existence of a "list" system in multiple-member constituencies and the order of placement of individual candidates on the list had major consequences for what candidates were elected and hence what sets of political attitudes might be directly represented in government.

The ways in which parties nominate candidates, the ability of nonparty groups to put candidates on the ballot through petition-gathering or other devices, laws regulating political money, the size of constituencies and the "fairness" with which they are drawn up, the number of offices filled by election and the extent to which different constituencies overlap one another, the mechanics of voting on election day—these and a host of other factors produce endless mixes of electoral arrangements. Effective political leaders must know how their election systems operate—and can be operated. And they must have a grasp of public opinion not only in its general form but in the way that it responds to particular electoral influences. In New Zealand this would mean recognizing the continued force of class voting despite the claim of many New Zealanders that theirs is a classless society. In Norway it would mean recognition of the special importance of the interaction of geography, climate, religion, social class, and an underlying disquiet about the role of central authority. In Sweden it would mean recognition of the importance of consumerism, modernism, and social planning. In Israel it would mean recognition of a peculiar mixture of religious, traditionalist, and modernist attitudes joined with an obsession for security. All these are perhaps recognitions of the obvious, but it is the ability to divine existing and latent opinion, to understand and perhaps influence election arrangements, and above all to combine the two that marks the great strategist of party, opinion, and election leadership.

Like lightning flashes in the night, elections suddenly illuminate the political battlefield and throw long-developing forces into shadowy relief. Political chieftains who have been drumming up support and perhaps boasting of their phalanxes of followers are put to the test. Leadership falls into the hands of combatants who, in a Tolstoyan murk of battle, joust with chosen opponents and try to bring into action huge, ill-informed rank and file who may or may not show up on the day of battle, election day.

Who are these electoral leaders? An important and hotly contested election will bring a broad spectrum of leadership into play. On the continuing assumption that political cleavages evolve out of shifting and sharpening wants, needs, and attitudes, leaders respond to and in turn intensify issue conflicts structured by these cleavages.

We can discern, first, leaders of strong but unorganized bodies of opinion that will deliver some votes to them on election day; second, leaders of organized groups that take positions on issues relevant to their groups' interests and opinions; third, leaders of minor parties, or of factions within major parties, who bring influence to bear on elections through marginal or balance-of-power tactics; fourth, major party leaders who seek to arouse rank-and-file support for their nominated candidates; and fifth, the candidates themselves, who try to build electoral majorities not only from the party rank and file but from any group they can win over. These several sets of leadership bring differing perceptions, goals, and interests to bear on one another in the electoral arena.

Public attention tends to fasten on the year-in, year-out election battles between the "ins" and the "outs." Far more significant, usually, are the struggles within parties and between party and nonparty leaderships over the makeup of the "ins" and the makeup of the "outs"—that is, over *what* wins, not simply *who* wins, the election decision. Such struggles usually revolve around a basic conflict between the *issue* leaders committed to some cause or program and the *party* leaders who head organizations that typically have existed for a long time, that have built up a heavy load of obligations and loyalties to extraparty and intraparty groups, that support a wide range of policies rather than concentrating on any one cause, and that have as their goal maintaining their own organization as well as using it for broader objectives. Sometimes the surge of a vital new cause may reinforce existing lines of conflict within a party or between parties. Occasionally the polarization of opinion that accompanies a transforming moral issue or burning cause cuts across, disrupts, and refashions dominant lines of cleavage—and this is the kind of event that "makes history." Slavery was such a cause in American history.

The interaction of goal or issue or "cause" leadership (as we shall call it) and party leadership is worth a closer look. Cause leaders differ among themselves depending on such factors as the intensity of their commitment to the cause; whether or not they espouse other, possibly conflicting causes; and their present or potential location or involvement in an attitudinal group oriented around the cause, or in an organized group supporting the cause (and perhaps other causes), or in a minor party committed to this and/or other causes, or in a major party (in power or out of power) attentive to the cause and interested in exploiting it. Party leaders hold differing perspectives and tactical positions depending on their estimate of the salience of the cause to leaders and followers in the party as a whole; depending on its salience to the party wing or territorial group with which the party leader is connected; on the extent and nature of the competition between the two major parties; on the continued strength of loyalty within the party to other causes that might conflict with the new cause; and on the extent to which the persons who really lead the party are not the organization leaders with long-run commitments to the party but candidates or officeholders who may use the party simply for their own opportunistic, short-run purposes.

Leaders of major parties may react to the rise of powerful and controversial new issues in different ways in their efforts to win elections and gain or regain office. Consider five major types of responses.

1. One or both major party leaderships may straddle the issue or absorb it, "morselize" it, tame it, and make it agree with other goals the party is committed to (as in the cases of health and housing in Britain).

2. The leadership of both major parties may fail to respond to the emerging cause to the point of not even trying to absorb it. In that event a new minor party leadership may try to ride to office with it. (Organized mainly over the slavery issue, the new Republican party followed this strategy in 1856.)

3. Burning issues may slice through long-frozen party leadership structures like a hot knife, bringing lasting realignment of the polar and centrist forces in either or both major parties as new leaders rise with new issues and old leaders decline with diminishing ones. (Such was the impact of slavery and civil war in the United States.)

Three types of leaders may respond to the new cause and cling to it, James Sundquist notes: zealots who are truly committed to the cause and may even subordinate their own interests to it, opportunists who may have little personal involvement in the issue but use it to benefit their own careers, and established political leaders in areas where the cause has its greatest appeal and who are thus compelled by constituency pressures to support it. The zealots must defeat, then, "not only their opponents on the issue, but also the straddlers and the policy of straddling. Indeed, they and their opponents have a mutual interest in a further polarization of the community that will discredit the straddlers and remove the basis of their support."

4. A great cause may gather such wide, intense, and persisting support that it overwhelms the leadership structure of one or both parties. In that event the party may decline and disappear (as in the case of the Whigs in the 1850s). On the other hand, *both* major party leaderships may respond to the supporters of such a cause or movement (as in the case of the reaction of both Democratic and Republican party leaders to the American Progressive movement of the first years of this century), though only with a good deal of backing and filling.

5. Perhaps the most significant type of response of party leadership to new issues develops when leaders of one major party are more responsive to the issue than those of the other. Polarizing forces are more likely to develop in the party out of power because that party is looking for new issues to upset the current party balance while the "ins" are broadly satisfied with the status quo. In this case leadership in one party may be realigned but not in the incumbent party, though in the long run the party that has picked up and exploited a persisting issue (as the Democrats did with the depression in the 1930s) will have a strategic advantage over the opposition.

The form of the realignment, Sundquist notes, is determined by the degree of difficulty encountered by the polar forces backing the new issue in gaining control of one of the major parties and by the extent of the development of the issue at the time that control is gained. Realignment reaches its peak in one or more critical elections that may resolve or block the realigning process.

Political historians have identified three major realigning periods in American history. The first came almost on the heels of the establishment and consolidation of a two-party system in the United States. By the 1830s and 1840s both the Democrats and the Whigs were national parties loosely aligned against each other over familiar issues like the tariff and internal improvements. The cause of abolitionism of slavery was barely a cloud on the horizon; indeed, in many Northern localities abolitionists were rejected, hated, and persecuted. Propelled by slowly developing religious, economic, and anti-establishment attitudes, antislavery feeling grew in New England and along the New England migration trails into the upper midwest. Rebuked by the major parties, the antislavery forces formed third parties—the Liberty party in 1840 and the Free Soil party eight years later. And they rediscovered the great strategic drawback of third-party action: the party tended to draw support from the major party closer to it in its position in the cause and thereby helped the most antagonistic party (in this case the Democrats).

Antislavery leaders met this dilemma by working increasingly in the Whig party, divided as it was between Conscience Whigs and Cotton Whigs but eager to find a winning issue against the generally dominant Democrats. Continued straddling of the slavery issue by most of the leaders in the two major parties—especially in the Compromise of 1850—produced a rapid strengthening of polar elements in both parties. Split north and south between militants and moderates, the Whig party fell into pieces; the Democratic party, split the same way, continued as a national coalition under "Northern leaders with Southern principles," but power in the party flowed more and more into the hands of the Southerners. In 1856 a new force, the Republican party, inherited much of the voting strength of the Free Soilers and the Conscience Whigs. By 1860 the now explosive impact of the slavery issue split the Democratic party in two, enabling the Republicans to win the presidency. The election of 1860 reflected and catalyzed forces that had been gathering for at least a generation.

Republicans, victorious in war as in politics, quickly developed a vested interest in exploiting the old slavery issue—now the secessionist issue—following the Civil War. "Vote as you shot," Union Army veterans were exhorted. The Republicans, embracing major elements of industry, labor, farming, and the Grand Army of the Republic, established themselves as the dominant party coalition. The Democrats fought their way back to major party status with remarkable speed; by the 1880s they were hotly contesting the Republicans for the presidency, and under Grover Cleveland they won popular-vote pluralities three times in a row (though failing to carry the Electoral College on the second occasion, in 1888). What could threaten a two-party system reestablished so strongly? The answer lay in the gathering unrest in the cities and on the farms. Panics, depressions, rising prices, labor exploitation, desperate strikes, low farm prices, tight money—these and other sources of unrest and protest seemed to set the stage for a new party alignment.

For a long time, the Democrats could not capitalize on discontent for several reasons: their leader, Grover Cleveland, had little appeal to aroused farmers and laborites; the party still suffered from the old stigma of "rum, Romanism, and rebellion"; and the Southern and rural elements of the party did indeed exercise undue influence in its councils. A series of third-party efforts—Greenbackers, workers, farmers, populists, and others—sharpened the issues without displacing either of the major parties. Both parties remained under conservative leadership while forces within them polarized. In 1896, aroused by the oratory of William Jennings Bryan, agrarian, Western, populist, Southern, and silverite leaders in the Democratic party wrested control from the Eastern conservatives and "gold bugs" at the party's national convention. The Democrats had absorbed and exploited the populist thrust, but at fearful cost. Bryan's geographical appeal was so limited that he lost every Northern state east of the Mississippi, every county in New England, and the bulk of labor in the industrial East. While sections of the Democratic party were permanently radicalized, or at least agrarianized, the Democrats were left as a minority party and would not win the presidency again until the Republicans split asunder in 1912. It was a partial realignment, with cold comfort for the G.O.P.'s opposition.

The first two realignments had been slow in the making, as the forces of protest gathered momentum, but each had come to a peak in one crucial realigning election. The third realignment came hard on the heels of a fast-changing economic and social situation but manifested itself in a series of elections over several decades. This was the "Roosevelt realignment" of the 1930s—and its dissimilarity with the first two realignments offers a major insight into the roles of party leaders and election leaders.

When the Great Depression began to grip the nation's economy at the end of the 1920s the leadership of both major parties was still in the hands of conservatives. Both parties had responded to the progressive impulse during the first two decades of the century, but now the dominant leadership elements in both parties endorsed the goals of limited national government, low taxes, government economy, rugged individualism, states' rights, and similar policies and shibboleths of the 1920s. In each major party a small group of leaders took a progressive stance. Liberal Republicans could boast of men like senators William Borah of Idaho and Charles L. McNary of Oregon and of governors of the Theodore Roosevelt tradition, Democrats of their Al Smiths and Franklin Roosevelts in governorships and the David Walshes and Robert F. Wagners in the Senate. As the opposition party looking for a winning issue, the Democrats might have seen some hope in combining progressives in all parties against the conservative Republicans, but the Democrats had neither the leadership nor the doctrine—and certainly not the unity—to accomplish such a strategic feat. The nomination of Smith in 1928 was a daring departure from the old politics, but the appeal of the Happy Warrior, like that of Bryan, was too narrow to pull together a winning combination.

The situation drastically changed in the early thirties, during three racking years of unemployment, despair, and unresponsive government. Roosevelt united the Democratic party behind his 1932 campaign, and he appealed also to "Bull Moose" Republicans. While Roosevelt's race was too cautious and calculated to bring over progressive Republicans *en masse,* it was shrewd enough to bring electoral victory. Then came the final months of economic paralysis under Hoover; Roosevelt's electrifying leadership during the "hundred days"; the first flush of recovery, psychological as well as economic; spreading tumult and upheaval as workers, farmers, old persons, the jobless, and other restive groups moved into political action behind new leaders like John L. Lewis, Huey Long, Father Coughlin; Roosevelt's shift to the left in the "second hundred days" of 1935; his passionate appeal to the great majority in the campaign of 1936 and his massive, nationwide victory.

The election of 1936 seemed to mark the high-point of a third great period of party realignment, with the Democrats becoming the clearly liberal party and the Republicans discarding their progressive wing for good. And to a degree, with the flow of "Roosevelt Republicans" into the New Deal ranks and the exodus of conservative Democrats, the parties were realigned. But it was a partial realignment, and therein lies its special interest. After his 1936 mandate Roosevelt proceeded with controversial reforms such as his Supreme Court-packing proposal and his effort to "purge" the Democratic ranks of anti-New Deal members of Congress, mainly from the South. But the realignment set in motion at the presidential level seemed to have little impact in the South and in a number of Northern states. The great majority of conservative Southern senators and representatives were wholly content to remain in the Democratic party even as the "socialistic" Roosevelt and his "left-wing brain trusters" seemed to be leading it on a sinister and dangerous course. Roosevelt for his part soon began conciliating the Southern Democrats on Capitol Hill after the failure of his "purge" so that by the end of the 1930s the Democratic party still seemed to be the awkward alliance of urban Northerners and rurally based Southerners that it had been for a century.

The reason for this nonalignment was in part the spreading aggression in Europe and Asia and Roosevelt's need for Southern support for his foreign policies, combined with the internationalist stance of most Democratic congressmen from the South. But the main reason lay in Roosevelt's brand of election and public-opinion leadership.

Roosevelt was a consummate manager of public opinion—probably, if one could measure these things, the most skillful and effective in American history. He showed a mastery of the techniques of communication, as in his use of the "fireside chat" to communicate directly with mass audiences, and in his ability to make press conferences serve his interests at least as much as those of the reporters. But he was not merely a technician; he influenced news largely because he *made* news in a never-ending stream of innovations, legislative proposals, little surprises, crisis actions, controversial reforms, and travels around the country and abroad. His personal charm helped him gain and hold the affection of an enormous variety of political and other leaders; his flair for persuading, yielding, advancing, retreating, demanding, compromising—as the immediate situation dictated—enabled him to keep the most diverse forces united, at least for a time, behind his programs.

One reason Roosevelt had a grasp on public opinion was that he studied public opinion; more than in any previous presidency, mail was analyzed, reports were collected from administrative agencies, and newspapers by the hundreds were clipped and digests compiled. The President also had more access to, and was more attentive to, opinion-polling data than was generally known at the time. Finally, Roosevelt had a superb sense of timing. He took care not to confront his political opponents when they were mobilizing; after waiting for the crest of the opposition effort to subside, he acted quickly. He recognized that at times the public wearied of reform and excitement and needed a breathing spell. Sometimes he moved very slowly in influencing public opinion, while his more militant lieutenants worried and grumbled; sometimes he moved very quickly. "I am like a cat," he said once. "I make a quick stroke and then I relax."

The acid test of opinion leadership is election victory, and Roosevelt rarely failed this test. In his long political career he won twice for state senator, twice for governor, four times for President; he failed only in an ill-conceived attempt to win a United States senatorial nomination over a Tammany-supported candidate and as James M. Cox's running mate in 1920 (a low point for the Democrats). Roosevelt won elections not only against redoubtable Republi-

can campaigners but against the election opposition of some of the most formidable opinion leaders of the day—not only Lewis, Coughlin, and Al Smith
(in 1936) but William Randolph Hearst, Burton K. Wheeler, Henry Luce, and
other leaders. And he pulled a host of other candidates into office on his broad
coattails.

Many of the same qualities that made Roosevelt a great mobilizer of
public opinion and harvester of votes made him less effective as a realigner of
parties. His day-to-day and election-to-election successes were so impressive
that there was less incentive to organize the Democratic party for the long run.
It was much easier to exploit his own personal skill for immediate needs than to
improve the rickety and sprawling party organization. To be sure, the President
did intervene in some state and local election struggles in 1938 against conservative Democratic candidates—a move that took some courage on the part of a
man who valued his personal friendships with politicians across the spectrum—
but the "purge" was a case in point: instead of devoting political resources to a
long-term building up of the grass-roots foundation for liberal Democrats, the
President intervened on a highly personal, unplanned, one-shot basis. The traits
that made Roosevelt a brilliant tactician—his dexterity, his command of a variety of roles, his personal charm and magnetism, his ability to manage public
opinion, his skillful and dramatic electioneering—were not the best traits for
hard, long-range, and purposeful building of a strong popular movement behind
a coherent political program.

All this might seem unexceptional—the natural tendency of a pragmatic
politician to deal with immediate, concrete problems—except that Roosevelt
himself was thoroughly aware of the fundamental weakness of the Democratic
party and the need for realignment. "Rex," he said to Rexford Tugwell one
night in 1932, "we shall have eight years in Washington. At the end of that
time we may or may not have a Democratic party; but we will have a Progressive one." He kept alive the hopes of Harold Ickes and other former Bull
Moosers as to the possibility of realignment. Then, in 1944, he raised the question explicitly, though indirectly, with Wendell Willkie, who by then had been
repudiated by centrists and conservatives in his own party. "I think the time
has come for the Democratic party to get rid of its reactionary elements in the
South, and to attract to it the liberals in the Republican party," Roosevelt said
to his counselor, Samuel Rosenman, in instructing him to talk with Willkie.
"We ought to have two real parties—one liberal and the other conservative. As
it is now, each party is split by dissenters." This was a long-range plan,
Roosevelt added, but "we can start building it up right after election this fall."
Willkie was interested but suspicious. He feared that Roosevelt might simply
be trying to win him over personally and to divide the Republican party at elec-

tion time. He decided to wait until after the election, but a month before the election Willkie died.

Succeeding Democratic presidents and Democratic presidential nominees inherited Roosevelt's strategic predicament but not always his flair for winning elections. They might have been willing to risk losing the support of conservative Southern Democrats in presidential elections in order to strengthen the Roosevelt coalition (including more and more Negro participation) in the North, since the "winner-take-all" mechanism of the Electoral College tended to favor the Northern or presidential Democrats. The Democratic nominees who won (save for Kennedy) did not need Southern support in the Electoral College; those who lost would not have been saved by it. Indeed, the South in this respect was lost anyway; starting with the anti-Catholic defection from Smith, and beginning again with the anti-civil rights defection from Truman, Southern states repeatedly withheld support from Democratic nominees and gave it to Republicans or third-party candidates, until its own favorite son, Jimmy Carter, won in 1976. Democratic presidents and nominees feared to repudiate the South less because of the election threat than because of the threat to their programs in Congress. Conservative Democrats often held the balance of voting power in both houses; and through the workings of congressional seniority their influence—especially their negative influence—was magnified.

So the great New Deal realignment era seemed stranded halfway through the realigning process, with the South supporting state and local Democratic tickets but not national ones, and with black and other liberal activists in the North denouncing the presidential Democrats for cowardice and hypocrisy and talking about a third-party movement of their own. Still, considerable realignment *did* take place, at the state and local levels, but mainly as a result of decisions made by state and local leaders and rank-and-file leaders, and it took place slowly. In the absence of national leadership, party realignment proceeded ponderously and erratically, but it proceeded. A host of rank-and-file leaders, rebelling against the liberalism of Truman, Kennedy, Johnson, and others, wrenched themselves away from their ancestral ties to the Democratic party. Many were young businessmen who increasingly preferred the Republican party and its doctrine of lower taxes, less spending, and minimal regulation of business. Others were segregationists who disliked the civil rights positions of both major parties but found the Republican a bit less unpalatable. Some officeholders and party officials, such as John Connally of Texas, abruptly switched major parties; others became political independents or joined third parties and then embraced Republicanism. The switching across the South was halting and uneven. Twenty-five years after the Democratic party's commitment to civil rights under Truman a large number of Southern seats in Congress were held by conservative Democrats, and they still benefited from seniority and from anti-majoritarian arrangements in Congress. But the straggling cross-over to the Republicans was continuing.

Why the sluggishness of the third great realigning period compared with the first two? The answer lay in part in the absence of the bold and transcending leadership of abolitionists and anti-abolitionists or progressives like Woodrow Wilson, Theodore Roosevelt, and Robert La Follette, Sr.—but only in part. The main reason lay in the change that had overcome the American party system during the twentieth century. Previously the parties were relatively so well organized and unified that considerable congruence existed between the national party and the state and local parties. "In the nineteenth century," according to Sundquist, "a man who was a Whig, a Democrat, or a Republican in presidential politics belonged automatically to the same party in state and local politics, and vice versa." Since 1932, however, voters have behaved very differently in presidential elections than in state and local.

The roots of this fundamental change lie, oddly enough, in the second realigning period, in the sharp geographical cleavage over Bryan in 1896. In many parts of the country the normal party balance was overturned when that election and subsequent elections left countless heavily one-party, noncompetitive districts in the "Solid North" as well as the "Solid South." Strong parties that almost always won, weak parties that never had a chance of winning—the combination encouraged a corrupt and flabby politics. This development coincided with and probably contributed to a powerful Progressive thrust against crude, unkempt party politics and in favor of nonpartisan, "independent" political behavior that could vanquish alike the ward boss and the trust, the machine and the monopolist.

On the premise that "the only cure for democracy is more democracy," the reformers proceeded, probably without fully understanding the implications of their actions, to dismantle party structures. The establishment of the direct primary in many states shifted control over nominations from the party organization to masses of voters far less responsive to party influence. Straight-ticket voting was discouraged in some states by abolishing party-column listings on the ballot. "Nonpartisan" elections—that is, elections in which candidates could not run as party nominees—were instituted in many cities. Civil service laws tried to eradicate party patronage. "Independence" was glorified as a civic virtue more concerned with issues and less devoted to personal leadership and party program. The vigorous partisan press of the nineteenth century gave way to the "independent," nonpartisan newspapers of the twentieth century. Later the advent of radio and television, both of which are determinedly nonpartisan and required by government to shun political bias, enabled candidates to make a direct appeal to the electorate without the intervention of party organization. State and local elections were set for years other than those of presidential elections in order to make "straight" party voting more difficult. Centralized party leadership was weakened in the House of Representatives with the overthrow of "Czar" Cannon.

These trends have produced an extensive decomposition of the American party system in many areas. "The political parties are progressively losing their hold upon the electorate," Burnham summarized. "The losses the two parties, particularly the Democrats, have suffered in this decade have largely been concentrated among precisely those strata in the population most likely to act through and in the political system out of proportion to their numbers. This may point toward the progressive dissolution of the parties as action intermediaries in electoral choice and other politically relevant acts." The sharp rise in split-ticket voting and the number of persons who classify themselves as independents are major indicators of this trend.

In the United States, as elsewhere, the leadership of opinion embraces many dimensions: needs, wants, attitudes; the structuring of opinions in varying degrees of ideological form and substance; parties in varying degrees of organization, realignments, and even dissolution; elections won or lost as a result of such variables—and ultimately the composition of government and the distribution of power. The most dynamic force making and shaking these interacting and balancing tendencies is the leadership of a mobilized public opinion in a situation of conflict where great leaders are taking opposing sides. Parties—essentially organizations of leaders and subleaders—can provide a base of organized opinion for great leadership. Ultimately it is the posing of great moral values that enables leaders to mobilize and direct opinion, organize, realign, and reorganize parties, and win not just an occasional election but enough elections to enable leaders to govern. Party opinion leadership is transactional leadership of a particularly significant type for it brings together fluid voluntary associations of leaders and followers committed to mutual goals.

The fact that leaders do not need merely to reflect superficial opinions and qualities in the electorate is dramatized by the extent that "great leaders" have arisen out of a hinterland or social enclave more than out of the heartlands of their countries. Napoleon came from Corsica, Lloyd George from Wales, MacDonald from Scotland, for example, even aside from Hitler's origins in Austria and Stalin's in Georgia. Disraeli, Franklin Roosevelt, de Gaulle, Lenin, Marx, Engels, to cite a few among hundreds of examples, were hardly sons of the proletariat, or even of the lower middle class. Some leaders have seemed in their own persons to violate everything their followers held dear. Thus Charles Stewart Parnell, as F. S. L. Lyons has noted, was an aristocrat leading a mainly middle-class party, a Protestant mobilizing Catholics, a landlord at the head of a party of landlord-haters. Jinnah, known to his Moslem followers as Qaid-e-Azam, or "Great Leader," violated in his personal demeanor some of the oldest customs of his movement. But what these leaders had was a powerful conviction of the rightness of their own and their followers' cause; the engagement of leaders and followers in such causes enabled leadership to transcend the conventional limits of superficial opinion-representation.

11

GROUP LEADERSHIP:
BARGAINERS AND BUREAUCRATS

The leader can be central to the cohesion and viability not only of nations and armies but of smaller, more ordinary groups. "The loss of the leader in some sense or other, the birth of misgivings about him, brings on the outbreak of panic," Sigmund Freud wrote in *Group Psychology and the Analysis of the Ego*. Freud observed that as a rule the ties between members of a group disappear at the same time that the tie with their leader is ended. The assassination of national leaders like Gandhi and John Kennedy produced psychic disorganization and social malaise in India and the United States. It has long been known, too, that the death of a unit commander on the battlefield can cause sudden demoralization and disintegration among his troops. The viability of less august groups may also hinge on their leadership.

Consider the case of the Norton Street boys, a Boston street-corner group of young men, all in their twenties, who might have struck a casual passerby as an amorphous collection of young drifters with little structure to their lives or to their friendships. As described in William F. Whyte's *Street Corner Society*, it was a group, and a most cohesive group, with stable interrelationships and a clear structure of leadership. At the top was Doc; beneath him were Mike and Danny and also Long John in a somewhat anomalous relationship; beneath Mike and Danny were Nutsy and Angelo and Frank and a half dozen other followers. Doc was the focal point for the organization of the group. "In his absence," an observer reported, "the members of the gang are divided into a number of small groups. There is no common activity or general conversation. When the leader appears, the situation changes strikingly. The small units form into one large group. The conversation becomes general, and unified action frequently follows. The leader becomes the central point in the discussion. A

287

follower starts to say something, pauses when he notices the leader is not listening, and begins again when he has the leader's attention. When the leader leaves the group, unity gives way to the divisions that existed before his appearance.''

Doc was born on Norton Street in the slums of Boston in 1908. His parents were among the thousands of Italian immigrants who during the late nineteenth century had settled in this area, only a step from the center of the city and the sites of celebrated revolutionary events. The youngest child in a large family, Doc was his mother's favorite. When Doc was three years old polio lamed his left arm, but through intensive exercise he regained almost the full use of it. During his early years his mother dressed him neatly and treated him as something of a model child. At the age of twelve Doc got into his first fight, at the instigation of an older brother, and won it. He found himself in a culture of physical competition and combat. Was it in compensation for the impaired arm that Doc fought his way to the top? He certainly discovered that once he had risen he could tell the boys on Norton Street what to do. "They listened to me. If they didn't, I walloped them." His part in the transaction was to give them protection; if one of his friends got beaten up, he would ask the victim to point out his oppressor—and he would wallop him, too.

Conflict with outsiders, and conflict within the group, helped create a stable network of interrelationships within the Norton Street gang. Corner boys developed their own norms, too. "We were the best street in Cornerville," Doc boasted. "We didn't lush [steal from a drunk] or get in crap games. Sometimes we stole into shows free, but what do you expect . . . ?" Doc did well enough in school, but after his third year in high school he left to take a job with a stained-glass firm. He lost his job when the firm collapsed during the Depression. Doc could find occasional work on the WPA but there were long layoffs. It was during these layoffs that he spent time with that most dependable and rewarding group he had ever known. Perhaps inevitably the group was involved in politics. Loyal to the "old country," it reacted defensively when Franklin Roosevelt denounced Mussolini's Italy, following the attack on France in 1940, as "the hand that held the dagger." Its main political role, however, was to serve as a somewhat independent unit at the foundation of large and extended campaign organizations. The stakes were small and personal. A Cornerville man could get ahead in politics either by supporting the Republican party, going into business, and, if successful, eventually moving out of the neighborhood, or by working with local Democratic "machines," delivering the Cornerville vote, and eventually rising through Democratic ranks—with probable involvement in the rackets. He could not go both routes. For the Corner boys the main reward from politics was some access to the machinery of local government and some protection from the harsher operations of the law.

Transactional leadership like this thrives in small groups. Formal or informal heads of groups act as brokers both within their groups and among groups. These transactions consist of mutual support and mutual promises, expectations, obligations, rewards. In retrospect the Wilsons and the Lenins, the Hitlers and the Gandhis appear as lofty figures towering over a shrunken political landscape peopled by masses of gray humanity and a few secondary and tertiary figures. In fact such giants were very much a product of, and remained always a part of, extended and complex structures of group relationships in which they not only influenced but were heavily influenced by these "lower" figures. The attention of biographers, however, diminishes as one descends the hierarchy of eminence. The renowned leader will typically be the subject of perhaps a hundred or more biographies. Lesser but still widely known leaders rate a handful of books—typically an "authorized" biography, a puff or two, a critical life that may take the form of a castigation or exposé, a revisionist treatment, and ultimately a more or less "definitive" account. Secondary figures such as cabinet members, leading parliamentarians, or minor dictators will be fortunate to gain a decent biography. (Dean Acheson is said to have been taken aback on reading a study that defined him as merely a dependent variable.) Beneath this level attention quickly dwindles; secondary and tertiary figures pass into the pages of history in the form of brief newspaper accounts, essentially autobiographical summations in *Who's Who,* and kindly obituaries. Yet to overlook these less eminent figures who allied with, influenced, and were influenced by the Wilsons and the Lenins is to overlook a crucial component of transactional leadership.

The Leadership of Small Groups

We know a good deal about the leadership of the Norton Street boys because in the late 1930s Whyte, then a young Harvard graduate student, settled in the heart of Boston to make a community study, enlisted the cooperation of Doc, and through Doc became a member of Norton Street society. Whyte's study, published in 1943, came at a time of intensifying interest in the structure and leadership of small groups. Observers had been aware of groups as the "foundations" of society since the days of classical political thought—Aristotle discussed bands and families—but the 1950s witnessed an explosion of interest in the subject, an interest that was both provoked and satisfied by intensive studies of bomber crews and other small groups during World War II and by the growing concern in business and industry with morale, compliance, and productivity on the part of clusters of workers.

Out of these studies, with their bias toward Western and particularly American experience, developed a relatively consistent definition of the small group—as a collection of persons with shared purposes and values; with face-to-face or otherwise physically close relations to one another; with extensive social contacts among themselves as a result of shared interests and influence on one another; and with some stabilization of roles.

Like the earlier studies of leadership and community, the analysis of small groups tended to exaggerate the importance of consensus and to minimize that of conflict within the group. The "group dynamics" school clung to an assumption that might be valid in the small group experimental situation but is not in an organizational context, Sidney Verba complained. "This may be called the 'no-conflict' assumption: that there is a single group goal or a single method of attaining a group goal that is in the best interests of all concerned—both leaders and followers." Interests of leaders and followers were assumed to be identical. Such an assumption has some validity for small experimental groups insulated from external pressures but not for complex social and political situations in which goals are in conflict.

Thus the group is assumed to be a collection of persons in a state of equilibrium. In this state, efforts to change the group to a new level or type of activity will bring pressures to return the group to its former equilibrium. The effort to change may generate hostility toward the leaders as the initiator of change, for it is their role to maintain a balance between the individual needs and wants of group members and the goal-oriented activity of the group as a whole.

This equilibrium rests on a structure of give and take. Small-group members talk with one another, laugh with one another, offer and receive advice, provide cues to one another, give and receive help, or, less typically, disagree and show antagonism. The more familiarity, the more interaction—and vice versa. A powerful factor is a sense of mutual obligation and a need for reciprocity. In some theories the group, as a system, is endowed with self-stabilizing, self-maintaining tendencies without significant internal strains and disturbed only by irritating forces from the outside. Whyte saw some of these phenomena of equilibrium in Cornerville. "Each individual has his own characteristic way of interacting with other individuals." The Norton Street gang had a remarkably fixed pattern of activity from day to day. Psychologically the Corner boys needed a stable and continuing group activity; materially they needed the benefits of a sense of mutual obligation, most notably in lending and borrowing money, in giving and receiving cigarettes or a cup of coffee.

A powerful tendency toward conformity develops in such small groups. Myriad experiments have demonstrated that individual perception of the most "objective" phenomenon is heavily influenced by group standards or judgments: the more ambiguous the phenomenon, the greater the conforming perception. The group tends to set standards not only for internal matters such as rates of productivity in an industrial plant but for activities outside the "jurisdiction" of the group; thus the choice of outside political leaders as well as of group leaders could be influenced by conformist tendencies. Conformity tends to increase with the attractiveness of the group (that is, its ability to reward its members in various ways) and with the amount of direct pressure from the group. "We do as the others do," Bernard Bass notes, "to avoid ostracism or censure from those we value, or to gain various rewards, such as encouragement, money, or friendship." Groups, like nation-states, may regard deviation as disloyalty, noncompliance as treason.

Conformity may be a mindless huddling up to one another, as in a herd, but typically the group coalesces around more or less explicit goals and norms. There is a *purpose* to the conformity or consensus. The standards of behavior with which group members are expected to comply are drawn from the explicit and implicit goals of the group. "Each person has within him a set of norms and goals which are a composite of his own idiosyncratic ideals, the expectations of the group in which he is participating at the moment, and the expectations of other groups of which he is also a member," A. Paul Hare writes. Some tension between individual needs and group expectations is almost inevitable. In the event of a conflict a kind of appeal may take place—an appeal to tradition, "group unity," the written or unwritten procedures, constitution, or declaration of purposes of the group, or to some "higher" moral code. To such a moral code dissenting members can also appeal. The deviating group member has four other resorts, according to Hare: to try to change the group norms, to remain a deviant, to leave the group, or to drop his opposition and conform.

Conformity does not depend on equal status among the members of the group; usually group statuses are closely perceived, and this may make for greater conformity, depending on the internal structure of the group and its extragroup relations. Members of groups usually rank one another informally on the basis of such factors as the recognized ability of the group member to relate to group goals, the extent to which the person lives up to group norms and follows group-approved procedures, and personal qualities that have no special relevance to the group but are highly valued in the culture. The process works both ways: as persons are valued for some quality close to group needs they tend to conform more and to raise their status even higher. In a group that has no clear goals or norms, members may be ranked on the basis of more general, amorphous criteria such as appearance or congeniality. The more certain and explicit the group goals, the more status will turn on competence or commitment to help achieve them; an athletic team will rank the star player higher in status (but not necessarily in popularity). Higher-status persons tend to be more centrally located in the communications network and to have a greater potential for group leadership—but the realization of this potential depends on a multitude of other factors.

The small group can be one of the most solid, durable, and highly structured entities in human society. Small groups have survived the most intense pressure and stress—indeed, have seemed to gain from such stress, as evidenced in the annals of countless military units. Many historians of war have attributed this brand of solidarity to the devotion of soldiers to a leader or a set of well-defined national goals. The portrait of German soldiers fighting in the name of their führer and an invincible German nation has become familiar; few small groups have exceeded the comradeliness, the solidarity, and the subordination to authority of the battalions that made up the German army during World War II. How explain this willingness to fight and die in the name of a remote leader or an abstract ideology? Edward Shils and Morris Janowitz interpreted the cohesion of the *Wehrmacht* as a direct result of soldiers' ability to identify their personal safety and survival with the advancement of Hitler and the Nazi cause on the battlefront. Observers found that the effectiveness of German troops depended little on their political or ideological concerns or even their concern for Germany's national survival; most of the soldiers knew little about the latest developments at the front. They were motivated instead by their dedication to Hitler as a strong, even immortal personality who would ensure their physical strength and protection. As long as the troops perceived their führer as a commanding figure, there was a high degree of solidarity and obedience to junior officers. Hitler was a brute power wielder, but his role was transactional for certain groups at certain times. When the image of a strong Hitler began to be discredited, the bonds between soldier and soldier and between soldiers and leaders weakened and military cohesion and effectiveness was undermined. The transaction ceased; there was no move upward to other levels of interchange.

In optimal conditions—for German soldiers, Hitler at the apex of his authority in 1940—group leadership will directly act for the group, enhance its solidarity, and steel it to its duties. So impressive are group unity, membership conformity, and leadership representativeness in both laboratory situations and real life, however, that a bias may result. Both groups and group leadership tend to be seen mainly as stable, unchanging systems of interaction structured around set tasks and clear goals, unmarred by conflict. Leaders emerge from the group; they are the agent of the group; they are at the center of group communication; they are the most conforming members of the group; to a large degree they are creations and captives of the group. But transactional leadership is also a force for intensifying group conflict, exercising power within the group, challenging and altering as well as conforming to group norms and values, and causing social change as well as preserving the status quo within and among small groups.

The main source of conflict in the small group is the affiliation of its members with more than one group. However central to persons may be their membership in a primary group such as family or work group, they do deal with members of other groups and must respond to other group needs and demands as the price of maintaining membership in those groups. Such overlapping group membership is a seedbed of potential conflict that becomes overt when group members, responding to competing group claims, challenge those of the central group. Such group members are taking roles, however briefly, as leaders. Overlapping group memberships precipitate conflicts not only between leaders but *within* them. Samuel Stouffer cites the familiar example of the noncommissioned officer caught in a conflict situation: "On the one hand, the noncom had the role of agent of the command and in case the orders from above conflicted with what his men thought were right and necessary he was expected by his superiors to carry out the orders. But he also was an enlisted man, sharing enlisted men's attitudes, often hostile attitudes, toward the commissioned ranks. Consequently, the system of informal controls was such as to reward him for siding with the men in a conflict situation and punish him if he did not." Such conflict situations can take the form of overlapping and competing group memberships, conflicting attitudes among group members toward the norms of different groups, and responsiveness of group members to contradictory expectations directed to them by different groups or group leaders.

Leaders tend to be more divided than other group members because they respond more intensively to external contacts than do other members. Some stabilization of conflict may result. Whyte notes the special status of the leader in relations outside the group: "The leader's reputation outside the group tends to support his standing within the group, and his position in the group supports his reputation among outsiders." The ability of the leader to relate the membership to the external environment also depends on the attitudes of the membership; the leader might lose out to a competitor.

Internal forces may produce conflict when the external ones are neutralized or in equilibrium, even in rare cases when the group exists in virtual isolation. Changing needs within a group—for example, a shift for members of a peasant family from physiological and safety needs to affection and esteem needs during a long period of rising agricultural prosperity and freedom from foreign invasion—could alter leadership composition and relations within the group. Conflict can develop around compelling problems such as a disparity between the group member's self-esteem and the esteem accorded by others. The more that members are esteemed by others in the group, the more they are likely to attempt leadership and to succeed; the higher their self-esteem, the more likely they will be to attempt leadership. A disparity between the two can lead to leadership conflict and a change in the leadership structure.

The same tendency prevails in a disparity between high status in the group and esteem by others. Bass summarizes: "If one's self-esteem is higher than the esteem he is accorded by other members, he is likely to attempt more leadership and succeed less than a member whose esteem matches (own) high self-esteem. Status and self-accorded status follow the same proposition. . . . Since status or esteem produces success as a leader, if the high-status member is not esteemed or vice versa, conflict is likely." Other dynamic forces within the group may make for conflict—for example, simple generational change, alterations in task assignment, and Oedipal relationships.

The extent to which group leaders exert power rather than merely symbolic authority turns on leaders' possession of resources that they can expend in tapping other group members' motive bases—wants, needs, motives, expectations, attitudes, and values—in order to induce or compel members (followers) to behave as the leaders wish them to. The group leaders' resources may be of many different types: formal authority, which can be converted into actual influence under certain conditions; their competence as related to tasks and goals the group members value; their centrality in the communications network, enabling them to control information; their anticipated ability to fulfill members' expectations. But the essence of the leaders' power is less the extent to which they can live up to general perceptions of leaders' style, role, and the like than the extent to which they can satisfy—or appear to satisfy—specific *needs* of the followers. These needs may be higher or lower, in A. H. Maslow's hierarchical formulation, but they are a continuing, dynamic, and variegated linkage between group leaders and followers. And they bring the followers strongly into the leadership process; if the leaders must ultimately satisfy followers' needs, the leaders' special role in the small group as well as in larger groups will embrace tasks from initiating to articulating to catalyzing action.

The more group leaders satisfy members' needs, the more political capital they accumulate to spend in the political marketplace. The leaders may threaten to deny members' "lower" needs. "No one is afraid of Caesar himself," Epictetus noted, "but he is afraid of death, loss of property, prison, disenfranchisement. Nor does anyone love Caesar himself, unless in some way Caesar is a person of great merit; but we love wealth, a tribuneship, a praetorship, a consulship. When we love and hate and fear these things, it needs must be that those who control them are masters over us.'' Similarly, when local party leaders (like the Democratic mandarins of Chicago) deliver their precincts, they are usually demonstrating less an ability to manipulate or steal than their effectiveness in meeting voters' needs by interceding with the welfare bureau, fixing a parking ticket, finding a job, or merely supplying recognition, affection, or esteem.

Typically the purpose of small groups is the achievement of these kinds of rather specific tasks. Group success and leader effectiveness are measured not only by the achievement of the task but by the extent to which the task embodies group values and the achievement furthers fundamental group goals. The goals may be multiple and, if so, should be hierarchically organized. One of the goals may be "meaningful social participation" by group members, as E. P. Hollander suggests, but this value might yield to a more fundamental one such as more equitable distribution of material and psychic income within the group or between groups. The test is the realization of "real change" as collectively determined by group leaders and followers, however small the political group may be.

Bureaucracy Versus Leadership

On the face of it, a bureaucratic organization would appear to embody leadership characteristics opposite to those of the small group and transactional leadership. The bureaucratic organization seems to be the product of a conscious decision by leadership to organize human and material resources for a carefully defined goal, while the small group is viewed as the more or less spontaneous, autonomous outgrowth of social conditions. Bureaucratic leadership would appear to have the formal and actual authority to organize and reorganize employees in hierarchical relations for both its continuing and its changing purposes. The small group may follow goals that may be ill-defined, conflicting, and susceptible to group change; its leadership may lack formal legitimacy and perhaps external credibility and be peculiarly vulnerable to the shifting loyalties and purposes of followers. It may be nonhierarchical. However tough and durable a small group may be, according to these perceptions, it draws these qualities from its own resources and not from formal or legal structures or authority. All this contrasts with stereotypes about bureaucracy.

Bureaucracy is the world of explicitly formulated goals, rules, procedures, and givens that define and regulate the place of its "members," a world of specialization and expertise, with the roles of individuals minutely specified and differentiated. Its employees are organized by purpose, process, clientele, or place. It is a world that prizes consistency, predictability, stability, and efficiency (narrowly defined) more than creativity and principle. Roles and duties are prescribed less by superiors (leaders) than by tradition, formal examinations, and technical qualifications. Careers and job security are protected by tenure, pensions, union rules, professional standards, and appeal procedures. The structure, Robert Merton notes, is one that "approaches the complete elimination of personalized relationships and nonrational considerations (hostility, anxiety, affectual involvements, etc.)." The more these personalized relationships are eliminated, the less potential there is for reciprocity, response to wants, needs, and values—that is, transactional leadership.

Bureaucratic behavior as characterized in this archetype is antithetical to leadership as defined in this volume. Through its methodical allotment of tasks, its mediating and harmonizing and "adjustment" procedures, its stress on organizational ethos, goals, and authority, bureaucracy assumes consensus and discounts and discredits clash and controversy, which are seen as threats to organizational stability. Bureaucracy discourages the kind of power that is generated by the tapping of motivational bases among employees and the marshaling of personal—as opposed to organizational—resources. Bureaucracy pursues goals that may as easily become separated from a hierarchy of original purposes and values as from human needs. And bureaucracy, far from directing social change or serving as a factor in historical causation, consciously or not helps buttress the status quo.

In this theoretical description of bureaucracy, authority is substituted for power. Bureaucratic authority is formal power that has been vested in persons by virtue of their holding certain positions, that is, vested in the positions themselves; the exercise of power under such authority is recognized both by rulers and decision makers and by those subject to the rules and decisions. The personal characteristics of superior and subordinate and the virtue or good sense of the rules or decisions are held to be irrelevant. Such authority may be used to influence subordinates under a system of rewards and penalties; but authority is typically accepted because the subordinate is motivated to respect its credibility and legitimacy. Formal authority does not acknowledge other motivational bases. Reliability and conformity are the hallmarks of bureaucracy; hence, Merton observes "the fundamental importance of discipline which may be as highly developed in a religious or economic bureaucracy as in the army."

Under this model "the bureaucratization of the world"—whether in democracies, dictatorships, or developing nations—has been so widely noted as to appear to be a universal or at least a dominant phenomenon. Max Weber observed, however, that bureaucratic authority historically was not the rule but the exception. Even in large political systems such as those of the ancient Orient, the Germanic and Mongolian empires of conquest, and many feudal structures of state, he noted, rulers carried out key measures through their inner circles of personal trustees, table companions, and servants of the court. In certain cultures, on the other hand, bureaucracies were the dominant basis of organization—as in Egypt during the new empire; the later Roman principate; the Roman Catholic Church, especially since the thirteenth century; China during most of its recent history; and the modern European state and the large complex capitalistic enterprise. To Weber, development of the money economy was a precondition for the establishment of pure bureaucratic organization. The shifting of the authority to tax and to allocate revenue from lord or satrap to central authority was crucial to the rise of central administration. The purchase of offices, commissions, and sinecures gave way to more impersonal, fixed, and "regular" ways of staffing governments. The most notable sphere of bureaucratization was *war*. As late as the Thirty Years' War the soldier still had personal ownership of his weapon, horses, and uniforms, the rank of officer was obtained through purchase of a commission, and the regiment served as an economic and managerial organization operating under the colonel as entrepreneur. War became bureaucratized when it was "nationalized" by the state, much as railways and utilities were later taken over by socialist governments.

Bureaucratization of society brought early reactions against its seeming impersonality and rigidity and against a collective arbitrariness that often exceeded the personal capriciousness of the ruler of old. Tocqueville warned of "an immense and tutelary power" that extended its arm over the whole community, covering "the surface of society with a network of small complicated rules, minute and uniform, through which the more original minds and the most energetic characters cannot penetrate, to rise above the crowd." The fact that this "humanitarian bureaucracy," as Robert Nisbet called it, was a product of mass democracy and egalitarianism made it seem no less threatening and insidious in the modern world.

Whether the reaction against bureaucracy takes the form of grumbling at the endless forms and waiting lines of Soviet officialdom, of complaining about the bottomless "paperwork" of large public and private bureaucracies in the United States, or of protesting the procedures in new nations associated with British and other colonial rule that are often exceeded by new native officials, that reaction is almost as universal as the process of bureaucratization itself. Reasoned repugnance toward bureaucracy is based mainly on two considerations. One is the fear that the individual is swallowed up in the machine, separated from tools, alienated from work, and ultimately, as Thorstein Veblen contended, trained into incapacity: Organization Man and Woman, anti-human, anti-individualistic, anti-their own real nature. The other fear, closely related, is that the original human *ends* of work or administration come to be submerged in organizational *means*. Once-rational procedure becomes foolish routine. Paperwork designed to enhance communication now blocks or distorts it. What was a considered hierarchy of ends and means is overturned as instrumental values are substituted for ultimate or terminal values. A change in motives on the part of the bureaucrat goes hand in hand with a displacement of goals, resulting in rigidity and ritualism.

These bureaucratic tendencies might seem far removed from the turbulent world of leadership, transformational or transactional, and especially of democratic politics. But one of the most searching dissections of bureaucracy took as its subject the seemingly most dynamic, popular, and goal-minded institution of democracy, the mass political party. Writing of trade unions as well as parties, Robert Michels enunciated a general rule that "the increase in the power of the leaders is directly proportional with the extension of the organization." Thus the "iron law of oligarchy" inverted the relation of leaders and led. The kind of political party that had been designed to challenge the old aristocratic or autocratic political organizations had itself bureaucratized political organization and stifled political action.

Michels' application of the iron law to political parties, Weber's thesis that the demos never "governs" larger associations but rather that the mass of people are governed by executives and administrators, the contention of a multitude of analysts that bureaucracy subordinates employees to rigid authority—such concepts pose a paradox for the study of leadership and bureaucracy. On the one hand, bureaucracy would seem to be, as we have noted, the very distillation of leadership, since administrative means are carefully organized to carry out explicit ends; if some of the directives may appear to be outmoded or anachronistic, leadership has the authority to change them. On the other hand, the classic stereotype of bureaucracy—rigidity, oligarchy, deference, impersonality, specialization, lack of reciprocal relationship of wants, needs, motives, and values between leaders and followers—would seem to represent the negation of leadership. To the extent that bureaucracy is *in practice* the simple application of authority from the top down, it is not leadership. To the extent that it exemplifies conflict, power, values, and change in accordance with leader-follower needs, it embodies leadership.

Even the outwardly most disciplined and unified bureaucracy may harbor latent and overt conflict. Analysis of an industrial organization will typically identify not only employer-employee tension but power struggles among top managers, between line and staff personnel, and among members with different professional affiliations or kinds of expertness, and other tensions that shade into the personal and the idiosyncratic. The most disciplined army is full of grumbling, jockeying, intramural competition, and criticism. Conflict is often sharper in public bureaucracies because of their legal obligations to respond to clientele groups which in turn exert pressures on them (e.g., taxpayer groups and contractors in relation to defense departments). Conflict between individual need systems and environmental demands, Warren Bennis postulates, occurs in all segments of organization; the degree of conflict "depends primarily on the level of aspiration of the individual as determined by his reference groups and personality factors, and of need satisfaction rather than the environmental conditions." Conflict may vary with the location of positions: Robert L. Kahn noted that positions deep in an organizational structure were relatively conflict-free, while positions located near the "skin or boundary" of the organization were likely to be conflict-ridden. Conflict within public bureaucracies is also affected by the political culture and climate—the extent, for example, to which the free play and combat of interests are stifled, permitted, or encouraged in the outside world. The question is not the existence of conflict within public bureaucracies but its character, intensity, and the manner in which it is expressed, channeled, or camouflaged.

At the root of bureaucratic conflict lies some kind of struggle for power and prestige. This struggle pervades the bureaucracy because it engages persons who tap one another's motivational and need bases and who have various power resources (withdrawal of services, denial of esteem to others, widening the area of conflict by such devices as giving "confidential" stories to the press, appeals up the line to superiors or unions or professional associations) that they can employ or mobilize in this process. This is the "real" authority that lies behind the "legitimate" authority of executives and foremen. The authorities are supposed to have a monopoly of sanctions and hence of formal power in bureaucracies, but since sanctions are as variegated as the human wants and needs that activate them, sanctions may be widely distributed throughout the bureaucracy. While the actual extent of the distribution will vary broadly from organization to organization depending on a host of internal and external factors, the analysis of power in bureaucracy cannot be confined within the boundaries of formal authority.

In bureaucracy, as in other social entities, power is arbitrary and feckless unless guided by purpose. What objectives, intentions, or goals, measured by what values, inform the uses of institutional power? The answers, again, are as varied as the motives of administrative leaders and followers. If bureaucracies were rationally organized and led, administrators would act according to a hierarchy of ends and means, a comprehensive and integrated scale of values. In actual behavior, Herbert A. Simon writes, "a high degree of conscious integration is seldom attained. Instead of a single branching hierarchy, the structure of conscious motives is usually a tangled web or, more precisely, a disconnected collection of elements only weakly and incompletely tied together, and the integration of these elements becomes progressively weaker as the higher levels of the hierarchy—the more final ends—are reached." This does not mean that bureaucrats are utterly lost in a maze of immediate motives and ultimate values. Particularly in public bureaucracies, where the agency is committed by statute to certain objectives, officials may make more than a token effort to realize those objectives.

Often we find in even sharper form the ambivalence noted between the pursuit of personal ends such as income and job security and the pursuit of broader, more collective ends such as the established goals of the agency. While every organization embraces both sets of values, usually in the same person, the allegiance to more general ends is typically greater in a public than in a private bureaucracy (such as a business enterprise) because in the latter the institutional ethic and the commercial subculture around it support an unembarrassed pursuit of higher profits, more pay, and better working conditions. To be sure, in public bureaucracies perhaps more than in private, rules originally conceived as means to ends become transformed into ends-in-themselves as Merton has pointed out, and instrumental values become terminal values, but at least the broader purposes and values remain there to be invoked by political authority and leadership. Ultimately, as both Weber and Parsons have insisted, organizations must be tested and defined by purpose.

And change? The stereotyped view of bureauracy is one of an institution braced against change. As a Harvard professor during the 1960s, Henry Kissinger wrote an article that lamented the stifling influence of the foreign policy bureaucracy on creative diplomacy. "Attention tends to be diverted from the act of choice—which is the ultimate test of statesmanship—to the accumulation of facts. Decisions can be avoided until a crisis brooks no further delay, until the events themselves have removed the element of ambiguity. But at that point the scope for constructive action is at a minimum. Certainty is purchased at the cost of creativity." Not surprisingly, when Kissinger became White House foreign policy adviser and then secretary of state, he circumvented the structure of department bureaucracy and process in a way some would castigate as "Lone Ranger diplomacy."

Certainly the great administrative agencies in virtually all societies encompass powerful forces that guard the ramparts against threats to the status quo. But this protective and rigidifying tendency is not universal and inevitable. If potential or actual conflict exists in the bureaucracy, if bureaucrats respond to wider sets of values than the narrow organization norms, if these dynamic forces engage persons' needs and motives and hence manifest themselves in new power patterns and alignments, then the bureaucracy may become more a seedbed for change than an arena for *stasis*.

This process will vary with the type of change. At the least the bureaucracy may respond to internal innovative forces, in the case of the coming to power of a new executive leader who can mobilize support within the bureaucracy on the basis of legitimacy as the new leader, the appeal of the program to some bureaucratic elements, and the power to reward friends and penalize foes in the agency. This was the case when Kissinger took the helm of the State Department in 1973. Yet as Kissinger and countless others have discovered, the administrator may find these powers inadequate in dealing with encrusted routines and widespread resistance and hence may have to find other ways of mobilizing administrative resources. More typically, even hostile bureaucrats change to at least some degree in response to external pressure because of the need to survive and the civil service ethic of neutrality. Radicals and revolutionaries may feel the need to transform the structure of the entire bureaucracy or to abolish it to fulfill their goals. Successful revolutionaries usually replace the old with a new form of bureaucracy.

Another type of change is generated internally. Certain bureaucratic elements, reflecting both their developing needs and external societal influences, serve as forces of change within some administrative enclaves, and the spirit of change may be contagious. Still another type of change is anticipatory; as Louis Gawthrop says, the force of change may be anticipated by the organization, which is then in a position to "respond" to the change even before an external or internal group makes the specific demand for the change. The test of change is not passive adaptation but policy and organizational innovation and creativity, and these depend, as Victor Thompson and others have contended, on the maintenance within bureaucracies of legitimized conflict and a "pluralized babble."

"Not I, but ten thousand clerks, rule Russia," sighed an eighteenth-century czar. In bureaucracy Weber saw the possibility for both freedom and despotism—for the liberation of humankind through collective reason, and for the dehumanization of people through the conversion of bureaucratic means into ends. Less grandiosely, we can see potentials for both ossification and innovation in most public bureaucracies. The potential for bureaucratic leadership is at its fullest when these forces are somewhat evenly balanced in conflict. By responding to this conflict, by engaging the forces that play on and in the organization, by remaining sensitive to the distribution of power within the agency, bureaucratic leadership can be an important part of the broader forces of party, legislative, and executive leadership that bring change to the entire society. Public bureaucracies participate in genuine leadership if, recognizing that they themselves are instrumentalities to external ends, they respond to reciprocal relationships with the individuals and groups they exist to serve.

Bureaucracy has had a bad name because the reciprocal relationship is often forgotten or distorted—bureaucracies may lead, but they are also followers, "servants of the people." Too often bureaucracies acknowledge only their internal reciprocity and the transactional relationship between managers and employees and in consequence respond to their own mutual wants, needs, motives, and values without acknowledging the *primary* relationship, which is external. Thus bureaucracies may make their own survival the terminal value rather than an instrumental one. Welfare recipients or "clients," students, patients, constituents of private and religious organizations, customers, often find themselves regarded as irrelevant nuisances by those hired to serve them. Public bureaucracies may be more vulnerable to this distortion than private retail business because they often lack competition, demand for accountability of performance, and dependency on the client for job security and advancement. Private business may also be vulnerable the further it gets from its customers and the more monopolistic it becomes.

Leadership in Political Interest Groups

"Leadership is not an affair of the individual leader. It is fundamentally an affair of the group," Arthur Bentley wrote in a signal attack on popular conceptions of leadership in a seminal work published in 1908. For Bentley the great phenomenon of leadership was not the leader but the spectacle of groups differentiated for the purpose of leading other groups, with one specialized group leading other groups in a particular phase of activity. Groups could not be called into life by mere clamor of leaders; the leader got his strength solely from the group. Ultimately, with Bentley, the group *was* leadership; leadership was simply the expression of the group.

This homage to groups over individual leaders found little acceptance among Americans during a decade that witnessed the leadership, emergent or full-blown, of Theodore Roosevelt, Wilson, La Follette, and a covey of popular reformers and muckrakers. Bentley's argument, when republished during the 1930s, was even less compelling in an era of Franklin Roosevelt, Stalin, Hitler, Gandhi, and other global leaders. But under the impact of the small-group emphasis that brought out such studies as that of the Norton Street gang and George Homans' work after World War II, Bentley's theory enjoyed a revival that helped precipitate searching studies of political interest groups in many polities. W. G. Carleton described this shift in scholarship as a trend away from a "formal, structural, static, deductive, rational and qualitative approach to one that is functional, realistic, evolutionary, quantitative, pluralist and relativist." But the question remained whether group analysis could capture the full dimensions of political leadership in interest groups.

The analysis of interest groups—in both its epistemology and its definitions—tended to begin with a static perception of interest groups and the way in which leadership emerged from them. This perception allowed little room for the analysis of conflict. It began with categorical groups, persons who (a) had some characteristic in common (such as age, color, sex, occupation, affliction or disability, high status) and (b) exhibited a "minimum frequency of interaction" based on the shared characteristic. Interest group, in a widely adopted definition by David Truman, denoted any group that "on the basis of one or more shared attitudes, makes certain claims upon other groups in the society for the establishment, maintenance, or enhancement of forms of behavior that are implied by the shared attitudes." Truman, like many other group theorists, recognized the role of leadership within interest groups. He defined the leader as the person who initiated relationships, verbal or otherwise, to which others in the group responded (the relationships must indicate some consistency over time). But this definition seemed more quantitative than qualitative; it said the leader simply initiated more relationships than did the follower. The most successful leaders might be those who responded in private to the actions of followers in their group—in which case, presumably, the followers became the leaders. This equation was summarized by some theorists as the ratio between the frequency with which an individual initiates actions in group situations and the frequency with which the person responds to the initiative of others; the ratio, it was said, would measure leadership in quantitative terms. While the emphasis on interrelation was valid, the theory reduced the process of leadership to a series of mere exchanges of roles that so-called leaders and so-called followers almost mechanically assumed. It was a circular theory that missed the unique and dynamic aspects of the leadership process. It was transactionalism with a vengeance.

To capture these aspects requires analysts of interest group leadership to start not with interrelationships within categorical groups, important though these be, but with the interaction among persons holding—or being gripped by—varying degrees and types of wants, needs, and expectations and exerting diverse claims and demands on other groups, other leaders, and government. Interest group theorists, including Bentley, assume the existence of potential groups, and "tendencies" and "stages" in the development of groups, but these generalities obscure the key aspects of interest group leadership. The fact that a want is strongly felt by certain persons may make them a more responsive target for leadership initiatives than the mere fact of their having that want. Poor people or victims of a natural disaster are defined by their common condition, but some may deny the condition. Like the semi-mythical Alger hero, not all the poor feel poor.

We assume that leaders initiate relationships with followers; what, then, is the nature of the relationships, the point at which they begin, and their effect on the leaders as well as the followers? If leaders intervene at the stage at which a sense of want is developing, they may influence the nature of that want as the followers mold it. Leaders can also help convert that want into a more explicit *need* related to resources that leaders and followers see as potentially available in their environment. As leaders persuade their followers not only to want but to deserve and *expect* certain goods they direct them into a more politically oriented posture; and when leaders in turn help convert these expectations into *demands,* they become leaders of interest groups that make claims of other interest groups, and on government.

This is not a simple linear process. Some members of a potential interest group may be unable to make the shift from their condition of want (such as hunger) to the appropriate state of need. Others may be unable to move from a sense of need to a relevant sense of expectation or to a posture of making relevant political demands. Thus members of a potential interest group may be at a variety of different "stages" or "tendencies." Skilled leadership may be necessary to help them move to the next "stage," and the changes may be erratic, uneven, and regressive.

Nor are leaders constant, unvarying factors in these changes; their own needs and expectations may be erratic or volatile. Implicated with the wants and needs of their followers, their own demands may be overly dependent on a response from followers that may in fact not come. They may simply lack the skills necessary to communicate, activate, mobilize, guide, and command. Their own wants—for recognition, for status, for power—may be more elevated or sophisticated than those of their followers and hence much harder to satisfy—it may be harder for them to know when they *are* satisfied. They may be ignored or rejected by their followers and thus lose their leadership status and with it their capacity to satisfy their own psychological and even physical needs.

These tendencies, moreover, often operate in a context of *conflict*. Leaders differ in perceptions of their own and others' wants and needs; so do followers. Leaders may clash over who among them will have the power to respond to followers' needs. To attempt to satisfy mass needs is inevitably to compete for scarce resources. In a large European trade union whose members pursue both ideological and bread-and-butter objectives, both followers and leaders will be split over government policy—over the question, for example, whether more political resources should be devoted to nationalization of industry or to improved welfare programs. Leaders may divide not only over who should take leadership positions but over the very definition of leadership. Norman Luttbeg and Harmon Zeigler found in a study of a teachers' association that the group leader accepted the premise that members should obey followers' wishes but could not refrain from jealousy over their autonomy. It seemed a classic case of Edmund Burke's view of the leader torn between the duty both to represent followers and to exercise independent judgment. The observers found that the leaders of the teachers' group were unable to resolve this problem. "The representative nature of the organization," the study concluded, "is not only meaningful to leaders but is also potentially divisive of the leadership."

One of the most troublesome questions for democratic politics is how to provide for or compensate for the unheard voices of the unorganized, inarticulate groups described first by Kenneth B. Clark as the "powerless." In the United States such groups have traditionally been the poor—the white poor in Appalachia, the black poor in urban enclaves, the native Americans on reservations—and the disenfranchised, including children, convicted felons, the mentally ill. Few of the organized interest groups, which are primarily middle class, effectively represent these people. Robert Kennedy's early sponsorship of ways to explore means of giving voice and power to the silent and the impotent, followed by Lyndon Johnson's onslaught on poverty through organized community activity, provided a beginning, but on the whole groups like the Welfare Rights Organization have been unable to exert significant impact on bureaucracies or legislatures, and their modest influence has declined. Most of these groups have turned to focus on traditional political power (as in the election of black sheriffs in the South) as a more likely transactional instrument if not an instrument of transforming social change.

Whether interest groups—and interest group leadership—exist in authoritarian societies depends on definition and ideology. In the Soviet Union the Communist party repudiates the legitimacy of groups formed outside the umbrella of the party. A party spokesman denied that there could be any social group in the Soviet state that "would have the privilege of evaluating its own activity otherwise than from the viewpoint of the aims and political interests of the working class." He denounced the free play of parliaments and oppositions. The chief guarantee of the unity of the Soviet society was not the "free play of forces" but the "intelligent delineation of functions for common coordinated work under the leadership of the Communist Party." The official leadership principle remained intact—officially.

The fact that the Soviets did not even recognize the existence of Western-style interest groups has handicapped the amassing of data on interest groups in Russia. Even more serious is the conceptual problem. Interest groups are traditionally viewed as collectivities of persons who make political demands and claims on the basis of a common set of attitudes, or through interaction among themselves, or both. It has been some time since one could measure the size and spread of interest groups in the Soviet Union, except for the big, formal organizations that serve essentially as one-way transmission belts from power wielders to followers. A tougher question is whether a genuine interest group can exist when there are shared grievances among the members (perhaps over repressive measures by the state) but when circumstances prevent group members from reacting overtly. A government act of repression provokes parallel but independent responses from writers all over the Soviet Union, for example, and the writers do not need to pass around mimeographed secret documents in order to express common reactions to the act. Does an interest group spring into being as soon as the writers react to the act? Or only when the writers are willing and able to act?

Such awkward questions can be resolved by viewing interest groups not as mere collections of "similar" persons or of common responses or of interactions but as persons who share common needs and respond to leaders who can evoke and help fulfill these needs. Under this definition, interest groups play an important if subtle role in authoritarian societies. In a study of Soviet politics, H. Gordon Skilling and Franklyn Griffiths concluded that since Stalin the Soviet Union has shown signs of incipient pluralism. Nonparty political organizations in Russia seldom enjoy the constitutional or even the practical sanctions that could enforce their interests, but interest groups—despite the official disparagement of the "free play of forces"—have influenced decisions and blocked the implementation of Soviet decree. The military protected its autonomy and strategic viewpoint from the hand of Khrushchev. Scientists succeeded in carrying through the reorganization of the Academy of Science and excluding engineers from it—against the apparent desires of the regime. Groups of lawyers have exerted some influence on the drafting of the Soviet legal codes, and economists have helped to shape government decisions on price formation.

And where there are genuine interest groups, with possibilities of conflict, there are potential interest group leaders. The traditional Western view of politics in the authoritarian state sees a facade of stability and behind that facade a continuing rough-and-tumble struggle between contending leaders. The contenders in the Soviet leadership struggle have not been a series of "followerless leaders" jockeying for position but candidates for power who draw on and are supported by interest groups and who adopt positions that reflect the needs and wants of the members of those groups. Contending Soviet leaders have drawn on institutions and interest groups in a fashion that seems strikingly Western. These groups include official agencies such as the army and the police, regional constituencies such as the citizens of Leningrad, Kiev, or Tbilisi, ideological constituencies that include the camps which make up the traditional Soviet split between liberal and conservative, and even personality cults—Lenin, Stalin, Khrushchev, and newer leaders have all had their actual or pretended protegés. Skilling and Griffiths found that in spite of the official Soviet position against them, the phenomenon of interest groups as an influence on government policy in the Soviet Union is waxing. They concluded that "on most issues, there are rival coalitions of forces facing each other—including vested interests seeking to preserve the status quo and innovative forces strong for change—and that the resolution of such conflicts may lead to the victory of some groups, the failure of others, or to a compromise of opposing viewpoints."

Group leadership—in small, informal groups like the Norton Street boys, in bureaucracies, in clearly articulated interest groups—is immanent in human society. In the natural conflict of human interests and ambitions, groups will clash with groups and leaders with leaders, but realizing common aspirations depends largely on that critical tie between the leader and followers who are members of groups. Group leaders mobilize followers as resources in larger contests for power or prestige. It is this linkage that can win influence for a group like the Norton Street boys, that can move a bureaucracy from routine to creative responsive action, that can convert the demands of interest groups into government policy. Transactional leadership is crucial to group leadership, and it is just as crucial to the more encompassing forces of party, legislative, and executive leadership. Rarely does it play a vital role in transforming leadership.

12 --

PARTY LEADERSHIP

After the elections in England in the summer of 1830—a period of gathering tension and polarization over prospects of electoral reform—the government and the opposition could not agree even as to which side had won or lost. For the benefit of Lord Peel, a young minister listed members of Parliament as Friends, Moderate Ultras, Doubtful Favorable, Very Doubtful, Foes, and Violent Ultras, among other designations. One wonders if Peel was impressed by this effort to clarify chaos. Western political parties originated typically in the recruitment of small groups of followers by leaders either in government or seeking to gain access to government. Often called parties, these groups were what some would term today circles, cliques, factions, cabals, combinations, camarrilla. Their roots in the country at large were truncated, extending mainly to local notables in aristocracy or squirearchy. Faction was fluid and ephemeral. Only the office of the whips, and later a few political clubs, according to R. T. McKenzie, provided a semblance of party organization and discipline.

American parties, too, germinated in groups forming around leaders. Party of any sort was in ill repute; "If I could not go to heaven but with a party," said Jefferson, who would go down in history as the main founder of the (first) Republican party, "I would not go there at all." But the impetus toward party was unquenchable as leaders differed over issues and policy and recruited more and more followers for support in legislatures or at the polls. Since President Washington was "above politics" and tried to conduct a nonpolitical administration, parties formed first around leaders in Washington's cabinet, notably Alexander Hamilton, and around leaders in Congress, notably James Madison. During this early period members of Congress usually won office through small, informal combinations of friends and neighbors, with practically no po-

308

litical organization in the modern sense. Increasingly they campaigned on the basis of wider appeals, using tickets with party labels. Politicians' minds were dominated in an expanding republic by the possibility of recruiting more support from an expanding electorate.

French parties also were born in groupings around parliamentary leaders, but their birth was more exotic—or at least more Parisian. When representatives to the Estates-General began to arrive at Versailles, according to Maurice Duverger, they felt confused and isolated and, under the leadership of older hands, naturally tended to group together in defense of their common interests. The Breton deputies hired a room in a café and organized regular meetings among themselves. They recruited deputies from other regions on the basis of shared political doctrines, and in this fashion the Breton Club became an ideological group. When the assembly was transferred from Versailles to Paris the club could not find a new café but hired the refectory of a convent and became famous under the new name, Jacobins. Sixty years later French parties, partly because their doctrines were still ill-defined, were taking their names from their meeting places; in the French Constituent Assembly of 1848 there were groups of the Rue de Poitiers (Catholic Monarchists) and of the Rue de Castiglione and the Rue des Pyramides (Left). Similar tendencies were evident in Germany in the Frankfurt and other parliaments.

The transformation of these early groups into parties in the modern sense took place as political combatants, while keeping their footing in the government, moved to mobilize masses that were slowly being enfranchised. The crucial change was less in the ambitions or motivations of leaders than in the conversion of millions of persons from political outsiders to political followers, among whom new local and national leadership was recruited. Thus parties in their modern image—organizations appealing to large numbers of persons to support candidates for office under a public label—had to wait for the spread of the franchise before they could evolve. As a result such parties are a relatively modern invention. Belgium, the Scandinavian countries, and France did not establish manhood suffrage until late in the last century or early in this one. And an equally vital development—the granting of woman's suffrage—is essentially a twentieth-century phenomenon.

Party leaders competed for the support of the newly enfranchised under their party labels and slogans, and as the electorate grew increasingly knowledgeable as a result of higher literacy and education, a sea change took place in the climate of Western politics. The masses were not simply vote fodder but human beings with needs and goals; their expectations were aroused as party leaders and candidates out-promised one another. Electoral committees and other organizations established by party leaders to recruit electoral support could also be used by voters to establish links with and controls over their leaders in parliament and ministry. The impetus was especially strong on the left. Those coming late into the electorate tended to be low-income persons, and they wanted more from government than the patronage proffered by older party elites to leaders of small groups that supported them. The big new electorates wanted *government policy,* and hence they wanted control over their leaders and parties in office.

Given these wants and needs, it was inevitable in the Western democracies that doctrinal and electoral forces would develop outside the intragovernmental or parliamentary parties and would attempt to subject parliament and government to external political controls. The two tendencies converged; parliamentary leaders were reaching out for electoral support while group leaders outside were moving into the governmental preserve, and often the efforts engaged, overlapped, or bypassed each other. Different origins put their stamp on the leadership of the developing parties, at least for a time. In Britain the Labour party rose directly out of a decision by the Trades Union Congress at the turn of the century to create a parliamentary and electoral association. An Independent Labour party had already been politically active, but its base was weak; only the involvement of the unions, with their considerable voting potential, could create a party with the power to influence directly or even control the government.

The British experience has been paralleled in other countries by labor and other interests. Farmers and workers organized parties in Scandinavia. Calvinists in the Netherlands organized the Anti-Revolutionary party to combat the Catholic Conservative party. In Belgium clerical and lay leaders established "Catholic school committees" across the country to oppose hated laws on secular teaching; later these committees were converted into sections of the Catholic party. Freemasons, ex-servicemen, nationalists, businessmen, and other groups organized parties elsewhere. Not all these parties were eminently successful at the polls, but they represented a successful effort to organize voters and to bring leadership into government from the outside.

The gradual emergence of a "country party" representing a wider public in opposition to the "court party"—to use the terms loosely—helped create the most visible and persistent of all political conflicts, the clash between the "ins" and the "outs." The notion of tolerating an *opposition*—especially an organized opposition—was hard for the court party to accept, and it spread slowly. The very term *party* had its etymological roots in the concepts of division and parting, but the word came to be used as much to ignore or suppress differences as to express and legitimate them. The "spirit of party" was, as noted, widely disfavored in the early years of the American Republic, and the rise of popular, competitive parties there was more the work of practicing politicians aspiring for office than of established thought. In Britain it was not until 1841, according to John Mackintosh, that the "opposition won a general election and the Crown accepted the decision at the polls." The acceptance of party conflict was closely related to the rise of modern liberalism. One could apply to tolerance of party opposition Ortega y Gasset's famous description of liberalism as "the supreme form of generosity; it is the right which the majority concedes to minorities and hence it is the noblest cry that has ever resounded in this planet. It announced the determination to share existence with the enemy; more than that, with an enemy which is weak. . . ."

If the fundamental party conflict is that between parties contending for power, also significant and often more illuminating are the conflicts *within* parties. Any party of size is an aggregate of group interests embracing all the conflicts endemic to groups—conflicts between skilled craftsmen and ordinary labor in trade unions, between affluent farmers and marginal tillers of the soil in agricultural organizations, between large and small businessmen, between sectarian and secular elements. As a widely based organization the party is rent also by competing regional interests and by parochial and provincial elements rebelling against centrist direction. As a staging area for present and future leaders the party attracts the politically ambitious; as an organization girded for perpetual battle it attracts the combative; as a visibly power-seeking enterprise it attracts both the pragmatic and the ideological, both the moderate and the extremist. Along the lines of such conflicts power within the party is channeled and distributed, creating transactional structures of political leadership.

Parties: Conflict and Leadership

The power of the political party stems from the capacity of party leaders at every level to identify and activate the wants, needs, and expectations of existing and potential party followers and to meet—or promise to meet—resulting demands by mobilizing economic, social, and psychological resources. This is to picture abstractly a process that is most human and earthy in its execution. No one described the human role of the party leader better than the famed Tammany underboss, George Washington Plunkitt. To hold your district, he preached from his pulpit, a bootblack stand, "you must study human nature and act accordin'. You can't study human nature in books. Books is a hindrance more than anything else. If you have been to college, so much the worse for you. . . . To learn real human nature you have to go among the people, see them and be seen. I know every man, woman, and child in the Fifteenth District. . . . I know what they like and what they don't like, what they are strong

at and what they are weak in, and I reach them by approachin' at the right side.
. . . I don't trouble them with political arguments. I just study human nature
and act accordin'.''

In understanding his people's wants and needs—''what they like and what
they don't like''—Plunkitt was of course appealing to a particular collection of
interests. As Tocqueville had noted earlier, ''a political aspirant in the United
States begins by discovering his own interest, and discovering those other interests which may be collected around and amalgamated with it. He then continues to find out some doctrine or principle which may suit the purposes of this
new association, and which he adopts in order to bring forward his party and
secure its popularity.'' In his political culture Plunkitt sought to meet the needs
of his followers for jobs, contracts, Christmas baskets, excursions, licenses,
handouts. In another culture the party leader meets the need for ideological
expression and response, for militant combat against the opposition, for politics
and programs from government, for assault on the status quo or defense of it.
In such a political culture the general doctrine, not personal or group interest,
may come first and may even be drawn from the very sources—books, manifestos, doctrinal tracts—that the Tammany boss spurned.

Whatever the political culture, the effectiveness of the political party
leader depended on an ability to offer material or psychic help, not abstract advice or sermons—as Plunkitt said, *help*. And the capacity of the political party
leadership to provide help depended on their ability to control first their own organization and ultimately the chief public distributor of goods, the government.

The relation of leaders to rank and file in political parties of democratic
tendencies is subject to a special tension. On the one hand, the doctrinal emphasis of the party on democratic goals and procedures compels leaders to heed
the needs and attitudes and sensitivities of the membership. Party constitutions
and procedures call for open debate in local meetings, election of party officials
by majority rule and often by secret ballot, the adoption of party planks by similar methods, and the deputizing of elected delegates to support the local party's
positions at higher party levels. The hierarchy of leadership, comprising typically a national chairman or president, a national executive committee or council, an annual or biennial national conference representing the whole party, and
a layer of state or regional committees or councils, is drawn directly or indirectly from the mass base. Controls on leaders are built into the party rules; for
example, decisions on organizational policy or party program may be subject to
a referendum of the party rank and file.

On the other hand, powerful forces propel the party toward strong leadership and even oligarchy. As heads of fighting organizations pitted against other
parties, leaders require disciplined support. In a multi-party polity the leader-

ship must compete with other party leaderships or bargain and coalesce with those leaderships. Leadership needs to be able to move quickly and with considerable flexibility and force. It cannot wait for long debates and ponderous decision-making at the lower extremities of the party. Even aside from interparty combat and cooperation the national leadership seeks to present a common visage to the people and hence seeks disciplinary powers to hold in line errant local or provincial sections of the party that might mar that image.

The outcome of these competing tendencies toward centralized and dispersed party leadership varies widely with party systems and, indeed, with individual parties. The final balance depends not only on intraparty and interparty forces but on the context of political culture and structure. A nation's ideology and traditions may oppose centralized control in party, government, or economy; a society sharply divided along regional, ethnic, class, racial, or linguistic lines may resist consolidated party leadership. Constitutional and electoral arrangements closely affect party organization. A federal form of government, with power divided among central, regional, and local authority, creates so many separate centers of public power that central party leadership is hard put to gain control of them. The constitutional separation of powers at any level of government, especially between the legislative and executive branches, not only may set up similar barriers to central party control but may have a reverse effect in activating potential cleavages within the party.

The range of possibilities is wide. At one extreme is the American party system, long noted for its decentralization of power and fragmented leadership. American parties developed in a society that valued individualism and to a marked degree protected states' rights and regional diversity. The Constitution institutionalized three layers of government that had the effect eventually of compelling the parties to stretch themselves thin to be effective at every level. Election to Congress and to state legislatures was based mainly on single-representative districts—an electoral arrangement that required parties to support somewhat different policies in different parts of the country. The populist and progressive movement around the turn of the century established a multitude of elective offices that overloaded party energy and organization; it blunted party power by instituting party primaries, thereby transferring the vital selection of candidates from party caucuses and conventions to open elections that were often beyond the control of party organization. There were exceptions to this general state of affairs. Centralized party leadership in the person of city and ward bosses dominated many a metropolitan area. A coalition of business and party leadership held sway in some states and one of rural and business interests in others. Most of the city machines are now long dead, and party power is typically as fragmented and even pulverized at the state level as it is at the national or local levels. The result of these and related tendencies is an extraordinary dispersion and attenuation of leadership through the entire party system.

Consider in contrast the pre-World War I Social Democratic party of Germany. Its leadership presided over an organization with a mass base embracing millions of industrial workers. The party had a large dues-paying, card-carrying membership, in doctrine and social makeup relatively homogeneous. The party leadership as an organization was strongly linked both vertically and horizontally. The party served as an effective means of recruiting political leadership in the trade unions and the working class. It established in Berlin a noted school that provided "mid-career training" for permanent party officials and prepared candidates for leadership in the party and the trade unions. At the height of the party's power, in the pre-World War I years, it supported a bureaucracy of three thousand permanent officials. Organized in opposition to the dominant aristocratic and bourgeois influences in German politics, the Social Democratic working-class movement became, as Leon Epstein notes, a subculture within the German community, a whole way of life in itself. "The fact that the labor movement became 'home, fatherland and religion' to hundreds of thousands," according to Guenther Roth, "points up their great alienation from the dominant system."

So tightly organized did the Social Democrats appear that they became a kind of model for Robert Michels' theory of the "iron law of oligarchy" in democratic associations. Michels' theory was no law, much less an "iron" law, but it was a powerful indictment of centralizing and bureaucratic tendencies in European left-wing parties. Parties that began with a radical or revolutionary (transforming) impetus, Michels argued, and that proclaimed the idea of democracy both as an end and a means, eventually deteriorated into oligarchical, anti-democratic (power-wielding) organizations. Once entrenched in the party officialdom, leaders drawn from the masses refused to give way to new aspirants who reflected new radical currents. Established leaders bought off or co-opted rising young rivals with favors and patronage, including appointment to ministries. If still threatened by the prospect of dislodgement, established leaders threatened to resign; the membership was so idolatrous of leadership and dependent on it that the rank and file would rally to its defense. To be sure, leaders sometimes fell out among themselves and hence were vulnerable to rebellious outsiders, but usually the leadership formed a "compact phalanx." The result of all this, according to Michels, was that officialdom took over, packing even "democratic" conferences and congresses. Bureaucratic timidity replaced the old daring and creativity. Party leaders indulged in bargaining, competing, and coalescing with rival parties instead of frontally attacking them. Opportunism won out over the strategy of principle. The party, essentially a means, became an end in itself. And ultimately social movements took on the qualities of conservatism, immobility, and oligarchy that characterized the very state they had originally been organized to combat.

Michels' thesis suffered from at least two fundamental flaws. One was his overgeneralization about the centralizing and dictatorial trends in Western democracies. Many political parties, especially centrist and conservative parties, were unlike the German Social Democrats. It was significant, for example, that when Michels drew on American political experience to support his thesis he cited boss rule in American cities and the Speaker's control over the House of Representatives; he ignored contrary tendencies in the already somewhat dispersed party system in the United States. Michels' other failing was his underestimating party leaders' legitimate need for extensive authority and discretion. The more the party leaders were slavishly representative of the party rank and file, the more they might be limited to the attitudes and needs of a narrow sector of the public, whereas party victory at the polls and success in putting through national programs depended largely on the ability of leaders to widen the party's vision, to expand its electoral base, to broaden its appeal to hostile or apathetic voters, and hence to augment its capacity to seize control of the government and put through its programs.

The great strength of Michels' thesis, in our terms, was his awareness of the conflict between transactional and transformational forces in Western parties. His work was a preface to understanding the power of other conflicts within and between political parties.

Party Leaders and Government Leaders

The most explosive party conflict is not between rival parties or between rivals within parties. It is between leaders of the party as an *organization* and leaders of the same party who hold positions of power in *government*. While conflict *between* and *within* parties is considered normal, predictable, and assuaged by time-honored understandings about good winners and good losers, majority rule, "to the victor belong the spoils," and so on, conflict between leaders of the party organization and party leaders or members who hold government positions is regarded with suspicion and disillusion as being abnormal—and hence it is governed by fewer rules and understandings. Organization leaders distrust government leaders because the latter appear to ignore party programs and party needs; because they flirt with, engage, and sometimes even appear to marry nonparty or opposition-party leaders; because they receive spoils—well-paid government jobs, public attention and adulation, ceremonial and royal awards (even peerages and knighthoods), and above all direct governmental *power*—that are denied to most party leaders. Government leaders distrust party leaders because the latter seek to restrict their independence; because they hold government leaders to their party commitments and promises; because they seem to underestimate the practical problems of wielding power (including the frequent need to compromise with opposition leaders); and because they want to share the spoils.

Conflict between organization leaders and government leaders is more disorderly and convoluted than the formal, visible, and accepted competition between parties or the somewhat structured multi-factional contests within parties. Relations between organization and government leaders turn on the interplay of conflict and power among (1) leaders of party organizations in constituencies that choose government officials; (2) party-affiliated government leaders (usually members of legislatures) chosen from those constituencies; (3) national organization leaders representing "the whole party"; (4) party-affiliated government leaders of "the whole nation." This is a simplified picture, for the leadership in any one of these groupings may be multi-dimensional and divided. Factional conflicts, for example, occur among national organization leaders and among government leaders—indeed, in each sector of party and government. The interplay is further complicated by interparty politics—that is, by the fact that relations within the party, especially between organization and government leaders, are closely affected by diverse estimates by party leaders as to how decisions *within* the party will affect contests *between* the parties. Add the ever-present features of all politics—conflicts between moderates and militants, between various ideologies and interests, between generations, and between ambitious contestants competing over nothing but personal advancement—and one has a sense of the endless combinations and permutations of power relationships. But the most durable conflict is between organization and government leaders in a context of either two-party or multi-party politics—a combination that allows four possibilities: (1) strong influence by organization leaders over government leaders in a two-party context; (2) the same in a multi-party context; (3) predominance of government leaders over organization leaders in a two-party context; and (4) the same in a multi-party context. British, French, Australian, and American party politics exemplify these four types of leadership relationships.

Since both the Conservative and Liberal parties in Britain grew out of factional politics within the Court and within Parliament, it is not surprising that both parties in the nineteenth century were dominated by the principle of parliamentary leadership and control by the party-leaders-in-government over the party rank and file—that is, the supremacy of government leaders over organization leaders. Despite intermittent grumbling by local Conservative party leaders, especially about aristocratic elements usually so influential in the national leadership of the party, the Tories have faced few systematic efforts by leaders of rank-and-file elements to challenge the control by Conservative leaders and members of Parliament over party strategy, recruitment, policy, and program. One exception was the campaign of Lord Randolph Churchill to "democratize" the Conservative party in the mid-1880s. With impeccable credentials as the son of a Tory duke, a Marlborough, Churchill could happily assault his fellow aristocrats and demand that the party give more representation to the workingmen and indeed adopt "of the people, for the people, by the people" as its motto. Partly because Churchill was widely viewed as a political adventurer intent only on his own advancement, but mainly because of the powerful traditions in the Conservative party, the effort at "democratization" failed. To this day the party proclaims the right of its leaders-in-government in London to make the key political decisions and to determine the program, while the job of the organization leaders is to arouse support and enforce discipline among party workers and adherents.

The parliamentary "leadership principle" was equally potent in the Liberal party in its years of greatness; its Whig leadership overcame a direct challenge to that principle. Then, as increasing numbers of middle-class and working-class men gained the vote, Liberal members of Parliament, like their Conservative counterparts, sought to protect and broaden their popular support without sacrificing their freedom of policy and maneuver in Westminster. They ran up against the inevitable dilemma: how to win the allegiance of the masses without granting them more power over party policy? The challenge to the Liberal establishment came in the person of Joseph Chamberlain, successful businessman turned Radical politician. Fresh from his feat of building in Birmingham a "caucus" system modeled (or so his critics said) after Tammany Hall, Chamberlain led in the creation of the National Liberal Federation as a nationwide, rank-and-file, democratically chosen organization to formulate a radical program for the Liberal party, to nominate candidates to run on that program, and to put pressure on the parliamentary party to enact the program. Chamberlain and the federation scored some brilliant political victories, but the effort to democratize the Liberal party ran afoul of Gladstone's continuing leadership, the Irish issue that divided the party, and the English tradition of parliamentary supremacy. At the height of Liberal party power in the twentieth century the leadership principle remained intact.

Was it inevitable that party leaders in government prevail over party organization leaders? Must the parliamentary wing control the entire movement? The rising labor leadership of the late nineteenth century in Britain said no. They derided the two established parties for allowing decisions to be made by small cliques of parliamentary politicians who assumed that the local organizations of the parties would support their programs and win elections for them. They noted with dismay and delight the failure of the Chamberlain and Churchill revolts against centralized power. The leaders of labor, emboldened and sustained by their belief in radical and socialist goals, resolved that their movement—and ultimately their party—would enthrone democracy and make government leaders subordinate to organization leaders democratically chosen by the rank and file. This was one of two key decisions made by the Labour party; the other was that trade-union, socialist, and radical organizations, after having attempted to work in coalition with the Liberals and at times with the Tories, and having failed, it was felt, to advance Labour's interests, must cast off from the two big parties and create a vehicle of their own. An independent, autonomous, democratic, representative, class-based, radical, and socialist party—a *transforming* movement: this was the fundamental goal of most Labour leaders at the turn of the century.

It was much easier for them to decide for "democratization" of their party and rank-and-file control over the parliamentary wing of the party than it would have been for Conservatives or Liberals to do so. Leadership of Labour emerged first in the country—in the reform, Chartist, trade-union, cooperative, socialist, and other movements—and *then* was "extended" into Parliament; it did not evolve outward from parliamentary faction into wider and wider circles of leadership. McKenzie notes that Labour decided to carry into Parliament, as it had into other sectors, its campaign for economic and social change. "It followed naturally that the Labour M.P.s and the Parliamentary Labour Party itself were from the beginning considered to be 'the servants of the movement.' . . . It became an article of faith in the Labour Party that the ultimate subservience of the Parliamentary Labour Party to the party outside Parliament was proof of the democratic structure of 'the Movement'." During long years of opposition, that doctrine was not squarely challenged because the party had no prime minister or cabinet minister faced with the responsibilities of governing, the imperative to compromise, and the seductions of power. During its periods of participating in coalition governments, in 1924 and in 1929–1931, however, leaders of the Labour party in Parliament asserted their independence from the rank-and-file organization. But despite much grousing in the ranks, the parliamentary leadership was not at that time overcome.

If any question about reality versus rhetoric remained by the end of World War II, the issue was clarified in the famous tilt between Conservative Prime Minister Winston Churchill and socialist intellectual Harold Laski. For years the Tories, baited by Labour about their "undemocratic" practices, had replied that for Labour to establish a party line over its members in Parliament was to threaten the ancient and revered doctrine of parliamentary supremacy. The issue came to a head when Churchill, presiding over a caretaker government, invited Clement Attlee as leader of the Labour opposition to accompany him to the Potsdam conference. Laski, who at the time was head of the party organization as chairman of the National Executive (Committee), declared that Attlee must attend in the role of observer only; Labour would not share responsibility without power. His party, Laski added provocatively, had not yet had the opportunity to discuss the decisions to be considered at Potsdam. Churchill then questioned the advisability of Attlee's attending the conference; the Labour party constitution, he noted acidly, "would apparently enable the Executive Committee to call upon a Labour Prime Minister to appear before them and criticize his conduct of the peace negotiations. . . ." Later Churchill broadened his attack and warned of the threat of "the dictatorship of the Labour caucus." Attlee refuted the charge; he admitted that the NEC must be consulted but asserted that the NEC would have no power to challenge the actions and conduct of a Labour prime minister. Attlee's behavior supported his words. At a victory celebration following Labour's electoral triumph Attlee announced that he had been invited by the king to form a government. He had not consulted with the NEC before accepting the commission. His associates were surprised by the announcement—most notably Laski himself, who was chairing the victory rally.

Once before the Labour party had had a prime minister—or thought it had, only to find that he was independent. Ramsay MacDonald's early life fostered independent action. He was born a bastard child in a two-room "but and ben" (kitchen and parlor) in a village of farmworkers and fishermen not far from the Scottish highlands. As a boy he had read omnivorously in Carlyle, Ruskin, and Henry George and then graduated to Marxism; after settling in Bristol to find work, he embraced the evangelical socialism of the Social Democratic Federation. He moved on to London, where he spent weeks looking for work while subsisting mainly on oatmeal sent from home. In the mid-1880s he became involved in electoral politics, joined the Fabian Society, and began to meet the politically active liberal, radical, and labor leadership of Britain. He married a woman who was both socialist and moneyed; she enabled him to entertain and to travel.

MacDonald's political horizons were expanding at the same time that labor was beginning to make itself felt as a political force in a nation dominated by Conservative and Liberal party politics. He became active in the Independent Labour party, founded in the early 1890s as an independent, socialist, and working-class organization. He stood for Parliament in Southampton, ending up at the bottom of the poll with fewer than one thousand votes. MacDonald recognized that the Independent Labour party lacked a base; it was scorned equally by the Marxists for its moderation and by trade unionists for its cloudy socialism. But it was a time for party-building. Representatives of unions, the Independent Labour party, socialist societies, and the Fabians met in 1900 in a summit conference and set up the Labour Representation Committee "in favour of establishing a distinct Labour group in Parliament who shall have their own Whips and agree upon their policy." MacDonald, who was deeply involved in these efforts, became the LRC's first secretary. In the same year he failed again in a campaign for Parliament, but the following year he became a London County Councilman and five years later finally won a seat. In 1906 he helped convert the LRC into a full-fledged Labour party.

MacDonald seemed a natural parliamentary leader and stood out in a labor bloc composed mainly of rough-hewn trade-union leaders. His ability to win the support of both moderate unionists and doctrinaire socialists gave him a commanding position in the labor movement; soon he was elected chairman of the parliamentary labor group. He opposed Britain's entrance into World War I and won both plaudits and opprobrium as a pacifist; once in the war Britain should win it, he believed, and he cooperated with the war effort. He was badly defeated in elections dominated by the war spirit, but in 1922 he was again elected to the House of Commons and in the same year was chosen chairman of the parliamentary Labour party.

With the once powerful Liberal party divided and broken and the Conservatives faltering in the face of postwar domestic problems, Labour felt ready for power and MacDonald for leadership. In the 1923 general election the Labourites replaced the Liberals as the second party. The Conservatives won the most parliamentary seats, but the other two parties together outnumbered them in the new House. MacDonald was asked to form a new government, which he did in coalition with the Liberals. Early in his political career Mac-Donald had campaigned in alliance with Liberals, only to turn to an independent third party; now he found doctrinal differences between the two parties still sharp. The Labour-Liberal coalition government yielded within a year to the Conservatives. In his few months in office MacDonald showed marked capacity for leadership, but he aroused suspicions on the part of back-benchers. For years Labour had insisted that if the party won office, the parliamentary leaders of the party must ultimately be responsible to the movement, but MacDonald chose his cabinet and decided on policy as independently of secondary leaders as Liberal and Conservative leaders had done. Already there was a grumbling among party rank and file that their old "socialist" leader was unduly susceptible to the seductions of fashionable London society and was running the risk of yielding to the "aristocratic embrace."

Whatever its wins and losses at the polls, Labour during these years was immensely strengthening itself as an organization under the gifted leadership of men like Arthur Henderson. In the general election of 1929 the hard organizational work paid off: Labour doubled its poll over the 1923 vote and at last outstripped the Tories in parliamentary victories. Once again MacDonald took office, this time without the need for coalition with the Liberals, and once again he chose his cabinet in consultation not with the organizational leadership of the party or even with the body of the parliamentary Labour party, but with a handful of close associates in the top leadership of the party. For a time in office MacDonald seemed to try to follow a middle line between Labour party militants, whose "flashy futilities" he was not reluctant to denounce, and the great trade-union ballast in the party. In fact the new Labour prime minister seemed more interested in foreign than domestic affairs (he had served as foreign secretary as well as prime minister in 1924).

As leader of the government MacDonald insisted on steadfast loyalty from the parliamentary Labour party and on loyalty and noninterference from the organized labor movement as a whole. Old Labourites wondered how much loyalty he would show the party. Almost from the start he seemed intent on conciliating rival party leaders and business interests. In his first speech to the House of Commons as prime minister in 1929 he talked about welcoming cooperation, putting ideas into a common pool, and about the duty of the M.P.s to act more as a "Council of State and less as arrayed regiments facing each other in battle." MacDonald desperately seized on this kind of support as Britain slid deeper into depression. In the face of spreading unemployment and heavy inroads on Britain's gold reserve, he did not take advantage of capitalist collapse to usher in the era of socialism but turned to businessmen and bankers and their conservative allies. The crisis came over the question of cutting spending, in particular spending on unemployment insurance, in order to save the pound. So strong was loyalty to the prime minister both in the parliamentary and the mass party that MacDonald almost brought his party around to his conservative fiscal policies. Finally the bulk of the party leadership dug in its heels. Balked in his own party, MacDonald tendered his resignation to the king; the monarch asked him to stay; and MacDonald abruptly and unceremoniously deserted his old Labour colleagues (except for a few who went over with him), dickered with the opposition parties, and formed a new "national" government. The organizational leadership of the Labour party stood by "helpless and horrified" as their old leader deserted them. As for MacDonald, he is alleged to have said as he formed his new government, "tomorrow every duchess in London will be wanting to kiss me."

Throughout his career MacDonald had moved sporadically from preaching transforming leadership to practicing transactional leadership. After flirting with Marxism he had risen to power with a party that made the strategic decision to advance a left-wing program and to stay clear of coalitions with "bourgeois" parties in order to maximize its transforming impact once it gained office on its own. But later he and other Labour party leaders agreed on coalition with the Liberals and again—in effect—with the Tories in 1931. He had defied the martial spirit in 1914 only to join the war effort soon after, attacked capitalism much of his life only to try to save it during its time of trial, and helped build a new party that preached the reconstruction of society but served more as political broker than social creator (at least before World War II). MacDonald's career thus embodied the dilemma of Western left-wing parties that ideologically want to transform society but in practice carry on political transactions just as bourgeois parties do—to the derision of Communist parties that solve that particular dilemma only by entangling themselves in even more serious ones. Labourites long would grumble about MacDonald's party treason, but they could not deny the need for party leadership.

Since World War II the supremacy of the parliamentary Labour party has been widely accepted in the Labour party, though the official rhetoric still stresses the ultimate sovereignty of the rank and file. Paradoxically, the party still exemplifies organizational influence, if only in contrast to other political parties in Western democracies. The reason for this is that Labour party policy is debated, and Labour party leadership recruited, in a context of extensive rank-and-file participation in decisions over candidates and program and intensive grass-roots leadership in these areas. This is bolstered by direct expression of local and regional attitudes and ideology in national party conferences and councils and, above all, by effective articulation among sectors of the national party leadership and between these sectors and the leadership structure in the parliamentary party. The rather extraordinary nature of the leadership structure of British parties, especially the Labour party, becomes clearer when this party system is compared to others.

The leadership of French parties of the center has long been noted for its freewheeling independence, doctrinal suppleness, and flair for private political enterprise. No party provided these qualities in greater abundance than the Radical Socialists, commonly called the Radicals. The oldest of France's formal political parties, the Radicals came into the period of their greatest influence in the fateful decade of the 1930s. Located strategically between the right-wing and left-wing parties, impelled by much of France's revolutionary tradition, and supported by many because of its impassioned anti-clerical stand in earlier decades, the party seemed potentially able to supply the political leadership that could cope with the domestic and foreign crises that overcame France in the thirties. But in the verdict of many it ended up as a politicians' party, one with leaders who had power but refused to lead. Government leaders in the party did hold ascendancy over organization leaders, however, in large part because the party organization was so weak. Local party committees had little control over deputies elected to the national Chamber of Deputies; the usual arrangement was that party activists allowed the deputies to vote as they pleased in the Chamber as long as the deputies intervened with the bureaucracy in Paris to assist the activists with local or individual problems. The membership of the party was fairly extensive but was neither large enough nor organized enough to support a strong national organization. The higher councils of the party were dominated by government leaders rather than organization leaders. In 1935, Peter Larmour reports, the party's national executive committee had 2,388 members, of whom 1,406 held or had held positions as deputy, senator (member of the upper house), mayor, or departmental councillor, or were former candidates for these positions. The national party congress was somewhat more equitable in representation, but its proceedings were usually arranged in advance by the national party leadership—and this, too, was heavily influenced by the parliamentarians. Occasionally revolts broke out in the executive committee of the party congress, but they were usually overcome through skillful compromise.

On the face of it this dispersion of power would seem to provide the parliamentary leadership with considerable autonomy. Yet that leadership was frustrated too. The Radical "group" in Parliament was divided into a host of ideological groupings and jesuitical distinctions that only by oversimplification could be classified as left wing, moderate left, moderate, and conservative. Historical, regional, and interest-group cleavages cut across this spectrum. Then, too, the same freedom from national and local organization that liberated the parliamentarians from party control thwarted any effort parliamentary leaders, ministers, or the prime minister made to apply discipline to the parliamentary rank and file. Party looseness, like party discipline, could cut several ways. Not only Radical party leaders in Parliament but leaders of Radical party factions lost control of their parliamentary followings as individual members chaffered and traded with leaders, peers, followers, other party leaders, local and national party organizations, and outside economic interests in an endless coupling, separating, and rejoining. But the main difficulty was that the Radical party was eternally a minority party and hence had to join with parties of the right or left if it was to share power. It was more tempting for Radical leaders to share in the political rewards and personal delights of ministerial membership than to accept the political punishment of isolation for doctrinal purity.

All these conditions put a premium on leadership as bargaining, as tactical maneuvering, as adjusting to political and institutional forces rather than overcoming them. It was a *politics* of great movement and delicate balances, but it ended as a *polity* of immobilism and stalemate. Ironically perhaps, many of the leaders themselves, as Larmour concluded, "were curiously admirable. Most were honest, many very earnest; some even had that frighteningly complete culture and competence of the polished Frenchman. . . . They were part of that republican aristocracy which, in spite of its surface futility, gave a tough and durable tone to the Republic. No political party could reasonably have had better personnel, and that makes the tragedy of their failure the more profound." The Radical party was revitalized after World War II, and it attracted some fresh, youthful leadership; but once again it exhibited its old weaknesses—divided leadership, plastic doctrine, lax discipline, excessive compromise—and inevitably the party became highly vulnerable to the Gaullists.

Almost the polar opposite of the French Radical party was the Australian Labor party in the fullness of its power and discipline following World War II. Drawn from militant trade unionism in a relatively small and homogeneous population, the Australian labor movement early in its history confronted the classic problem of the power of the leaders of the whole party organization versus the power of its members in the state legislatures and especially in the national parliament. In a long struggle in which parliamentarians repeatedly fought off Labor discipline by deserting the party and allying with Liberal and other opposition elements, the party organization won out and clamped a policy of severe discipline on the parliamentary members. Candidates for Parliament must be members of their local Labor party branch. Their candidacy must be cleared with state and national party authority. Failing of nomination, they must undertake to support the successful Labor party nominee; if nominated, they must campaign on the basis of the party program. If elected, they become members of a parliamentary Labor party that meets in caucus, discusses issues on the basis of the party platform, and decides its position by majority vote—to which the member must yield. Remarkably, the labor movement showed itself willing again and again to enforce discipline and solidarity at the price of short-run political defeat, on the theory that the party eventually would come into office and that when it did so it would have a foundation of organization and discipline that would enable it to transform the society.

Essential to the working credo of the Australian Labor party was the doctrine that its leaders in government, like its leaders of party, were servants of the movement. Its parliamentary candidates were required to sign a pledge that had been adopted only after long and sharp controversy in the party: "I hereby pledge myself not to oppose any selected and endorsed candidate of the Australian Labor Party, New South Wales Branch. I also pledge myself, if returned to Parliament, on all occasions to do my utmost to ensure the carrying out of the principles embodied in the Labor Platform and on all such questions, and especially on questions affecting the fate of a Government, to vote as a majority of the Labor Party may decide at a Caucus meeting.''

The enforcement of this pledge depended on more than the candidate's willingness to observe the pledge; it turned on the party's capacity to discipline its candidates and members of Parliament and ultimately on the capacity of the labor movement to overcome regional, doctrinal, and religious differences among its members and to capitalize on the old-time fear of labor socialists and radicals that once persons had attained parliamentary power and perquisites they would desert their class. A Labor member in Queensland reflected this view. ''The friends are too warm, the whiskey too strong, and the cushions too soft. My place is out among the shearers on the billabongs.''

Few political parties in Western democracies have matched the ''iron discipline'' of the Australian Laborites, but the impetus to discipline is ever-present and has brought interesting variations in various liberal, labor, and socialist parties. The Belgian Christian Social party and the Italian Christian Democratic party prohibited government leaders (i.e., ministers) from membership in the national committees of the party organization. Various socialist parties have sought to limit the power of parliamentary parties to coalesce with nonsocialist parties in parliament. The Belgian and Austrian socialist parties sought to curb the party organization leadership of members who were also parliamentary leaders. These arrangements tended to have limited effect because they related only to part of the power structure of the party and because the crucial decisions were typically made by government leaders rather than organization leaders. Many left-wing or moderate-left parliamentary parties exhibited marked parliamentary cohesion in a multi-party context (the French parties seemed to be exceptions to this generalization). But this cohesion within minority parties emanated more from basic doctrinal agreement on the part of the mass membership and from the need to maintain unity in opposing and coalescing with opposition parties than from party rules and organization. Epstein summarized the situation: ''Any parliamentary government, in order successfully to stabilize executive authority and so endure in the modern world, must produce cohesive parties regardless of the number of competing parties.'' Many parties did not demonstrate such cohesion, of course, and very few matched the solidarity and discipline of the Australian Laborites.

We must conclude that, on the whole, *government* leaders (party leaders who are holding elective or appointive office in parliaments and ministries) wield far more power in government and even in party than do *organization* leaders (leaders elected by the party organization). This is broadly true in Western-type parliamentary democracies. The influence of the party-leaders-in-government in most of these countries is dwarfed in comparison with the domination of government leaders over party organization leaders in the United States. The difference would not seem a marked one on organization charts. American parties, like their Western democratic counterparts, exhibit a nice vertical structure. The party is bottomed in thousands of precinct, ward, town, and city committees; it rises through county and state committees to a national committee much like the executive committees of other parties, and to its ultimate source of national authority, the national presidential convention, which resembles the usual party conference except that it meets quadrennially rather than annually.

In fact this is a most misleading picture. A more penetrating analysis of the distribution of real power (as opposed to formal authority) in the American political structure would demonstrate that, with few exceptions, power in persuading, organizing, and activating the voters is exercised far more by organized but highly personal groups that revolve around officeholders and candidates for office than by party organization leaders. This imbalance was slow to be perceived by many European observers, and even by Americans, because a myth persisted for many decades that the American party system was the apotheosis of boss control of candidates, caucus rule of legislative parties, party dictation to mayors, governors, and on occasion even to presidents. There was just enough truth in this portrait during the late nineteenth century to make it plausible. City bosses did, in effect, hire and sack some mayors and aldermen; economic oligarchs did exercise enormous influence over some governors, senators, and officials of lower status; and certain presidents cooperated with party leaders on matters of patronage if not on larger issues.

But even as European publicists painted lurid pictures of boss rule in America and even as European party politicians warned that adopting stronger party discipline would mean importing "Tammany bossism" into Belgian or Dutch or Scandinavian parties, party power and responsibility were dissolving in the United States. Despite the impetus of the Jeffersonian, Jacksonian, and post-Civil War Republican movements, parties achieved little national organization, discipline, or solidarity outside the centralizing influence of the President or occasionally a few nationally oriented senators. The causes of party disorganization and decentralization were manifold: a tradition of individualism that thwarted efforts to build the kind of working-class solidarity achieved abroad; a system of federalism that dispersed power through several levels of government and hindered parties from securing a firm grip on government machinery; a nation of many regions and localities, religious and racial differences, that bred disunity at the heart of the party system and illuminated strong national personalities; the adoption of the party primary for choosing candidates—a device that on balance, as we have seen, transferred power over candidate selection from the party organization to more numerous, diverse, and less party-oriented voters; the adoption, mainly during the early twentieth century, of the ''long ballot,'' which created so many elective offices at the lower and middle levels of government that the party as an organization could not easily fulfill its obligation to help elect—and thereby exercise some influence over—candidates for the many offices; and the growing respectability—in part a result of these factors—of ''independence'' from party and involvement in a host of ''nonpartisan,'' nonaffiliated ''voluntary'' organizations, such as the League of Women Voters or (more recently) Common Cause, that operate above, around, or apart from party organizations.

The upshot is that in the United States, behind the facade of party activity and organization, politicians gain office and stay in office largely on the strength of the personal organizations they have been able to build inside and outside the party and across party lines. A vastly greater amount of political money is raised and spent by individual candidates than by party organizations. Campaigns are typically managed by candidates' staffs rather than party committees. Once nominated, candidates either exploit party organization or ignore it, depending on their need. Once elected, they dominate the party organization—to the extent that they bother with it at all—to a far greater degree than party can influence them. And the federal government subsidizes candidates far more than parties.

Parties retained strength in one major respect. Most of the voters considered themselves Democrats or Republicans, in varying degrees of intensity, so it was important in most elections for candidates to gain a major-party nomination that would guarantee them a large stock of votes on election day. But they secured the party nomination on their own while the party organization usually remained neutral, and hence they were more indebted to their personal organizations than to party organization for obtaining that stock. In election campaigns the party sometimes failed to identify itself actively with the party nominee when the omens for victory seemed poor, putting time and money instead into local candidacies more directly dependent on and thus loyal to party leadership. Once elected, politicians were essentially free from party control over their policy positions. When officeholders deserted their party and ignored the party platform on which they (presumably) had been elected, or failed to provide the patronage expected, the party rarely deprived them of renomination for the simple reason that party organizations could not overcome the office-holders' personal organizations in the final electoral showdown.

The most graphic demonstration of the supremacy of government leaders over organization leaders in the American system was the relation of the President to the national chairman of the party. It came to be a tradition that once a presidential candidate was elected, no matter what his party credentials or his party commitment, he had the automatic and absolute right to demand the resignation of the existing chairman and to replace him with his own man. Few seemed to find anything strange in a great national party, a century or a century and a half old, with its own organization and tradition, abjectly subjecting itself as a national entity to the new nominee. Rarely did the presidential candidate appoint a politician of high national standing to the position; and if elected President he would treat the national chairman as a kind of staff assistant, and the national committee more as a nuisance than a source of party direction and political talent.

The relationship between Richard Nixon and the Republican national party exemplified this imbalance. For years Nixon cultivated all sectors of the party in order to gain the party's presidential nomination in 1960 and again in 1968. But having achieved the nomination, he depended in his 1968 campaign on his personal organization; once elected, he chose men of ordinary stature to head the party and largely ignored them thereafter. Nixon's bypassing of the Republican party in his 1972 re-election campaign and his reliance on a personal organization that indulged in illegal and scandalous campaign deeds was of course a caricature and a perversion of the relationship, but it also was an extension of the subordination of the national organization of both parties to the "strong" presidents of the past. The national leadership of the Republican party was too weak to dream of challenging Nixon over Watergate. On the other hand, the party leadership was quick to remind the voters of the fact that it had been bypassed by Nixon—and thus to argue that it should not be tainted by his misdeeds.

The ascendancy of government leaders over organization leaders on the American party scene did not lead to the rise of "government bosses" as replacement for the "party bosses" of nineteenth-century fame. Government leaders found it no easier than had organization leaders to overcome the political and institutional forces that fragmented power; they, too, had to overcome the divisive impact of checks and balances, federalism, primaries, the long ballot, and public attitudes. The main effect was not to create new power structures (save in one instance) but to disintegrate and pulverize political power. If specialists in the American party system detected striking signs of party decay and dissolution in the late twentieth century, one could find similar disintegration in other sectors of the political system.

The exception to decay, of course, was the presidency. The power of this institution was in large part a response to the power vacuum that surrounded other American political institutions. The President was, to be sure, "party" chief as well as "chief" legislator and commander-in-chief, but his subordination of his party role and responsibilities to other priorities exhibited in marked form a condition that existed throughout virtually all levels and sectors of the American system: the subordination of organization leaders to those in government.

One-Party Leadership

As socialist and labor parties grew in membership and electoral influence during the early years of this century, left-wing leaders watched with sardonic amusement while chairmen of "bourgeois" parties struggled with the problem of electing their candidates to parliament and then maintaining control over those candidates in office. The left-wing leaders consciously and explictly had faced the enigmas and dilemmas of leadership and power. They were for the most part committed to the need for fundamental social change; hence they spurned the transactional and parliamentary politics of brokers exchanging favors and jobs with one another and called for a strategy of *transforming* underlying conditions. But transformation could not be accomplished by will or fiat. How then to create a political organization and a political strategy that could overcome the lethargy, parochialism, shortsightedness, and conservatism of the masses, that could recruit and indoctrinate cadres, that could maintain discipline among militants committed to change, that above all could hold in line those who won parliamentary leadership and became vulnerable to the temptations of opportunism, careerism, and ultimately some kind of sellout to the enemy and betrayal of the cause?

The answer of Lenin and many other revolutionaries to this question was the small, unified, dedicated, ideological, disciplined party that could serve as the Vanguard of the Masses. "If we have a strongly organized party," Lenin wrote in the first issue of *Iskra* in December 1900, "a single strike may grow into a political demonstration, into a political victory over the regime." For years he fought down those in the Social Democratic party who wanted a broad democratic movement that might support social reform rather than revolution, while the party endured years of division and demoralization, until World War I gave the revolutionaries their great opportunity. A few months before taking power in 1917 Lenin was still denouncing the Social Democratic party leaders who had deserted the masses and the "parliamentary-bourgeois republic" that "restricts the independent political life of the masses, hinders their direct participation in the democratic upbuilding of the state from bottom to top. . . . What we want is to build the whole world over again." To dramatize the need for a sharp break with the past, Lenin favored dropping the name Social Democratic Labor party in favor of the name Communist party, as the instrument of the new Soviets of Workers' and Soldiers' Deputies.

Lenin would have served the interests of clarity, if not those of the new Communist party, had he dropped the word *party* rather than the term *Social Democratic*. For the organization he brought into power in the new Soviet Union as a "party" bore little relation to the parties of Western Europe with their provision for ultimate rule by the dues-paying membership, their electoral responsibility of higher party committees and authorities to the rank and file, and their careful separation of the powers of organization leaders from those of party leaders in government (whatever the violations in practice). The new Communist party was less a party in the accepted sense than a doctrine, a vocation, a strategy, and an empowering of *leadership*. It was a *system* of leadership that vested power neither in the rank and file nor in the party leaders in government nor indeed in the national party councils and congresses but in a select body of men and women operating at every level and directed from small circles within the vast, gray bureaucracy. It was a *leadership apparatus* operating behind a party facade.

The new Communist party in the Soviet Union provided the arena for this apparatus. In form the apparatus resembled the traditional party. After many expansions and contractions (or purgings) for reasons of state, there was, by the fiftieth anniversary year of the Soviet regime, a mass membership of twelve million members and candidates for membership. This membership was organized in almost half a million units that ranged in number from a handful of members to several hundred and were grounded either in geographical areas such as wards or election districts or in economic bodies such as offices, farms, and factories. These local organizations chose delegates to city or district conferences, which in turn selected delegates to regional (*oblast*) conferences, which elected delegates to the party congresses of the republics, which chose delegates to the All-Union Party Congress. But every level and sector of party activity was dominated by bureaus, committees, or small groupings of leaders who made up the control system of the whole apparatus.

Despite these trappings of "democratic centralism," the party's propaganda agencies acknowledged the leadership structure of the party. "The Communist Party of the Soviet Union," according to the revised statutes adopted at the twenty-second party congress in 1961, "is the tried and tested militant vanguard of the Soviet people, which unites, on a voluntary basis, the more advanced, the politically more conscious section of the working class, collective-farm peasantry and intelligentsia of the USSR. . . . The Party . . . is the leading and guiding force of Soviet society. . . . The CPSU bases its work on the unswerving adherence to the Leninist standards of party life—the principle of collective leadership, the comprehensive development of inter-party democracy, the activity and initiative of the Communists, criticism and self-criticism." All "manifestations of factionalism and clique activity" were barred.

Thus the leadership apparatus was legitimized, but where was power to be found within that apparatus? "Few groups of power-holders," Schuman notes, "have excelled the Russian Marxists in confusing shadow with substance, solemnly proclaiming 'rules' which are subsequently ignored, devising procedures on paper which are widely at variance with human realities, and revising, reshuffling, renouncing, and renovating all sorts of agencies of Party and Government alike at a dizzy tempo." In general, political leadership is exercised in the Communist party of the Soviet Union by those who recognize—within the boundaries drawn by the Kremlin—the wants, needs, expectations, and attitudes of the mass public, party rank and file, socio-economic interests, ideological groups, bureaucratic organizations (including most notably the armed forces), and party hierarchs, and who are able to marshal appropriate resources to meet, or appear to meet, those wants and needs. One detects some dispersion of leadership. In a highly centralized, corporate, and bureaucratic society, power to mobilize resources turns on the capacity to have ties with and some influence over leaders of key ministries, propaganda agencies, the Red Army, the secret police, and party bureaucracies in the larger republics and in key sectors of the national party. The particular strategies of employing force, fraud, and favors vary with changes in national needs, public moods, foreign relations, and power relations within the party apparatus.

To this extent leadership is transactional. But to a remarkable degree power and leadership are concentrated in the general secretary of the national party, in the dominant faction in the party Presidium, and in little-known, almost faceless functionaries in the party bureaucracy. To the extent that generalization is possible, Frederick Barghoorn has captured well the persisting power structure in the Kremlin. The top rulers, according to Barghoorn, consist of "clusters of powerful individuals rather than a homogeneous inner core; and, judging from the earlier political struggles within the system, apparently power groups at the top levels usually cut across functional lines, for powerful party leaders have friendships and alliances not only within the party organization in the narrow sense but also within the economic bureaucracy, the armed forces, and the secret police. The ruling vigilance, and ruthless terror, has always been able to break up tendencies of these various chains of command to act as units against the party center; but this problem has never been finally and completely solved.'' Some flux is possible within the system, as indicated by the shift from Lenin's relatively open party to Stalin's iron control and merciless purges and back to the more relaxed centralism of Khrushchev and his successors so we can identify *leadership* tendencies in Russia, in our sense of the term. But the power of the apparatus remains virtually unchallenged.

One-party dictatorship in the Soviet Union set the pattern for Communist party domination in the Eastern European satellites of Russia following World War II. Like the Bolsheviks, the Eastern European Communists had had to survive as clandestine, illegal associations; like the Bolsheviks they got their chance to seize power in wartime. Unlike the Bolsheviks, however, these Communist parties won power—or held on to it—largely because of the military intervention of an external force, the Soviet Union. Hence the satellite parties have not had to confront the dilemmas of coexisting with independent parties in a multi-party polity. The Communist parties in western Europe *have* had to face this dilemma. On the one hand, as consecrated Communists the leaders sought to bring about fundamental social change through a Leninist type of apparatus. The second Congress of the Communist International warned all parliamentary representatives that they were not legislators ''seeking a basis of understanding with other legislators'' but *party agitators* ''sent among the enemy to apply the party's decisions.'' On the other hand, Communist leaders must live in and off enemy territory—parliamentary societies in which political power is shared by several parties and distributed through fragmented institutions. And the lot of Communist leaders in Western democracies was made harder by the fact that Moscow pressured them at times to collaborate with the bourgeois parties, at other times to battle with them—and the party line could change quickly and with little warning. ''Eurocommunism'' has had to cope with such pressures.

Communist party leaders in the West responded to this dilemma by building or maintaining organizations with considerable political autonomy that were yet capable of operating in pluralistic politics. The parties were centrally led but encouraged rank-and-file participation in organizational and tactical decision-making. The Communist parties in western Europe had the usual party structure of local organizations or branches, district and regional committees, national bureaucracies, central committees, and party congresses, but they were much more than electoral organizations. With their party schools, sports clubs, cultural groups, and recreational activities they sustained a semi-autonomous society in which party members and adherents could lead much of their lives.

External influences were, therefore, reduced. The parties sponsored youth organizations that served as a source of recruitment and a means of indoctrination. These seemingly representative institutions and rich group associations could not conceal the omnipresent control of central leadership.

The French Communist party demonstrated its capacity to enforce discipline in what was allegedly a nation of extreme heterogeneity and redoubtable individualism. Delegates to the national congress did not actually choose members of the party's Central Committee; they ratified the nominations of the party leadership. The French Communists in particular had to confront the need to maintain discipline over members of the party taking seats in a parliament notorious for its political free enterprise, fluid party lines, and temptations to barter for favors and offices. They were familiar with Robert de Jouvenel's observation: "Two deputies of different parties have more in common than a deputy and a militant member of the same party."

The party, therefore, maintained schools for deputies, provided research facilities for its parliamentarians, prepared the bills introduced by them on the floor, and granted them the services of the party's secretariat in lieu of private secretarial help. By Communist tradition the deputies were supposed to turn over their parliamentary salaries to the party in exchange for party pay and perquisites. What the party granted, however, the party could take away—and sometimes did. Willing to lose some voting support if necessary to secure the loyalty of its deputies, the national party ran "foreign" candidates in some localities because it feared that a local person might build a separate local organization; indeed, the party "rotated" candidates to combat excess localism. The Communists did make some concessions to *personalismo*. On the fiftieth birthday of its noted leader Maurice Thorez, the party circulated special membership cards printed in the form of a letter headed "J'adhère au Parti de Maurice THOREZ" and including a birthday tribute to the party chieftain. But Thorez was an organization leader, not just a *government* leader.

Fascism abominated Communist ends but embraced Communist means, especially that of the disciplined party apparatus. In German Nazism, and to a lesser extent in Italian fascism, there was the same centralized organization the Communists used, with strong vertical linkage to put down disunity and rebellion; the same emphasis on youth organizations and intensive recruitment; the same concern with direct action—propaganda, turmoil, protest, violence—and with electoral efforts as a secondary priority; the same demands on the total loyalty and full-time service of party members; the same subordination of party parliamentarians to party organization. The fascist party, however, was more prone to violence for its own sake; to obsession with devil-hunting and racial "purity" (with the Jews seen as devils); to a mystical solidarity and communion of the party elite; to almost continuous purges of officials and members; in sum, to a totalitarian control of the party that did not even admit of the pretense of direct and indirect election of party leaders.

The Nazis proclaimed and practiced power in its most extreme, perverted, and brutish form. The power wielder was supreme over the people, the party, the government, the constitution—indeed, over the state itself. As "terrible simplifiers," the Nazis did not admit of the complexities that even the Communists had to accommodate. The power wielder's rule was absolute. Much has been written about the totalitarian *Führerprinzip,* but it was never described more starkly or simply than by Rudolf Hess when he proclaimed at the Nazi party rally in Nuremberg in 1934: "Adolf Hitler is the Party. The Party is Adolf Hitler." Nothing transactional there.

Nowhere was the rise of party leadership more dramatic, yet more complex and mysterious, than in the so-called developing nations. Traditional leadership was centered in family authority, village elders, tribal chiefs; it was usually highly structured but also widely dispersed. Local authority was clothed with extraordinary and even magical powers when it acted as an instrument of royal or aristocratic authority. Thus Lloyd Fallers pictured a Busoga chieftaincy: "The authority of the ruler, as representative of the royal group, extended over members of all clans; the royal ancestors were in a sense 'national' ancestors and the royal group, through the ruler, had interests in all the land of the state and its products. The royal group was . . . the structural manifestation and the symbolic embodiment of the unity of the whole state. . . . [The chief's] special relationship with the royal ancestors and nature spirits served both to support the ruler's position and to prevent his misuse of power, for these supernatural forces were believed to favour the general welfare and to punish rulers who became cruel or tyrannical."

The structure of political leadership in such societies would seem to be rigid and unchanging. Maternal or paternal authority, tribal rule, decision-making by elders, ideological control by religious leaders (local or missionary) both reflected and fortified class, caste, and geographical alignments; and all this might be underpinned with guns, money, and laws by colonial rulers. How could an entirely new form of political leadership, based on aggregating interests across wide populations, emerge out of such traditional systems? The answer lay in the slow, steady, but sometimes explosive interaction of conflict and change. The same colonial, class, caste, and attitudinal forces that seemed locked in mutual support in the villages and provinces could be the source of tensions that waited to be activated. In the nineteenth and twentieth centuries even the more remote villages could not escape the impact of world wars, the spread of religious and lay ideology, international depressions and recoveries, changes in trading routes, and the remorseless rise and fall in the demand and price of raw materials. The origin of change might be as obscure as the source of a great river in some forested mountain range. But the mutterings in a trading center, the gossip along a camel route, an encounter with a health center, the books that came into a missionary school, the shifts of perceived needs on the part of suppressed peoples—all these could precipitate changes in political attitude and behavior that could erupt in a mighty transforming movement.

The new leaderships that emerged from the tension points of change and conflict were largely controlled by ineluctable circumstances in shaping new party and other political institutions. At least they had a good deal of experience or observation to go by. Just as colonial Americans had "gone to school" in Locke and Blackstone whether or not they had ever attended Oxford or Cambridge, just as affluent young Latin Americans in the last century were educated in the courts of Spanish and other kings or fell under the spell of republican or revolutionary ideas in Paris or Rome, so the new leaders were often schooled in the political ideas or government systems of the English, the Americans, the French, or more recently the ideologies and revolutions of the Russians, the Chinese, and the Cubans. They witnessed, that is, the workings of one-party, two-party, and multi-party systems, of centralized and decentralized parties, of revolutionary apparatuses come to power—and from their observations (and occasionally their participation) they could draw lessons that might apply to their own developing polities.

The political systems that emerged from these forces, both deterministic and volitional, defy easy generalization. Not only did a wide variety of party systems develop from society to society, but the same nation might undergo major changes in its systems of political leadership. Turkey illustrates the point. Emulating Western monarchs in earlier centuries, Mahmud II centralized power in the ancient Ottoman empire over Janissaries, Islamic religious leaders, and landowners and inaugurated a program of reform and modernization in the early nineteenth century. A brief period of parliamentary rule was followed by another period of sultanate autocracy, followed by a second phase of constitutionalism by the original Young Turks. Periods of military dictatorship and allied occupation during World War I were climaxed by the abolition of the sultanate in the early 1920s. For a generation Turkey experienced one-party rule under Mustafa Kemal—and her famed Atatürk—and later Ismet Inönü. Following World War II a competitive party system developed out of the struggling party movements of the earlier period. The Democratic party split off from the dominant party under Kemal and Inönü, the Republican People's party. As Jeffersonian Republicans had done in the early 1800s and British Labourites in the early 1900s, the Democrats aroused support in areas the governing party had been unable to tap, and in 1950 the Democrats in Turkey won a sweeping victory, converting the Republicans into the opposition. The Republicans were stimulated into effective counterorganization, and by the late 1950s Turkey could boast of two competitive, well-organized, vigorously led parties. Some observers concluded that Turkey had at last achieved a mature and stable system of party leadership. But the new decade brought a military coup, extensive martial law, and further periods of authoritarian government.

Significant patterns could be detected among the "undeveloped" nations. The vast majority had various forms of one-party leadership. In a pioneering and sophisticated series of studies in the late 1950s, Gabriel Almond and James Coleman and their associates classified political systems in underdeveloped areas by the criteria "degree of competitiveness" and "degree of political modernity." Of the seventy-four nations analyzed, only twelve were classified as possessing competitive political systems. Of the balance, twenty-six were classified as "authoritarian" and the rest as "semi-competitive." The countries were also classified by area: Southeast Asia, South Asia, Near East, Africa, and Latin America. There were no sharply different area patterns; the three degrees of competitiveness were well represented in all areas—except that Africa at that time could boast of no competitive polities.

The criterion of political modernity in this study was that of quality and complexity rather than competitiveness. The most general characteristic of a modern political system, according to Almond and Coleman, "is the relatively high degree of differentiation, explicitness, and functional distinctiveness of political and governmental structures, each of which tends to perform, for the political system as a whole, a regulatory role for the respective political and au-thoritative functions." By any reasonable criteria only Israel, Chile, and Uruguay, in the Almond and Coleman study, could boast both a competitive and a modern political system; and only nine other countries—Malaya, the Philippines, Ceylon, India, Lebanon, Turkey, Argentina, Brazil, and Costa Rica—had a competitive political system with a "mixed" degree of political modernity.

Political party leadership may play varying roles in the processes of politi-cal modernization that Almond and Coleman summarize. As an instrument of socialization, the party, with its array of activists and its techniques of pro-paganda, can penetrate families, tribes, villages, and other primary organiza-tions, can excite attention, challenge existing values, inculcate new attitudes, transform loyalties, and ultimately shape political behavior. As a recruiting agency, the party can draw persons out of their ethnic, class, religious, and other subcultures and, in the style of Boss Plunkitt, enlist them in a political cause and organize them in a political apparatus—in short, convert the apathetic into followers and the followers into leaders. As articulator and aggregator of interests, the party identifies major needs and claims, promises to respond to them, casts them in programmatic form, establishes priorities among them, and takes responsibility for consideration of them and action on them by the government leaders over whom the party claims to exert some influence. As an instrument of communication, the party may act as a vital link in informing party and government leaders of the wants, claims, and expectations of the party rank and file and the general public, and it may at the same time communicate the leaders' promises, exhortations, achievements, and excuses to the people.

Is the dominant single party more effective in these modernizing and mobilizing functions than the competitive two-party or multi-party system? It depends of course on the particular political context and on what is meant by "effective," but it has been widely believed that one-party leadership can arouse and convert without the requirement of adapting or truckling to popular attitudes, that it can challenge parochial, conservative, and traditional social and political structures and bring about redistribution of income and even transformation of society as a result of its continuous, intensive, militant indoctrination of followers and mustering of power—and that it can do this in part because such one-party leadership has the political field to itself and is not curbed or weakened by competition. Other observers disagree. "Some scholars have suggested that while mobilist one-party systems facilitate national integration," Myron Weiner and Joseph LaPalombara observe, "they inhibit effective participation and thereby facilitate the development of oligarchical systems primarily concerned with political survival, national aggrandizement, or personal gain rather than, say, economic growth, social welfare, or democratic political values." According to this view, one-party mobilization resembles bureaucracy in the confusing of ends with means. It may bring simply a circulation of power-holding rather than a transactional progression to new levels of expectation and fulfillment or a transforming leadership that leads to basic social change.

Party Leadership: Power and Change

Parties are the vehicles of collective leadership. Whether the party leaders are world-famous personalities or obscure local committee members, their political vocation is to recognize the wants and needs of present and potential constituencies, to arouse and intensify expectations, to enlist more persons in the party cause, to win elections—and then to mobilize the party's influence within and outside government to satisfy rising demands, thereby winning more elections and remaining in office. With their feet in the grass roots, their fingers close to the levers of government, and their minds attuned to shifting popular attitudes and expectations as well as to changes in the political system itself, party leaders ideally are superbly equipped to serve as part of a giant apparatus that links popular need to government response and government action back to popular response that in turn sustains the party's grip on government.

Two questions arise from the role of party as collective leadership. One concerns the capacity of the party to produce change consistent with party program, goals, or ideology—whether the party is merely the reflection of more fundamental forces operating outside it, the passive receptacle for such forces, or a prime cause itself of purposeful, transforming social change. The other question asks where *in* the party, particularly among the various leadership sectors, power is exerted.

We must be clear what kind of party system we are analyzing—an authoritarian one-party system, a competitive two-party system, an adaptive multiparty system, or others. And we must be clear what kind of change we are looking for—psychological, social, economic, political, governmental, or other. There can be little doubt that highly programmatic or ideological parties coming to power in countries undergoing the nation-building process have a major impact on the shape of the political system. Dynamic party leaders break through tight, parochial group memberships and affiliations; they activate new wants and aspirations; they challenge old loyalties and replace them with new ones; they recruit followers who become new leaders; they broaden participation, strengthening linkages horizontally between previously separate localities and regions and vertically between localities and the center; they combine varied interests, build party institutions, and eventually take over and recast government institutions. Such new parties may also have a major impact in a negative way by overthrowing old party structures and repressing other new parties that threaten their hegemony.

Still, transactional strategies may predominate. James Coleman and Carl Rosberg have drawn a distinction in "uniparty or one-party states" between the "pragmatic-pluralistic pattern" and the "revolutionary pattern." In tropical Africa the more pragmatic-pluralistic party has a more limited preoccupation with ideology and is more adaptive and aggregative and tolerant of a "controlled pluralism" in the scope, depth, and tempo of its modernization strategy. The more revolutionary-centralizing party is constant, preoccupied, and even compulsive in ideology and anti-traditional, transformative, and even revolutionary in its approach to modernization. The degree of political mobilization and of popular commitment expected from followers is partial and intermittent with the first kind of party and high and constant with the second. In pragmatic-pluralistic parties the degree of intraparty hierarchism and discipline ranges from the more centralized to the more pluralistic; the degree of "associational monopoly and fusion" is generally looser, and assimilation of political institutions into "party government" is limited; whereas the revolutionary-centralizing parties rated high and even "total" on all these degrees of hierarchy, discipline, fusion, and assimilation.

Political parties that developed in the Western tradition also showed marked variations—especially between the two-party and multi-party systems—but in general tended to adapt to the existing government institutions rather than seek to transform them. Even the British Labour party had to bow to the British tradition of parliamentary sovereignty. American parties had some success in unifying the fragmented governmental system but tended to be fragmented themselves as they tried to influence and act through a structure of federalism and separation of powers; they are now mainly transactional agencies. French politics tended toward multi-partyism, in part because the legislative chambers offered political rewards to party coalition builders and to party independents, in contrast to the tendency toward two-party polarization in American presidential politics and British parliamentary politics.

In many polities the manipulation of electoral representation provided a virtual laboratory exercise in the manner in which institutional arrangements could affect party organization. A system of proportional representation was almost certain to encourage multi-partyism because proportional representation, with its slavishly accurate reproduction of minority groups, encouraged splinter and transactional parties to enter the political arena in the hope that their tiny number of seats would at least furnish them with some trading capital. An electoral system providing for single-member constituencies would tend in a relatively homogeneous country to distort the results by magnifying the number of legislative seats won by the largest national party (and to some degree that of the second largest party); single-member constituencies have the opposite effect in heterogeneous societies and hence foster multi-partyism. The American type of presidential government tended to encourage a two-party politics on the national level because the presidency was such a lucrative political prize that diverse interests and regions sought to pool their supporters and voters tended to become polarized in defense of one or the other's presidential leader or presidential candidate.

Political parties, then, may have significant impacts on political systems. But political change may not mean fundamental change—the kind of *transformation* that the mass of people can see and feel and taste and that can reshape their lives. How significant are parties in causing real change? Here the answer may be even more tentative. To begin, the question must be clarified. What is the measure of change? Is it change promised by party leaders or is it change measured by more objective standards?

As for promised change, rough appraisals can be made of the extent to which party goals have been realized. The protection of national security, the extension of safeguards for individual liberty, the redistribution of national income in more egalitarian ways, the overcoming of a depression, for example, all can be appraised in relation to the promises made by the party winning power. This kind of measurement is even more possible in respect to specific policies on matters that people can directly experience—jobs, medical care, housing, education, poverty programs, environmental control, and the like. Many people are highly skeptical that parties will carry out such programs and meet their commitments, but the party record in many nations is not one of failure. The rejuvenated Liberal party in Britain during the early years of the century realized the promises it had made on vital matters. A study of American major-party platforms and the ensuing legislative records indicated that far more of the parties' promises had been carried out than the cynics had been prepared to admit.

The supreme test of the militant, ideological, monolithic party is whether it can bring about the transformations it promised. Here again the record would vary enormously from nation to nation. The Communist party of the Soviet Union clearly was the vanguard in bringing about extensive changes in the common lives of the Russian people. Yet anyone closely observing Russian society may be as much impressed by the continuities in the lives of Russians as by the discontinuities. A Russian Rip Van Winkle returning to a Russian village twenty years after the Revolution might find that living conditions had not changed all that much, aside perhaps from health and nutrition. In other nations—Yugoslavia, for example—the Communist party was a great innovating and transforming force. Perhaps the most striking success of militant ideological parties is not so much in transforming society as it is in setting and fulfilling priorities. To win a war, to collectivize agriculture, to manufacture atomic and nuclear weapons, to control the sources of information of the people—these more specific and explicit types of goals could be achieved in many cases. But to alter fundamentally the behavior of masses of people—this was something else. As a leader of the risorgimento in Italy said after national unification had been achieved to some degree, "Having made Italy, we must now make Italians."

What is the role of leadership within political parties? Can interrelations or processes be identified that imply a distinctive role for such party leadership? Leadership is generated in and between parties along the lines of *conflict* that develop among group interests and political factions ramifying throughout the polity. In most societies these conflicts are complex and multiple—between militants and moderates, between generations, between nationalists and parochialists, between groups supporting clashing policies, and many others. The conflict comes to a head, as we have noted, in the struggle between leaders of the party organization and leaders of the same party who hold government responsibilities. This struggle actually produces a four-way conflict as local organization leaders variously combine and contend with national organization leaders and as locally elected party leaders in government variously cooperate and clash with national party leaders responsible for running the government. Any one of these four leadership collectivities may combine or contest with any of the others, thereby producing multiple leadership commixtures.

In the hundreds of major parties and the many more hundreds of minor parties active in over one hundred nations, the interrelations among these party leadership sectors take too many forms to allow generalization. The ways in which leadership clusters within the party cooperate and contend with one another can best be seen in those situations in which the intraparty struggle spills outside the confines of secret party councils and becomes an open conflict in which each side mobilizes its supporters and draws on all its resources. The British Labour party was racked after World War II by dissension over both domestic and foreign policy. One of the sharpest critics of the Labour government under Prime Minister Attlee was K. Zilliacus, Member of Parliament, who had been readopted by his Gateshead (East) Constituency Labour party as their parliamentary candidate for the next election. After much agitation the National Executive Committee of the Labour party (composed of the prime minister, twelve trade-union heads, six ministers, and others) decided to withhold endorsement of Zilliacus' candidature and so informed the local Gateshead party. Zilliacus, however, had developed close ties with some leaders of the Gateshead party, which defiantly voted to support him. When Zilliacus stepped up his left-wing activities in defiance of party policy, the NEC voted to expel him from the party. Instructed by the NEC to drop Zilliacus and select another candidate, the Gateshead party took its case to the annual party conference and lost it in a vote supporting the NEC. Later the Gateshead party was "reformed" and ran a candidate sanctioned by the national party leadership. Zilliacus stood in the general election as an independent and lost to the regular Labour candidate. The lesson of all this was not lost on other potentially rebellious Labour M.P.s.

Contrast this exercise of central party discipline with a somewhat comparable effort in the United States. In 1938 President Franklin D. Roosevelt confronted deep divisions within the Democratic ranks in Congress, especially between Northern New Dealers and Southern and border-state conservatives. He embarked on his notorious "purge," in which, acting explicitly as head of the Democratic party, he urged voters in a number of Democratic primaries to repudiate their incumbent Democratic senator and choose a dependable New Dealer instead. The local party organizations—to the extent that they existed at all—rallied to the defense of their men in the Senate and the Democratic voters followed suit. What Roosevelt lacked was precisely what the central leadership of the Labour party possessed: a well-organized local party over which the national organization could exert some discipline. Lacking such an organization, Roosevelt improvised; had he planned his strategy well in advance and built up a local New Deal organization within the Democratic party, he might have succeeded in some of his purge attempts, at least outside the Deep South.

Actual purges, however, are the exception in centrally but democratically organized parties. A more typical example of the resolution of leadership rivalries in the British parties was the effort of the Attlee government to enact a conscription bill over the opposition of Labour M.P.s who preferred to "keep left." After Attlee announced the proposed bill to a private meeting of the parliamentary Labour party, that group was divided, and some weeks later seventy or eighty Labourites signed an agreement asking the party to reject the bill and then proceeded to vote against the bill. Two days later the government reduced the proposed period of service under the bill from eighteen to twelve months. This transaction succeeded; the government won passage of the bill the following month by a top-heavy vote and later won endorsement of it at the Labour party conference.

It is the capacity of the party to tolerate and to resolve such internal power and policy conflicts that defines it as an institution of collective leadership. Most conflicts in most parties do not reach the point of open defiance, threatened rebellion, and purges; discerning leadership heads off the crisis through skillful mixtures of discipline and compromise. The power of various factions to protest and that of the party leadership both to yield and to stand firm suggests that leadership is distributed throughout the party. Even in the Labour party—where in the Zilliacus and other cases government leaders of the party were able to work closely with national organization leaders of the party to use the local party organization to discipline a local government leader (the errant M.P.)—the government leaders must adopt policy with a keen sense of how not only the members of Parliament but the party rank and file will react. Most decisions by both organization and government party leaders are made by anticipation of support and opposition. Local leaders exert power without having to operationalize it, perhaps without even seeing it. Central and local leadership, government and organization leadership—these leadership elements not only tolerate leadership from opposing elements, they exact it. The party operation assumes a balance of leadership, vertically and horizontally. In this sense the party becomes a *structure of leadership*.

We can conclude that party leadership is generally transactional, but it has vast transforming potential. As a structure of leadership in a competitive political situation the party activates leaders throughout the structure; it also converts followers into leaders as conflict over policy and position draws in more and more of the rank and file. That conflict draws in great numbers of people previously outside the party organization as leaders try to mobilize voters in support of the leaders' efforts. Hence the ultimate test of the power of party leadership is its capacity to mobilize millions of followers, to align and realign voters, to shape and reshape public opinion. For these processes create more millions of leaders whose individual power may be slight but whose collective power makes the leaders more subordinate to followers than controlling of them, and potentially makes party leadership, thus broadly defined, into a powerful instrument of social transformation and historical causation.

13 --

LEGISLATIVE LEADERSHIP:
THE PRICE OF CONSENSUS

The classic seat of transactional leadership is the "free" legislature. With an assured degree of formal influence over lawmaking and a power base in the electorate "back home," members interact on a plane of rough equality. Typically the chamber becomes a trading arena in which members' individual interests and goals are harmonized through age-old techniques of bargaining, reciprocity, and payoff. The trading system is not necessarily self-sustaining. Modal values of fairness, tolerance, and trust (e.g., keeping one's word) guide legislative action. Leadership is necessary for the initiating, monitoring, and assured completing of transactions, for settling disputes, and for storing up political credits and debits for later settlement.

Not all legislatures embody transactional leadership. Just as certain parties in certain nations serve as key agencies for *transforming* leadership, so legislatures such as the Supreme Soviet in Russia have served as conspicuous parts of a system of mobilizing and modernizing leadership. The parliaments in some liberal democracies can serve as agencies of party or majority action designed to "transform" society, as many British Labourites hoped to do through the House of Commons in the late 1940s. But the tradition, the ethic, the organization, the spirit of the Western parliamentary enterprise is that of transaction and brokerage. No legislature lives up to that tradition and ethic more faithfully than the United States Senate. On occasion that chamber has been an instrument of party or majority action, but far more often it has been a place of exchange.

Individual leaders, like institutions, can embrace various kinds of leadership at various times and under varied conditions. During his years as majority leader in the Senate, Lyndon B. Johnson was the consummate transactional leader of legislation. So many channels of obligation, expectation, and exchange radiated through his towering and glowering presence that the source of his power was called the "Johnson network." Johnson had a considerable power base in the Senate that consisted mainly of decisive influence over prized committee appointments and certain chairmanships, allotments of congressional campaign funds, Senate services and perquisites, junkets, and more. He also gained from the close cooperation and collective leadership of a group of highly loyal lieutenants. But his greatest power resources consisted of his own skills in recognizing senators' needs and motives, amassing and disbursing credits, mixing techniques of deference and domination, and employing the Johnson "treatment," the tone of which has been defined as the powerful application of varying concoctions of "supplication, accusation, cajolery, exuberance, scorn, tears, complaint, the hint of threat."

Three years after leaving his Senate leadership post Johnson was President. He brought many of his old legislative techniques with him to the White House. But now he enjoyed the far greater resources of the presidency, and he exploited them to the hilt. We can measure this augmented power by the legislative results he gained and by their later impact on the country. As Senate Democratic leader during the Eisenhower years, and as Kennedy's vice president, Johnson helped put through a number of compromise civil rights bills that all but exhausted his reservoirs of transactional power yet helped bring only marginal improvements for blacks and others at the end of the policy process. On becoming President he salvaged and strengthened the moderate Kennedy proposals of 1963. The big Johnson civil rights package passed Congress in 1964 with the remarkable grass-roots support that the White House, along with party, civil rights, and religious leaders, was able to mobilize. Most symbolic of the alteration in the leadership structure was Johnson's role in the breaking of a long Senate filibuster—the very weapon that conservative senators had used to water down earlier civil rights bills. The next year the President and congressional liberals pushed through a sweeping voting rights bill that directly expanded the black electorate and would have a lasting transforming impact on the pattern of Southern politics.

Some contend that legislators can produce similar results without executive leadership, and they can cite arresting cases in point. In general, however, Western-style legislatures in this century have failed to act decisively on the central and rending political issues of our time. Internal legislative leadership has failed to overcome—except when backed up by powerful executive or party sanctions—the slowness of legislative deliberation, the often archaic lawmaking machinery and procedures, the devices for minority obstruction and delay, and, behind all this, the fragmentation innate in the relationships of legislators representing separated constituencies and the multi-party or multi-faction systems that divide legislators into not simply an action-minded majority opposing an opposition-minded minority but numberless factions equipped with absolute or partial veto powers.

The Legislator as Leader

On the occasion of the inauguration of a new constitution for Nigeria in 1952, members of a British parliamentary delegation made a side trip to the Gold Coast to make a presentation to the Gold Coast Assembly on behalf of the "mother of parliaments." The presentation consisted of a copy of Erskine May's *Parliamentary Practise,* alleged to be the enshrinement of six centuries of British parliamentary wisdom. The volume was suitably inscribed by Winston Churchill and Clement Attlee. In making the presentation a Conservative member of Parliament, Sir Edward Keeling, told the Assembly that according to popular understanding Parliament could do anything but change man to woman and vice versa. But, he added, in practice many other things were *not* done. The sovereign's name was never mentioned, for example, the civil service was not involved politically, and the rights of the opposition were carefully observed.

It was a nostalgic moment of cross-cultural indulgence on the part of a nation that was soon to be undergoing its own political ordeal—in which not all the parliamentary niceties would be observed. Members of the Gold Coast Assembly might have reflected, too, that the "Mother of Parliaments" was not the sovereign body in political practice that it was in constitutional theory. The House of Commons, indeed, had come to be perceived as one of the most drilled and regimented assemblies on earth for all the hullabaloo of parliamentary debating style. The loyal opposition was tolerated but essentially cut off from power—at least until the next election. And the great number of members of Parliament were seen as "vote fodder" for party whips who, after the sounding of bells, as in a Pavlov experiment, herded the members past tellers and pursued the culprit who failed to attend or who, on attending, failed to vote correctly.

By such perceptions, which are widely shared in many countries about most parliaments, the very concept of legislative leadership would seem to be self-contradictory. On the one hand, heirs to the Western parliamentary tradition recall the glorious moments in history when "representatives of the people" (even if self-appointed) gathered in solemn assembly to protest monarchical and other forms of executive absolutism or even tyranny. The rise of legislative power had been closely linked to the expansion of individual liberty and popular rule, consecrated in bills of rights written and unwritten. Legislatures formed and flowered, especially during the late eighteenth and nineteenth centuries, when popular assemblies expressed both the negative concept of liberty as opposition to arbitrary acts of government that improperly restricted the rights of businessmen, workers, and others, and the positive concept of freedom expressed in the use of government to expand the social and economic rights of man to a secure income, decent housing, protection in old age, and more. The first half of the twentieth century, however, witnessed the pulverizing of traditional legislative authority under the impact of fascism, Communism, and other forms of totalitarianism. The famous German Reichstag was reduced under the Nazis to a crowd of robots who slavishly approved Hitler's acts when called on to act at all.

Even in nations where parliaments still held some power, the old ethic of men "sprung fresh from the people" coming together for free and independent expression of popular needs and wants had given way to disillusioned views of legislators as puppets controlled by forces within or outside the legislature. The individual legislator is seen to be under several types of restraints.

One of these consists of *local forces*. The legislator is perceived as representing a constituency so unified in its attitudes toward the central regime or toward other areas of the nation that the representative's freedom of action is sharply limited. Thus the member of the British Parliament from Ulster, the member of the Indian Parliament from an area such as Madras, with its linguistic and other forms of separatism, or the member of the French Parliament from the "Red Belt" of Paris, all would seem rigidly bound to dominant attitudes in their constituencies if they wished to retain their seats in the next election. The only kind of leadership the legislator could display under these conditions, it would seem, consists of thinking up new and more ingenious ways of dramatizing the compacted attitudes of the people back home.

A second perception of legislators is of persons bound hand and foot to organized interests in their constituency, in the whole polity, or both. According to this view, such interests through their power to influence and activate voters in the constituency and through their skill in manipulating money, propaganda, and other forms of influence in the capitol, virtually take over the lawmaking process, at least in their area of interest. Thus the process of tariff-making in the American Congress has been studied as an almost mathematical conversion of the economic power of industrial and commercial interests into decision-making influences in House and Senate committees.

If lawmakers are not seen as puppets of interests, they may be viewed as pawns of a third force—of political party rule in their districts, in the legislature, or both. According to this view, legislators may owe their nomination to a constituency party organization or party "machine" that has the power to deprive them of renomination or, should they win renomination, to throw its weight effectively against them at the general election. Often such a local party organization is articulated with the national party, whose leaders in the legislature keep tabs on such legislators and hold them in line through judicious combinations of carrot and stick applied at both the national and the local levels through the party machinery.

These perceptions of the legislator's leadership role have been validated by extensive empirical data. But a broader concept of that role—or potential role—emerges from different perceptions, especially the legislators' perceptions of their own role. They may see the legislature itself as a more viable entity than many of its critics do; however decrepit or anachronistic it may appear to outsiders, to these lawmakers it is at least a place for conducting political and governmental business and at most a dynamic source of leadership in the nation. They can note, too, that whatever the "decline" of parliament in the West, the doctrine of parliamentary supremacy remains a compelling one. Parliaments constitutionally retain supreme lawmaking power; symbolically they are the supreme representative institution. And it is noteworthy that even in nations where the legislature simply ratifies party decision, as in the case of the Supreme Soviet in Russia, *constitutionally* the legislature does remain supreme; the same is true with legislatures in many other authoritarian societies. Individual members may properly feel that they control a significant portion of autonomous power.

More important, there are countless opportunities for the individual member to exercise leadership within the machinery of parliamentary institutions and in relations with his constituents and with party and governmental leadership. Members can maximize their independence—and hence their potential capacity for leadership—in several ways in their relations to their district. Even when constituents are united and extremist in their attitudes toward an issue, those constituents ordinarily expect their representatives to show some flexibility in dealing with leaders of opposing groups—that is, most constituents understand the requirements of bargaining. More typically the voters themselves will be divided on a pressing question or vary in the degree of their support of some widely agreed on policy; the legislator can play off these differences against one another. Then, too, legislators can depend on a significant number of constituents being willing to grant them some independence because voters feel that independent action is part of the job; the voters do not need to have read Edmund Burke's speech to the electors of Bristol to understand that they hire not a puppet but a representative who offers his "unbiased opinion, his mature judgement, his enlightened conscience." Even more, legislators often have the opportunity to shape constituents' attitudes by taking strong positions in the legislature and in the district. Some voters use them as a guide to their own thinking, in part because they trust them and know that they are far better informed about most questions. The very fact that large numbers of constituents are usually uninformed or uninterested in policy questions may give the legislators more leverage.

Some of these same considerations apply to the legislator's relations with party organizations and leaders and with organized interests. However extensive the discipline or influence party leaders may bring to bear on them, party and group leaders must recognize that ultimately the legislators hold independent power in a constitutionally independent assembly. For their term of office, they each hold, moreover, a vital power—one vote in lawmaking—and party and group leaders will need that vote on future roll calls. Thus members have a constantly renewable chip to throw on the legislative gaming table. They may also win influence by demonstrating expertise on issue areas, by parliamentary eloquence, by dint of long experience in the chamber with its consequent perquisites, by skill in applying personal influence to other legislators, by mastery of legislative technique, or by a simple capacity to make trouble and throw up roadblocks (as Huey Long did). The greatest source of influence and potential leadership, though, is found less in individual efforts than in membership in the numerous groups that spring up in a highly politicized environment. "One way in which individual Diet members can try to get more voice in party decisions is to organize semi-formal groups within the Diet," writes Nobutaka Ike in his study of Japanese politics. "Freshmen Diet members of a party, for instance, will often form freshmen clubs and meet fairly regularly to exchange views." Japanese party leaders have extensive power, but they must anticipate rank-and-file attitudes to retain it.

The influence of party leaders over individual legislators is strong also in India, but the rank and file there cannot be pushed too hard, as the following parliamentary repartee suggests. The Speaker was remarking on the distrust exhibited even by members of the government party toward their leaders.

> Members should not jump to the conclusion that the Government wants to keep anything away from them. . . . That seems to me to be a remnant of old memories, ignoring the character of the Government we have now. . . . We must change our approach towards the Government. (An Hon. Member: What about the Government changing its approach?) Whatever may be the mistakes of Government, we are now a sovereign House and the Government is responsible to the House. (An Hon. Member: It is not.) If they are not, I should say the House is weak not to drive them out. (An Hon. Member: It is for you.) It is not for the Speaker. It is for the majority to be strong and insistent, and I am sure that any

government which claims to be democratic and responsible to the House is bound to respond to what the House says.

The subtle influence of the back-bencher in the British House of Commons illustrates the possible extent of the individual legislator's leadership, and the restrictions on it, in a parliament that has been widely emulated in the British dominions and beyond. In Westminster the back-benchers may enlarge their influence by taking part in a multitude of party, regional, issue, and ideological groups, some of which cross party lines. They may abstain from voting on an important party question or even vote against their party leadership on matters of grave conscience. Occasionally party leaders in Parliament permit "free votes" on which back-benchers can take independent action and seek to mobilize support from other members. Back-benchers vitally interested in controversial issues on which the major parties prefer not to take a stand have been able to take advantage of the procedures for private members' bills to steer key reform measures successfully through the House, as in the case of A. P. Herbert's reform of the divorce laws in the Marriage Act of 1937 and Sydney Silverman's success, after many attempts, in gaining almost single-handedly the abolition of capital punishment. Individual members sometimes openly rebel against their party leadership and defy the whips; sometimes they are penalized and even lose their seats, but more often they survive politically. More commonly it is the threat of rebellion or disaffection that forces the leadership to modify their position in advance. Back-benchers, who are often far more independent and critical in their remarks on and off the House floor than they are in the final "division," help set the tone and temper of the House and contribute to an environment of dissensus that establishes wide perimeters within which the party leadership must act.

A trend toward broader back-bench influence has been noted in recent years. "Members have obtained major improvements in the facilities available to them; executive action is now subject to much fuller scrutiny by select committees. . . . Private members' legislation has become more important; members have displayed more independence in the division lobbies," Peter Richards has summed it up. The development should not be overdrawn; the trend may be short-lived. But the enlargement of the private member's discretion and influence at least enhances his *potential* for legislative leadership.

The degree to which individual legislators actually realize their potential for legislative leadership turns on a number of factors: (1) the conflict situation in which they act, in their constituency and in the legislature; (2) the roles they assume in the face of varied claims, demands, and expectations; (3) the values they hold and the goals derived from them; and (4) the extent to which they can manipulate conflict situations and roles to obtain legislation or other parliamentary action that helps realize their goals.

Conflict lies all about the legislator in the typical constituency; the question is how the member perceives it and acts on it. Conflict reflects the customary differences between producer and consumer, labor and capital, farmer and wholesaler, Hindu and Moslem, immigrant from one part of the homeland and immigrant from another, and endless combinations and subdivisions of these and other differences. Conflict also pervades the attitudes of individuals who feel "cross-pressured" by the competing and antagonistic forces that play on them. Legislators may perceive only conventional types of conflict and may ignore more subtle but perhaps more important conflicts within the minds of the voters. Sensing even the gross differences among or within individuals would be difficult for the legislator who was not equipped with sophisticated polling techniques—a resource sometimes available to presidents and prime ministers but rarely to representatives of small districts. Legislators usually act by rule of thumb on the basis of face-to-face contact, their mail, previous election results, rumors and tales, and hunch.

Legislators may have considerable latitude in the manner in which they respond to conflict. One of the classic dilemmas—or opportunities—is the choice between trying to represent the aggregated needs, wants, attitudes, and interests of their whole constituency against external claims and (turning the axis of conflict) representing certain interests within the constituency against others within it. Legislators may seek to mute each of these conflicts—and indeed all conflicts—in order to reduce the immediate pressure and their vulnerability at the next election. The extent to which they can mute conflict will turn both on their skills and on the degree to which intradistrict conflict is not easily conciliated as a result of historic circumstance and the efforts of other political leaders to keep the conflict alive for their own purposes. Thus a "conflict over conflict" is carried on by the legislator, by present or potential election opponents, by national and local parties, by nationally and locally organized interests, and by other political entities.

Similar conditions of conflict may dominate the legislative arena, though with heightened intensity. Individual legislators will have some choice between playing up their areal responsibilities and demands as opposed to those of other members and involving themselves with parties or groups whose interests cut across intraconstituency solidarity. The legislature by definition is a political marketplace where representatives disagree over policy and ideology and compete for restricted resources. On some questions, such as a public works bill that distributes highways, schools, and other benefits to all constituencies with polished and unassailable impartiality, the legislator may submerge conflict in a flood of favors for the people back home. Other issues, fought over with burning intensity both in the legislature and in the country, polarize the legislature and offer the lawmaker no haven.

Most parliamentary conflict falls somewhere between the great polarizing issues and the bland and harmonizing ones; how legislators deal in considered and self-protective fashion with the ceaseless rush of these conflicts turns in part on their assumption of leadership roles in their districts and in the legislature.

To view legislators' choices of roles through their eyes, in terms of the political context as they see it, is to move beyond the simple alternative of *delegate* role versus *trustee* role. A locally elected representative serving in a legislature that covers a much broader area will inevitably be divided between national and local responsibilities as he or she sees them. But each of these responsibilities (and opportunities) takes so many different forms, and the local and national duties and opportunities overlap to such a degree, that legislators are likely to think and act not in response to two great alternatives but in response to a spectrum of choices—choices that vary as the legislators encounter new political openings and closures. Consider the role of delegate. If legislators decide to give first priority to this role, they encounter a host of thorny questions. Should they respond to the vocal needs and wants of their constituents or should they try to legislate for their constituents' strong but less articulated "real" needs as the legislators perceive them? They can never represent all the interests of all the members of their constituency; how then do they define the local interests that they must serve?

It is easy to pose "local" interests versus "national" ones, but the two are intertwined. Legislators may seek a high tariff for some commodity, the production of which represents the "economic life blood" of their district; if they gain such a tariff as a result of bargaining with other representatives and agreeing to *other* higher tariffs, and their constituents as a result are inflicted with a general price rise, have they been true delegates of their district? What about the constituents who prefer that their representatives act in the legislature as "national tribunes" rather than as local agents—do legislators serve the interests of those voters by taking the delegate's role?

Similar questions plague legislators who seek to "serve the nation"; it is harder to define the nation's interest than it is the district's. National forces are even more variegated: there are party pressures from various personalities and wings in the national party, exhortations and criticisms of the press and other media, and ideological and policy influences. By definition legislators are single voices but taken together they cry out that they speak for the entire nation even when they are in fact locally attuned. Some legislators do indeed become national leaders: witness the long struggle of Senator George Norris of Nebraska to protect Muscle Shoals from private takeover and his leadership in the establishment of the Tennessee Valley Authority. But national leadership may exact a price from the legislator who remains dependent on his constituency, and Norris eventually paid the price. Witness the dilemma of Senator James W. Fulbright of Arkansas, who held national leadership in Senate foreign policy but was blocked from possible appointment as secretary of state because of his conservative votes on civil rights measures, which he believed necessary in order to hold his Senate seat.

Faced with such perplexities, legislators in Western-style democracies do not make strategic choices; they "play it as it lays." "There is a line of demarcation between what they want at home and what you think is good for them," an American state legislator says. "I haven't been too disturbed by that yet but it could become a major problem. I don't think I could ever settle just where the line is. It is too flexible. Each piece of legislation must be considered individually to determine it." Another says, "Uniformly, I have not taken either one position—sometimes one, sometimes the other. . . . The evidence of success is that I'm still here."

Such representatives cannot clearly define their role in terms of whether they should serve local or national interest and whether they should follow the will of the people (locally or nationally) or legislate as the legislator thinks best on the basis of superior information, experience, and exposure. Eventually, however, it may prove more difficult for legislators to flit from role to role than to define the kind of general posture they wish to assume, if only because role-taking itself confronts them with endless choices, and life is easier when they can establish and follow some rough guidelines. They might have a choice of one or more of several broadly defined roles.

Ideologues speak for doctrines that may be supported widely throughout their district but more typically are held by a small but highly articulate minority. The doctrine may be economic, religious, nationalistic, linguistic, regionalistic, revolutionary, reactionary, xenophobic, anti-centrist. In the legislature ideologues are likely to find allies of similar doctrinal disposition. They often vote—and talk—across party and other established lines.

Tribunes (the term is used by John Wahlke and associates to denote the legislator who "may primarily perceive himself as the discoverer, reflector, advocate, or defender of popular needs and wants") may view themselves as representing primarily the people back home or the polity as a whole; in any case they see themselves as a strong link between popular aspirations and governmental action. "The tribune may express one or more of three conceptions of his role,'' according to Wahlke et al. "He may perceive himself as the discoverer or connoisseur of popular needs, as the defender of popular interests, or as the advocate of popular demands.'' Sensitive to popular feeling, they are not necessarily subservient to it.

Careerists look on their career in the legislature as a value in itself or as a stepping-stone to higher office inside the legislature or outside but not as a means of serving broader goals or interests. To advance their career they oblige those public or private groups that can best help them. Careerists are not necessarily harmful to the general welfare; it depends on how they define their goals. They may simply try to do such an outstanding job in the legislature that they will impress their constituents and close observers in the capitol. John F. Kennedy clearly looked on the House of Representatives and later the Senate as stepping-stones to the presidency. "We were just worms there,'' he said about the House when he was senator, and he was equally uncomplimentary about his role in the Senate once he had become President. But he knew that he had to do a decent job as legislator, in most respects at least, if he was to win the credentials to run for President.

Parliamentarians play one or both of two roles. One is that of *technician*, who becomes an expert in parliamentary procedure and has a major part in expediting or obstructing legislation. The other is the *institutionalist*, who seeks to protect the parliamentary institution itself. Perhaps they succumb to the seductive charms, genteel ways, and historic lore of parliament; perhaps they believe that the survival and health of the legislature are crucial to the British, Japanese, or Italian way of life. As ''institutional patriots'' (Donald Matthews' term) they cherish the indoctrination, the mutual forbearance and protection, the traditionalism, and the courtesy that make up the way of life in an ancient and proud institution such as the United States Senate.

Brokers, perhaps the most universally recognized of legislative types, see themselves as playing an indispensable role in mediating among antagonistic lawmakers, balancing interests, weighing all sides, tempering conflict, and finally creating legislative unity and action, if only at the level of the lowest common denominator. They are often, in Carl Friedrich's words, specialists in diagnosing group opinion in their constituencies, and they know "just how far to go in order to strike a balance between the pressure from various special groups and the resistance (passive pressure) from the group as a whole.''

Other legislative roles can be identified: *party loyalists* act as the agents of a strong party organization in their constituency or in the legislature; *policy generalists* work for a broad program, often a party program; *policy specialists* focus their legislative efforts on one problem, on which the specialist becomes recognized as something of an expert, something of an enthusiast, and perhaps something of a bore. Some of these roles are incompatible with one another; it would be difficult for one legislator to try to play consistently the roles, say, of both ideologue and broker. Others can easily coexist in the same person—for example, careerist, parliamentarian, and broker. What determines the kind of role legislators will play and the potential leadership for which they will position themselves? The main factor is their perception of the conditions that structure their legislative situation in a (usually) competitive situation: the electoral and opinion forces pressing on them from their district and the institutional restraints and political pressures facing them in the legislature. Their immediate instinct may be one of sheer political survival and their principal role that of the opportunist. Given a modicum of security, however, and given the possibility of playing off roles against one another—using their effectiveness in one role to strengthen their effectiveness in another—and given the possibility of "banking" goodwill and influence over time so that they will have a reservoir of power to draw on as needed—given all these conditions, legislators will be in a position to seek more than simple survival. The role or roles they play will then turn largely on the goals or purposes they set for themselves. These may be highly self-regarding and careerist; they may relate more to their constituency or their party; they may serve a great cause. The goals may reflect a disposition, in Max Weber's sense, to live *off* politics as opposed to living *for* politics—that is, for certain general purposes far beyond and above the legislator's individual well-being or success. These goals will vary enormously from legislator to legislator and legislature to legislature, but they will take on some pattern, and some common implications for the study of parliamentary leadership, as lawmakers become involved more deeply in the legislative structure and in the collective purposes of interest and party.

Group Leadership and Legislative Structure

The dominant view of legislative groups and factions is one of a collection of legislators essentially controlled by outside interests—in short, a flock of followers. "What are the different classes of legislators," James Madison asked, "but advocates and parties to the causes which they determine"—and which, one might add, determine them. For decades the popular picture of the legislature (and not only in the United States) has been one of "the inert part of a cash register, ringing up the additions and withdrawals of strength, a mindless balance pointing and marking the weight and distribution of power among the contending groups," in Earl Latham's words. But Latham goes on to say that "legislatures are groups also and show a sense of identity and consciousness of kind that unofficial groups must regard if they are to represent their members effectively." We are reminded once again that leadership and followership are inseparable and that neither role can be imputed to a politician on the basis of outward appearance alone or of a single episode.

The role of legislative groups and factions in the British Parliament is especially deceptive. Parliamentary tradition in Westminster frowns on the naked play of interest and pressure. "Parliamentarism ruled out 'authoritative instructions' and 'mandates' from the electorate," Samuel Beer states. "It also ruled out associations formed outside Parliament for the purpose of determining what Parliament ought to do and for pressing these decisions on it as coming from a higher authority." Cabinet influence over the Commons and strong party discipline also would seem to discourage faction. In fact Parliament supports a vigorous group life that directly reflects the clash of organized interests outside. Members of Parliament organize permanent, semi-permanent, and short-lived committees around economic, ideological, foreign-policy, veterans', single-issue, and other interests just as do members of less august legislatures. It is not unusual for the Trades Union Congress to sponsor at least one hundred successful Labour candidates for Parliament. The sitting M.P.s work together not only in the parliamentary Labour party but in connection with specific questions of importance to the TUC. On the business side, members—mostly Conservatives—have been associated with insurance, banking, brewing, publishing, and much else.

The extent to which members of Parliament may act for a specific interest with which they are connected is shrouded in the kind of ambiguity that allows politicians considerable scope but discourages the overstepping of certain boundaries. Members may not use their parliamentary status for their own financial benefit or that of their business associates; but they may—and are expected to—act in behalf of the broader interests that sponsored them. "If an ex-miner speaks on the need for safety in mines or if an ex-teacher argues that teachers should have higher pay—this can be regarded as part of the process of representation," Richards explains. "But if a Member takes some action in Parliament as a result of a specific payment then his behavior is unethical." The line is drawn as much in subtle conventions and understandings as in written rules.

The remarkable capacity of a parliamentary group to serve both as part of the government and as a source of pressure on the government is illustrated by the British Legion, the nation's largest veterans' organization. The president of the legion for many years was Sir Ian Fraser, a blinded veteran of World War I and a Conservative M.P. The legion had the usual interests and goals of a veterans' organization, mainly higher disability pensions and other government benefits. In Parliament the legion was organized as a "House of Commons Branch" comprising all legion members in the house and boasting of the Speaker as honorary president. Fraser sought to toe the line delicately between his party, his parliamentary, and his legion obligations. He directed both approbation and mild complaint against his own government when the Conservatives brought in a small improvement in the basic pension. He had to cope with Labour opposition members in the legion's branch in the Commons who accused him of yielding to his party masters, with activists in the British Legion who questioned whether he should continue as head of the organization, and with competing organizations such as the British Limbless Ex-Servicemen's Association. When the chips were down in a House roll call Fraser stuck with his party's whips, but on one occasion he walked into the opposition lobby. Somehow he managed to keep his standing in the Conservative party, the legion, and the legion's branch in the Commons, all the while providing adroit leadership of the veterans' forces in Parliament.

The factional leadership in Westminster of the British Legion branch and its Conservative chief represents an extreme case of "free-floating" leadership allowed by the cabinet and the party whips. In general the parliamentary and party leaderships are extremely wary of the claims and demands of factional leaders, and they have means of curbing their activities. Far more leeway to factional and group leadership is allowed in the United States, in Congress and in most state legislatures. Groupings based on area, which are central to the American national legislature, are not unknown in Britain with its Scottish and Welsh nationalists both within and outside the two major parties, but in the United States sectionalism has been more variegated and even more intense. Groupings like the midwestern bloc, the New England bloc, and above all the Southern bloc are sometimes formally organized but the power of region when region seems to be challenged is so ready and omnipresent that formal leadership and structure is unnecessary—leaders spring to the microphone with little organizational prompting.

Factions and factional leadership in Congress and the American state legislatures are usually grounded in organized interests in the constituencies, and it is this relation that has produced the simplistic view of one-way pressures exerted by group interests and their lobbyists. In fact the relation is very much a two-way transactional one, and legislative leaders often take more initiative and play a stronger role than do group interest leaders. The former are usually on the scene, they may be the first to uncover a threat to the group, they have means of communication and protest immediately at hand, and they can claim attention with more credibility than lobbyists often can. The roles may be interchangeable; sometimes it will be the factional leader in the legislature more than the interest-group leader who alerts the group's membership, arouses their concern, mobilizes their political potential, instructs them on the strategy to be used with the legislature, unites them over the issue at hand, and plays down other divisive matters. We hear much about the stream of letters and telegrams that pours into legislators' offices when a group interest such as that of labor, veterans, or anti-vivisectionists is aroused; we hear much less about the initiatives legislative factions have taken to precipitate the inundations of their own and other members' offices. The stream runs both ways. Charles Clapp has found a widely held view in Congress that the most potent lobby is the built-in lobby of the congressmen themselves.

In these two-way transactions—really multi-way, since conflicting subfactions are usually involved both in the legislature and outside—much depends on the role that factional leaders assume. They may see their role in the legislature as that of neutral umpire or detached arbitrator; far more often, at least in the less disciplined parliaments, factional legislative leaders see themselves as the proper representatives of group interest—indeed, can hardly perceive issues outside the frame of reference of their group affiliations. "A legislator-politician no less than any other man," David Truman notes, ". . . lived his life in a series of environments, largely group-defined. These have given him attitudes, frames of reference, points of view, which make him more receptive to some proposals than to others." Many legislators will insist "in all sincerity that they vote as their own consciences dictate," but "their 'consciences' are creatures of the particular environments in which they have lived and the group affiliations they have formed."

Ordinarily the legislative-faction leader and the interest-group leader do not follow prescribed roles but respond to specific political situations. Their relation to one another is explicitly transactional. Interest-group leaders and their lobbyists can provide the legislator with money, staff assistance, and above all support in the state or district. But, as Matthews has pointed out, legislators can influence lobbyists. One way is by noncooperation. "The senators have what the lobbyists want—a vote, prestige, access to national publicity, and the legislative 'inside dope.' Moreover, the lobbyist wants this not just once but many times over a number of years. The senators are in a position to bargain." Senators also cultivate with lobbyists friendships that may make the lobbyists protective of the senators' interest, Matthews observes, and the senator can through various devices build up a long-term "credit" with the lobbyist that the senator can bring into play on a crucial issue.

It has long been observed that legislators tend to become socialized by their parliamentary institutions, indoctrinated in their myths, folkways, unwritten rules, as they spend more and more of their days in the loving and perhaps insidious embrace of their legislative home. Ardent newcomers, spurred by some sweeping and moralistic mandate from their constituency, learn that the price of parliamentary effectiveness is to mute their voices, listen to their elders, and above all observe the norms and customs. "If you want to get along, go along," is the advice of transactional legislative leaders that is heard in the parliamentary languages of many nations. Carried to an extreme, this tendency would produce legislators who were slaves to institutions, perhaps decrepit or even defunct institutions. Less commonly recognized is the capacity of some legislators not to be controlled by the legislative environment but to exploit it for their own purposes—or, perhaps more typically, to yield to institutional demands and claims in certain respects in order that they may exercise leadership over the institution and its legislative output in other respects.

The degree and quality of leadership that can be exercised in these respects will depend in part on the role the legislator assumes. Parliamentarians spend years learning procedures that provide them with a decisive advantage in expediting action on their own bills and in delaying or devitalizing the measures of political opponents. Skillful brokers could take advantage of countless opportunities for mediating among hostile factions as bills are worked through the legislative maze, and they could exert a "broker's fee" of added influence in the process. Institutionalists in general, as noted above, value the legislative way of life not only because they enjoy it but because they benefit from it. On the other hand, in the legislature with a dispersed power system, the ideologue may attract much attention but have little legislative impact, while the policy generalist may have to settle for incrementalism rather than breakthrough programs.

The most significant, persistent, and visible part of the legislative system is usually the committee structure. It may be of some significance that parliaments that were created or re-created in several of the larger nations following World War II established strong committee systems, often with chairmanships that could accommodate effective leaders. In Japan the prewar Diet had several standing committees, but leadership was exercised to a great degree in each chamber sitting as a "committee of the whole." In the postwar Diet there was a full set of standing committees, each covering a major policy area such as education, finance, foreign affairs, or transportation. Much of the legislative work of the present Diet is shouldered by these committees, which also have investigative powers. The committee system strengthens a legislature that reflects the decision of the American framers of the postwar Japanese constitution to make the new Diet the heart of the new governmental system. Perhaps the American constitutionalists in Tokyo in the late 1940s, like their predecessors in Philadelphia in 1787, underestimated the potential role of party.

The legislative committees in the Indian lower house, the House of the People, provide opportunity for significant policy leadership. The powerful standing committees inherited from the prewar assemblies were abolished by the government in the early 1950s in a political struggle against a system that was considered hostile both to the government and to the British parliamentary tradition. However, two significant financial committees, the Public Accounts Committee and the Estimates Committee, were allowed to exert at least negative influence. Of the Estimates Committee W. H. Morris-Jones has observed: "The indirect influence of the Committee—working through the House and the parties as well as through public opinion generally—is probably even more important than its direct influence on the Government." The Public Accounts Committee serves as a vigilant watchdog over expenditures.

The West German Bundestag embraces a system of relatively strong and autonomous committees with chairmen who exercise considerable initiative and discretion. The chamber has become heavily dependent on the substantive work of the committees. Whether or not this situation was influenced by American experience, the significance of the present German committee system pales in comparison with that of the standing committee structure in both houses of the American Congress.

The standing committees of both houses would seem to offer ample opportunity for legislative leadership. The committees have long been perceived as "little legislatures" that had full authority to generate legislation on their own and to approve, reject, or sharply modify legislative proposals by the executive, by individual members of Congress, or by members of the committee themselves. Perhaps the most impressive feature of the committees has been their stability: they represent small structures of durable and predictable power, structures that are a solid part of the overall legislative system. Thus the old Foreign Relations Committee of the Senate and the House Rules Committee had a political standing, a reputation for independence, a visibility (or invisibility when they preferred), a linkage with other power centers on Capitol Hill, a breadth of substantive jurisdiction, and an accumulation of legislative experience that together gave these committees the kind of influence that persists despite changes in the political climate, despite the coming of new presidents who might threaten committee autonomy, and despite reforms and reorganizations of the legislative system itself. It is notable that Congress in its life of almost two centuries has repeatedly restructured and "reformed" its committees without (for the most part) fundamentally altering their influence and autonomy.

On the secure grounding of such committees the formal leaders of the committees—chairpersons, ranking majority and minority party members of the committees, and subcommittee chairpersons—can establish spheres of group and individual influence that have qualities of durability and predictability. This tendency takes on marked importance in Congress because of the committee seniority system that, despite occasional departures, is almost certain to reward the individuals with the longest consecutive tenure on the committee with the committee chair or the ranking minority leadership. The seniority rule in turn is linked with the tendency toward one-partyism in many Senate seats and most House seats. Those who become chairpersons are often members of Congress from "safe" seats that they have cultivated over the years, that are noncompetitive between the two major parties, and that discourage challenges to the incumbents' renomination as well as threats to their re-election. Inevitably, given a modicum of ability, committee chairpersons come to dominate legislative substance and procedure in their committees; they also possess a legislative resource that they can use as political currency in dealing with other power centers in Congress. Committee power lies at the heart of the whole transactional system of reciprocity, brokerage, and exchange on Capitol Hill, and the chairpersons command the most resources.

Nowhere is this kind of influence displayed more persistently and predictably than in the financial committees of Congress—the Senate Finance Committee, the House Ways and Means Committee, and the appropriations committees of both chambers. And nowhere do the chairpersons have a greater potential for influence. In the House the Appropriations Committee chairman, according to Richard Fenno, "is expected to call meetings of the Committee, fix its agenda, and preside over its meetings. He is expected to create subcommittees as he thinks necessary and to appoint the majority party members to each subcommittee. . . . He is expected to suggest (subject to formal appointment by the Speaker) the House conferees on appropriation bills. . . . He is expected to exercise surveillance over the flow of Committee work, from hearings to markup, to full Committee. . . . He decides when an appropriation bill will go to the House floor, and he negotiates with the Senate on the timing of conference committee meetings." These powers and expectations are fixed by the traditions of the House, Fenno notes; they could be modified by a committee majority, but drastic change would challenge the "most hallowed norms" of the chamber.

The House Appropriations Committee provides an extreme example of the kind of committee power Woodrow Wilson described and denounced a century ago as "government by the Standing Committees." He compared the "disintegrate ministry" of the chairmen of the committees with the system of central, responsible party government in the British Parliament. It is not accidental that the British Parliament, in contrast with the American, the French, and numerous legislatures for which it otherwise serves as a model, has been steadfast over the decades in not granting great power to its standing committees. House of Commons committees cannot kill measures or delay them indefinitely. They work on the specifics and technicalities rather than the overall substance of legislation. The cabinet and party leadership simply will not allow the committees to threaten their authority.

The influence of substantive committees and of committee chairmen in some legislative systems is therefore considerable. Nevertheless it should not be exaggerated. That kind of influence may be essentially negative, used mainly to block or cripple other leaders' projects, and useful for positive action only to the extent that committee leaders can "bank" and focus their accumulated influence. Committee leaders' power also may seem appreciable mainly because power otherwise is so invisibly dispersed throughout the legislature. But the main limitation on committee leadership is the overall institutional structure and political environment of the parliament. However ingenious, shrewd, and manipulative committee leaders may be, however adept at banking and brokerage, they rarely can free themselves of the institutional incubus to the extent that they can exercise broad and imaginative leadership that can transcend immediate political forces. That is why Wilson insisted that, despite the tremendous power lodged in committees and their chairmen, there were in Congress no "authoritative leaders," no national leaders embodying grand principles, but rather a host of "court-barons" and "lord-proprietors." In appearance a feudalistic system, this dispersionary power made for a transactional system, and in many legislatures still does.

Even with the most potent chairpersons the institutional and environmental weight can be overwhelming. The House Appropriations Committee chairperson, Fenno says, has a great potential for influence, but the degree to which this potential is realized turns on the degree to which the role is played in accordance with congressional norms. The chairperson must observe the seniority rule, avoid unduly aggrandizing his own position, compromise with his peers, consult in advance in making key decisions, and tone down partisanship whenever possible. Thus he has leadership influence only if "he can handle people and play his cards right," as one subcommittee chairman observed of the committee chairman. If this is true of Appropriations, it is far more significant in the case of lesser committees in Congress and in many other legislatures.

The legislative structure does not naturally make for positive, comprehensive, principled—that is, transforming—leadership; it makes for an accommodating, brokering, incremental—that is, transactional leadership. When committees do seem to exercise significant influence, either it is based on obstruction or it represents affirmative power granted to the committee by higher parliamentary or party authority—power that can be revoked at will by that authority.

Central Legislative Leadership

It seems likely that the leadership potential of most legislatures can be achieved neither through the actions of individual legislators nor through the collective efforts of group-involved lawmakers active in factions and ensconced in committee structures. Brokerage and compromise, yes; transforming leadership, no. This view, however, is very much the product of twentieth-century experience and perception. A century ago, people—at least in the parliamentary democracies—looked on the legislature as the seat of collective leadership in the nation. They watched the performances of the brilliant oratorical gladiators; little boys wanted to grow up to be the scintillating pleader, defender, and wit who held the rapt attention of his fellow legislators and the fashionable ladies in the visitors' gallery. And it was not just a performance; the parliamentarians were often able to produce. In the face of the breaking of ties between North and South, senators Clay and Webster were able to achieve comprehensive, if rather temporary, settlements; in the face of industrial exploitation and turmoil Disraeli and Gladstone won passage of major social legislation in parliaments that were not packed with the socially conscious. And they mobilized the necessary support for such measures without much help from disciplined, aggregating parties as we know them.

In most Western democracies today the parliamentary leadership must summon the power of party to insure rank-and-file support of the mass of legislative proposals that the leadership puts forth. The old parliamentary ways—the informality, the amiable debate on the floor and off, the shifting group coalitions, the respect for rank-and-file independence, the concern for tradition—have had to yield to systems of discipline that could maximize party support. India is fairly typical of the more recently modernizing nations. Following independence, there were years of uncertainty as to how leadership and power should be distributed between national party organizations and party members in a Parliament that, like that of the British, was viewed as sovereign. The dominant Congress party finally dealt with the question by arranging for members of its parliamentary party—that is, sitting members of Parliament—to be closely integrated with party organization at both district and national levels, by seeing to it that in particular the leading Congress M.P.s had important posts in the party hierarchy, and by setting up the usual methods for enforcing party discipline, including whips. There were charges, especially in the press, that the government would be taking its orders not from a "sovereign Parliament" but from a dictatorial party clique. The issue was resolved partly through the skill and firmness of Nehru, who on one occasion forced a Hindu "of the old school" out of the organizational party leadership because Nehru feared that he might use his party position unduly to encourage conservative policies in the legislature. Various devices, including a score or more of party standing committees, were instituted to help educate and "socialize" rank-and-file members of the parliamentary party, but the iron hand of party was usually visible in the velvet glove.

Such party discipline could not have been effective in Parliament, of course, had not the parliamentarians shared a common doctrine or ideology. Stanley Kochanek notes that, save for the Harijans (untouchables) and the Tribals, Indian voters, like most electorates, have sought not a leadership reflecting exactly their social composition but a leadership representing their perception of their needs and interests. The parliamentary party leadership is drawn from middle-class and upper-class backgrounds, from the professions, and from landowners. They were welded together doctrinally and emotionally in their struggles against the British; a jail sentence was both a badge of honor and a certificate of movement loyalty. Recruitment patterns are changing as memories of the struggles recede, but the parliamentary party leadership is still able to command a considerable degree of party doctrinal support from new candidates for the Congress party. Other parties in India also show these tendencies toward discipline, with varying degrees of effectiveness.

Legislative leadership in many parliaments elsewhere has a strong foundation in party solidarity and discipline. The parliamentary leadership of the Convention People's party in Ghana—a leadership dominated by lawyers, journalists, and youth spokesmen—drew much of its influence from its earlier solidarity in the fight against colonialism and from party discipline, as well as from the charismatic leadership of Kwame Nkrumah. In Bonn, according to Gerhard Loewenberg, party groups in Parliament developed increasingly complex internal organizations as the number of significant parties fell and as the mobilizing of rank-and-file support in the chamber became more imperative. In Japan, Chitoshi Yanaga could write a decade after the end of World War II that voting in the Diet was strictly controlled by political parties, that the party caucus was the center of "practical party politics" and was used constantly, and that "Members of the Diet are rigidly bound by the decisions of the caucus and few dare to disregard them." Party discipline varied within parliaments, of course, and was often stronger with parties toward the left and right of the political spectrum.

Once again it is in the "Mother of Parliaments" that one finds the most significant practice of parliamentary party discipline, if only because of the wide emulation of the House of Commons in other polities. It was rather ironic that Churchill should have faulted the Labourites in 1945 for alleged domination of the parliamentary party by the party organization when the Conservatives have long kept their parliamentary steeds in close-fitting though sometimes camouflaged harness. To be sure, the Tories would not accept extensive control of the parliamentary party by the "external organization," but within the parliamentary party the leadership has considerable power. The ordinary member of Parliament was virtually impotent, complained a Conservative M.P.; the "member is the obedient servant of the party machine." Acting through the parliamentary party and the party organization, the Conservative leaders hold the ultimate power to oust the erring member from the party, but this is a weapon rarely used, for expulsion from the party would appear as unseemly as expulsion from a club. The leadership prefers to depend on the natural solidarity emerging from class, school, occupation, and club; on its ability to reward obedience with the promise of a safe parliamentary seat, a junior ministership, and honors of various sorts; and on the widespread recognition among Tory back-benchers that leadership is imperative and requires disciplined support.

In the light of the widespread recognition of the failures of French parliamentary leadership before World War II, some expected that postwar reforms would provide more institutional support for leadership strength and stability. Efforts made in this direction failed to overcome the old intellectual, social, and political forces that led to instability and *immobilisme*. In the Fourth Republic, as in the Third, divisions in the lower chamber were so acute that forming a cabinet was, as Roy Macridis noted, like trying to sign a treaty among warring nations. The main source of weakness was still the power of any party in the coalition to drop out and thereby threaten a collapse of the cabinet—and the bargaining power it drew from its ability and willingness to drop out. A second source of weakness was the uncertainty of parliamentary party leaders about their ability to retain the support of their rank-and-file parliamentarians. It was easy for back-benchers to abstain or to vote with another party that might be seated next to them, cheek by jowl, in the assembly. On the whole the parliamentary parties maintained a rough solidarity, but the extent of it varied from time to time and from party to party, depending on the issue, the parliamentary rewards and penalties at the disposition of the leadership, and the extent to which the parliamentary leadership could depend on the party organization in the constituencies to reward good behavior and penalize bad. Since the relation of parliamentary party leadership to local party organization leadership was generally tenuous, the premier and his ministers usually had to bargain for support and could rarely be sure of the outcome.

It may be argued that the effectiveness of *parliamentary party* leadership is not a fair test of the potential of *legislative* leadership because the power of the former emanates from forces outside the legislature—from the executive, the national party organization, the local or district party organization, or combinations thereof. Is there a brand of authentic parliamentary leadership that emanates from the legislature itself—from its procedures and institutions, heritage and authority, internal dynamic or human resources, or combinations thereof? American legislatures offer some insight into this problem.

All these legislatures, national and state, are organized on a rough party basis; virtually all are organized on a two-party (Democratic versus Republican) basis. The formal legislative leadership is chosen by party; it is almost unheard of for United States senators or representatives not to vote for their nominated party leaders in the interparty balloting for the top positions (Speaker of the House and majority leader of the Senate) and other majority and minority leadership positions. On this score party solidarity is near-absolute. Committees are organized on a party basis, with the majority power being given more seats than the minority; members are seated on the floor of House and Senate according to party; party whips are appointed; majority party leaders are granted considerable control of the agenda, subject to due consultation with minority party leaders.

The party beat is more palpable than real. When it comes to *policy,* the substance of legislation, party influence is much smaller than it is on procedural and organizational matters. The lack of party solidarity varies widely from state legislature to state legislature and within the Congress from time to time, issue to issue, and circumstance to circumstance, but the norm is party regularity strongly modified by regional, ideological, interest-group, and personal forces. Party serves as a guide, a touchstone, and sometimes as a rallying point, but it is easy to desert party; indeed, party rebels can flaunt their "party independence" in the constituencies and often gain politically thereby. "The constituency orientation of the legislators," Judson James notes, "is reinforced by the contemporary disruption and decline of party organization."

Party organization in some states and districts is relatively strong; the key question is who controls the local organization? If the congressional party leadership had direct influence over the local party, or even a direct link with it, that leadership might prevail, at least in the nomination process. Such influence rarely exists. The local party is usually either autonomous or captive to a mayor or governor or some other local or state officeholder who has little involvement with the national party. Indeed, at the key points of nomination and election Congress has barricaded itself against the influence of national party organization. The Hatch Act of 1940 was not simply a measure to segregate civil servants from the temptation of party politics; it was in part a calculated means of diminishing the allocation by President and national party organization of federal patronage to local political adversaries of the congressmen. Moreover, Democrats and Republicans in both houses have established congressional campaign committees to mobilize money and other political resources for congressional candidates.

In the light of this weakness of party, and in the light of the limited influence of executives over legislators locally and independently selected, the American legislature would seem to offer a useful testing of the potential of autonomous legislative leadership. And so it does—but the results do not suggest the existence or the potential of great leadership. In the absence of executive leadership from outside or party leadership from outside or inside, legislatures do not seem to generate their own *parliamentary* leadership capable of aggregating support behind legislation, setting the lines of conflict, mobilizing support in the country, and enacting measures into law. One can find exceptions where great parliamentary leaders are able to dominate legislatures through the power of personality and principle, but in the twentieth century the examples are few. If the ultimate test of leadership is *action,* parliamentary leaders without party or executive resources cannot in the long run pass that test; they cannot concert the efforts of several hundred autonomously elected legislators, over whose political fortunes they have little influence, in such a way as to produce comprehensive and systematic legislative results.

Nor in France could one cancel out the influence of party in the national legislature and find the makings of great parliamentary leadership. Under the Third Republic in the 1930s the French unwittingly conducted a kind of experiment not only in a multi-party system but in weak parties (at least outside the left); the leaders that emerged on this terrain were skillful brokers and coalition builders but were hardly the source of innovation, creativity, or transforming social change. "You have debased everything by fixing, intrigue, and slickness," Léon Blum cried out to Pierre Laval in the Chamber of Deputies, and he could have said this to many other parliamentarians; Blum himself was able to build an unusually effective coalition in the Popular Front, but that, too, failed. Most governments rose and fell not on the basis of compelling issues and alternatives but to a large degree on the buying and selling of honors, subsidies, favors, and special electoral arrangements. To the end the chamber remained a "republic of pals" among whom responsibility, authority, and leadership were so splintered and eroded that the regime came to serve as a symbol of instability, immobility, and inaction in the face of growing crisis.

Could a parliament even under the best of circumstances—that is, with strong executive, party, and parliamentary leadership possessing direct connections with party organization nationally and in the constituencies—could such a parliament serve as an institutional foundation for the kind of leadership that directs effectively the processes of peaceful but transforming social change? Ralph Miliband has cast doubt even on this possibility. The absolute commitment of the British Labour party to *parliamentary* constitutional socialism had brought the movement's leaders into the smothering embrace of Westminster. Life there offered temptations toward diluting the socialist program in favor of a spurious national unity, toward sticking with parliamentary leaders— like MacDonald—even when they deserted the cause, and toward subjecting the program to the conservative attrition inevitable in any parliament and fortified there by the diversions and obstructions thrown up by the Lords, the Crown, and the social life of London. To be sure, Miliband's evidence suggests that British socialism was stranded in more than the parliamentary shoals—that the moderation of the Labour party reflected the force of parliamentary tradition in the country, the attenuation of class attitudes among workers, and the moderation and the lack of radical militance among most Labour party and trade-union leaders. Labour members of Parliament at the turn of the century had read in their youth not Marx, Miliband notes, but Shakespeare, Ruskin, and Dickens; still, Labour's parliamentary leadership did not liberate the movement from these tendencies but sharpened them. Even Aneurin Bevan's parliamentary group fell back under his leadership on the politics of maneuver and transaction and served to blunt and blur the impact of the left. The alluring alternative of direct action tempted sections of the Labour movement, including some who went over to the Communist party, to seize it. But for millions of persons on the left or right, and for their leaders, the easiest, the most available alternative to legislative or party action was executive leadership.

Legislative structure, like small or informal group leadership or larger hierarchical bureaucracies, exemplifies transactional leadership. It rests on reciprocal responses of leader and led to perceived wants, needs, expectations, and values. It, too, depends on conflict for movement; to the extent that conflict is either suppressed or permitted to break up into fragments, stalemate or chaos results and the transactional process will have failed. Conflict that leads to resolution of conflict by majority victory or by factional compromise may lead to higher levels of expectation and social change. To the extent that legislatures are not responsive to their constituencies, transaction also fails, as it fails when interest groups submerge leadership. But legislatures cannot on their own exercise transforming leadership.

14

EXECUTIVE LEADERSHIP

No twentieth-century leader has exercised, personified, and symbolized executive leadership in a democracy more dramatically than Charles de Gaulle. Nor has any leader more consciously defined the role for himself. He made it clear at the start of his climactic reign as president that he considered himself to be "France's guide and head of the Republican State" and that he was prepared to "exercise supreme power to the full." Within a few years he was advancing the claim that the French people must understand that "the indivisible authority of the State is confided in its entirety to the President by the people who have elected him, that no other authority exists, neither ministerial nor civil nor military, nor judicial, which is not conferred and maintained by him. . . ." Molded by his early years as an army officer, hardened by his leadership in exile during World War II, tempered by his long observation of party politics, and seasoned by Algeria and other post-World War II crises in France, his notions of executive leadership fortified him as he dealt with rival institutions, constitutional restraints, and sectional politics and as he appealed directly to the French people for support.

De Gaulle had no parliamentary background. Of the sixteen presidents of the Third and Fourth Republics, all had been members of one or the other of the two chambers of parliament; ten had been president of one or the other chamber. Powerful parliamentarians could have confidence in such chief executives. De Gaulle had long despised the brokerage and trading of the parliamentary counting houses. He had equal disdain for the ballet of the parties, with their endless coalition and cleavage, compromise and improvisation, resulting in "hair-trigger" government that could explode at the slightest pressure. Squabbling parties and parliamentarians could not provide the solidarity, the purpose, and the grandeur that de Gaulle sought for France.

"It goes without saying," he proclaimed shortly after World War II, "that executive power should not emanate from Parliament—a Parliament which should be bi-cameral and should exercise legislative power—or the result will be a confusion of powers which will reduce the Government to a mere conglomeration of delegations. . . . The unity, cohesion and internal discipline of the French Government must be held sacred, if national leadership is not to degenerate rapidly into incompetence and impotence."

De Gaulle drew his political power not from traditional political institutions but from his own resources of self-confidence and indomitability and from direct, personal contact with the French people. He depended first on sheer exploitation of his personality. This exploitation—later called the "style" of the general—"involved certain conceptions of the dignity of the office," according to Dorothy Pickles, "a belief in Presidential pomp and ceremony, a visible occupancy of the chair of State, whether in his capacity as President of the Council of Ministers, as President of the Community, as the representative of his country on visits abroad, or as its chief spokesman in foreign affairs, either at home or abroad." De Gaulle's use of the press conference epitomized his personal approach. In a vast hall used for galas, before six hundred journalists and two or three hundred cabinet members, officials, diplomats, and guests, and in the blaze of television lights, the general would enter through red curtains held apart by ushers in white tie and tails. Answering mainly anticipated questions, de Gaulle used the conferences less for the edification of the press than to inform and reassure his public.

His personal relationship with the people was epitomized in the shift to election of the president by direct popular vote. De Gaulle sponsored the change from the old system of indirect election in which the officials of small towns had an undue advantage. Election by direct vote, he said, would provide presidents with the "explicit confidence of the Nation." Direct election also provided the president with political legitimacy and credibility in dominating Parliament and the parties.

At a minimum de Gaulle's political and symbolic powers enabled him to be a powerful arbitrator in keeping the components of government in their place and insuring the supremacy of the president. At most those powers made him an elected near-absolute monarch at least in the exercise of executive leadership. At first de Gaulle favored leaving routine budgetary and administrative powers with the cabinet ministers and the permanent bureaucracy, but this proved impracticable as people and Parliament turned to the general for action in times of crisis and distress. De Gaulle had been determined to concentrate on strategic matters and to avoid being diverted to "quarter-master business," Philip Williams and Martin Harrison note, but this conception "was tenable only in the situation de Gaulle had known in his previous spell in office, during and just after the war, when victory and economic reconstruction were objectives common to all political groups, however bitterly they might quarrel over their separate ideologies and interests.'' Crises such as Algeria demanded action, but action cost money and posed executive problems of spending and taxation. De Gaulle had wanted to be chief executive; he also had to be, to a degree, chief administrator.

The executive leadership of Charles de Gaulle culminated in his exercise of emergency powers. The nation tended to unite behind him; opposition shrank in the constitutional sectors and retreated to the streets and the ramparts outside. His emergency powers could be employed in phony as well as true crisis. Despite much grumbling, the once powerful French legislature capitulated in the face of executive action and crisis management. In his later years as president, with the lessening of crisis, he depended less on emergency power, but the precedents had been established.

Assumption of personal authority, marked self-confidence and political skill, the diminution of legislative and party opposition, personal and dramatic links with the people, the enhancement of executive function and responsibility, the exploitation of emergency powers—these are qualities of executive leadership, and most of these qualities de Gaulle displayed. In looking back a generation later, however, we can ask what fundamental alterations he wrought during his many years in power in the period of sweeping change within and among nations following World War II. That he produced or presided over significant advances during the period cannot be gainsaid. His fatherhood of the Fifth Republic, his call to the French people to reassert their national pride and honor, his skillful liquidation of the old colonial structure in Algeria and elsewhere were memorable deeds. But the great achievements of his final years in office were essentially negative achievements, as David Schoenbrun has contended. No fundamental change, no transformation, occurred in the lives of millions of ordinary Frenchmen, despite the summonses to renewal and greatness. De Gaulle created a unifying atmosphere of drama in a nation struggling to redeem itself from the ambivalence and shame of the war. It was a theatrical episode but not a period of substance in achievement of social change.

The de Gaulle experience raises questions about the problems and the potential of executive leadership—above all, its capacity to relate to and act on the real needs, aspirations, and values of potential followers.

The Political Executive: Power and Purpose

The distinguishing characteristics of executive leaders, in contrast with party or parliamentary leaders, are their lack of reliable political and institutional support, their dependence on bureaucratic resources such as staff and budget, and most of all their use of *themselves*—their own talent and character, prestige and popularity, in the clash of political interests and values. Party leaders in a power contest can mobilize political apparatuses that, ideally, reach throughout the country and activate rank-and-file party sentiment in their support. Parliamentary leaders may fall back on legislators who themselves represent constituencies that can be mobilized behind the leadership. Executive leaders in a power struggle may appeal to public opinion but lack the machinery to activate it, shape it, channel it, and bring it to bear on the decision-making process. Hence they, in contrast with the others, must depend more on personal manipulation and executive management than on institutional support.

If executive leaders compete in a more confined arena, however, the conflict is no less intense and consequential. Not only do they confront the *extraorganizational* influences of ramifying ideologies, personality differences, and clashing interest-group affiliations that engage and divide the officials under them; not only must they preside over administrators who belong to various parties, religious denominations, professional organizations, trade unions; they must also cope with the conflicts that are generated *within* any large organization. Rooted in technological forces and proliferating through complex organizations, these conflicts are functions of such phenomena as specialization, the status system and its inequalities, and a lack of shared values. Staff persons contend with line persons both because of varied perspectives and duties and because of differences in age, education, status, career hopes, ambition ladders. Experts with diverse educational backgrounds and present functions struggle to protect and expand their jurisdictions. The relations within executive organizations reflect tensions between occupational and family roles. Tension may also rise from the clash between orientations toward personal goals and orientations toward organizational goals. Internal interest groups form naturally in large-scale organizations, Philip Selznick notes, since the total enterprise is a kind of polity embracing a number of suborganizations. Finally, there is the phenomenon of executives intentionally cultivating conflict among their staffs for purposes of their own—usually to maintain better control over the staff. No organizations, of course, are free of power problems and conflicts. The question is how power, in a context of latent and overt conflict, is mobilized, organized, and managed by political executives—and to what ends.

Different kinds of power have been identified in organizations: legitimate power, reward power, punishment power, referent power, and expert power. Referent power is influence stemming from one's affective regard for, or identification with, another person. Legitimate power, and to some degree expert power, are closely linked to the concept of authority in organizations. Leaders are said to possess bureaucratic authority when they are accorded the formal right to demand compliance with their wishes from another person—not necessarily a subordinate—who has the duty to obey. Authority also has a psychological dimension: Usually people simply accept authority because of a predisposition to do so rather than a conscious decision to defer to formal legitimacy. Thus many executive leaders carry the clout of authority as part of the trappings and equipment, the rewards and responsibilities, of the office; it comes with the job.

These notions are useful but inadequate for understanding the bases of the power of executive leadership in large, complex organizations. Executive leaders have effective power (rather than merely formal authority) to the degree that they can activate the need and motivational bases of other leaders and subordinates in the organization. This power in essence is the traditional power to reward and penalize—but what do the respondents or power recipients consider to be rewards and penalties? In a large organization these motivations are likely to be as varied as human needs can be—not only for security, higher income, and better working conditions but for affection, recognition, deference, esteem, and for both autonomy toward and dependence on the executive leader, for both conformity and individuality—traits that can exist in the same person. Other things being equal, the stronger the motivational base the leader taps, the greater control over that person the leader can exercise.

The process is by no means purely mechanical or quantitative. Executive leaders must estimate the motivation of members of their inner circle of subordinates and that of rival leaders, and they must do so with some accuracy. They must sense where attitudes within their organization may be deeply anchored in basic predispositions, and hence virtually invulnerable to leadership authority or persuasion, and where beliefs may be superficial. A study of outpatient departments in a large city hospital, for example, disclosed that the effectiveness of supervisors' influence over nurses was diminished simply by incorrect perceptions on the part of the supervisors of what rewards the nurses wished. Formal communication and information channels may be clogged or snarled by misinformation and bias; executives may resort to establishing their own intelligence apparatus for their own unique purposes. And in calculating other persons' needs, executives must calculate their own—including the distorted perceptions their own needs bring to their calculation of others' needs.

The main determinant of the extent and exercise of executive leaders' power within organizations is the extent of their institutional and personal resources. Whether they have essential control of hiring, work assignments, job security, promotion, pay increases, suspending, firing, and the like or must share such powers with party organizations, legislatures, courts, unions, professional associations, and informal leaders closely affects executive control over penalties and rewards. At the higher levels of organization—at the level of top staff and management positions—crude economic rewards and penalties are typically less efficacious and leadership depends more on executives' personal resources such as their capacity to grant or withdraw respect, recognition, and affection. People need appreciation, recognition and a feeling of accomplishment, and the confidence that people who are important to them believe in them. But meeting such psychological needs, as opposed to satisfying merely material ones such as more pay, calls for the sophisticated use of human skills.

Leaders' effectiveness in handling power turns on their skills in activating their resources as well as the relevant value of those resources. They must be able to communicate with a variety of people of widely different background, temperament, interest, and attitude. The key elements in this process may be neither the message nor the medium but the source and the target. Much of the leaders' influence will turn on their own qualities of character, expertise, prestige, intelligence, charm, and creditability, but these will have little impact unless they engage relevant needs and motivations in the person being influenced. Hence the strong emphasis, in modern organizations, less on formal authority or automatic compliance than on techniques of persuasion drawn not from manuals on how to influence people but from authentic sources of individual character and genuine human need.

Finally, executive leaders consider costs involved in the exercise of effective leadership. Overcoming resistance to plans, adjusting plans to prevailing values by identifying them with value symbols, securing compliance through a variety of techniques—all these can be costly to executives' personal and institutional resources. The strategy is to use these resources without using them up, but the point at which the bank account of influence may be overdrawn is not easy to estimate. Another cost is time. Almost any kind of leadership influence may be possible if the effort can be prepared in advance and continued long enough. But the expense of doing so—the slow process of gaining followers' confidence, the careful attention to their real as well as their felt needs, the hard thought and planning required in sorting out ends and means—may simply be too high, and executives are tempted to fall back on short-run, expedient decisions that can bring dependable if fleeting results.

Few executive leaders have better exemplified the strengths and weaknesses of personal management than Franklin Roosevelt. He had a discerning—some said intuitive—grasp of the needs and motivations of the cabinet members and agency chiefs he dealt with. One of his many techniques—difficult for a man who loved to talk and dominate the scene—was simply to listen sympathetically to those who poured out their woes and frustrations (often caused in large part by the President himself), as in the case of Joseph Kennedy. He knew how to persuade one person by argument, another by charm, another by a display of self-confidence, another by flattery, another by an encyclopedic knowledge. While Roosevelt doubtless paid a price for his supple management, since it encouraged him to follow short-run expedient goals rather than long-run political strategy, he demonstrated the extent to which executive leaders can exploit their own personal as well as institutional resources.

To dwell on executives' capacity for management and manipulation, however, is to risk exaggerating their causal role in the overall movement of events and to minimize that of subordinate executives and followers. For if the assumption of the key central role of need has validity, we cannot be content with assessing only the personal motives of leaders and followers, important though these motivations be. We must also consider the more general goals and values that influence members of organizations—especially public organizations and especially at the middle-to-higher administrative and political levels.

It was long assumed that the fundamental, if not the sole, meaning and justification of organization was purpose, mission, task, or goal. The organization was in essence a means to an end, and the end was a purpose anchored in, and measured by, values defined as preferred end-states that served as both calls to action and guides to behavior. Talcott Parsons, drawing from Max Weber and others, conceived goal as defining organization. From this concept certain conclusions followed. To reach general goals a number of subgoals or instrumental goals had to be established, and these had to be institutionalized in a structure of programs, policies, offices, administrators, and specialized tasks.

This classical view has yielded in recent times to the remonstrances of "organization theorists." Goal assumes some kind of *intent,* and the nature of intent—its subjective quality, its conscious or unconscious motivation, and its somewhat problematic relation to goal and goal realization—makes for obscurity. "In reality," William Gore writes, "goals are always surrounded by a thick, sticky coating of ambiguity. They are presented to us in a number of forms: regulations, interests, aversions, concerns, purposes, and commitments. . . ." While the concept of goal is indispensable to the theory and practice of leadership, if only to enable us to measure leadership effectiveness, the concept must be broken down into meaningful categories. And goals may be pursued with varying degrees of intensity and commitment. Goals may represent end-values such as peace, individualism, or equality, or they may be instrumental to such goals. Goals may be displaced onto one another; they may be substituted for one another. Traditional values, for example, may be displaced by a marketing ethic of self-promotion, status borrowing, and false conviviality, as Robert V. Presthus has noted. The extreme displacement is the outright substitution of means for ends as instrumental goals of an organization as loyalty or seniority come to be cherished in themselves. (We have noted this problem in our discussion of bureaucracies.)

Most organizations lack central, unifying goals, critics of the abstraction say—and I share their objections. Instead, numberless members of the organization hold numberless combinations of goals. There is no single "organization goal" just as there is no single "group mind." The usual goal clusters, Robert Tannenbaum, Irving R. Weschler, and Fred Massarik note, "contain elements that have differential weight in the attainment of still 'higher' goals in a hierarchy. An industrial organization, for example, may have many goals: high employee morale, labor peace, high productivity, contribution to community welfare, etc." The larger and more complex the organization, the greater the number of goals pursued. A complicating factor is the element of time. A new organization established to carry out a definite mission may be largely defined in terms of that central goal; as time passes and the original goal is achieved, modified, or forgotten, new instrumental goals may succeed the original.

The array of goals must have some form and coherence or the organization will fall to pieces. How assess the influence of goals on the political impact, long-run influence, and leadership of the organization? First, by discriminating between individual and collective goals: Darwin Cartwright and Alvin Zander distinguish among the goals of a person in a group, the goal of an individual for a group, and the goal of a group. Once again we face the problem of dualism: many organization members may have goals that are unrelated to the organization (though affecting it) or that *are* relevant yet may frustrate collective goals. Second, by conceiving goals as arrayed in a hierarchy consisting at the base of the more personalized, discrete individual goals in all their immense plurality and complexity and at the top of the more generalized, collective, value-laden goals expressed and legitimated by authoritative organization spokesmen. It is exceedingly difficult for the observer to rate and rank this medley of goals because of their subjectivity and ambiguity, but failure to rate—or at the very least to separate out the trivial and ephemeral from the predominant and persisting and, in Lawrence Mohr's terms, the transitive (externally oriented) from the reflexive (internally oriented) organization goals—would be to thwart any real understanding of the relation of individual and organizational goals. Rough techniques have indeed been developed to identify goals and gain information about their relative importance.

Above all, the pursuit of goals has a dynamic quality, and goals pursued can best be evaluated not as stable elements in organizational structures but as elements that can be activated within and outside the organization. Depending on their own skills in manipulating power resources (including communication techniques) relevant to the needs and motivations of officials and employees of their agencies, executive leaders can instill their own purposes into the agency and suppress or modify competing or conflicting purposes; or they will need to modify their own purposes in the face of contrary goals sought by agency personnel; or (more typically) they will trade off. In fact the executive leader deals with executive subleaders with needs of their own and power resources and skills of their own. All sets of leaders and subleaders will typically draw on outside sources of support such as parties and legislatures, but here we stress executive relationships within the executive apparatus.

Consider the classic case of the young zealot, a rising leader of a new reform or left-wing cabinet, who is appointed head of a ministry of education. He comes into the ministry, let us assume, pledged to the egalitarian values, purposes, and goals his party embraced in seeking votes. He has not only purposes but a hierarchy of purposes: he is committed (in order of declining importance) to extension of educational equality and opportunity to poor or disadvantaged children, to better education for all schoolchildren, and to better conditions for teachers. Let us put aside for the moment the thorny problem that the execution of these purposes, even when the generalities are agreed on, will produce endless conflicts over suitable means. Let us also put aside the inevitable foot-dragging and genteel sabotage on the part of those who have no priority of purpose aside from personal advancement or sticking to their niches in the existing order. A clash over goals will exist when the new executive leader confronts (in various operating units of the department) subleaders who hold purposes similar but ordered differently (perhaps in reverse sequence). Probably the order of priorities will vary among departmental units as permanent bureaucratic leaders adhere to their long-run commitment to the second purpose and unit leaders oriented toward unions and professional organizations of teachers put teachers' pay and working conditions first.

Conflicts over priorities are seated in, and probably exacerbated by, a pluralism of personal needs and motivations that may seem irrelevant to the public goals of the department but in fact enlarge the tangle of commitments, loyalties, and purposes. Coming from the world of party and parliamentary politics, the new minister may be tempted to exert his purpose by "rational" argument and persuasion. But the executive subleaders have long debated these same purposes; they have built their lives on them and their livings off them, and they are not easily converted. Hence the minister may need to fall back on bargaining, exchange, and trade-offs.

Contrast this situation—an executive leader entering into an already structured administrative organization—with the opportunity facing leaders who can create their own institutions. Such an opportunity, so familiar in private business and industry when the Krupps and the Fords established the institutions that carried their own names and purposes, is less common in public institutions. New government bureaucracies have usually been created in military crises, where existing peacetime organizations could not be converted to war tasks; during revolutions, when new regimes suspected the loyalties and purposes of those manning existing bureaucracies; and in reform governments that sought to achieve priority goals through newly organized agencies, as in the case of the New Deal administration of Franklin Roosevelt. With a new institution executive leaders can define their purposes within the mandate given them, install their own personal staff, select key executive personnel, delegate authority as they choose, set up channels of communication and command appropriate to their purposes, and organize the basic structure of subunits. Under such circumstances the new agency might indeed become, in Selznick's words, the "institutional embodiment of purpose"—*their* purpose.

Whether "statesman-leaders" can accomplish all this, even when the decks have been cleared for them, is another matter. They may accomplish and exhaust their original purpose, after which the organization may turn to new goals under their leadership, or they may be deflected to new purposes by a new government, or they may dissolve into a pursuit of many goals under many leaders. An original set of priority purposes and structure of ends and means may become deranged or turned upside down. Commitment and direction may give way to specialization and routine. Whether executive leaders can force their organization to adhere to original goal priorities or can substitute new ones of equal legitimacy and moral and political validity will depend largely on their capacity to marshal *external political resources*. Lacking these, they may be forced back on their own reserves, their skill at converting subordinates' needs into administrative energy, and ultimately on their own character—their drive, vision, dedication, tenacity, commitment—to the degree that they possess these qualities.

The Executive Leader as Decision Maker

When he was deputy quartermaster general at Simla, Sir Ian Hamilton would toil far into the night composing lengthy minutes supporting his decisions of the day. His chief, the quartermaster general, also toiled far into the night writing minutes supporting or disapproving these decisions. When his chief sickened and left for home, Hamilton took over his work while retaining his own former responsibility, for a stingy government would not provide him with a deputy. Hamilton dreaded the prospect of holding both impossible jobs at the same time, but to his surprise and delight the job became much easier. "I studied the case as formerly,'' he wrote, ''but there my work ended; I had not to persuade my own subordinates. . . . I just gave an order—quite a simple matter unless a man's afraid: 'Yes,' I said, or 'No!' ''

To concentrate authority in one office, to insulate decision-making against outside appeal, to assume single responsibility, to reduce alternatives to yes or no—these are hallowed and orthodox goals of the executive decision maker. Concepts of decision-making have been closely influenced by the military, which created its own administrative apparatus, personnel system, headquarters, and executive leadership apart from the civilian bureaucracy. Classical thinking about executive decision-making has viewed the process as an essentially orderly and rational one. A problem is defined and isolated; information is gathered; alternatives are set forth; an end is established; means are created to achieve that end; a choice is made. The ''constant refinement of purpose,'' according to Chester Barnard, ''is the effect of repeated decisions, in finer and finer detail, until eventually detailed purpose is contemporaneous accomplishment.'' The essence of the executive's function is the specialization of the process of making organizational decisions.

Such a pat and logical theory could hardly escape critical revision in the light of modern experience. Administration does not take place in a vacuum, revisionists contended, but in the context of the political and psychological forces, rational and irrational, operating through it. The stately procession of ends and means usually became displaced and deranged in practice. The human materials of executive decision-making were not standardized and replicable but unpredictable combinations of enthusiasts, foot-draggers, expediters, empire builders, adjusters, and others who brought to bear their own motivations, attitudes, and goals. People responded to unseen ideologies and mythologies, to distant bugle calls and drumbeats. Executive decision-making was filled with unanticipated and dysfunctional activities. The new theory concentrated on what decision makers actually did rather than what they ought to do. But was there any pattern in all this activity?

Executive decision-making is not a series of single, linear acts like baking a pie. It is a process, a sequence of behavior, that stretches back into a murky past and forward into a murkier future. It is associated with other basic social processes: the division of labor, group relations, reward and penalty systems and other social control mechanisms, and—as we have seen—the holding of single or plural needs, motivations, goals, and values. Organization theorists see the process as a turbulent stream rather than as an assembly-line operation—as ''a twisted, unshapely, halting flow of interactions between people,'' in Gore's words, ''interactions that shift constantly from a rational to a heuristic mode and back again.''

In this turgid complexity the key ordering factor is executive decision makers' calculations, however subconscious, impressionistic, or faulty, on how to use and adapt chains of cause and effect relevant to their goals. Executives are typically surrounded by opportunities and constraints. Their position and their skill and the needs of the organization and of client groups and constituencies provide them with the basic resources for exercising influence over the allocation of resources. Typically they will be operating amid streams of causal factors that close off multitudinous possibilities while opening up others. There is a vital dimension of time in this process. Executive leaders cannot undo history; they inherit situations in which predecessor leaders, rival leaders, and cooperating leaders have created flow lines of decision that circumscribe and envelop their own decision-making. And, like all politicians and public performers, they must anticipate how various groups and publics will react to different decisions and modify their own actions accordingly. Information, communication, analysis, and forecasting may all be spotty and deficient. As a result executives operate by feel and by feedback. They grope their way into the future, moving one step at a time, ready always to fall back as they encounter obstacles. Or they may "work backward," studying used paths and relating them to desired ends. Feedback may be more reliable than prediction, but it may come haltingly and in ambiguous form.

All this is endemic in executive decision-making in pluralistic societies in which the stream of cause and effect is shifting and multi-channeled. But we must not overgeneralize. Types of executive decision-making vary from the most independent and autonomous (like Sir Ian Hamilton's) on the one hand to the most restricted and dependent on the other. Of the former the best examples are usually found in the military—as in a situation in which a commander is considering attacking a strongpoint or launching an invasion. Granted that he is restricted by the strategic situation (embracing a host of earlier decisions), by logistics, by the morale, equipment, training, and other characteristics of his troops, and by unforeseen contingencies of weather and enemy action. Still, within his domain he has extensive power over causal factors. He can distribute military resources, shuffle and reorganize lower units, promote and displace commanders, set and reset tactical plans, schedule sequences. Higher and lower commanders, poor communication and information, crossed purposes, and the like may thwart him, but with luck his only true adversary may be the enemy.

Another example of extensive decision-making autonomy is the post-revolutionary situation. Revolutions are designed to sweep away "archaic" institutions and procedures that would hinder the realization of revolutionary goals. Old ministries and bureaus give way to revolutionary cadres and commissariats. Bureaucrats of the old regime are dismissed and regulations changed as the sons and daughters of the revolution take over the apparatus of state. Difficulties abound. Specialists are still needed in the intricate policy-making of diplomacy, finance, and war, and specialists may not be automatons capable of shedding one set of doctrines and loyalties and taking on another. Old bureaucrats with precise duties and goals may be replaced by new zealots with cloudy ones. The locomotive of history cannot be switched onto a new track all that easily. But revolutionary strategy may provide at least the possibility of a new roadbed.

Reform governments too may seek to install executive leaders with ample decision-making discretion. A common technique in this century is nationalization, through which the state assumes ownership and "control" of an industry. But many a socialist has found that the victory was pyrrhic; running up the Union Jack over a nationalized coal pit did not bring a ready transformation of habit and procedure. Decision makers struggled with many of the same old ineluctable forces of union resistance, archaic techniques, a technology too outmoded to improve efficiency but too valuable to be scrapped, and settled customs and routines. Compromise with the past and concessions to external and internal forces of resistance are almost inevitable.

In the United States the Tennessee Valley Authority was created by the Roosevelt administration in order to establish comprehensive controls over a disorderly river and its impoverished river basin; another objective was to decentralize administration and delegate authority from Washington to the region. The TVA was a striking success in achieving its central objectives, but a price was paid. Lacking close-in support from the White House, it was compelled to cultivate support and discourage resistance in the field. In particular TVA cooperated with the extension service of the land-grant colleges in the seven valley states; the old extension service became in effect an operating arm of the new agency. The TVA had to compromise with the rural "courthouse politics" long influential in local agricultural activities, with established and somewhat conservative farm organizations like the American Farm Bureau Federation, and with the more prosperous and established farmers at the expense of farm tenants. "In addition," according to Selznick, "the TVA's commitment to the Extension Service involved it in the national struggle for control of the U.S. agricultural programs, drawing it into the Farm Bureau camp."

If executive leaders are significantly restricted even in optimum situations, decision makers typically seem far more creatures of restraint than creators of opportunity. Their role is essentially one of choosing among set options—often rather narrow and short-run options—in a causal flow already established for them by earlier decision makers. Ends have previously been established in such multiplicity that decision is restricted to the more limited choices of specific means. In this situation narrow critera of utility are likely to prevail. Probability curves, Julian Feldman and Herschel Kanter suggest, are estimated from one set of choices and used to analyze a second set of decisions. In Charles Lindblom's terms, leadership is incremental movement, accommodation, and adjustment. Progress, such as it is, is achieved more by coping than by planning, deciding, and solving.

If an ultimate test of leadership is transforming change, executive decision-making is only one step, however crucial, in a long chain of causation. Chester Barnard, who was both a pioneering theorist of organization and a practitioner as head of the New Jersey Bell Telephone Company, observed that if a telephone company president ordered two telephone poles removed from one side of a street to the other, the order would involve perhaps ten thousand decisions of one hundred men located at fifteen points, "requiring successive analyses of several environments, including social, moral, legal, economic, and physical facts of the environment, and requiring 9000 redefinitions and refinements of purpose, and 1000 changes of purpose. . . ." Tracing this stream of decisions to the completion of the pole relocation, however, would take us only part way along the stream of causal episodes. Depending on the purpose of the shift in poles—better service, aesthetic improvement, public relations, whatever—one would need to inquire how much actual change had occurred in the quality of service or in the appearance of the street.

For the executive leader, a major decision relevant to a definite goal activates a structure of decision-making. The major decision is typically made in a context of knowledge of past decisions and their consequences and anticipation of future decisions and their consequences. The decision can be implemented through an organization, carried through a "decision tree" of more and more specific decisions. The basic decision in pursuit of a general goal is broad in scope and potential impact. It sets in force a number of more specific alternatives and precludes a great many others. One may be chosen, which in turn blocks off certain alternatives and activates still others. The decision becomes more and more specific (though probably affecting more and more persons) until the ultimate decisions are actions that can be properly considered the actual ingredients of real change.

Our zealous young minister of education, for example, pursuing his ultimate goal of equality, decides that educationally disadvantaged children must receive more and better education. This decision excludes a number of other choices, such as diversion of resources toward better education for affluent middle-class children. It sets up a new array of alternatives: more educational attention to children in rural areas or in big cities, to children in certain racial or ethnic groups, or perhaps to children in all these groups. A decision for the last alternative would open up a number of options concerning definitions of eligibility based on financial need, intelligence test scores, medical (physical and/or psychiatric) diagnoses. Such decisions might be made at the national level by the central government. As the decisions become more specific and of more limited scope, discretion and choice may be delegated to provincial or municipal governments, where the "funnel of specificity" would continue to operate, subject to regional or local conditions. The process finally comes down to the most concrete decisions about a schoolchild's daily life—remedial reading, special tuition, summer camps, medical care, recreation, exposure to television, psychiatric counseling, time with and away from parents, and so on. Ultimately the process ends with at least two other factors: the changes registered not simply *around* the schoolchild but *in* him and *by* him on his own volition, so that he becomes part of the causal process; and the element of *time,* for months and years may have to pass before one can conclude whether or not the original decision of the minister of education produces actual change congruent with his goal—to conclude, in effect, whether he actually did make a *decision.*

All this does not mean that the executive leader must intervene at every level to supervise and guarantee the effectiveness of subdecision-making relevant to goals. Executive leaders command subleaders who, if conscious of goal hierarchies and committed to them, can monitor the chain of ends-means relations. Moreover, they have the benefit of a vast amount of control and energy-saving because of the "decision packages" available. Thus if a decision is made for more visual education, the securing of technology and information embodies decision-making programmed earlier into the technology and services. There may be a danger here to original purpose, if the means are not properly related or adaptable to that purpose. The visual education "package" might turn out to be adapted to the needs of middle-class children rather than youngsters from working-class or ethnic backgrounds. But with a fair degree of knowledge and control, a strategy for change, using not only technology but administrative knowledge, financial resources, community clientele groups, teacher training, and other factors, can be made to serve the leader's purpose.

Favorable circumstances for implementation of strategy may not be present. Executive leaders' purposes may not be clear; or they may have a host of purposes without priority; or they may have no purposes save self-advancement or enhancement. Subordinate executives may misunderstand those purposes; or they may understand them and disagree; or, not caring, they may let things drift. As decision-making becomes more specific along the decision tree or merges into administrative structures outside the organization, purpose becomes more attenuated, more easily deflected into channels dominated by parochial institutions and purposes and by group and individual pressures. Hence, as Barnard has observed, "repeated decisions involving constant determination of new strategic factors are necessary to the accomplishment of broad purposes or any purpose not of immediate attainment."

The task of executive leaders is hard enough when they pursue long-accepted goals, such as national defense or social welfare for the elderly, through organizations that are subject to the usual quota of misunderstanding, inefficiency, miscommunication, and excess group and individual self-interest. They may become more the victim of their organization than the directors of it for public ends. But their task is more difficult if they wish to be innovative and creative. In the past, as Victor Thompson has written, innovation in society largely took place through the birth of new or innovative organizations and the death of old or tradition-bound ones, but given the capital requirements of today's technology, this method seems wasteful—or at least expensive. The question is whether *existing* organizations can learn to innovate. It is much easier for executive leaders searching for alternatives to make small variations from existing situations, for then the search for alternatives can be more easily measured and limited. Hope for innovation depends on the capacity of executive leaders to provide a role for generalists as well as specialists in the organization; to tolerate the kind of apparently aimless, slow, even erratic behavior that sometimes produces intellectual breakthroughs; to legitimize the kind of conflict that often provokes innovation; and to cultivate new ideas even when they threaten the power and status of subordinate leaders or the leaders themselves. Ultimately, Thompson contends, creativity may call for "self-actualization through work"—a convergence, perhaps, between Maslow's higher needs and the work ethic.

Is the executive leader helpless in the face of all the constraints and difficulties? Barnard suggests the "theory of the strategic factor," the factor "whose control, in the right form, at the right place and time, will establish a new system or set of conditions which meets the purpose." Effective decision is always the control of the changeable strategic factors in relation to the restatement and effectuation of purpose. Hence the process of decision is one of successive approximations—of continuous refinement of purpose and closer determination of fact over time. On the basis of his study of French bureaucracy Michel Crozier concludes that organizational progress can be achieved—or at least organizational stalemate broken—only through major crises of regime. Gore sees organizational survival, if not effectiveness, as turning on essentially ideological or even psychological qualities. In all these cases one wonders if the test is control of the organization itself rather than control of the long chain of human behavior to which the organization is supposed to be merely instrumental.

It may be that organization theorists are groping for a power that cannot exist—the power of executive decision makers under given conditions to mobilize in themselves and their organizations enough control of causal factors both to imbue their organizations with purpose and to lead them in bringing about actual causal social change. The only alternative may be a change in the conditions. One way to alter conditions is Selznick's—achieving the "institutional embodiment of purpose" through strategic and tactical planning—but that alternative calls for such a massive effort at organizational renovation as to leave, one fears, little energy for the creation of actual social change; or it calls for a revolution that might clear out the administrative scenery but have ominous and uncontrollable side effects. Another way to alter conditions is to enable the executive leader to mobilize political resources in groups, parties, public opinion, and legislatures—that is, to enable the executive leader to become a *transforming* leader in the fullest sense of the term.

The American President as Executive Leader

The American presidency was not designed to be the center of leadership in the new republic. If any branch of government was to serve as a positive and innovative force in a system of carefully intermingled powers, it was the legislative. Certainly the President was not expected to be either a legislative leader or a party leader. He was to be the chief *executive*—"The executive power shall be vested in a President of the United States of America," the Constitution decreed—but he was not to be the executive *leader*. It was expected, partly because it was assumed that General George Washington would be the first President, that presidents would be judicious chief executives and high-minded chief magistrates somewhat removed from the turbulence of factional strife. The alchemy of time transformed the role of the President into what has more recently been called the imperial and even the omnipotent presidency.

The most vain of the framers' hopes was that the President would be "above" political conflict. By dexterously mixing, dividing, and merging powers among separated institutions, by making these institutions directly or indirectly responsible to different combinations of interests and constituencies, they built conflict into the very structure of American government, including the presidency. Washington had hardly taken office when cleavages in interests and ideologies began to develop within his administration. As the presidency became more directly responsive to the people through constitutional and political changes, the office came to confront and embody the most fundamental conflicts in American life. For decades the great conciliators, like Daniel Webster and Henry Clay, were legislative leaders, while it was the President—notably Jefferson, Jackson, and Lincoln—who came to embody and to articulate the passionate political causes of the first century of the new nation. As the office became more "democratized," the winner of the presidential sweepstakes tended to be increasingly the product of party strife and political rough-and-tumble.

Presidents were the product of conflict, not the advocates of it. Once installed in the White House they typically called for an adjournment of partisan hostility, a new solidarity of the American people, and a cessation of party politics at the water's edge (if not nearer to Washington). It has not been recorded that these pieties had any significant effect on political behavior. Every convening of Congress brought scores of dedicated party foes into the nation's capital, along with the sunshine warriors of the President's own party. Elections were rigidly scheduled for every two and four years, and not even the fiercest of civil wars or the gravest of world wars brought a suspension of the quadrennial presidential bloodletting. As the national government took on more and more responsibility for domestic prosperity, social justice, and national security, more and more of the most intense and divisive issues forced their way into the White House (or the White House reached out to seize them). A presidential aide could say, 175 years after the planning of the nonpartisan, magisterial presidency, that if he were to name the one quality that characterized most issues reaching the President, "I would say it was conflict—conflict between departments, between the views of various advisers, between the Administration and Congress, between the United States and another nation, or between groups within the country: labor versus management, or race versus race, or state versus nation." But no matter how widespread and divisive the conflict came to be—even in the case of the war in Vietnam—sonorous utterances about bipartisan unity continued.

Conflict centered in the White House because there the power stakes were highest. Presidential power, like all political power, is a function of the leader's will to arouse and tap the needs and wants of followers and his capacity to mobilize resources to meet those needs and wants, thereby contriving to retain followers' support and to continue in power. Almost from the start American presidents showed an extraordinary capacity to divine popular sentiment and to dramatize the White House as the "people's office." After popular heroes—party builders like Jefferson, successful generals like Jackson, homespun, rustic politicians like Lincoln—entered or emerged from the White House, they became the stuff of popular legend and were ushered into the nation's pantheon.

As the presidency became more visible and "popular," disaffected voters turned to it to satisfy their needs and aspirations and a powerful symbiotic relationship developed between the people and their President. The rise of the popular press, radio, and television simply broadened and intensified this symbiosis.

It is in the expansion of the President's resources relevant to popular need, however, that the presidency has undergone almost revolutionary changes. The framers endowed the office with enough authority to administer the executive branch and to protect the executive against depredations by what was considered to be the predominant branch in a republic, the legislative. Thus the presidential power to veto acts of Congress was viewed as essentially a negative power. For decades it was used sparingly and self-protectively. But in this century the veto has become one of the most formidable positive powers of the President. With it presidents can not only block congressional enactments (unless overriden by a two-thirds vote in both houses), they can use their right to veto as a bargaining device to gain other legislation or to induce Congress to revise measures under threat of veto. The President has supplemented the formal veto power with an expanded power to impound large sums of money appropriated by Congress and to refuse to implement legislation enacted by Congress, as in the case of President Nixon, who simply made Title VI of the Civil Rights Act of 1964 "inoperative."

The President's war-making power was originally to be that of a commander-in-chief exercising control over the organization and deployment of land and sea forces and determining their temporary and localized engagement against border intrusions or against pirates preying on American shipping on the high seas. This authority has become transformed into the power of the President to conduct vast and interminable wars in remote areas of the globe. The President's power to make executive agreements with other nations was originally conceived as a means of arranging immediate, ad hoc, temporary agreements over a single problem. Gradually, "in a way that neither historians nor legal scholars have made altogether clear," as Arthur Schlesinger, Jr., says, the executive agreement began to emerge as a more general power. Eventually it came to be used for the most momentous decisions—for example, Franklin Roosevelt's exchange of American destroyers for the lease of British bases after the fall of France in 1940. The number of executive agreements grew first arithmetically, then geometrically. According to the calculations of Senator Sam J. Ervin, Jr., as recently as 1930 the United States had concluded twenty-five treaties and only nine executive agreements. In 1968 alone, the President concluded sixteen treaties and 266 executive agreements. By 1972 the United States had a total of 947 treaties and 4,359 executive agreements. No longer were these agreements merely ad hoc and temporary; they had the same standing under international law as did treaties, and they dealt with equally portentous matters. The President's power in domestic policy and decisions has expanded with almost equal force. While presidential authority over fiscal and monetary policy is partial and uneven, by merging and manipulating economic powers the White House can directly influence private and public decision-making throughout the national economy.

The President's power has expanded enormously in other areas as well. But the more we dwell on this expansion, the more directly we encounter a fundamental paradox. The presidential power that seems so vast and indeed excessive to many outside the White House appears all too small and shrunken to presidents and their aides when compared to the stupendous burdens put on the White House. They keenly feel the lack of assured, dependable power that chief executives in some other nations draw from their extensive legislative and party resources. To them the President is very much alone, isolated, thrown back on a limited power base, pitted against Congress and other institutions and the ambitious power seekers inhabiting them, in a conflict in which the President's power base is a sharply delimited one.

From these perceptions has emerged a theory of presidential power as essentially the power to dicker and transact. "The power to persuade is the power to bargain," according to Richard Neustadt, a onetime White House aide. "Status and authority yield bargaining advantages. But in a government of 'separated institutions sharing power,' they yield them to all sides. With the array of vantage points at his disposal, a President may be far more persuasive than his logic or his charm could make him. But outcomes are not guaranteed by his advantages. There remain the counter pressures those whom he would influence can bring to bear on him from vantage points at their disposal. Command has limited utility; persuasion becomes give-and-take. It is well that the White House holds the vantage points it does. In such a business any President may need them all—and more."

To the marketplace of bargaining presidents bring whatever resources they possess—influence over public opinion, veto and the threat of veto, party and legislative influence if any, power to make prestigious appointments, and other established political assets. They must bring something more, Neustadt contends: reputations as skillful bargainers, power wielders, leaders. Presidents must have a will to power or they will not be successful presidents. They must constantly search for power, building it, if necessary, out of every scrap of formal authority and personal influence they can locate. They must constantly guard whatever power they have achieved. They must hoard power so that it will be available in the future. To bargain effectively means to make the right choices, and the right choices are those that win concessions from rivals and at the same time bolster the President's power posture and resources.

Endless presidential bargaining, persuading, power-hoarding, managing, manipulating—is this executive *leadership?* It all depends on the stakes of the struggle. The bargaining-reciprocity model of presidential strategy has been criticized as being not only excessively Machiavellian in its precepts but lacking connection with goals and values. Divorced from ethics, leadership is reduced to management and politics to mere technique. When presidents enter the political marketplace to negotiate with minority interests, they in effect legitimate those interests and yield partially to them as part of the bargaining process; they may do this at the expense of raising the issues, the stakes, and the purposes to a much higher, more inclusive, more general welfare-oriented level. Broader, more "popular" and egalitarian values may be sacrificed to the benefit of organized interests that can put their best bargainers into the trading arena and mobilize support behind them. Presidents, as bargainers for a more inclusive public interest, may be unduly handicapped. Their strategic situation is much inferior to that of the *political* leader who can lift the issues in conflict out of the narrow arena of bargaining to the level of program, purpose, and even ideology.

To perceive that a President has the strategic alternative of pursuing a general public purpose instead of merely negotiating with a host of less inclusive ones is to assume that some kind of *national purpose* exists and can be identified. Many deny this. "The history of the formulation of the national purpose, in America as elsewhere," according to Hans Morgenthau, "is the story of bad theology and absurd metaphysics, of phony theories and fraudulent science, of crude rationalizations and vulgar delusions of grandeur." Americans never witnessed an "end to ideology," in this view; they never had an ideology.

Ideology no, but purposes yes. Behind the glittering rhetoric, the cloudy generalities, the empty bombast of politicians, preachers, and publicists, we have discerned two fundamental values that over the years, in varying degrees, have informed the American purpose. One is the pursuit of liberty as apotheosized in the Declaration of Independence, protected in the Bill of Rights, appealed to by the abolitionists, encoded and guaranteed, after many diversions and vagaries, by the Supreme Court. The other is equality, also proclaimed in the Declaration, reaffirmed by the struggle for emancipation, protected, as to race, in the Fourteenth and Fifteenth Amendments, appealed to by workers, farmers, and other disadvantaged groups during the nineteenth and early twentieth centuries, and embodied, more or less successfully, in the domestic programs of Woodrow Wilson, Franklin Roosevelt, and succeeding liberal Democratic presidents. These values have been in conflict with one another, as in the long struggle between concepts of liberty that stressed the rights of property and defensive concepts of liberty that protected "human" rights of individuals against arbitrary public and private power. The values have been also in *internal* conflict, as in the twentieth-century struggle between the egalitarian concept of equal *opportunity* and the egalitarian concept of equal *condition*. There has taken place a rough convergence within and between these values, however, exemplified most dramatically by Roosevelt's explicit broadening of the Bill of Rights from an emphasis on negative liberties *against* government to the achieving of positive liberty (including equality) *through* government, in his State of the Union message in January 1944.

Most presidents, as practical men and accomplished bargainers, have resisted ideological and even program commitment. But the compulsion of events has forced them to make choices among values. That compulsion changed Lincoln from the Whiggish, conservative, moderate egalitarian of the 1840s and 1850s to one who assumed the role of Great Emancipator. It forced him, as a Jeffersonian libertarian, to suspend basic liberties during the Civil War. He made his classic defense of his usurpations: "Was it possible to lose the nation and yet preserve the Constitution? By general law, life and limb must be protected, yet often a limb must be amputated to save a life, but a life is never wisely given to save a limb." The question of ultimate purpose remained. *What was one saving in saving the nation?* It was the Supreme Court that most aptly answered Lincoln, in a post-Civil War decision rebuking the late President for his theory of presidential war power: "A country preserved at the sacrifice of all the cardinal principles of liberty, is not worth the cost of preserving it." Wars, depressions, domestic unrest, great moral issues like Vietnam and Watergate have posed the most urgent questions of value and purpose for pragmatic politicians, however much they have sought to evade them.

The capacity of presidents to transcend their everyday role as bargainers and coalition builders and to confront the overriding moral and social issues facing the country gives rise not only to questions of principle, purpose, and ethics but to considerations of sheer presidential effectiveness—of presidential impact on social change and causation. Critics of the bargaining-persuading model of the presidency contend that as a result of this strategy chief executives limit their influence on policy to what can be squeezed out of their negotiations with bargainers for group interests. To be sure, the President may be the more skillful trader, and his power resources usually match if they do not surpass the combined influence of those of his rivals and competitors. But by bargaining in the trading arena, by implicitly accepting the assumptions of the negotiating game, by consenting to considerable compromise in advance as part of the terms of the restricted conflict, presidents enormously narrow their options both in number and importance. Carter is only the most recent case. *They have a choice only of options relevant to the context in which they bargain.* They do not have the option of changing the rules and assumptions of the game, of shifting the plane of combat from one set of issues to a wholly new or redefined set of issues, or of immensely broadening the stakes by lifting the struggle out of the trading arena to the level of compelling national issue, broad popular choice, and great public conflict.

This question of the effectiveness of presidents as executive leaders—indeed, of the very definition of their effectiveness, measured by the moral and practical criteria of the values espoused and exemplified—may be examined in the context of several modern presidencies. The first modern President, in several respects, was Lincoln, who came to exert extensive power under the press of dire civil strife that required the social and economic mobilization of persons and resources and led to centralizing tendencies in government. His administration was a high-water mark in the exercise of executive power in the United States. For months he ruled without calling Congress into session. He increased the army and navy beyond the limits set by law, proclaimed that the slaves of those in rebellion were emancipated, declared martial law and suspended habeas corpus, and spent millions without congressional appropriation. Lincoln acted in a wholly "pragmatic" and operational manner in overriding his old Whig anti-presidential power views in order to fight the war.

Lincoln was also opportunistic and expedient in his attitude toward slavery during the early part of the war. He made clear that he was not conducting the war in order to interfere with slavery in the seceded states, for those states could return to the Union with slavery intact; he still favored colonization of American Negroes in other parts of the world; his Emancipation Proclamation was issued perhaps as much for immediate military and practical purposes as for moral reasons; and, above all, he continued strongly to defend states' rights. Perhaps one cannot fault Lincoln for conducting a colossal balancing act between abolitionists and border-state moderates, between congressional radicals and conservatives, to win the war. But there was a price to pay after his death, for the moral issue of the Civil War became the very practical problem of war's end—the problem of Reconstruction.

Here Lincoln's operationalism broke down. So cautious had he been not to interfere with military necessities, and so orthodox had he been about the powers of the states, that the North ended the war without clear guidance from the fallen leader with regard to postwar policies that might carry out the great moral commitment of the nation to the freedmen. States' rights, moderation, and compromise would stand in the way of enacting and enforcing federal guarantees of land for the freedmen, the right to vote, and education for their children. Perhaps Lincoln recognized how severely limited his options were within the context in which he operated. "I claim not to have controlled events but confess plainly that events have controlled me."

Not until the new century was there another President who exploited his executive power to the hilt and had no hesitation in proclaiming the fact. He believed in the theory, Theodore Roosevelt said, "that the executive power was limited only by specific restrictions and prohibitions appearing in the Constitution or imposed by the Congress under its Constitutional powers. My view was that every executive officer . . . was a steward of the people bound actively and affirmatively to do all he could for the people, and not to content himself with the negative merit of keeping his talents undamaged in a napkin. . . . I did not usurp power, but I did greatly broaden the use of executive power." He believed, he said, that the efficiency of the American governmental system depended on its possessing a "strong central executive," so wherever he could he established precedents for strength in the executive. Theodore Roosevelt was an activist but not a governmental reformer. He accepted the system of checks and balances essentially as it was and bargained even with persons he considered "idiots" and "cranks" in order to extract what he could from the system. He was, in short, essentially an executive leader rather than a political or legislative leader.

It remained for Theodore Roosevelt's distant cousin Franklin to demonstrate the power that could be wielded by the chief executive in a time of harrowing domestic crisis. As politician-in-chief Roosevelt demonstrated a grasp of public opinion in all its subtlety and complexity as well as its potential power, a sense of timing—both in moving quickly and in delaying prudently—that kept his adversaries off balance, an attention to political detail, a skill at mediating among group factions and playing them off one against the other, an ability to separate opposition leaders from the rank and file (as he did with John L. Lewis and his coal miners), an ability to choose his own battleground and make his foes fight on it, a mixture of personal charm and political craft—all qualities that together made him probably the most effective political tactician of this century.

To these political skills were allied unorthodox, highly personalized, and altogether formidable executive methods. Roosevelt managed to stay on top of his restless, bickering, and ambitious executive subordinates by drawing fully on his formal and informal powers as chief executive; by raising goals, creating momentum, inspiring personal loyalty, getting the best out of people; by skillful timing, now waiting endlessly while his aides chafed, sometimes moving quickly before his staff had been informed, but usually choosing a time when his target—a foot-dragging agency or a bovine official—was most vulnerable;

by deliberately fostering among his aides a sense of competition and a clash of wills that led to disarray, heartbreak, and anger but also set off pulses of executive energy and sparks of creativity; by maintaining an extremely wide "span of control"—or at least one of attention, encouragement, and intervention; by handing out one job to several persons and several jobs to one person, thereby strengthening his own position as a court of appeals, a depository of information, and a tool of coordination; by ignoring or bypassing collective decision-making agencies such as the cabinet and dealing instead with varying combinations of persons from different agencies; by often delving into specific, even tiny matters that some officials had assumed were far below or beyond the chief executive's reach; by sometimes withholding information, sometimes supplying it, to keep aides and officials in line; by maintaining his own private storehouse of intelligence drawn from countless letters, memos, and gossip and fed by contending subordinates; by retiring behind the protection of rules, customs, and conventions when they served his needs and evading them when they did not—and always by persuading, flattering, juggling, improvising, reshuffling, harmonizing, conciliating, manipulating.

To what values and purposes were these great skills harnessed? Roosevelt entered office as a Wilsonian Democrat with no systematic program or ideology save for a generalized belief in liberty and equality. Within this rubric, and under the intense pressure of an economy in crisis, he proclaimed three more specific goals during his first months in office: recovery, relief, and reform. A spate of reform legislation brought long-needed changes in the relations of employer and worker, seller and buyer, big business and small business, farmer and middleman, utility user and investor and utility practice. Relief was provided to the needy of all sorts: industrial workers, tenant farmers, professional people, artists of all kinds, businessmen. But the supreme immediate goal, the one to which Roosevelt was most committed and for which the people had given him his main mandate, was economic recovery, and progress here was halting. Unemployment dropped some during Roosevelt's first term but shot up again during his second, and it was only with the coming of World War II and its enormous spending requirements that real recovery was achieved.

Roosevelt's fine tactical qualities undoubtedly broadened his options. He was unusually effective in leading Congress during his first term. This was partly due to his vast popularity and to his having started his term, as Neustadt said, "with vivid demonstrations of tenacity and skill in every sphere, thereby establishing a reputation sure to stand the shocks of daily disarray until he was prepared to demonstrate again." It is highly significant, though, that despite his mammoth re-election victory of 1936 Roosevelt did not possess the scope of power he felt he needed. He tried to "pack" and modernize the Supreme

Court, and the attempt failed in Congress. He tried to rejuvenate and liberalize the Democratic party, but he largely failed in the Democratic party primaries of 1938, when he intervened to back pro-Roosevelt candidates over anti-New Deal ones. In the congressional elections of 1938 he lost support in both House and Senate. By the end of his second term he had lost much of his potency in domestic policy. Reputation, skill, and popularity continued; he simply lacked the stable sources of power that could make possible strong leadership.

Roosevelt was a Grand Improviser who frankly prided himself on his ability to move one foot at a time, feinting, parrying, withdrawing, seizing on every opportunity, using every jot and tittle of his day-to-day power. His reputation as a bargainer was unequaled. In the end it was not enough; it was necessary but not adequate. He simply could not find the resources within his executive power to bring about the fundamental changes—real recovery for the entire nation, fundamental and long-run improvement in the lot of the one-third who were ill-fed, ill-housed, and ill-clad, basic change in either equal opportunity or equal condition—that many felt the New Deal stood for. Roosevelt disdained set programs and ideology; he did not favor basic government reform; both his attempted Court purge and his intervention in the primaries were essentially ventures in the manipulation of personal influence. Still he kept feeling the limits of his power; the fact that throughout his life he kept returning to the possibility of a party realignment under which the Democrats would become a dependably and programmatically liberal party suggests the sharp limits to executive power, no matter how gifted the improviser.

No president since Woodrow Wilson has entered the White House with as clear and considered a conception of presidential power and responsibility as did John F. Kennedy in 1961. This was partly because he had studied the manner in which the "great" presidents had exercised power—and he approved of it. "I am no Whig," he liked to proclaim. "I want to be a President," he said in his campaign, "who acts as well as reacts—who originates programs as well as study groups—who masters complex problems as well as one-page memorandums. I want to be a President who is a Chief Executive in every sense of the word—who responds to a problem, not by hoping his subordinates will act, but by directing them to act—a President who is willing to take the responsibility for getting things done, and take the blame if they are not done right. . . ." Kennedy had a somewhat more systematic set of policies than had Roosevelt, but like the great chief executives he proposed to exploit his executive powers to the hilt.

The trouble was that these powers were wholly inadequate. Kennedy had neither Roosevelt's influence in Congress nor his big popular margins in the polls and public opinion surveys, and he appeared to use up his political resources in getting even a minimal program through the legislature. By the 1960s the Democratic party was in even greater disarray than it had been in the 1930s, so the party was unable to provide Kennedy with stable and predictable support. His ardor for the bold execution of presidential power seemed to cool. A book by a close presidential aide, Theodore Sorensen, published during Kennedy's third year in office and given a foreword by Kennedy himself, seemed to reflect the President's sense of deflation—or perhaps of a new realism. The President's authority was not as great as his authority, Sorensen wrote. He had extraordinary but sharply limited power. His political resources—whether money, manpower, time, credibility, or patronage—often seemed meager.

Some wondered why Kennedy did not make a bolder or more imaginative effort to break out of the near-impasse in which he found himself. The President did intervene to help Democrats in the congressional elections of 1962 (until he was compelled to return to Washington to confront the Cuban missile crisis) and he used every ounce of "blarney, bludgeon, and boodle" to influence Congress. But he did not seek to alter the system within which he operated. Doubtless this was partly because he felt that his big opportunity would come in the election of 1964, when he might sweep into Congress with Democratic majorities big enough to put through his program and perhaps adopt at least minor governmental reforms. But the main reason for Kennedy's diffidence was probably intellectual; he felt that, like most chief executives, he could extract enough influence from his executive powers to provide the leadership that was needed. He dared not attempt reforms that might fail and might also arouse the barons of Capitol Hill. And perhaps he was not temperamentally up to it or intellectually in favor of it. He was acutely aware, according to Sorensen, of Jefferson's dictum that "Great innovations should not be forced on slender majorities." Assassination put an end to any chance of finding out what he could have done if he had been given more time.

Nixon's administration is still too recent to afford a reliable perspective on his role as executive leader. A tentative judgment, however, might be that he represented both a culmination and a caricature of the resort to the powers and precedents of the executive leader. Faced with Democratic majorities in both houses of Congress, he resorted to bargaining rather than moral leadership. Inheriting a federal judiciary largely appointed by Democratic predecessors, he filled vacancies with conservatives to provide ideological balance, but not all Nixon judges acted like Nixon men. Presiding over a Republican party shrunken in size and organized almost as poorly as the Democratic party, he largely ignored the GOP and ran for office, as we have noted, on the basis of his own personal organization built up over the years. If Roosevelt was the supreme improviser, Nixon was the utter opportunist, shifting ideological stances, repudiating (making "inoperative") previous positions, raising campaign funds by the tens of millions to guarantee re-election, sabotaging the Democratic party, visiting Peking and Moscow while bombing Southeast Asia to stop the spread of militant Communism, adopting economic controls after having flatly opposed them. Finally cornered and trapped, he seemed to make a last desperate effort to retrieve what scraps of influence he could from the inner recesses of the executive. It was not enough.

Thus the dilemma of executive power remains. In protecting themselves—their reputations, choices, resources—what are chief executives guarding? If they constantly protect themselves, to what extent are they also guarding the *purpose* they are supposed ultimately to be serving? How do they draw the line between preserving power for themselves and expending it for broader goals? If they follow a strategy of opportunism and expediency, are they not tempted to yield to its beguilements rather than sacrifice glory and reputation in a quixotic quest for great ends, as Wilson is supposed to have done?

Graver questions portend. If presidents continually draw from their narrower powers as chief executive, and if they lack broader legislative and party resources, do they not put themselves in a position, in the long run, where they have only a choice among limited options rather than the capacity to broaden immensely their options and opportunities? If problems remain unsolved because neither President nor Congress can confront them, does this not lead to a crisis at home or abroad, in economics, politics, world stability, or national morality? And if government by crisis is both the inevitable product of executive leadership and its ultimate mechanism, is there a price to be paid for a democratic society?

The implication of European and American experience is clear: executive leadership in itself is inadequate for sustained and planned social transformation. Executive leadership is indispensable for crisis situations and effective in accomplishing specific and limited goals. But loss of direction and control within the structure of executive leadership; the continuing weight of conflicting commitments, motives, and goals; the restraints inherent in the executive process; the limited time accorded to most executive systems combined with the inability of leaders to marshal ideological and political resources outside the system—all these inhibit executive leaders who, on the face of it and for short periods, seem effective, practical, on top of things. It is significant that the enduring New Deal emerged not out of Roosevelt's "hundred days" of 1933, when he gave a brilliant demonstration of executive leadership, but out of the "second hundred days" of 1935, which emerged out of decades of intellectual ferment, political action, and legislative as well as executive policy-making; it is significant too that, to the degree that the Labour party brought fundamental change to Britain during the late 1940s, these achievements had their source in decades of intellectual creativity, ideological ferment, policy conflict, and political organizing—especially party-building. Executive leadership, to produce intended real change, must be solidly founded in power and principle.

PART V

IMPLICATIONS: THEORY AND PRACTICE

15

DECISION AND CHANGE

Wearing a Red Guard armband, Mao Tse-tung greeted a million Red Guards at a colossal rally in Peking's Tien-an-men Square in mid-August 1966—the first of eight impassioned rallies during which he gave his personal blessing to ten million or more young revolutionaries who had made pilgrimages to the capital. Throughout China huge character posters, perennial symbol and means of protest, enlivened hundreds of walls in public places, providing vivid backdrops for demonstrations in which "capitalist roaders" in the party were publicly chastised and deposed. In the following months Red Guards by the millions, enjoying free transportation on trains, crossed the country, exchanged experiences, and set up liaison committees to plan and carry out joint action.

Toward the end of the year Mao officially widened the scope of the Cultural Revolution to include industry and agriculture. He alerted workers and peasants simultaneously to "grasp revolution and promote production," thus once again subtly restricting mass action at the same time that he was expanding it. The great mass of peasants were still not playing a significant role in the Cultural Revolution except to the extent that they participated as soldiers. But urban workers, who called themselves "revolutionary rebels," had begun spontaneous protests earlier in the year and soon became the vanguard of the revolutionary upheaval. The motives of the young workers, many of them well-educated, were broadly similar to those of equally rebellious students. Both were fighting against the inequality, authoritarianism, and capitalist tendencies and corruption they believed to be embodied in factory managers. The goal of the workers was equality, their target, "capitalistic" incentives.

During this tumultuous period, Mao, his party associates, and leaders of

401

the mass organizations defined the limits of mass action and created new structures of power to carry out their goals. It was evident by the end of 1966 that Mao wanted the revolution to move further and faster to the left. The "Revolutionary Rebel" workers in the "Revolutionary Rebel General Headquarters" in Shanghai, China's largest city, took over the city's newspapers, ousted the local party committee, and seized political power. Mao enthusiastically applauded. "Internal rebellions are fine," he told Cultural Revolution leaders. "This is one class overthrowing another. This is a great revolution." Encouraged, the editors of *Red Flag,* the voice of the Cultural Revolution leadership, put out a call to workers and students everywhere to "resolutely seize power."

Some time during this period Mao underwent a change of heart. Early in 1967 he and Defense Minister Lin Piao ordered the People's Liberation Army, hitherto neutral, to intervene in the revolution, ostensibly in support of the left. This portentous decision, which would markedly change the nature of the struggle, led to a more moderate shift of power in two provinces. PLA troops, party cadres, and radical activists from mass organizations joined in "triple alliances" to form revolutionary committees to exercise power. Mao made it clear that the province and city-level revolutionary committees were the correct form for the new structures of power in China and that mass organization would be encouraged to seize and exercise power though not independently. When the revolutionary momentum continued, and when the revolutionaries proclaimed the birth of the Shanghai Commune (inspired by the ill-fated Paris Commune of 1871) Mao denounced its "extreme anarchism." He demanded that the radicals work within the triple alliances with soldiers and party cadres. The radicals resisted. It was a "counterrevolutionary adverse current" that would restore the "capitalist roaders" to power, they protested. Guerrilla warfare and open battles broke out between Red Guards and PLA troops in a number of provinces.

The Red Guards had gone too far; Mao had lost control. He knew he must call a halt to the revolution he had instigated. The unruly Red Guards would have to be disciplined and brought under control by the revolutionary workers, who had mainly stayed in the factories to "grasp revolution and promote production." One hundred thousand workers from sixty Peking factories, organized into Mao Tse-tung Propaganda Teams, were told to occupy the Peking universities. Summoning student leaders, Mao reproached them for anarchism and factionalism. "You have let me down and, moreover, you have disappointed the workers, peasants, and soldiers of China." Working-class activists took over and radically reorganized the educational system. By the end of 1968 the Communist party bureaucracy had been shattered, tripartite revolutionary committees were in power throughout China, and the People's Liberation Army had become the "main pillar of the dictatorship of the proletariat." The demise of the Great Proletarian Cultural Revolution was signaled most clearly when Mao at the end of 1968 directed millions of educated youth, especially Red Guard elements, to the countryside for re-education by the peasants.

To thousands of delegates to the Ninth Congress of the Chinese Communist party in April 1969 Mao declared the Cultural Revolution over—at least for a time. Now was a time for consolidation. Yet the revolution was incomplete; there must be revolutions again. In the following years the party was largely rebuilt and the mass base of the party broadened, doubling in size and admitting millions of workers and peasants, especially women. Countless cadre schools conducted massive re-education campaigns in the rural areas. Both the "Down to the Countryside Movement" and the cadre schools were radical measures to restore peace in the cities, to consolidate the Cultural Revolution, and—one of Mao's deepest concerns—to alleviate the "three great distinctions" between city and countryside, workers and peasants, and mental and manual labor.

What was the outcome of all this? The extent of real social change, as we define it, was rather mixed. Admission of workers and peasants to the educational system was immensely broadened. Some concrete move toward eliminating inequalities and material incentives in industry and agriculture has been reported, but the change has not been dramatic. Various reforms in the bureaucracy, such as reducing its size and combining separate state and party agencies into unified structures, has brought some democratization of authority. Yet Mao's chief target, bureaucratization, has been alleviated but not halted.

The change brought about by the Cultural Revolution was motivational and spiritual rather than material or structural—a "qualitative jump in consciousness," as K. S. Karol summed it up—a radical transformation in the attitudes and behavior of the Chinese people. This revolution in consciousness was most pronounced in promoting egalitarian and fraternal aspirations and values. Collectivism and concern for the common welfare had been elevated over individualism and elitism. The "three great distinctions" and the four "olds"—old ideas, customs, manners, and habits—had been curbed to some degree. Mass participation and criticism—within limits—had been encouraged. Whether this change in spirit will lead to a significant transformation of the norms, institutions, and behavior of the Chinese people—that is, to *real* change—remains to be seen. Most Chinese still lived in poverty in the 1960s; nevertheless they had enough food, shelter, and medical care to satisfy subsistence wants and could therefore generate newer motivations on a higher level. The new motives were the needs and aspirations for community and cooperation; for participation in a collective life larger than one's personal existence; and, on a higher level, for the universal values of freedom, equality, democracy, and justice. Because Mao tapped these powerful and intensifying motives, he opened the floodgates to an outpouring of suppressed resentments and grievances; he channeled the protest to serve his own ends and, to varying degrees, the ends of his followers. In anticipating and preparing for the "second round," the transformation of needs and motives engendered by the "first round" of socialist revolution, and in initiating a grand strategy of implementing decisions in response to these new motivations, Mao demonstrated his genius as a transforming leader.

Most extraordinary was the evidence of Mao's power of decision in the flux of change. It is one thing to help found and then guide a vast revolutionary movement through dictatorship, world war, and civil war to final power; it is much more unusual to alter radically and even to reverse the currents of revolutionary action and consolidation. The source of Mao's power was not magic but his uncanny insight into the new motivations of the Chinese people.

The Leader as Policy Maker

Unlike Mao, few Western leaders in the established bureaucratic politics of the West have the heady prospect of making decisions that might transform their societies. More than any other leaders, policy makers in large, heavily institutionalized political systems must be conscious of the web of interrelated means and ends within which they act. Institutions press too closely and the wider political environment is too intrusive, hostile, and intractable to permit indulgence in utopianism. As leaders they must avoid those pressures that would reduce their role to that of mere agent of the narrow and short-run purposes that engage most administrators, high and low. To pursue wider goals they must avoid being drawn into and "morselized" by existing administrative arrangements, with their multifarious institutional demands.

Even transition holds its perils for the leader bent on new policies. Elected President in 1932 amid deepening economic prostration, Franklin D. Roosevelt confronted a repudiated Herbert Hoover intent on committing the president-elect to the administration's foreign policy on arms control, war debts, and the gold standard. Hoover and Roosevelt and their advisers recognized that the public wanted some show of concord and continuity between the two regimes. Yet Hoover and Roosevelt deeply distrusted each other. Hoover was convinced that the election of Roosevelt was responsible for further economic downturn. In what Frank Freidel calls "one of the strangest struggles in the history of the presidency," the lame-duck President tried to draw Roosevelt into the Administration's embrace and the president-elect fought to escape it. Roosevelt offered every kind of cooperation except involvement in Hoover's policies and responsibility for federal action that had occurred before March 1933. Despite bitter criticism in the press and in Republican circles—Secretary of State Henry Stimson said Hoover's dignity "made Roosevelt look like a peanut"— Roosevelt stuck to his position. He entered office and the "hundred days" free of the awkward embrace of a repudiated administration.

Roosevelt's was an extreme case: he was acting in a critical transitional period and he possessed unusual self-confidence. Most institution-bound policy makers, in Burma or Britain, the Soviet Union or the United States, or elsewhere, operate among a multitude of constraints. They may have only scanty knowledge of their situation and of the alternatives; hence they move cautiously, hoping to generate enough information to guide them to the next phase. Discussing decision-making as it is defined and employed by certain psychologists and decision theorists, Raymond Bauer notes that the "model assumes a single decision-making unit with a single set of utility preferences; knowledge of a reasonably full range of action alternatives and of their consequences; this intention of selecting that course of action of maximum utility; and the opportunity, disposition, and capacity to make the appropriate calculations. In the process of policy formation every one of these assumptions is violated." The costs of action will often be unclear, the benefits over the longer run even less predictable. Perhaps policy makers could exert more influence if they had more and better information, but the cost of gaining that information, the time and resources spent, is high; the economist Lionel Robbins noted the "marginal utility of not thinking about marginal utility." Above all, policy makers act amid a plethora of values, goals, interests, and needs which may have an order of hierarchy they cannot always recognize.

Institution-bound policy makers grope along, operating "by feel and by feedback." They concentrate on method, technique, and mechanisms rather than on broader ends or purposes. They protect, sometimes at heavy cost to overall goals, the maintenance and survival of their organization because they are exposed daily to the claims of persons immediately sheltered by that organization. They extrude red tape even as they struggle with it. They transact more than they administer, compromise more than they command, institutionalize more than they initiate. They fragment and morselize policy issues in order better to cope with them, seeking to limit their alternatives, to delegate thorny problems "down the line," to accept vague and inconsistent goals, to adapt and survive. Thus they exemplify the "satisficing" model, as economists call it, far more than the "maximizing" one.

Can policy makers then really "make policy"? Can they control final administrative action and actually produce change? Can they, indeed, exert *leadership?* If so, how is it done?

They can and do produce real change, as *public* policy makers, if they keep the wants and purposes of the great public in mind as representing the most compelling claim. As we have seen, those public wants and purposes typically are no errant or vagrant collection of interests and attitudes and tendencies; they have form, order, structure, and a set of priorities of their own. Public policy makers are effective to the extent that they can make their policies and the institutions to which they have access responsive to public needs and goals. This is extraordinarily hard to accomplish. Needs and aspirations "out there" seem remote, inchoate, fugitive, opaque; the needs and expectations "in here"—in the legislative, administrative, or judicial policy-making entity—are familiar, intimate, palpable. Not only is it a long way from out there to in here; but the goals and needs differ. Leaders are entangled in collective leadership institutions, administrative, legislative, or judicial, that limit their capacity to appeal over the heads of peers to broader but more remote publics.

To reach those remote publics, legislators and administrators receive reports from subordinates and representatives "closer to the field"; they may be peppered with mail and other communications from hopeful or disgruntled constituents; they read critical editorials in the press and elsewhere; they are accosted on the street or by telephone. Some policy makers take the initiative, through opinion polling, assigned field investigations, or other means, to divine public attitudes and wishes. The most conspicuous of all testing methods is of course the election—with the ever-threatening possibility of repudiation at the polls. But none of these methods can mobilize the full potential responsiveness of the major publics.

The devices of contact with these publics are crude, inevitably selective and distorted; the attitudes measured are superficial and volatile. It is not enough to administer to the visible, immediate, and undifferentiated needs and purposes of large numbers of people. Effective policy makers—those working for real change—must move on directly and purposefully to the "second round"—that is, the reorganization of popular needs and goals *following* the effectuation of the first round of policy-making. Most notably, they must assess the impact of policies that, in satisfying existing and recognizable need, alter the motivations not simply by extinguishing them and returning to some kind of equilibrium *but that in the very act of satisfaction create further wants and demands.* And they must calculate, if they can, what hierarchical order of needs and values may activate "higher" stages. The policy maker must anticipate reactions from informal and unofficial leaders as well as from formal ones and in a variety of settings and circumstances, not only the structured and traditional ones. Thus it was necessary for Roosevelt to move on from the economic "survival" needs of the "first" New Deal of 1933 to the egalitarian and reformist requirements of the "second" New Deal of 1935.

Many policy makers fail in the second and subsequent rounds; failure is less surprising than accomplishment. The occasional success of some, and the repeated successes of a few, appear to depend in part on their trust in intuition. Mystical explanations can provide little help for understanding policy leadership; the concept of *empathy* is more useful, for it reinterprets the apparently extrarational as the ability of some policy makers to comprehend and to respond to the cognitive and emotional structures of needs and the values that lie behind them. Empathy understands the needs of wider publics and their reactions when their needs are *satisfied*. Such a feat might be accomplished by a policy leader whose antennae have been sensitized by experience or by a novice who can see through the posture and defense of public attitudes to the real needs and values behind the protective facade.

Decision and Dissent

Typically leaders as policy makers operate in relatively settled and even structured political situations, within broadly agreed on boundaries and constraints, governed by established and legitimating traditions, precedents, and pronouncements. Party leaders act within the mythology of popular heroes and symbols, party platforms and procedures, external competition and internal pressure. Legislative leaders respond to constitutional and political restraints and opportunities. Judicial policy makers take account of statutes and precedents that, even in their ambiguous and contradictory legitimations, establish directions and guidelines. In a relatively stable political system leaders will also be bound by their own previous commitments.

The American President, Theodore Sorensen points out, "need not make a fetish of consistency but he must avoid confusion or the appearance of deception. He will in most cases, therefore, adopt his own policies as precedents and consider his own statements as binding, whether they were contained in an informal answer to a press conference question or in a formal document of state. . . ."

We can generalize with a measure of confidence about the behavior of leaders who undergo common socializing experiences, act within a relatively fixed and predictable political system, confront common policy questions, and deal with broadly similar policy constraints and supports. Can we also generalize about behavior under stress in leaders who must make swift decisions in crisis situations, often without guidelines or even authorization? In the 1950s and 1960s the Supreme Court felt impelled to make binding decisions on the most delicate and pressing issues of civil rights, electoral processes, and relations of religion and state, with only the most general of constitutional sanctions, beset by a host of conflicting precedents, and in a social context of accelerating tension and conflict. In the 1970s Congress had to establish specific impeachment procedures in an almost unprecedented environment of popular anxiety and attention. In all societies leaders must deal with sudden catastrophes like earthquakes or hurricanes or epidemics as well as with economic and political crises few could have predicted.

Often leaders do not behave like leaders—they do not because they cannot. To take the lead is to act in terms of certain values and purposes; leaders assume initiatives and organize support on the basis of the structure of wants, needs, expectations, and demands that lies beneath value and purpose. To be overwhelmed by a sudden imperative call to make a decision among various alternatives when the popular response to alternatives is, at best, ambiguous, and at a time and in circumstances not of a leader's choosing, is to have surrendered power to earlier decision makers. That was Stalin's plight after the Nazi invasion of Russia in June 1941. Hitler's decision to invade immediately closed off a host of options that had still lain open to the Kremlin in the spring of that year. The attack opened up a new set of options for Moscow, but only one seemed viable: to defend Mother Russia. If it is true that Stalin was psychologically immobilized for some days following the attack, his inertness may have reflected the plight of a man who had been accustomed to act on his own initiative in conditions of his own choosing.

In a world of ideally rational thought and action, the decision-making leader responds to unexpected events by analysis of the relevant facts and reassessment of ends and means. A classic decision-making sequence was defined by John Dewey: feeling a difficulty, locating and defining it, proposing possible solutions, rationally developing the implications of the alternatives, and "making further observations and experiments that lead to acceptance or rejection of each suggestion." Sorensen states that White House decision-making "ideally" encompasses "first: agreement on the facts; second: agreement on the overall policy objective; third: a precise definition of the problem; fourth: a canvassing of all possible solutions, with all their shades and variations; fifth: a list of all the possible consequences that would flow from each solution; sixth: a recommendation and final choice of one alternative; seventh: the communication of that selection; and eighth: provision for its execution." But Sorensen grants that such procedure is exceptional. Steps cannot be taken in proper order; facts are disputed; judgments over ends and means differ; goals are imprecise; all "available choices may be difficult mixtures of both good and evil.'' And so Yehezkel Dror concludes in a wide-ranging study, that when making decisions, ''individuals almost never *spontaneously* use such elements of 'rational' decision-making as searching widely for alternatives, elaborating operational goals, and setting down explicit expectations, or such rigorous concepts and tools of optimal decision-making as probabilities, logic, information search, and randomization. . . . Many decisions fulfill personality functions that are not directly related to the issue ostensibly to be decided. Consequently, the full significance of a decision often cannot be understood without depth analysis, and the 'effectiveness' of a decision in serving such deep needs is very difficult to evaluate.''

The reaction against the rationalistic analysis of the decision-making process has found expression in another famous theory of decision and change, ''the science of muddling through.'' Muddling through is the making of public policy by small adjustments, piecemeal responses, wrong turns, marginal innovations, short steps, limited action—all leading to only gradual change. These actions of transactional leadership react to immediate situations and pressures, strike bargains with allies and adversaries, follow limited and short-run goals, and seek to maintain equilibrium and to avoid fundamental change. Such leadership does not respond to more generalized, more deep-rooted, more dynamic, and more changeable wants and needs.

The resort to incrementalist, transactional types of decision-making leadership underlines again the plight of party, legislative, executive, and other decision makers facing crises they cannot fully comprehend, under circumstances of other leaders' making, at times they cannot control, and without the opportunity or even the ability to exploit information sources fully, to keep clear operating goals in mind, or to consider long-term implications and to respond to popular needs, wants, and values. In a traditional leadership process they could fit their decisions into an ''operational code'' drawn from and supporting a hierarchy of values—and hence inflict some order onto the decision-making process. But fresh and novel problems and crises cannot be fed into a decision-making machine.

Decision makers may respond to new problems and crises by old techniques of delay. Legislative decision makers, hoping to defuse issues, are adept in setting up investigating or deliberating bodies that can report at a later time when, it is hoped, public feeling will have lost some of its intensity. Courts may resort to technicalities to find a case moot or may return a case to a lower court for reconsideration as a device for postponing decision on a controversial constitutional question until public attitudes have ''matured'' or tension eased. The success of this endeavor will often turn on factors beyond the leaders' control. A court may be saved from a difficult decision by the action of a legislature in extending the compass of law. Decision-making can also be avoided by instituting a search for information or authority supporting positions already taken or desired, thereby avoiding different and challenging alternatives. Ole Holsti has documented various "reconstructing strategies" that John Foster Dulles, Eisenhower's secretary of state, employed to avoid "cognitive dissonance" when he confronted "discrepant information" that challenged his views of the Soviet Union as expansionist and belligerent. Decision makers may evade major value-freighted decisions by making small ones, as "practical" and "pragmatic" measures. They may brush off their previously proclaimed sympathy for those who might be severely affected by nondecision. They may resort to acts of confession or expiation to resolve their dilemmas in ways personally satisfying to them but not conducive to decision. Although these devices tend to relieve conflict and strain within the decision maker, in the long run they may identify the problem or crisis, or at the least make more dense the thicket of complexity of choice and serve mainly to shift decision-making power to lower levels in the legislative, administrative, or judicial hierarchies, or to entities wholly outside these hierarchies.

A second type of response by decision makers is far more rare: surrender. President Warren G. Harding once burst out to a friend, "John, I can't make a damn thing out of this tax problem. I listen to one side and they seem right, and then God! I talk to the other side and they seem just as right, and there I am where I started. I know somewhere there is a book that would give me the truth, but hell, I couldn't read the book. I know somewhere there is an economist who knows the truth, but I don't know where to find him and haven't the sense to know him and trust him when I did find him. God, what a job." This would be the nadir of leadership in decision-making.

A more effective way to handle choice in the face of conflicting advice and division in popular attitudes is to use conflict deliberately to protect decision-making options and power, and, even more, to use conflict to structure political environment so as to maximize "constructive" dissonance, thus allowing for more informed decision-making. Perhaps the chief means of doing this is to create a system of "multiple access" and "multiple advocacy" around the decision maker. Some decision-making institutions are initially established on this principle; legislatures and legislative committees, for example, may be organized on the basis of a two-party or multi-party system. Collegial courts and juries, and the adversary basis on which trials are conducted in many countries, embrace the idea of conflict in their very foundation. Courts, as in some tough school-desegregation cases, may appoint "masters" or an advisory panel to provide analysis of alternatives. Executive branches are usually established on a different basis—that is, one of single-minded judgment and execution—

but multiple access and advice can—and I believe must—be built into the advisory system around the executive, too.

To build systems of multiple access and advocacy establishes a pluralistic and conflicted advisory system; more, it makes probable the access of decision makers to a wide range and variety of wants and needs and, especially, demands, values, and purposes. Even advisers who are mere technical specialists will have ties to groups of experts—agronomists, nuclear scientists, economists, educators, media technicians—with not inconsiderable influence over opinion-forming agencies and in their own professional associations. And gifted advisers on broader political matters will deal with and respond to political constituencies that connect them with potent popular movements and other forces.

These linkages may provide political decision makers with considerable leverage. Through advisers, decision-making leaders can mobilize networks of leaders and followers, each with roots in empowering constituencies. The impetus of interacting and conflicting advice will be outward as well as inward. The more varied the access and the advocacy, the more varied the specialized and supporting groups that can be reached and perhaps mobilized. A decision of Soviet party officials to emphasize investment of producer goods, of Indian authorities to alter public policy on population control, of Polish Communists to raise prices of consumer goods, of the British Labour party to speed up the nationalization of industry, will bring clusters of experts and supporting constituencies and interests into conflict with one another, and the sharper the conflict and the more explicit it becomes, at least within certain channels, the more the "outlying" interests will be mobilized and capable of putting pressure on government from the outside. If decision makers "inside" can win support in certain networks, they can use this support as leverage in dealing with other experts and their constituencies by co-opting them, by citing opposing authority against them, by enlisting broader constituencies through them in situations of conflict.

Using experts as leverage assumes, however, that the political decision makers themselves are assured and collected personages who can distance themselves from multiple advocates and exploit their differences rather than be further divided by them—or overcome by them, as in the case of Harding. Occasionally we identify leaders of such self-confidence or set purpose; thus in World War II Churchill (for military advice), de Gaulle, and Roosevelt seemed to possess these qualities. Roosevelt, in particular, could subject himself to the most conflicting kinds of advice—conversing animatedly with alleged monetary quacks, for example, during a period when he was receiving advice from prestigious bankers—without appearing to lose his direction, but even Roosevelt seemed for a time immobilized by conflicting advice, and by the warring interests his advisers tapped, as the nation headed into the "recession" of 1937–1938. Plural decision-making bodies are even more subject to the paralysis induced by multiple advocacy because multiple advocates and the interests they represent are built into the heart of their operation.

The divisive and immobilizing impact of multiple access and advocacy may be all the more severe when the sources of decision conflict within leaders are psychological as well as political and intellectual. "Internalized moral standards, ego ideals, and basic components of the person's conscious self-image tend to be implicated by every important decision," Irving Janis says. "Often these considerations are fleetingly thought about or perhaps occur only in daydream fantasies about consequences which do not manifestly refer to the decision itself. Nevertheless, it is assumed that for every vital decision some identifiable thought sequences occur that refer, at least in derivative form, to disturbing questions about changes in self-esteem (e.g., 'Will I feel that my action is moral or immoral? Will I feel proud of myself or ashamed and guilty? Will I be living up to my ideals or letting myself down?'). All such considerations are referred to as *anticipations of self-approval or disapproval.*"

To some degree decision makers can organize multiple access and advocacy to encourage or to block off conflict. Describing President Nixon's handling of his National Security Council, Alexander George notes that Nixon contended after he took office in 1968 that his system was "designed to make certain that clear policy choices reach the top, so that various positions can be fully debated in the meetings of the Council." Differences of view, he said, "are identified and defended, rather than muted or buried." He refused, the President said, "to be confronted with a bureaucratic consensus that leaves me no options but acceptance or rejection, and that gives me no way of knowing what alternatives exist." One might almost have concluded that Nixon had set up a pluralistic legislature within the executive office. George concludes that the roles of cabinet officials and other senior officials had been seriously weakened for multiple advocacy, that Nixon's version of the National Security Council could seriously overburden the top-level decision maker, and that in fact the Nixon administration had "resorted to a centrally directed, depoliticized system of policy making." This conclusion is a reminder that dissent, if it is not quelled or nullified entirely, can be so reorganized and concentrated as to minimize its effect; and that for maximum effect conflict must be encouraged and diffused through every level and enclave of decision-making bodies.

In the Bay of Pigs crisis, John F. Kennedy had seemed to pay the price of inheriting a decision ready-made by the previous administration and of executing it without the benefit of full multiple access and advocacy. Following the disaster, Arthur Schlesinger noted, Kennedy knew "that he would have to broaden the range of his advice, make greater use of generalists in whom he had personal confidence and remake every great decision in his own terms. . . ."

The Cuban missile crisis gave Kennedy an opportunity to redeem the errors of the Bay of Pigs. The Executive Committee (ExCom) of the National Security Council, charged with responsibility for considering alternatives, solicited divergent views, encouraged advocacy of a variety of proposals, and encouraged lower-ranking officials to offer their recommendations even when these were opposed to those of superiors. But perhaps the most significant aspect of both crises was the constraints more remote publics imposed on leaders of superpowers. Robert Kennedy remembered his brother brooding about "the specter of the death of the children of this country and all the world —the young people who had no role, who had no say, who knew nothing, even, of the confrontation, but whose lives would be snuffed out like everyone else's. They would never have a chance to make a decision." A secret letter from Khrushchev to the President during the missile crisis was even more eloquent and poignant: "If you have not lost your self-control and sensibly conceive what this might lead to, then, Mr. President, you and I ought not now to pull on the ends of the rope in which you have tied the *knot of war,* because the more the two of us pull, the tighter the knot will be tied. And a moment may come when that knot will be tied so tight that even he who tied it will not have the strength to untie it, and then it will be necessary to cut that knot, and what that would mean is not for me to explain to you. . . ." Because Kennedy assumed responsibility for decision in the missile crisis, he saved later leaders much harder ones. And the children Robert Kennedy mentioned of another generation—a remote, "non-voting" public—did not have to suffer far harsher decisions. Because Khrushchev was able to make the decision to withdraw, a catastrophe was averted—the knot was untied. But both leaders were operating in situations where the range of decision had been dangerously narrowed, not only by their own action but by earlier choices of less "responsible" leaders and by the tyranny of circumstance.

The Test: Real, Intended Change

Most of the world's decision makers, however powerful they may appear in journalistic accounts, must cope with the effects of decisions already made by events, circumstances, and other persons and hence, like Khrushchev and Kennedy, must act within narrow bounds. Decision-making opportunities typically come to them in the form of a few limited options. The advisers and institutions and procedures that once upon a time might have been organized to empower them often turn out to have become sources of restraint. The main function—even of those labeled radicals or reformers or revolutionaries—is often to maintain existing political arrangements and hence to contribute to continuity, equilibrium, and stability. Such decision makers are defensive and palliative rather than creative. Occasionally they act at such critical turning points in the great affairs of nations that their tiny leverage tips affairs toward one course of action rather than another or holds matters in balance or in suspension until decisions can be made at a later time. But those later decisions may be even more constrained as a result of intervening events.

Napoleon, it is said, could look upon a battle scene of unimaginable disorder and see its coherence for his own advantage. If some decision makers seem to have enormous influence on history and are thrust into the pantheon of world heroes, this may be in part the result of miscalculation by the chroniclers of their actual impact on the shank of history and their glorification as heroes by panegyrists. Even more the reason may be a faulty or inadequate conception of the nature of change. Dramatic decision-making may lead only to cosmetic change, or to temporary change, or to the kind of change in symbols and myths that will preserve the existing order rather than transform or undermine it. Such seemed to be true of de Gaulle's regime. A realistic and restricted definition of policy and decision leadership is necessary to a serviceable concept of social change.

By social change I mean here *real change*—that is, a transformation to a marked degree in the attitudes, norms, institutions, and behaviors that structure our daily lives. Such changes embrace not only "new cultural patterns and institutional arrangements" and "new psychological dispositions," in the terms used by Herbert Kelman and Donald Warwick, but changes in material conditions, in the explicit, felt existence, the flesh and fabric of people's lives. Such changes may be a far cry from the "changes" that legislative, judicial, and executive decisions are supposed to bring automatically. The leadership process must be defined, in short, as carrying through from the decision-making stages to the point of concrete changes in people's lives, attitudes, behaviors, institutions. Even the sweep of this process is not enough, however, for we must include another dimension: *time*. Attitude and behavior can change for a certain period; as in a war, popular fads and emotional political movements change only to revert later. Real change means a continuing interaction of attitudes, behavior, and institutions, monitored by alterations in individual and collective hierarchies of values.

Leadership brings about real change that leaders *intend*, under our definition. Leaders may seem to cause the most titanic of changes—such as the human and physical wreckage left in the wake of civil war—but that wreckage itself presumably was not the central purpose of the leaders. It would be idle here to measure the extent and character of social change unless we also examine the intentions of those who make the decisions that were intended to bring about change. Such an examination is necessary if we are to find purpose and meaning, rather than sheer chance or chaos, in the unfolding of events. A definition that demands so much from leadership also requires that we consider the totality of decision-making by leaders at all levels and in all the interstices of the polity. For actions or changes that might seem errant or vagrant in relation to visible leaders may be the planned outcome of decisions by less conspicuous and less "legitimate" leaders far down the line. The test is purpose and intent, drawn from values and goals, of leaders, high and low, resulting in policy decision and real, intended change.

Social change is so pervasive and ubiquitous in the modern world, and often so dramatic and menacing, as to attract intensive scholarly investigation. It has become an intellectual growth industry. Hegel and Marx are not the only celebrated theorists who have dealt with it as a central phenomenon in social analysis and historical fact. In surveying the vast literature on change, one remarks once again on the absence of a clear concept of the role of artistic or intellectual or political or social leadership in the processes of change, on the absence in most works of references to leadership in theory or practice. Often the process of *innovation* is explored but not in a broad framework of the leadership motivations, goals, and processes within which innovation takes on meaning and direction. It is as though change took place mechanically, apart from human volition or participation. What then, in a preliminary way, can be said about the role of policy and decision-making leadership in the process of real social change?

This question can be answered only in the context of the conditions of stability, continuity, persistence, and inertia that grip most of humankind. We of the modern era hear and see so much of what is called dizzying change—the rise and fall of leaders, dynasties, and whole nations, the continuing eruptions and disruptions of technology, massive migrations, the "population explosion," rapid alterations in economic conditions, the flux of artistic, literary, and other fashions—that we tend to underplay the fixity in human affairs. "Social interaction is to be found in social fixity and persistence as well as in social change," Robert Nisbet observes. "That is why, if we are to answer the question of causation in change, we are obliged to deal with, first, *the nature of social persistence* and, then, with *variables, not constants,* when we turn to the matter of what causes the observed change in structure, trait, or idea." Systems, once established, generate countless forces and balances to perpetuate themselves.

Our very assumption of change is culture-bound. "For most of the world's people, who have known only the changelessness of history, such stress on the difficulty of change would not be necessary," according to Robert Heilbroner. "But for ourselves, whose outlook is conditioned by the extraordinary dynamism of our unique historical experience, it is a needed caution. Contrary to our generally accepted belief, change is not the rule but the exception in life." And Leonard Meyer says, at the start of a chapter headed "The Probability of Stasis": "The presumption that social-cultural development is a necessary condition of human existence is not tenable. The history of China up to the nineteenth century, the stasis of ancient Egypt, and the lack of cumulative change in countless other civilizations and cultures make it apparent that stability and conservation, not change, have been the rule in mankind generally. . . ."

What then is all the activity? Much of it is the appearance of multitudinous readjustments as the system absorbs small variations in the basic pattern and maintains its own pace and direction. The anthropologist Alfred R. Radcliffe-Brown noted the changes within structures that did not affect the structural form of society. He made a sharp distinction between *system maintenance,* the kind of readjustment that was essentially an adjustment of the equilibrium of a social structure, and what he called *system change* or "change of type," which he defined as "a change such that when there is sufficient of it, the society passes from one type of social structure to another." The vast proportion of the decisions of decision makers, high and low, is readjustment that maintains the equilibrium of the social structure.

A system can appear dynamic in guarding its own statics. A leader who departs from system or group norms in some decision will suffer undue attention, pressure, sanctions, and perhaps rejection or exclusion. To cite one of innumerable laboratory experiments, F. Merei demonstrated that a child with evident leadership qualities was nevertheless forced to abide by the established play norms of a small kindergarten group. If a change in one part of a system seems to threaten other parts, it is sealed off; at most it is not allowed to change much faster than the others. A host of institutional safeguards, some of them vested with sacrosanct status or mystification, is built around stabilizing decision-making processes. Outsiders and outside ideas are smoothly rejected. One of the most common tendencies in the history of arms development and change has been the resistance of military decision makers to weapons innovations that much later, after being adopted in crisis or catastrophe, took on their own institutional protection.

A number of strategies have been developed to overcome resistance to change: coercive strategies, normative strategies (achieving compliance by invoking values that have been internalized), utilitarian strategies (control over allocation and deprivation of rewards and punishments), empirical-rational strategies (rational justification for change), power-coercive strategies (application of moral, economic, and political resources to achieve change), and reeducative strategies (exerting influence through feeling and thought). Coercive strategies need not detain us here, since we exclude coercion from the definition of leadership; the majority of the other strategies provide for deprivation of group support for the beliefs, attitudes, values, and concepts of self that combine to tie a person to the status quo. A common thread—perhaps the only common thread—running through these diverse strategies is their difficulty. Most seem to be aimed not so much at altering the attitudes and behavior of the ultimate targets of change—citizens in their daily lives—but at the subordinate decision makers in government or business or other collectivities who are supposed to *administer* the change. Even if top policy makers were able to exert control down the line over subordinate policy makers, a huge gap remains between their operating decisions and real change in the behavior of the greater public. "In here" is still sharply different from "out there." All this simply confirms in theory what decision-making leaders find in practice: that breaks and erosions and disturbances in the "line of command" produce attenuation of purpose and of action at the grass roots and that, even when they do not, the target publics may not respond. Decisions are rarely self-implementing. Many of the administrative devices intended to communicate command and direction from the top become means for blunting or distorting the chain of decision.

Grand policy-making and decision-making leadership, in short, can wither at the most crucial phase—that of influence over popular attitudes and behavior. Is there any way out of this dilemma?

The answer to this question ultimately turns on the nature of the goals of decision-making leadership. These, of course, vary enormously. On the most personal and individual level policy makers may seek small changes that affect only themselves. This may be a service from a government bureau, exemption from a regulation, some honor or special recognition from the state. Frustrated by the regular bureaucratic decision-making machinery, they may "walk their papers" through the administrative labyrinth. In realizing their own specific and perhaps narrow goal, in effecting a small change for themselves, they leave the decision-making process itself hardly touched. They have "beaten the system," but the system in the long run beats them, for their very success lowers pressure to improve the machinery—at least on their part and for the short run—hence it may continue to operate poorly for the great number of persons it services. Some individual efforts, however narrowly and self-servingly motivated, may implicate others in a beneficial way, but those benefits will rarely rise above the "satisficing" level.

At the general or collective level, on the other hand, the goal of a leader may be such comprehensive social change that the existing social structure cannot accommodate it. Hence, in the eyes of certain leaders, that structure must be entirely uprooted and a whole new system substituted, probably through revolutionary means. Revolutions do not always succeed, however, and when they do succeed, revolutionary action, in disrupting existing structures and mobilizing new social forces, incidentally arouses new needs and establishes new goals. Real change may take forms very different from the revolutionary goals originally sought. The most violent revolution, no matter how far-reaching its professed desire for reconstructing society, typically falls short of complete real change. The notion of "a *complete* change in the structural form of a society is . . . incoherent," Ernest Nagel says.

Between the extremes of planning discrete individual change and planning comprehensive and drastic change lies *middle-range* planning, responding to shared needs and other motivations and aimed at collective goals that represent the main planning effort of political leadership in most societies. This kind of *planning leadership* seeks genuine social change for collective purposes, though not necessarily at the same pace, or on so wide a front, as that of revolutionary action. The task of this kind of leadership is political and governmental planning for real social change.

The critical problem concerns the implication of planned ends for planning ways and means, the demands that comprehensive real change puts on existing social and political systems (which we will label here "social structures"). We are defining planning here not only as the establishment of definite social and economic goals to meet popular wants, needs, and expectations, but as the considered and deliberate reshaping of means necessary for the realization of comprehensive real change. Lewis Coser, like Radcliffe-Brown, has made a useful distinction between changes *of* systems and changes *in* systems. He refers to a change *of* system "when all major structural relations, its basic institutions, and its prevailing value system have been drastically altered." Changes *in* system take place more slowly and affect smaller sectors of a system. Given enough time, however, changes in system, through mutual stimulation and adjustment, can produce extensive change if not fundamental transformation of system. The accumulated changes in the British political system over the past two centuries have substantially altered the political structure, but these changes (such as extension of the suffrage) appeared at the time to be changes within the system.

Changes *in* system would seem far more system-transforming than changes *of* systems, if only because the latter type of change comes so hard. Yet the extent of change *of* political systems since 1800 has been remarkable. Ted Gurr has found that the incidence of "system-transforming political change" has been high and pervasive both in the Third World and in the European zone of influence. The median duration of historical Latin and Afro-Asian polities and of European nations during that period was about the same: twelve years. The incidence of abrupt political change had increased markedly from the nineteenth to the twentieth centuries, Gurr found. "Of the 150 historical polities in the sample which were established before 1900," according to Gurr, "half survived for 20 years; but for the 117 historical polities established after 1900, the 'half-life' was only nine years." The extent to which these transformations took place as a result of collective and comprehensive planning by leaders varied widely, but these findings underline the vulnerability and impermanence of social structures that may appear to be well established.

Planning for structural change, whether of the system or in the system, is the ultimate moral test of decision-making leadership inspired by certain goals and values and intent on achieving real social change; it is also the leader's most potent *weapon*. It is a test in that planning calls for thinking and acting along a wide battlefront of complex forces, institutions, and contingencies; if the planners really "mean it," they must plan for the reshaping of means as required by the ends to which they are committed. It is a weapon in that a well-conceived plan, along with available planning technology, supplies leaders with an estimate of the human, material, and intellectual resources necessary to draw up and drive through a plan for substantial social change. Planning is designed to anticipate and to counter the myriad factors that impair the line of decision and action between the policy-making of planning leaders and real change in the daily lives of great numbers of people.

Still, the best laid plans of mice and men go aft agley. Why? In part because the plans are poorly drawn or badly executed. In part because plans encounter "chance" developments no mortal could possibly predict. And in large part because most planners focus on technical and administrative factors, minimizing the psychological and the structural forces. At a certain point following the Bolshevik revolution, Alex Inkeles observes, the "political and economic development of the revolution had now run far ahead of the more narrowly 'social.' In the haste of revolutionary experiment, no systematic attention had been given to the congruence of the newly established institutional forms with the motivational systems, the patterns of expectation and habitual behavior, of the population. Furthermore, as the new institutions began to function they produced social consequences neither planned nor anticipated by the regime." The problem was exacerbated for the Bolsheviks, Inkeles adds, by a Marxist ideology that predisposed leaders to assume that basic changes in the pattern of human relations, which they viewed only as part of the "dependent" superstructure of society, must automatically follow from changes in the political and economic system.

Planners elsewhere have encountered similar problems of human motivation. A British Labour government, in nationalizing the coal mines, misconceived the reactions of the very miners whose lot it was mainly designed to ameliorate. For many miners the change seemed to amount to the substitution of one bureaucracy for another. Indian population planners miscalculated the principal motive of Indian villagers, which was to raise children who would be available for labor and for family income—a motive that overrode the effect of propaganda in favor of limited families for the sake of other goals. American political planners in 1787 shaped a superb political structure for pitting faction against faction and thus breaking the force of faction in government, but they underestimated the popular and egalitarian forces that would threaten such balanced and stabilized government from outside. In the light of planning mishaps, it is not surprising that planners often seek to isolate their new structures from unpredictable psychological forces operating through a political system. Thus the leaders of the Tennessee Valley Authority established their own planning mechanism "in the field" and resented efforts by Washington decision makers to intervene. Autonomy was a two-bladed sword, however; it protected sectoral planners against bureaucratic aggression in the central government, but it did so at the expense of contracting the scope and power of leadership planning.

To note that effective planning must consider motives and values is to return to our central emphasis on a general theory of political leadership. Planning leaders, more than other leaders, must respond not simply to popular attitudes and beliefs but to the fundamental wants and needs, aspirations and expectations, values and goals of their existing and potential followers. Planning leadership must estimate not only initial responses from the public but the extent to which successful plans will arouse new wants and needs and aims in the second and succeeding "rounds" of action. Planning leaders must perceive that consensus in planning would be deceptive and dangerous, that *advocacy and conflict* must be built into the planning process in response to pluralistic sets of values. Planning leaders must recognize *purpose*—indeed, planning is nonexistent without goals—and recognize that different purposes will inform the planning process. Plans must recognize means or modal values too, especially in procedures providing for expression of majority attitudes without threatening rights of privacy and self-expression. And planning must recognize the many faces of power; ultimately the authority and credibility of planning leadership will depend less on formal position than on the capacity to recognize basic needs, to mobilize masses of persons holding sets of values and seeking general goals, to utilize conflict and the adversary process without succumbing to it, and to bring about real social change either through existing social structures or by altering them.

"Increasingly," Karl Mannheim wrote shortly before his death, "it is recognized that real planning consists in coordination of institutions, education, valuations and psychology. Only one who can see the important ramifications of each single step can act with the responsibility required by the complexity of the modern age." It is the leaders who preeminently must see in this way. But to *see* alone is insufficient; they must *act* too, and of all the tasks proposed by Mannheim and in this book, the changing of institutions is the most difficult. For institutions are encapsulated within social structures that are themselves responses to earlier needs, values, and goals. In seeking to change social structures in order to realize new values and purposes, leaders go far beyond the politicians who merely cater to surface attitudes. To elevate the goals of humankind, to achieve high moral purpose, to realize major intended change, leaders must thrust themselves into the most intractable processes and structures of history and ultimately master them.

16 --

TOWARD A GENERAL THEORY

Late in the winter of 1968, in response to my request that I interview President Johnson about his memories of Franklin Roosevelt, I received an invitation from the President and Mrs. Johnson to an informal family dinner. Making my way across Lafayette Park toward the White House a few days later, I was struck by the appearance of the imposing old building. The place now seemed dark, cold, diminished. Was it my imagination that it appeared to be under siege?

After close inspection of my credentials by guards at the gate, I was escorted into the mansion, taken in the little elevator to the second floor, and ushered into the family living room. In addition to the President and First Lady only a staff member and an ex-governor of Texas and their wives were present. The conversation was guarded and subdued, with everyone avoiding the subject that lay over the White House like a shroud, until one of the President's daughters flounced into the room in a housecoat, sat in her father's lap, then beside him on the floor, and suddenly started talking about Vietnam. Most of her friends and those of her husband were military men, she said, but she understood the feelings of young people who hated the war. She then presented those feelings, as simply and eloquently as I could remember having heard. The President listened, saying nothing.

During a lull I turned to my host and inquired about a meeting between Johnson and Franklin Roosevelt during the war years. The President dealt briefly and uninterestedly with the query, then began to reminisce about his boyhood years in Texas. He talked until dinner—about his parents, his mother's expectations of him, his father's discipline, his brothers and sisters. He talked during dinner, hardly bothering to eat, about his life and troubles growing up. He talked on and on after dinner, while his wife and friends listened with apparent interest to stories they must have heard many times. Finally, exhausted by the flow of words and overcome with a feeling of guilt over the presidential time I was monopolizing, I managed to rise to my feet and murmur my apologies. The President accompanied me halfway to the elevator, then announced and conducted a tour of the family living quarters, including a look at the presidential bedside piled with memoranda and reports.

Next day I happened to be standing outside the office of a presidential aide when the tall figure loomed again. The President led me to a tiny room off the oval office, where he produced a bound collection of the messages exchanged between Washington and Moscow during the Arab-Israeli hostilities of 1967. A large finger pointed to an ominous message from the Kremlin that virtually threatened war, then pointed proudly to the President's de-escalating response. Once again I made my escape. I left with no illusions as to the role I was expected to serve. Deserted by large portions of the constituencies that had given him his landslide victory of 1964, the President was seeking a final victory before the bar of history. Even this academic might have a vote to cast in the ultimate verdict. Every juror would count.

I reflected on the vagaries of power and leadership. Here was a President who had his hand on all the alleged levers of influence. The party he headed enjoyed majorities in both houses of Congress. After five years in the White House he had the constitutional right to run for four more. He had billions to budget and spend. He commanded a huge staff, talent, presidential attention, television screens, planes, cars. Only his finger could pull the nuclear trigger. Yet the man was almost impotent. He could not run again, for reasons of both bodily and political health. His congressional majorities were no longer dependable. He could not win in Southeast Asia with conventional war tactics and dared not employ nuclear strategy. Looking at him, especially from afar, people saw a man of vast power; looking out at the people, he felt lonely and powerless.

At night, I learned later, Johnson dreamed a recurring dream of impotence. He dreamed that he was lying in bed in the Red Room of the White House, paralyzed from the neck down, listening to his aides in the next room quarreling over the division of power. He could hear them but could not speak to them. Waking from his sleep after such a dream, the President would make his way through the empty corridors of the White House to the place where Woodrow Wilson's portrait hung. It soothed him to touch Wilson's portrait, for Wilson had been paralyzed and now was dead but Johnson was still alive and active. In the morning the fears would return—of paralysis of the body, paralysis of his presidency. And soon he would quit.

He would do so with a wrenching sense of damaged self-esteem. He felt that he had been, above all, a leader—of the poor, the blacks, the sick, the alienated. Perhaps he did not comprehend that the people he had led—as a result in part of the impact of his leadership—had created their own fresh leadership, which was now in some ways outrunning his. In sensing black wants, recognizing black needs, arousing black aspirations, legitimating black expectations, meeting black demands, Johnson had not only helped focus the effort and reinvigorate the organization of the old Negro groups like the NAACP. He had mobilized in the South and in the ghettos a new breed of militant black who was brassy, noisy, assertive, and moving far beyond the reach of that long presidential arm. Leadership had begat leadership and hardly recognized its offspring. Vietnam was more than perplexing to him, it was sickening. He had followed the responsible, the moderate strategy of Truman, Eisenhower, and Kennedy; he had learned from earlier wars that if you clung to your course and persevered, victory would come. But victory would not come in Vietnam; and now young men were resisting the draft, religious leaders were demonstrating at the White House gates, college students were so hostile that there was hardly a campus he could visit. And a brash young rival, Bobby Kennedy, and others waited offstage. Political leadership had simply passed out of the President's hands, and with it had gone political power. Followers had become leaders.

On the face of it, there was nothing unusual about Johnson's loss of power. Winston Churchill, Chiang Kai-shek, Nikita Khrushchev, Sukarno, and later Richard Nixon, de Gaulle, Indira Gandhi all suddenly slid—or were pushed—down the "greasy pole." But Johnson's plight was especially poignant and significant. On the one hand, in meeting to some degree the economic needs of blacks and others he had unwittingly aroused higher needs and values that he could neither comprehend fully nor gratify. On the other hand, in *not* meeting the demands of the anti-Vietnam militants he had generated new dimensions and intensities of conflict, thereby producing a whirlwind he could not control. His "abdication" a few weeks after I visited him was simple recognition of that fact.

If leaders who seemed to wield power often lacked it, followers who seemed impotent might unexpectedly exert influence. The Maoist demand that leaders struggle against self-advancement and privilege has been traced to the Taoist insistence that the sage must make himself lower than the people in order not to offend them. Few would seem more powerless and passive than slaves, but in the American antebellum South slaves were not mere recipients of power; the masters' paternalism aroused expectations other than those intended. "By developing a sense of moral worth and by asserting rights,"

Eugene Genovese concluded, "the slaves transformed their acquiescence in paternalism into a rejection of slavery itself."

We need not look so far back to glimpse the interlocking of leadership and followership, of power-wielding and power-receiving. The programs of private television are mainly financed by advertisers who make a massive effort to gauge the wants and needs of buyers, whose buying habits in turn are closely influenced by the messages on the tube. Politicians organizing revolutionary movements or planning to run for office take soundings in the villages or through opinion polls to see what the people want—but what the people want is mightily affected by the promises and preachings of politicians. Next to me as I write hangs a cartoon published in London in 1830 showing a frock-coated John Bull reading *The Times,* with a chain running from the *Times* masthead to his nose. The cartoon is captioned, "The man wot is easily led by the nose." But the editors of the newspaper, ever needful of readers, faced the threat of competing papers.

So again the paradox: Who are the leaders and who the led? Who is leading whom to where? For what purposes? With what results?

Leadership and Collective Purpose

To answer such questions we must proceed to the formidable task of seeing the role of leadership, as we have defined it, in historical causation. Let us take stock of the definition. Leadership is the reciprocal process of mobilizing, by persons with certain motives and values, various economic, political, and other resources, in a context of competition and conflict, in order to realize goals independently or mutually held by both leaders and followers. The nature of those goals is crucial. They could be separate but related; that is, two persons may exchange goods or services or other things in order to realize independent objectives. Thus Dutchmen (colonists in America) give beads to Indians in exchange for real estate, and French legislators trade votes in the Assembly on unrelated pieces of legislation. This is *transactional* leadership. The object in these cases is not a joint effort for persons with common aims acting for the collective interests of followers but a bargain to aid the individual interests of persons or groups going their separate ways.

Leaders can also shape and alter and elevate the motives and values and goals of followers through the vital *teaching* role of leadership. This is *transforming* leadership. The premise of this leadership is that, whatever the separate interests persons might hold, they are presently or potentially united in the pursuit of "higher" goals, the realization of which is tested by the achievement of significant change that represents the collective or pooled interests of leaders and followers.

Both forms of leadership can contribute to human purpose. If the *transactions* between leaders and followers result in realizing the individual goals of each, followers may satisfy certain wants, such as food or drink, in order to realize goals higher in the hierarchy of values, such as aesthetic needs. The chief monitors of transactional leadership are *modal values,* that is, values of means—honesty, responsibility, fairness, the honoring of commitments—without which transactional leadership could not work. Transformational leadership is more concerned with *end-values,* such as liberty, justice, equality. Transforming leaders "raise" their followers up through levels of morality, though insufficient attention to means can corrupt the ends.

Thus both kinds of leadership have moral implications. How can we define that morality? Summoned before the "bar of history," Adolf Hitler would argue that he spoke the true values of the German people, summoned them to a higher destiny, evoked the noblest sacrifice from them. The most crass, favor-swapping politician can point to the followers he helps or satisfies. Three criteria must be used to evaluate these claims. Both Hitler and the politician would have to be tested by modal values of honor and integrity—by the extent to which they advanced or thwarted fundamental standards of good conduct in humankind. They would have to be judged by the end-values of equality and justice. Finally, in a context of free communication and open criticism and evaluation, they would be judged in the balance sheet of history by their impact on the well-being of the persons whose lives they touched.

Because our emphasis is on collective purpose and change we stress the factors that unite leaders and followers as well as those that differentiate them. This distinction may be elusive to an observer who sees leaders leading followers but does not understand that leaders may modify their leadership in recognition of followers' preferences, or in order to anticipate followers' responses, or in order to harmonize the actions of both leader and follower with their common motives, values, and goals. Leaders and followers are engaged in a common enterprise; they are dependent on each other, their fortunes rise and fall together, they share the results of planned change together.

So defined, leadership—especially transforming leadership—is far more pervasive, widespread—indeed, common—than we generally recognize; it is also much more bounded, limited, and uncommon. *Common,* because acts of leadership occur not simply in presidential mansions and parliamentary assemblies but far more widely and powerfully in the day-to-day pursuit of collective goals through the mutual tapping of leaders' and followers' motive bases and in the achievement of intended change. It is an affair of parents, teachers, and peers as well as of preachers and politicians. *Uncommon,* because many acts heralded or bemoaned as instances of leadership—acts of oratory, manipulation, sheer self-advancement, brute coercion—are not such. Much of what commonly passes as leadership—conspicuous position-taking without followers or follow-through, posturing on various public stages, manipulation without general purpose, authoritarianism—is no more leadership than the behavior of small boys marching in front of a parade, who continue to strut along Main Street after the procession has turned down a side street toward the fairgrounds. Also, many apparent leaders will be only partial leaders. They may tap followers' motives or power bases; or they may take value-laden positions; or they may sharpen conflict; or they may operate at the final policy-making or implementation stages; or they may do some or all of these. The test of their leadership function is their contribution to change, measured by purpose drawn from collective motives and values.

Even if we exclude acts of nonleadership from our analysis, we must include an enormous variety and range of actions that in themselves constitute complete leadership acts—that is, the process and achievement of intended change—or that consciously make up significant links in the total process of achieving intended change. Not only the building of a new political party aimed at mobilizing tribal groups for the sake of social change, or a campaign against illiteracy, or a community development program, but a mother consciously acting in such a way that her small son's sensitivity to others will be improved, a taxi driver deliberately setting an example of considerate driving, a Red Guard leader making sure that food and drink are equally shared on a work project in the country—all these are parts of the totality of the leadership process. Leadership begins earlier, operates more widely, takes more forms, pervades more sectors of society, and lasts longer in the lives of most persons than has been generally recognized.

In the billions of acts that comprise the leadership process, or parts of it, a pattern can be discerned that makes possible generalizations about leadership, generalizations that in turn would underlie an effective general theory and serve as a guide to the successful practice of leadership. The answer will not be found in conventional wisdom and the hoary adages about leadership—that leaders are born and not made, or made and not born, that they must be trained, or cannot be trained, that they have to exhibit certain physical qualities like imposing height or unusual endurance or commanding voice, or mental qualities like memory for faces and names or unusual intelligence, or magical qualities. We have seen that leadership, as we have defined it, is a function of complex biological, social, cognitive, and affective processes, that it is closely influenced by the structures of opportunity and closure around it, that it may emerge at different stages in different peoples' lives, that it manifests itself in a variety of processes and arenas—in short, we have seen that the usual generalizations are without foundation (or at best apply only to highly specific subcultures). Can we *generalize* about leadership across polities and over time?

We of this generation can so generalize because of the concepts and data now available from those working in the field of moral development. These scholars have concluded that all persons in all cultures are not mere internalizers of specific values and beliefs and opinions that surround them, nor are they simply passive inheritors of parental ideology or reflectors of situationist ethics. These scholars believe that they "have rather firmly established a culturally universal invariant sequence of stages of moral judgment." This is a bold claim, and it awaits further systematic examination and verification. But one need not accept the claims of absolute invariance and irreversibility and universality to see the vital implications of these findings for a general theory of leadership. The emphasis on the developmental nature of human values and behavior is in accord with the work of Adler, Maslow, Piaget (especially the development of intelligence), Erikson, Rokeach, Kohlberg, and others who see the powerful role of growth and change in humankind.

The hierarchy of needs, the structure of values, the stages of moral development have been presented in earlier pages; we now need to analyze these developmental processes more closely and to see their implications for a general theory of leadership. The main question concerns the role of leaders in helping to move followers up through the levels of need and the stages of moral development. Just as leadership processes convert Maslow's "static" model into a dynamic one of ever-evolving deprivations and satisfactions, so these processes convert the structure of moral behavior into a structure of change and development. The central process involved, as we have emphasized, is one of *conflict* and *choice*. As children move through the stages of moral development they are caught between "natural" wants and needs and the necessity of obeying rules in order to avoid punishment; between idiosyncratic impulses and desires and the incentive to conform in order to receive awards, the return of favors, and the approval of others; between the desire to explore deviant kinds of behavior and the avoidance of unacceptable behavior because of guilt instigated by censure from legitimate authorities; between conflicting sets of personal values; and ultimately between condemnation by others and self-condemnation. Such conflicts are the main "motor" or condition for "upward" movement. They are worked out and movement is spurred not simply by reasoning about higher modes of thinking but by day-to-day exposure to concrete choices that reflect moral conflicts. Often the conflicts can be resolved not in the circumstances of a particular moral stage but in the reorganized perspective of the next stage above, in role-taking, or in the resort to leadership.

Dominating and personifying these alternatives are grass-roots leaders: parents, teachers, peers, priests, gang leaders, party officials, village elders. The sharper the conflict, the larger the role of leaders will tend to be. Children move through stages of moral development only in part as a result of the teachings of parents, preachers, teachers, and others; they are influenced by what the teachers *are* as well as by what they teach. Children may internalize the values of parents, school, and culture—the social matrix—and move to "higher" stages only as they see the linkages between those values and the widening social environment through which they proceed. Their growth is a continuous process of stages of response. Assuming new roles as they deal with new social pressures, children gain perspectives on themselves by imaginatively taking the view of their own actions held by their partners in role relationships. Role-taking demands an appreciation of others' situations and perspectives, empathy for others' needs and goals. Children, parents, teachers, and others variously and transiently become leaders and followers. Those with stronger and clearer motivations and purposes as "legitimate" teachers have the greater influence. In most cultures those teachers are parents.

We find two powerful leadership forces operating. Leaders and followers are locked into relationships that are closely influenced by particular local, parochial, regional, and cultural forces. In the progression of both leaders and followers through stages of needs, values, and morality, leaders find a broadening and deepening base from which they can reach out to widening social collectivities to establish and embrace "higher" values and principles. This broader, more principled kind of leadership—the kind of leadership that tends to be visible, formal, and legitimate—is usually expressed at the higher stages of moral development. Gandhi and Wilson and Tito and Franklin Roosevelt are prime examples in this century.

The process is not a simple or smooth one, nor is it predetermined. Leaders constantly come up against the intense, highly structured "situationist ethics" of particular groups and localities. What may seem to some principled leaders to be parochialism, inertia, perversity, or apathy may be, in fact, highly charged leader-follower relationships with their own tradition, structure, logic, and morality. Only with time, determination, conviction, and skill—and with the indispensable element of conflict—can followers be drawn out of these narrower collectivities and into "higher" purpose and principle validated by the most enduring criteria of justice and humanity and forged in an open and continuing conflict of values.

These higher principles and purposes comprise values that earlier we termed *modal values* and *end-values*. Typical modal values, such as honesty, responsibility, courage, and simple fairness, in the sequence of moral stages take on increasingly the qualities of more broadly and socially defined morality. At preconventional levels modal values are defined by rewards and penalties. Avoidance of punishment is a value in its own right. Fairness is valued, but only on the basis of reciprocity or mutual back-scratching, not on the higher level of fidelity or justice, at which level modal values become end-values. At conventional levels valued behavior is viewed as that which helps or pleases others and meets their approval. Good intentions—"meaning well"—are esteemed. Conformity to dominant opinion, to established rules, authority, and the demands of the social order is necessary and desirable within limits. The postconventional levels put greater emphasis on adhering to standards that conform to the agreed-on principles of the whole society and to the fundamental constitutional arrangements of its political system. Law is emphasized on the condition that law can be changed. *At the highest level* modal values are rights defined on the basis of a conscience that expresses the broadest, most comprehensive, and universal principles; hence they merge with the end-values of justice, equity, and human rights.

The fact that modal values involve individual *conduct* more than change, *style* more than *substantive results* (real change), does not diminish their significance. Fairness, civility, tolerance, openness, and respect for the dignity of others undergird and legitimate the elaborate system of due process that characterizes decent relations among human beings and informs constitutional democracies at their best. However, while these qualities have important implications for political and governmental systems, they are largely shaped in environments such as school and family that are not *overtly* political. While they are affected by conflicts and dilemmas within and between persons, moreover, they are not especially controversial. Indeed, investigators have found considerable similarity as well as differences in the manner in which persons in different cultures adhere to modal values. The dynamics of such values are dynamics chiefly of *personal* leadership.

Personal leadership becomes heavily politicized—becomes *political* leadership—as it relates to purposes issuing from and addressed to end-values such as security and order, liberty and equality, freedom and justice. If differences over modal values in personal conduct persist in some respects among persons and localities, among regions and cultures, one might expect that conflict on a truly grand scale dominates people's attachment to end-values. Within nations liberals and conservatives, leftists and rightists, socialists and Tories, struggle with one another over the essential purposes and goals of government; violent differences over explicit substantive ends feed the ideological battles that in turn embitter relations among nations. Often the conflict pits not value against value but *definitions* of values against one another. Both Roosevelt and Hitler made the symbol "freedom" the great object for which their nations fought during World War II; it was conflict over the *substance* of freedom that radically separated the two men and their ideologies.

Just as investigators have identified a "culturally universal" sequence of stages of moral judgment about personal conduct, there is considerable evidence of a large degree of commonality across cultures of consensus and conflict over end-values held by both leaders and followers. In a massive investigation of popular attitudes in more than a dozen countries, Hadley Cantril found a strong pattern across cultures of human concerns and aspirations; he found also common sequences of intensifying responses to deprivation that proceeded in developmental steps from acquiescence in miserable conditions (as in India) to an awakening of potentialities, to a grasping of means of realizing goals, and finally to self-reliance and self-assertion leading to action. A more common aspect of diverse cultures was the evident desire of large numbers of people for the freedom to exercise choice, to assert their own identity, to achieve personal respect and dignity. Milton Rokeach found a pattern in the development of values that responded to human need and correlated with Maslow's and Erikson's developmental sequences in a method of investigation that, he concluded, could be employed cross-culturally. The four-nation study concluded that relationships among leaders' values in different countries were highly comparable and that leaders differed more among themselves within the same community than they did from country to country.

These are preliminary findings; much more data must be collected and analyzed. If the findings hold up, however, a profoundly important hope may begin to be justified—that principles can be identified that to a marked degree transcend national and cultural borders, that these principles constitute both modal values and end-values, that political leaders and followers can mutually shape their purposes on the sustaining basis of these values, and that—because of the sequential and developmental forces at work—political leadership will elevate followership as followers sustain their leaders. This is not to minimize the force of conflict that divides persons over values. Yet much depends on the *alignment* of conflict—that is, on whether conflict isolates people in their nations, regions, or localities or whether conflict *cuts through* these entities and arrays human beings by purpose and principle rather than by geography or ethnocentricity. Conflict over purpose and principle compels political leadership to divide forcibly and responsibly over the most significant values in terms of potential for change—that is, over end-values that emerge directly out of the wants and needs, aspirations and expectations, of humankind.

Dare we speculate about these end-values and ultimate purposes? Only to a degree. Probably the worldwide debate over principle and purpose will focus even more directly, over the decades ahead, on the mutually competing and supporting values, the paradoxical trade-offs, of *liberty* and *equality*. Conflict over freedom of political and literary and artistic expression will probably sharpen within the Communist nations and the developing nations, just as it will continue to be a central political issue in the Western democracies. The claim of unfulfilled egalitarian promises will be asserted in "bourgeois" democracies and will continue and perhaps escalate in Communist societies that make equality their central tenet. How these values will be defined; how they will relate to one another in hierarchies of principles or priorities of purposes; how "subvalues"—liberty as privacy, for example, or equality as opportunity—will support or contradict related subvalues; how idiosyncratic talent and freedom of innovation will be protected under the doctrine of liberty of expression—these and many other questions can only be roughly answered. Fortunately, analysts can proceed on the basis of reason and logic as well as empirical data collection and analysis. One of the remarkable intellectual developments of recent years has been the rise in the quality and quantity of the investigation across national borders of peoples' needs, aspirations, and values at the same time that scholars have been reanalyzing concepts of equality in terms of the principles of "justice."

The debate over liberty and equality and related values, in the contemporary worldwide arena of discourse, is a debate not over the Good and the Bad but over concepts and priorities. Some—John Rawls, for example, and this author—would grant priority to *liberty* over any other social good, assuming it be equal liberty. (The only value, I believe, that might be elevated over liberty is security, but security would decline in desirability if it guaranteed only survival and not the values such as liberty that make life worth living.) Others would make *equality* the archstone of their hierarchy of values. We can see the implications for leadership in the process of choice and priority-making. Leaders who appeal to followers with simplistic slogans such as Equality, Progress, Liberty, Justice, Order are neither offering a guide to followers on where leaders really stand nor mobilizing followers to seek explicit objectives; they are seeking the widest possible consensus on the basis of the thinnest—or least thoughtful—consensus. They are not acting as leaders as we have defined leadership. Leaders who act under conditions of conflict within hierarchies of needs and values, however, must act under the necessity of choosing between certain *kinds* of liberties, equalities, and other end-values. They both exploit purpose and are guided by it.

Out of the varying motives of persons, out of the combat and competition between groups and between persons, out of the making of countless choices and the sharpening and steeling of purpose, arise the elevating forces of leadership and the achievement of intended change.

Leadership as Causation

To define leadership in terms of motivation, value, and purpose is to glimpse its central role in the processes of historical causation. That definition may help us to right certain imbalances and to sort out certain misplaced priorities that have plagued the search for causal explanations.

The definition allows us to make crucial distinctions between historical events without purpose and human acts that have purpose, between intended and unintended acts of persons, and between acts of *power* and acts of *leadership*. By starting with a totally inclusive concept of historical causation, we can successively narrow the scope of our definition of causal influence so as to identify and isolate the role of leadership. Each succeeding concept will serve as a subset of the preceding, more generalized concept.

1. *Historical causation* is the totality of forces, human and nonhuman, affecting the behavior of persons directly or indirectly. It includes *all* causal interrelations: the effects on human beings of physical environment, biological evolution, climate, natural disasters, insect and animal life, epidemics, and famine, as well as persons' decisions and actions. Historical causation includes the phenomena of both the spread of a disease like typhus and the reactions of human beings to it. Personal and impersonal forces together produce combinations of intended and unintended change.

2. *Social causation* embraces those processes and effects of historical causation that are produced by the decisions and nondecisions, the intended and unintended efforts of *persons*. Wars, migrations, technological inventions, decisions to run for office, and planning to counter the effects of anticipated catastrophe such as drought are examples of social causation, as is a decision *not* to act. Decisions of human beings do not always produce intended effects or planned change, of course; they may even produce intended effects that in turn produce unintended and undesired effects. Thus rulers take purposeful action (e.g., to win a battle) that helps set off chains of intended and unintended interactions (e.g., to lose the war and succumb to revolution). Social causation is that part of history that is caused by human action.

3. *Power* consists of those processes and effects of social causation that are produced by the intended, purposeful efforts of persons with power resources (power base)—the efforts stemming from the motives of the power wielder *regardless of whether or not the motives of power wielders are congruent with those of power recipients*. The actual extent of the exercise of power is measured by the extent that intended results are realized. Power is *intended* social causation.

4. *Political power* comprises those processes and effects of power that relate to the "authoritative allocation of values"—that are considered legitimate uses of power under existing conventions, traditions, understandings, or constitutional processes. This legitimacy is usually linked to formal authority and the established government, but it need not be. Revolutionary leaders too are seen as legitimate by their supporters; theirs is a different kind of legitimacy, one stemming from their perceived recognition and satisfaction of popular wants, needs, and aspirations, either in a context—unless and until the new revolutionary regime cracks down—or in a relatively free and spontaneous expression of opinion.

5. *Political leadership* is those processes and effects of political power in which a number of actors, varying in their composition and roles from situation to situation, spurred by aspirations, goals, and other motivations, appeal to and respond to the needs and other motives of would-be followers with acts for reciprocal betterment or, in the case of transforming leaders, the achievement of real change in the direction of "higher" values. Political leadership is tested by the extent of real and intended change achieved by leaders' interactions with followers through the use of their power bases. Political leadership is *broadly intended "real change."* It is *collectively purposeful causation.*

These definitions are designed to enlarge the usefulness of the concept of political leadership in the analysis of collectively motivated political acts. They will also aid us in dealing with the age-old analytic "dichotomy" between behavioral and structural factors. The dichotomy takes many forms, but typically the structuralist approach emphasizes systemic, institutional, "functional" aggregations, such as class alignments, legal systems, educational bureaucracies, political organizations (parties, interest groups, electoral machinery), and other "external" forces. The behavioralist focuses on "internal" influences, such as motivations, perceptions, and understanding and knowledge as reflected in behavior, some of which can be measured by polls, surveys, and election results. This dichotomy, which has been simplistically but usefully described as the difference between pressures "on" persons and pressures "in" persons, this dialectical interplay between the socially derived "me" and a biologically based "I" (as Robert Friedrichs has termed it in a different context) can be resolved if we see the leader as empowered or constrained not by some cloudy or ephemeral entity such as class support or party opposition but by an estimate (accurate or not) of the political resources (votes, money) the leader can find in that entity, *as modified by leaders' and supporters' motivations.* The "structure" (a union, corporation, regional party, politicized church) is judged by its potential for constraining or blocking possible alternative courses by the leader.

The leader is dealing with persons—potential followers—who have their own power bases, however small, and their own hierarchies of motives.

In this process *both* behavioral and structural variables are converted into two sets: (1) the *motive bases*—hierarchies of want, need, aspiration, etc.—that can be mobilized by competing leaders and (2) the *actual power* that can be mustered through these motive bases—power that rests in economic, social, and other resources centered in institutions, technology, coalitions, constitutions, rules, traditions, ballots, money, information, intelligence, genius, skills. The leader eternally must deal with the double and interrelated question: what *can* these persons do for (or against) me in a pursuit of collective goals and what *will* these persons do for (or against) me? Hence leaders must assess collective motivation—the hierarchies of motivations in both leaders and followers—as studiously as they analyze the power bases of potential followers and rival leaders. Thus the power of a big corporation, which may appear to the casual observer (or to the ideologue) to wield massive political power because of its financial, skill, and organizational resources, must be tested by the acts and decisions of corporation leaders relevant to their own motives, to the motives of others that relate to available choices, to the power bases of specific persons inside and outside the corporation as they relate to those choices, to the convertibility of the corporation's economic power into political power (requiring recomputation of leaders' and followers' power bases), and to the degree to which preferred choices can be acted on. The largest restriction on the corporate leader in this regard may not be the difficulty of mobilizing the power bases of leaders and followers within the corporation but that of identifying and aligning commonalities between leader and follower hierarchies of motivations, especially in the transfer of those motivations to the *political* sphere.

All this can also be said about the "powerful" labor union. The relations between the New Deal and the United Mine Workers, between Franklin Roosevelt and mine workers chief John L. Lewis, illustrate the fascinating connections and degree of convertibility of respective sets of motive and power bases. In 1933 the New Deal administration proposed and Congress passed the National Recovery Act with the prime goal of putting people back to work, not of aiding and abetting unionism. Lewis, exploiting Roosevelt's popularity in the pits, plastered posters throughout the mining areas proclaiming, PRESIDENT ROOSEVELT WANTS YOU TO JOIN THE UNION. Roosevelt belatedly supported the Wagner Act in 1935, which also boosted labor's power to organize, especially in industrial unions. In 1936 Lewis and his newly formed Committee for Industrial Organization supported Roosevelt's re-election bid. Lewis walked into Roosevelt's office with a check for $250,000 and a photographer to put the donation on record. Roosevelt, aware of the possible impact of this transaction on some of his own followers' motivations, genially waved away the check. "No, John," he said. "Just keep it, and I'll call on you if and when any small need arises." In the following weeks campaign requests quietly extracted almost half a million dollars from Lewis' treasury. During Roosevelt's second term, however, Lewis broke with him over labor, political, and foreign policy. The union leader called the President weak, tricky, and lacking in conviction. In 1940 Lewis announced that he would resign as CIO president if Roosevelt won a third term. It was a test of Roosevelt's and of Lewis' political power in coal mining areas, and Roosevelt won. Later, during the war years, mine workers "voted" for Lewis when the President appealed to miners not to strike or to return to work if they had struck. Exploiting the motive bases and power bases of their followers to the hilt, the rival leaders failed or succeeded in varying degrees in transferring their support into a common battleground. Certainly neither the New Deal nor the mine workers union was "monolithic."

Another advantage of this view of leadership is that it enables us to sort out, at least in a preliminary way, the multiple forces at work and to shun explanations that turn on such a multitude of causes and so many different kinds of causes as to end up as nonexplanations. At the same time it avoids further search for *the* single cause. Certain causal factors can be converted into common, comparable, and potentially measurable and quantifiable scales. It is impossible to compare the political effect on persons of their unemployment, affiliation with a noneconomic interest group, general interest in public affairs, Oedipal tendencies, ethnic attitude, and late socialization experiences unless factors can be converted into common elements of power and motivational bases that permit identification and possible measurement. A single factor that might superficially be seen as crucial—membership in the "working class," for example, or possession of a million pounds—can be discounted until converted into power and motive bases relevant to leaders' choices and decisions.

Possessing a million pounds *may* be a crucial fact, but only if it is congruent with other power-base elements in a situation relevant to leadership. Possessing the right to hire and fire *may* be a crucial fact, but only in relation to employees' desires to keep their jobs, the interest of others in getting jobs, attitudes within the corporation and within the community as to the proper exercise of the right to hire and fire, union rules and attitudes, local or national newspaper reporters looking for "issues," legal rights and the ease and difficulty of invoking them, and—always—employees' and bosses' hierarchies of motivations relevant to the issue. In numerous situations "naked power" *is* exercised. An oligarchic corporation boss in a company-controlled town with no competing centers of power such as a newspaper or an independent church, with considerable control over company funds for paternalistic uses in meeting employees' wants and needs, with a plant "security" unit and perhaps a vigilante group among the citizenry, and with the capacity to appeal to the "nigger issue" in helping influence employee solidarity—such an oligarch is a power wielder, not a leader. A jail keeper may control the persons in his cells, but his would be acts of coercive power, not of leadership, for leadership always assumes some commonality of hierarchies of motives between leader and follower, and some degree of choice in a context of conflict or competition.

To perceive the working of leadership in social causation as motivational and volitional rather than simply as "economic" or "ideological" or "institutional" is to perceive not a lineal sequence of stimulus-response "sets" or "stages," nor even a network of sequential and cross-cutting forces, but a rich and pulsating *stream* of leadership-followership forces flowing through the whole social process. The living tissue is unimaginably complex. Much that is causal must be inferred, as apparent "leaders" react to anticipated motivations of apparent "followers" before initial action is taken and as followers react in advance to expected leadership actions. The actual interplay and conflict of countless and infinitely varied motive and power bases produce a density of relationships beyond full comprehension, although the hierarchical and developmental organization of motives, values, and purposes imparts some order and direction.

To handle this complexity analytically we may follow heuristically a "clean sheet" device of observing the leadership-followership process at a starting point where a Moses or a Joseph Smith has led his flock to a new life in a promised land, or a politician has mobilized a new popular movement, or a bureaucrat has set up a new agency in a city remote from the capital. The clean sheet is hypothetical, of course, since the leaders will carry with them socializing experiences and sets of motives and values acquired in previous habitats, and a rough leadership structure will have developed before or during the "exodus." But the new home will at least provide a more isolated context, one with fewer influences to track.

The signal aspect of the new situation will be the creation of new leadership as "exodus" leaders infuse their flock with heightened motivations, purpose, and missionary spirit. Followers become proselytizers who act on their own raised consciousness and arouse motivations in others. "Whatever the source of the leader's ideas," David McClelland says, "he cannot inspire his people unless he expresses vivid goals which in some sense they want. Of course, the more closely he meets their needs, the less 'persuasive' he has to be; but in no case does it make sense to speak as if his role is to force submission. Rather it is to strengthen and uplift, to make people feel that they are the origins, not the pawns, of the socio-political system." Such proselytizing will not assume consensus. Establishment of goals will be surer and firmer in a context of conflict, which at first may lie between the exodus group and hostile forces (in both its former and new environments) and later will develop within the exodus group.

As the new movement or organization expands and stabilizes, its structure takes on institutional and bureaucratic form, generating new motives and behaviors associated with careerism, professional recognition, organizational status, financial betterment. In the process original purpose may become blurred. The influence of the movement or organization on leaders and followers and on the wider public will be largely determined, however, by the thrust and appeal of the purpose established by the leadership at all levels within it. To maintain discipline, militance, and purpose and to counter the diffusion of energy, leadership will use psychological and institutional resources. The movement or organization will be separated from former environments insofar as possible, as in the exodus; hierarchical relationships will be developed; communication will be centralized; discipline will be maintained. Military forces, with their physical and geographical autonomy, separate identification achieved through distinctive uniforms and other symbols, and internal reward and discipline systems, are extreme examples of the attempted coordination of purpose, organization, and operation, in part through isolation. Such leadership structures are designed for maximum causal effect.

If concert of purpose provides direction for leadership-followership, then power bases of leaders and followers are social energies forceful enough to bring about real change. In the competition among leaders and in the mobilization of followers by leaders, the parties will seek to exploit their power bases so as to realize particular goals. The nature of these power resources will vary enormously: economic, ideological, military, political (personal popularity, access to voters, control of communication), skills, traditions, rules, friendship networks, access to decision-making centers, ability to appeal to wider publics through the press, certain persons' desire for publicity and others' fear of it. Would-be leaders ascertain the distribution of power resources *relevant to the purpose at hand.* Crucial in this process is accurate judgment of the capacity and willingness of various power holders using specific resources for specific purposes. *Purpose and power are commingled.* And in this process motive is, or should be, central. Power bases of followers that leaders hope to mobilize on behalf of their own purposes may be used by followers *against* the leaders. There is a time dimension too: leaders and followers may hoard power resources in order to fight different battles at later times.

To catalogue the power bases in one polity or even in one political organization of some size would be impossible, both because of the variety of the types and locations of resources and because those resources would need to be inventoried not for their abstract or reputed significance but for their causal influence *in specific situations relevant to the motivational and power bases of other specific actors involved.* To propose this concept, we must again insist, is not to assume a radically pluralistic distribution of power; it is not to contend that power bases and motive hierarchies are so varied, intransitive, and noncomparable that concentrated power is a myth. It is only to repeat that such power must be *analyzed* rather than assumed, viewed in its specific motivational contexts rather than hypothesized in advance. In some cases it will be found that countervailing motivation tendencies on the part of would-be followers are so weak, the motivations of power holders are so strong and congruent, their power resources are so ample and assured and relevant to the goal at hand, and the followers have so few avenues of appeal to public opinion, escape, defiance, sabotage, counterorganization (as in unions), legal assistance, judicial intervention, support from guerrilla or revolutionary groups, resort to tradition, "rights," constitutional guarantees—that in the light of the absence or presence of such factors a "power elite" may exist. If certain "leaders" held such power, however, the situation would be coercive and hence outside the bounds of our definition of leadership.

Paradoxically, it is the exercise of *leadership* rather than that of "naked power" that can have the most comprehensive and lasting causal influence as measured by real change. This is so because leaders engaging with the motivations of followers and of other leaders at all levels of movements and organizations are able to exploit the massed social energies of all the persons consciously involved in a joint effort. There is nothing so power-full, nothing so effective, nothing so causal as common purpose if that purpose informs all levels of a political system. Leadership *mobilizes,* naked power *coerces.* To be sure, leaders, unlike power holders, will have to adjust their purposes in advance to the motive bases of followers, but this still leaves a wide field for leadership, innovation, and action. Moreover, unity of purpose and congruence of motivation foster causal influence far down the line. Nothing can substitute for common purpose, focused by competition and combat, and aided by *time.*

Leadership and Change

The ultimate causal impact of leadership can be understood only in the flow of specific leadership-followership interactions emerging from the clash and congruence of hierarchies of motivations. In some theories of historical causation the movement of causal forces is pictured as a series of discrete acts or thrusts or stages, giving the impression that history resembles—to return to our earlier metaphor—a group of croquet players swinging mallets that knock croquet balls through a succession of wickets. But even if we hypothesize that causal influences are set in motion when leaders take the initiative in linking themselves with followers to fulfill mutual purposes, we cannot identify discrete steps in the process. We always find a stream of evolving interrelationships in which leaders are continuously evoking motivational responses from followers and modifying their behavior as they meet responsiveness or resistance, in a ceaseless process of flow and counterflow.

Consider a common Third World experience of this century. A left-wing, anti-colonial party, with strong and purposeful leadership, responding to mass wants and needs and aspirations as articulated by party leaders, throws out the old colonial regime and sets up a nationalist and socialist one. Nationalizing industry is a top priority. The new regime puts a bill through parliament to take over the mines, sets up a new coal board, dispossesses the colonial owners, establishes new management, and assumes "control" of the enterprise. Mobilization of mass needs and aspirations has thus created a power base for the new regime in a series of "steps." Responses, however, vary. Native managers and foremen, who had actually run the mines under the colonial masters, object to the new dispensation and perhaps turn to the courts, which have retained a measure of independence. Technical problems require consultation with the former colonial owners or managers. Adjoining "new nations" cut official imports in order to develop their own resources. Mine development requires more capital from domestic and foreign sources, and not every source may be motivated to cooperate. Life in the mines, set in the molds of routine, rules, tradition, long-established expectations and personal relationships, managerial rights and obligations, technical and technological imperatives, hardly changes. Production fails to increase and perhaps falters.

Little change has in fact been accomplished. But the process does not end there. Conflict over the situation is engendered among national leaders, new managers, management and employees, party and revolutionary organizations, national and local government officials, the employed and the jobless. Out of these conflicts new purposes are fashioned, new goals set, new procedures and institutions established. But the extent of real change in the working lives of the miners, in the rules they live under, in the distribution of power around them, in their lives at home, *must be investigated, not assumed.*

Processes such as these can be treated with some sophistication by the "field theoretical approach," which rejects the "genetic" conception of causality in favor of emphasis on the cause and effect of closely related events; "the field at the present moment is seen as a product of the field in the immediate neighborhood at a time just past." Attention is concentrated on measuring behavior at points close to succeeding and dependent behavior. The difficulty is that long-term psychological and social forces are embedded in the motive bases, and often in the power bases, of the actors in the field. The field theory encourages attention to movement among multilateral sequences of causal action; for example, voters may be affected by a number of simultaneous events, such as a depression, the advent of a new regime, and guerrilla action; voters may simultaneously be exposed to different channels of communication; voters may react in terms of affiliations held at the same time, such as union membership, party allegiance, religious choice, sex, and age; resulting acts may include voting in a certain way or not voting, turning to direct action or deciding on individual betterment as against taking part in a collective effort. Even these multilateral factors, however, will have a certain mechanical quality—will be like mallets hitting croquet balls—unless attention is paid to the interplay among both sequential and simultaneous forces, and that interplay cannot but draw into account the effects of needs, expectations, goals, and other motivational factors.

So causal influences as finally concretized in visible, tangible social change will be a product of the motivational interactions as they in turn mobilize leaders' and followers' power bases. This is a continuous, seamless set of processes as policy is made in party congresses, interest-group headquarters, legislative chambers, and executive offices and as policy is executed at the final action end of collective effort. Politicians will be tapping power bases—mobilizing interest groups, calling in credits, appealing to traditions and rules that help their cause, evoking party platforms or the farewell addresses of founding fathers as legitimations, calling on talent and expertise relevant to the policy issue. At the "final stage" of implementation the tapping of power bases will continue, but here the resources to be used may be more tangible: funds from treasuries and budget officers, personnel taken from other agencies or freshly recruited authority to issue rules and regulations, bureaucratic facilities such as communication and transportation. These entities do not sit around ready for the taking; bureaucrats have their own motivations and power bases.

We speak of final stages, but of course there are no final stages. The combinations of means and instrumental ends constantly open up new possibilities as others are foreclosed. Real change means the creation of new conditions that will generate their own changes in motivations, new goals, and continuing change.

Leadership analysis, with its emphasis on motivation, improves explanation by enabling the analyst to identify *purpose* among all the eddies and crosscurrents of the many forces at work—purpose that can be measured in itself to some degree and compared to intended results (real change). Consider a simple example: (a) Jones dies from arsenic; (b) he drank it in a glass of port; (c) Smith put the arsenic into the glass of port; (d) Smith wanted to kill Jones; (e) Smith wanted to do so because he would benefit from Jones' will. All these are causal, but as a factor of significance in both common sense and theory, Smith's *motivation* for wanting to kill Jones towers over causal relations a, b, and c. The motive is the paramount object of the police investigation; it is the factor that gives us food for thought as to whether we can prevent such murders; the other factors are matters of mere personal or technical interest (Jones likes port; arsenic kills). We might even conclude that arsenic should be made harder to procure and yet recognize that the dominant cause lies in human motivation, in this case greed. It is persons' *intent,* along with skill in exploiting power bases, that signalizes the most *human* factor in all the economic, social, military, and other "deterministic" forces that are said to make history. It is purpose that puts man into history.

Restoring the role of purposeful leadership to theories of history moves us from the world of abstraction to the world of day-to-day relationships, to what Peter Berger and Thomas Luckmann have called the "reality of everyday life" in discussing the "social construction of reality," the commonsense knowledge that people share with other people. It enables us, in the fashion of modern historians, to look at history from the bottom up and not merely at the "great men" and from the top down. It enables us to see history, in Isaiah Berlin's words, as "the sum of the actual experience of actual men and women *in their relation to one another* and to an actual, three-dimensional, empirically experienced, physical environment."

Traditional conceptions of leadership tend to be so dominated by images of presidents and prime ministers speaking to the masses from on high that we may forget that the vast preponderance of personal influence is exerted quietly and subtly in everyday relationships. The Indian shopkeeper who reads the newspaper, the uncle who travels, the local party zealot returned from a gathering of the faithful, the newspaper editor who transmits messages from far-off leaders (or suppresses them or garbles them), the village scrivener, the itinerant preacher, the bartender, the elevator operator, the most articulate of the women washing clothes in the nearby stream—these are the people who, with their more or less independent sets of hopes and goals, pass on to the "masses" the messages from on high—but at a price. Local, unofficial, unrecognized leaders of opinion, themselves motivated by needs such as self-esteem and esteem from others, they understand what motivates the people they see face to face, day after day, to a degree and with an accuracy that the leaders outside cannot match.

The role of the "great man" need not be diminished in this analytical process; he is only de-mythicized and de-mystified. That role is all the more legitimate and powerful if top leaders help make their followers into leaders. Only by standing on *their* shoulders can true greatness in leadership be achieved.

17

POLITICAL LEADERSHIP
AS PRACTICAL INFLUENCE

For a time the manuscript circulated quietly from hand to hand in Florence and seemed to excite no special interest. Then in 1532, five years after the author's death, it was published in Rome and the floodgates of outrage and reprobation opened. Moralists were appalled. Here was a tract that frankly put expediency over morality. It advised leaders to use craft and deceit, and worse, to use naked power and exert their will. Advice to princes had always been clothed in moralistic and theological dressing. Surely this new tract—flagrantly titled *The Prince*—must be a product of the devil. After some years it was condemned by the Church of Rome and placed on the Index. Today, more than half a millennium after the author's birth, *The Prince* still stands as the most famous—and infamous—of books of practical advice to leaders on how to win and wield power.

It seemed odd to some that such a tract should have come from the pen of Niccolò Machiavelli, for the Florentine had not seemed to benefit from his own practical wisdom. He had been one of those bright young operational types who swim rapidly to the surface during times of ferment and change. At twenty-nine he was granted an influential post in the recently established republican government of Florence. For more than a decade he served as a high-ranking diplomat, foreign policy adviser, domestic administrator, and military planner and organizer. In 1512 his newly formed militia broke ranks in the face of Spanish and German troops, the Florentine republic fell, and the Medicis returned. Machiavelli was ousted from office, arrested for treason, tortured on the rack, freed, exiled. He was then forty-three.

On his small ancestral farm a day's journey from Florence he supervised the work in the fields, and in the evening "I take off my peasant clothes, dirty

444

and spotted with mud, and don royal and festive garments,'' he reportedly said. "Thus worthily dressed, I step among the men of antiquity and, feeling no weariness, forgetting all my troubles, and neither fearing poverty nor dreading death, I live wholly among them." He evidently worked first on what would become his *Discourses,* a defense of democratic republicanism, a call for leadership, and a plea for military strength. Soon, however, he fell to work on *The Prince.* In twenty-six short chapters he laid out his mordant maxims. It is necessary for a prince who wishes to maintain himself to learn how not to be good. A prince must imitate the fox and the lion, for the lion cannot protect himself from traps and the fox cannot defend himself from wolves. One must therefore be a fox to recognize traps and a lion to frighten wolves. Those that wish to be only lions do not understand this. Therefore a prudent ruler ought not to keep faith when by so doing it would be against his interest or when the reasons which made him bind himself no longer exist. If men were all good, this precept would not be a good one; but as they are bad, and would not observe their faith with you, so you are not bound to keep faith with them. If one has to choose between inflicting severe injuries and inflicting light ones, he ought to inflict severe injuries. Princes ought to murder their opponents rather than take their property, since those who have been robbed, but not those who are dead, can plan revenge.

So shocking were these teachings that many doubted the Florentine meant them seriously. It was not clear whether he was analyzing how rulers *should* behave or how they *did* behave. What was he really trying to do? Was he a realist who described facts as he saw them, clinically? Was he a political scientist looking behind forms for general patterns of political behavior, studying evil as impersonally as a scientist analyzes epidemics? Was he a nationalist defending the methods patriots must use to unify Italy? Was he simply a man of his time, reflecting the morality of his day and his place? Or was he, on the contrary, a brilliant harbinger of realpolitik, the cornerstone of the modern state? Was he a summoner of progressive forces against the dying feudal aristocracy? Or—the most provocative political speculation of all—was he a superb political satirist intending *The Prince* to be a taunt and a challenge to the Medicis and a tocsin to the people of Florence, but so camouflaged as to avoid exposing the author to the rack?

None of the theories explain the strangest fact of all: Machiavelli's practical advice was not at all practical. Even amid the murderous rivalries of the Italian boot, princes behaving so wickedly and selfishly would win only short-run victories. Nor could interstate relations long be conducted on many of his principles. The Florentine had dramatized a profound half-truth—that men are essentially selfish, self-regarding, self-protective. But selfishness could take many forms, some of them benign. Machiavelli had projected some notions that were only locally applicable at best into an ideology of ruthlessness and selfishness.

More than mere selfishness; at the core of Machiavellianism lay the most pernicious and inhuman concept of all: the treatment of other persons, other leaders, as *things*. With Machiavelli, Richard Christie and Florence Geis wrote, it seemed "that success in getting others to do what one wishes them to do would be enhanced by viewing them as objects to be manipulated rather than as individuals with whom one has empathy. The greater the emotional involvement with others, the greater the likelihood of identifying with their point of view." But it is precisely that—identifying with the point of view of followers —that makes the transforming leader, in the long run, far more effective than manipulators.

Teaching Leadership or Manipulation?

Machiavelli has had countless imitators. The vogue of the "how to" manual still thrives today: How to gain power. How to influence people. How to win office. How to take over an organization. How to organize a people's movement. Most of these guides are promoted as being wholly practical—buy and peruse them and you really will win that election to the legislature, run your party organization more efficiently, raise yourself in the boss's eyes, and—can we doubt it?—rise in Russia from head of your *oblast* committee to leadership in the Central Committee of a union republic. Such manuals may be useful for gaining and exercising leadership in highly predictable and structured situations such as commanding a submarine, winning office in British working-class areas, advising a South American junta, gaining influence in a Middle Eastern sheikdom. They may also be useful in situations of personal interaction dominated by set needs, aspirations, values, and ethics. But they can be impractical and misleading for training leaders in wider and more complex collectivities. Situation-specific, they are directed so intensively at concrete circumstances that they may positively handicap persons who wish to advance beyond those circumstances.

The main failure of these manuals is more pernicious. While few of them today emulate the master in offering Machiavellian advice on how to coerce, control, or deceive other persons, many do seek to train persons to manage and manipulate other persons rather than to *lead* them. The technique is usually that of the marketplace manipulation: to play on low-order wants and needs and to create hopes and aspirations where none existed before, through the use of saturation promotion and propaganda. Worse, the manuals treat persons as *things*, as tools to be used or objects to be stormed like a castle. At best they search for the lowest common denominator of motives among persons and within persons and exploit those motives for the benefit of the power wielder, not the target. At best they teach transactional—not transforming—leadership.

Probably the most widely read primer on personal influence in modern times is Dale Carnegie's *How to Win Friends and Influence People.* The copy in front of me is from the "113th printing"; the jacket proclaims "over 9,533,500 copies" sold (and this was in 1964). The book has been translated into twenty-eight languages, and I have no doubt that it was a best seller in all of them. It has indeed an international flavor, for incidents were collected from the lives of great men—and some women—from throughout the Western world. Carnegie also conducted workshops where thousands heard lectures and stories on ways of exercising practical influence.

It would be easy to dismiss Carnegie as merely the most noted in a long line of teachers of salesmen's tricks: how to get the foot in the door, how to disarm the customer, how to beat out the competition. In fact the book had higher pretensions than this, and it largely realized them. The essential tactic was not to outwit or deceive target persons but to persuade them to do something that the influencer wanted them to do. The salesperson—or vote seeker—could do this by remembering first names, exhibiting deference, flattering targets in such a way as not to arouse their suspicions—above all, by talking about them and their interests or beliefs. Carnegie quoted James Harvey Robinson: "The little word 'my' is the most important one in human affairs, and properly to reckon with it is the beginning of wisdom." He quoted Harry A. Overstreet: "Action springs out of what we fundamentally desire . . . and the best piece of advice which can be given to would-be persuaders, whether in business, in the home, in the school, in politics, is: first, arouse in the other person an eager want." He quoted William James: "The deepest principle in human nature is the craving to be appreciated."

Could anything be more human and benign, as well as practical, than this? It was almost as though Dale Carnegie had been brought up on Maslow (or Maslow on Carnegie). First his salesman meets the customers' basic need by selling them something to eat or drink or keep warm with or provide security in the home. Then he meets a "higher" need by massaging their self-esteem through the simple device of admiring their children or home or dog. Carnegie tells story after story of difficult targets—mean-spirited landlords, angry customers, hard-fisted moneylenders, crabby bureaucrats—disabled by graduates of the Dale Carnegie course in human relations, master persuaders who find ways to identify and placate egos. "First, arouse in the other person an eager want"—then satisfy it.

When one puts these techniques of persuasion into a wider context, however, and considers their implications for the political arena, doubts set in. How significant and how durable is the stroking that led to the sale of, say, a washing machine? If the salesman was relying on his sweet-talking rather than the quality of the product, will the washer wear out before the memories of the sweet talk wear thin? In satisfying "lower" needs was the salesman arousing "higher" ones? And could he do anything about *those?* Applying the question to the world of politics, we find the familiar problem of the candidate who offers personality and charisma instead of substance. The transaction is a fleeting one—and only a transaction. The voter receives recognition, a smile, the remembrance of his name; the candidate receives a vote. The transaction may supplement a more enduring exchange over public policy, or it may supplant it.

Still, it is evident that the technique of influencing people under certain circumstances and in certain ways can be taught. Can *leadership* be taught?

The most practical way to begin to answer this question is also the most theoretical: to define both education and leadership in the broadest and most fundamental way and to understand the vital relationship of the one to the other. We have conceived of leadership in these pages as the tapping of existing and potential motive and power bases of followers by leaders, for the purpose of achieving intended change. We conceive of education in essentially the same terms. So viewed, education is not merely the shaping of values, the imparting of "facts" or the teaching of skills, indispensable though these are; it is the total teaching and learning process operating in homes, schools, gangs, temples, churches, garages, streets, armies, corporations, bars, and unions, conducted by both teachers and learners, engaging with the total environment, and involving influence over persons' *selves* and their opportunities and destinies, not simply their minds. Persons are taught by shared experiences and interacting motivations within identifiable physical, psychological, and sociopolitical environments. Ultimately education and leadership shade into each other to become almost inseparable, but only when both are defined as the reciprocal raising of levels of motivation rather than indoctrination or coercion.

The search for wholeness—that is, for this kind of *full, sharing, feeling* relationship—between "teachers" and "students," between leaders and followers, must be more than merely a personal or self-regarding quest. Fully sharing leaders perceive their roles as shaping the future to the advantage of groups with which they identify, an advantage they define in terms of the broadest possible goals and the highest possible levels of morality. Leaders are taskmasters and goal setters, but they and their followers share a particular space and time, a particular set of motivations and values. If they are to be effective in helping to mobilize and elevate their constituencies, leaders must be whole persons, persons with fully functioning capacities for thinking and feeling. The problem for them as educators, as leaders, is not to promote narrow, egocentric self-actualization but to extend awareness of human needs and the means of gratifying them, to improve the larger social situation for which educators or leaders have responsibility and over which they have power. Is it too much to believe that it is "the grand goal of all leadership—to help create or maintain the social harbors for these personal islands?" Gandhi almost perfectly exemplified this.

What does all this mean for the teaching of leadership as opposed to manipulation? "Teachers"—in whatever guise—treat students neither coercively nor instrumentally but as joint seekers of truth and of mutual actualization. They help students define moral values not by imposing their own moralities on them but by positing situations that pose hard moral choices and then encouraging conflict and debate. They seek to help students rise to higher stages of moral reasoning and hence to higher levels of principled judgment. Throughout, teachers provide a social and intellectual environment in which students can *learn*. None of this favors "permissiveness" or laissez-faire in the home or classroom; rather, students are helped to respect the fairness, equity, honesty, responsibility, and justice for which they speak. Nor is it to deprecate the importance of teaching and learning specific skills. The possession of a "marketable" skill is not only useful for transaction, it is vital to a person's self-esteem, a source of self-actualization, and a means of livelihood. It is a power base that, along with other power resources such as the right to vote, to speak, and to protest, equips persons to throw their weight into the economic and political arena—and massively so, if they can combine with others. One cannot strike if one has no job to strike, just as one cannot dispute the teacher if one has no teacher.

Clearly this kind of education is not restricted to school; it starts in the home and exists potentially in every major sector and institution of society. Much debate has been heard on the question of whether home or school or workplace or pub has the most influence educationally on the growing child and developing adult. The answer will vary from place to place and era to era. A study of Israeli children suggested that "in general, kibbutz-reared adults appear to fill positions of moral responsibility equivalent to those of nonkibbutz reared persons. The kibbutz data, then, seem to suggest that an intense relationship to parents may not be necessary for the level of moral conduct and judgment expected in western societies." The United States pioneered in the development of free public schools; curiously for a people supposedly devoted to free enterprise, it made a heavy commitment (through the individual states) to a socialistic educational system, with the school buildings owned by the government and the teachers and administrators hired, paid, and fired by it. Perhaps because the schools seemed to hold such colossal potential influence over the minds and manners of the young, however, schools were devitalized as a means of overt value clarification and dissemination. Hence in many respects leadership may have been nurtured and shaped more in the home, in churches, on the athletic field, and on the job than in the schools.

We are discussing the teaching of leadership in circumstances where democratic procedures and values are not frills, fads, or facades but are essential to moral education. We cannot infer, however, that leadership of this sort abounds in democracies and languishes in dictatorships. One will find enclaves of educational indoctrination and manipulation in democracies and enclaves of dissent and conflict in dictatorships. Democratic societies may tend toward a special vice of their own: teachers who, lacking strong ideological commitment, are unprepared to overcome irksome intellectual and pedagogical problems of dealing with critical questions of moral values and hence may convert moral issues like fairness and considerateness into matters of administrative conformity or teacher convenience, such as rules about "neatness" or "quiet." These small virtues have their own place, but they do not substitute for moral judgments and values.

In considering the implications of moral education of leadership for the public and civic life, we are talking about much more than teaching technique in home, classroom, and other schools. We are talking about the broader subject of the *political education* of all citizens in democratic environments. The intimate relationship of moral and political education has been a central concern of philosophers from Plato to Dewey. Such concern has long seemed "theoretical" and "impractical" to practitioners trying to get through one lesson and survive one unruly class. But failures of political education have immensely "practical" results. Democratic and constitutional processes are heavily dependent on the extent to which modal values and end-values are debated in all sectors of society and made clear and salient and present throughout the citizenry. Richard Nixon would never have been closely threatened with impeachment if that long dormant procedure had not been brought squarely before the public as a result of intense discussion and debate—and above all by a concern with justice and morality—throughout the land. The investigation of Watergate and its attendant immoralities was a profound educational experience for the American public—and for publics elsewhere who saw that the democratic process of critical review could work without destroying the fabric of the society.

Long before the crisis of the Weimar Republic and the rise of Hitler, Max Weber noted in Wilhelm II's Germany an ominous lack of political education stemming from a number of factors: Bismarck's cultivation of a "completely nonpolitical kind of hero worship''; the discouragement of autonomous power among persons and groups and political parties; bureaucratic power lacking in grasp of broader public values; a weak and negative Parliament; manipulative executive leadership. Without the symbiosis of strong leadership and an active citizenry, Weber saw a crisis of *both* leadership and citizenship. The task, he concluded, was (in the words of Lawrence A. Scaff) ''to teach citizens to evaluate speech and action intelligently, and at the same time create a system that would make political leadership *possible*. Germany had done neither; consequently it lived with the worst imaginable combination: irresponsible demagoguery from above, emotional pressures from below, but without parliament, responsible leadership, or democracy—that is, without the only institutions capable of ending this condition and channeling political conflict in a constructive direction.'' England provided a sharp contrast, with its robust party system, active opposition, constitutionally sovereign parliament, and unique organizations like the Workers Educational Association, which taught tens of thousands of British workers not only vocations and skills but philosophy, history, sociology, politics, and other avenues to considered moral judgments and to a broader conception of citizenship.

The Armament of Leadership

The call for leadership is one of the keynotes of our time. Commencement platforms echo with appeals for high-minded public service—to young graduates, most of whom are worried about finding a job. The summons to leadership seems most urgent in eras (such as the present) that follow periods of ''great leadership.'' In few nations is the appeal made more often than in the United States—ironically, in view of its political system designed to fragment and hobble leadership. The head of a large bank, otherwise moderate in his views, proclaims that the fate of the Republic depends on whether Americans can recover a profound belief in the democratic process and that in order to do that ''we must have leaders.'' A journalist remarks that if Martian spacemen were to land and demand, ''Take me to your leader,'' Earthlings would be at a loss to direct them.

   Two themes often characterize these summonses. One is that we do not really know just what leadership is. Why are the ''leaders'' not leading? asks a university president and expert on organization. ''One reason, I fear, is that many of us don't have the faintest concept of what leadership is all about. Leading does not mean managing.'' The ''nature of leadership in our society is very imperfectly understood,'' John Gardner observes, ''and many of the public statements about it are utter nonsense.'' The other theme is the need for moral, uplifting, transcending leadership, a leadership of large ideas, broad direction, strong commitment. Leaders must offer moral leadership, Gardner says. "They can express the values that hold the society together. Most important, they can conceive and articulate goals that lift people out of their petty preoccupations, carry them above the conflicts that tear a society apart, and unite them in the pursuit of objectives worthy of their best efforts." Presumably one can lead others *downward*—down the primrose path or down the road to barbarism. Yet leadership has—quite rightly, in my view—the connotation of leading people upward, to some higher values or purpose or form of self-fulfillment.

Certainly few have been recorded as opposing leadership, least of all moral leadership. Yet one observes a curious ambivalence when the press examines a particular leader, especially one who has gained some reputation for holding elevated and principled views. We are assured that the leader is not dogmatic, doctrinaire, or ideological, but is really a practical person. The leader even makes bookcases in the basement, rebuilds cars in the garage, or grows herbs in the garden. It is a matter of getting things done and making things work. The leader is in short a "pragmatist," sometimes even—the ultimate tribute—a *hard-nosed* pragmatist.

The calls for leadership, the uncertainties as to just what it is, the ambivalent attitudes toward moral leadership and principled leaders—all these, I think, reflect deep ambiguity and confusion over the place of leadership in political life—at least in the democracies where leaders are expected to lead the people while the people are supposed to lead the leaders. The confusion will continue as long as we fail to distinguish leadership from brute power, leadership from propaganda, leadership from manipulation, leadership from pandering, leadership from coercion. It has been contended in these pages that by clarifying the definition of leadership we can enormously broaden its utility as a tool for causal analysis and its potential for realizing modal values and end-values. It remains to put some of the characteristics of leadership so defined in summary form and to note some possible implications, practical and otherwise.

Leadership is collective. "One-man leadership" is a contradiction in terms. Leaders, in responding to their own motives, appeal to the motive bases of potential followers. As followers respond, a symbiotic relationship develops that binds leader and follower together into a social and political collectivity. Cadres form; hierarchies evolve; structure hardens. Responding to leaders' initiatives, followers address their hopes and demands to politicians who use their power resources relevant to those hopes and demands to satisfy them. Leaders seek to mobilize existing social collectivities, whether class, nationalistic, ethnic, or other.

A critical consideration is the form or structure that collective leader-follower relationships assume. The emotional connection between heroic leaders and the vast numbers of followers who relate to them in mass meetings or on television is a form of collective leadership. But the absence of "layers" of grass-roots activists, cadres, subleaders (save for the small circle of aides and advisers surrounding the charismatic leader) makes for imbalances between leaders' and followers' powers, a certain instability and precariousness in their relationships, and potential derangements of political and constitutional processes. Hence the vital necessity of political movements that metamorphose into the kind of political party that over the years helps leaders to satisfy peoples' valid needs. "The labor parties in Northwestern Europe," according to Gunnar Myrdal, "are . . . the final outcome of much more than a century of great and influential people's movements, the temperance movement, the nonconformist religious movements, the cooperative movement, the trade union movement, the adult education movement and the movement for general suffrage." The absence in the United States of a major party firmly based in a social movement has impaired the linkage between Americans and their leaders, especially the President.

Leadership is dissensual. The dynamo of political action, meaningful conflict, produces engaged leaders, who in turn generate more conflict among the people. Conflict relevant to popular aspirations is also the key democratizer of leadership. It causes leaders to expand the field of combat, to reach out for more followers, to search for allies. It organizes motives, sharpens popular demands, broadens and strengthens values. Much depends on the organization of conflict—whether, for example, the axis of conflict is shifted from national boundaries, or from regional boundaries within nations, to class or interest group or doctrinal cleavages *within* nations or regions.

Dissensus and conflict run up against the ethic of "unity" in many democracies. Political leaders call for harmony and cooperation, though they practice the opposite as they compete for office. In particular, party politics is supposed to "stop at the water's edge." Except perhaps in time of war, such calls for national unity can be a danger sign in a democracy. Vietnam for the Americans, Suez for the British, Pearl Harbor for the Japanese, demonstrated that party politics—that is, conflictive politics—should not stop short of *any* major concern of people. It would probably be better for most organizations, including corporations, unions, and university faculties, for dissensus to be built into their structures. A two-party or two-faction system could keep alive a kind of "loyal opposition" to the establishment, a goad to complacent doctrine, a steady drumfire of criticism. The scope and nature of this kind of conflict—which must not be allowed to override other kinds—would need to be spelled out in some type of charter.

The paramount question facing all the peoples of the world is the *global* organization and management of conflict—how to shift the axis of conflict so that needs and aspirations could be appealed to and aggregated on a worldwide basis, so that right-wing as well as socialistic and other left-wing parties could be organized on a world scale, and so that rival leaders of global parties and movements could build links among like-minded people across national boundaries. Conflict unifies people just as it divides them. The only long-run hope for world peace is to realign the foundations of political combat and consensus so that conflicts are managed peacefully within nations rather than by force between nations. This was the noble vision of the pre-World War I European socialists. It remains a utopian hope, given the political fragmentation of the globe.

Leadership is causative. True leadership is not merely symbolic or ceremonial, nor are "great men" simply the medium or mechanism through which social forces operate. The interaction of leaders and followers is not merely transactional or a process of exchange. The result of the interactive process is a change in leaders' and followers' motives and goals that produces a causal effect on social relations and political institutions. That effect ranges from the small and hardly noticed to the creative and historic. The small changes are more numerous, of course, and collectively and cumulatively they bring about the "gradual change" that permanently alters the course of history. The role of the leader may be differentiated between the event-full and event-making, in Sidney Hook's term, or between the Mosaic (calculating, bureaucratic) and the Alexandrian (heroic, revolutionary) in James Reichley's. Hook's event-making man is our transforming leader, provided that the event makers are moral leaders—that they are both responding to and elevating the wants and aspirations and values of those affected by the events.

The most lasting tangible act of leadership is the creation of an institution—a nation, a social movement, a political party, a bureaucracy—that continues to exert moral leadership and foster needed social change long after the creative leaders are gone. An institution, it is said, is but the lengthened shadow of a man, but it takes many men and women to establish lasting institutions. The establishment of a new system of government embracing a structure of divided and fragmented powers by the framers of 1787—and by their supporters and adversaries in the various states and by the political theorists who inspired them—was perhaps the most creative and durable act of political planning in modern history. It was ironic that such brilliant leadership would found a system that so hobbled leadership; yet it was a system that could meet, albeit partially and with all deliberate slowness, the moral challenge of slavery in the 1860s and that of black rights a century later.

The most lasting and pervasive leadership of all is intangible and noninstitutional. It is the leadership of influence fostered by ideas embodied in social or religious or artistic movements, in books, in great seminal documents, in the memory of great lives greatly lived.

Leadership is morally purposeful. All leadership is goal-oriented. The failure to set goals is a sign of faltering leadership. Successful leadership points in a direction; it is also the vehicle of continuing and achieving purpose. Where leadership is necessary, Philip Selznick writes, "the problem is always *to choose key values and to create a social structure that embodies them.*" Purpose may be singular, such as the protection and enhancement of individual liberty, or it may be multiple, in which case it will be expressed in a set of priorities. Both leaders and followers are drawn into the shaping of purpose. "Our dilemma, then, is not an absence of leaders," Benjamin Barber observes, "but a paucity of values that might sustain leaders; not a failure of leadership but a failure of followership, a failure of popular will from which leadership might draw strength. . . ." But the transforming leader taps the needs and raises the aspirations and helps shape the values—and hence mobilizes the potential—of followers.

Transforming leadership is elevating. It is moral but not moralistic. Leaders engage with followers, but from higher levels of morality; in the enmeshing of goals and values both leaders and followers are raised to more principled levels of judgment. Leaders most effectively "connect with" followers from a level of morality only one stage higher than that of the followers, but moral leaders who act at much higher levels—Gandhi, for example—relate to followers at all levels either heroically or through the founding of mass movements that provide linkages between persons at various levels of morality and sharply increase the moral impact of the transforming leader. Much of this kind of elevating leadership asks sacrifices *from* followers rather than merely promising them goods.

The most dramatic test in modern democracies of the power of leaders to elevate followers and of followers to sustain leaders was the civil rights struggle in the United States. Myrdal recognized presciently that this was a moral struggle, a struggle for the soul of America. There were those who pandered to the base instincts of persons—the very negation of leadership—but many more who appealed to the spirit of a "moral commitment of the American nation to high ideals," Myrdal said years later. "In spite of all the conspicuous and systematic gross failures of compliance, America of all countries I knew had come to have the most explicitly formulated system of general ideals in reference to human interrelations, shared, on one level of valuations, by all its citizens." Shared by all its citizens—that was the crux of the struggle. The battle was won at lunch counters, on highways, in classrooms, in front of courthouses by followers who had become leaders. On the other side of the globe, the pacific and egalitarian values taught by Mohandas Gandhi were proving to be an elevating force in an even harsher struggle for social justice.

On the other side of the world stands, too, the leadership heritage of Mao. For many years Westerners comfortably assumed that the choice of democratic leadership models lay between the British parliamentary system, with its emphasis on majority rule, cabinet (collective) leadership, and loyal opposition, and the American "presidential" system, with its provisions for presidential leadership, checks and balances, minority rights, and shifting majority and minority coalitions in legislatures and in elections. A kind of constitutional sweepstakes took place as partisans of either of the two forms watched anxiously to see which model the new nations of Africa or Asia would adopt. As it turned out, many of the developing nations that bothered to adopt either of the models created oligarchic structures behind the democratic forms. Most of their rulers were not leaders but power wielders (including a few despots); hence they taught us little about principled leadership except its vulnerability and disposability.

Mao's alternative looms as a far greater practical and moral challenge to the West, especially in its attraction for new nations and for dissident Communists in Eastern Europe and perhaps even in Russia. That model is not one of the alternation of leadership projected into power by parties vying for election victories but of a leadership *that both renews and challenges its own institutions* by mobilizing the masses against their own bureaucracies in party and government. It is Jefferson's notion of the tree of liberty being watered by revolution every twenty years or so, transported to another culture. Like the commanders of a guerrilla army, Mao and his associates alternated between spurring the masses on to act, to seize power, and to extend democracy, and restraining the grass-roots activists and putting limits on mass action. They led a fluid, shifting coalition of leaders closely linked to followers, and they acted as brokers between the conflicting interests of the vast, multi-faceted constituencies that they had mobilized. To some it seemed that Mao and his associates were swinging back and forth like a pendulum, from left to right, from anarchy to order, from democracy to dictatorship. On closer analysis it appears that Mao's actions were dictated by his ideology, that his complicated, zig-zag course can be explained by his determination to chart an ideological and strategic course that at the same time incorporated *both* poles of the contradiction between centralism and diffusion of power.

His strategy was based solidly in Mao Tse-tung Thought with its theory of conflict—the "unity of opposites"—in every contradiction, its Leninist discipline and organization balanced by mass spontaneity and participation. The new constitution of the Communist party, adopted in 1969, called for "both centralism and democracy, both discipline and freedom, both unity of will and personal ease of mind and liveliness." To a large extent Mao failed to reshape the institutional means in order to achieve his ultimate aims. The People's Communes were repudiated, the tripartite revolutionary committees were awkward and undemocratic, and the reformed party was unable to eradicate bureaucratization and revisionism. The erosion of personal liberty and privacy was enormous. But he did succeed in fashioning another instrument, more intangible but more powerful, to move closer toward his goal—raising consciousness and transforming values on a vast scale, mobilizing the higher aspirations of the Chinese people, reconstructing political institutions, producing substantial and real change, the nature of which cannot yet be fully evaluated.

"Here I stand, I can do no other!" Luther cried. It is the power of a person to become a leader, armed with principles and rising above self-interest narrowly conceived, that invests that person with power and may ultimately transform both leaders and followers into persons who jointly adhere to modal values and end-values. A person, whether leader or follower, girded with moral purpose is a tiny principality of power. In all my observations of men of practical affairs making policy, I remember most vividly a meeting of men of "power" and a quixotic woman who was very much present though not there. She had opposed a construction project that, in her view, threatened environmental and aesthetic damage. Again and again the meeting returned to the question, what would Mrs. Lowell accept? She had armed herself with a moral issue—and with a power base in a band of mobilized followers. That impractical woman had turned out to be practicality itself.

Leadership: Of Whom? To What?

When a leader or a teacher seeks to influence a person by appealing to that person's motive base, the implicit question is: to *what* specific motives is one appealing? Who is the true "I" that is appealing, the true "me" that is being appealed to? With what resources, or power base, is one appealing? For what end and for *whose* end? In what social environment—that is, in relation to the motives and resources of what wider groups and publics and leader-follower relationships? And over time span?

To ask these questions is to raise again the crucial but difficult problem of who is the leader, who is the led. We have long known that persons are complex bundles of motivations. *Manipulators* can appeal to such of these as meet their own wants and needs and then forget them. Yet we also know that there is typically some unity, congruence, harmony within persons' structures of motivations. For the manipulator to play on one motive, to inflate it and perhaps abuse it, as did Joe McCarthy in playing on people's fears of domestic Communists, is to risk disturbing effects on other motives, if only by neglecting or minimizing them. But more than this, motives tend to be organized in some kind of hierarchy. To thwart the realization of some motives will have major effects, to *satisfy* some may have even more significant effects. Again the question: who is the *who* whom someone is seeking to lead? And to what or where? Both leader and led must deal with these questions.

To appeal solely to "lower" or artificially sustained and intensified needs is to subject followers to manipulation. It has equally serious consequences for *leaders*. Essentially they manipulate themselves in manipulating others. In concentrating on a particular "lower" need of the follower they concentrate as well on their own particular motivations that prompt them to arouse that need in a follower (student, customer, voter). The more the follower's need is aroused and satisfied, the more the manipulator's motive to satisfy that need is sustained and perpetuated. Leader and led come to be locked into a symbiotic maintenance of each other's lower needs. A gun merchant may arouse in a prospective customer a fear of personal danger by conjuring up exaggerated worries about domestic enemies or foreign invaders. It is one thing to help liberate persons from a basic need, such as food or safety, so that they might be free to move up the hierarchy of needs to a level where those needs can be fulfilled, something quite different to pinion a person to an artificial need through exclusive access to that person's motive base. What is a lower and higher need, an artificial and authentic need? Only *followers* can determine that, and they can do so only if they have a fair, free, and open choice, in a context of full information and conflicting or competing alternatives, and with enough time.

All this applies to collective as well as individual needs and values. Politicians have long been accused of "pandering" to the lowest instincts of the voters. In Russia the czar—Little Father—was criticized for catering to the most primitive psychological needs of his people. Lloyd George was charged with fawning to British *revanchists* when he allegedly promised to "squeeze the Huns until the pips squeak." Franklin Roosevelt was attacked for truckling to the jobless and the shiftless. If these politicians were pandering, were they pandering only to their followers or to something in themselves? We cannot wait for the verdict of the "bar of history"; that court has a disconcerting habit of issuing different verdicts in different eras. And future verdicts rarely influence the leadership practices of "pragmatic politicians."

No, a means must be found to distinguish true leadership from manipulation at a time when such distinctions can make a difference for other leaders and for voters. That distinction must be made by *followers* at every level, from aides and advisers in circles immediately around the leaders, across a range of persons, the activists and opinion leaders and cadres in the political movement or party, to the leaders of a host of group interests, to the great number of voters and other political participants. Because followers will make these judgments, one can hope that they will evaluate rulers and politicians on the basis of potential for humane and responsible leadership. However, followers can do this—we repeat—only when leaders competing with one another have full and free opportunity to appeal to followers' "hearts and minds," that is, to various levels in their hierarchies of motives, under conditions of free speech and open conflict.

So viewed, the struggle to exert practical influence is a *competitive* struggle to reach out and activate various motivations of followers. Voters are not just manipulable puppets. The seemingly quick and easy way to appeal to those levels of motivations—by "pandering" to the lowest and biggest and most accessible level of motivation—may also be the quick and easy way for leaders to lose contact with followers as they "really" are or as they "really" may come to be—and hence to lose power. But in variously mobilizing and satisfying and helping reshape followers' needs and other motives, the leader is entering into a full relation with followers, one that combines their motive and power bases and may cause them *both* to move to higher motivational levels. Henri Peyre has rightly emphasized the ability both to experience the emotions of a group and to voice their aspirations as qualities vital to leadership.

This view has major implications for the representative as well as the elective process in a democracy. The conventional view is that leaders (politicians) must represent followers (voters). Yet we are seeing that there is no single unitary voter or follower but bundles of motive and power bases. Leaders cannot possibly "re-present" and act on those bundles in all their multi-variety. They must determine what *in* the follower they will recognize and represent, and what they will *not*. One of the oldest questions for representative democracies is whether leaders should take stands they believe in when they know their constituents do not support them. Democratic theory seems ambivalent on the matter: leaders must be representative but not too representative. John F. Kennedy wrote a book that apotheosized great Americans who were great because they did *not* follow their followers, did *not* represent the represented (or at least certain elements among the represented). While these brave leaders also tended not to fare very well at the polls, they later attracted the votes of historians, including Kennedy; but it was Edmund Burke who said, after he had been much praised for his eloquent statement about not slavishly catering to the electors of Bristol (and had then been defeated in an election), that he thought perhaps his sentiment had been praised too much. The theory, of course, is that

the voter "hires" representatives not just to reflect the voter's wants and demands but to exercise their independent judgment—after which the voters may
determine how that judgment worked out (if it is not too late) and then rehire
them or sack them. In thus being engaged with followers *over time,* leaders
must face the test of whether they have indeed tapped authentic needs of followers.

How, then, do we exert influence as a leader? First, by clarifying within
ourselves our own personal goal. If that goal is *only* to secure a livelihood or
advance a career, our tactic need only be calculatedly self-serving and manipulative—at least until our career or prominence is assured. We will at least know
who has been led where. Alternatively, we may link our career with a cause
that rises above considerations of personal success and may provide some
social good. In practice leaders so intertwine their motives that they are hard to
separate, as leaders variously support causes that in turn support them. But
what happens at the fateful moment when career diverges from cause? Students
over the years have told their teachers that they first would "make their million" and then go into politics or the public service. A few, like Jeb Magruder,
manage the transition, though not always with happy results; most fail to amass
their million or do amass it and then concentrate on keeping it or amassing
another. *Decide on whether we are really trying to lead anyone but ourselves,
and what part of ourselves, and where, and for what purposes.*

The second question is *whom* are we seeking to lead? This is not a matter
of defining merely the voters or coalitions we wish to mobilize, but of the motives, aspirations, values, and goals that are to be mobilized within the followers, within their groups. Authentic leadership is a collective process, I contend, and it emerges from the clash and congruence of motives and goals of
leaders and followers. It requires neither that leaders slavishly adapt their own
motives and goals to those of followers nor vice versa. It means that, in the
reaching out by leaders to potential followers, broader and higher ranges of motivation come into play and that both goals and means of achieving them are informed by the force of higher end-values and modal values. Leaders' goals at
the start may be only bread and circuses, but as those goals are reached or
blocked, their purpose may be converted to the realization of higher needs like
esteem, recognition, and fulfillment for both leaders and led. *Define our potential followers, not in the manipulative sense of how to persuade them to our
own ends, such as they are, but in terms of mutuality and of future motives that
may be stimulated as present motives are variously realized or blocked.*

Third, where are we seeking to go? The answer usually seems obvious: the
goal consists of immediate, short-run, easily definable, step-by-step objectives.
But often these calculations of tangible objectives fail to allow for the likeli-

hood that goals will be changed as intermediate steps are taken; that targets will be transformed and perhaps elevated as more followers become involved; that conflict will develop and alter outcomes. Above all, the absorption with short-run, specifiable goals may dilute attention to the likely final outcome of a long and complex process of leadership-followership interaction. Attention may continue to center in the predictable, visible matters of technique and process and personality rather than in the prospects and nature of fundamental, substantive alterations in people's lives and welfare and opportunities—of "real change." Political leadership, however, can be defined only in terms of, and to the extent of the realization of, purposeful, substantive change in the conditions of people's lives. *The ultimate test of practical leadership is the realization of intended, real change that meets people's enduring needs.*

Fourth, how do we overcome obstacles to realizing our goals? Only two generalizations can we apply to the hundreds of specific situations a political leader may face. One is to recognize the motivations of potential followers in all their fullness and complexity (and enough has been said above about that). The other is never to assess at face value, or by reputation, or by easy quantification, the power bases of a rival or possible obstructionist (or of possible supporters). Those power bases—which may look so impressive in the form of the presidency of an institution or the possession of money or the command of armies or the availability of weapons or the support of millions of persons—*must always be assessed in terms of the motivations of those leaders and followers,* as those motivations relate to the disposition of power resources. The question is always one of convertibility, and political power, unlike electric power, is not easily convertible. *Watch out for the towering giant with feet of clay, especially if we are the giant.*

These "rules" for practical influence may seem impractical in some instances, perhaps even utopian. But what is proposed is not all that different from what we do daily and automatically as we make approaches to people and anticipate their reactions—and perhaps anticipate our own reactions to their reactions. The function of leadership is to *engage* followers, not merely to activate them, to commingle needs and aspirations and goals in a common enterprise, and in the process to make better citizens of both leaders and followers. To move from manipulation to power-wielding is to move from the arithmetic of everyday contacts and collisions to the geometry of the structure and dynamics of interaction. It is to move from checkers to chess, for in the "game of kings" we estimate the powers of our chessmen and the intentions and calculations and indeed the motives of our adversary. But democratic leadership moves far beyond chess because, as we play the game, the chessmen come alive, the bishops and knights and pawns take part on their own terms and with their own motivations, values, and goals, and the game moves ahead with new momentum, direction, and possibilities. In real life the most practical advice for leaders is not to treat pawns like pawns, nor princes like princes, but all persons like *persons*.

Woodrow Wilson called for leaders who, by boldly interpreting the nation's conscience, could lift a people out of their everyday selves. That people can be lifted *into* their better selves is the secret of transforming leadership and the moral and practical theme of this work.

ACKNOWLEDGMENTS

SOURCES

INDEX

ACKNOWLEDGMENTS

Since intellectual effort, like leadership itself, is dependent on both collective and critical collaboration, I feel exceptionally fortunate in the quality of the assistance I have received in writing this book. Alexander George, Fred I. Greenstein, and M. Brewster Smith rigorously criticized an earlier draft of the work, on the basis of their broad backgrounds and researches in political psychology and analysis of personality. Elizabeth Léonie Simpson assisted me on several drafts, sharing with me her general background in humanistic psychology and her particular interest in teaching as an act of leadership. Jeanne N. Knutson made both critical and constructive comments on my treatment of early socializing influences on leaders. James C. Davies, long a student of human nature in politics and especially of the role of needs and wants, advised me especially on the early chapters. Benjamin Barber provided wise and timely advice on theoretical aspects. Philippa Strum criticized especially the latter chapters, on the basis of her own work on American political leadership.

At Williams College my colleagues Raymond W. Baker, David A. Booth, George R. Goethals II, George E. Marcus, Kurt Tauber, and Robert G. L. Waite were typically generous with their assistance. I am especially pleased to have been associated, in a political leadership course, with students who exemplified my view that the taught teach the teacher. In particular, Michael Beschloss shared with me his findings on the relationship of Franklin D. Roosevelt and Joseph P. Kennedy and other subjects, and helped me in innumerable ways. John Simpson subjected my work to the kind of critical scrutiny expected of more senior reviewers. Michael Golden provided indispensable and unflappable assistance on technical aspects of the manuscript, as did Wendy Parmet at an earlier stage. Repeated revisions of certain chapters made me especially

465

dependent on the efficiency and patience of the faculty secretarial office. Sarah J. Midgley, Anna J. Morris, and Jeffrey P. Trout assisted indispensably in final preparation of the manuscript. I was fortunate to have in Sydney Wolfe Cohen an indexer with special competence and interest in the study of leadership.

I have had the benefit of the incomparable critical and collaborative talents of my editor, Jeannette E. Hopkins, who has made her own distinct intellectual contribution to the work. Stewart Burns worked closely with me in analyzing certain problems and helping draft some significant passages that lay within his areas of special competence. And once again my wife, Joan Simpson Burns, gave me unending support and encouragement, on the basis of her professional skills and her special understanding of my wants and needs.

SOURCES

PROLOGUE: THE CRISIS OF LEADERSHIP

Plutarch on philosophers' obligations: Plutarch, *Moralia,* Vol. 10, Harold North Fowler, tr. (London: William Heinemann, 1936), pp. 27ff, 75ff. Shakespeare's borrowing from Plutarch: D. A. Russell, *Plutarch* (London: Duckworth, 1973).

Major introductions to the study of leadership are Glenn D. Paige, *The Scientific Study of Political Leadership* (New York: Free Press, 1977); Alvin W. Gouldner, ed., *Studies in Leadership* (New York: Harper & Brothers, 1950), especially the editor's introduction. Dankwart A. Rustow, ed., *Philosophers and Kings: Studies in Leadership* (New York: George Braziller, 1970), especially the editor's introduction, reprinted in "The Study of Leadership," Reprint Series No. 19, Research Center in Comparative Politics and Administration, Brooklyn College of the City University of New York, n.d.; Lester G. Seligman, "The Study of Political Leadership," *American Political Science Review* (December 1950), 904–915; T. N. Whitehead, *Leadership in a Free Society* (Cambridge, Mass.: Harvard University Press, 1936).

1. THE POWER OF LEADERSHIP

Samuel Butler on authority: Samuel Butler, *Miscellaneous Thoughts,* quoted in Harold D. Lasswell, *Power and Personality* (New York: Norton, 1976), p. 7.

John Speke on the incident at Mtésa's court: John Hanning Speke, *Journal of the Discovery of the Source of the Nile* (New York: Harper & Brothers, 1864), pp. 289–290.

Frederick William and son: Ludwig Reiners, *Frederick the Great* (New York: Putnam, 1960); Edith Simon, *The Making of Frederick the Great* (Boston: Little, Brown, 1963).

Power (and leadership) as personal and motivational: Kenneth B. Clark, *Pathos of Power* (New York: Harper & Row, 1974), esp. ch. 4; Adolf A. Berle, *Power* (New York: Harcourt, Brace & World, 1967), pp. 18, 59.

The Two Essentials of Power

Russell on power as fundamental concept: Bertrand Russell, *Power, A New Social Analysis* (New York: Norton, 1938), p. 1.

"Power of A over B": John R. P. French, "A Formal Theory of Social Power," *Psychological Review,* Vol. 63, No. 3 (May 1956), 181–194.

Banishing the concept of power: William H. Riker, "Some Ambiguities in the Notion of Power," *American Political Science Review,* Vol. 58, No. 2 (June 1964), 341–349.

Weber on power: Max Weber, *The Theory of Social and Economic Organization,* Talcott Parsons, ed. (Glencoe, Ill.: Free Press, 1957), p. 152, quoted by Robert A. Dahl, "Power," *International Encyclopedia of the Social Sciences* (New York: Macmillan and Free Press, 1968), Vol. 12, p. 406.

McClelland on goal of power holders: David C. McClelland, *Power: The Inner Experience* (New York: Irvington, 1975), p. 17; see also D. G. Winter, *The Power Motive* (New York: Free Press, 1973).

Impact of Kennedy Inaugural film: McClelland, p. 15.

Sources of strength in oneself: McClelland, p. 16.

Effectance: Robert W. White, "Motivation Reconsidered: The Concept of Competence," *Psychological Review,* Vol. 66, No. 5 (July 1959), 297–333.

The ubiquity of power: Alfred McClung Lee, "Power-Seekers," in Gouldner, ed., *Studies in Leadership,* p. 668.

Dahl on the dimensions of power: Dahl, pp. 407–408.

Lasswell and Kaplan on power: Harold D. Lasswell and Abraham Kaplan, *Power and Society* (New Haven: Yale University Press, 1950), ch. 5.

Lehman on micropower: Edward W. Lehman, "Toward a Macrosociology of Power," *American Sociological Review,* Vol. 34, No. 4 (August 1969), 453–465.

Leadership and Followership

Lasswell and Kaplan on power: Lasswell and Kaplan, *Power and Society,* p. 77.

Janda on power: Kenneth F. Janda, "Towards the Explication of the Concept of Leadership in Terms of the Concept of Power," in Glenn D. Paige, ed., *Political Leadership* (New York: Free Press, 1972), pp. 45–68, quoted at p. 57.

McFarland on leadership: Andrew S. McFarland, *Power and Leadership in Pluralist Systems* (Stanford: Stanford University Press, 1969), p. 174.

Bell et al. on power as a relationship: Roderick Bell, David V. Edwards, and R. Harrison Wagner, *Political Power* (New York: Free Press, 1969), p. 4.

Hitler treating persons as things: Richard Hughes, *The Fox in the Attic* (New York: Harper & Row, 1962), p. 266.

Russian linguist on the Soviet government: Hedrick Smith, *The Russians* (New York: Ballantine, 1976), p. 339.

Complex aspects of power: Steven Lukes, *Power: A Radical View* (London: Macmillan, 1976); John R. Champlin, "On the Study of Power," *Politics and Society,* Vol. 1, No. 1 (November 1970), 91–111; Geoffrey Debnam, "Nondecisions and Power: The Two Faces of Bachrach and Baratz," *American Political Science Review,* Vol. 69, No. 3 (September 1975), 889–904 (see also rejoinders); and works on power cited above.

What Leadership Is Not: Closing the Intellectual Gap

Plato's parable of the ship: *The Republic of Plato,* B. Jowett, trans., (Oxford: Clarendon Press, 1888), Book VI, pp. 185–186.

Hooker on the need for authority: Richard Hooker, *Laws of Ecclesiastical Polity,* quoted in Charles W. Hendel, "An Exploration of the Nature of Authority," in Carl J. Friedrich, ed., *Authority* (Cambridge, Mass.: Harvard University Press, 1958), p. 8.

Hobbes on authority: cited in *ibid.,* p. 17.

Hannah Arendt on the decline of the concept of authority: Hannah Arendt, "What Was Authority?" in Friedrich, ed., passim.

Weber on authority: Max Weber, *The Theory of Social and Economic Organization,* Talcott Parsons, ed. (New York: Oxford University Press, 1947), esp. Pt. III.

Friedrich on modern authority: Carl J. Friedrich, *Man and His Government* (New York: McGraw-Hill, 1963).

Pareto on the circulation of the elites: Vilfredo Pareto, *Mind and Society,* Arthur Livingston, ed. (New York: Harcourt, Brace, 1935).

The Plymouth counterpart to Plato's parable of the ship: Norman Jacobson, "Knowledge, Tradition, and Authority: A Note on the American Experience," in Friedrich, ed., *Authority,* pp. 117–118.

Engels on leadership as administrative management: Friedrich Engels, "On Authority," in Robert C. Tucker, ed. *The Marx-Engels Reader* (New York: Norton, 1972), quoted at p. 664.

American historians and political scientists on the presidency: James MacGregor Burns, *Presidential Government* (Boston: Houghton Mifflin, 1966), ch. 3.

On more recent concepts of authority, see Clarke E. Cochran, "Authority and Community: The Contributions of Carl Friedrich, Yves R. Simon, and Michael Polanyi," *The American Political cal Science Review* (June 1977), 546–558.

Frederick the Great on the passion of princes: quoted from his *Memorabilia.*

2. THE STRUCTURE OF MORAL LEADERSHIP

Plato on needs and wants: *The Republic of Plato,* B. Jowett, trans. (Oxford: Clarendon Press, 1888), Book II, pp. 49–53.

Critical analysis of moral development theory: Elizabeth Léonie Simpson, "Moral Development Research: A Case Study of Scientific Cultural Bias," *Human Development,* Vol. 17 (1974), 81–106; Jane Loevinger, *Ego Development* (San Francisco: Jossey-Bass, 1976), esp. chs. 9, 10.

Girvetz on moral dogmatism: Harry K. Girvetz, *Beyond Right and Wrong* (New York: Free Press, 1973), p. 3.

Bertolt Brecht, "Die Dreigroschenoper" in *Stücke für das Theater am Schiffbauer damm* (Berlin: Suhrkamp Verlag, 1962).

The Power and Sources of Values

Tapping Lake Sevan: *New York Times,* May 29, 1977, p. 9.

Sycamore tree incident: *New York Times,* May 25, 1976, p. 33.

John Adams on studying politics and war: James Truslow Adams, *The Adams Family* (Boston: Little, Brown, 1930), p. 67.

Thai boy scout and his ideology: *New York Times,* November 29, 1976, p. 8.

The relationship of Franklin D. Roosevelt and Joseph P. Kennedy: Michael R. Beschloss, "Joseph Kennedy and Franklin Roosevelt: A Study in Power and Leadership," Williams College, 1977. Joseph Kennedy's Lend Lease testimony: Richard J. Whalen, *The Founding Father* (New York: New American Library, 1964), pp. 352–355.

Piaget on children's internalization of values: Jean Piaget, *The Moral Judgment of the Child* (New York: Harcourt, Brace, 1932).

Jung on ends: C. C. Jung, *Collected Papers on Analytical Psychology* (London: Baillière, Tindall and Cox, 1922), pp. x, xiv.

Huxley on the superego: T. H. Huxley and J. S. Huxley, *Touchstone for Ethics* (New York: Harper & Brothers, 1947), p. 256.

Erikson on conscience: Erik H. Erikson, *Identity: Youth and Crisis* (New York: Norton, 1968), p. 119.

Parsons on Freud's view: Talcott Parsons, *Social Structure and Personality* (New York: Free Press, 1964), passim.

Conflict and Consciousness

Influence of Pareto, Durkheim, Weber, etc.: Clinton F. Fink, "Some Conceptual Difficulties in the Theory of Social Conflict," *Journal of Conflict Resolution,* Vol. 12, No. 4 (December 1968), 425; see also Anthony Oberschall, *Social Conflict and Social Movements* (Englewood Cliffs, N.J.: Prentice-Hall, 1973), esp. pp. 1–8.

Simmel: Georg Simmel, "The Sociology of Conflict," *American Journal of Sociology,* Vol. 9, No. 4 (1903–04), 490–525; Simmel, *Conflict and the Web of Group Affiliations,* Kurt H. Wolff and Reinhard Bendix, trs. (Glencoe, Ill.: Free Press, 1955.)

Recent scholarly interest in conflict: Lewis A. Coser, *The Functions of Social Conflict* (Glencoe, Ill.: Free Press, 1956); Ralf Dahrendorf, *Class and Class Conflict in Industrial Society* (Stanford: Stanford University Press, 1959); Louis Kriesberg, *The Sociology of Social Conflicts* (Englewood Cliffs, N.J.: Prentice-Hall, 1973).

Simmel on group harmony: Paraphrased by Coser, p. 31, from opening pages of Simmel, *Conflict.*

Conflict within individuals: see, for example, Muzafer Sherif, *An Outline of Social Psychology* (New York: Harper & Brothers, 1948), esp. chs. 10, 15–17.

Malinowski on conflict in small groups: Bronislaw Malinowski, "An Anthropological Analysis of War," *Magic, Science and Religion* (Glencoe, Ill.: Free Press, 1948), p. 285, quoted by Coser, p. 63. See also Fink, pp. 445–456.

Schattschneider on scope of conflict: E. E. Schattschneider, *The Semi-Sovereign People* (New York: Holt, Rinehart and Winston, 1960), pp. 2–3.

Madison on conflict: *The Federalist,* Jacob E. Cooke, ed. (Middletown, Conn.: Wesleyan University Press, 1961), No. 10, pp. 58–59.

Leaders and their followings: cf. Andrew McFarland, *Power and Leadership in Pluralist Systems* (Stanford: Stanford University Press, 1969), pp. 189–191.

For other sources on conflict see Peter W. Sperlich, *Conflict and Harmony in Human Affairs* (Chicago: Rand McNally, 1971); Anthony de Reuck and Julie Knight, eds., *Conflict in Society* (Boston: Little, Brown, 1966); *Journal of Conflict Resolution,* Vol. 12 (1968), passim; Walter Korpi, "Conflict, Power and Relative Deprivation," *American Political Science Review,* Vol. 68, No. 4 (December 1974), 1569–1578.

Hegel, Feuerbach, and Marx on consciousness and on needs: Gyorgy Márkus, *The Marxian Concept of Consciousness, Political Science Syllabus;* Henri Lefebvre, *Dialectical Materialism* (London: Jonathan Cape, 1968); A. James Gregor, *A Survey of Marxism* (New York: Random House, 1965). Marx on "fresh needs": from Karl Marx and Friedrich Engels, *The German Ideology* (New York: International Publishers, 1947), as summarized in Lefebvre, p. 70.

On consciousness see also Pratima Bowes, *Consciousness and Freedom* (London: Methuen, 1971).

Sorel on violence and class identity: Georges Sorel, *Reflections on Violence,* T. E. Hulme, tr. (New York: B. W. Huebsch, 1914).

The Elevating Power of Leadership

Need of safety and security as counterparts of conforming to and maintaining the social order: Lawrence Kohlberg "The Cognitive-Developmental Approach to Moral Education," *Phi Delta Kappan* (June 1975), 671; cf. Elizabeth Simpson, "A Holistic Approach to Moral Development and Behavior," in T. Lickona, ed. *Moral Development and Behavior* (New York: Holt, Rinehart and Winston, 1976), passim.

Simpson on relation of esteem needs and natural-law values: Elizabeth Léonie Simpson, *Democracy's Stepchildren* (San Francisco: Jossey-Bass, 1971), p. 126.

Four-nation study on transformations of values: *Values and the Active Community* (New

York: Free Press, 1971), pp. 13, 72–79. The four nations studied are India, Poland, the United States, and Yugoslavia.

Rokeach on imbalance within value systems: Milton Rokeach, *The Nature of Human Values* (New York: Free Press, 1973), p. 217.

Rokeach on contradictions and self-conception: Rokeach, pp. 226, 229–233.

Experimenters as leaders: Bernard M. Bass, *Leadership, Psychology and Organizational Behavior* (New York: Harper & Brothers, 1960), p. 97.

Susanne Langer on consciousness: quoted in Simpson, *Democracy's Stepchildren,* p. 73.

Erikson's eight stages of man: Erik H. Erikson, "The Problem of Ego Identity," *Journal of the American Psychoanalytic Association,* Vol. 4 (1956), 56–121.

Studies on irreversibility of movement toward four general values: cited in Rokeach, p. 328.

Myrdal on higher valuations: Gunnar Myrdal, *An American Dilemma* (New York: Harper & Brothers, 1944), p. 1029.

Max Weber's two ethics: Max Weber, "Politics as a Vocation," reprinted in H. H. Gerth and C. Wright Mills, *From Max Weber: Essays in Sociology* (New York: Oxford University Press, 1953), pp. 77–128.

3. THE PSYCHOLOGICAL MATRIX OF LEADERSHIP

Power and hierarchy among primates: Fred H. Willhoite, Jr., "Primates and Political Authority: A Biobehavioral Perspective," *American Political Science Review,* Vol. 70, No. 4 (December 1976), 1110–1126, which includes abundant references to the literature; Lionel Tiger and Robin Fox, *The Imperial Animal* (New York: Holt, Rinehart & Winston, 1971); Erik H. Erikson, *Identity: Youth and Crisis* (New York: Norton, 1968), pp. 279–280.

Primate leadership behavior at the Delta Regional Primate Research Center: Emily Hahn, "On the Side of the Apes," Part II, *The New Yorker,* April 24, 1971, pp. 64–65 (emphasis added); the basic source is E. W. Menzel, Jr., "A Group of Young Chimpanzees in a One-Acre Field," in Allan M. Schrier and Fred Stollnitz, eds., *Behavior of Nonhuman Primates* (New York: Academic Press, 1974), Vol. 5, pp. 83–153.

Goat behavior: Jeannie C. Stewart and J. P. Scott, "Lack of Correlation between Leadership and Dominance Relations in a Herd of Goats," *Journal of Comparative and Physiological Psychology* (August 1947), 255–264.

Imprinting: Konrad Z. Lorenz, *King Solomon's Ring* (London: Methuen, 1952); Howard Moltz, "Imprinting: Empirical Basis and Theoretical Significance," *Psychological Bulletin* (July 1960), 48–58.

Finder bees: Karl von Frisch, *Bees: Their Vision, Chemical Senses and Language* (Ithaca: Cornell University Press, 1950).

Stereotyping of women's political and leadership roles: J. Jaquette, ed., *Women in Politics* (New York: Wiley, 1974); Martin Gruberg, *Women in American Politics* (Oshkosh, Wisc.: Academic Press, 1968); Paula Johnson, "Women in Power: Toward a Theory of Effectiveness," *Journal of Social Issues,* Vol. 32, No. 3 (1976), 99–110; Wilma Rule Krauss, "Political Implications of Gender Roles: A Review of the Literature," *American Political Science Review,* Vol. 68, No. 4 (December 1974), 1706–1723.

Keniston quotation: Kenneth Keniston, "Psychological Development and Historical Change," *Journal of Interdisciplinary History,* Vol. 2, No. 2 (Autumn 1971), 329–345, at 342.

The Cocoon of Personality

Psychoanalytical aspects of Gandhi's childhood: M. K. Gandhi, *Gandhi's Autobiography: The Story of My Experiments with Truth* (Washington, D.C.: Public Affairs Press, 1948); Erik H. Erikson, *Gandhi's Truth* (New York: Norton, 1969); E. Victor Wolfenstein, *The Revolutionary Person-*

ality (Princeton: Princeton University Press, 1967); Sebastian de Grazia, "Mahatma Gandhi: The Son of His Mother," *Political Quarterly,* Vol. 19 (1948), 336–348.

The Erikson observation on Gandhi's "spoiling" is from Erikson, p. 106; Gandhi's Oedipal conflict: Erikson, p. 129.

The Wolfenstein quotation: Wolfenstein, pp. 82–83; Gandhi's is from his *Autobiography,* p. 13. For extensive biographical data see Pyarelal, *Mahatma Gandhi,* Vol. 1, *The Early Phase* (Ahmedabad: Navajivan, 1956); Ved Mehta, *Mahatma Gandhi and His Apostles* (New York: Viking Press, 1977).

Sources on Lenin: Bertram D. Wolfe, *Three Who Made a Revolution* (New York: Dial Press, 1948); Adam B. Ulam, *The Bolsheviks* (New York: Macmillan, 1965); David Shub, *Lenin* (Garden City, N.Y.: Doubleday, 1948); Wolfenstein, pp. 33–49.

The Wolfe warning is from Wolfe, p. 42; the Wolfenstein quotation from Wolfenstein, p. 39.

Hitler's memories of his family life: Adolf Hitler, *Mein Kampf* (Boston: Houghton Mifflin, 1943), pp. 3, 4, 28; see also pp. 31–32.

Psychoanalytical sources on Hitler: Walter C. Langer, *The Mind of Adolf Hitler* (New York: Basic Books, 1972), the report prepared for the United States Office of Strategic Services during World War II; a critique of Langer, Hans W. Gatzke, "Hitler and Psychohistory," *American Historical Review,* Vol. 78, No. 2 (April 1973), 394–401; and three studies by Robert G. L. Waite: "Adolf Hitler's Anti-Semitism: A Study in History and Psychoanalysis," in Benjamin B. Wolman, ed., *The Psychoanalytic Interpretation of History* (New York: Basic Books, 1971); "Adolf Hitler's Guilt Feelings: A Problem in History and Psychology," *Journal of Interdisciplinary History,* Vol. 1, No. 2 (Winter 1971), 229–249; and an afterword to the Langer volume, pp. 215–238. The Langer quotation is from Langer, pp. 150–151; the Waite quotation is from the same work, p. 227; see also Robert G. L. Waite, *The Psychopathic God: Adolf Hitler* (New York: Basic Books, 1977); I also had the benefit of personal consultation with Robert Waite.

Bismarck on his parents is cited in Otto Pflanze, "Toward a Psychoanalytic Interpretation of Bismarck," *American Historical Review,* Vol. 77, No. 2 (April 1972), 419–444, at 429; Pflanze's comment on the drive to power, p. 420.

Schumacher: Lewis J. Edinger, *Kurt Schumacher* (Stanford: Stanford University Press, 1965), pp. 10–11.

Eleanor Roosevelt: Joseph P. Lash, *Eleanor and Franklin* (New York: Norton, 1971); she is quoted on the death of her father at p. 59.

Richard M. Nixon: Bruce Mazlish, *In Search of Nixon* (New York: Basic Books, 1972), esp. pp. 20–26.

The Wellsprings of Want

Heredity and inheritance: George Gaylord Simpson, *The Meaning of Evolution* (New Haven: Yale University Press, 1949).

Klineberg on motives: Otto Klineberg, *Social Psychology* (New York: Holt, Rinehart and Winston, 1954).

Nash on satisfying needs: John Nash, *Developmental Psychology* (Englewood Cliffs, N.J.: Prentice-Hall, 1970).

Stages of childhood: Erik H. Erikson, *Childhood and Society,* 2nd ed., (New York: Norton, 1963), esp. ch. 7; Erikson, *Identity: Youth and Crisis* (New York: Norton, 1968), esp. ch. 3.

Albert Bandura and Richard Walters on learning: Jerome Kagan and Ernest Havemann, *Psychology: An Introduction* (New York: Harcourt, Brace & World, 1968).

Davies on wants and needs: James C. Davies, *Human Nature in Politics* (New York: Wiley, 1963).

Smith on intentionality: M. Brewster Smith, "Metapsychology, Politics, and Human Needs," in R. Fitzgerald, ed., *Human Needs and Politics* (Rushcutters Bay, South Australia: Pergamon Press, 1977) pp. 124–141.

Hanna Pitkin, *The Concept of Representation* (Berkeley: University of California Press, 1967) p. 209.

I have drawn heavily on Jeanne N. Knutson, *The Human Basis of the Polity* (Chicago: Aldine, 1972), an effort to explore the psychological roots of political leadership on the basis of aggregative data explicitly organized for, and tested to meet, hypotheses about the origins of leadership. The first two quotations from her are from pp. 181 and 190.

Maslow on leadership needs: Knutson, p. 26.

Maslow on the holistic theory of change and growth: A. H. Maslow, "Dynamics of Personality Organization: I," *Psychological Review,* Vol. 50, No. 5 (September 1943), 514-539.

Maslow on higher needs: A. H. Maslow, *Motivation and Personality* (New York: Harper & Brothers, 1954), passim.

Maslow on child's need for routine: Maslow, *Motivation and Personality,* p. 87.

Lane on Rapuano's loss of identity: Robert E. Lane, *Political Ideology* (New York: Free Press, 1962), p. 111.

Maslow on safety-deprived persons' search for a stronger person: Maslow, *Motivation and Personality,* p. 88.

Knutson's conclusions on their shrinking from leadership roles: Knutson, p. 198.

Barber on Connecticut legislators: James David Barber, *The Lawmakers* (New Haven: Yale University Press, 1965), p. 25.

Participation in bureaucratic organizations: Rufus Browning and Herbert Jacob, "Power Motivation and the Political Personality," *Public Opinion Quarterly,* Vol. 28, No. 1 (Spring 1964), 75-90.

Wilson and Tumulty: John Morton Blum, *Joe Tumulty and the Wilson Era* (Boston: Houghton Mifflin, 1951), p. 121; also see Gene Smith, *When the Cheering Stopped* (New York: Morrow, 1964), pp. 205-207.

The Transmutation of Need

Smith on wants: Smith, "Metapsychology, Politics, and Human Needs."

Arendt on necessity: Hannah Arendt, *On Revolution* (New York: Viking Press, 1963), pp. 129, 53.

Roosevelt on necessitous men: quoted in James MacGregor Burns, *Roosevelt: The Soldier of Freedom* (New York: Harcourt Brace Jovanovich, 1970), p. 425.

Starvation experiments: Ancel Keys, J. Brozek, A. Henschel, O. Mickelson, and H. L. Taylor, *The Biology of Human Starvation* (Minneapolis: University of Minnesota Press, 1950).

Davies on effect of food and affection deprivation: James C. Davies, "Where from and Where to?" ch. 1 in Jeanne N. Knutson, ed., *Handbook of Political Psychology* (San Francisco: Jossey-Bass, 1973), p. 7; see also Davies, *Human Nature in Politics* (New York: Wiley, 1963), esp. ch. 1.

Need hierarchy: A. H. Maslow, " 'Higher' and 'Lower' Needs," *Journal of Psychology,* Vol. 25 (1948a), 433-436, included as ch. 8 in Maslow, *Motivation and Personality* (New York: Harper & Brothers, 1954); see also other works of Maslow, and Ledford J. Bischof, *Interpreting Personality Theories* (New York: Harper & Row, 1964), ch. 15.

Horney on security needs: Karen Horney, *The Neurotic Personality of Our Time* (New York: Norton, 1937).

Davies on popular response to threats against their needs: Davies, *Human Nature in Politics,* p. 10. On the definition of "safety" and "security," James C. Davis has shown me his correspondence with Abraham H. Maslow: Davies to Maslow, July 19, 1966; Maslow to Davies, July 26, 1966.

Smith on Maslow's hierarchy: Smith, "Metapsychology," p. 18.

Politics of sex: F. A. Beach, cited in C. N. Cofer and M. H. Appley, *Motivation: Theory and Research* (New York: Wiley, 1964), p. 175.

The Hierarchies of Need and Value

Erikson on moralities and ethics: Erikson, *Identity: Youth and Crisis* (New York: Norton, 1968), p. 119.

Kohlberg on stages of moral development: Lawrence Kohlberg, "The Cognitive-Developmental Approach to Moral Education," pp. 670–677, esp. p. 671; Kohlberg, "The Claim to Moral Adequacy of a Highest Stage of Moral Judgment," *The Journal of Philosophy*, Vol. 70, No. 18 (October 25, 1973), 630–646.

Interview of Judith: Fred I. Greenstein, *Children and Politics* (New Haven: Yale University Press, 1965), p. 25.

Erikson on the adolescent mind: Erikson, *Childhood and Society*, pp. 262–263; Erikson on adolescence as a normative crisis: Erikson, *Identity*, p. 163.

Research on normative and factual values: Henry Margenau, "The Scientific Basis of Value Theory," in Abraham H. Maslow, ed., *New Knowledge in Human Values* (Chicago: Regnery, 1959), pp. 38–39.

Values as goals and end states: Alvin W. Gouldner, *The Coming Crisis of Western Sociology* (New York: Basic Books, 1970), pp. 190–191.

Concepts of opportunistic rule-playing versus stage of conscience: Jane Loevinger, "The Meaning and Measurement of Ego Development," *American Psychologist*, Vol. 21, No. 3 (March 1966), 195.

Rokeach on internalized values: Milton Rokeach, *Beliefs, Attitudes, and Values* (San Francisco: Jossey-Bass, 1972), p. 160.

Peer influence: Richard M. Merelman, "The Development of Policy Thinking in Adolescence," *American Political Science Review*, Vol. 65, No. 4 (December 1971), 1033–1047; see also sources cited therein.

Kohlberg on levels of moral development: Lawrence Kohlberg, "Moral Development and Identification," ch. 7 in Harold W. Stevenson, ed., *Child Psychology* (62nd Yearbook of the National Society for the Study of Education), (Chicago: University of Chicago Press, 1963), pp. 277–332.

Simpson on congruence of need theory and value theory: Elizabeth Léonie Simpson, "A Holistic Approach to Moral Development and Behavior," in T. Lickona, ed., *Moral Development and Behavior* (New York: Holt, Rinehart and Winston, 1976). I am indebted to Elizabeth Simpson for further discussion of this subject.

Study of Italian youth: Joseph LaPalombara and Jerry B. Waters, "Values, Expectations, and Political Predispositions of Italian Youth," *Midwest Journal of Political Science*, Vol. 5, No. 1 (February 1961), 39–58; the sample consisted of 3,000 respondents, 18 to 25 years old.

Toki study of Japanese schoolchildren: K. Toki, "The Leader-Follower Structure in the School-Class," *Japanese Journal of Psychology*, Vol. 10 (1935), 27–56, cited and reported in Eugene L. Hartley and Ruth E. Hartley, *Fundamentals of Social Psychology* (New York: Knopf, 1961), pp. 631–633.

Whyte study of street-corner leadership: William F. Whyte, *Street Corner Society* (Chicago: University of Chicago Press, 1943), p. 260.

Greenstein on culture-and-personality distinctions: Fred I. Greenstein, "Personality and Political Socialization: The Theories of Authoritarian and Democratic Character," *Annals of the American Academy of Political and Social Science*, Vol. 361 (September 1965), 81–95, at 95. See also Roberta Sigel, ed., *Political Socialization: Its Role in the Political Process* (Philadelphia, 1965).

4. THE SOCIAL SOURCES OF LEADERSHIP

Hobbes on the family as a small *Leviathan:* Richard Allen Chapman, *"Leviathan* Writ Small: Thomas Hobbes on the Family," *American Political Science Review,* Vol. 69, No. 1 (March 1975), 76–90.

Tocqueville on infant behavior: Alexis de Tocqueville, *Democracy in America,* Vol. 1 (New York: Vintage Books, 1945), pp. 27–28.

Anaclitic relation: Walter Mischel, *Introduction to Personality* (New York: Holt, Rinehart and Winston, 1971), pp. 36–37, 234–236.

The primal horde: see, for example, Sigmund Freud, *Totem and Taboo* (New York: Vintage Books, 1946).

Lidz on the family as a leadership system: Theodore Lidz, *The Person* (New York: Basic Books, 1968), p. 58.

Kohlberg on influence of the father in most cultures: Lawrence Kohlberg, "Moral Development and Identification," ch. 7 in Harold W. Stevenson, ed., *Child Psychology* (Chicago: University of Chicago Press, 1963), p. 309.

Presumption of lesser political influence of father on children in America as compared to other cultures, see also M. Jennings and Richard Niemi, *The Political Character of Adolescence* (Princeton: Princeton University Press, 1974), pp. 24–25, 46, 105.

The Family as Imperium

Erikson on the interplay of generations: *Insight and Responsibility,* p. 114.

Erikson on children's play: *Insight and Responsibility,* p. 120.

Exploratory curiosity: Anne Roe and L. Z. Freedman, "Evolution and Human Behavior," in Anne Roe and George Gaylord Simpson, eds., *Behavior and Evolution* (New Haven: Yale University Press, 1958).

Piaget on new experience: Jean Piaget, *The Origins of Intelligence in Children* (New York: International Universities Press, 1952).

Persistence of values: Richard E. Dawson and Kenneth Prewitt, *Political Socialization* (Boston: Little, Brown, 1969), pp. 22–23. See also Talcott Parsons, *Social Structure and Personality* (Glencoe, Ill.: Free Press, 1964), p. 86.

Dollard on person as a collected whole: John Dollard, *Criteria for the Life History* (New Haven: Yale University Press, 1935), p. 27.

Langton on diverse household patterns: Kenneth P. Langton, *Political Socialization* (New York: Oxford University Press, 1969), p. 30.

Five-nation study: Gabriel A. Almond and Sidney Verba, *The Civic Culture* (Boston: Little, Brown, 1965).

Parental overprotection: Frank A. Pinner, "Parental Overprotection and Political Distrust," *Annals of the American Academy of Political and Social Science,* Vol. 361 (September 1965), 58–70.

Caribbean study: Langton, *Political Socialization,* p. 26.

Cambridge study: Eleanor E. Maccoby, Richard Mathews, and Anton Morton, "Youth and Political Change," *Public Opinion Quarterly,* Vol. 18, No. 1 (Spring 1954), 23–29. See also Kent L. Tedin, "The Influence of Parents on the Political Attitudes of Adolescents," *American Political Science Review,* Vol. 68, No. 4 (December 1974), 1579–1592.

Political Schooling

Merriam on the influence of schools: Charles E. Merriam, *The Making of Citizens* (Chicago: University of Chicago Press, 1931), p. 273. More recent conclusion on same: Kenneth P. Langton and M. Kent Jennings in Langton, *Political Socialization,* ch 4; Almond and Verba, p. 316.

Relation between civics courses and political interest: Langton, p. 97. Japanese school indoctrination: Herbert Passin, "Japan," in James S. Coleman, ed., *Educational and Political Development* (Princeton: Princeton University Press, 1965), pp. 310–311; cf. Joseph A. Massey, "The Missing Leader: Japanese Youths' View of Political Authority," *American Political Science Review,* Vol. 69, No. 1 (March 1975), 31–48.

Soviet indoctrination: Jeremy R. Azrael, "Soviet Union," in Coleman, *Education and Political Development,* p. 356; cf. Hadley Cantril, *Soviet Leaders and Mastery Over Man* (New Brunswick: Rutgers University Press, 1960); and, in another context, Charles Price Ridley, Paul H. B. Godwin, and Dennis J. Doolin, *The Making of a Model Citizen in Communist China* (Stanford: Hoover Institution Press, 1971).

Bennington study: Theodore M. Newcomb, *Personality and Social Change* (New York: Dryden Press, 1943).

See generally M. Kent Jennings and Richard G. Niemi, "The Transmission of Political Values from Parent to Child," *American Political Science Review,* Vol. 62, No. 1 (March 1968), 169–184.

Adolescents as patriots: Robert D. Hess and Judith V. Torney, *The Development of Political Attitudes in Children* (Chicago: Aldine, 1967), ch. 2 and passim, quoted at p. 23.

New Haven children's perception of leadership: Greenstein, *Children and Politics,* ch. 3. Chicago: Hess and Torney, p. 213.

Idealization of the President: Hess and Torney, pp. 2, 32; Greenstein, ch. 3; Robert D. Hess and David Easton, "The Child's Changing Image of the President," *Public Opinion Quarterly,* Vol. 24, No. 4 (Winter 1960), 632–644.

Death of President Kennedy: Greenstein, pp. 48–50; Roberta S. Sigel, "Image of a President: Some Insights into the Political Views of School Children," *American Political Science Review,* Vol. 62, No. 1 (March 1968), 216–226, at 216, 219, 226.

Learning adult role differences: Hess and Easton, p. 642.

Sequence of learning: Greenstein, pp. 71–84; Hess and Torney, passim.

Socio-economic and sex differences: Hess and Torney, chs. 7 and 8; Greenstein, chs. 5 and 6.

See in general Seymour Martin Lipset, *Political Man: The Social Bases of Politics* (Garden City, N.Y: Doubleday, 1960).

Political efficacy: David Easton and Jack Dennis, "The Child's Acquisition of Regime Norms: Political Efficacy," *American Political Science Review,* Vol. 61, No. 1 (March 1967), 25–38, and sources cited therein; Easton and Dennis quoted at p. 33.

Erikson on leadership and followership: Erik H. Erikson, *Identity: Youth and Crisis* (New York: Norton, 1968), p. 187.

Gandhi's adolescence: *Gandhi's Autobiography,* Part One, passim; Wolfenstein, pp. 78–88; Erik H. Erikson, *Gandhi's Truth* (New York: Norton, 1969), Part Two, ch. 1.

Cultural context: Thomas J. Hopkins, *The Hindu Religious Transition* (Encino, Calif.: Dickenson, 1971); Max Weber, *The Religion of India* (Glencoe, Ill.: Free Press, 1958).

Gandhi's comment on the "blot" on him after his father's death is from his *Autobiography,* p. 45; the quotation from Erikson is from *Gandhi's Truth,* pp. 128, 129.

P. Spratt, *Hindu Culture and Personality* (Bombay: Manaktalas, 1966), a psychoanalytical study, includes an appendix on Gandhi. See also Mehta, *Mahatma Gandhi and His Apostles,* passim, on this period.

Quotations from *Mein Kampf* are from pp. 5, 10, 18, 22, 76–83.

Langer on Hitler's guilt feelings on deaths of father and brother: Langer, p. 178. See also Waite, *The Psychopathic God,* passim.

Vienna in Hitler's day and his relation to it: William A. Jenks, *Vienna and the Young Hitler* (New York: Columbia University Press, 1960).

Lenin's adolescence: Louis Fischer, *The Life of Lenin* (New York: Harper & Row, 1964); Leon Trotsky, *Lenin* (New York: Minton, Balch & Co., 1925); Shub, ch. 2; Wolfe, ch. 3. Wolfenstein quotations: Wolfenstein, p. 43.

Robert Payne, *The Life and Death of Lenin* (New York: Simon and Schuster, 1964), emphasizes Lenin's early reading.

Self-esteem, Social Role, and Empathy

Heinz L. Ansbacher and Rowena R. Ansbacher, eds., *The Individual Psychology of Alfred Adler* (New York: Basic Books, 1956), pp. 103–119, 126–142.

Maslow on esteem needs: A. H. Maslow, *Motivation and Personality* (New York: Harper & Brothers, 1954), p. 90; see also Abraham H. Maslow, *The Farther Reaches of Human Nature* (New York: Viking Press, 1971), Appendix D, an "extension and improvement" of his earlier presentation of the instinctoid nature of basic needs.

Wilson's need for esteem: George and George, *Woodrow Wilson and Colonel House,* pp. 8–9.

William James on self-esteem: Muzafer Sherif and Hadley Cantril, *The Psychology of Ego-Involvements* (New York: Wiley, 1947), p. 119.

Lane on person disappointed in his status: Robert E. Lane, *Political Ideology* (New York: Free Press, 1962), pp 106–107.

Mischel quotation: Mischel, *Introduction to Personality,* pp. 413–414, 416, and sources cited therein.

English public schools: Rupert Wilkinson, *Gentlemanly Power: British Leadership and the Public School Tradition* (London: Oxford University Press, 1964); see also W. L. Guttsman, *The British Political Elite* (London: Macgibbon & Kee, 1963).

Parsons on manpower allocation: Parsons, *Social Structure and Personality,* p. 131.

Piaget on child's preoperational phase: Lidz, *The Person,* p. 84.

Erikson on adolescent roles and role confusion: Erikson, *Childhood and Society,* pp. 261–262; see also Erikson, *Insight and Responsibility,* p. 92, and V. Flavell, *The Development of Role-Taking and Communicative Skills in Children* (Huntington, N.Y.: Krieger, 1975).

The definition of role is drawn largely from Daniel J. Levinson, "Role, Personality, and Social Structure in the Organizational Setting," *Journal of Abnormal and Social Psychology,* Vol. 58 (1959), reprinted in Greenstein and Lerner, *A Source Book for the Study of Personality and Politics* (Chicago: Markham, 1971), pp. 61–74.

Levinson on apathetic conformity: Levinson, pp. 72–73.

William James on social selves: quoted in Harold D. Lasswell and Abraham Kaplan, *Power and Society* (New Haven: Yale University Press, 1950), p. 12.

Knutson on relation of need for esteem and socio-economic status: Knutson, p. 207; see, however, V. Wylie, *The Self-Concept* (Lincoln: University of Nebraska Press, 1961).

Coopersmith on effect of degrees of self-esteem: Stanley Coopersmith, *The Antecedents of Self-Esteem* (San Francisco: Freeman, 1967), p. 46.

Bass's summary of investigations of self-esteem and leadership: Bernard M. Bass, *Leadership, Psychology and Organizational Behavior* (New York: Harper & Brothers, 1960), p. 299; Bass also reports the Stogdill and Barber findings, pp. 299–300.

Prewitt on social status and political power: Kenneth Prewitt, "Political Socialization and Leadership Selection," *Annals of the American Academy of Political and Social Science,* Vol. 361 (September 1965), 100.

I have drawn from the work of the worthy biographers Woodrow Wilson has attracted: George and George, *Woodrow Wilson and Colonel House,* is a pioneering personality study; the remarkable partnership of Sigmund Freud and William C. Bullitt, *Thomas Woodrow Wilson* (Boston: Houghton Mifflin, 1967), a psychological study; John Morton Blum, *Woodrow Wilson and the Politics of Morality* (Boston: Little, Brown, 1956); Woodrow Wilson, *Leaders of Men,* T. H. Vail Motter, ed. (Princeton: Princeton University Press, 1952); John Maynard Keynes, *Essays and Sketches in Biography* (New York: Meridian, 1956).

The quotation from the Georges is from their volume, p. 114, as is the observation of William Allen White, p. xxi.

The basic source of factual information on Wilson is the set of authoritative biographies by Arthur S. Link and the papers of Woodrow Wilson edited by Professor Link and associates, all published by Princeton University Press.

Thomas A. Bailey's studies, *Woodrow Wilson and the Lost Peace* (New York: Macmillan, 1944) and *Woodrow Wilson and the Great Betrayal* (New York: Macmillan, 1945), thoroughly cover the League battle.

On the institutionalized opposition to Wilson see James MacGregor Burns, *The Deadlock of Democracy* (Englewood Cliffs, N.J.: Prentice-Hall, 1963), ch. 6. The Georges are quoted on Wilson's need for adulatory friends from p. 43 of their work. Tucker on Wilson's moving to new leadership roles: Robert C. Tucker, "The Georges' Wilson Reexamined: An Essay on Psychobiography," *The American Political Science Review* (June 1977), 617; see also Karen Horney, *Neurosis and Human Growth* (New York: Norton, 1950).

5. THE CRUCIBLES OF POLITICAL LEADERSHIP

Freud on his youthful ambition: Sigmund Freud, *The Interpretation of Dreams* (London: Hogarth, 1953), as quoted in Erik Erikson, *Insight and Responsibility* (New York: Norton, 1964), p. 194.

Philip E. Vernon, *Personality Tests and Assessments* (London: Methuen, 1953).

Heinz L. and Rowena R. Ansbacher, eds., *The Individual Psychology of Alfred Adler* (New York: Basic Books, 1956) pp. 103–107, 125–129.

Abraham H. Maslow: *Motivation and Personality* (New York: Harper & Brothers, 1954).

The Spur of Ambition

Gandhi on his ambition is from Erik H. Erikson, *Gandhi's Truth* (New York: Norton, 1969), p. 144. Gandhi on his reflections in the station waiting room: Mohandas K. Gandhi, *Gandhi's Autobiography: The Story of My Experiments with Truth* (Washington, D.C.: Public Affairs Press, 1948), p. 141. Erikson's comment on this episode: *Gandhi's Truth,* p. 166. See also Mehta, pp. 99–130.

Hitler's reaction to the defeat of Germany: Walter C. Langer, *The Mind of Adolf Hitler* (New York: Basic Books, 1972), pp. 186–189. Hitler on his own reaction: Adolf Hitler, *Mein Kampf* (Boston: Houghton Mifflin, 1943), p. 223.

On the thematic unity in Hitler's speeches over time see Raoul de Roussy de Sales, ed., *My New Order* (New York: Reynal & Hitchcock, 1941), a compendium of Hitler's speeches beginning in April 1922.

On the beer hall putsch and its aftermath see Harold J. Gordon, Jr., *Hitler and the Beer Hall Putsch* (Princeton: Princeton University Press, 1972).

Lenin's early manhood: David Shub, *Lenin* (Garden City, N.Y.: Doubleday, 1948); Bertram D. Wolfe, *Three Who Made a Revolution* (New York: Dial Press, 1948); E. Victor Wolfenstein, *The Revolutionary Personality* (Princeton: Princeton University Press, 1967).

Adam B. Ulam, *The Bolsheviks* (New York: Macmillan, 1965), portrays Lenin's shift to the principle of leadership and is the source, p. 182, of the quotation about the dictatorial implications of his position. V. I. Lenin, *Selected Works* (New York: International Publishers, 1967), pp. 97–256, contains the text of *What Is to Be Done?*

Hamilton on fame: quoted by Larry Peterman, in review of Trevor Colburn, ed. *Fame and the Founding Fathers: Essays by Douglas Adair* (New York: Norton, 1974), in *American Political Science Review* (June 1977), 678.

The Need for Gratification

Maslow on subsidiary sets of needs: Abraham H. Maslow, *Motivation and Personality* (New York: Harper & Brothers, 1954), p. 90.

Knutson on power as linked directly to only one of Maslow's needs: Jeanne Knutson, *The Human Basis of the Polity* (Chicago: Aldine-Atherton, 1972), p. 68.

Edwin O'Connor, *The Last Hurrah* (Boston: Little, Brown, 1956), a novel written directly out of the personalities and conditions of Boston politics, is the source (p. 101) of the Garvey-Hennessey dialogue.

The Browning and Jacob study: Rufus P. Browning and Herbert Jacob, "Power Motivation and Political Personality," *Public Opinion Quarterly,* Vol. 28, No. 1 (Spring 1964), 75–90, reprinted in Greenstein and Lerner, pp. 443–454 (quotation from pp. 452–453).

Knutson is quoted from Knutson, pp. 47–48; and Barber from *The Lawmakers,* (New Haven: Yale University Press, 1965), as quoted in Knutson, p. 48.

On Bismarck's drive to power see Otto Pflanze, "Toward a Psychoanalytic Interpretation of Bismarck," *The American Historical Review,* Vol. 77, No. 2 (April 1972), 419–444, passim.

Significance of how persons cope with their problems: Smith, Bruner, and White, pp. 281ff.

Hargrove on Roosevelt: Erwin C. Hargrove, *The Power of the Modern Presidency* (New York: Knopf, 1974); see also James MacGregor Burns, *Roosevelt: The Lion and the Fox* (New York: Harcourt, Brace Jovanovich, 1970), passim.

Kurt Goldstein, *Human Nature in the Light of Psychopathology* (Cambridge, Mass.: Harvard University Press, 1940). The need for self-actualization: Maslow, *Motivation and Personality,* esp. pp. 91–92, 149, 183.

Higher needs: Maslow, pp. 146–150.

Knutson on self-actualization: Knutson, pp. 86–87ff.

White on competence or "effectance": Robert W. White, "Motivation Reconsidered: The Concept of Competence," *Psychological Review,* Vol. 66, No. 5 (September 1959), 297–333.

On self-actualization see also Lane, *Political Thinking and Consciousness* (Chicago; Markham, 1969), pp. 44–45.

Political skills and political selection: Fred I. Greenstein, *Personality and Politics* (Chicago: Markham, 1969), p. 45; see also Kenneth Prewitt, "Political Socialization and Leadership Selection" *Annals of the American Academy of Political and Social Science,* Vol. 361 (September 1965), 96–111.

Maslow's "biologistic" approach to self-actualization: A. H. Maslow, *Toward a Psychology of Being,* 2nd ed. (Princeton: Van Nostrand Reinhold, 1968), p. 160, cited by Smith, below.

Further aspects of self-actualization, especially in its potential for leadership: M. Brewster Smith, "On Self-Actualization," ch. 9 in his *Humanizing Social Psychology* (San Francisco: Jossey-Bass, 1974), pp. 164–179; and Jeanne N. Knutson, *The Human Basis of the Polity,* pp. 86–102.

Definition, intensity, variety, and worldwide scope of popular aspirations: Hadley Cantril, *The Pattern of Human Concerns* (New Brunswick: Rutgers University Press, 1965).

Davies on violence: James C. Davies, "Aggression, Violence, Revolution, and War," in Jeanne N. Knutson, ed., *Handbook of Political Psychology* (San Francisco: Jossey-Bass, 1973), p. 247.

Ted Robert Gurr on value expectations: cited in Knutson, p. 248; cf. Charles Tilly, "Revolutions and Collective Violence," ch. 5 in Fred I. Greenstein and Nelson W. Polsby, *Handbook of Political Science,* Vol. 3 (Reading, Mass.: Addison-Wesley, 1975). "Objective" and "felt" needs of migrant poor in Latin America: Wayne A. Cornelius, "Urbanization and Political Demand Making: Political Participation Among the Migrant Poor in Latin American Cities," *American Political Science Review,* Vol. 68, No. 3 (September 1974), 1125–1146. But see Abraham H. Miller, Louis H. Bolce, and Mark Halligan, "The J-Curve Theory and the Black Urban Riots; An Empirical Test of Progressive Relative Deprivation Theory," *American Political Science Review,* Vol. 71, No. 3 (September 1977), 964–982.

Openings and Closures: The Structure of Political Opportunity

Major sources on this subject are Joseph A. Schlesinger, *Ambition and Politics* (Chicago: Rand McNally, 1966); Lester G. Seligman, *Recruiting Political Elites* (New York: General Learning Press, 1971); Gordon S. Black, "A Theory of Political Ambition: Career Choices and the Role of Structural Incentives," *American Political Science Review,* Vol. 66, No. 1 (March 1972), 144–159; Kenneth Prewitt, *The Recruitment of Political Leaders: A Study of Citizen-Politicians* (Indianapolis: Bobbs-Merrill, 1970).

Namier on the House of Commons and on rotten boroughs: Lewis Namier, *The Structure of Politics at the Accession of George III,* 2nd ed. (London: Macmillan, 1957), pp. 1, 63; Chesterfield is quoted at p. 1.

Of the immense literature on the effects of the first and second reform bills in Britain, W. L. Guttsman, ed., *The English Ruling Class* (London: Weidenfeld and Nicolson, 1969) provides some useful selections.

The Weber quotation is from H. H. Gerth and C. Wright Mills, eds. and trs., *From Max Weber: Essays in Sociology* (New York: Oxford University Press, 1946), p. 105.

Soviet opportunity structure: Raymond A. Bauer, Alex Inkeles, and Clyde Kluckhohn, *How the Soviet System Works* (Cambridge, Mass.: Harvard University Press, 1957); W. W. Rostow, *The Dynamics of Soviet Society* (New York: Norton, 1953); Frederick L. Schuman, *Government in the Soviet Union* (New York: Crowell, 1967).

Alexander Hamilton on the attractiveness of the new constitutional system to men of ambition: Jonathan Elliot, ed., *The Debates in the Several State Conventions on the Adoption of the Federal Constitution* (Philadelphia: Lippincott, 1836), pp. 306, 364.

The "steam kettle effect": Thomas R. Herwitz, Harry J. Kelly, and Maryfrances Tyler, "Democratic Politics and Party Regeneration in the Massachusetts Third Congressional District" (Williamstown, Mass.: 1976), pp. 31–33.

Classic works on the education of princes: Desiderius Erasmus, *The Education of a Christian Prince* (New York: Columbia University Press, 1936), Lester K. Born, translator; Juan de Mariana, *The King and the Education of the King* (Chevy Chase, Md.: Country Dollar Press, 1948); G. A. Moore, translator; Machiavelli's *The Prince.*

The quotations from Erasmus are from pp. 31, 33–34.

Rupert Wilkinson, *Gentlemanly Power* (London: Oxford University Press, 1964) describes British leadership and the public school tradition, with an illuminating comparison of Confucian education; Wilkinson is quoted on his comparison of the two systems at pp. 125–126.

Groton as a training ground for political leadership: Frank D. Ashburn, *Peabody of Groton* (New York: Coward, McCann, 1944), and Burns, *Roosevelt: The Lion and the Fox,* pp. 10–16, 496.

On education for leadership in ancient Greece, see Werner Jaeger, *Paideia: The Ideals of Greek Culture* (Oxford: Blackwell, 1939).

I have drawn my account of political education in developing countries largely from the studies of different countries in James S. Coleman, ed., *Education and Political Development* (Princeton: Princeton University Press, 1965).

The Creation of Followers

Schumpeter quotation: J. Schumpeter, *Capitalism, Socialism and Democracy* (New York: Harper & Brothers, 1947), p. 269.

Erikson quotation: Erikson, *Gandhi's Truth,* p. 408.

On political participation the coverage is vast; I have used especially Sidney Verba and Norman H. Nie, *Participation in America* (New York: Harper & Row, 1972); Lester W. Milbrath, *Political Participation* (Chicago: Rand McNally, 1965); Norman H. Nie, G. Bingham Powell, Jr., and Kenneth Prewitt, "Social Structure and Political Participation: Developmental Relationships," *American Political Science Review,* Vol. 63, No. 2 (June 1969), 361–378, and Vol. 63, No. 3 (September 1969), 808–832; Gabriel A. Almond and Sidney Verba, *The Civic Culture* (Princeton: Princeton University Press, 1963); Kenneth Prewitt, *The Recruitment of Political Leaders* (Indianapolis: Bobbs-Merrill, 1970).

Stein Rokkan, "The Comparative Study of Political Participation: Notes Toward a Perspective on Current Research," in Austin Ranney, ed., *Essays on the Behavioral Study of Politics* (Urbana: University of Illinois Press, 1962), pp. 47–90; Giuseppe Di Palma, *Apathy and Participation* (New York: Free Press, 1970); and Almond and Verba are important for international comparisons.

Face-to-face influence: Paul Lazarsfeld et al., *The People's Choice,* 2nd ed. (New York: Columbia University Press, 1948), passim.

Five-nation study: Nie, et al.

Key on intensity: V. O. Key, Jr., *Public Opinion and American Democracy* (New York: Knopf, 1961), p. 227.

Key on the attentive and inattentive public: Key, ch. 11.

Electorate divisions: Lazarsfeld, et al.; Milbrath, passim.

Two-step flow: Lazarsfeld; Key; see also for the marginal but significant role of party workers, Phillips Cutright and Peter H. Rossi, "Grass Roots Politicians and the Vote," *American Sociological Review,* Vol. 23, No. 2 (April 1958), 171–179.

Participation in China: John Wilson Lewis, *Party Leadership in Communist China* (Ithaca: Cornell University Press, 1963); James R. Townsend, *Political Participation in Communist China* (Berkeley: University of California Press, 1967); K. S. Karol, *China: The Other Communism* (New York: Hill and Wang, 1967); John Wilson Lewis, ed., *Party Leadership and Revolutionary Power in China* (Cambridge, England: Cambridge University Press, 1970).

The Mao statement is quoted in Lewis, *Party Leadership in Communist China,* p. 184.

Overlap of activism: Verba and Nie.

Most of the works cited above on political participation are relevant to questions of apathy. Key's conclusions about voters: V. O. Key, Jr., *The Responsible Electorate* (Cambridge, Mass.: Harvard University Press, 1966), p. 7.

On apathy see especially Herbert McClosky, "Political Participation," *International Encyclopedia of the Social Sciences,* Vol. 12, pp. 252–265; on alienation, Murray B. Levin, *The Alienated Voter* (New York: Holt, Rinehart and Winston, 1960); on anomie, L. Srole, "Social Integration and Certain Corollaries: An Exploratory Study," *American Sociological Review,* Vol. 21, No. 6 (December 1956), 709–716; and Knutson's comments thereon, in Knutson, pp. 150–153.

Cantril on apathy in India: Hadley Cantril, *The Pattern of Human Concerns* (New Brunswick: Rutgers University Press, 1965), p. 303.

On anomie I have used also Herbert McClosky and John H. Schaar, "Psychological Dimensions of Anomy," *American Sociological Review,* Vol. 30, No. 1 (February 1965), 14–40.

On the extension of the franchise see Rokkan's excellent tables in Ranney, *Essays,* esp. p. 75.

6. INTELLECTUAL LEADERSHIP: IDEAS AS MORAL POWER

Aron on defining the intellectual: Raymond Aron, *The Opium of the Intellectuals* (New York: Doubleday, 1957), p. 203.

Schumpeter on the same: Joseph A. Schumpeter, *Capitalism, Socialism, and Democracy* (New York: Harper & Brothers, 1942, 1947), p. 145.

Hofstadter on the intellectual: Richard Hofstadter, *Anti-Intellectualism in American Life* (New York: Knopf, 1963), p. 25.

Nettl's definition of intellectuals: J. P. Nettl, "Ideas, Intellectuals, and Structures of Dissent," in Philip Rieff, ed., *On Intellectuals* (Garden City, N.Y.: Doubleday, 1969), p. 81.

Intellectual activity as response to societal need: Edward A. Shils, "Intellectuals," *International Encyclopedia of the Social Sciences,* Vol. 7, p. 44.

On the early lives of some of the French thinkers see Frank E. Manuel, *The Prophets of Paris* (Cambridge, Mass.: Harvard University Press, 1962), passim.

Mill's melancholia: Michael St. John Packe, *The Life of John Stuart Mill* (New York: Macmillan, 1954), pp. 74–81.

Quarrel between the ancients and the moderns: Ira O. Wade, *The Intellectual Origins of the French Enlightenment* (Princeton: Princeton University Press, 1971), pp. 624–631.

Intellectuals at the Tension Points

Pessimistic view of man: Lester G. Crocker, *An Age of Crisis: Man and World in Eighteenth Century French Thought* (Baltimore: Johns Hopkins Press, 1959), esp. ch. 8.

Crocker on the Age of Enlightenment: Crocker, p. 455.

Robespierre and the revolution: Crocker, pp. 462–463.

Making the rounds of salons: Kingsley Martin, *French Liberal Thought in the Eighteenth Century* (Boston: Little, Brown, 1929), p. 109.

Diderot and Montesquieu on the salons: quoted in Martin, p. 105.

Coser on the "literature of sociality": Lewis A. Coser, *Men of Ideas* (New York: Free Press, 1965), p. 15.

Censorship and the diffusion of ideas: Coser, pp. 83–97 and passim; Ira O. Wade, *The Clandestine Organization and Diffusion of Philosophic Ideas in France from 1700 to 1750* (New York: Octagon Books, 1967).

Frankel on the true intellectual: Charles Frankel, *The Faith of Reason* (New York: King's Crown Press, 1948), p. 9.

D'Alembert on men of letters: quoted in Frankel, p. 10.

Cassirer on Taine: Ernst Cassirer, *The Philosophy of the Enlightenment* (Princeton: Princeton University Press, 1951), p. 267.

Tocqueville on eighteenth-century French writers: Alexis de Tocqueville, *The Old Regime and the French Revolution,* quoted in de Huszar, p. 18.

Liberty and Power

Nedham on freedom: quoted in W. B. Gwyn, *The Meaning of the Separation of Powers* (New Orleans: Tulane University Press, 1965), p. 22.

Sydney and Hobbes on the need to contain power: quoted in Gwyn, p. 23. English ideas after the Civil War: Gwyn, p. 37.

Laslett on Locke: Peter Laslett, ed., *Locke's Two Treatises of Government* (Cambridge, England: Cambridge University Press, 1970), p. 70.

Plato on balance in government: B. Jowett, translator, *Laws,* III, *The Dialogues of Plato* (Chicago: Encyclopedia Britannica, 1952), Vol. 7. pp. 671–672.

Aristotle on Proportion: Aristotle, *Politics* (Oxford: Oxford University Press, 1962), Ernest Barker, translator, Book V, ch. 9, p. 232.

Vile on separation of powers as subordinate theory taking on a life of its own: M. J. C. Vile, *Constitutionalism and the Separation of Powers* (Oxford: Clarendon Press, 1967), p. 98.

English coffee-houses: Aytoun Ellis, *The Penny Universities* (London: Secker & Warburg, 1956).

The London clubs: Robert J. Allen, *The Clubs of Augustan London* (Cambridge, Mass.: Harvard University Press, 1933), esp. chs. 2 and 4.

Bailyn on liberty and power as opposites: Bernard Bailyn, *The Ideological Origins of the American Revolution* (Cambridge, Mass.: Harvard University Press–Belknap Press, 1967), pp. 57–58.

Madison on granting of charters: quoted in Bailyn, p. 55.

Tory critic of American ''heroes'': quoted in Bailyn, p. 281.

Madison on factions and conflict: *Federalist* No. 10.

Curbing the effects of faction: *Federalist* No. 51.

Bailyn on the Constitution as the culmination of a long development: Bailyn, p. 285.

Intellectuals and the Nature of Liberty

Cartwright on the cabinet: John Cartwright, *An Appeal on the Subject of the English Constitution* (Boston, Lincolnshire, 1797), pp. 46, 51, quoted in Vile, pp. 117–118.

Recognition of balanced power and equilibrium as leading to governmental deadlock: Vile, p. 106.

Bentham on government as an evil: Jeremy Bentham, *An Introduction to the Principles of Morals and Legislation* (New York: Columbia University Press, 1945), p. 170.

On Bentham generally: Crane Brinton, *English Political Thought in the Nineteenth Century* (London: Benn, 1933); John Stuart Mill, ''Bentham,'' in Gertrude Himmelfarb, ed., *John Stuart Mill, Essays on Politics and Culture* (Garden City, N.Y.: Doubleday, 1963).

Himmelfarb on Mill's liberty: Gertrude Himmelfarb, *On Liberty and Liberalism* (New York: Knopf, 1974).

John Stuart Mill: H. J. McCloskey, *John Stuart Mill: A Critical Study* (London: Macmillan, 1971); Maurice Cowling, *Mill and Liberalism* (Cambridge, England: Cambridge University Press, 1963); Michael St. John Packe, *The Life of John Stuart Mill* (New York: Macmillan, 1954); Isaiah Berlin, *Two Concepts of Liberty* (London: Oxford University Press, 1958), esp. pp. 7–16.

The Fabians: A. M. McBriar, *Fabian Socialism and English Politics 1884–1918* (London: Cambridge University Press, 1962), from which H. G. Wells is quoted at p. 346; E. J. Hobsbawm, *Laboring Men* (New York: Basic Books, 1964); Royden Harrison, *Before the Socialists* (London: Routledge & Kegan Paul, 1965). I have also had the opportunity to read a preliminary draft of the manuscript of Norman MacKenzie and Jeanne MacKenzie on the Fabians, from which I have quoted Beatrice Webb (from her *Diary*, March 12, 1893).

The Intellectual Test of Transforming Power

Hartz on the American fear of majority rule: Louis Hartz, *The Liberal Tradition in America* (New York: Harcourt, Brace and Co., 1955), p. 129.

William Graham Sumner: Richard Hofstadter, *Social Darwinism in American Thought* (New York: Braziller, 1959), ch. 3; Robert G. McCloskey, *American Conservatism in the Age of Enterprise* (Cambridge, Mass.: Harvard University Press, 1951), chs. 2 and 3.

Stephen J. Field: McCloskey, chs. 4 and 5; Carl B. Swisher, *Stephen J. Field* (Washington: Brookings, 1930).

Andrew Carnegie: John C. Van Dyke, ed., *Autobiography of Andrew Carnegie* (Boston: Houghton Mifflin, 1948); Andrew Carnegie, *Triumphant Democracy* (New York: Scribner, 1893).

The feting of Herbert Spencer: Hofstadter, pp. 48–49.

Lester Ward: Hofstadter, ch. 4; Ralph H. Gabriel, *The Course of American Democratic Thought* (New York: Ronald Press, 1940), chs. 14 and 17.

Woodrow Wilson quoted respectively from Woodrow Wilson, *The New Freedom* (Garden City, N.Y.: Doubleday, Page, 1913), pp. 64–65; Woodrow Wilson, "Cabinet Government in the United States," *International Review,* Vol. 7 (August 1879), 150; see also Austin Ranney, *The Doctrine of Responsible Party Government* (Urbana: University of Illinois Press, 1962).

Franklin Roosevelt's brains trust: Rexford G. Tugwell, *The Brains Trust* (New York: Viking Press, 1968); Raymond Moley, *After Seven Years* (New York: Harper & Brothers, 1939); Eric Goldman, *Rendezvous with Destiny* (New York: Knopf, 1952).

Franklin Roosevelt on the economic bill of rights: Samuel I. Rosenman, ed., *The Public Papers and Addresses of Franklin D. Roosevelt* (New York: Harper & Brothers, 1950), 1944–45 volume, pp. 40–41.

Works on intellectual leadership in American politics other than those cited above: Daniel J. Boorstin, *The Genius of American Politics* (Chicago: University of Chicago Press, 1953); Richard Hofstadter, *The Age of Reform* (New York: Knopf, 1955); Charles Edward Merriam, *American Political Ideas* (New York: Macmillan, 1929), esp. chs. 11 and 12.

The Commager study is Henry Steele Commager, *Majority Rule and Minority Rights* (New York: Oxford University Press, 1943).

The Lerner study is Max Lerner, *Ideas Are Weapons* (New York: Viking Press, 1939).

Harrison on necessary conditions for political influence by intellectuals: Royden Harrison, *Before the Socialists* (London: Routledge & Kegan Paul, 1965), pp. 254–255.

Peter Gay, *The Enlightenment: An Interpretation* (New York: Knopf, 1966).

7. REFORM LEADERSHIP

Kallen: Horace M. Kallen, *Encyclopedia of the Social Sciences,* Vol. 7 (New York: Macmillan, 1934), p. 194.

Grey's early life and character: George Macaulay Trevelyan, *Lord Grey of the Reform Bill* (New York: Longmans, Green, 1920), quoted (on Eton) at p. 4.

Butler on Eton as political educator: J. R. M. Butler, *The Passing of the Great Reform Bill* (New York: Longmans, Green, 1914), p. 233.

Addington on Grey: quoted in Trevelyan, *Lord Grey of the Reform Bill,* p. 15; for a different attitude see Earl Giles Ilchester, ed., *The Journal of Elizabeth, Lady Holland* (London: Longmans, Green, 1908), Vol. I, p. 100.

On Grey generally, see *Dictionary of National Biography,* Vol. 29, pp. 178–179; Earl Charles Grey, *Correspondence with King William IV and Sir Herbert Taylor* (London, J. Murray, 1867), 2 vols.; and Grey, *Correspondence with Princess Lieven,* G. LeStrange, tr. (London: Bentley and Son, 1890), 2 vols.

Great Britain: The Insistent Particularists

Reform as animating force: Butler, p. 3.

Butler on no need for reform in 1770s and 1780s: Butler, p. 12.

Trevelyan on split in Whig party: Trevelyan, p. 48.

Grey on Whigs as defenders of liberty: Grey to Lambton, January 3, 1820, cited in Butler, pp. 35–36.

Grey's prescience at thirty: Spencer Walpole, *History of England* (London: Green and Co., 1878–1905), ch. 13.

Grey on need for major reform: Speech on the Reform Bill, October 3, 1831, *Hansard Parliamentary Debates,* 3rd series, Vol. 7 (London: T. C. Hansard, 1832), pp. 934, 935.

On passage of the reform bill I have used Butler and Trevelyan; see also G. M. Trevelyan,

British History in the Nineteenth Century and After, 1782–1919 (New York: Harper & Row, 1966); Elie Halévy, *History of the English People in the Nineteenth Century,* (New York: Harcourt, Brace, 1924), Vols. 2, 3; J. A. R. Marriott, *England Since Waterloo* (London: Methuen, 1913); G. D. H. Cole, *A Short History of the British Working Class Movement, 1789–1927* (London: George Allen and Unwin, 1927); Asa Briggs, *The Age of Improvement* (London: Longmans, Green, 1959); G. D. H. Cole, *The British Common People, 1746–1946* (New York: University Paperbacks, 1961).

Of the biographies of leaders in collaboration or competition with Grey see especially Graham Wallas, *The Life of Francis Place* (New York: Franklin, 1898); Frances Hawes, *Henry Brougham* (New York: St. Martin's Press, 1958); G. D. H. Cole, *The Life of William Cobbett* (London: W. Collins Sons, 1924); John W. Osborne, *William Cobbett: His Thought and His Times* (New Brunswick: Rutgers University Press, 1966).

Mather on anti-leadership attitudes of Chartists: F. C. Mather, *Chartism* (London: Historical Association, 1965), pp. 29–30; Mather is also the source, p. 30, of the quotation of William Lovett.

Remarks of Robert Hartwell: quoted in M. Beer, *A History of British Socialism* (London: George Allen and Unwin, 1940), III, pp. 25–26.

Briggs on Chartist followership: Asa Briggs, "National Bearings," in Asa Briggs, ed., *Chartist Studies* (London: Macmillan, 1959), pp. 292–294.

Propaganda efforts of Anti-Corn League: Donald Grove Barnes, *A History of the English Corn Laws from 1660–1846* (New York: Augustus M. Kelley, 1965), p. 259.

On the anti-corn law movement, and especially its leadership, see also C. R. Fay, *The Corn Laws and Social England* (London: Cambridge University Press, 1932); G. M. Trevelyan, *The Life of John Bright* (Boston: Houghton Mifflin, 1925); John Morley, *The Life of Richard Cobden* (Boston: Roberts Brothers, 1881).

The problems of party and reform leadership are brilliantly developed by D. A. Hamer, *Liberal Politics in the Age of Gladstone and Rosebery* (Oxford: Clarendon Press, 1972). Gladstone to Bright on shaping issue: John Morley, *The Life of William Ewart Gladstone* (New York: Macmillan, 1903), Vol. 2, p. 87. Chamberlain: James L. Garvin and Julian Amery, *The Life of Joseph Chamberlain* (London: Macmillan, 1932–1969), esp. Vols. 1 and 2.

Russia: Reform from Above

The czar as Czar of Freedom: Stephen Graham, *Tsar of Freedom* (New Haven: Yale University Press, 1935).

Alexander on his father: quoted in Alfred J. Rieber, *The Politics of Autocracy* (Paris: Mouton, 1966), p. 20.

Chamberlin on Slavophiles: William Henry Chamberlin, *The Russian Revolution* (New York: Grosset & Dunlap, 1965), Vol. I, p. 21.

On Alexander's reasons for undertaking emancipation see especially Rieber; and E. Lampert, *Sons Against Fathers* (Oxford: Clarendon Press, 1965), esp. Part One.

Elena Pavlovna as reformer: Rieber, p. 41.

Alexander II's address to the Moscow gentry leadership: quoted in Michael T. Florinsky, *Russia: A History and an Interpretation* (New York: Macmillan, 1953), Vol. II, p. 883; see also Lampert, pp. 10–11.

Rieber on reform implementation: Rieber, p. 54.

Lampert on the effect of emancipation on the peasantry: Lampert, pp. 23–24.

Turgenev on Russians' needs: Ivan S. Turgenev, *Fathers and Sons* (New York: Modern Library, 1961), p. 68.

Alexander on the bond of sovereign to people: Letter to A. I. Bariatinskii, July 7, 1858, quoted in Rieber, p. 34.

Lampert on social conflict: Lampert, p. 52.

Other sources on Alexandrine reformism aside from those cited above: Terence Emmons, *The Russian Landed Gentry and the Peasant Emancipation of 1861* (London: Cambridge University Press, 1968); Bernard Pares, *Russia and Reform* (London: Archibald, Constable, 1907).

Pobedonostsev: Robert F. Byrnes, *Pobedonostsev: His Life and Thought* (Bloomington: Indiana University Press, 1968), quoted at p. 324.

Alexander on Bismarck and liberalism: quoted in Florinsky, p. 1090.

Liberals in politics: George Fischer, *Russian Liberalism from Gentry to Intelligentsia* (Cambridge, Mass.: Harvard University Press, 1958), p. 6; this discussion draws heavily from this work.

Liberals as empiricists: Fischer, p. 14, quoting Aleksandr Potresov in *Obshchestvennoe dvizhenie v Rossii,* I, p. 242.

Small deeds versus senseless dreams is a theme of Fischer, passim.

Useful sources for the period, aside from those quoted above, are Richard Hare, *Pioneers of Russian Social Thought* (Oxford: Oxford University Press, 1951); Hugh McLean, Martin E. Malia, and George Fischer, *Russian Thought and Politics,* Harvard Slavic Studies, Vol. IV (The Hague: Mouton, 1957), esp. Part Two; Marc Raeff, ed., *Russian Intellectual History: An Anthology* (New York: Harcourt, Brace & World, 1966); Hans Kohn, ed., *The Mind of Modern Russia* (New York: Harper & Brothers, 1955).

Reform in America: Dilemmas of Transforming Leadership

Emerson on reform: Ralph Waldo Emerson, *Miscellanies: Embracing Nature, Addresses, and Lectures* (Boston: Osgood, 1876), pp. 186, 187, 200.

Nevins on reform: Allan Nevins, *Ordeal of the Union* (New York: Scribner, 1947), p. 113.

Phillips on the reformer and the politician: quoted in Richard Hofstadter, *The American Political Tradition* (New York: Vintage Books, 1954), p. 138.

James Russell Lowell quotation: Nevins, Vol. 1, p. 147.

Sumner on true politics: David Donald, *Charles Sumner and the Coming of the War* (New York: Knopf, 1960), p. 219.

Lincoln on the radicals: Fawn Brodie, *Thaddeus Stevens* (New York: Norton, 1959), p. 199.

Hofstadter on abolitionist millennialism: Hofstadter, *American Political Tradition,* p. 145.

Reformers' attitudes toward organized labor: John G. Sproat, *The Best Men* (New York: Oxford University Press, 1968), p. 208.

Reform leadership among Republicans and independents: Earle Dudley Ross, *The Liberal Republican Movement* (New York: Henry Holt, 1919), esp. ch. 3.

On the period and the movement generally, aside from sources cited above, see Ralph Korngold, *Thaddeus Stevens* (New York: Harcourt, Brace, 1955); Ellis Paxson Oberholtzer, *A History of the United States Since the Civil War* (New York: Macmillan, 1922, 1926), Vols. 2 and 3.

Theodore Roosevelt on mossbacks and on reformers: Elting E. Morison, ed., *The Letters of Theodore Roosevelt* (Cambridge, Mass.: Harvard University Press, 1951–1954), esp. vols. 2–4, passim.

Hofstadter on reform division over organization: Hofstadter, *The Age of Reform,* p. 255.

White on breaking the machine: William Allen White, *The Old Order Changeth* (New York: Macmillan, 1911), pp. 39, 121, quoted in Hofstadter, pp. 256–257.

Hofstadter on disinterested need: Hofstadter, p. 257.

Ostrogorski on single-issue parties: M. I. Ostrogorski, *Democracy and the Organization of Political Parties* (New York: Macmillan, 1902), Vol. 2, pp. 664–665.

Ford's views on party and president: Henry Jones Ford, *The Rise and Growth of American Politics* (New York: Macmillan, 1898).

Ford on presidency and party: Ford, pp. 292, 356.

Croly on executive leadership: Herbert Croly, *Progressive Democracy* (New York: Macmillan, 1914), pp. 304, 305.

See generally Austin Ranney, *The Doctrine of Responsible Party Government* (Urbana: University of Illinois Press, 1962) on the analyses by leading academic and other critics of the relation of political organization and the individual citizen.

For a nineteenth-century attack on the "evil of party" see Albert Stickney, *A True Republic* (New York: Harper & Brothers, 1879). Two twentieth-century works that criticized or denigrated the role of party in reform leadership: John Dewey, *The Public and Its Problems* (New York: Henry Holt, 1927), and Dewey, *Liberalism and Social Action* (New York: Putnam, 1935).

8. REVOLUTIONARY LEADERSHIP

Louis' remark and Arendt's comment: Hannah Arendt, *On Revolution* (New York: Viking Press, 1963), p. 41.

The definition of revolution: Mark N. Hagopian, *The Phenomenon of Revolution* (New York: Dodd, Mead, 1974), pp. 1, 3.

Martin Luther: I have used especially Owen Chadwick, *The Reformation* (Baltimore: Penguin Books, 1964); Richard Friedenthal, *Luther,* John Nowell, tr. (London: Weidenfeld and Nicolson, 1967), quoted at pp. 96–97; Erik H. Erikson, *Young Man Luther* (New York: Norton, 1962).

General treatments of revolution, aside from those referred to below: Arendt; Hagopian; Ted Robert Gurr, *Why Men Rebel* (Princeton: Princeton University Press, 1970); James V. Downton, Jr., *Rebel Leadership* (New York: Free Press, 1973); James Chowning Davies, ed., *When Men Revolt and Why* (New York: Free Press, 1971); Bob Jessop, *Social Order, Reform and Revolution* (New York: Herder and Herder, 1973).

France: The Maelstrom of Leadership

Events of 1787–1789: Georges Lefebvre, *The Coming of the French Revolution* (Princeton: Princeton University Press, 1947); M. J. Sydenham, *The French Revolution* (London: Batsford, 1965).

Occupations of the crowd that stormed the Bastille: George Rudé, *The Crowd in the French Revolution* (Oxford: Clarendon Press, 1959), p. 57.

Le Bon on the irrationality of crowd leaders: Gustave Le Bon, *The Crowd* (New York: Viking Press, 1960), p. 118 (originally published in 1895); cf. Rudé, pp. 219–221.

Rudé on the effect of the food situation: Rudé, p. 208.

Conditions of the French peasantry: Alexis de Tocqueville, *The Old Regime and the Revolution* (New York: Harper & Brothers, 1856), esp. ch. 12.

On the French revolution as a European movement: R. R. Palmer, *The Age of the Democratic Revolution,* Vol. I, *The Challenge* (Princeton: Princeton University Press, 1959).

Palmer on the Declaration of the Rights of Man and Citizen: Palmer, I, pp. 486–487.

Text of Declaration of the Rights of Man and Citizen: Lefebvre, pp. 221–222.

Text of draft provision in 1793 Declaration: Sydenham, p. 165; statement of Saint-Just on liberty: Sydenham, p. 164. Arendt on French and American revolutions: Hannah Arendt, *On Revolution* (New York: Viking Press, 1963), p. 49.

Arendt on price of solving the social question through political means: Arendt, p. 108.

For a critique of Arendt's views of revolution see Hagopian, pp. 66–67.

Robespierre on missing the moment of found freedom: quoted in Arendt, p. 55.

Brissot on disorganizers: quoted in Sydenham, p. 133.

Sydenham on the tragedy of the Revolution: Sydenham, p. 237.

See also Clarence Crane Brinton, *The Jacobins* (New York: Macmillan, 1930); M. J. Sydenham, *The Girondins* (London: Athlone, 1961); R. R. Palmer, *Twelve Who Ruled* (Princeton: Princeton University Press, 1969).

Russia: The Vocation of Leadership

Treadgold on the nature of revolutionary journalism: Donald W. Treadgold, *Lenin and His Rivals* (New York: Praeger, 1955), p. 69.

Marx and Engels on the working class as a political party: Resolution relative to the General Rules (adopted at the Hague Congress of the International Workingmen's Association, September 1872), in *The International Herald,* London, December 14, 1872, cited by Monty Johnstone, "Marx and Engels and the Concept of the Party," *The Socialist Register* (1967), pp. 121, 145.

Rossanda on Marx-Lenin theory of revolution: Rossana Rossanda, "Class and Party," *The Socialist Register* (1970), p. 219.

Lenin on spontaneity: V. I. Lenin, *What Is to Be Done?* (New York: International Publishers, 1929), p. 41.

Lenin on spontaneous birth of new social order: Lenin, pp. 50–51.

Lenin on the role of the working class and on the Mensheviks' leading badly: quoted in Treadgold, p. 170.

Miliukov: Thomas Riha, *A Russian European* (Notre Dame: University of Notre Dame Press, 1969).

On the revolution of 1905 and the period immediately preceding see especially Ulam, *The Bolsheviks,* ch. 4.

Trotsky on the dead revolution and the new one: quoted in Michael T. Florinsky, *Russia: A History and an Interpretation,* Vol. II (New York: Macmillan, 1953), p. 1183.

Florinsky on liberals and self-government: Florinsky, p. 1184.

Lenin on skipping the capitalistic phase: V. I. Lenin, *Two Tactics,* quoted in Shub, p. 113.

Ulam on Lenin's isolation: Ulam, p. 270.

Deutscher on the differences between Lenin and Trotsky: Isaac Deutscher, *The Prophet Armed* (New York: Oxford University Press, 1954), p. 291.

Ulam on the fear of repudiating Lenin as leader: Ulam, p. 365.

Wolfenstein on leader as fulfilling a father's role: Wolfenstein, pp. 227, 233–234.

Lenin's rules for uprisings: quoted from Payne, p. 363.

See also Louis Fischer, *The Life of Lenin* (New York: Harper & Row, 1965); Marx-Engels-Lenin Institute, *Vladimir I. Lenin: A Political Biography* (New York: International Publishers, 1943).

China: The Cult of Leadership

Lewis on leadership doctrine in Communist China: John W. Lewis, *Leadership in Communist China* (Ithaca: Cornell University Press, 1963), p. vii.

Lenin on imperialism: quoted in Fischer, p. 97.

Greene on the failure of reform leadership in prerevolutionary China: Fred Greene, *The Far East* (New York: Holt, Rinehart, 1957), p. 102.

Sun Yat-sen and the Kuomintang in its early years: Li Chien-nung, *The Political History of China, 1840–1928* (Princeton: Van Nostrand, 1956); Lucian W. Pye, *China: An Introduction* (Boston: Little, Brown, 1972); Harold Z. Schiffrin, *Sun Yat-sen and the Origins of the Chinese Revolution* (Berkeley: University of California Press, 1968); Greene.

Stalin on squeezing out the Kuomintang: Ulam, p. 276; Bukharin on Canton as "red Moscow": Stephen F. Cohen, *Bukharin and the Bolshevik Revolution* (New York: Knopf, 1973), p. 260.

Ulam on Chiang's tactics: Ulam, p. 276.

Personal and political background of Mao Tse-tung: Benjamin I. Schwartz, *Chinese Communism and the Rise of Mao* (Cambridge, Mass.: Harvard University Press, 1951); Stuart Schram, *Mao Tse-tung* (New York: Simon and Schuster, 1966).

Mao's report on the peasantry: partial text in Stuart R. Schram, *The Political Thought of Mao Tse-tung* (New York: Praeger, 1963), pp. 179–188.

Mao's relation to the kidnapping of Chiang Kai-shek: James Pinckney Harrison, *The Long March to Power* (New York: Praeger, 1972), pp. 268–270.

Mao's study of the peasantry: Lewis, pp. 11–12.

Mao on physical exercise: "A Study of Physical Education," *Hsin Ch'ing Nien* (April 1917), quoted in Schram, pp. 98–102.

Mao on contradictions: quoted in Schram, pp. 134, 236.

Schurmann on Mao's theory of contradictions: Franz Schurmann, *Ideology and Organization in Communist China* (Berkeley: University of California Press, 1966), pp. 103–104.

People's Daily on leadership and contradictions: quoted in Lewis, pp. 90–91.

Party organization and propaganda: Alan P. L. Liu, *Communications and National Integration in Communist China* (Berkeley: University of California Press, 1971); Frederick T. C. Yu, *Mass Persuasion in Communist China* (New York: Praeger, 1964).

Lewis on Mao's emphasis on followers' interaction with leaders: Lewis, p. 22.

Mao on learning from subordinates: excerpt from speech of March 13, 1949, at the Second Plenum of the Seventh Central Committee, quoted in Schram, p. 219.

Schurmann on Communist party as leadership structure: Schurmann, p. xlii.

Demands of party life: A. Doak Barnett, *Cadres, Bureaucracy, and Political Power in Communist China* (New York: Columbia University Press, 1967), pp. 434–435.

I have also used Ping-ti Ho and Tang Tsou, eds., *China in Crisis,* Vol. 1, *China's Heritage and the Communist Political System* (Chicago: University of Chicago Press, 1968), Books 1 and 2; A. Doak Barnett, *Communist China: The Early Years, 1949–55* (New York: Praeger, 1964); John Wilson Lewis, ed., *Party Leadership and Revolutionary Power in China* (London: Cambridge University Press, 1970); K. S. Karol, *China: The Other Communism* (New York: Hill and Wang, 1967). See also Frederick Wakeman, Jr., *History and Will: Philosophical Perspectives of Mao Tse-tung's Thought* (Berkeley: University of California Press, 1973).

Stalin's self-idealization: Robert C. Tucker, *Stalin as Revolutionary, 1879–1929* (New York: Norton, 1973), esp. pp. 425–461; see also Milovan Djilas, *Conversations with Stalin* (New York: Harcourt, Brace & World, 1962), passim.

9. HEROES AND IDEOLOGUES

Freud on Michelangelo's "Moses": Sigmund Freud, "The Moses of Michelangelo," originally published anonymously in *Imago,* III, 1914, reprinted in Sigmund Freud, *On Creativity and the Unconscious* (New York: Harper & Brothers, 1958), pp. 11–41.

Jones on Freud's identification with Michelangelo: Ernest Jones, *The Life and Work of Sigmund Freud* (New York: Basic Books, 1953) Vol. 2, pp. 366–367.

Freud on his "love-child": Jones, p. 367. Freud on Moses as "great man": Sigmund Freud, *Moses and Monotheism* (New York: Knopf, 1939), pp. 168–175.

Moses as leader: Martin Buber, *Moses* (Oxford: East & West Library, 1946); Max Weber, *Ancient Judiasm* (Glencoe, Ill.: Free Press, 1952); Wayne A. Meeks, *The Prophet-King* (Leiden: Brill, 1967); Gerhard von Rad, *Moses* (London: Butterworth Press, n.d.); André Neher, *Moses and the Vocation of the Jewish People* (London: Longmans, Green, 1959). I have used also Aaron Wildavsky, "What Moses Learned About Leadership," Brooklyn College, 1977.

Joan of Arc as heroic leader: Charles Wayland Lightbody, *The Judgements of Joan* (Cambridge, Mass.: Harvard University Press, 1961), quoted at p. 27; Jules Michelet, *Joan of Arc* (Ann Arbor: University of Michigan Press, 1957); Régine Pernoud, *Joan of Arc* (New York: Grove Press, 1961); Alice Buchan, *Joan of Arc and the Recovery of France* (London: Hodder & Stoughton, 1948); Henri Guillemin, *Joan, Maid of Orléans* (New York: Saturday Review Press, 1973). Joan's voices and visions as congruent with a well-known hallucinatory pattern: Edward Lucie-Smith, *Joan of Arc* (New York: Norton, 1976), pp. 15–17.

Heroic Leadership

Max Weber's "pure" types of authority and theory of charisma: Max Weber, *Theory of Social and Economic Organization* (New York: Oxford University Press, 1947); H. H. Gerth and C. Wright Mills, *From Weber: Essays in Sociology* (London: Routledge and Kegan Paul, 1948); see also Carl J. Friedrich, "Political Leadership and the Problem of Charismatic Power," *Journal of Politics,* Vol. 23, No. 1 (February 1961), 3–24; Peter M. Blau, "Critical Remarks on Weber's Theory of Authority," *American Political Science Review,* Vol. 57, No. 2 (June 1963), 305–315.

Davies on traditionalist rule: James C. Davies, *Human Nature in Politics* (New York: Wiley, 1963), p. 298, from which the story about Peter the Great is also taken.

Absence of conflict in theory of charisma: Daniel Katz, "Patterns of Leadership," in Jeanne N. Knutson, ed., *Handbook of Political Psychology,* pp. 215–218, quoted at p. 216.

The account of the Mahdi of the Sudan is taken wholly from Richard H. Dekmejian and Margaret J. Wyszomirski, "Charismatic Leadership in Islam: The Mahdi of the Sudan," *Comparative Studies in Society and History,* Vol. 14, No. 2 (March 1972), 193–214, quoted at pp. 203, 212–214.

Tucker on heroic leadership as fulcrum: Robert C. Tucker, "The Theory of Charismatic Leadership," in Dankwart A. Rustow, ed., "Philosophers and Kings: Studies in Leadership," *Daedalus,* Vol. 97, No. 3 (Summer 1968), 731–756, quoted at p. 734.

Pye on bond between idolized leader and follower: Lucian W. Pye, *Politics, Personality, and Nation Building: Burma's Search for Identity* (New Haven: Yale University Press, 1962), passim.

Rustow on Ataturk: Dankwart A. Rustow, *A World of Nations: Problems of Political Modernization* (Washington, D.C.: Brookings, 1967).

Apter on Nkrumah: David Apter, *The Politics of Modernization* (Chicago: University of Chicago Press, 1965), pp. 298–299.

Hoffer on "true believers": Eric Hoffer, *The True Believer: Thoughts on the Nature of Mass Movements* (New York: Harper & Brothers, 1951), passim.

Philip Rosenberg, *The Seventh Hero: Thomas Carlyle and the Theory of Radical Activism* (Cambridge, Mass.: Harvard University Press, 1974), esp. ch. 9.

Ideological Leadership

Significant works on ideology that I have used: Karl Mannheim, *Ideology and Utopia* (New York: Harcourt, Brace & World, Harvest ed., n.d.); Richard Lichtman, "Marx's Theory of Ideology," *Socialist Revolution,* Vol 5, No. 1 (April 1975), 45–76; Robert E. Lane, *Political Ideology* (Glencoe, Ill.: Free Press, 1962); Willard A. Mullins, "On the Concept of Ideology in Political Science," *American Political Science Review,* Vol. 66, No. 2 (June 1972), 498–510.

"End of Ideology": Daniel Bell, *The End of Ideology: On the Exhaustion of Political Ideas in the Fifties* (Glencoe, Ill.: Free Press, 1965); Joseph LaPalombara, "Decline of Ideology: A Dissent and an Interpretation," *American Political Science Review,* Vol. 60, No. 1 (March 1966), 5–16.

Schlesinger on ideology: Arthur M. Schlesinger, Jr., and Morton White, *Paths of American Thought* (Boston: Houghton Mifflin, 1963), p. 532.

Brzezinski on ideology: Zbigniew K. Brzezinski, *Ideology and Power in Soviet Politics* (New York: Praeger, 1962), p. 5.

Four-nation study: *Values and the Active Community,* passim.

Lane on questions of ideology: Lane, pp. 14–15.

Mullins on ideology as agency of change: Mullins, p. 504.

I have used some phrases and sentences from James MacGregor Burns, "Political Ideology," in Norman MacKenzie, ed., *A Guide to the Social Sciences* (London: Weidenfeld & Nicolson, 1966), pp. 205–223.

Mao to Edgar Snow on need for personality cult: Lucian W. Pye, *Mao Tse-tung* (New York: Basic Books, 1976), p. 12.

Leadership as Transformation

Mao on arousing emotions in others: quoted in Pye, p. 14.

Mao on the true, the good, etc.: quoted in Lowell Dittmer, "Thought Reform and Cultural Revolution: An Analysis of the Symbolism of Chinese Polemics," *American Political Science Review*, Vol. 71, No. 1 (March 1977), 72.

Chiang Ch'ing's role: Roxane Witke, *Comrade Chiang Ch'ing* (Boston: Little, Brown, 1977), as quoted in John K. Fairbank, "Mrs. M. and the Masses," *The New York Review*, May 12, 1977, p. 21.

Mao's comments on his long swim: Edgar Snow, *The Long Revolution* (New York: Random House, 1971), p. 169.

Mao's doctrine of "from the masses": Mao Tse-tung, *Selected Works*, Vol. 3 (Peking: Foreign Languages Press, 1965), p. 119.

Mao's tactics in the Cultural Revolution: Parris H. Chang, *Power and Policy in China* (University Park: Pennsylvania University Press, 1975), p. 175.

Mao on exploiting the negative example: Han Suyin, *Wind in the Tower: Mao Tse-tung and the Chinese Revolution, 1949–1975* (Boston: Little, Brown, 1976), p. 276.

Pye on Mao's understanding of emotions of others: Pye, p. 308.

Mao on anarchy and the need for chiefs: Dittmer, p. 82.

Stewart Burns drafted a major part of this treatment of Mao's ideological leadership.

10. OPINION LEADERSHIP: THE MISSING PIECE OF THE PUZZLE

Key's "incomparable" study was V. O. Key, Jr., *Southern Politics* (New York: Knopf, 1949); his public opinion study was *Public Opinion and American Democracy* (New York: Knopf, 1961); and his last book, in which he concluded that "Voters are not fools," was *The Responsible Electorate* (Cambridge, Mass.: Harvard University Press, 1966).

Transactional opinion leadership: George C. Homans, *Social Behavior: Its Elementary Forms* (New York: Harcourt, Brace & World, 1961), esp. chs. 3 and 4, and sources cited in ch. 4; Bob Jessop, *Social Order, Reform and Revolution* (New York: Herder and Herder, 1973), esp. chs. 2 and 3; James V. Downton, Jr., *Rebel Leadership* (New York: Free Press, 1973), ch. 4.

Clark on opinion research: Kenneth B. Clark, *Pathos of Power* (New York: Harper & Row, 1974), p. 68.

Arousal: The Mobilization of Political Opinion

Communications transmission: Elihu Katz and Paul F. Lazarsfeld, *Personal Influence* (New York: Free Press, 1964), pp. 29–30; see also V. O. Key, Jr., *Public Opinion and American Democracy*, pp. 73–74.

The leader and inconsistent opinions or multiple cleavages: Key, *Public Opinion and American Democracy*, pp. 177–178.

Perceptual distortion: Bernard R. Berelson, Paul F. Lazarsfeld, and William N. McPhee, *Voting: A Study of Opinion Formation in a Presidential Campaign* (Chicago: University of Chicago Press, 1954), p. 200; see also Philip K. Hastings, "The Independent Voter in 1952: A Study of Pittsfield, Massachusetts," *American Political Science Review*, Vol. 47, No. 3 (September 1953), 805–810.

Reduction of dissonance: Robert Lane and David Sears, *Public Opinion* (Englewood Cliffs, N.J.: Prentice-Hall, 1964), pp. 47–51.

Definition of opinion leadership: Katz and Lazarsfeld, p. 138.

The 1940 presidential campaign study relating to opinion leadership: Paul F. Lazarsfeld, Bernard Berelson, and Hazel Gaudet, *The People's Choice* (New York: Columbia University Press, 1948).

Communication in Kalos, Greece: J. Mayone Stycos, "Patterns of Communication in a Rural Greek Village," *Public Opinion Quarterly,* Vol. 16, No. 1 (Spring 1952), 59–70.

The Russian Communist party agitator as opinion leader: Alex Inkeles, *Public Opinion in Soviet Russia* (Cambridge, Mass.: Harvard University Press, 1950), pp. 88–89.

Concept of the attentive public: Gabriel A. Almond, *The American People and Foreign Policy* (New York: Harcourt, Brace, 1950); Donald J. Devine, *The Attentive Public* (Chicago: Rand McNally, 1970).

The latent public: Key, *Public Opinion and American Democracy,* ch. 11.

Two-step flow of information and opinion: Katz and Lazarsfeld, passim.

Complexity of multifold flow of leadership-followership opinion: Katz and Lazarsfeld, p. 322.

Key on public opinion as a system of dikes: Key, *Public Opinion and American Democracy,* p. 552.

Aggregation: The Alignment of Opinion

Public opinion as conflict: William Albig, *Public Opinion* (New York: McGraw-Hill, 1939), p. 1; Kimball Young, *Social Psychology* (New York: Crofts, 1944), pp. 430–431; Clarence Schettler, *Public Opinion in American Society* (New York: Harper & Brothers, 1960), Part I.

In Latin America, the patrón relation between leaders and followers in government: Arpad von Lazer, *Latin American Politics: A Primer* (Boston: Allyn & Bacon, 1971), p. 24.

Analysis of the transferability of the Vargas vote in Brazil and the Perón vote in Argentina: Paul H. Lewis, "The Durability of Personalist Followings: The Vargas and Peronist Cases," *Polity,* Vol. 5, No. 3 (Spring 1973), 401–414.

Class membership, class attitudes, class consciousness, class behavior: studies of the interrelations of these phenomena are countless; see (aside from the classic treatments of Karl Marx and his disciples and critics) Giovanni Sartori, "The Sociology of Parties: A Critical Review," in Committee on Political Sociology of the International Sociological Association, *Party Systems, Party Organization, and the Politics of New Masses* (Berlin: Institut für politische Wissenschaft an der Freien Universität, 1968), and sources cited therein; see also Erik Allardt and Yrjö Littunen, eds., *Cleavages, Ideologies, and Party Systems* (Helsinki: The Academic Bookstore, 1964), passim; Seymour H. Lipset and Stein Rokkan, eds., *Party Systems and Voter Alignments* (New York: Free Press, 1967), passim; and other sources cited in notes for ch. 7.

Influence on polling results of association of issue with party or leader: Key, *Public Opinion and American Democracy,* pp. 450–452.

Key on leader-mass opinion interaction: Key, p. 454.

Luis Muñoz Marín and the Popular Democratic party: Robert W. Anderson, *Party Politics in Puerto Rico* (Stanford: Stanford University Press, 1965), passim.

Mandel and two-party realignment: John M. Sherwood, *Georges Mandel and the Third Republic* (Stanford: Stanford University Press, 1970).

Basic political, economic, and social trends in Britain: Richard Rose, "Party Systems, Social Structure and Voter Alignments in Britain," in Committee on Political Sociology of the International Sociological Association, *Party Systems, Party Organizations, and the Politics of New Masses,* pp. 318–384.

Conservative party and working-class opinion: Robert T. McKenzie and Allan Silver, *Angels in Marble* (Chicago: University of Chicago Press, 1963); Robert T. McKenzie and Allan Silver, "The Delicate Experiment: Industrialism, Conservatism, and Working-Class Tories in England," in Lipset and Rokkan, pp. 115–125; see also James Cornford, "The Adoption of Mass Organization by the British Conservative Party," in Allardt and Littunen, pp. 400–424.

Labour party strategy vis-à-vis the Liberals: see the excellent discussion in Samuel H. Beer, *British Politics in the Collectivist Age* (New York: Knopf, 1965), pp. 137–143.

See generally G. D. H. Cole, *A History of the Labour Party from 1914* (London: Routledge & Kegan Paul, 1948), chs. 2, 3; Dean McHenry, *The Labor Party in Transition,* passim.

Definition of realignment: Walter Dean Burnham, *Critical Elections and the Mainsprings of American Politics* (New York: Norton, 1970), p. 10; see also James L. Sundquist, *Dynamics of the Party System* (Washington, D.C.: Brookings, 1973), pp. 5–9.

Voting: The Conversion of Opinion

Elections as tests of public opinions: James Bryce, *The American Commonwealth* (New York: Macmillan, 1931), Vol. 2, p. 274, as cited in Marbury Bladen Ogle, Jr., *Public Opinion and Political Dynamics* (Boston: Houghton Mifflin, 1950), p. 55.

Dominant political attitudes in New Zealand: Alan D. Robinson, "Class Voting in New Zealand: A Comment on Alford's Comparison of Class Voting in the Anglo-American Political Systems," in Lipset and Rokkan, pp. 95–114; in Norway: Stein Rokkan, "Geography, Religion, and Social Class: Crosscutting Cleavages in Norwegian Politics," in Lipset and Rokkan, pp. 367–444; see also Stein Rokkan and Henry Valen, "Regional Contrasts in Norwegian Politics: A Review of Data from Official Statistics and from Sample Surveys," in Allardt and Littunen, pp. 162–238.

Sundquist on responses of types of leaders within parties to emerging causes: James L. Sundquist, *Dynamics of the Party System* (Washington, D.C.: Brookings, 1973), pp. 285–286.

Realignment summarized: Sundquist, pp. 293–294 (italics deleted from the original).

Party realignment during the 1840s and 1850s: Robert V. Remini, *Martin Van Buren and the Making of the Democratic Party* (New York: Columbia University Press, 1959); Clement Eaton, *Henry Clay and the Art of American Politics* (Boston: Little, Brown, 1957); David H. Donald, *Charles Sumner and the Coming of the Civil War* (New York: Knopf, 1960); R. F. Nichols, *The Disruption of American Democracy* (New York: Macmillan, 1948); Sundquist, chs. 4 and 5 and sources cited therein; and of course the works of Allan Nevins.

Late nineteenth-century party developments: Solon J. Buck, *The Granger Movement* (Cambridge, Mass.: Harvard University Press, 1913); John D. Hicks, *The Populist Revolt* (Minneapolis: University of Minnesota Press, 1931); Allan Nevins, *Grover Cleveland: A Study in Courage* (New York: Dodd, Mead, 1932); Paxton Hibben, *The Peerless Leader, William Jennings Bryan* (New York: Farrar and Rinehart, 1929); V. O. Key, Jr., "A Theory of Critical Elections," *Journal of Politics,* Vol. 17, No. 1 (February 1955), 3–18.

Franklin Roosevelt and the early New Deal: Arthur M. Schlesinger, Jr., *The Coming of the New Deal* (Boston: Houghton Mifflin, 1959); Schlesinger, *The Politics of Upheaval* (Boston: Houghton Mifflin, 1960); Frank Freidel, *Franklin D. Roosevelt: Launching the New Deal* (Boston: Little, Brown, 1973); William E. Leuchtenburg, *Franklin D. Roosevelt and the New Deal* (New York: Harper & Row, 1963).

Roosevelt as manager of public opinion: Elmer E. Cornwell, Jr., *Presidential Leadership of Public Opinion* (Bloomington: Indiana University Press, 1965), esp. ch. 6; Samuel I. Rosenman, *Working with Roosevelt* (New York: Harper & Brothers, 1952).

Roosevelt on his catlike quality: quoted in James MacGregor Burns, *Roosevelt: The Lion and the Fox* (New York: Harcourt, Brace & World, 1956), p. 285.

Roosevelt to Tugwell on party realignment: Schlesinger, *The Coming of the New Deal*, p. 504; to Rosenman on same: James MacGregor Burns, *Roosevelt: The Soldier of Freedom* (New York: Harcourt Brace Jovanovich, 1970), p. 511.

Sundquist on divergence between national voting and state and local voting: Sundquist, p. 213.

Walter Dean Burnham, *Critical Elections and the Mainsprings of American Politics* (New York: Norton, 1970), p. 130.

Lyons on Parnell: F. S. L. Lyons, *The Fall of Parnell* (London: Routledge & Kegan Paul, 1960), p. 32.

11. GROUP LEADERSHIP: BARGAINERS AND BUREAUCRATS

Freud on loss of the group leader: Sigmund Freud, *Group Psychology and the Analysis of the Ego* (London: Hogarth Press, 1949), p. 49.

The Norton Street boys: William F. Whyte, *Street Corner Society* (Chicago: University of Chicago Press, 1955).

The Leadership of Small Groups

Rising interest in small groups: Fred L. Strodtbeck, "The Case for the Study of Small Groups," *American Sociological Review,* Vol. 19, No. 6 (December 1954), 651–657; A. Paul Hare, *Handbook of Small Group Research* (New York: Free Press, 1962), pp. vi–vii.

Useful definitions of small groups are Hare, p. 10; Bernard Berelson and Gary A. Steiner, *Human Behavior: Shorter Edition* (New York: Harcourt, Brace & World, 1964), p. 55.

"No-conflict" assumption: Sidney Verba, *Small Groups and Political Behavior* (Princeton: Princeton University Press, 1961), p. 222.

The leader's role in group change: Kurt Lewin, *Field Theory in Social Science* (New York: Harper & Brothers, 1951), pp. 202–207.

Interaction in small groups: George Homans, *The Human Group* (New York: Harcourt, Brace & World, 1950), passim; Robert T. Golembiewski, *The Small Group* (Chicago: University of Chicago Press, 1962), pp. 64–65; Clavis R. Shepherd, *Small Groups* (San Francisco: Chandler, 1964), pp. 27–36; for a philosophical critique see Alvin Gouldner, *The Coming Crisis of Western Sociology* (New York: Basic Books, 1970), pp. 231–232; Whyte is quoted from *Street Corner Society,* p. 263.

Conformity: Bernard M. Bass, *Leadership, Psychology and Organization Behavior* (New York: Harper & Brothers, 1961), pp. 239ff, and the many conformity studies reported therein, pp. 31ff; Hollander, chs. 14–19; Bass: quoted from Bass, p. 241.

Group norms and goals: Barry E. Collins and Harold Guetzkow, *A Social Psychology of Group Processes for Decision-Making* (New York: Wiley, 1964), esp. pp. 158ff; Hare, pp. 24–25 (Hare quoted at p. 24); Berelson and Steiner, pp. 56–58.

Status of members in groups: Hollander, p. 11; Berelson and Steiner, pp. 60–61; Bass, passim.

Edward Shils and Morris Janowitz, "Cohesion and Disintegration in the Wehrmacht," in Bernard Berelson and Morris Janowitz, eds., *Public Opinion and Communication* (New York: Free Press, 1953), pp. 407–422.

The static conception of small-group leadership is presented in Bass, Homans, and Shepherd, and in much of the literature cited therein.

External sources of conflicting group leadership: Verba, pp. 155ff.

Example of noncommissioned officer in conflict: Samuel A. Stouffer, "An Analysis of Conflicting Social Norms," *American Sociological Review,* Vol. 14, No. 6 (December 1949), 707 (cited by Verba, p. 154).

Whyte on leaders' internal-external relations: Whyte, p. 260.

The discussion of leadership conflict within small groups is drawn largely from Bass, chs. 16 and 20; he is quoted at p. 457.

Epictetus is quoted in Bass, pp. 226–227, from Epictetus, *On Freedom,* in C. G. Starr, *Civilization and the Caesars* (Ithaca: Cornell University Press, 1954), p. 144.

Hollander on leader effectiveness: Hollander, pp. 237–238.

Bureaucracy Versus Leadership

Study of bureaucracy in the Western tradition: Gerth and Mills, *From Max Weber;* Robert K. Merton, Ailsa P. Gray, Barbara Hockey, and Hanan C. Selvin, *Reader in Bureaucracy* (Glencoe, Ill.: Free Press, 1952); Herbert A. Simon, *Administrative Behavior* (New York: Macmillan, 1947); Dwight Waldo, *The Administrative State* (New York: Ronald Press, 1948), inter alia.

Structure of impersonality: Robert K. Merton, "Bureaucratic Structure and Personality," in Merton et al., *Reader in Bureaucracy,* p. 363; see also Gerth and Mills, p. 202.

Irrelevance of personal characteristics: Peter M. Blau, *Bureaucracy in Modern Society* (New York: Random House, 1956), pp. 75ff; cf. Daniel Katz and Robert L. Kahn, *The Social Psychology of Organizations* (New York: Wiley, 1966), pp. 202ff.

Merton on bureaucratic discipline: Merton et al., p. 365.

Weber on the relation of bureaucracy to the rise of money income: Gerth and Mills, pp. 204–209, 223.

Tocqueville quoted on bureaucratization: Robert A. Nisbet, *The Sociological Tradition* (New York: Basic Books, 1966), pp. 129–130; Nisbet is quoted at p. 130.

Michels on party oligarchy: Robert Michels, *Political Parties: A Sociological Study of Oligarchical Tendencies of Modern Democracy* (New York: Free Press, 1949), pp. 32ff and passim.

Bureaucracy and conflict: Warren G. Bennis, "Leadership Theory and Administrative Behavior: The Problem of Authority," *Administrative Science Quarterly,* Vol. 4, No. 3 (December 1959), 259–301, at 281; Melville Dalton, "Staff and Line Relationships—A Study of Conflicts," in Robert Dubin, ed., *Human Relations in Administration: The Sociology of Organization* (New York: Prentice-Hall, 1951), pp. 128–138.

Location of conflict: Katz and Kahn, p. 192.

Struggle for power within bureaucracy: Merton, Blau, Dubin, Crozier, passim.

Simon on lack of integration: Simon, *Administrative Behavior,* p. 63; see also Peabody and Rourke, pp. 805–807.

Henry Kissinger, "Domestic Structure and Foreign Policy," *Daedalus,* Vol. 95 (Spring 1966), 503–529, quoted at 507–508.

Bureaucracy and change: Seymour Martin Lipset, "Bureaucracy and Social Change," in Merton et al., *Reader in Bureaucracy,* pp. 221–232; Crozier, pp. 201–202.

Gawthrop on anticipatory change: Louis C. Gawthrop, *Bureaucratic Behavior in the Executive Branch* (New York: Free Press, 1969), p. 179.

On maintaining a "pluralistic babble": Victor A. Thompson, *Modern Organization* (New York: Knopf, 1961), esp. ch. 5.

On innovation: Victor A. Thompson, *Bureaucracy and Innovation* (University: Alabama University Press, 1969).

See generally: F. William Howton, *Functionaries* (Chicago: Quadrangle, 1969); and Robert Presthus, *The Organizational Society* (New York: Knopf, 1962).

Leadership in Political Interest Groups

Quotation from Bentley: Arthur F. Bentley, *The Process of Government* (Chicago: University of Chicago Press, 1908), quoted at p. 223; see ch. 8, passim.

Influence of small-group analysis on leadership theory: David B. Truman, *The Governmental Process* (New York: Knopf, 1951), pp. 189–193.

Homans' work: see especially George C. Homans, *The Human Group.*

Carleton on the shift of emphasis to group studies: W. G. Carleton, "Political Science and the Group Process," *South Atlantic Quarterly* (Durham, N.C.: Duke University Press, 1955), Vol. 54, pp. 340–350.

Definition of categorical and of interest groups: Truman, ch. 2, quoted at p. 33.

Truman on measuring leadership: Truman, ch. 7, quoted at p. 191.

Conflict over leadership role: Norman R. Luttbeg and Harmon Zeigler, "Attitude Consensus and Conflict in an Interest Group; An Assessment of Cohesion," *American Political Science Review,* Vol. 60, No. 3 (September 1966), 655–666, quoted at p. 658.

Official Soviet view of leadership and interest groups: Kirill Mazurov, *Pravda,* November 7, 1968, December 4, 1968, cited in H. Gordon Skilling and Franklyn Griffiths, eds., *Interest Groups in Soviet Politics* (Princeton: Princeton University Press, 1971), pp. 35–36, 44–45, 390–416.

12. PARTY LEADERSHIP

The listing of party factions is summarized in R. T. McKenzie, *British Political Parties* (London: Heinemann, 1955), p. 2; McKenzie on whips' organization: McKenzie, p. 3.

Jefferson on parties: Nathan Schachner, *Thomas Jefferson,* 2 vols. (New York: Appleton, 1951), pp. 343–346.

Origin of parties in parliamentary leadership: Maurice Duverger, *Political Parties* (London: Methuen, 1954), pp. xxiv–xxv.

Parties and the spread of suffrage: Leon D. Epstein, *Political Parties in Western Democracies* (New York: Praeger, 1967), p. 25.

Emergence of groups out of extragovernmental groups in Western democracies: examples drawn chiefly from Duverger, pp. xxx–xxxiv.

Etymology of "party": *Oxford English Dictionary* (New York: Oxford University Press, 1971), p. 2088.

Acceptance of opposition in Britain: John P. Mackintosh, *The British Cabinet* (London: Stevens, 1962), p. 17, cited in Dahl, *Political Oppositions in Western Democracies* (New Haven: Yale University Press, 1966), p. 7.

Liberalism as the supreme form of generosity: José Ortega y Gasset, *The Revolt of the Masses* (New York: Norton, 1932), p. 83.

Parties: Conflict and Leadership

Boss Plunkitt on human nature: W. L. Riordan, *Plunkitt of Tammany Hall* (New York: McClure, Phillips, 1905), pp. 33–34.

Tocqueville: quoted in Burns, *Deadlock of Democracy* (Englewood Cliffs, N.J.: Prentice-Hall, 1967), p. 213.

Epstein on the prewar Social Democratic party: Epstein, p. 136; Roth on same: Guenther Roth, *The Social Democrats in Imperial Germany* (Totowa, N.J.: Bedminster Press, 1963), p. 11.

On the Social Democratic party experience and comparable party organization and leadership see Duverger, passim.

Michels' "iron law of oligarchy": Robert Michels, *Political Parties* (New York: Hearst's International Library, 1915), passim; see also C. W. Cassinelli, "The Law of Oligarchy," *American Political Science Review,* Vol. 47, No. 3 (September 1953), 773–784.

See in general Kay Lawson, *The Comparative Study of Political Parties* (New York: St. Martin's Press, 1976), esp. pp. 112–136.

Party Leaders and Government Leaders

A basic source on efforts to develop rank-and-file strength and influence in the Conservative and Liberal parties in the late nineteenth century remains the opinionated but richly factual classic, M. Ostrogorski, *Democracy and the Organization of Political Parties* (New York: Macmillan, 1902), Vol. 1, parts 2 and 3; see also J. L. Garvin, *The Life of Joseph Chamberlain* (London: Macmillan, 1932), Vol. 1; McKenzie, passim.

Parliamentary Labour party as emanation of labour movement: McKenzie, p. 13.

Distribution of power within the Labour party: McKenzie, esp. chs. 1, 6, 7; see also Michels, passim, and Samuel H. Beer, *British Politics in the Collectivist Age* (New York: Knopf, 1965), chs. 3–6.

Ramsay MacDonald as party leader: G. D. H. Cole, *British Working Class Politics, 1832–1914* (London: George Routledge & Sons, 1941); G. D. H. Cole, *A History of the Labour Party from 1914* (London: Routledge & Kegan Paul, 1948); "James Ramsay MacDonald," *Dictionary of National Biography,* 1931–1940 (London: Oxford University Press, 1949); Clement R. Attlee, *As It Happened* (London: Heinemann, 1954); M. Beer, *A History of British Socialism* (London: George Allen and Unwin, 1940).

MacDonald's alleged address to House of Commons: *Hansard,* Vol. 229, col. 65, July 2, 1929.

On the leadership and organization of the French Radical party I have drawn heavily from Peter J. Larmour, *The French Radical Party in the 1930's* (Stanford: Stanford University Press, 1964); I have quoted him on the National Executive Committee's membership at p. 25, and on the party's leadership at p. 55; see also Duverger, esp. pp. 183–186, and Avery Leiserson, *Parties and Politics* (New York: Knopf, 1958), p. 217.

The Radical party after World War II: Philip M. Williams, *Crisis and Compromise* (Hamden, Conn.: Archon Books, 1964), ch. 9; Duncan MacRae, Jr., *Parliament, Parties and Society in France, 1946–1958* (New York: St. Martin's Press, 1967), passim.

Geoffrey Warner, *Pierre Laval and the Eclipse of France* (New York: Macmillan, 1968) portrays the pre-World War II parties from the perspective of a politician who journeyed through the party continuum from left to right.

Solidarity and discipline in Australian labor politics: Louise Overacker, *The Australian Party System* (New Haven: Yale University Press, 1952), esp. chs. 2–5; the candidate's pledge is reproduced on p. 337 and the labor member's observation on p. 113.

Relations of organization leadership and government leadership in other nations: Duverger, passim; Epstein on party cohesion in multi-party societies: Leon D. Epstein, *Political Parties in Western Democracies* (New York: Praeger, 1967), pp. 339–340.

See generally Sigmund Neumann, ed., *Modern Political Parties* (Chicago: University of Chicago Press, 1956).

This discussion of the American leadership and party system is drawn largely from James MacGregor Burns, *The Deadlock of Democracy* (Englewood Cliffs, N.J.: Prentice-Hall, 1963), and from the sources cited therein, pp. 343–368; major, more recent sources are: Walter Dean Burnham, *Critical Elections and the Mainsprings of American Politics* (New York: Norton, 1972); William Nisbet Chambers and Walter Dean Burnham, eds., *The American Party System: Stages of Political Development* (New York: Oxford University Press, 1967); Charles Hardin, *Presidential Power and Accountability* (Chicago: University of Chicago Press, 1974). Other major sources are John S. Saloma III and Frederick H. Sontag, *Parties* (New York: Knopf, 1972); James L. Sundquist, *Dynamics of the Party System* (Washington, D.C.: Brookings, 1973); Robert J. Huckshorn, *Party Leadership in the States* (Amherst: University of Massachusetts Press, 1976).

One-Party Leadership

Lenin on party organization and on the Social Democratic moderates: Shub, pp. 61–62, 222.

The Communist party of the Soviet Union, according to party statutes: Frederick L. Schuman, *Government in the Soviet Union* (New York: Crowell, 1967), p. 75; Schuman on the obscurity of Soviet power location: Schuman, p. 81.

Barghoorn on the Soviet power structure: Frederick C. Barghoorn, "The U.S.S.R.: Monolithic Controls at Home and Abroad," in Neumann, *Modern Political Parties,* p. 227.

East European Communist parties: Andrew Gyorgy, "Satellite Parties in Eastern Europe," Neumann, pp. 284–301.

Warning of Communist International to Communist parliamentarians is quoted from Duverger, p. 197.

Leadership and discipline in Western European Communist parties: Duverger, esp. ch. 3; Neumann, passim; see also Mario Einaudi, Jean-Marie Domenach, and Aldo Garosci, *Communism in Western Europe* (Ithaca: Cornell University Press, 1951).

The Thorez membership card is reproduced in Duverger, p. 181.

Busoga leadership: Lloyd A. Fallers, *Bantu Bureaucracy* (Chicago: University of Chicago Press, 1965), p. 127, as cited in Gabriel A. Almond and James S. Coleman, *The Politics of Developing Areas* (Princeton: Princeton University Press, 1960), pp. 327–328.

Turkish political development: C. H. Dodd, *Politics and Government in Turkey* (Berkeley: University of California Press, 1969); Kemal H. Karpat, *Turkey's Politics* (Princeton: Princeton University Press, 1959).

Classification of political systems in underdeveloped areas by degree of competitiveness and by degree of political modernity: Almond and Coleman, pp. 532ff, especially Table 1, p. 534.

The criteria of political modernity: Almond and Coleman, pp. 532–533.

One-party systems as mobilizing instruments: Myron Weiner and Joseph LaPalombara, "The Impact of Parties on Political Development," in LaPalombara and Weiner, eds., *Political Parties and Political Development* (Princeton: Princeton University Press, 1966), p. 425.

Party Leadership: Power and Change

"Pragmatic-pluralizing" parties versus revolutionary-centralizing parties: James S. Coleman and Carl G. Rosberg, Jr., eds., *Political Parties and National Integration in Tropical Africa* (Berkeley: University of California Press, 1964), p. 5.

The disciplining of K. Zilliacus: James MacGregor Burns, "The Parliamentary Labor Party in Great Britain," *American Political Science Review*, Vol. 44, No. 4 (December 1950), 867–868.

For the view that Labour party government leaders have compromised and betrayed the basic principles of the party, see Ralph Miliband, *Parliamentary Socialism* (London: George Allen and Unwin, 1961).

13. LEGISLATIVE LEADERSHIP: THE PRICE OF CONSENSUS

Lyndon B. Johnson as legislative and executive leader: James L. Sundquist, *Politics and Policy* (Washington, D.C.: Brookings, 1968); Rowland Evans and Robert Novak, *Lyndon B. Johnson: The Exercise of Power* (New York: New American Library, 1966); Harry McPherson, *A Political Education* (Boston: Little, Brown, 1972); W. W. Rostow, *The Diffusion of Power* (New York: Macmillan, 1972); Eric F. Goldman, *The Tragedy of Lyndon Johnson* (New York: Knopf, 1969).

The Legislator as Leader

The presentation of Erskine May to the Gold Coast Assembly was reported in *The Times* (London), March 3, 1952, as quoted in David E. Apter, *The Gold Coast in Transition* (Princeton: Princeton University Press, 1955), p. 184.

Tariff-making in the American Congress as expression of economic power: E. E. Schattschneider, *Politics, Pressures and the Tariff* (New York: Prentice-Hall, 1935).

Freshman legislators' clubs in Japanese Diet: Nobutaka Ike, *Japanese Politics* (New York: Knopf, 1957), p. 185; see also Nobutaka Ike, "Japan," in George McTurnan Kahin, ed., *Major Governments of Asia* (Ithaca: Cornell University Press, 1963), passim.

Indian parliamentary colloquy: Indian Parliamentary *Debates,* December 20, 1950, quoted by W. H. Morris-Jones, *Parliament in India* (Philadelphia: University of Pennsylvania Press, 1957), pp. 151–152.

Private members' bills: A. P. Herbert, *Holy Deadlock* (Garden City, N.Y.: Doubleday, 1934);

A. P. Herbert, *Independent Member* (London: Methuen, 1950); see generally Peter G. Richards, *Parliament and Conscience* (London: Allen and Unwin, 1970).

Richards on back-benchers' influence: Peter G. Richards, *The Backbenchers* (London: Faber and Faber, 1972), p. 9.

Role-taking by the individual legislator: the most useful source is John C. Wahlke, Heinz Eulau, William Buchanan, and LeRoy C. Ferguson, *The Legislative System* (New York: Wiley, 1962); the comments of the state legislators are from p. 279 of this work (italics deleted from original).

Wahlke on the Tribune: Wahlke et al., pp. 252, 253; I have used certain concepts and terms such as "the Tribune" as found in this seminal work.

Kennedy on his House and Senate careers: interviews with the author, 1959.

The "institutional patriot" in the United States Senate: Donald R. Matthews, *U.S. Senators and Their World* (Chapel Hill: University of North Carolina Press, 1960), esp. chs. 4 and 5.

Friedrich on the specialist in group opinion: Carl J. Friedrich, *Constitutional Government and Democracy,* rev. ed. (Boston: Ginn, 1964), p. 319.

Group Leadership and Legislative Structure

Latham on legislative groups: Earl Latham, *The Group Basis of Politics* (Ithaca: Cornell University Press, 1952), p. 37.

"Instructions" to Parliament: Samuel H. Beer, *British Politics in the Collectivist Age* (New York: Knopf, 1965), p. 16.

Richards on proper and improper representation: Richards, p. 180.

Sir Ian Fraser and the British Legion in Parliament: John H. Millett, "The Role of an Interest Group Leader in the House of Commons," *Western Political Quarterly,* Vol. 9, No. 4 (1956), 915–926.

Clapp on congressmen as lobbyists: Charles L. Clapp: *The Congressman: His Work as He Sees It* (Washington, D.C.: Brookings, 1963), p. 179.

Truman on legislators' group affiliations: David B. Truman, *The Governmental Process* (New York: Knopf, 1951), pp. 338–339.

Matthews on senators' influence over lobbyists: Donald R. Matthews, *U.S. Senators and Their World* (New York: Vintage Books, 1960), pp. 188–190.

Legislative committee system in Japan: Kahin, pp. 190–193; see also Ike, pp. 181–182.

Parliamentary committee system in India: W. H. Morris-Jones, *Parliament in India* (Philadelphia: University of Pennsylvania Press, 1957), ch. 6, quoted at pp. 309–310; Kahin, pp. 325–327.

In Western Germany: Gerhard Loewenberg, *Parliament in the German Political System* (Ithaca: Cornell University Press, 1967), pp. 143–153, 326–335.

Committees and committee chairman in the American legislative system: Bertram M. Gross, *The Legislative Struggle* (New York: McGraw-Hill, 1953); William L. Morrow, *Congressional Committees* (New York: Scribner, 1969); William J. Keefe and Morris S. Ogul, *The American Legislative Process,* 2nd ed. (Englewood Cliffs, N.J.: Prentice-Hall, 1968).

On the fiscal committees: Richard F. Fenno, Jr., *The Power of the Purse* (Boston: Little, Brown, 1966); Aaron Wildavsky, *The Politics of the Budgetary Process* (Boston: Little, Brown, 1964).

Fenno quotation: Fenno, pp. 136–137.

Wilson on power of congressional committees: Woodrow Wilson, *Congressional Government,* 15th ed. (Boston: Houghton Mifflin, 1885), passim.

Fenno on restrictions on Appropriations Committee chairman: Fenno, pp. 137–138.

Central Legislative Leadership

Parliamentary party discipline in India: Kahin, ch. 11; Park and Tinker, ch. 4; Morris-Jones, ch. 4.

Congress party doctrine and recruitment: Stanley A. Kochanek, *The Congress Party of India* (Princeton: Princeton University Press, 1968), p. 382.

Parliamentary party leadership in Ghana: Apter, chs. 10 and 11; in West Germany: Loewenberg, ch. 4; in Japan: Chitoshi Yanaga, *Japanese People and Politics* (New York: Wiley, 1956), p. 267.

Conservative parliamentary party discipline and leadership: Beer, passim; Richards, passim; Leon D. Epstein, "Cohesion of British Parliamentary Parties," *American Political Science Review,* Vol. 50, No. 2 (June 1956), 360–377.

Postwar parliamentary leadership and discipline in France: Roy C. Macridis and Robert E. Ward, eds., *Modern Political Systems: Europe* (Englewood Cliffs, N.J.: Prentice-Hall, 1963); Peter Campbell, "Discipline and Loyalty in the French Parliament," Wahlke and Eulau, pp. 143–149.

James on constituency orientation of legislators: Judson L. James, *American Political Parties in Transition* (New York: Harper & Row, 1974), p. 202.

Party and parliamentary leadership in American legislatures: David B. Truman, *The Congressional Party* (New York: Wiley, 1959); Randall B. Ripley, *Party Leaders in the House of Representatives* (Washington, D.C.: Brookings, 1967); Wahlke, Eulau, Buchanan, and Ferguson, esp. chs. 8, 15; James, passim; Nelson W. Polsby, "The Institutionalization of the U.S. House of Representatives," *American Political Science Review,* Vol. 62, No. 1 (March 1968), 144–168; David J. Rothman, *Politics and Power: The United States Senate, 1869–1901* (Cambridge, Mass.: Harvard University Press, 1966); Lewis A. Froman, Jr., *Congressmen and Their Constituencies* (Chicago: Rand McNally, 1963); Ralph Huitt, "Democratic Party Leadership in the Senate," *American Political Science Review,* Vol. 55, No. 2 (June 1961), 333–344; Walter J. Oleszek, "Party Whips in the United States Senate," *Journal of Politics,* Vol. 33, No. 4 (November 1971), 955–979; Barbara Hinckley, *The Seniority System in Congress* (Bloomington: University of Indiana Press, 1971); David R. Mayhew, *Party Loyalty Among Congressmen* (Cambridge, Mass.: Harvard University Press, 1966); Robert L. Peabody, "Party Leadership Change in the United States House of Representatives," *American Political Science Review,* Vol. 61, No. 3 (September 1967), 675–693.

Blum to Laval: quoted in Geoffrey Warner, *Pierre Laval and the Eclipse of France* (New York: Macmillan, 1968), p. 126; on the Fourth Republic, see Nathan Leites, *On the Game of Politics in France* (Stanford: Stanford University Press, 1959), with a suggestive foreword by D. W. Brogan.

Miliband on socialism and legislative leadership: Ralph Miliband, *Parliamentary Socialism* (London: George Allen and Unwin, 1961).

14. EXECUTIVE LEADERSHIP

Charles de Gaulle as executive leader: see generally Charles de Gaulle, *Mémoires d'espoir:* Vol. 1, *Le renouveau, 1958–1962* (Paris: Plon., 1970); Vol. 2, *L'effort, 1962* (Paris: Plon., 1971).

De Gaulle's view of presidential power: broadcasts of December 28, 1958, and January 29, 1960, quoted in Dorothy Pickles, *The Fifth French Republic* (New York: Praeger, 1962), p. 138, and in Philip M. Williams and Martin Harrison, *Politics and Society in de Gaulle's Republic* (Garden City, N.Y.: Doubleday, 1972), p. 172.

De Gaulle on executive versus parliamentary power: Pickles, p. 33.

Pickles' view of the presidential office: Pickles, p. 136.

De Gaulle's press conferences: Pierre Viansson-Ponté, *The King and His Court* (Boston: Houghton Mifflin, 1965), pp. 44–47; David Schoenbrun, *The Three Lives of Charles de Gaulle* (New York: Atheneum, 1966), pp. 344–345.

Direct election of president: Williams and Harrison, pp. 172–173 (De Gaulle quoted on p. 173).

De Gaulle's hope to avoid routine administrative direction: Williams and Harrison, p. 174.

On the political and institutional aspects of the Fifth Republic see Roy C. Macridis and Bernard E. Brown, *The De Gaulle Republic* (Homewood, Ill.: Dorsey Press, 1960); on De Gaulle himself: Alexander Werth, *De Gaulle* (New York: Simon and Schuster, 1965).

See also review article by John C. Cairns, "De Gaulle as President: First Triumphs and Last Memoirs," *American Historical Review,* Vol. 78, No. 5 (December 1973), 1406–1420, and works cited therein.

Schoenbrun on de Gaulle's negative achievements: Schoenbrun, p. 364.

The Political Executive: Power and Purpose

The executive leader and conflict: Barnard, pp. 270–278; William J. Gore, *Administrative Decision-Making* (New York: Wiley, 1964), pp. 38f; Victor A. Thompson, *Bureaucracy and Innovation* (University: University of Alabama Press, 1969), passim; Philip Selznick, *Leadership in Administration* (New York: Harper & Brothers, 1957), pp. 63–64; Melville Dalton, "Staff and Line Relationships—A Study of Conflicts," in Robert Dubin, *Human Relations in Administration* (New York: Prentice-Hall, 1951), pp. 128–138; Presthus, passim; Crozier, p. 139.

Five types of organizational power: Katz and Kahn, ch. 11. Acceptance of authority: Herbert A. Simon, Donald W. Smithburg, and Victor A. Thompson, *Public Administration* (New York: Knopf, 1950), ch. 8. See also Donald C. Stone on executive influence: Waldo, ed., *Ideas and Issues in Public Administration* (New York: McGraw-Hill, 1953), p. 339.

Franklin Roosevelt's personal management: Richard E. Neustadt, *Presidential Power* (New York: Wiley, 1950), passim; James MacGregor Burns, *Roosevelt: The Lion and the Fox* (New York: Harcourt, Brace & World, 1956), pp. 264–265, 371–375.

Organizational purpose and goal: Talcott Parsons, *Politics and Social Structure,* pp. 318–319, 341–342; Chester Barnard, *The Functions of the Executive* (Cambridge, Mass.: Harvard University Press, 1945), passim (indexed as purpose); William J. Gore, *Administration Decision-Making: A Heuristic Model* (New York: Wiley, 1964), pp. 37ff; Victor A. Thompson, *Modern Organization,* ch. 6; Presthus, passim.

Gore quotation: Gore, p. 37.

Organization theorists on goals: see especially Lawrence B. Mohr, "The Concept of Organizational Goal," *American Political Science Review,* Vol. 67, No. 2 (June 1973), 470–481; see also Tannenbaum, Weschler, and Massarik, pp. 28–29; Cartwright in March, *Handbook of Organization,* pp. 10–11.

Displacement of goals on one another: Presthus, pp. 195–196, 218–219, 320.

Goal clusters: Tannenbaum et al., p. 30.

Time element: Amitai Etzioni, *Modern Organizations* (Englewood Cliffs, N.J.: Prentice-Hall, 1964), pp. 5, 13.

Differentiating goals: Dorwin Cartwright and Alvin Zander, *Group Dynamics,* 3rd ed. (New York: Harper & Row, 1968), pp. 403f.

Techniques for identifying goals and measuring goal importance: Mohr, p. 478, and works listed therein.

Institutional embodiment of purpose: Selznick, ch. 4.

The Executive Leader as Decision Maker

Sir Ian Hamilton's decision-making: Sir Ian Hamilton, *The Soul and Body of an Army* (London: Arnold, 1921), pp. 235–236, cited by Stein, p. 237.

Classic conceptions of executive decision-making: Barnard, passim; Whyte, *Organizational Behavior* (Homewood, Ill.: Irwin, 1968), pp. 686–687; Gore, pp. 3ff; Barnard, p. 196. Contemporary, more contextual approach: James G. March and Herbert A. Simon, *Organizations* (New York: Wiley, 1958); Whyte, p. 687.

Gore on stream of interactions: Gore, p. 21.

Decision maker operating "forward and backward": Julian Feldman and Herschel E. Kanter,

"Organizational Decision Making," in March, *Handbook of Organizations,* pp. 615–617; Whyte, pp. 697–699.

The Tennessee Valley Authority as an "autonomous" organization: Philip Selznick, *TVA and the Grass Roots* (Berkeley: University of California Press, 1949); see also Philip Selznick, *Leadership in Administration* (New York: Harper & Brothers, 1957), pp. 42–45, from which Selznick is quoted at pp. 43–44.

Probability curves: Feldman and Kanter, p. 625.

Lindblom on incrementalism: Charles Lindblom, *The Intelligence of Democracy* (New York: Free Press, 1965), p. 148 and passim; see also David Braybrooke and Charles E. Lindblom, *A Strategy of Decision* (New York: Free Press, 1963).

Barnard on telephone pole decision-making: Barnard, p. 198; see also Simon, pp. 226–227.

Concept of the "decision tree": McFarland, esp. ch. 6.

Barnard on repeated decision-making: Barnard, pp. 205–206.

Thompson on innovation: Victor A. Thompson, *Bureaucracy and Innovation* (University: University of Alabama Press, 1969), p. 4.

Thompson on "self-actualization through work": Thompson, p. 106.

Theory of the "strategic factor": Barnard, pp. 202–206.

Crozier on organizational progress through crisis: Michel Crozier, *The Bureaucratic Phenomenon* (Chicago: University of Chicago Press, 1964), pp. 116, 310.

Gore on organizational survival: Gore, pp. 20–21.

Selznick on institutional embodiment of purpose: Selznick, *Leadership in Administration,* ch. 4.

The American President as Executive Leader

Presidential aide on White House conflict: Theodore C. Sorensen, *Decision-Making in the White House* (New York: Columbia University Press, 1963), p. 14.

Classic treatments of the constitutional background of presidential power are Edward S. Corwin, *The President: Office and Powers,* rev. ed. (New York: New York University Press, 1957); Clinton Rossiter, *The American Presidency* (New York: Harcourt, Brace, 1956); William Howard Taft, *Our Chief Magistrate and His Powers* (New York: Columbia University Press, 1916); Woodrow Wilson, *Constitutional Government in the United States* (New York: Columbia University Press, 1908).

Presidential politics and popularity: Thomas A. Bailey, *Presidential Greatness: The Image and the Man from George Washington to the Present* (New York: Appleton, 1966); Wilfred Binkley, *The Man in the White House* (Baltimore: Johns Hopkins Press, 1959); Elmer E. Cornwell, *Presidential Leadership of Public Opinion* (Bloomington: Indiana University Press, 1965); Stuart Gerry Brown, *The American Presidency: Leadership, Partisanship, and Popularity* (New York: Macmillan, 1966).

Presidential power: Herman Finer, *The Presidency: Crisis and Regeneration* (Chicago: University of Chicago Press, 1960); Louis W. Koenig, *The Chief Executive* (New York: Harcourt Brace & World, 1964); Richard Neustadt, *Presidential Power* (New York: Wiley, 1960); Harold J. Laski, *The American Presidency* (New York: Harper & Brothers, 1940); Arthur M. Schlesinger, Jr., *The Imperial Presidency* (Boston: Houghton Mifflin, 1973).

Rise of executive agreements: Schlesinger, pp. 85–86. Recent proliferation of executive agreements: Sam J. Ervin, Jr., "Separation of Powers and Foreign Affairs," paper prepared for the Center for the Study of Democratic Institutions, Santa Barbara, California, October 1973, p. 10.

Neustadt on presidential bargaining: Neustadt, pp. 36–37. Critique of bargaining model: William T. Bluhm, *Theories of the Political System* (Englewood Cliffs, N.J.: Prentice-Hall, 1965). Raising presidential bargaining to more inclusive levels: Peter W. Sperlich, "Bargaining and Overload: An Essay on *Presidential Power,*" in Wildavsky, ed., *The Presidency,* pp. 168–192.

Lack of national purpose: Hans J. Morgenthau, *The Purpose of American Politics* (New York:

Vintage Books, 1964), p. 7; see also Louis Hartz, *The Liberal Tradition in America* (New York: Harcourt, Brace, 1955); and Boorstin, *The Genius of American Politics* (Chicago: University of Chicago Press, 1953); Herbert McClosky, "Consensus and Ideology in American Politics," *American Political Science Review,* Vol. 58, No. 2 (June 1964), 361–382.

Lincoln on limb versus life: John G. Nicolay and John Hay, eds., *Complete Works of Abraham Lincoln* (Lincoln Memorial University, 1894), Vol. 10, p. 66. The Supreme Court's response: *ex parte Milligan* (4 Wall. 120–121, 126, 1866). This discussion of Lincoln is drawn from a somewhat more extended comment in James MacGregor Burns, *Presidential Government: The Crucible of Leadership* (Boston: Houghton Mifflin, 1966), pp. 34–45. Lincoln's remark on being controlled by events is quoted in Richard Hofstadter, *The American Political Tradition* (New York: Vintage Books, 1954), p. 130.

Theodore Roosevelt on his use of executive power: Theodore Roosevelt, *An Autobiography* (New York: Macmillan, 1921), p. 395; see also Clinton Rossiter, *Alexander Hamilton and the Constitution* (New York: Harcourt, Brace & World, 1964), p. 248.

Franklin Roosevelt as political tactician: drawn from James MacGregor Burns, *Roosevelt: The Lion and the Fox* (New York: Harcourt, Brace & World, 1956), pp. 284–287 and passim; Franklin Roosevelt as chief executive: quoted directly from James MacGregor Burns, *Roosevelt: The Soldier of Freedom* (New York: Harcourt Brace Jovanovich, 1970), pp. 347–348.

Neustadt on Roosevelt's reputation-building: Neustadt, p. 63. For a somewhat different perspective on Franklin Roosevelt, see Arthur M. Schlesinger, Jr., *The Age of Roosevelt,* esp. Vol. 2, *The Coming of the New Deal,* and Vol. 3, *The Politics of Upheaval* (Boston: Houghton Mifflin, 1959, 1960).

Kennedy on presidential performance: "Speeches, Remarks, Press Conferences and Statements of Senator John F. Kennedy, Aug. 1 through Nov. 7, 1960," *Final Report of the Senate Committee on Commerce,* 87th Congress, 1st Session, 1961, p. 904. Sorensen's book is *Decision-Making in the White House.* See also Emmet John Hughes, *The Living Presidency* (New York: Coward, McCann & Geoghegan, 1973), pp. 57–58.

Jefferson on slender majorities: Sorensen, p. 48.

Nixon presidency: Schlesinger, *The Imperial Presidency,* esp. ch. 8; Jules Witcover, *The Resurrection of Richard Nixon* (New York: Putnam, 1970); Garry Wills, *Nixon Agonistes* (Boston: Houghton Mifflin, 1970); Bruce Mazlish, *In Search of Nixon* (New York: Basic Books, 1972).

15. DECISION AND CHANGE

Mao Tse-tung leading and altering the Cultural Revolution: Stuart Schram, ed., *Authority, Participation and Cultural Change in China* (London: Cambridge University Press, 1973).

The "qualitative jump in consciousness": K. S. Karol, *The Second Chinese Revolution* (New York: Hill & Wang, 1973), p. 455.

See also Han Suyin, Karnow, and Snow in source notes for Chapter 9. Stewart Burns drafted the material on Mao and the Cultural Revolution jointly with the author.

The Leader as Policy Maker

Interregnum relations between Hoover and Roosevelt: Frank Freidel, *Franklin D. Roosevelt: Launching the New Deal* (Boston: Little, Brown, 1973), p. 18.

Roosevelt as "peanut": Freidel, p. 45.

Bauer on a model of decision-making requirements: Raymond A. Bauer and Kenneth J. Gergen, *The Study of Policy Formation* (New York: Free Press, 1968), p. 11.

Robbins on marginal utility: Bauer and Gergen, p. 92.

On "extra-rationality" in public policy-making see Yehezkel Dror, *Public Policymaking Reexamined* (San Francisco: Chandler, 1968), chs. 12, 13.

Decision and Dissent

Sorensen on presidential policy constancy: Theodore C. Sorensen, *Decision-Making in the White House* (New York: Columbia University Press, 1963), p. 34.

On generalizing about leaders and decision-making see also: Victor H. Vroom and Philip W. Yetton, *Leadership and Decision-Making* (Pittsburgh: University of Pittsburgh Press, 1973).

John Dewey on rational decision-making: adapted and quoted from Dror, pp. 79–80.

Sorensen on decision-making: Sorensen, pp. 18–20.

Dror on limitations of decision-making: Dror, p. 79.

The "science of muddling through": see in general Charles E. Lindblom, *The Intelligence of Democracy* (New York: Free Press, 1965).

Holsti on Dulles' "restructuring strategies": Ole R. Holsti, "Cognitive Dynamics and Image of the Enemy: Dulles and Russia," in D. J. Finlay, O. R. Holsti, and R. R. Fagen, *Enemies in Politics* (Chicago: Rand McNally, 1967), pp. 25–96.

Harding on decision-making: Richard F. Fenno, *The President's Cabinet* (Cambridge, Mass.: Harvard University Press, 1959), pp. 40–41.

Janis on leaders' internal reactions and anticipations: Irving L. Janis, "Decisional Conflicts: A Theoretical Analysis," *Journal of Conflict Resolution,* Vol. 3 (1959), 6–27, quoted at 15.

Richard Nixon on his National Security Council system of advice: Richard Nixon, *U.S. Foreign Policy for the 1970's: A New Strategy for Peace,* A Report to the Congress, February 18, 1970 (Washington, D.C.), p. 22.

George on National Security Council decision-making under Nixon: Alexander L. George, "The Case for Multiple Advocacy in Making Foreign Policy," *American Political Science Review,* Vol. 66, No. 3 (September 1972), 751–785, quoted at 761; see also comment by I. M. Destler and rejoinder by George: George, pp. 786–795.

Kennedy after the Bay of Pigs: Arthur M. Schlesinger, Jr., *A Thousand Days* (Boston: Houghton Mifflin, 1965), p. 296; see also Theodore C. Sorensen, *Kennedy* (New York: Harper & Row, 1965), p. 305.

Kennedy and Khrushchev on the missile crisis: Graham T. Allison, *Essence of Decision* (Boston: Little, Brown, 1971), pp. 211, 212 (emphasis added).

The Test: Real, Intended Change

Kelman and Warwick on types of changes: Herbert C. Kelman and Donald P. Warwick, "Bridging Micro and Macro Approaches to Social Change: A Social-Psychological Perspective," in Gerald Zaltman, ed., *Processes and Phenomena of Social Change* (New York: Wiley, 1973), pp. 20–21.

Nisbet on persistence and change: Robert Nisbet, ed., *Social Change* (New York: Harper & Row, 1972), p. 5.

Heilbroner on change: Robert Heilbroner, *The Future As History* (New York: Harper & Row, 1968), p. 195.

Meyer on change: Leonard B. Meyer, *Music, the Arts, and Ideas: Patterns and Predictions in Twentieth Century Culture* (Chicago: University of Chicago Press, 1967), p. 134.

Both Heilbroner and Meyer are quoted in Nisbet, pp. 11–12; Radcliffe-Brown on two types of change: Alfred R. Radcliffe-Brown, *A Natural Science of Society* (New York: Free Press, 1957), p. 87.

Kindergarten experiment: F. Merei, "Group Leadership and Institutionalization," *Human Relations,* Vol. 2 (1939), 23–39.

Strategies for overcoming resistance to change: Zaltman, p. 4, drawn in turn from Garth N. Jones, *Planned Organizational Change* (New York: Praeger, 1969); Robert Chin and Kenneth Benne, "General Strategies for Effective Changes in Human Systems," in W. G. Bennis, K. D. Benne, and R. Chin, eds., *The Planning of Change* (New York: Holt, Rinehart and Winston, 1969); Gerald Zaltman, Philip Kotler, and Ira Kaufman, *Creating Social Change* (New York: Holt, Rinehart and Winston, 1972).

Other sources of social change and its blockage: Everett E. Hagen, *On the Theory of Social Change* (Homewood, Ill.: Dorsey Press, 1962); Wilbert E. Moore, *Social Change* (Englewood Cliffs, N.J.: Prentice-Hall, 1963); Gouldner, *The Coming Crisis of Western Sociology.*

Nagel on change: Ernest Nagel, *The Structure of Science* (New York: Harcourt, Brace & World, 1961), p. 529.

Coser on changes of system and changes in systems: Lewis A. Coser, *Continuities in the Study of Social Conflict* (Glencoe, Ill.: Free Press, 1967), p. 28.

Gurr on political system transformation: Ted Robert Gurr, "Persistence and Change in Political Systems, 1800–1971," *American Political Science Review,* Vol. 68, No. 4 (December 1974), 1500–1501.

Inkeles on Bolshevik planning: Alex Inkeles, *Social Change in Soviet Russia* (Cambridge, Mass.: Harvard University Press, 1968), pp. 14, 15).

Mannheim on planning: Karl Mannheim, *Freedom, Power, and Democratic Planning* (New York: Oxford University Press, 1950), p. xviii.

16. TOWARD A GENERAL THEORY

Lyndon Johnson's dream: Doris Kearns, *Lyndon Johnson and the American Dream* (New York: Harper & Row, 1976), p. 342.

Taoist and Maoist emphasis on self-expression by the masses: Robert Jungk et al., *China and the West: Mankind Evolving* (New York: Humanities Press, 1971).

Slaves' resistance: Eugene D. Genovese, *Roll, Jordan, Roll* (New York: Pantheon Books, 1974).

Leadership and Collective Purpose

Transactions between leaders and followers: note discussion in Bernard M. Bass, *Leadership, Psychology, and Organization Behavior* (New York: Harper & Brothers, 1960), pp. 94ff.

Quotation on the establishment of "a culturally invariant sequence of stages of moral judgment": Lawrence Kohlberg, "The Claim to Moral Adequacy of a Highest Stage of Moral Judgment," *Journal of Philosophy,* Vol. 70, No. 18 (October 25, 1973), 630–631; see also Elizabeth Léonie Simpson, "A Holistic Approach to Moral Development and Behavior," ch. 9 in T. Lickona, ed., *Moral Development and Behavior* (New York: Holt, Rinehart and Winston, 1976), pp. 159–170.

Other sources of development theory: Lawrence Kohlberg, "Moral Development and Identification," ch. 7, in Harold W. Stevenson, ed., *Child Psychology* (62nd Yearbook of the National Society for the Study of Education), Part I (Chicago: University of Chicago Press, 1963), pp. 277–332; Kohlberg, "Development of Moral Character and Moral Ideology," in Martin L. Hoffman and Lois Wladis Hoffman, eds., *Review of Child Development Research,* Vol. 1 (New York: Russell Sage Foundation, 1964), pp. 383–431; Kohlberg, "Stage and Sequence: The Cognitive-Developmental Approach to Socialization," in David A. Goslin, *Handbook of Socialization Theory and Research* (Chicago: Rand McNally, 1969), pp. 347–480; and other apposite articles in these collections.

See generally Theodore Mischel, ed., *Cognitive Development and Epistemology* (New York: Academic Press, 1971).

Roosevelt's and Hitler's definitions of freedom: James MacGregor Burns, "Hitler, Roosevelt, and the Battle of Symbols," *Antioch Review,* Vol. 2 (1942), 407–421; see also Ralph K. White, "Hitler, Roosevelt and the Nature of War Propaganda," *Journal of Abnormal and Social Psychology,* Vol. 44 (1949), 157.

Cantril: Hadley Cantril, *The Pattern of Human Concerns* (New Brunswick: Rutgers University Press, 1965), pp. 14–16, 327–328.

Four-nation study of differences among leaders: International Studies of Values in Politics, *Values and the Active Community* (New York: Free Press, 1971), esp. pp. 10, 149ff; see also Florence Rockwood Kluckhohn and Fred L. Strodtbeck, *Variations in Value Orientations* (Evanston, Ill.: Row, Peterson, 1961).

Rawls on justice: John Rawls, *A Theory of Justice* (Cambridge, Mass.: Harvard University Press, 1971); Norman Daniels, ed., *Reading Rawls* (New York: Basic Books, 1974).

Leadership as Causation

"Dichotomy" between structural and behavioral variables: McFarland, pp. 125–128.

Friedrichs on the interplay between the socially derived "me" and biologically based "I": Robert W. Friedrichs, *A Sociology of Sociology* (New York: Free Press, 1970), p. 227.

Transferability of power between Roosevelt and Lewis: James MacGregor Burns, *Roosevelt: The Lion and the Fox* (New York: Harcourt, Brace, 1956), pp. 216–217, 286–287, 449–450.

McClelland on leaders' arousing motivations of followers: David C. McClelland, *Power: The Inner Experience* (New York: Irvington, 1975), p. 260.

I have found useful on aspects of historical causation: R. M. MacIver, *Social Causation* (Boston: Ginn, 1942); Erich Kahler, *The Meaning of History* (Cleveland: World Publishing, 1964); Edward Hallett Carr, *What Is History?* (New York: Knopf, 1962); Hans Meyerhoff, ed., *The Philosophy of History in Our Time* (Garden City, N.Y.: Doubleday, 1959).

Leadership and Change

Field theory analysis: Kurt Lewin, *Field Theory in Social Science* (New York: Harper & Brothers, 1951).

My example of Jones and Smith was suggested by a somewhat similar example in Morton White, *Foundations of Historical Knowledge* (New York: Harper & Row, 1965), pp. 144–145.

Berger and Luckmann on the reality of everyday life: Peter L. Berger and Thomas Luckmann, *The Social Construction of Reality* (Garden City, N.Y.: Doubleday, 1967), pp. 21–28; see also the work of Erving Goffman.

Berlin on the actual experience of men and women: Isaiah Berlin, *The Hedgehog and the Fox* (New York: Simon and Schuster, 1970), p. 11 (emphasis added).

17. POLITICAL LEADERSHIP AS PRACTICAL INFLUENCE

From the enormous bibliography on Machiavelli I have used especially: Max Lerner, ed., *The Prince and the Discourses of Machiavelli* (New York: Random House, 1950), including introduction by the editor; Benedetto Croce, *Elementi di politica* (Bari: Lius, Laterza & Figli, 1925); Leo Strauss, *Thoughts on Machiavelli* (Glencoe, Ill.: Free Press, 1958); Anthony Parel, ed., *The Political Calculus* (Toronto: University of Toronto Press, 1972); Garrett Mattingly, "Machiavelli's *Prince*: Political Science or Political Satire," *American Scholar*, Vol. 27, No. 4 (Autumn 1958), 482–491; and De Lamar Jensen, ed., *Machiavelli* (Lexington, Mass.: Heath, 1960).

Machiavelli on his evening writing: Valeriu Marcu, *Accent on Power: The Life and Times of Machiavelli* (New York: Farrar & Rinehart, 1939), p. 257.

Machiavelli and conflict: Fred R. Dallmayr, "Beyond Dogma and Despair: Toward a Critical Theory of Politics," *American Political Science Review*, Vol. 70, No. 1 (March 1976), 64–79.

Machiavelli's view of persons as things: Richard Christie and Florence L. Geis, *Studies in Machiavellianism* (New York: Academic Press, 1970), pp. 3–4, cited in Robert E. Lane, "Interpersonal Relations and Leadership in a 'Cold Society,'" paper prepared for delivery at the Congress of the International Political Science Association, Edinburgh, August 1976, p. 15.

On Machiavelli's intention see also Irving Howe, *Politics and the Novel* (New York: Avon Books, 1970), esp. pp. 44–46.

Teaching Leadership or Manipulation?

Carnegie's book is Dale Carnegie, *How to Win Friends and Influence People* (New York: Simon and Schuster, 1936); Robinson is quoted at p. 113, Overstreet at p. 40, James at p. 30.

The "grand goal of leadership": David Loye, *The Leadership Passion* (San Francisco: Jossey-Bass, 1977), p. 76.

Main sources on moral development and moral education: Lawrence Kohlberg, "Indoctrination Versus Relativity in Value Education," *Zygon: Journal of Religion and Science,* Vol. 6, No. 4, (December 1971), 285–310; Kohlberg, "The Cognitive-Developmental Approach to Moral Education," *Phi Delta Kappan,* June 1975, 670–677; Kohlberg, "Stages of Moral Development as a Basis for Moral Education," ch. 1 in Beck, Crittenden and Sullivan.

See also Anne Colby, review of works on teaching and clarification of values, *Harvard Educational Review* Vol. 45, No. 1 (February 1975), 134–143; John S. Stewart, "Clarifying Values Clarification: A Critique," *Phi Delta Kappan,* June 1975, p. 684–688; R. S. Peters, "Moral Development: A Plea for Pluralism," in Theodore Mischel, ed., *Cognitive Development and Epistemology* (New York: Academic Press, 1971), pp. 237–267.

Study of kibbutz-raised children in Israel: cited in Lawrence Kohlberg, "Development of Moral Character and Moral Ideology," in Martin L. Hoffman and Lois Wladis Hoffman, *Review of Child Development Research,* Vol. 1 (New York: Russell Sage Foundation, 1964), p. 415.

Max Weber on deficiencies in political education in pre-World War I Germany: Lawrence A. Scaff, "Max Weber's Politics and Political Education," *American Political Science Review,* Vol. 67, No. 1 (March 1973), 128–141; Weber is quoted at p. 132.

Elizabeth Léonie Simpson collaborated in the drafting of this section.

The Armament of Leadership

Call that "we must have leaders": Walter B. Wriston, "Liberty, Leadership and License," University of Chicago Graduate School of Business, Chicago, March 11, 1976, p. 5.

Journalist's remark: Brock Brower, quoted in *Time,* July 15, 1974, p. 21.

Statement of university president: Warren G. Bennis, "Where Have All the Leaders Gone?" Federal Executive Institute, 1975, pp. 1, 11.

Gardner on leadership: John W. Gardner, "The Antileadership Vaccine," *Annual Report of the Carnegie Corporation of New York,* New York, 1965, pp. 3, 12.

Myrdal on the labor parties of Europe: Gunnar Myrdal, "Race and Class in a Welfare State," Columbia University, October 28, 1976, p. 29.

Event-full and event-making leadership: Sidney Hook, *The Hero in History* (Boston: Beacon Press, 1955).

Reichley on Mosaic and Alexandrian leadership: A. James Reichley, "Our Critical Shortage of Leadership," *Fortune,* September 1971, pp. 90–91.

Selznick on the social embodiment of purpose: Philip Selznick, *Leadership in Administration* (New York: Harper & Brothers, 1957), p. 60.

Barber on failure of followership: Benjamin Barber, "Command Performance," *Harper's,* April 1975, p. 53.

Myrdal on American values: Myrdal, "Race and Class in a Welfare Society."

The Chinese Constitution of 1969: Edgar Snow, *The Long Revolution* (New York: Random House, 1971), p. 255.

On Mao's strategy cf. Phillip Bridgham, "Mao's Cultural Revolution in 1967: The Struggle to Seize Power," *China Quarterly,* Vol. 34 (April–June 1968), 6; Edward Rice, *Mao's Way* (Berkeley: University of California Press, 1972), esp. pp. 298–317.

Leadership: Of Whom? To What?

Henri Peyre on ingredients of leadership: *Time,* July 15, 1974, p. 23.

Leadership of the global community: Robert C. Tucker, "Personality and Political Leadership," *Political Science Quarterly,* Vol. 92, No. 3 (Fall 1977), 383–393, esp. p. 393.

INDEX

509

About the Author

Leadership represents a culmination—to date—and a synthesis of James MacGregor Burns's distinguished career as teacher, writer, scholar, and activist, combining his insights as historian and political scientist and, for the first time, broadening his scope to examine political process and power all over the world.

Burns's study of leadership—transactional and transformational—has roots in his definitive two-volume biography of Franklin Roosevelt, *Roosevelt: The Lion and the Fox* (winner of the Woodrow Wilson Foundation award, the Tamiment Prize and the Francis Parkman award) and *Roosevelt: The Soldier of Freedom* (winner of the Pulitzer Prize and the National Book Award), as well as in his study of top leadership, *Presidential Government: The Crucible of Leadership,* and biographies of two Kennedys, *John Kennedy: A Political Profile,* published before the nomination in 1960, and *Edward Kennedy and the Camelot Legacy*. His first book was on Congress (*Congress on Trial*); he has written on the American party system (*The Deadlock of Democracy*), a best-selling textbook, with Jack Peltason (*Government by the People*), and a prophetic diagnosis of American leadership (*Uncommon Sense*).

Burns has had field experience on the American political scene as delegate to several Democratic national conventions, as candidate for Congress from western Massachusetts, and as political reformer, both in his native Berkshire County, Massachusetts, and on the national level. A graduate of Williams College, he went to Washington as a congressional assistant, worked on the National War Labor Board and as an army historian in World War II, and returned to earn his Ph.D. at Harvard. He is Woodrow Wilson Professor of Government at Williams College and recent president of the American Political Science Association.